Course	Introduction to Business
Course Number	**Business 100**
	FULLERTON COLLEGE
	BUSINESS ADMINISTRATION

http://create.mheducation.com

ISBN-10: 1308265700   ISBN-13: 9781308265704

Contents

Credits

Business in a Changing World

chapter one

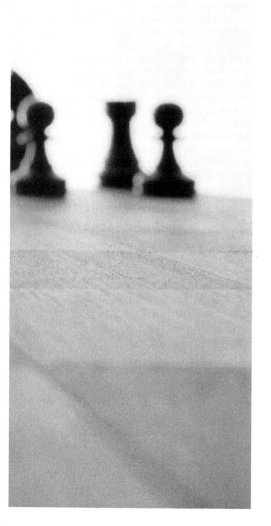

the dynamics of business + economics

We begin our study of business in this chapter by examining the fundamentals of business and economics. First, we introduce the nature of business, including its goals, activities, and participants. Next, we describe the basics of economics and apply them to the United States' economy. Finally, we establish a framework for studying business in this text.

LEARNING OBJECTIVES

L01 Define basic concepts such as business, product, and profit.

L02 Identify the main participants and activities of business and explain why studying business is important.

L03 Define economics and compare the four types of economic systems.

L04 Describe the role of supply, demand, and competition in a free-enterprise system.

L05 Specify why and how the health of the economy is measured.

L06 Trace the evolution of the American economy and discuss the role of the entrepreneur in the economy.

business individuals or organizations who try to earn a profit by providing products that satisfy people's needs

product a good or service with tangible and intangible characteristics that provide satisfaction and benefits

profit the difference between what it costs to make and sell a product and what a customer pays for it

nonprofit organizations organizations that may provide goods or services but do not have the fundamental purpose of earning profits

stakeholders groups that have a stake in the success and outcomes of a business

THE NATURE OF BUSINESS

A **business** tries to earn a profit by providing products that satisfy people's needs. The outcome of its efforts are **products** that have both tangible and intangible characteristics that provide satisfaction and benefits. When you purchase a product, you are buying the benefits and satisfaction you think the product will provide. A Subway sandwich, for example, may be purchased to satisfy hunger, while a Chevrolet Camaro may be purchased to satisfy the need for transportation and the desire to present a certain image.

Most people associate the word *product* with tangible goods— an automobile, computer, phone, coat, or some other tangible item. However, a product can also be a service, which occurs when people or machines provide or process something of value to customers. Dry cleaning, a checkup by a doctor, a performance by a basketball player—these are examples of services. Some services, such as Flickr, an online photo management and sharing application, do not charge a fee for use but obtain revenue from ads on their sites. A product can also be an idea. Accountants and attorneys, for example, generate ideas for solving problems.

The Goal of Business

The primary goal of all businesses is to earn a **profit**, the difference between what it costs to make and sell a product and what a customer pays for it. If a company spends $8.00 to manufacture, finance, promote, and distribute a product that it sells for $10.00, the business earns a profit of $2.00 on each product sold. Businesses have the right to keep and use their profits as they choose—within legal limits—because profit is the reward for the risks they take in providing products. Earning profits contributes to society by providing employment, which in turn provides money that is reinvested in the economy. Not all organizations are businesses, however. **Nonprofit organizations**, such as the Red Cross, Special Olympics, and other charities and social causes, do not have the fundamental purpose of earning profits, although they may provide goods or services and do engage in fund raising.

To earn a profit, a person or organization needs management skills to plan, organize, and control the activities of the business and to find and develop employees so that it can make products consumers will buy. A business also needs marketing expertise to learn what products consumers need and want and to develop, manufacture, price, promote, and distribute those

Seventh Generation is a leading brand of environmentally friendly household products. Its Natural 4X Laundry Detergent is packed in a bottle made from 100 percent recycled fiber.

products. Additionally, a business needs financial resources and skills to fund, maintain, and expand its operations. Other challenges for businesspeople include abiding by laws and government regulations; acting in an ethical and socially responsible manner; and adapting to economic, technological, political, and social changes. Even nonprofit organizations engage in management, marketing, and finance activities to help reach their goals.

To achieve and maintain profitability, businesses have found that they must produce quality products, operate efficiently, and be socially responsible and ethical in dealing with customers, employees, investors, government regulators, the community, and society. Because these groups have a stake in the success and outcomes of a business, they are sometimes called **stakeholders**. Many businesses, for example, are concerned about how the production and distribution of their products affect the environment. Concerns about landfills becoming high-tech graveyards plague many electronics firms. Best Buy offers recycling of electronics at all of its stores. The stores take cell phones, DVD players, and most other electronic products in their green program, regardless of where they were purchased. Other businesses are concerned about the quality of life in the communities in which they operate. For example, the Kansas City Chiefs have raised millions for charitable organizations over the past 10 years. One of the franchise's philanthropic activities is the Chiefs Charity game, which raises over $500,000 annually for local charities.[1] Others are concerned with promoting business careers among African American, Hispanic, and Native American students. The Diversity Pipeline Alliance is a network of national organizations that work toward preparing students and professionals of color for leadership and management in the 21st-century workforce. The Pipeline assists individuals in getting into the appropriate college, pursuing a career in business, or earning an advanced degree in business.[2] Other companies, such as Home Depot, have a long history of supporting natural disaster victims, relief efforts, and recovery. Still other companies have a long history of supporting natural disaster victims from Hurricane Katrina to relief efforts and earthquake recovery for Haiti.

The People and Activities of Business

Figure 1.1 shows the people and activities involved in business. At the center of the figure are owners, employees, and customers; the outer circle includes the primary business activities—management, marketing, and finance. Owners have to put up resources—money or credit—to start a business. Employees are responsible for the work that goes on within a business. Owners can manage the business themselves or hire employees to accomplish this task. The president, chief executive officer (CEO), and board chair of Procter & Gamble, Robert A. McDonald, does not own P&G, but is an employee who is responsible for managing all the other employees in a way that earns a profit for investors, who are the real owners. Finally, and most importantly, a business's major role is to satisfy the customers who buy its goods or services. Note also that people

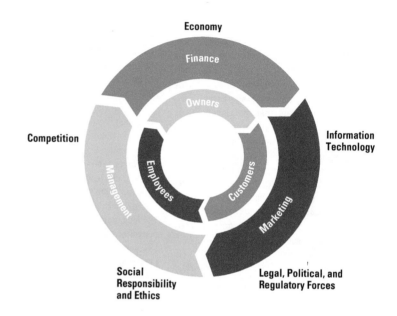

FIGURE 1.1
Overview of the Business World

and forces beyond an organization's control—such as legal and regulatory forces, the economy, competition, technology, the political environment and ethical and social concerns—all have an impact on the daily operations of businesses. You will learn more about these participants in business activities throughout this book. Next, we will examine the major activities of business.

Management

Notice that in Figure 1.1 management and employees are in the same segment of the circle. This is because management involves coordinating employees' actions to achieve the firm's goals, organizing people to work efficiently, and motivating them to achieve the business's goals. NASCAR has been a family-run business since its inception. Brian France, current chair and CEO, is following in the footsteps of his father and grandfather in providing leadership for the sport. NASCAR is now the second most popular spectator sport in the country, outperforming fan numbers and viewership for the Indy Racing League. NASCAR is also the second biggest television draw in sports, behind the NFL.[3] Management is also concerned with acquiring, developing, and using resources (including people) effectively and efficiently. The Campbell Soup Company enlists its workers to help squeeze more efficiency out of its plants. Operating efficiency comes from saving time, money, and effort.[5]

STARBUCKS MANAGING GLOBAL SUCCESS

After years of large-scale expansion, Howard Schultz returned as Starbucks' CEO to energize and grow the company. The plan involved closing nearly 1,000 stores and other aggressive cost-cutting. Realizing that the United States has become a saturated market, Starbucks is now focusing more on international growth.

One lucrative market is Japan. Japan is the largest coffee consuming country globally. Starbucks has been involved in Japan since 1995 and now runs close to 900 stores throughout the country. Starbucks has succeeded in part by adapting its products to Japanese tastes. For example, the Japanese tend to drink less coffee per sitting, so serving sizes have been reduced.

However, not all countries are as accepting as Japan. For example, when Starbucks first entered Great Britain, it moved quickly—perhaps too quickly. British consumers did not take to Starbucks' signature stores or its premium high-priced coffee, especially since Great Britain was more of a tea-driven market. Starbucks has therefore begun renovating its stores, creating a unique look for each that fits the local culture. With over 600 stores in Britain, Starbucks is currently making a profit.

Starbucks is now turning its attention toward expansion in China. Starbucks first entered China in 1999 and now operates 700 stores. Finding the right approach in China is difficult, and reaching profitability may take years of trial and error. The company has recently entered into the Chinese tea market to respond to local consumer demand.

Starbucks is ready to grow in a healthier fashion by remodeling its current stores and modifying its products to local tastes. It continues to be ranked among the world's most ethical companies, which helps boost Starbucks' reputation. The company hopes that its emphasis on individuality and global expansion will become additional drivers for further success.[4]

Discussion Questions

1. How has Starbucks been able to be successful outside the United States?
2. How has Howard Schultz's (founder and past CEO) return to the company impacted Starbucks' success?
3. What role does maintaining an ethical organizational culture play in Starbucks' success?

Production and manufacturing is another element of management. At Campbell Soup, for example, a 20-person work team was created to determine how best to cut costs in some plants. In essence, managers plan, organize, staff, and control the tasks required to carry out the work of the company or nonprofit organization. We take a closer look at management activities in Parts 3 and 4 of this text.

Consider different management approaches by Samsung Electronics and Sony. Samsung believes it is important to manufacture its own TV sets. The firm believes that not manufacturing is to abandon the quality of your brand. Sony is hiring others to build 40 percent of its TVs to reduce costs. In contrast, Samsung is the only TV maker that produces its own computer chips used in digital TVs. Samsung is managing manufacturing, design, and marketing to gain efficiencies.[6] Consequently, making decisions to ensure the business achieves its short- and long-term goals is a vital part of management.

Marketing

Marketing and consumers are in the same segment of Figure 1.1 because the focus of all marketing activities is satisfying customers. Marketing includes all the activities designed to provide goods and services that satisfy consumers' needs and wants. Marketers gather information and conduct research to determine what customers want. Using information gathered from marketing research, marketers plan and develop products and make decisions about how much to charge for their products and when and where to make them available.

In response to growing concerns over childhood obesity, Kellogg's has agreed to phase out advertising to children under the age of 12, unless those cereals are healthy (low calorie, low sugar and salt). In addition, Kellogg's will stop using cartoon and licensed characters such as Shrek to promote its products to children.[7] Other food producers have responded to consumer health concerns by modifying their products to make them healthier. Unilever, for example, announced that it was eliminating all hydrogenated oils, which contain trans-fats, from its soft-spread brands. I Can't Believe It's Not Butter will be one of several Unilever brands to have its hydrogenated oils replaced with palm and plant oils. Such a move reduces the risk of heart disease for consumers, while simultaneously allowing Unilever to market its brands as healthier.[8] Marketers use promotion—advertising, personal selling, sales promotion (coupons, games, sweepstakes, movie tie-ins), and publicity—to communicate the benefits and advantages of their products to consumers and increase sales. Nonprofit organizations also use promotion. For example, the National Fluid Milk Processor Promotion Board's "milk mustache" advertising campaign has featured Brooke Shields, Beyonce Knowles, Sheryl Crow, Elizabeth Hurley, Serena Williams, and even animated "celebrities" such as Garfield.[9] We will examine marketing activities in Part 5 of this text.

Finance

Owners and finance are in the same part of Figure 1.1 because, although management and marketing have to deal with financial considerations, it is the primary responsibility of the owners to provide financial resources for the operation of the business. Moreover, the owners have the most to lose if the business fails to make a profit. Finance refers to all activities concerned with obtaining money and using it effectively. People who work as accountants, stockbrokers, investment advisers, or bankers are all part of the financial world. Owners sometimes have to borrow money from banks to get started or attract additional investors who become partners or stockholders. Owners of small businesses in particular often rely on bank loans for funding. Part 6 of this text discusses financial management.

Why Study Business?

Studying business can help you develop skills and acquire knowledge to prepare for your future career, regardless of whether you plan to work for a multinational *Fortune* 500 firm, start your own business, work for a government agency, or manage or volunteer at a nonprofit organization. The field of business offers a variety of interesting and challenging career opportunities throughout the world, such as marketing, human resources management, information technology, finance, production and operations, wholesaling and retailing, and many more.

Studying business can also help you better understand the many business activities that are necessary to provide satisfying goods and services—and that these activities carry a price tag. For example, if you buy a new compact disk, about half of the price goes toward activities related to distribution and the retailer's expenses and profit margins. The production (pressing) of the CD represents about $1, or a small percentage of its price. Most businesses charge a reasonable price for their products to ensure that they cover their production costs, pay their employees, provide their owners with a return on their investment, and perhaps give something back to their local communities. Bill Daniels founded Cablevision, building his first cable TV system in Casper, Wyoming, in 1953, and is now considered "the father of cable television." Prior to Daniels' passing in 2000, he had established a foundation that currently has funding of $1.1 billion and supports a diversity of causes from education to business ethics. During his career, Daniels created the Young American Bank, where children could create bank accounts and learn about financial responsibility, and this remains the world's only charter bank for young people. He created the Daniels College of Business through a donation of $20 million to the University of Denver. During his life, he affected many individuals and organizations, and his business success has allowed his legacy to be one of giving and impacting communities throughout the United States.[10] Thus, learning about business can help you become a well-informed consumer and member of society.

Business activities help generate the profits that are essential not only to individual businesses and local economies but also to the health of the global economy. Without profits, businesses find it difficult, if not impossible, to buy more raw materials, hire more employees, attract more capital, and create additional products that in turn make more profits and fuel the

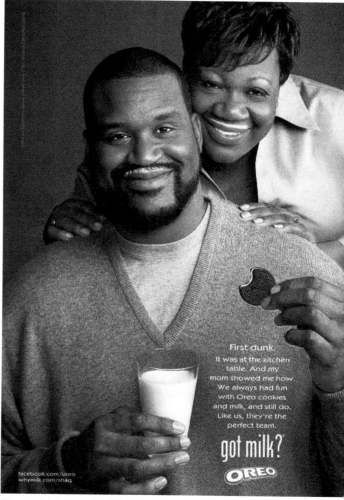

Famous athlete Shaquille O'Neal and his mother sport milk mustaches in the "Got Milk?" campaign.

world economy. Understanding how our free-enterprise economic system allocates resources and provides incentives for industry and the workplace is important to everyone.

THE ECONOMIC FOUNDATIONS OF BUSINESS

To continue our introduction to business, it is useful to explore the economic environment in which business is conducted. In this section, we examine economic systems, the free-enterprise system, the concepts of supply and demand, and the role of competition. These concepts play important roles in determining how businesses operate in a particular society.

economics the study of how resources are distributed for the production of goods and services within a social system

natural resources land, forests, minerals, water, and other things that are not made by people

human resources the physical and mental abilities that people use to produce goods and services; also called labor

financial resources the funds used to acquire the natural and human resources needed to provide products; also called capital

economic system a description of how a particular society distributes its resources to produce goods and services

Economics is the study of how resources are distributed for the production of goods and services within a social system. You are already familiar with the types of resources available. Land, forests, minerals, water, and other things that are not made by people are **natural resources. Human resources**, or labor, refers to the physical and mental abilities that people use to produce goods and services. **Financial resources**, or capital, are the funds used to acquire the natural and human resources needed to provide products. Because natural, human, and financial resources are used to produce goods and services, they are sometimes called *factors of production*. The firm can also have intangible resources such as a good reputation for quality products or being socially responsible. The goal is to turn the factors of production and intangible resources into a competitive advantage.

Economic Systems

An **economic system** describes how a particular society distributes its resources to produce goods and services. A central issue of economics is how to fulfill an unlimited demand for goods and services in a world with a limited supply of resources. Different economic systems attempt to resolve this central issue in numerous ways, as we shall see.

Although economic systems handle the distribution of resources in different ways, all economic systems must address three important issues:

1. What goods and services, and how much of each, will satisfy consumers' needs?

2. How will goods and services be produced, who will produce them, and with what resources will they be produced?

3. How are the goods and services to be distributed to consumers?

Communism, socialism, and capitalism, the basic economic systems found in the world today (Table 1.1), have fundamental differences in the way they address these issues. The factors of production in command economies are controlled by government planning. In many cases, the government owns or controls the production of goods and services. Communism and socialism are, therefore, considered command economies.

Communism Karl Marx (1818–1883) first described **communism** as a society in which the people, without regard to class, own all the nation's resources. In his ideal political-economic system, everyone contributes according to ability and receives benefits according to need. In a communist economy, the people (through the government) own and operate all businesses and factors of production. Central government planning determines what goods and services satisfy citizens' needs, how the goods and services are produced, and how they are distributed. However, no true communist economy exists today that satisfies Marx's ideal.

On paper, communism appears to be efficient and equitable, producing less of a gap between rich and poor. In practice, however, communist economies have been marked by low standards of living, critical shortages of consumer goods, high prices, and little freedom. Russia, Poland, Hungary, and other Eastern European nations have turned away from communism and toward economic systems governed by

▼ **TABLE 1.1** Comparison of Communism, Socialism, and Capitalism

	Communism	Socialism	Capitalism
Business ownership	Most businesses are owned and operated by the government.	The government owns and operates major industries; individuals own small businesses.	Individuals own and operate all businesses.
Competition	None. The government owns and operates everything.	Restricted in major industries; encouraged in small business.	Encouraged by market forces and government regulations.
Profits	Excess income goes to the government.	Profits earned by small businesses may be reinvested in the business; profits from government-owned industries go to the government.	Individuals are free to keep profits and use them as they wish.
Product availability and price	Consumers have a limited choice of goods and services; prices are usually high.	Consumers have some choice of goods and services; prices are determined by supply and demand.	Consumers have a wide choice of goods and services; prices are determined by supply and demand.
Employment options	Little choice in choosing a career; most people work for government-owned industries or farms.	Some choice of careers; many people work in government jobs.	Unlimited choice of careers.

Source: "Gross Domestic Product or Expenditure, 1930–2002," *InfoPlease* (n.d.), www.infoplease.com/ipa/A0104575.html (accessed February 16, 2004).

communism first described by Karl Marx as a society in which the people, without regard to class, own all the nation's resources

socialism an economic system in which the government owns and operates basic industries but individuals own most businesses

capitalism, or free enterprise an economic system in which individuals own and operate the majority of businesses that provide goods and services

free-market system pure capitalism, in which all economic decisions are made without government intervention

mixed economies economies made up of elements from more than one economic system

supply and demand rather than by central planning. However, their experiments with alternative economic systems have been fraught with difficulty and hardship. Cuba continues to apply communist principles to its economy, but Cuba is also experiencing economic and political change. Countries such as Venezuela are trying to incorporate communist economic principles. Hugo Chavez, Venezuela's president, has developed a partnership with Cuba, but 85 percent of his citizens surveyed do not want their country to be like Cuba.[11] Consequently, communism is declining and its future as an economic system is uncertain. When Fidel Castro stepped down as president of Cuba, his younger brother Raul formally assumed the role and eliminated many of the bans, including allowing the purchase of electric appliances, microwaves, computers, and cell phones. The communist country appears more open to free enterprise now.[12] There is a plan to shift hundreds of thousands of workers from the public sector to the private sector. Similarly, China has become the first communist country to make strong economic gains by adopting capitalist approaches to business. Economic prosperity has advanced in China with the government claiming to ensure market openness, equality, and fairness.[13]

Socialism

Socialism is an economic system in which the government owns and operates basic industries—postal service, telephone, utilities, transportation, health care, banking, and some manufacturing—but individuals own most businesses. For example, in France the postal service industry La Posta is fully owned by the French government and makes a profit. Central planning determines what basic goods and services are produced, how they are produced, and how they are distributed. Individuals and small businesses provide other goods and services based on consumer demand and the availability of resources. Citizens are dependent on the government for many goods and services.

Most socialist nations, such as Sweden, India, and Israel, are democratic and recognize basic individual freedoms. Citizens can vote for political offices, but central government planners usually make decisions about what is best for the nation. People are free to go into the occupation of their choice, but they often work in government-operated organizations. Socialists believe their system permits a higher standard of living than other economic systems, but the difference often applies to the nation as a whole rather than to its individual citizens. Socialist economies profess egalitarianism—equal distribution of income and social services. They believe their economies are more stable than those of other nations. Although this may be true, taxes and unemployment are generally higher in socialist countries. Perhaps as a result, many socialist countries have also experienced economic difficulties.

Capitalism

Capitalism, or free enterprise, is an economic system in which individuals own and operate the majority of businesses that provide goods and services. Competition, supply, and demand determine which goods and services are produced, how they are produced, and how they are distributed. The United States, Canada, Japan, and Australia are examples of economic systems based on capitalism.

There are two forms of capitalism: pure capitalism and modified capitalism. In pure capitalism, also called a **free-market system,** all economic decisions are made without government intervention. This economic system was first described by Adam Smith in *The Wealth of Nations* (1776). Smith, often called the father of capitalism, believed that the "invisible hand of competition" best regulates the economy. He argued that competition should determine what goods and services people need. Smith's system is also called *laissez-faire* ("let it be") *capitalism* because the government does not interfere in business.

Modified capitalism differs from pure capitalism in that the government intervenes and regulates business to some extent. One of the ways in which the United States and Canadian governments regulate business is through laws. Laws such as the Federal Trade Commission Act, which created the Federal Trade Commission to enforce antitrust laws, illustrate the importance of the government's role in the economy. In the most recent recession, the government provided loans and took ownership positions in banks such as Citigroup, AIG (an insurance company), and General Motors. These actions were thought necessary to keep these firms from going out of business and creating a financial disaster for the economy.

Mixed Economies

No country practices a pure form of communism, socialism, or capitalism, although most tend to favor one system over the others. Most nations operate as **mixed economies,** which have elements from more than one economic system. In socialist Sweden, most businesses are owned and operated by private individuals. In capitalist United States, an independent federal agency operates the postal service and another independent agency operates the Tennessee Valley Authority, an electric utility. In Great Britain and Mexico, the governments are attempting to sell many state-run businesses to private individuals and companies. In Germany, the Deutsche Post is privatized and trades on the stock market. In once-communist Russia, Hungary, Poland, and other Eastern European nations, capitalist ideas have been implemented, including private ownership of businesses. Communist China allows citizens to invest in stocks and permits some private and foreign ownership of businesses.

demand the number of goods and services that consumers are willing to buy at different prices at a specific time

supply the number of products—goods and services—that businesses are willing to sell at different prices at a specific time

The Free-Enterprise System

Many economies—including those of the United States, Canada, and Japan—are based on free enterprise, and many communist and socialist countries, such as China and Russia, are applying more principles of free enterprise

3. Individuals and businesses must have the right to make decisions that determine the way the business operates. Although there is government regulation, the philosophy in countries like the United States and Australia is to permit maximum freedom within a set of rules of fairness.

4. Individuals must have the right to choose what career to pursue, where to live, what goods and services to purchase, and more. Businesses must have the right to choose where to locate, what goods and services to produce, what resources to use in the production process, and so on.

> "Demand is the number of goods and services that consumers are willing to buy at different prices at a specific time."

to their own economic systems. Free enterprise provides an opportunity for a business to succeed or fail on the basis of market demand. In a free-enterprise system, companies that can efficiently manufacture and sell products that consumers desire will probably succeed. Inefficient businesses and those that sell products that do not offer needed benefits will likely fail as consumers take their business to firms that have more competitive products.

A number of basic individual and business rights must exist for free enterprise to work. These rights are the goals of many countries that have recently embraced free enterprise.

1. Individuals must have the right to own property and to pass this property on to their heirs. This right motivates people to work hard and save to buy property.

2. Individuals and businesses must have the right to earn profits and to use the profits as they wish, within the constraints of their society's laws, principles, and values.

Without these rights, businesses cannot function effectively because they are not motivated to succeed. Thus, these rights make possible the open exchange of goods and services. In the countries that favor free enterprise, such as the United States, citizens have the freedom to make many decisions about the employment they choose and create their own productivity systems. Many entrepreneurs are more productive in free-enterprise societies because personal and financial incentives are available that can aid in entrepreneurial success. For many entrepreneurs, their work becomes a part of their system of goals, values, and lifestyle. Consider Barbara Corcoran, who built one of New York's largest real estate companies. She is now a panelist on an ABC program, *Shark Tank*, which gives entrepreneurs a chance to receive funding to realize their dreams.

The Forces of Supply and Demand

In the United States and in other free-enterprise systems, the distribution of resources and products is determined by supply and demand. **Demand** is the number of goods and services that consumers are willing to buy at different prices at a specific time. From your own experience, you probably recognize that consumers are usually willing to buy more of an item as its price falls because they want to save money. Consider handmade rugs, for example. Consumers may be willing to buy six rugs at $350 each, four at $500 each, but only two at $650 each. The relationship between the price and the number of rugs consumers are willing to buy can be shown graphically, with a *demand curve* (see Figure 1.2).

Supply is the number of products that businesses are willing to sell at different prices at a specific time. In general, because the potential for profits is higher, businesses are willing to supply more of a good or service at higher prices. For

▼**FIGURE 1.2**
Equilibrium Price of Handmade Rugs

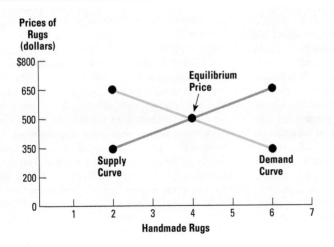

equilibrium price the price at which the number of products that businesses are willing to supply equals the amount of products that consumers are willing to buy at a specific point in time

competition the rivalry among businesses for consumers' dollars

pure competition the market structure that exists when there are many small businesses selling one standardized product

monopolistic competition the market structure that exists when there are fewer businesses than in a pure-competition environment and the differences among the goods they sell are small

oligopoly the market structure that exists when there are very few businesses selling a product

example, a company that sells rugs may be willing to sell six at $650 each, four at $500 each, but just two at $350 each. The relationship between the price of rugs and the quantity the company is willing to supply can be shown graphically with a *supply curve* (see Figure 1.2).

In Figure 1.2, the supply and demand curves intersect at the point where supply and demand are equal. The price at which the number of products that businesses are willing to supply equals the amount of products that consumers are willing to buy at a specific point in time is the **equilibrium price**. In our rug example, the company is willing to supply four rugs at $500 each, and consumers are willing to buy four rugs at $500 each. Therefore, $500 is the equilibrium price for a rug at that point in time, and most rug companies will price their rugs at $500. As you might imagine, a business that charges more than $500 (or whatever the current equilibrium price is) for its rugs will not sell many and might not earn a profit. On the other hand, a business that charges less than $500 accepts a lower profit per rug than could be made at the equilibrium price.

If the cost of making rugs goes up, businesses will not offer as many at the old price. Changing the price alters the supply curve, and a new equilibrium price results. This is an ongoing process, with supply and demand constantly changing in response to changes in economic conditions, availability of resources, and degree of competition. For example, the price of oil can change rapidly and has been between $35 and $145 a barrel over the last five years. Prices for goods and services vary according to these changes in supply and demand. This concept is the force that drives the distribution of resources (goods and services, labor, and money) in a free-enterprise economy.

Critics of supply and demand say the system does not distribute resources equally. The forces of supply and demand prevent sellers who have to sell at higher prices (because their costs are high) and buyers who cannot afford to buy goods at the equilibrium price from participating in the market. According to critics, the wealthy can afford to buy more than they need, but the poor may be unable to buy enough of what they need to survive.

The Nature of Competition

Competition, the rivalry among businesses for consumers' dollars, is another vital element in free enterprise. According to Adam Smith, competition fosters efficiency and low prices by forcing producers to offer the best products at the most reasonable price; those who fail to do so are not able to stay in business. Thus, competition should improve the quality of the goods and services available or reduce prices. For example, thanks to smart design and excellent timing, Apple dominates the market for downloadable music with its iTunes online service, iPod MP3 player, and iPhone. However, many companies have set their sights on capturing some of the firm's market share with new products of their own. Therefore, Apple must constantly seek to remain competitive by creating new innovations to maintain its market share—and sometimes capture market share from other companies. Its iPad 2 device, released in 2011, combines the smartphone and the laptop into one product. The iPad also contains an interface that allows users to read books as well as take pictures, which will capture some of the e-reader market dominated by Amazon's Kindle.[14]

Within a free-enterprise system, there are four types of competitive environments: pure competition, monopolistic competition, oligopoly, and monopoly.

Pure competition exists when there are many small businesses selling one standardized product, such as agricultural commodities like wheat, corn, and cotton. No one business sells enough of the product to influence the product's price. And, because there is no difference in the products, prices are determined solely by the forces of supply and demand.

Monopolistic competition exists when there are fewer businesses than in a pure-competition environment and the differences among the goods they sell is small. Aspirin, soft drinks, and vacuum cleaners are examples of such goods. These products differ slightly in packaging, warranty, name, and other characteristics, but all satisfy the same consumer need. Businesses have some power over the price they charge in monopolistic competition because they can make consumers aware of product differences through advertising. Dyson, for example, attempts to differentiate its vacuum cleaners through product design, quality, and advertising. Consumers value some features more than others and are often willing to pay higher prices for a product with the features they want. For example, Advil, a nonprescription pain reliever, contains ibuprofen instead of aspirin. Consumers who cannot take aspirin or who believe ibuprofen is a more effective pain reliever may not mind paying a little extra for the ibuprofen in Advil.

An **oligopoly** exists when there are very few businesses selling a product. In an oligopoly, individual businesses have control over

> Competition, the rivalry among businesses for consumers' dollars, is another vital element in free enterprise.

monopoly the market structure that exists when there is only one business providing a product in a given market

economic expansion the situation that occurs when an economy is growing and people are spending more money; their purchases stimulate the production of goods and services, which in turn stimulates employment

inflation a condition characterized by a continuing rise in prices

their products' price because each business supplies a large portion of the products sold in the marketplace. Nonetheless, the prices charged by different firms stay fairly close because a price cut or increase by one company will trigger a similar response from another company. In the airline industry, for example, when one airline cuts fares to boost sales, other airlines quickly follow with rate decreases to remain competitive. Oligopolies exist when it is expensive for new firms to enter the marketplace. Not just anyone can acquire enough financial capital to build an automobile production facility or purchase enough airplanes and related resources to build an airline.

When there is one business providing a product in a given market, a **monopoly** exists. Utility companies that supply electricity, natural gas, and water are monopolies. The government permits such monopolies because the cost of creating the good or supplying the service is so great that new producers cannot compete for sales. Government-granted monopolies are subject to government-regulated prices. Some monopolies exist because of technological developments that are protected by patent laws. Patent laws grant the developer of new technology a period of time (usually 20 years) during which no other producer can use the same technology without the

agreement of the original developer. The United States granted its first patent in 1790. Now its patent office receives hundreds of thousands of patent applications a year, although it is estimated that China will soon overtake the United States in patent filings.[15] This monopoly allows the developer to recover research, development, and production expenses and to earn a reasonable profit. An example of this type of monopoly is the dry-copier process developed by Xerox. Xerox's patents have expired, however, and many imitators have forced market prices to decline.

Economic Cycles and Productivity

Expansion and Contraction Economies are not stagnant; they expand and contract. **Economic expansion** occurs when an economy is growing and people are spending more money. Their purchases stimulate the production of goods and services, which in turn stimulates employment. The standard of living rises because more people are employed and have money to spend. Rapid expansions of the economy, however, may result in **inflation**, a continuing rise in prices. Inflation can be harmful if individuals' incomes do not increase at the same pace as rising prices, reducing their buying power. Zimbabwe suffered from hyperinflation so severe that its inflation rate rose into the hundreds of millions. With the elimination of the Zimbabwean dollar and certain price controls, the inflation rate began to decrease, but not before the country's economy was virtually decimated.[16]

Economic contraction occurs when spending declines. Businesses cut back on production and lay off workers, and the economy as a whole slows down. Contractions of the economy

PATAGONIA SHINES DURING RECESSION

Patagonia founder and owner Yvon Chouinard proves that ethical business practices and product quality can lead to profitability, even during periods of economic contraction. In fact, during the latest recession, Patagonia had its best two years ever. What was Patagonia's secret to success? Dedicated employees, loyal customers, and products built to last. Patagonia's values are minimalistic and reflect those of a business founded by climbers and surfers.

Based upon these values, Patagonia's goal is to create durable outdoor gear and clothing. Since it specializes in environmental gear, the company is dedicated to environmentally friendly practices. Its

adoption of organic cotton and its recycling efforts are a few of the reasons consumers are fiercely loyal. Since the inception of its "cradle to cradle" Common Threads recycling program, most of its products, when they do reach the ends of their life spans, may be returned to Patagonia and made into new products. These efforts help drive environmentally concerned consumers to pay more for its products. Consumers, who often opt for long-lasting products during periods of economic contraction, began purchasing from Patagonia to get the most out of their money.

Patagonia is also debt free and creates quality relationships with stakeholders. To maintain its debt-free status, Chouinard carefully monitors Patagonia's growth. This allows him to assist suppliers in tough times and to keep business running smoothly. It also gives Patagonia

freedom to retain its strong values. Patagonia treats its employees with respect and promotes a strong balance between work and personal life. The company provides flex time, on-site child care, paid maternity/paternity leave, and paid leave for volunteering. Patagonia's success epitomizes what can happen when high ethical standards and sound business strategies are implemented.[17]

Discussion Questions

1. Why has Patagonia been successful during the latest recession?

2. Describe why consumers tend to be more loyal to "green," environmentally friendly companies?

3. How do Patagonia's employee policies improve its bottom-line success?

lead to **recession**—a decline in production, employment, and income. Recessions are often characterized by rising levels of **unemployment**, which is measured as the percentage of the population that wants to work but is unable to find jobs. Figure 1.3 shows the overall unemployment rate in the civilian labor force over the past 80 years. Rising unemployment levels tend to stifle demand for goods and services, which can have the effect of forcing prices downward, a condition known as *deflation*. The United States has experienced numerous recessions, the most recent ones occurring in 1990–1991, 2002–2003, and 2008–2011. The most recent recession (or economic slowdown) was caused by the collapse in housing prices and consumers' inability

economic contraction a slowdown of the economy characterized by a decline in spending and during which businesses cut back on production and lay off workers

recession a decline in production, employment, and income

unemployment the condition in which a percentage of the population wants to work but is unable to find jobs

to stay current on their mortgage and credit card payments. This caused a crisis in the banking industry, with the government bailing out banks to keep them from failing. This in turn caused a slowdown in spending on consumer goods and a reduction in employment. Unemployment reached 10 percent of the labor force. Don't forget that personal consumption makes up almost 70 percent of gross domestic

▼**FIGURE 1.3**
Annual Average Unemployment Rate, Civilian Labor Force 16 Years and Over

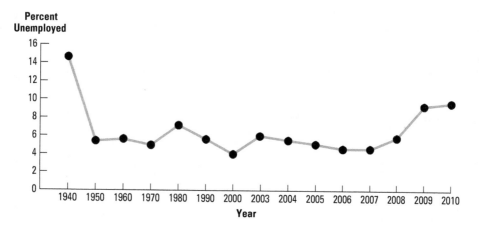

Sources: "Employment status of the civilian noninstitutional population, 1940 to date," Bureau of Labor Statistics, www.bls.gov/cps/cpsaat1.pdf (accessed February 11, 2010); "Where can I find the unemployment rate for previous years?," Bureau of Labor Statistics, www.bls.gov/cps/prev_yrs.htm (accessed February 11, 2011).

You can see what the U.S. government currently owes—down to the penny—by going to the website for the Bureau of the Public Debt, www.publicdebt.treas.gov/.

depression a condition of the economy in which unemployment is very high, consumer spending is low, and business output is sharply reduced

gross domestic product (GDP) the sum of all goods and services produced in a country during a year

budget deficit the condition in which a nation spends more than it takes in from taxes

product, so consumer behavior is extremely important for economic activity. A severe recession may turn into a **depression**, in which unemployment is very high, consumer spending is low, and business output is sharply reduced, such as what occurred in the United States in the early 1930s. The most recent recession is often called the Great Recession because it was the longest and most severe economic decline since the Great Depression.

Economies expand and contract in response to changes in consumer, business, and government spending. War also can affect an economy, sometimes stimulating it (as in the United States during World Wars I and II) and sometimes stifling it (as during the Vietnam, Persian Gulf, and Iraq wars). Although fluctuations in the economy are inevitable and to a certain extent predictable, their effects—inflation and unemployment—disrupt lives and thus governments try to minimize them.

Measuring the Economy Countries measure the state of their economies to determine whether they are expanding or contracting and whether corrective action is necessary to minimize the fluctuations. One commonly used measure is **gross domestic product (GDP)**—the sum of all goods and services produced in a country during a year. GDP measures only those goods and services made within a country and therefore does not include profits from companies' overseas operations;

it does include profits earned by foreign companies within the country being measured. However, it does not take into account the concept of GDP in relation to population (GDP per capita). Figure 1.4 shows the increase in GDP over several years, while Table 1.2 compares a number of economic statistics for a sampling of countries.

Another important indicator of a nation's economic health is the relationship between its spending and income (from taxes). When a nation spends more than it takes in from taxes, it has a **budget deficit**. In the 1990s, the U.S. government eliminated its long-standing budget deficit by balancing the money spent for social, defense, and other programs with the amount of money taken in from taxes.

In recent years, however, the budget deficit has reemerged and grown to record levels, partly due to defense spending in the aftermath of the terrorist attacks of September 11, 2001. Massive government stimulus spending during the most recent recession also increased the national debt. Because Americans do not want their taxes increased, it is difficult for the federal government to bring in more revenue and reduce the deficit. Like consumers and businesses, when the government needs money, it borrows from the public, banks, and other institutions. The national debt (the amount of money the nation owes its lenders) exceeded $13.5 trillion in 2010 due largely to increased spending by the government and an economic stimulus package to help stave off the worst effects of the Great Recession.[18] This figure is especially worrisome because, to reduce the debt to a manageable level, the government either has to increase its revenues (raise taxes) or reduce spending on social, defense, and legal programs, neither of which is politically popular. The national debt figure changes daily and can be seen at the

▼**FIGURE 1.4**
Growth in U.S. Gross Domestic Product

Sources: "Table D1. Population, U.S. Gross Domestic Product, and Implicit Price Deflator, 1949–2008," EIA, www.eia.doe.gov/aer/txt/ptb1601.html (accessed February 3, 2010); "Spending As Percent of GDP," usgovernmentspending.com, www.usgovernmentspending.com/downchart gs.php?year=1900_2010&units=p&title=Spending%20as%20percent%20of%20GDP (accessed January 4, 2011).

Department of the Treasury, Bureau of the Public Debt, website. Table 1.3 describes some of the other ways we evaluate our nation's economy.

▼ **TABLE 1.2** A Comparative Analysis of a Sampling of Countries

Country	Population (in millions)	GDP (Purchasing Power Parity)	Unemployment Rate (%)	Inflation (% change)
Argentina	41.343	596	8.0	11.00
Australia	21.515	889.6	5.192	2.90
Brazil	201.1	2,194	7.200	4.90
Canada	33.8	1,335	7.991	1.60
China	1,330	9,854	4.100	5.00
France	64.768	2,160	1.640	1.50
Germany	82.282	2,951	7.053	1.00
India	1,173	4,046	9.4	11.70
Israel	7.353	217.1	7.400	2.60
Japan	126.8	4,338	5.145	−0.90
Mexico	112.5	1,560	5.000	4.10
Russia	139.4	2,229	7.500	6.70
South Africa	49.1	527.5	24.800	4.50
United Kingdom	62.348	2,189	7.876	3.30
United States	310.2	14,720	9.730	1.40

Sources: International Monetary Fund, www.imf.org/external/pubs/ft/weo/2010/02/weodata/index.aspx (accessed January 3, 2011); "Unemployment around 10 per cent, very thin social safety net," AsiaNews. it, November 15, 2010, www.asianews.it/news-en/Unemployment-around-10-per-cent,-very-thin-social-safety-net-19993.html (accessed January 3, 2011); The CIA, *The World Fact Book*, https://www.cia.gov/library/publications/the-world-factbook/rankorder/rankorderguide.html (accessed January 28, 2011).

▼ **TABLE 1.3** How Do We Evaluate Our Nation's Economy?

Unit of Measure	Description
Trade balance	The difference between our exports and our imports. If the balance is negative, as it has been since the mid-1980s, it is called a trade deficit and is generally viewed as unhealthy for our economy.
Consumer Price Index	Measures changes in prices of goods and services purchased for consumption by typical urban households.
Per capita income	Indicates the income level of "average" Americans. Useful in determing how much "average" consumers spend and how much money Americans are earning.
Unemployment rate	Indicates how many working age Americans are not working who otherwise want to work.*
Inflation	Monitors price increases in consumer goods and services over specified periods of time. Used to determine if costs of goods and services are exceeding worker compensation over time.
Worker productivity	The amount of goods and services produced for each hour worked.

*Americans who do not work in a traditional sense, such as househusbands/housewives, are not counted as unemployed.

THE AMERICAN ECONOMY

As we said previously, the United States is a mixed economy based on capitalism. The answers to the three basic economic issues are determined primarily by competition and the forces of supply and demand, although the federal government does intervene in economic decisions to a certain extent. To understand the current state of the American economy and its effect on business practices, it is helpful to examine its history and the roles of the entrepreneur and the government.

A Brief History of the American Economy

The Early Economy Before the colonization of North America, Native Americans lived as hunter/gatherers and farmers, with some trade among tribes. The colonists who came later operated primarily as an *agricultural economy*. People were self-sufficient and produced everything they needed at home, including food, clothing, and furniture. Abundant natural resources and a moderate climate nourished industries such as farming, fishing, shipping, and fur trading. A few manufactured goods and money for the colonies' burgeoning industries came from England and other countries.

As the nation expanded slowly toward the West, people found natural resources such as coal, copper, and iron ore and used them to produce goods such as horseshoes, farm implements, and kitchen utensils. Farm families who produced surplus goods sold or traded them for things they could not produce themselves, such as fine furniture and window glass. Some families also spent time turning raw materials into clothes and household goods. Because these goods were produced at home, this system was called the domestic system.

The Industrial Revolution The 19th century and the Industrial Revolution brought the development of new technology and factories. The factory brought together all the resources needed to make a product—materials, machines, and workers. Work in factories became specialized as workers focused on one or two tasks. As work became more efficient,

FOOD TRUCKS GIVE RESTAURANTS A RUN FOR THEIR MONEY

Mobile food trucks are using entrepreneurship adapted to our fast-paced and Internet-based economy to challenge the dominancy of local cuisine. Long known for their prepackaged sandwiches and snacks, many food truck businesses are adapting to consumer demand by offering gourmet food at affordable prices. These mobile entrepreneurs are also masters of digital media, using sites such as Facebook and Twitter to alert their fans of their ever-changing locations and menu selections. The food truck has become so popular that The Food Network launched *"The Great Food Truck Race,"* a reality television show in which mobile food operators drive cross-country to see who can sell the most food.

This is not to say that the life of a food truck entrepreneur is easy. Government regulations require food truck operators to obtain a number of permits, and restaurants sometimes resort to lobbying to keep food trucks away from their areas. Still, by offering consumers new, affordable options for dining out, mobile food trucks are becoming a formidable competitor for brick-and-mortar restaurants.[19]

productivity increased, making more goods available at lower prices. Railroads brought major changes, allowing farmers to send their surplus crops and goods all over the nation for barter or for sale.

Factories began to spring up along the railways to manufacture farm equipment and a variety of other goods to be shipped by rail. Samuel Slater set up the first American textile factory after he memorized the plans for an English factory and emigrated to the United States. Eli Whitney revolutionized the cotton industry with his cotton gin. Francis Cabot Lowell's factory organized all the steps in manufacturing cotton cloth for maximum efficiency and productivity. John Deere's farm equipment increased farm production and reduced the number of farmers required to feed the young nation. Farmers began to move to cities to find jobs in factories and a higher standard of living. Henry Ford developed the assembly-line system to produce automobiles. Workers focused on one part of an automobile and then pushed it to the next stage until it rolled off the assembly line as a finished automobile. Ford's assembly line could manufacture many automobiles efficiently, and the price of his cars was $200, making them affordable to many Americans.

The Manufacturing and Marketing Economies

Industrialization brought increased prosperity, and the United States gradually became a *manufacturing economy*—one devoted to manufacturing goods and providing services rather than producing agricultural products. The assembly line was applied to more industries, increasing the variety of goods available to the consumer. Businesses became more concerned with the needs of the consumer and entered the *marketing economy*. Expensive goods such as cars and appliances could be purchased on a time-payment plan. Companies conducted research to find out what products consumers needed and wanted. Advertising made consumers aware of differences in products and prices.

Because these developments occurred in a free-enterprise system, consumers determined what goods and services were

DID YOU KNOW?

Approximately 60 percent of adult women work.[21]

produced. They did this by purchasing the products they liked at prices they were willing to pay. The United States prospered, and American citizens had one of the highest standards of living in the world.

The Service and New Digital Economy

After World War II, with the increased standard of living, Americans had more money and more time. They began to pay others to perform services that made their lives easier. Beginning in the 1960s, more and more women entered the workforce. The United States began experiencing major shifts in populations. The U.S. population grew 9.7 percent in the past decade to almost 309 billion. This is the slowest pace of growth since the Great Depression, with the South leading the population gains. While the birth rate in the United States is declining, new immigrants help with population gains. The United States is growing at about the same rate as Mexico and Brazil.[20] The profile of the family also began to change: Today there are more single-parent families and individuals living alone, and in two-parent families, both parents often work.

One result of this trend is that time-pressed Americans are increasingly paying others to do tasks they used to do at home, like cooking, laundry, landscaping, and child care. These trends have gradually changed the United States to a *service economy*—one devoted to the production of services that make life easier for busy consumers. Service industries such as restaurants, banking, health care, child care, auto repair, leisure-related industries, and even education are growing rapidly and may account for as much as 80 percent of the U.S. economy. These trends continue with advanced technology contributing to new service products based on Internet-based e-business and digital media that provide smartphones, social networking, and a virtual world. Table 1.4 provides evidence that the new digital economy is changing how we use information and the service industry. More about the Internet, business, and new online social media can be found in Chapter 13.

The Role of the Entrepreneur

An **entrepreneur** is an individual who risks his or her wealth, time, and effort to develop for profit an innovative product or way of doing something. Wolfgang Puck, although an Austrian by birth, is a true American entreprenuer. He moved to Los Angeles to be a chef and opened Spago, an Italian-style trattoria that served good food that attracted movie stars. When people found his pizza so good that they took home extras to place in their freezers, he decided to build his frozen pizza into a multi-million-dollar business. Today, he has over 20 restaurants and Wolfgang Express bistros in 80 locations.[22]

The free-enterprise system provides the conditions necessary for entrepreneurs to succeed. In the past, entrepreneurs were often inventors who brought all the factors of production together to produce a new product. Thomas Edison, whose inventions include the record player and lightbulb, was an early American entrepreneur. Henry Ford was one of the first persons to develop mass assembly methods in the automobile industry. Other entrepreneurs, so-called captains of industry, invested in the country's growth. John D. Rockefeller built Standard Oil out of the fledgling oil industry, and Andrew Carnegie invested in railroads and founded the United States Steel Corporation. Andrew Mellon built the Aluminum Company of America and Gulf Oil. J. P. Morgan started financial institutions to fund the business activities of other entrepreneurs. Although these entrepreneurs were born in another century, their legacy to the American economy lives on in the companies they started, many of which still operate today. Milton Hershey began producing chocolate in 1894 in Lancaster, Pennsylvania. In 1900, the company was mass producing chocolate in many forms, lowering the cost of chocolate and making it more affordable to the masses, where it had once been a high-priced, luxury good. Early advertising touted chocolate as "a palatable confection and most nourishing food." Today, the Hershey Company employs more than 13,000 employees and sells almost $5 billion in chocolates and candies annually throughout the world.[23]

Entrepreneurs are constantly changing American business practices with new technology and innovative management techniques. Bill Gates, for example, built Microsoft, a software company whose products include Word and Windows, into a multibillion-dollar enterprise. Frederick Smith had an idea to deliver packages overnight, and now his FedEx Company plays an important role in getting documents and packages delivered all over the world for businesses and individuals. Entrepreneurs have been associated with such uniquely American concepts as Dell Computers, Ben & Jerry's, Levi's, Holiday Inns, McDonald's, Dr Pepper, Apple, Google, and Walmart. Walmart, founded by entreprenuer Sam Walton, was the first retailer to reach $100 billion in sales in one year and now routinely passes

that mark, with more than $408 billion in 2010. Sam Walton's heirs own about 40 percent of the company.[24] We will examine the importance of entrepreneurship further in Chapter 5.

> **entrepreneur** an individual who risks his or her wealth, time, and effort to develop for profit an innovative product or way of doing something

The Role of Government in the American Economy

The American economic system is best described as modified capitalism because the government regulates business to preserve competition and protect consumers and employees. Federal, state, and local governments intervene in the economy with laws and regulations designed to promote competition and to protect consumers, employees, and the environment. Many of these laws are discussed in the Chapter 2 Appendix.

Additionally, government agencies such as the U.S. Department of Commerce measure the health of the economy (GDP, productivity, etc.) and, when necessary, take steps to minimize the disruptive effects of economic fluctuations and reduce unemployment. When the economy is contracting and unemployment is rising, the federal government through the Federal Reserve Board (see Chapter 14) tries to spur growth so that consumers will spend more money and businesses will hire more employees. To accomplish this, it may reduce interest rates or increase its own spending for goods and services. When the economy expands so fast that inflation results, the government may intervene to reduce inflation by slowing down economic growth. This can be accomplished by raising interest rates to discourage spending by businesses and consumers. Techniques used to control the economy are discussed in Chapter 14.

The Role of Ethics and Social Responsibility in Business

In the past few years, you may have read about a number of scandals at a number of well-known corporations, including Enron, Tyco, Arthur Andersen, BP, Bear Stearns, AIG, and

▼ **TABLE 1.4** Volume of Traffic on the Internet

Application	Traffic Share
Data	28.1%
Online Video	26.2%
P2P File Sharing	24.9%
Other File Sharing	18.7%
Voice and Video Communications	1.7%
PC Gaming	0.7%
E-mail and Instant Messaging	0.3%
Gaming Console	0.2%

Source: Cisco, reproduced in *Bloomberg Businessweek Year in Review,* 2010, p. 24.

BUSINESS ETHICS GENERALLY REFERS TO THE STANDARDS AND PRINCIPLES USED BY SOCIETY TO DEFINE APPROPRIATE AND INAPPROPRIATE CONDUCT IN THE WORKPLACE.

Lehman Brothers. In many cases, misconduct by individuals within these firms had an adverse effect on current and retired employees, investors, and others associated with these firms. In some cases, individuals went to jail for their actions. Top executives like Enron's Jeffrey Skilling and Tyco's Dennis Kozlowski received long prison sentences for their roles in corporate misconduct. These scandals undermined public confidence in corporate America and sparked a new debate about ethics in business. Business ethics generally refers to the standards and principles used by society to define appropriate and inappropriate conduct in the workplace. In many cases, these standards have been codified as laws prohibiting actions deemed unacceptable.

Society is increasingly demanding that businesspeople behave ethically and responsibly toward not only their customers but also their employees, investors, government regulators, communities, and the natural environment. "Intel helped establish a goal for PFCs (perfluorocompounds) that the entire industry could support," stated Intel President and CEO Paul Otellini. "It came together before Kyoto and was the first worldwide, industry-wide goal to address climate change. We view our environmental strategies as integral to the way we do business. We strive to lead by example, and to be trusted stakeholders to governments worldwide."[25] Green business strategies create long-run relationships with all stakeholders by maintaining, supporting, and enhancing the natural environment.

▼**FIGURE 1.5**
The Organization of This Book

Economy
(Chapter 1)

Finance
(Chapters 14, 15, 16)

Owners

Competition
(Chapter 1)

(Chapters 7, 8, 9, 10, 11, 12)
Management

Employees

Customers

(Chapters 11, 12, 13)
Marketing

Information
Technology

Legal, Political, and
Regulatory Forces
(Chapter 2 Appendix)

Business Ethics and
Social
Responsibility
(Chapter 2)

Special Topics:
Global Business (Chapter 3)
Forms of Ownership (Chapter 4)
Small Business, Entrepreneurship, and Franchising (Chapter 5)

One of the primary lessons of the scandals of the past decade has been that the reputation of business organizations depends not just on bottom-line profits but also on ethical conduct and concern for the welfare of others. Consider that in the aftermath of these scandals, the reputations of every U.S. company suffered regardless of their association with the scandals. However, there are signs that business ethics is improving. One respected survey reported that well-implemented formal ethics and compliance programs dramatically increase reporting of observed misconduct and also help decrease the rate of misconduct.[26] Although these results suggest that ethics is improving, the fact that employees continue to report observing misconduct and experiencing pressure to engage in unethical or illegal acts remains troubling and suggests that companies need to continue their efforts to raise ethical standards. In fact, beginning in 2007 and 2008, ethical questions surfaced about lending practices in the mortgage industry. Mortgage lenders had been making adjustable rate mortgage loans in previous years to people who were not necessarily good credit risks. The brokers

SO YOU WANT A JOB // in the Business World /

When most people think of a career in business, they see themselves entering the door to large companies and multinationals that they read about in the news and that are discussed in class. In a national survey, students indicated they would like to work for Google, Walt Disney, Apple, and Ernst & Young. In fact, most jobs are not with large corporations, but are in small companies, nonprofit organizations, the government, and even self-employed individuals. There are 20 million individuals who the Small Business Administration says own their businesses and have no employees. In addition, there are nearly 5 million small businesses that employ 10 or fewer workers. With more than 75 percent of the economy based on services, there are jobs available in industries such as health care, finance, education, hospitality, entertainment, and transportation. The world is changing quickly and large corporations replace the equivalent of their entire workforce every four years.

The fast pace of technology today means that you have to be prepared to take advantage of emerging job opportunities and markets. You must also become adaptive and recognize that business is becoming more global, with job opportunities around the world. If you want to obtain such a job, you shouldn't miss a chance to spend some time overseas. As you get started on the path to thinking about job opportunities, consider all of the changes in business today that might affect your possible long-term track and that could bring you lots of success. You may want to stay completely out of large organizations and corporations and put yourself in a position for an entrepreneurial role as a self-employed contractor or small-business owner. However, there are many who feel that experience in larger businesses is helpful to your success later as an entrepreneur.

You're on the road to learning the key knowledge, skills, and trends that you can use to be a star in business. Businesses' impact on our society, especially in the area of sustainability and improvement of the environment, is a growing challenge and opportunity. Green businesses and green jobs in the business world are provided in this book to give you a glimpse at the possibilities. Along the way, we will introduce you to some specific careers and offer advice on developing your own job opportunities. Research indicates that you won't be that happy with your job unless you enjoy your work and feel that it has a purpose. Since you spend most of your waking hours every day at work, you need to seriously think about what is important to you in a job.[27]

earned fees for making the loans, and the fees were not contingent on the ability of the borrower to pay. It was later revealed that some mortgage lenders even knew that the borrowers were inflating their income to secure loans they could not afford. As interest rates rose and the monthly cost of the mortgage was adjusted upward, many borrowers were unable to make their monthly payments and so ended up defaulting on their loans and losing their homes. Many faulted the lenders for a lack of ethical behavior. The burst of this housing bubble helped contribute significantly to what many now refer to as the "Great Recession." We take a closer look at ethics and social responsibility in business in Chapter 2.

CAN YOU LEARN BUSINESS IN A CLASSROOM?

Obviously, the answer is yes, or there would be no purpose for this textbook! To be successful in business, you need knowledge, skills, experience, and good judgment. The topics covered in this chapter and throughout this book provide some of the knowledge you need

TEAM EXERCISE

Major economic systems including capitalism, socialism, and communism, as well as mixed economies, were discussed in this chapter. Assuming that you want an economic system that is best for the majority, not just a few members of society, defend one of the economic systems as the best system. Form groups and try to reach agreement on one economic system. Defend why you support the system that you advance.

to understand the world of business. The boxes and examples within each chapter describe experiences to help you develop good business judgment. The Team Exercise at the end of each chapter will help you develop skills that may be useful in your future career. However, good judgment is based on knowledge and experience plus personal insight and understanding. Therefore, you need more courses in business, along with some practical experience in the business world, to help you develop the special insight necessary to put your personal stamp on knowledge as you apply it. The challenge in business is in the area of judgment, and judgment does not develop from memorizing an introductory business textbook. If you are observant in your daily experiences as an employee, as a student, and as a consumer, you will improve your ability to make good business judgments.

Figure 1.5 is an overview of how the chapters in this book are linked together and how the chapters relate to the participants, the activities, and the environmental factors found in the business world. The topics presented in the chapters that follow are those that will give you the best opportunity to begin the process of understanding the world of business. ■

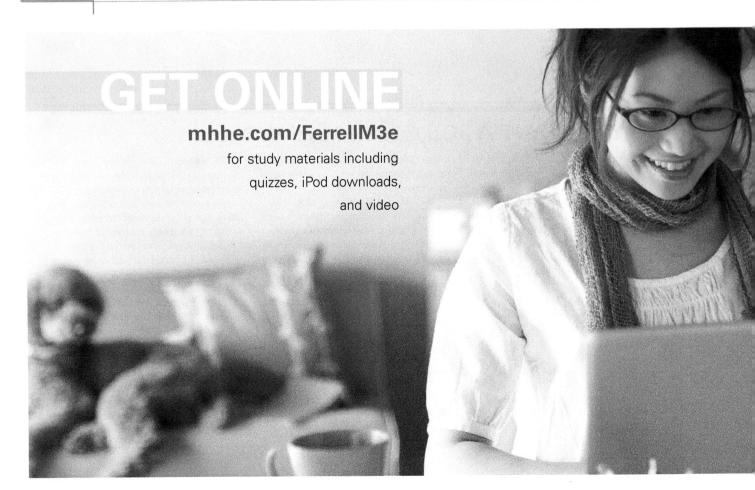

GET ONLINE

mhhe.com/FerrellM3e

for study materials including
quizzes, iPod downloads,
and video

chapter one

in a
nutshell

Goals, activities, and participants make up the fundamentals of business. Understanding the basics of economics and applying them to the United States' economy will further your understanding of how business works and provide a framework for learning about business.

The following statements will test your take-away knowledge from this chapter. Do your best to explain each one in the space provided below.

LO.1 Define basic concepts such as business, product, and profit.

LO.2 Identify the main participants and activities of business and explain why studying business is important.

LO.3 Define economics and compare the four types of economic systems.

LO.4 Describe the role of supply, demand, and competition in a free-enterprise system.

LO.5 Specify why and how the health of the economy is measured.

LO.6 Trace the evolution of the American economy and discuss the role of the entrepreneur in the economy.

Did your answers include the following important points?

LO.1. Define basic concepts such as business, product, and profit.

- A business is an organization or individual that seeks a profit by providing products that satisfy people's needs.
- A product is a good, service, or idea that has both tangible and intangible characteristics that provide satisfaction and benefits.
- Profit, the basic goal of business, is the difference between what it costs to make and sell a product and what a customer pays for it.

LO.2. Identify the main participants and activities of business and explain why studying business is important.

- The three main participants in business are owners, employees, and customers, but others—government regulators, suppliers, social groups, etc.—are also important.
- Management involves planning, organizing, and controlling the tasks required to carry out the work of the company.
- Marketing refers to those activities—research, product development, promotion, pricing, and distribution—designed to provide goods and services that satisfy customers.
- Finance refers to activities concerned with funding a business and using its funds effectively, and studying business can help you prepare for a career and become a better consumer.

LO.3. Define economics and compare the four types of economic systems.

- Economics is the study of how resources are distributed for the production of goods and services within a social system, and an economic system describes how a particular society distributes its resources.
- Communism is an economic system in which the people, without regard to class, own all the nation's resources, while in a socialist system, the government owns and operates basic industries but individuals own most businesses.

- Under capitalism, individuals own and operate the majority of businesses that provide goods and services.
- Mixed economies have elements from more than one economic system; most countries have mixed economies.

LO.4. Describe the role of supply, demand, and competition in a free-enterprise system.

- Supply is the number of goods or services that businesses are willing to sell at different prices at a specific time.
- Demand is the number of goods and services that consumers are willing to buy at different prices at a specific time.
- Competition is the rivalry among businesses to persuade consumers to buy goods or services.

LO.5. Specify why and how the health of the economy is measured.

- A country measures the state of its economy to determine whether it is expanding or contracting and whether the country needs to take steps to minimize fluctuations.
- One commonly used measure is gross domestic product (GDP), the sum of all goods and services produced in a country during a year.
- A budget deficit occurs when a nation spends more than it takes in from taxes.

LO.6. Trace the evolution of the American economy and discuss the role of the entrepreneur in the economy.

- The American economy has evolved through the early economy, the Industrial Revolution, the manufacturing economy, the marketing economy, and the service- and Internet-based economy of today.
- Entrepreneurs play an important role because they risk their time, wealth, and efforts to develop new goods, services, and ideas that fuel the growth of the American economy.

Practical Application

LO.1.

- When purchasing a product, the consumer is actually buying its anticipated benefits and _____.
- If a business is to be successful in the long run, it must treat its customers, employees, and community with social

  _____.

- The goal of business is to earn _____.

LO.2.

- _____ involves activities designed to provide goods and services that fulfill needs and desires of consumers.
- When a business fails or does not make a profit, _____ have the most to lose.
- Advertising, personal selling, coupons, and sweepstakes are forms of _____ .

LO.3.

- Private property, profits, independent business decisions, and choice are rights associated with _____.
- In _____ consumers have a limited choice of goods and services and prices are usually high.
- Most countries operate as _____, which have elements from more than one economic system.

LO.4.

- In _____ there are many small businesses selling one standardized product.
- The market structure that exists when there are very few businesses selling a product is called a(n) _____.
- The quantity of products that businesses are willing to sell at different prices at specific times is called _____.

LO.5.

- During _____ there is a decline in production, employment, and income.
- _____ is the sum of all goods and services produced in a country during a year.
- A(n) _____ occurs when a nation spends more than it takes in from taxes.

LO.6.

- The Industrial Revolution changed the United States from an agricultural economy to a(n) _____ one.
- _____ industries account for almost 80 percent of the American economy today.
- A person who risks his or her wealth and time to develop an innovative product or idea for profit is called a(n)

  _____.

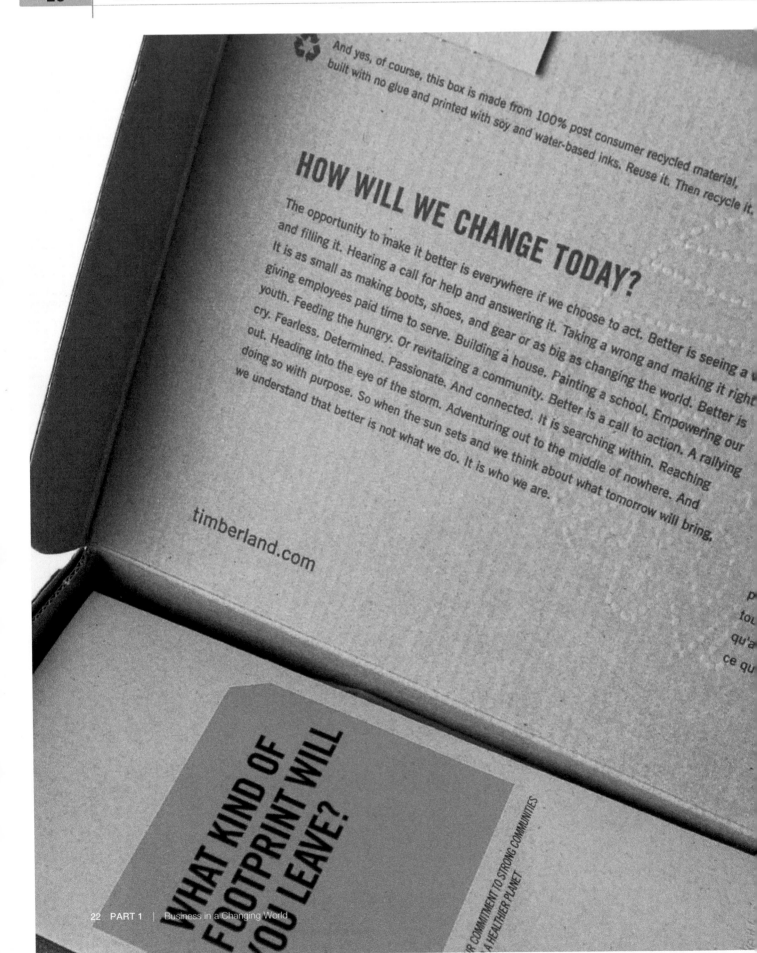

And yes, of course, this box is made from 100% post consumer recycled material, built with no glue and printed with soy and water-based inks. Reuse it. Then recycle it.

HOW WILL WE CHANGE TODAY?

The opportunity to make it better is everywhere if we choose to act. Better is seeing a w and filling it. Hearing a call for help and answering it. Taking a wrong and making it right It is as small as making boots, shoes, and gear or as big as changing the world. Better is giving employees paid time to serve. Building a house. Painting a school. Empowering our youth. Feeding the hungry. Or revitalizing a community. Better is a call to action. A rallying cry. Fearless. Determined. Passionate. And connected. It is searching within. Reaching out. Heading into the eye of the storm. Adventuring out to the middle of nowhere. And doing so with purpose. So when the sun sets and we think about what tomorrow will bring, we understand that better is not what we do. It is who we are.

timberland.com

WHAT KIND OF FOOTPRINT WILL YOU LEAVE?

R COMMITMENT TO STRONG COMMUNITIES
A HEALTHIER PLANET

chapter two

Any organization, including nonprofits, has to manage the ethical behavior of employees and participants in the overall operations of the organization. Misconduct can take on many forms within the business environment, including deceptive business practices and the withholding of important information from investors or consumers. Wrongdoing by some businesses has focused public attention and government involvement on encouraging more acceptable business conduct. Any organizational decision may be judged as right or wrong, ethical or unethical, legal or illegal.

In this chapter, we take a look at the role of ethics and social responsibility in business decision making. First, we define business ethics and examine why it is important to understand ethics' role in business. Next, we explore a number of business ethics issues to help you learn to recognize

continued on p. 24

business ethics + social responsibility

LEARNING OBJECTIVES

LO1 Define business ethics and social responsibility and examine their importance.

LO2 Detect some of the ethical issues that may arise in business.

LO3 Specify how businesses can promote ethical behavior.

LO4 Explain the four dimensions of social responsibility.

LO5 Debate an organization's social responsibilities to owners, employees, consumers, the environment, and the community.

business ethics principles and standards that determine acceptable conduct in business

social responsibility a business's obligation to maximize its positive impact and minimize its negative impact on society

such issues when they arise. Finally, we consider steps businesses can take to improve ethical behavior in their organizations. The second half of the chapter focuses on social responsibility. We survey some important responsibility issues and detail how companies have responded to them.

BUSINESS ETHICS AND SOCIAL RESPONSIBILITY

In this chapter, we define **business ethics** as the principles and standards that determine acceptable conduct in business organizations. Personal ethics relate to an individual's values, principles, and standards of conduct. The acceptability of behavior in business is determined by not only the organization but also stakeholders such as customers, competitors, government regulators, interest groups, and the public, as well as each individual's personal principles and values. The publicity and debate surrounding highly visible legal and ethical lapses at a number of well-known firms, including AIG, Countrywide Financial, and Enron, highlight the need for businesses to integrate ethics and responsibility into all business decisions. The most recent global financial crisis took a toll on consumer trust of financial services companies. Words used to describe these companies in a survey were "greedy," "impersonal," "opportunistic," and "distant." Most unethical activities within organizations are supported by an organizational culture that encourages employees to bend the rules.

On the other hand, organizations that exhibit a high ethical culture encourage employees to act with integrity and adhere to organizational values. Many experts agree that ethical leadership, ethical values, and compliance to maintain appropriate conduct are important in creating good business ethics. T-Mobile USA constantly reviews ethics training and all communications. It makes sure employees understand company values and regularly creates new compliance and ethics initiatives to address

Many consumers and social advocates believe that businesses should not only make a profit but also consider the social implications of their activities. We define **social responsibility** as a business's obligation to maximize its positive impact and minimize its negative impact on society. Although many people use the terms *social responsibility* and *ethics* interchangeably, they do not mean the same thing. Business ethics relates to an *individual's* or a *work group's* decisions that society evaluates as right or wrong, whereas social responsibility is a broader concept that concerns the impact of the *entire business's* activities on society. From an ethical perspective, for example, we may be concerned about a health care organization overcharging the government for Medicare services. For example, Abbot Laboratories Inc., Roxane Laboratories Inc., and B. Braun Medical Inc. paid $421 million to settle allegations that they committed Medicare and Medicaid fraud. The claim stated that the companies had reported false prices in order to receive larger reimbursements for doctors who chose their drugs.[2] From a social responsibility perspective, we might be concerned about the impact that this overcharging will have on the ability of the health care system to provide adequate services for all citizens.

The most basic ethical and social responsibility concerns have been codified by laws and regulations that encourage businesses to conform to society's standards, values, and attitudes. For example, after accounting scandals at a number of well-known firms in the early 2000s shook public confidence in the integrity of corporate America, the reputations of every U.S. company suffered regardless of their association with the scandals.[3] To help restore confidence in corporations and markets, Congress passed the Sarbanes-Oxley Act, which criminalized securities fraud and stiffened penalties for corporate fraud. After the financial crisis occurred in the most recent recession, the Dodd-Frank Act was passed to reform the financial industry and offer consumers protection against complex and/or deceptive financial products. At a minimum, managers are expected to obey all laws and regulations. Most legal issues arise as choices that society deems unethical, irresponsible, or otherwise unacceptable. However, all actions deemed unethical by society are not necessarily illegal, and both legal and ethical concerns change over time (see Table 2.1). Business law refers to the laws and regulations that govern the conduct of business. Many problems and conflicts in business can be avoided if owners, managers, and employees know more about business law and the legal system. Business ethics, social responsibility, and laws together act as

> "Many consumers and social advocates believe that businesses should not only make a profit but also consider the social implications of their activities."

problems or risk concerns. The senior leadership sets the tone by consistently communicating the message that integrity, compliance, and values are essential ingredients to the firm's performance.[1]

a compliance system, requiring that businesses and employees act responsibly in society. In this chapter, we explore ethics and social responsibility; The Appendix addresses business law, including the Sarbanes-Oxley Act and the Dodd-Frank Act.

▼ TABLE 2.1 A Timeline of Ethical and Socially Responsible Concerns

1960s	1970s	1980s	1990s	2000s
• Environmental issues • Civil rights issues • Increased employee-employer tension • Honesty • Changing work ethic • Rising drug use	• Employee militancy • Human rights issues • Covering up rather than correcting issues • Discrimination • Harassment	• Bribes and illegal contracting practices • Influence peddling • Deceptive advertising • Financial fraud (e.g., savings and loan scandal) • Transparency issues	• Sweatshops and unsafe working conditions in third-world countries • Rising corporate liability for personal damages (e.g., cigarette companies) • Financial mismanagement and fraud • Formalizing business ethics	• Employee benefits • Privacy issues • Financial mismanagement • Intellectual property theft • Responsible consumption • The role of business in promoting sustainable development

Source: Adapted from "Business Ethics Timeline," Copyright © 2003, *Ethics Resource Center* (n.d.), www.ethics.org, updated 2010. Used with permission.

The Role of Ethics in Business

You have only to pick up *The Wall Street Journal* or *USA Today* to see examples of the growing concern about legal and ethical issues in business. For example, the Department of Justice filed a lawsuit against MasterCard, Visa, and American Express for anticompetitive practices. The three companies forbade merchants from revealing processing fees to customers and offering discounts to those who had cards with lower fees. With merchants paying approximately $35 billion annually in credit card fees, the Justice Department claimed that forcing merchants to keep this information from consumers put retailers at a financial disadvantage. MasterCard and Visa agreed to settle the lawsuit.[4] Regardless of what an individual believes about a particular action, if society judges it to be unethical or wrong, whether correctly or not, that judgment directly affects the organization's ability to achieve its business goals.[5]

Well-publicized incidents of unethical and illegal activity—ranging from accounting fraud to using the Internet to steal another person's credit card number, from deceptive advertising of food and diet products to unfair competitive practices in the computer software industry—strengthen the public's perceptions that ethical standards and the level of trust in business need to be raised. Author David Callahan has commented, "Americans who wouldn't so much as shoplift a pack of chewing gum are committing felonies at tax time, betraying the trust of their patients, misleading investors, ripping off their insurance companies, lying to their clients, and much more."[6] Often, such charges start as ethical conflicts but evolve into legal disputes when cooperative conflict resolution cannot be accomplished. Headline-grabbing scandals like those associated with executive compensation and benefits packages create ethical concerns. In the United States, Charles O. Prince III, former CEO of Citigroup; Stanley O'Neal, former CEO of Merrill Lynch; and Angelo Mozilo, founder and former CEO of Countrywide Financial, rejected suggestions that they reaped lavish compensation packages while engaging in highly risky subprime lending associated with an international financial crisis. While O'Neal was fired for Merrill Lynch's poor performance, he was given a $161 million severance package on top of the $70 million he earned during four years as CEO.[7]

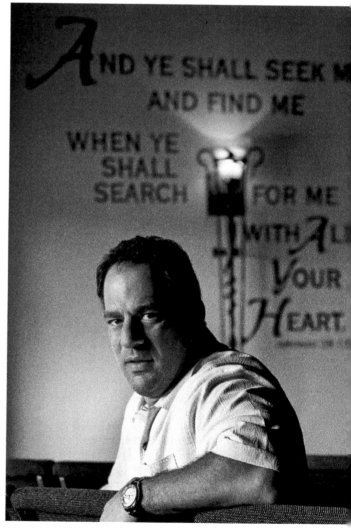

As a young man, Barry Minkow spent seven years in jail for fraudulent activities. In March 2011, Minkow pled guilty to securities fraud and admitted to using his fraud investigation company to make false accusations against Lennar Corporation.

ethical issue an identifiable problem, situation, or opportunity that requires a person to choose from among several actions that may be evaluated as right or wrong, ethical or unethical

However, it is important to understand that business ethics goes beyond legal issues. Ethical conduct builds trust among individuals and in business relationships, which validates and promotes confidence in business relationships. Establishing trust and confidence is much more difficult in organizations that have reputations for acting unethically. If you were to discover, for example, that a manager had misled you about company benefits when you were hired, your trust and confidence in that company would probably diminish. And if you learned that a colleague had lied to you about something, you probably would not trust or rely on that person in the future.

Ethical issues are not limited to for-profit organizations either. Ethical issues include all areas of organizational activities, including government. In government, several politicians and some high-ranking officials have faced disciplinary actions over ethical indiscretions. Former House Majority Leader Tom DeLay was sentenced to three years in prison after he was found guilty of money-laundering and conspiracy. DeLay was accused of channeling $190,000 of corporate money into the Republican National Committee.[8] Even sports can be subject to ethical lapses. At many universities, for example, coaches and athletic administrators have been put on administrative leave after allegations of improper recruiting practices came to light. After Tiger Woods's marital infidelity scandal broke, he was dropped by a number of major sponsors including Gatorade, AT&T, Gillette, and Tag Heuer. Tiger Woods lost an estimated $20 million in endorsements within one year because he lost the high integrity reputation that companies require for an endorser.[9] Across the world, a match-fixing scandal involving

Nobody likes a cheater, not even in the sports business. Although Mark McGwire broke baseball's home run record in 1998, he later admitted to taking steroids.

Recognizing Ethical Issues in Business

Recognizing ethical issues is the most important step in understanding business ethics. An **ethical issue** is an identifiable problem, situation, or opportunity that requires a person to choose from among several actions that may be evaluated as right or wrong, ethical or unethical. In business, such a choice often involves weighing monetary profit against what a person considers appropriate conduct. The best way to judge the ethics of a decision is to look at a situation from a customer's or competitor's viewpoint: Should liquid-diet manufacturers make unsubstantiated claims about their products? Should an engineer agree to divulge her former employer's trade secrets to ensure that she gets a better job with a competitor? Should a salesperson omit

> ## Many business issues seem straightforward and easy to resolve on the surface, but are in reality very complex.

Pakistan cricket shocked the country and caused some to question the integrity of the sport. Three Pakistani cricket players allegedly accepted payments in exchange for underperforming at a match in England.[10] Thus, whether made in science, politics, sports, or business, most decisions are judged as right or wrong, ethical or unethical. Negative judgments can affect an organization's ability to build relationships with customers and suppliers, attract investors, and retain employees.[11]

Although we will not tell you in this chapter what you ought to do, others—your superiors, co-workers, and family—will make judgments about the ethics of your actions and decisions. Learning how to recognize and resolve ethical issues is a key step in evaluating ethical decisions in business.

facts about a product's poor safety record in his presentation to a customer? Such questions require the decision maker to evaluate the ethics of his or her choice.

Many business issues seem straightforward and easy to resolve on the surface, but are in reality very complex. A person often needs several years of experience in business to understand what is acceptable or ethical. For example, if you are a salesperson, when does offering a gift—such as season basketball tickets—to a customer become a bribe rather than just a sales practice? Clearly, there are no easy answers to such a question. But the size of the transaction, the history of personal relationships within the particular company, and many other factors may determine whether an action will be judged as right or wrong by others. Companies

ONE OF THE PRINCIPAL CAUSES OF UNETHICAL BEHAVIOR IN ORGANIZATIONS IS OVERLY AGGRESSIVE FINANCIAL OR BUSINESS OBJECTIVES.

across the United States are starting to prevent access to Internet-video services at work. At issue is the theft of time by employees. For example, many employees spend an average of one hour each work day using social networking sites.[12] Another issue is the use of company resources to provide personal Internet access.

Ethics is also related to the culture in which a business operates. In the United States, for example, it would be inappropriate for a businessperson to bring an elaborately wrapped gift to a prospective client on their first meeting—the gift could be viewed as a bribe. In Japan, however, it is considered impolite *not* to bring a gift. Experience with the culture in which a business operates is critical to understanding what is ethical or unethical.

To help you understand ethical issues that perplex businesspeople today, we will take a brief look at some of them in this section. Ethical issues can be more complex now than in the past. The vast number of news-format investigative programs has increased consumer and employee awareness of organizational misconduct. In addition, the multitude of cable channels and Internet resources has improved the awareness of ethical problems among the general public. The National Business Ethics Survey found that workers witness many instances of ethical misconduct in their organizations (see Table 2.2).

One of the principal causes of unethical behavior in organizations is overly aggressive financial or business objectives. Many of these issues relate to decisions and concerns that managers have to deal with daily. It is not possible to discuss every issue, of course. However, a discussion of a few issues can help you begin to recognize the ethical problems with which businesspersons must deal. Many ethical issues in business can be categorized in the context of their relation with abusive and intimidating behavior, conflicts of interest, fairness and honesty, communications, misuse of company resources, and business associations.

Misuse of Company Resources

Misuse of company resources has been identified by the Ethics Resource Center as the leading issue in observed misconduct in organizations (see Table 2.2). Misconduct can range from firing workers for excessive use of e-mail at work to unauthorized use of equipment and computer systems to embezzling of company funds. In the retail area, internal employee

theft is a much larger problem than consumer shoplifting. Time theft costs can be difficult to measure but are estimated to cost companies hundreds of billions of dollars annually. It is widely believed that the average employee "steals" 4.5 hours a week with late arrivals, leaving early, long lunch breaks, inappropriate sick days, excessive socializing, and engaging in personal activities such as online shopping and watching sports while on the job. All of these activities add up to lost productivity and profits for the employer—and relate to ethical issues in the area of abusing company resources.

Because misuse of company resources is such a widespread problem, many companies, like Boeing, have implemented official policies delineating acceptable use of company resources. Boeing's policy states that use of company resources is acceptable when it does not result in "significant added costs, disruption of business processes, or any other disadvantage to the company."[13] The policy further states that use of company resources for noncompany purposes is acceptable only when an employee receives explicit permission to do so. This kind of policy is in line with that of many companies, particularly large ones that can easily lose millions of dollars and thousands of hours of productivity to these activities.

Abusive and Intimidating Behavior Abusive or intimidating behavior is the second most common ethical problem for employees. These concepts can mean anything from physical

▼ **TABLE 2.2** Percentage of U.S. Workforce Observing Specific Forms of Misconduct, 2007–2009

Behaviors	2009	2007
Company resource abuse	23%	n/a
Abusive behavior	22	21%
Lying to employees	19	20
Email or Internet abuse	18	18
Conflicts of interest	16	22
Discrimination	14	12
Lying to outside stakeholders	12	14
Employee benefit violations	11	n/a
Health or safety violations	11	15
Employee privacy breach	10	n/a
Improper hiring practices	10	10
Falsifying time or expenses	10	n/a

Source: Ethics Resource Center, *2009 National Business Ethics Survey: Business in the Recession*, www.ethics.org, p. 32.

bribes payments, gifts, or special favors intended to influence the outcome of a decision

threats, false accusations, profanity, insults, yelling, harshness, and unreasonableness to ignoring someone or simply being annoying; and the meaning of these words can differ by person—you probably have some ideas of your own. Abusive behavior can be placed on a continuum from a minor distraction to a disruption of the workplace. For example, what one person may define as yelling might be another's definition of normal speech. Civility in our society is a concern, and the workplace is no exception. The productivity level

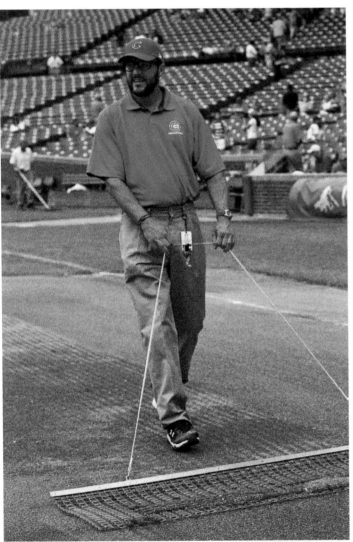

The show "Undercover Boss" gives managers the chance to understand how their subordinates feel as they take on the responsibilities of their employees. Many develop a stronger appreciation for their employees' challenging jobs, as Todd Rickets, co-owner of the Chicago Cubs, did after spending time working as part of the janitorial staff and grounds crew.

of many organizations has been diminished by the time spent unraveling abusive relationships.

Abusive behavior is difficult to assess and manage because of diversity in culture and lifestyle. What does it mean to speak profanely? Is profanity only related to specific words or other such terms that are common in today's business world? If you are using words that are normal in your language but that others consider to be profanity, have you just insulted, abused, or disrespected them?

Within the concept of abusive behavior, intent should be a consideration. If the employee was trying to convey a compliment but the comment was considered abusive, then it was probably a mistake. The way a word is said (voice inflection) can be important. Add to this the fact that we now live in a multicultural environment—doing business and working with many different cultural groups—and the businessperson soon realizes the depth of the ethical and legal issues that may arise. There are problems of word meanings by age and within cultures. For example, an expression such as "Did you guys hook up last night?" can have various meanings, including some that could be considered offensive in a work environment.

Bullying is associated with a hostile workplace when a person or group is targeted and is threatened, harassed, belittled, verbally abused, or overly criticized. Bullying may create what some consider a hostile environment, a term generally associated with sexual harassment. Although sexual harassment has legal recourse, bullying has little legal recourse at this time. Bullying is a widespread problem in the United States, and can cause psychological damage that can result in health endangering consequences to the target. Surveys indicate that approximately one in three adults have experienced bullying in the workplace, and one in seven workers witness bullying. Many victims and bystanders do not report bullying for fear of reprisals.[14] As Table 2.3 indicates, bullying can use a mix of verbal, nonverbal, and manipulative threatening expressions to damage workplace productivity. One may wonder why workers tolerate such activities. The problem is that 81 percent of workplace bullies are supervisors. A top officer at Boeing cited an employee survey indicating 26 percent had observed abusive or intimidating behavior by management.[15]

Conflict of Interest A conflict of interest, the most common ethical issue identified by employees, exists when a person must choose whether to advance his or her own personal interests or those of others. For example, a manager in a corporation is supposed to ensure that the company is profitable so that its stockholder-owners receive a return on their investment. In other words, the manager has a responsibility to investors. If she instead makes decisions that give her more power or money but do not help the company, then she has a conflict of interest—she is acting to benefit herself at the expense of her company and is not fulfilling her responsibilities as an employee. To avoid conflicts of interest, employees must be able to separate their personal financial interests from their business dealings. In the wake of the 2008 meltdown on Wall

▼ **TABLE 2.3** Actions Associated with Bullies

1. Spreading rumors to damage others
2. Blocking others' communication in the workplace
3. Flaunting status or authority to take advantage of others
4. Discrediting others' ideas and opinions
5. Use of e-mails to demean others
6. Failing to communicate or return communication
7. Insults, yelling, and shouting
8. Using terminology to discriminate by gender, race, or age
9. Using eye or body language to hurt others or their reputation
10. Taking credit for others' work or ideas

Source: © O. C. Ferrell, 2011.

▼ **TABLE 2.4** Least Corrupt Countries

Rank	Country	CPI Score*
1	Denmark/New Zealand/Singapore	9.3
4	Finland/Sweden	9.2
6	Canada	8.9
7	Netherlands	8.8
8	Australia/Switzerland	8.7
10	Norway	8.6
11	Iceland/Luxembourg	8.5
13	Hong Kong	8.4
14	Ireland	8.0
15	Austria/Germany	7.9
17	Barbados/Japan	7.8
19	Qatar	7.7
20	United Kingdom	7.6
21	Chile	7.2
22	Belgium/United States	7.1

*CPI score relates to perceptions of the degree of corruption as seen by businesspeople and country analysts and ranges between 10 (highly clean) and 0 (highly corrupt).

Source: "Corruption Perceptions Index 2010," Transparency International, www.transparency.org/policy_research/surveys_indices/cpi/2010/results (accessed January 6, 2011).

Street, stakeholders and legislators pushed for reform of the credit rating industry. Many cited rampant conflicts of interest between financial firms and the companies that rate them as part of the reason no one recognized the impending financial disaster. Conflict of interest has long been a serious problem in the financial industry because the financial companies pay the credit raters money in order to be rated. Because different rating companies exist, financial firms can also shop around for the best rating. There is no third-party mediator who oversees the financial industry and how firms are rated.[16]

As mentioned earlier, it is considered improper to give or accept **bribes**—payments, gifts, or special favors intended to influence the outcome of a decision. A bribe is a conflict of interest because it benefits an individual at the expense of an organization or society. Companies that do business overseas should be aware that bribes are a significant ethical issue and are, in fact, illegal in many countries. For example, the Merchant Bank in New York admitted to making unlawful payments to a government official in the Republic of Kazakhstan in order to secure business within the country. This payment, or bribe, was in clear violation of the U.S. Foreign Corrupt Practices Act.[17] While bribery is an increasing issue in many countries, it is more prevalent in some countries than in others. Transparency International has developed a Corruption Perceptions Index (Table 2.4). Note that there are 21 countries perceived as less corrupt than the United States.[18]

Fairness and Honesty Fairness and honesty are at the heart of business ethics and relate to the general values of decision makers. At a minimum, businesspersons are expected to follow all applicable laws and regulations. But beyond obeying the law, they are expected not to harm customers, employees, clients, or competitors knowingly through deception, misrepresentation, coercion, or discrimination. Honesty and fairness can relate to how the employees use the resources of the organization. A survey by Kelton research revealed that 56 percent of employed Americans pilfer products from their employers for personal use.[19] Although the majority of office supply thefts involve small things such as pencils or Post-it Notes, some

workers admit to stealing more expensive equipment such as laptops, PDAs, and cell phones. Employees should be aware of policies on taking items and recognize how these decisions relate to ethical behavior. Figure 2.1 provides an overview of the most pilfered office supplies.

One aspect of fairness relates to competition. Although numerous laws have been passed to foster competition and make monopolistic practices illegal, companies sometimes gain control over markets by using questionable practices that harm competition. Bullying can also occur between companies that are intense competitors. Even respected companies such as Intel have been accused of monopolistic bullying. A competitor, Advanced Micro Devices (AMD), claimed in a lawsuit that 38 companies, including Dell and Sony, were strong-arming customers (such as Apple) into buying Intel chips rather than those marketed by AMD. In many cases, the alleged misconduct not only can have monetary and legal implications but also can threaten reputation, investor confidence, and customer loyalty. A front-cover *Forbes* headline stated "Intel to ADM: Drop Dead." The intensely competitive atmosphere and Intel's ability to use its large size won it the high-profile Apple account, displacing IBM and Freescale. ADM claims it had no opportunity to bid because Intel had offered to deploy 600 Indian engineers to help Apple software run more smoothly on Intel chips.[20] The U.S. Federal Trade Commission joined in on the antitrust accusations against Intel by alleging

FIGURE 2.1
Office Supplies Reported Missing Most Often

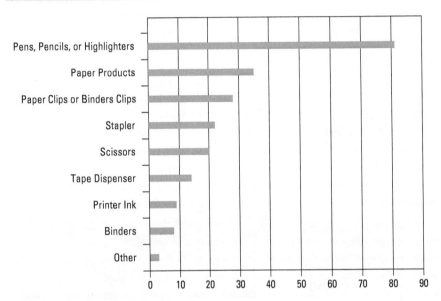

Source: "The Truth Behind Disappearing Office Supplies," OfficeMax, May 2010, multivu.prnewswire.com/mnr/officemax/44541/docs/44541-Report OfficeMaxWorkplaceUncoveredSurvey.pdf (accessed January 6, 2011).

at least once, 36 percent confessed to copying documents from the Internet, and 28 percent admitted to shoplifting.[23] If today's students are tomorrow's leaders, there is likely to be a correlation between acceptable behavior today and tomorrow. This adds to the argument that the leaders of today must be prepared for the ethical risks associated with this downward trend. According to a poll by Deloitte and Touche of teenagers aged 13 to 18, when asked if people who practice good business ethics are more successful than those who don't, 69 percent of teenagers agreed.[24] The same poll found only 12 percent of teens think business leaders today are ethical. On the other hand, another survey indicated that many students do not define copying answers from another students' paper or downloading music or content for classroom work as cheating.[25]

that Intel used illegal inducements and threats of retaliation to discourage computer makers from buying competitor AMD's chips. The FTC also claimed that Intel corrupted software built on Intel compilers to make it run slower on computers using AMD processors. Intel agreed to pay AMD $1.25 billion to settle the 2005 lawsuit. Intel also settled with the FTC by agreeing not to engage in payments or other anticompetitive practices to drive out competitors. The company created a $10 million fund to assist customers in recompiling the corrupted software. Intel's fines and the damage to its reputation may have a considerable impact on the way it operates in the market.[21]

Another aspect of fairness and honesty relates to disclosure of potential harm caused by product use. For example, many stakeholder groups have become increasingly concerned about the health effects of additives in food and manufactured products. The widespread use of plastic products have caused a number of stakeholder groups to raise questions about possible health problems associated with additives like Bisphenol A (BPA), which is suspected of causing health problems in infants and children. Many businesses, however, continue to include BPA in their products until research proves more conclusive on whether it is harmful.[22] While it is not mandatory to disclose whether a product contains BPA, some companies have turned a potential problem into a competitive advantage by labeling their BPA-free products to ease the fears of consumers.

Dishonesty has become a significant problem in the United States. A survey of nearly 25,000 high school students revealed that 64 percent of the students admitted to cheating on an exam

Perhaps even more troubling was the revelation that several FBI agents had cheated on a test covering FBI procedures for the surveillance of Americans. An investigation showed that several agents, including some FBI supervisors, took the test together or had access to the answer sheets in advance. Such cheating by adult government workers highlights a disturbing trend within the professional world.[26]

Communications Communications is another area in which ethical concerns may arise. False and misleading advertising, as well as deceptive personal-selling tactics, anger consumers and can lead to the failure of a business. Truthfulness about product safety and quality are also important to consumers. Claims about dietary supplements can be particularly problematic. VMG Global, a sports nutrition company, pleaded guilty to illegally putting steroids in two of its body-building supplements. For four years, the company knowingly spiked Tren Xtreme and Mass Xtreme, products that generated more than $5.6 million in revenue for the company. The company agreed to pay $500,000 in penalties and destroy all remaining inventory of the products.[27]

Some companies fail to provide enough information for consumers about differences or similarities between products. For example, driven by high prices for medicines, many consumers are turning to Canadian, Mexican, and overseas Internet sources for drugs to treat a variety of illnesses and conditions. However, research suggests that a significant percentage of these imported pharmaceuticals may not actually contain the labeled drug, and the counterfeit drugs could even be harmful to those who take them.[28]

Another important aspect of communications that may raise ethical concerns relates to product labeling. The Food and Drug Administration mandated that by 2012 all cigarette packs must include warnings and graphic images that show the consequences of smoking. The plans are for these images to cover half the space on packages and supplement all cigarette advertisements.[29] In Europe, at least 30 percent of the front side of product packaging and 40 percent of the back needs to be taken up by the warning. The use of descriptors such as "light" or "mild" has been banned.[30] However, labeling of other products raises ethical questions when it threatens basic rights, such as freedom of speech and expression. This is the heart of the controversy surrounding the movement to require warning labels on movies and videogames, rating their content, language, and appropriate audience age. Although people in the entertainment industry claim that such labeling violates their First Amendment right to freedom of expression, other consumers—particularly parents—believe that labeling is needed to protect children from harmful influences. Similarly, alcoholic beverage and cigarette manufacturers have argued that a total ban on cigarette and alcohol advertisements violates the First Amendment. Internet regulation, particularly that designed to protect children and the elderly, is on the forefront in consumer protection legislation. Because of the debate surrounding the acceptability of these business activities, they remain major ethical issues.

Business Relationships The behavior of businesspersons toward customers, suppliers, and others in their workplace may also generate ethical concerns. Ethical behavior within a business involves keeping company secrets, meeting obligations and responsibilities, and avoiding undue pressure that may force others to act unethically.

Managers in particular, because of the authority of their position, have the opportunity to influence employees' actions. For example, a manager might influence employees to use pirated computer software to save costs. The use of illegal software puts the employee and the company at legal risk, but employees may feel pressured to do so by their superior's authority. The National Business Ethics Survey found that employees who feel pressure to compromise ethical standards view top and middle managers as the greatest source of such pressure.[31]

It is the responsibility of managers to create a work environment that helps the organization achieve its objectives and fulfill its responsibilities. However, the methods that managers use to enforce these responsibilities should not compromise employee rights. Organizational pressures may encourage a person to engage in activities that he or she might otherwise view as unethical, such as invading others' privacy or stealing a competitor's secrets. The firm may provide only vague or lax supervision on ethical issues, creating the opportunity for misconduct. Managers who offer no ethical direction to employees create many opportunities for

manipulation, dishonesty, and conflicts of interest.

Plagiarism—taking someone else's work and presenting it as your own without mentioning the source—is another ethical issue. As a student, you may be familiar with plagiarism in school; for example, copying someone else's term paper or quoting from a published work or Internet source without acknowledging it. In business, an ethical issue arises when an employee copies reports or takes the work or ideas of others and presents it as his or her own. A manager attempting to take credit for a subordinate's ideas is engaging in another type of plagiarism.

> **plagiarism** the act of taking someone else's work and presenting it as your own without mentioning the source

Making Decisions about Ethical Issues

Although we've presented a variety of ethical issues that may arise in business, it can be difficult to recognize specific ethical issues in practice. Whether a decision maker recognizes an issue as an ethical one often depends on the issue itself. Managers, for example, tend to be more concerned about issues that affect those close to them, as well as issues that have immediate rather than long-term consequences. Thus, the perceived importance of an ethical issue substantially affects choices. However, only a few issues receive scrutiny, and most receive no attention at all.[32]

Table 2.5 lists some questions you may want to ask yourself and others when trying to determine whether an action is ethical. Open discussion of ethical issues does not eliminate ethical problems, but it does promote both trust and learning in an organization.[33] When people feel that they cannot discuss what they are doing with their co-workers or superiors, there is a good chance that an ethical issue exists. Once a person has recognized an ethical issue and can openly discuss it with others, he or she has begun the process of resolving that issue.

Improving Ethical Behavior in Business

Understanding how people make ethical choices and what prompts a person to act unethically may reverse the current trend toward unethical behavior in business. Ethical decisions in an organization are influenced by three key factors: individual moral standards, the influence of managers and co-workers, and the opportunity to engage in misconduct (Figure 2.2).

▼ **TABLE 2.5** Questions to Consider in Determining Whether an Action Is Ethical

Are there any potential legal restrictions or violations that could result from the action? Does your company have a specific code of ethics or policy on the action?

Is this activity customary in your industry? Are there any industry trade groups that provide guidelines or codes of conduct that address this issue?

Would this activity be accepted by your co-workers? Will your decision or action withstand open discussion with co-workers and managers and survive untarnished?

How does this activity fit with your own beliefs and values?

BP DISASTER LEADS TO QUESTIONS ABOUT ETHICS AND SOCIAL RESPONSIBILITY

British Petroleum (BP) has become synonymous with the worst oil leak disaster in U.S. waters to date. Simply put, BP failed to adequately prepare for a worst case scenario. When the *Deepwater Horizon* oil rig exploded, killing eleven workers and pouring millions of gallons of oil into the Gulf of Mexico, BP had no effective contingency plan. The crisis immediately spun out of control.

Not only did BP underestimate the risks, but some suggest it willfully cut corners to save money. A rig technician accused BP of knowing that the rig's blowout preventer was leaking weeks prior to the explosion. Similar accusations of risky or negligent behavior soon followed. Two months into the disaster, it was revealed that one-third of BP's deep water oil rig designs were deemed risky by government inspectors—a higher percentage than those of other oil companies.

Effective business ethics requires firms to identify risks and educate employees to deal with issues related to the risks. BP did not adequately acknowledge the risks despite warnings from industry experts. It also had no effective crisis management plan in place. BP did have a spill-response plan; however, its plan proved ineffective to handle the situation.

The disaster has undermined BP's reputation, and its ethics and social responsibility has been questioned by stakeholders. Many consumers responded by boycotting BP gas stations and products. The disaster has overshadowed BP's positive multimillion dollar investments in renewable energy. BP has implemented a $20 billion Deepwater Horizon Oil Spill Trust to pay out claims and a $500 million Gulf of Mexico Research Initiative to fund the study of the impacts of the disaster, among other initiatives. BP has a long history of environmental disasters and safety violations. What will it take to improve the reputation of BP?[34]

Discussion Questions

1. Are BP's attempts at compensation enough to change the company's reputation in the eyes of consumers?

2. What are the ethical considerations that BP failed to recognize in its management of risks?

3. How important is BP's reputation for business success?

While you have great control over your personal ethics outside the workplace, your co-workers and superiors exert significant control over your choices at work through authority and example. In fact, the activities and examples set by co-workers, along with rules and policies established by the firm, are critical in gaining consistent ethical compliance in an organization. If the company fails to provide good examples and direction for appropriate conduct, confusion and conflict will develop and result in the opportunity for misconduct. If your boss or co-workers leave work early, you may be tempted to do so as well. If you see co-workers engaged in personal activities such as shopping online or watching YouTube, then you may be more likely to do so also. In addition, having sound personal values contributes to an ethical workplace.

Because ethical issues often emerge from conflict, it is useful to examine the causes of ethical conflict. Business managers and employees often experience some tension between their own ethical beliefs and their obligations to the organizations in which they work. Many employees utilize different ethical standards at work than they do at home. This conflict increases when employees feel that their company is encouraging unethical conduct or exerting pressure on them to engage in it.

> ## Many employees utilize different ethical standards at work than they do at home.

It is difficult for employees to determine what conduct is acceptable within a company if the firm does not have established ethics policies and standards. And without such policies and standards, employees may base decisions on how their peers and superiors behave. Professional **codes of ethics** are formalized rules and standards that describe what the company expects of its employees. Codes of ethics do not have to be so detailed that they take into account every situation, but they should provide guidelines and principles that can help employees achieve organizational objectives and address risks in an acceptable and ethical way. The development of a code of ethics should include not only a firm's executives and board of directors, but also legal staff and employees from all areas of a firm.[35] Table 2.6 lists some key things to consider when developing a code of ethics.

Codes of ethics, policies on ethics, and ethics training programs advance ethical behavior because they prescribe which

▼**FIGURE 2.2**
Three Factors That Influence Business Ethics

| Individual Standards and Values | + | Managers' and Co-workers' Influence | + | Opportunity: Codes and Compliance Requirements | = | Ethical/Unethical Choices in Business |

activities are acceptable and which are not, and they limit the opportunity for misconduct by providing punishments for violations of the rules and standards. Codes and policies on ethics encourage the creation of an ethical culture in the company. According to the National Business Ethics Survey (NBES), employees in organizations that have written codes of conduct and ethics training, ethics offices or hotlines, and systems for reporting are more likely to report misconduct when they observe it. The survey found that a company's ethical culture is the greatest determinant of future misconduct.[36]

The enforcement of ethical codes and policies through rewards and punishments increases the acceptance of ethical standards by employees. For example, employees at Granite Construction are highly encouraged to engage in ethical behavior. Granite Construction holds six mandatory training sessions to manage risks, offers computer-based training for employees, provides ethics training for board members, and uses Field Compliance Officers to monitor compliance through all levels of the company. Granite's strong ethical culture inspired the creation of the Construction Industry Ethics and Compliance Initiative, consisting of a network of construction firms dedicated to supporting ethics and compliance throughout the industry.[37]

misconduct—with reduced fines and penalties when violations occur. Congress has also taken steps to close a legislative loophole in whistleblowing legislation that has led to the dismissal of many whistleblowers. In 2010 Congress passed the Dodd-Frank Act, which includes a "whistleblower bounty program." The Securities and Exchange Commission can now award whistleblowers between 10 and 30 percent of monetary sanctions over $1 million. The hope is that incentives will encourage more people to come forward with information regarding corporate misconduct.[39]

The current trend is to move away from legally based ethical initiatives in organizations to cultural- or integrity-based initiatives that make ethics a part of core organizational values. Organizations recognize that effective business ethics programs are good for business performance. Firms that develop higher levels of trust function more efficiently and effectively and avoid damaged company reputations and product images. Organizational ethics initiatives have been supportive of many positive and diverse organizational objectives, such as profitability, hir-

codes of ethics
formalized rules and standards that describe what a company expects of its employees

whistleblowing
the act of an employee exposing an employer's wrongdoing to outsiders, such as the media or government regulatory agencies

> "The current trend is to move away from legally based ethical initiatives in organizations to cultural- or integrity-based initiatives that make ethics a part of core organizational values."

One of the most important components of an ethics program is a means through which employees can report observed misconduct anonymously. Although the risk of retaliation is still a major factor in whether an employee will report illegal conduct, the NBES found that whistleblowing has increased in the past few years. Approximately 63 percent of respondents said they reported misconduct when they observed it.[38] **Whistleblowing** occurs when an employee exposes an employer's wrongdoing to outsiders, such as the media or government regulatory agencies. However, more companies are establishing programs to encourage employees to report illegal or unethical practices internally so that they can take steps to remedy problems before they result in legal action or generate negative publicity. Unfortunately, whistleblowers are often treated negatively in organizations. The government seeks to discourage this practice by rewarding firms that encourage employees to report

ing, employee satisfaction, and customer loyalty.[40] Conversely, lack of organizational ethics initiatives and the absence of workplace values such as honesty, trust, and integrity can have

▼ **TABLE 2.6** Key Things to Consider in Developing a Code of Ethics

- Create a team to assist with the process of developing the code (include management and nonmanagement employees from across departments and functions).
- Solicit input from employees from different departments, functions, and regions to compile a list of common questions and answers to include in the code document.
- Make certain that the headings of the code sections can be easily understood by all employees.
- Avoid referencing specific U.S. laws and regulations or those of specific countries, particularly for codes that will be distributed to employees in multiple regions.
- Hold employee group meetings on a complete draft version (including graphics and pictures) of the text using language that everyone can understand.
- Inform employees that they will receive a copy of the code during an introduction session.
- Let all employees know that they will receive future ethics training that will, in part, cover the important information contained in the code document.

Source: Adapted from William Miller, "Implementing an Organizational Code of Ethics," *International Business Ethics Review* 7 (Winter 2004), pp. 1, 6–10.

corporate citizenship the extent to which businesses meet the legal, ethical, economic, and voluntary responsibilities placed on them by their stakeholders

a negative impact on organizational objectives and employee retention. According to one report on employee loyalty and work practices, 79 percent of employees who questioned their bosses' integrity indicated that they felt uncommitted or were likely to quit soon.[41]

THE NATURE OF SOCIAL RESPONSIBILITY

There are four dimensions of social responsibility: economic, legal, ethical, and voluntary (including philanthropic) (Figure 2.3).[42] Earning profits is the economic foundation of the pyramid in Figure 2.3, and complying with the law is the next step. However, a business whose *sole* objective is to maximize profits is not likely to consider its social responsibility, although its activities will probably be legal. (We looked at ethical responsibilities in the first half of this chapter.) Finally, voluntary responsibilities are additional activities that may not be required but which promote human welfare or goodwill. Legal and economic concerns have long been acknowledged in business, but voluntary and ethical issues are more recent concerns.

Corporate citizenship is the extent to which businesses meet the legal, ethical, economic, and voluntary responsibilities placed on them by their various stakeholders. It involves the activities and organizational processes adopted by businesses to meet their social responsibilities. A commitment to corporate citizenship by a firm indicates a strategic focus on fulfilling the social responsibilities expected of it by its stakeholders. Corporate citizenship involves action and measurement of the extent to which a firm embraces the corporate citizenship philosophy and then follows through by implementing citizenship and social responsibility initiatives. One of the major corporate citizenship issues is the focus on preserving the environment. Consumers, governments, and special interest groups such as The Nature Conservancy are concerned about greenhouse gases and carbon emissions that are contributing to global warming. The majority of people agree that climate change is a global emergency, but there is not agreement on how to solve the problem.[43] Another example of a corporate citizenship issue might be animal rights—an issue that is important to many stakeholders. As the organic and local foods movements grow and become more profitable, more and more stakeholders are calling for more humane practices in factory farms as well.[44] Large factory farms are where most Americans get their meat, but some businesses are looking at more animal-friendly options in response to public outcry.

Part of the answer to the climate change crisis is alternative energy such as solar, wind, biofuels, and hydro applications. The American Solar Energy Society estimates that the number of "green" jobs could rise to 40 million by 2030.[45] The drive for alternative fuels such as ethanol from corn has added new issues such as food price increases and food shortages. More than 2 billion consumers earn less than $2 a day in wages. Sharply increased food costs have led to riots and government policies to restrict trade in basic commodities such as rice, corn, and soybeans.[46]

To respond to these developments, most companies are introducing eco-friendly products and marketing efforts. Even Walmart is taking advantage of the interest in the environment. The company is developing a new labeling system that shows consumers the carbon output of every product carried in Walmart's stores. Americans as consumers are generally concerned about the environment, but only 47 percent trust companies to tell them the truth in environmental marketing.[47] This is because most businesses are promoting themselves as green-conscious and concerned about the

▼**FIGURE 2.3**
The Pyramid of Social Responsibility

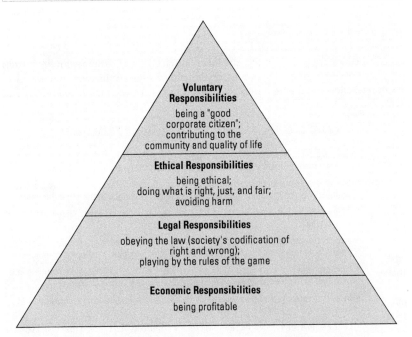

Source: Reprinted with permission from A. B. Carroll, "The Pyramid of Corporate Social Responsibility: Toward the Moral Management of Organizational Stakeholders," *Business Horizons,* July/August 1991. Copyright © 1991 by the Board of Trustees at Indiana University, Kelley School of Business.

environment without actually making the necessary commitments to environmental health. Even employees feel their employers aren't doing enough to protect the environment, with nearly 60 percent feeling that more needs to be to done to reduce, recycle, and support green policies.[48]

The Ethisphere Institute selects an annual list of the world's most ethical companies based on the following criteria: Corporate Citizenship and Responsibility; Corporate Governance; Innovation that Contributes to the Public Well Being; Industry Leadership; Executive Leadership and Tone from the Top; Legal, Regulatory and Reputation Track Record; and Internal Systems and Ethics/Compliance Program.[49] Table 2.7 shows the top 20 from that list.

Although the concept of social responsibility is receiving more and more attention, it is still not universally accepted. Table 2.8 lists some of the arguments for and against social responsibility.

Social Responsibility Issues

As with ethics, managers consider social responsibility on a daily basis. Among the many social issues that managers must consider are their firms' relations with owners and stockholders, employees, consumers, the environment, and the community. For example, Indra Nooyi, CEO of PepsiCo, believes that companies must embrace "purpose," not just for financial results, but also for the imprint they leave on society. She goes on to say that stakeholders, including employees, consumers, and regulators, "will leave no doubt that performance without purpose is not a long-term sustainable formula."[50]

Social responsibility is a dynamic area with issues changing constantly in response to society's demands. There is much evidence that social responsibility is associated with improved business performance. Consumers are refusing to buy from businesses that receive publicity about misconduct. A number of studies have found a direct relationship between social responsibility and profitability, as well as a link that exists between employee commitment and customer loyalty—two major concerns of any firm trying to increase profits.[51] This section highlights a few of the many social responsibility issues that managers face; as managers become aware of and work toward the solution of current social problems, new ones will certainly emerge.

▼ **TABLE 2.7** A Selection of the World's Most Ethical Companies

Hewlett-Packard Co.	Xerox
Trader Joe's	Nike
General Mills, Inc.	Salesforce.com
UPS	Barrett Jackson Auction Company
Patagonia	Dow Corning Corporation
General Electric	Ford Motor Company
Best Buy	ARAMARK
Kao	Caterpillar
Gap, Inc.	Aflac
International Paper	Whole Foods Market
IKEA	Google
AstraZeneca	Starbucks Coffee Co.
Pepsico Inc.	Target

Source: "2010 World's Most Ethical Companies," *Ethisphere*, Q4, pp. 30–31.

▼ **TABLE 2.8** The Arguments For and Against Social Responsibility

For:

1. Business helped create many of the social problems that exist today, so it should play a significant role in solving them, especially in the areas of pollution reduction and cleanup.
2. Businesses should be more responsible because they have the financial and technical resources to help solve social problems.
3. As members of society, businesses should do their fair share to help others.
4. Socially responsible decision making by businesses can prevent increased government regulation.
5. Social responsibility is necessary to ensure economic survival: If businesses want educated and healthy employees, customers with money to spend, and suppliers with quality goods and services in years to come, they must take steps to help solve the social and environmental problems that exist today.

Against:

1. It sidetracks managers from the primary goal of business—earning profits. Every dollar donated to social causes or otherwise spent on society's problems is a dollar less for owners and investors.
2. Participation in social programs gives businesses greater power, perhaps at the expense of particular segments of society.
3. Some people question whether business has the expertise needed to assess and make decisions about social problems.
4. Many people believe that social problems are the responsibility of government agencies and officials, who can be held accountable by voters.

Relations with Owners and Stockholders Businesses must first be responsible to their owners, who are primarily concerned with earning a profit or a return on their investment in a company. In a small business, this responsibility is fairly easy to fulfill because the owner or owners personally manage the business or know the managers well. In larger businesses, particularly corporations owned by thousands of stockholders, ensuring responsibility becomes a more difficult task.

Lady Gaga poses at an a M·A·C AIDS Fund event to promote VIVA GLAM lipstick. Money from the lipstick goes toward combating the AIDS virus.

consumerism the activities that independent individuals, groups, and organizations undertake to protect their rights as consumers

A business's obligations to its owners and investors, as well as to the financial community at large, include maintaining proper accounting procedures, providing all relevant information to investors about the current and projected performance of the firm, and protecting the owners' rights and investments. In short, the business must maximize the owners' investment in the firm.

Employee Relations

Another issue of importance to a business is its responsibilities to employees. Without employees, a business cannot carry out its goals. Employees expect businesses to provide a safe workplace, pay them adequately for their work, and keep them informed of what is happening in their company. They want employers to listen to their grievances and treat them fairly. In an effort to make Ford more competitive with foreign car companies, the United Auto Workers union agreed to allow the company to hire new workers at half the pay and with reduced benefits. This was a major concession on the part of the union, but was deemed a necessary step in keeping the company afloat. However, hiring new workers to do the same job as established ones for half the pay can result in dissatisfied employees and low morale.[52]

Congress has passed several laws regulating safety in the workplace, many of which are enforced by the Occupational Safety and Health Administration (OSHA). Labor unions have also made significant contributions to achieving safety in the workplace and improving wages and benefits. Most organizations now recognize that the safety and satisfaction of their employees are critical ingredients in their success, and many strive to go beyond what is legally expected of them. Healthy, satisfied employees also supply more than just labor to their employers. Employers are beginning to realize the importance of obtaining input from even the lowest-level employees to help the company reach its objectives.

A major social responsibility for business is providing equal opportunities for all employees regardless of their sex, age, race, religion, or nationality. Women and minorities have been slighted in the past in terms of education, employment, and advancement opportunities; additionally, many of their needs have not been addressed by business. For example, Outback Steakhouse agreed to pay nearly $1.9 million to settle a class-action lawsuit that alleged sexual discrimination against thousands of its female employees. The suit accused Outback of denying women the best job assignments, which prevented them from gaining the requisite experience to be eligible for upper-level management jobs.[53] Women, who continue to bear most child-rearing responsibilities, often experience conflict between those responsibilities and their duties as employees. Consequently, day care has become a major employment issue for women, and more companies are providing day care facilities as part of their effort to recruit and advance women in the workforce. In addition, companies are considering alternative scheduling such as flex-time and job sharing to accommodate employee concerns. Telecommuting has grown significantly over the past 5 to 10 years as well. Many Americans today believe business has a social obligation to provide special opportunities for women and minorities to improve their standing in society.

Consumer Relations

A critical issue in business today is business's responsibility to customers, who look to business to provide them with satisfying, safe products and to respect their rights as consumers. The activities that independent individuals, groups, and organizations undertake to protect their rights as consumers are known as **consumerism**. To achieve their objectives, consumers and their advocates write letters to companies, lobby government agencies, make public service announcements, and boycott companies whose activities they deem irresponsible.

Many of the desires of those involved in the consumer movement have a foundation in John F. Kennedy's 1962 consumer bill of rights, which highlighted four rights. The *right to safety* means that a business must not knowingly sell anything that could result in personal injury or harm to consumers. Defective or dangerous products erode public confidence in the ability of business to serve society. They also result in expensive litigation that ultimately increases the cost of products for all consumers. The right to safety also means businesses must provide a safe place for consumers to shop. In recent years, many large retailers have been under increasing pressure to improve safety in their large stores. Walmart faced serious scrutiny after the death of a guard during an early morning Black Friday stampede at a store on Long Island. The company was faced with lawsuits, bad press, and negative allegations related to the incident. In response, it implemented new measures such as staying open 24 hours on Thanksgiving. The tragic occurrence led other companies, such as Best Buy, to improve their safety plans as well.[54]

The *right to be informed* gives consumers the freedom to review complete information about a product before they buy it. This means that detailed information about ingredients, risks, and instructions for use are to be printed on labels and packages. The *right to choose* ensures that consumers have access to a variety of products and services at competitive prices. The assurance of both satisfactory quality and service at a fair price is also a part of the consumer's right to choose. Some consumers are not being given this right. Many are being billed for products and services they never ordered. According to the Federal Trade Commission, complaints about unordered merchandise and services jumped 169 percent over a two-year period. The *right to be heard* assures consumers that their interests will receive full and sympathetic consideration when the government formulates policy. It also ensures the fair treatment of consumers who voice complaints about a purchased product.

The role of the Federal Trade Commission's Bureau of Consumer Protection exists to protect consumers against unfair,

sustainability
conducting activities in a way that allows for the long-term well-being of the natural environment, including all biological entities. Sustainability involves the assessment and improvement of business strategies, economic sectors, work practices, technologies, and lifestyles so that they maintain the health of the natural environment.

deceptive, or fraudulent practices. The bureau, which enforces a variety of consumer protection laws, is divided into five divisions. The Division of Enforcement monitors legal compliance and investigates violations of laws, including unfulfilled holiday delivery promises by online shopping sites, employment opportunities fraud, scholarship scams, misleading advertising for health care products, and more.

Sustainability Issues Most people probably associate the term *environment* with nature, including wildlife, trees, oceans, and mountains. Until the 20th century, people generally thought of the environment solely in terms of how these resources could be harnessed to satisfy their needs for food, shelter, transportation, and recreation. As the earth's population swelled throughout the 20th century, however, humans began to use more and more of these resources and, with technological advancements, to do so with ever-greater efficiency. Although these conditions have resulted in a much-improved standard of living, they come with a cost. Plant and animal species, along with wildlife habitats, are disappearing at an accelerated rate, while pollution has rendered the atmosphere of some cities a gloomy haze. How to deal with these issues has become a major concern for business and society in the 21st century.

Although the scope of the word *sustainability* is broad, in this book we discuss the term from a strategic business perspective. Thus, we define **sustainability** as conducting activities in such a way as to provide for the long-term well-being of the natural environment, including all biological entities. Sustainability involves the interaction among nature and individuals, organizations, and business strategies and includes the assessment and improvement of business strategies, economic sectors, work practices, technologies, and lifestyles, so that they maintain the health of the natural environment. In recent years, business has played a significant role in adapting, using, and maintaining the quality of sustainability.

Environmental protection emerged as a major issue in the 20th century in the face of increasing evidence that pollution, uncontrolled use of natural resources, and population growth were putting increasing pressure on the long-term sustainability of these resources. Governments around the globe responded with environmental protection laws during the 1970s. In recent years, companies have been increasingly incorporating these issues into their overall business strategies. Some nonprofit organizations have stepped forward to provide leadership in gaining the cooperation of diverse groups in responsible environmental activities. For example, the Coalition for Environmentally Responsible Economies (CERES)—a

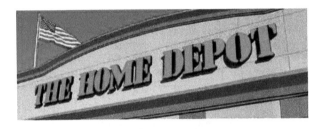

Values
The Home Depot's values guide the beliefs and actions of all associates on a daily basis. Our values are the fabric of the Company's unique culture and are central to our success. In fact, they are our competitive advantage in the marketplace. Associate pride and our "orangeblooded" entrepreneurial spirit are distinctive hallmarks of our culture.

1. **Taking care of our people:**
   The key to our success is treating people well. We do this by encouraging associates to speak up and take risks, by recognizing and rewarding good performance and by leading and developing people so they may grow.

2. **Giving back to our communities:**
   An important part of the fabric of The Home Depot is giving our time, talents, energy and resources to worthwhile causes in our communities and society.

3. **Doing the right thing:**
   We exercise good judgment by "doing the right thing" instead of just "doing things right." We strive to understand the impact of our decisions, and we accept responsibility for our actions.

4. **Excellent customer service:**
   Along with our quality products, service, price and selection, we must go the extra mile to give customers knowledgeable advice about merchandise and to help them use those products to their maximum benefit.

5. **Creating shareholder value:**
   The investors who provide the capital necessary to allow our company to grow need and expect a return on their investment. We are committed to providing it.

6. **Building strong relationships:**
   Strong relationships are built on trust, honesty and integrity. We listen and respond to the needs of customers, associates, communities and vendors, treating them as partners.

7. **Entrepreneurial spirit:**
   The Home Depot associates are encouraged to initiate creative and innovative ways of serving our customers and improving the business and to spread best practices throughout the company.

8. **Respect for all people:**
   In order to remain successful, our associates must work in an environment of mutual respect, free of discrimination and harassment where each associate is regarded as a part of The Home Depot team.

Home Depot has adopted eight core values as the foundation for its ethical culture, including a strong emphasis on sustainability.

union of businesses, consumer groups, environmentalists, and other stakeholders—has established a set of goals for environmental performance.

In the following section, we examine some of the most significant sustainability and environmental health issues facing business and society today, including animal rights, pollution, and alternative energy.

Pollution. Another major issue in the area of environmental responsibility is pollution. Water pollution results from dumping toxic chemicals and raw sewage into rivers and oceans, oil spills, and the burial of industrial waste in the ground where it may filter into underground water supplies. Fertilizers and insecticides used in farming and grounds maintenance also run off into water supplies with each rainfall. Water pollution problems are especially notable in heavily industrialized areas. Medical waste—such as used syringes, vials of blood, and HIV-contaminated materials—has turned up on beaches in New York, New Jersey, and Massachusetts, as well as other places. Society is demanding that water supplies be clean and healthful to reduce the potential danger from these substances.

Air pollution is usually the result of smoke and other pollutants emitted by manufacturing facilities, as well as carbon monoxide and hydrocarbons emitted by motor vehicles. In addition to the health risks posed by air pollution, when some chemical compounds emitted by manufacturing facilities react with air and rain, acid rain results. Acid rain has contributed to the deaths of many forests and lakes in North America as well as in Europe. Air pollution may also contribute to global warming; as carbon dioxide collects in the earth's atmosphere, it traps the sun's heat and prevents the earth's surface from cooling. It is indisputable that the global surface temperature has been increasing over the past 35 years. Worldwide passenger vehicle ownership has been growing due to rapid industrialization and consumer purchasing power in China, India, and other developing countries with large populations. The most important way to contain climate change is to control carbon emissions. The move to green buildings, higher-mileage cars, and other emissions reductions resulting from better efficiency have the potential to generate up to 50 percent of the reductions needed to keep warming at no more than 2°C above present temperatures—considered the "safe" level.[55] The 2007 U.S. Federal Energy bill raised average fuel economy (CAFE) standards to 35 mpg for cars by 2020, while Europe has the goal of a 40 mpg standard by the same deadline. Because buildings create half of U.S. greenhouse emissions, there is tremendous opportunity to develop conservation measures. For example, some utilities charge more for electricity in peak demand periods, which encourages behavioral changes that reduce consumption. On the positive side, there are more than 100 million bicycles produced annually worldwide, more than double the passenger vehicles produced.[56]

Land pollution is tied directly to water pollution because many of the chemicals and toxic wastes that are dumped on the land eventually work their way into the water supply. A study conducted by the Environmental Protection Agency found residues of prescription drugs, soaps, and other contaminants in virtually every waterway in the United States. Effects of these pollutants on humans and wildlife are uncertain, but there is some evidence to suggest that fish and other water-dwellers are starting to suffer serious effects.[57] Land pollution results from the dumping of residential and industrial waste, strip mining,

BIO-PLASTICS ARE A GROWING BUSINESS, BUT DO THEY LIVE UP TO THE HYPE?

Environmental issues can be addressed through alternatives such as bio-plastics. For instance, regular plastic has several problems—it stays around forever, and it contains a compound which has recently been accused of releasing harmful chemicals into food products. As a result, companies are working to create plastic that biodegrades (degrades naturally). Currently, two different types exist—both composed of fermented corn sugar. One is polylactic acid (PLA), which is 20 percent more expensive than regular plastic. The other is known as PHA plastic, which is twice as expensive as regular plastic.

These new bio-plastics are excellent in theory, but they require commitment on the part of consumers. Paper Mate's new biodegradable pens, made out of the more expensive PHA, must have their internal ink filters removed before the outer case can be buried to biodegrade. PLA plastics require composting, an activity that many consumers do not currently do. Even consumers that engage in composting might encounter difficulties. There are a number of differences between commercial composting and home-based composting. One lab conducted an experiment in which four biodegradable plastic products were placed in both types of composting situations for 25 weeks. Of the four in the home-based compost, only one began to biodegrade, indicating that home compost conditions are not right for many products. All but one did begin to break down in the commercial setting, but very few commercial composting sites in the United States currently accept plastics.

Consumer convenience is another problem. Many consumers want to be environmentally friendly, but only if it is convenient. This was clearly revealed after SunChips discontinued its initial biodegradable bags because consumers were complaining that the new bags were loud (SunChips has since released quieter biodegradable bags). Given all these stumbling blocks, will bio-plastics really make much of a difference?[58]

Discussion Questions

1. Do you think consumers will pay more for biodegradable packages?

2. What are the problems of trying to find and use biodegradable products?

3. What are the consumer issues associated with biodegradable packaging and products?

forest fires, and poor forest conservation. In Brazil and other South American countries, rain forests are being destroyed—to make way for farms and ranches, at a cost of the extinction of the many animals and plants (some endangered species) that call the rain forest home. Large-scale deforestation also depletes the oxygen supply available to humans and other animals.

Related to the problem of land pollution is the larger issue of how to dispose of waste in an environmentally responsible manner. Americans use 100 billion plastic bags each year,

which is between 10 and 20 percent of the total global usage (estimated at 500 billion to 1 trillion bags).[59] It takes 1,000 years for the bags to decompose. San Francisco has banned plastic bags; Ireland is now charging a nationwide tax of 15 cents on all supermarket shopping bags; and Australia and China are planning a similar program.[60] Whole Foods, the nation's leading natural and organic supermarket, ended its use of plastic bags on Earth Day 2008.[61] Whole Foods estimates that this move will keep 150 million new plastic grocery bags out of the environment each year.

Alternative Energy. With ongoing plans to reduce global carbon emissions, countries and companies alike are looking toward alternative energy sources. Traditional fossil fuels are problematic because of their emissions, but also because stores have been greatly depleted. Foreign fossil fuels are often imported from politically and economically unstable regions, often making it unsafe to conduct business there. The United States spends over $1 billion a day on foreign oil.[62] With global warming concerns and rising gas prices, the U.S. government has begun to recognize the need to look toward alternative forms of energy as a source of fuel and electricity. There have been many different ideas as to which form of alternative energy would best suit the United States' energy needs. These sources include wind power, solar power, nuclear power, biofuels, electric cars, and hydro and geothermal power. As of yet, no "best" form of alternative fuel has been selected to replace gasoline. However, the U.S. government has begun to recognize the need to reduce the nation's dependence on fossil fuels. It allocated billions of dollars toward renewable energy as part of President Obama's stimulus package.[63] Table 2.9 provides some facts regarding energy consumption.

Response to Environmental Issues. Partly in response to federal legislation such as the National Environmental Policy Act of 1969 and partly due to consumer concerns, businesses are responding to environmental issues. Many small and large companies, including Walt Disney Company, Chevron, and Scott Paper, have created a new executive position—a vice president of environmental affairs—to help them achieve their business goals in an environmentally responsible manner. A survey indicated that 83.5 percent of *Fortune* 500 companies have a written environmental policy, 74.7 percent engage in recycling efforts, and 69.7 percent have made investments in waste-reduction efforts.[64] Some companies are finding that environmental consciousness can save them money. DuPont saved

Wind power is growing in popularity as an alternative to traditional fuel sources.

?

DID YOU KNOW?

In one year, Americans generated 230 million tons of trash and recycled 23.5 percent of it.[65]

more than $3 billion through energy conservation by replacing natural gas with methane in its industrial boilers in many of its plants.[66]

Many firms are trying to eliminate wasteful practices, the emission of pollutants, and/or the use of harmful chemicals from their manufacturing processes. Other companies are seeking ways to improve their products. Utility providers, for example, are increasingly supplementing their services with alternative energy sources, including solar, wind, and geothermal power. Environmentalists are concerned that some companies are merely *greenwashing*, or "creating a positive association with environmental issues for an unsuitable product, service, or practice."

▼ **TABLE 2.9** Facts Related to Reducing Energy Consumption

- Keep your tires inflated at the recommended pressure. Not only is it safer, it can improve your gas mileage by more than 3 percent.
- The next time you buy a refrigerator, choose an ENERGY STAR model. If everyone buying a new refrigerator chose an ENERGY STAR model, it could save 914 million kilowatt-hours of electricity and more than $101 million in energy bills each year.
- Turn off your electronics when not in use. Stand-by power can account for up to 20 percent of energy use in the home.
- Use ENERGY STAR CFL light bulbs. If every home in America replaced just one light bulb with a CFL bulb, it could save as much as 6 billion kilowatts a year. This would save consumers more than $600 million in energy costs per year and reduce greenhouse gases by the equivalent of almost 750,000 cars.
- More than 50 percent of energy used in American homes is used for space heating and cooling. By properly sealing and insulating your attic, you can save up to 10 percent per year on your energy bills.

Source: "Make Every Day Earth Day," U.S. Department of Energy, www.energy.gov/energytips.htm (accessed January 25, 2010).

In many places, local utility customers can even elect to purchase electricity from green sources—primarily wind power—for a few extra dollars a month. Austin Energy of Austin, Texas, has an award-winning GreenChoice program that includes many small and large businesses among its customers.[67] Indeed, a growing number of businesses and consumers are choosing products, packaging, and processes more environmentally friendly have been labeled "green" business or marketing by the public and media. New Belgium, for instance, started selling aluminum cans of its beers because aluminum is easily recyclable and creates less waste. Lumber products at Home Depot may carry a seal from the Forest Stewardship Council to

> "Environmentalists are concerned that some companies are merely *greenwashing*, or 'creating a positive association with environmental issues for an unsuitable product, service, or practice.'"

green power sources where available. New Belgium Brewing, the third-largest craft brewer in the United States, is the first all-wind-powered brewery in the country. Many businesses have turned to *recycling*, the reprocessing of materials—aluminum, paper, glass, and some plastic—for reuse. Such efforts to make indicate that they were harvested from sustainable forests using environmentally friendly methods.[68] Likewise, most Chiquita bananas are certified through the Better Banana Project as having been grown with more environmentally and labor-friendly practices.[69]

MAJORA CARTER GROUP LLC BRINGS GREEN LIVING TO DISTRESSED COMMUNITIES

Sadly, many polluting factories and waste management facilities are located in lower-income communities. Majora Carter Group LLC wants to change all that. Founded by environmental advocate Majora Carter, the organization serves as a consultancy for clients interested in creating sustainability and green job growth within their communities. Majora Carter was inspired several years ago to take action to bring environmentally healthy practices to *all* communities, not just those in upper-class neighborhoods. The nonprofit organization she subsequently founded created a successful urban green-collar job training and placement system in the South Bronx. With her consulting firm, Carter now wants to go even further. Currently, Majora Carter is working to launch a national brand of locally grown, fresh produce under a cooperative structure. She is testing the concept in Detroit, a city hit hard by the recent recession and job loss. If Majora Carter has her way, distressed communities will be transformed into healthy areas offering opportunities for sustainability.[70]

It is important to recognize that, with current technology, environmental responsibility requires trade-offs. Society must weigh the huge costs of limiting or eliminating pollution against the health threat posed by the pollution. Environmental responsibility imposes costs on both business and the public. Although people certainly do not want oil fouling beautiful waterways and killing wildlife, they insist on low-cost, readily available gasoline and heating oil. People do not want to contribute to the growing garbage-disposal problem, but they often refuse to pay more for "green" products packaged in an environmentally friendly manner, to recycle as much of their own waste as possible, or to permit the building of additional waste-disposal facilities (the "not in my backyard," or NIMBY, syndrome). Managers must coordinate environmental goals with other social and economic ones.

Community Relations A final, yet very significant, issue for businesses concerns their responsibilities to the general welfare of the communities and societies in which they operate. Many businesses simply want to make their communities better places for everyone to live and work. The most common way that businesses exercise their community responsibility is through donations to local and national charitable organizations. Corporations contribute more than $14 billion each year to charitable causes.[71] For example, Safeway, the nation's fourth-largest grocer, has donated millions of dollars to organizations involved in medical research, such as Easter Seals and the Juvenile Diabetes Research Foundation International. The company's employees have also raised funds to support social causes of interest.[72] Avon's Breast Cancer Awareness Crusade has helped raise $700 million for breast cancer programs worldwide. Avon, a marketer of women's cosmetics, is also known for employing a large number of women and promoting them to top management; the firm has more female top managers (86 percent) than any other *Fortune* 500 company.[73] Even small companies participate in philanthropy through donations and volunteer support of local causes and national charities, such as the Red Cross and the United Way.

After realizing that the current pool of prospective employees lacks many basic skills necessary to work, many companies have become concerned about the quality of education in the United States. Recognizing that today's students are tomorrow's employees and customers, firms such as Kroger, Campbell Soup, Kodak, American Express, Apple, Xerox, and Coca-Cola are donating money, equipment, and employee time to help improve schools in their communities and around the nation. They provide scholarship money, support for teachers, and computers for students, and they send employees out to tutor and motivate young students to stay in school and succeed. Target, for example, contributes significant resources to education, including direct donations of $100 million to schools as well as fund-raising and scholarship programs that assist teachers and students. Through the retailer's Take Charge of Education program, customers using a Target Guest Card can designate a specific school to which Target donates 1 percent of their total purchase price. This program is designed to make customers feel that their purchases are benefiting their community while increasing the use of Target Guest Cards.[74]

Another tactic taken by some companies is to let consumers decide whether they want to contribute to socially responsible activities. What if Dell sold one notebook computer for $1,000 and the same computer for $1,150, with the understanding that the purchase of *this* computer would support the fight against AIDS around the world? Dell and Microsoft created

Many companies encourage their employees to volunteer for charitable organizations such as Habitat for Humanity.

products for the Product(Red) campaign, joining other large corporations such as The Gap, Apple, and Motorola in support of The Global Fund, an international organization fighting AIDS, tuberculosis, and malaria. The Product(Red) computer sold by Dell is significant to consumers and communicates their support to others.

Business is also beginning to take more responsibility for the hard-core unemployed. These are people who have never had a job or who have been unemployed for a long period of time. Some are mentally or physically disabled; some are homeless. Organizations such as the National Alliance of Businessmen fund programs to train the hard-core unemployed so that they can find jobs and support themselves.

TEAM EXERCISE

Sam Walton, founder of Walmart, had an early strategy for growing his business related to pricing. The "Opening Price Point" strategy used by Walton involved offering the introductory product in a product line at the lowest point in the market. For example, a minimally equipped microwave oven would sell for less than anyone else in town could sell the same unit. The strategy was that if consumers saw a product, such as the microwave, and saw it as a good value, they would assume that all of the microwaves were good values. Walton also noted that most people don't buy the entry-level product; they want more features and capabilities and often trade up.

Form teams and assign the role of defending this strategy or casting this strategy as an unethical act. Present your thoughts on either side of the issue.

In addition to fostering self-support, such opportunities enhance self-esteem and help people become productive members of society.

Finally, another way that many businesses are supporting philanthropy is through employee volunteerism programs. Salesforce.com, for example, strongly emphasizes community service within its corporate culture. Salesforce.com believes that the most effective community service is through the donation of money, time, and product. To encourage company employees to give of their time, Salesforce.com allows employees 1 percent time to volunteer in their communities. Studies have indicated that company support for employee volunteerism not only benefits communities but tends to increase employee morale as well.[75] ▪

SO YOU WANT A JOB // in Business Ethics and Social Responsibility /

In the words of Kermit the Frog, "It's not easy being green." It may not be easy, but green business opportunities abound. A popular catch phrase, "Green is the new black," indicates how fashionable green business is becoming. Consumers are more in tune with and concerned about green products, policies, and behaviors by companies than ever before. Companies are looking for new hires to help them see their business creatively and bring insights to all aspects of business operations. The American Solar Energy Society estimates that the number of green jobs could rise to 40 million in the United States by 2030. Green business strategies not only give a firm a commercial advantage in the marketplace, but help lead the way toward a greener world. The fight to reduce our carbon footprint in an attempt against climate change has opened up opportunities for renewable energy, recycling, conservation, and increasing overall efficiency in the way resources are used. New businesses that focus on hydro, wind, and solar power are on the rise and will need talented businesspeople

to lead them. Carbon emissions' trading is gaining popularity as large corporations and individuals alike seek to lower their footprints. A job in this growing field could be similar to that of a stock trader, or you could lead the search for carbon-efficient companies in which to invest.

In the ethics arena, current trends in business governance strongly support the development of ethics and compliance departments to help guide organizational integrity. This alone is a billion-dollar business, and there are jobs in developing organizational ethics programs, developing company policies, and training employees and management. An entry-level position might be as a communication specialist or trainer for programs in a business ethics department. Eventually there's an opportunity to become an ethics officer that would have typical responsibilities of meeting with employees, the board of directors, and top management to discuss and provide advice about ethics issues in the industry; developing and distributing a code of ethics; creating and maintaining an anonymous, confidential service to answer questions

about ethical issues; taking actions on possible ethics code violations; and reviewing and modifying the code of ethics of the organization.

There are also opportunities to support initiatives that help companies relate social responsibility to stakeholder interests and needs. These jobs could involve coordinating and implementing philanthropic programs that give back to others important to the organization or developing a community volunteering program for employees. In addition to the human relations function, most companies develop programs to assist employees and their families to improve their quality of life. Companies have found that the healthier and happier employees are, the more productive they will be in the workforce.

Social responsibility, ethics, and sustainable business practices are not a trend, they are good for business and the bottom line. New industries are being created and old ones are adapting to the new market demands, opening up many varied job opportunities that will lead to not only a paycheck, but to the satisfaction of making the world a better place.[76]

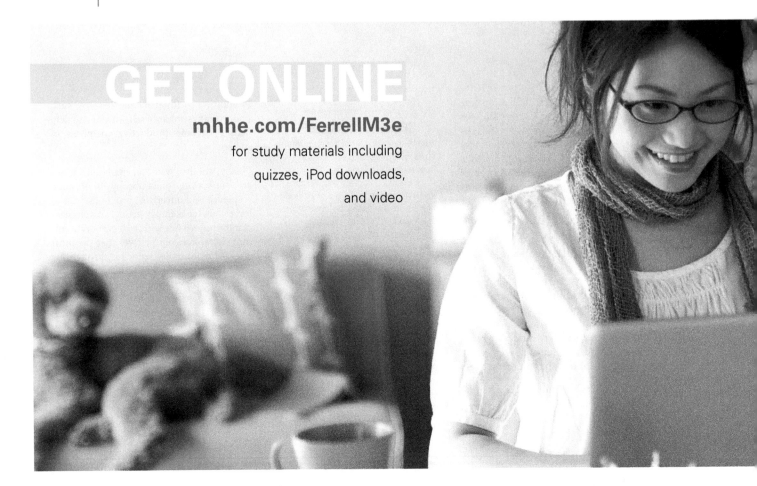

GET ONLINE

mhhe.com/FerrellM3e

for study materials including
quizzes, iPod downloads,
and video

chapter two appendix

the legal and regulatory environment

Business law refers to the rules and regulations that govern the conduct of business. Problems in this area come from the failure to keep promises, misunderstandings, disagreements about expectations, or, in some cases, attempts to take advantage of others. The regulatory environment offers a framework and enforcement system in order to provide a fair playing field for all businesses. The regulatory environment is created based on inputs from competitors, customers, employees, special interest groups, and the public's elected representatives. Lobbying by pressure groups that try to influence legislation often shapes the legal and regulatory environment.

SOURCES OF LAW

Laws are classified as either criminal or civil. *Criminal law* not only prohibits a specific kind of action, such as unfair competition or mail fraud, but also imposes a fine or imprisonment as punishment for violating the law. A violation of a criminal law is thus called

> "The primary method of resolving conflicts and business disputes is through lawsuits, where one individual or organization takes another to court using civil laws."

Marcia and Bill Baker found Heinz was underfilling their 20-oz. ketchup bottles by 1.5 oz. Heinz paid civil penalties and costs of $180,000 and had to overfill all ketchup bottles in California by 1/8 oz. for a year.

a crime. *Civil law* defines all the laws not classified as criminal, and it specifies the rights and duties of individuals and organizations (including businesses). Violations of civil law may result in fines but not imprisonment. The primary difference between criminal and civil law is that criminal laws are enforced by the state or nation, whereas civil laws are enforced through the court system by individuals or organizations.

Criminal and civil laws are derived from four sources: the Constitution (constitutional law), precedents established by judges (common law), federal and state statutes (statutory law), and federal and state administrative agencies (administrative law). Federal administrative agencies established by Congress control and influence business by enforcing laws and regulations to encourage competition and protect consumers, workers, and the environment. The Supreme Court is the ultimate authority on legal and regulatory decisions for appropriate conduct in business.

COURTS AND THE RESOLUTION OF DISPUTES

The primary method of resolving conflicts and business disputes is through **lawsuits**, where one individual or organization takes another to court using civil laws. The legal system, therefore, provides a forum for businesspeople to resolve disputes based on our legal foundations. The courts may decide when harm or damage results from the actions of others.

Because lawsuits are so frequent in the world of business, it is important to understand more about the court system where such disputes are resolved. Both financial restitution and specific actions to undo wrongdoing can result from going before a court to resolve a conflict. All decisions made in the courts are based on criminal and civil laws derived from the legal and regulatory system.

A businessperson may win a lawsuit in court and receive a judgment, or court order, requiring the loser of the suit to pay monetary damages. However, this does not guarantee the victor will be able to collect those damages. If the loser of the suit lacks the financial resources to pay the judgment—for example, if the loser is a bankrupt business—the winner of the suit may not be able to collect the award. Most business lawsuits involve a request for a sum of money, but some lawsuits request that a court specifically order a person or organization to do or to refrain from doing a certain act, such as slamming telephone customers.

The Court System

Jurisdiction is the legal power of a court, through a judge, to interpret and apply the law and make a binding decision in a particular case. In some instances, other courts will not enforce the decision of a prior court because it lacked jurisdiction. Federal courts are granted jurisdiction by the Constitution or by Congress. State legislatures and constitutions determine which state courts hear certain types of cases. Courts of general jurisdiction hear all types of cases; those of limited jurisdiction hear only specific types of cases. The Federal Bankruptcy Court, for example, hears only cases involving bankruptcy. There is some combination of limited and general jurisdiction courts in every state.

In a **trial court** (whether in a court of general or limited jurisdiction and whether in the state or the federal system), two tasks must be completed. First, the court (acting through the judge or a jury) must determine the facts of the case. In other words, if there is conflicting evidence, the judge or jury must decide who to believe. Second, the judge must decide which law or set of laws is pertinent to the case and must then apply those laws to resolve the dispute.

An **appellate court**, on the other hand, deals solely with appeals relating to the interpretation of law. Thus, when you hear about a case being appealed, it is not retried, but rather reevaluated. Appellate judges do not hear witnesses but instead base their decisions on a written transcript of the original trial. Moreover, appellate courts do not draw factual conclusions; the appellate judge is limited to deciding whether the trial judge made a mistake in interpreting the law that probably affected the outcome of the trial. If the trial judge made no mistake (or if mistakes would not have changed the result of the trial), the appellate court will let the trial court's decision stand. If the appellate court finds a mistake, it usually sends the case back to the trial court so that the mistake can be corrected. Correction may involve the granting of a new trial. On occasion, appellate courts modify the verdict of the trial court without sending the case back to the trial court.

Alternative Dispute Resolution Methods

Although the main remedy for business disputes is a lawsuit, other dispute resolution methods are becoming popular. The schedules of state and federal trial courts are often crowded; long delays between the filing of a case and the trial date are common. Further, complex cases can become quite expensive to pursue. As a result, many businesspeople are turning to alternative methods of resolving business arguments: mediation and arbitration, the mini-trial, and litigation in a private court.

Mediation is a form of negotiation to resolve a dispute by bringing in one or more third-party mediators, usually chosen by the disputing parties, to help reach a settlement. The mediator suggests different ways to resolve a dispute between the parties. The mediator's resolution is nonbinding—that is, the parties do not have to accept the mediator's suggestions; they are strictly voluntary.

Arbitration involves submission of a dispute to one or more third-party arbitrators, usually chosen by the disputing parties, whose decision usually is final. Arbitration differs from mediation in that an arbitrator's decision must be followed, whereas a mediator merely offers suggestions and facilitates negotiations. Cases may be submitted to arbitration because a contract—such as a labor contract—requires it or because the parties agree to do so. Some consumers are barred from taking claims to court by agreements drafted by banks, brokers, health plans, and others. Instead, they are required to take complaints to mandatory arbitration. Arbitration can be an attractive alternative to a lawsuit because it is often cheaper and quicker, and the parties frequently can choose arbitrators who are knowledgeable about the particular area of business at issue.

A method of dispute resolution that may become increasingly important in settling complex disputes is the **mini-trial**, in which both parties agree to present a summarized version of their case to an independent third party. That person then advises them of his or her impression of the probable outcome if the case were to be tried. Representatives of both sides then attempt to negotiate a settlement based on the advisor's recommendations. For example, employees in a large corporation who believe they have muscular or skeletal stress injuries caused by the strain of repetitive motion in using a computer could agree to a mini-trial to address a dispute related to damages. Although the mini-trial itself does not resolve the dispute, it can help the parties resolve the case before going to court. Because the mini-trial is not subject to formal court rules, it can save companies a great deal of money, allowing them to recognize the weaknesses in a particular case.

In some areas of the country, disputes can be submitted to a private nongovernmental court for resolution. In a sense, a **private court system** is similar to arbitration in that an independent third party resolves the case after hearing both sides of the story. Trials in private courts may be either informal or highly formal, depending on the people involved. Businesses typically agree to have their disputes decided in private courts to save time and money.

REGULATORY ADMINISTRATIVE AGENCIES

Federal and state administrative agencies (listed in Table A.1) also have some judicial powers. Many administrative agencies, such as the Federal Trade Commission, decide disputes that involve their regulations. In such disputes, the resolution process is usually called a "hearing" rather than a trial. In these cases, an administrative law judge decides all issues.

Federal regulatory agencies influence many business activities and cover product liability, safety, and the regulation or deregulation of public utilities. Usually, these bodies have the power to enforce specific laws, such as the Federal Trade Commission Act, and have some discretion in establishing operating rules and regulations to guide certain types of industry practices. Because of this discretion and overlapping areas of responsibility, confusion or conflict regarding which agencies have jurisdiction over which activities is common.

Of all the federal regulatory units, the **Federal Trade Commission (FTC)** most influences business activities related to questionable practices that create disputes between businesses and their customers. Although the FTC regulates a variety of

TABLE A.1 The Major Regulatory Agencies

Agency	Major Areas of Responsibility
Federal Trade Commission (FTC)	Enforces laws and guidelines regarding business practices; takes action to stop false and deceptive advertising and labeling.
Food and Drug Administration (FDA)	Enforces laws and regulations to prevent distribution of adulterated or misbranded foods, drugs, medical devices, cosmetics, veterinary products, and particularly hazardous consumer products.
Consumer Product Safety Commission (CPSC)	Ensures compliance with the Consumer Product Safety Act; protects the public from unreasonable risk of injury from any consumer product not covered by other regulatory agencies.
Interstate Commerce Commission (ICC)	Regulates franchises, rates, and finances of interstate rail, bus, truck, and water carriers.
Federal Communications Commission (FCC)	Regulates communication by wire, radio, and television in interstate and foreign commerce.
Environmental Protection Agency (EPA)	Develops and enforces environmental protection standards and conducts research into the adverse effects of pollution.
Federal Energy Regulatory Commission (FERC)	Regulates rates and sales of natural gas products, thereby affecting the supply and price of gas available to consumers; also regulates wholesale rates for electricity and gas, pipeline construction, and U.S. imports and exports of natural gas and electricity.
Equal Employment Opportunity Commission (EEOC)	Investigates and resolves discrimination in employment practices.
Federal Aviation Administration (FAA)	Oversees the policies and regulations of the airline industry.
Federal Highway Administration (FHA)	Regulates vehicle safety requirements.
Occupational Safety and Health Administration (OSHA)	Develops policy to promote worker safety and health and investigates infractions.
Securities and Exchange Commission (SEC)	Regulates corporate securities trading and develops protection from fraud and other abuses; provides an accounting oversight board.

OF ALL THE FEDERAL REGULATORY UNITS, THE FEDERAL TRADE COMMISSION (FTC) MOST INFLUENCES BUSINESS ACTIVITIES RELATED TO QUESTIONABLE PRACTICES THAT CREATE DISPUTES BETWEEN BUSINESSES AND THEIR CUSTOMERS.

business practices, it allocates a large portion of resources to curbing false advertising, misleading pricing, and deceptive packaging and labeling. When it receives a complaint or otherwise has reason to believe that a firm is violating a law, the FTC issues a complaint stating that the business is in violation.

If a company continues the questionable practice, the FTC can issue a cease-and-desist order, which is an order for the business to stop doing whatever has caused the complaint. In such cases, the charged firm can appeal to the federal courts to have the order rescinded. However, the FTC can seek civil penalties in court—up to a maximum penalty of $10,000 a day for each infraction—if a cease-and-desist order is violated. In its battle against unfair pricing, the FTC has issued consent decrees alleging that corporate attempts to engage in price fixing or invitations to competitors to collude are violations even when the competitors in question refuse the invitations. The commission can also require companies to run corrective advertising in response to previous ads considered misleading.

The FTC also assists businesses in complying with laws. New marketing methods are evaluated every year. When general sets of guidelines are needed to improve business practices in a particular industry, the FTC sometimes encourages firms within that industry to establish a set of trade practices voluntarily. The FTC may even sponsor a conference bringing together industry leaders and consumers for the purpose of establishing acceptable trade practices.

Unlike the FTC, other regulatory units are limited to dealing with specific products, services, or business activities. The Food and Drug Administration (FDA) enforces regulations prohibiting the sale and distribution of adulterated, misbranded, or hazardous food and drug products. For example, the FDA outlawed the sale and distribution of most over-the-counter hair-loss remedies after research indicated that few of the products were effective in restoring hair growth.

The Environmental Protection Agency (EPA) develops and enforces environmental protection standards and conducts research into the adverse effects of pollution. The Consumer Product Safety Commission (CPSC) recalls about 300 products a year, ranging from small, inexpensive toys to major appliances. The commission's website provides details regarding current recalls.

The CPSC has fallen under increasing scrutiny in the wake of a number of product safety scandals involving children's toys.

The most notable of these issues was lead paint discovered in toys produced in China. Other problems have included the manufacture of toys that include small magnets that pose a choking hazard, and lead-tainted costume jewelry.[77]

IMPORTANT ELEMENTS OF BUSINESS LAW

To avoid violating criminal and civil laws, as well as discouraging lawsuits from consumers, employees, suppliers, and others, businesspeople need to be familiar with laws that address business practices.

The Uniform Commercial Code

At one time, states had their own specific laws governing various business practices, and transacting business across state lines was difficult because of the variation in the laws from state to state. To simplify commerce, every state—except Louisiana—has enacted the Uniform Commercial Code (Louisiana has enacted portions of the code). The **Uniform Commercial Code (UCC)** is a set of statutory laws covering several business law topics. Article II of the Uniform Commercial Code, which is discussed in the following paragraphs, has a significant impact on business.

Sales Agreements Article II of the Uniform Commercial Code covers sales agreements for goods and services such as installation but does not cover the sale of stocks and bonds, personal services, or real estate. Among its many provisions, Article II stipulates that a sales agreement can be enforced even though it does not specify the selling price or the time or place of delivery. It also requires that a buyer pay a reasonable price for goods at the time of delivery if the buyer and seller have not reached an agreement on price. Specifically, Article II addresses the rights of buyers and sellers, transfers of ownership, warranties, and the legal placement of risk during manufacture and delivery.

Article II also deals with express and implied warranties. An **express warranty** stipulates the specific terms the seller will honor. Many automobile manufacturers, for example, provide three-year or 36,000-mile warranties on their vehicles, during which period they will fix any and all defects specified in the warranty. An **implied warranty** is imposed on the producer or seller by law, although it may not be a written document provided at the time of sale. Under Article II, a consumer may assume that the product for sale has a clear title (in other words, that it is not stolen) and that the product will both serve the purpose for which it was made and sold as well as function as advertised.

The Law of Torts and Fraud

A **tort** is a private or civil wrong other than breach of contract. For example, a tort can result if the driver of a Domino's Pizza delivery car loses control of the vehicle and damages property or injures a person. In the case of the delivery car accident, the injured persons might sue the driver and the owner of the company—Domino's in this case—for damages resulting from the accident.

Fraud is a purposeful unlawful act to deceive or manipulate in order to damage others. Thus, in some cases, a tort may also represent a violation of criminal law. Health care fraud has become a major issue in the courts.

An important aspect of tort law involves **product liability**— businesses' legal responsibility for any negligence in the design, production, sale, and consumption of products. Product liability laws have evolved from both common and statutory law. Some states have expanded the concept of product liability to include injuries by products whether or not the producer is proven negligent. Under this strict product liability, a consumer who files suit because of an injury has to prove only that the product was defective, that the defect caused the injury, and that the defect made the product unreasonably dangerous. For example, a carving knife is expected to be sharp and is not considered defective if you cut your finger using it. But an electric knife could be considered defective and unreasonably dangerous if it continued to operate after being switched off.

Reforming tort law, particularly in regard to product liability, has become a hot political issue as businesses look for relief from huge judgments in lawsuits. Although many lawsuits are warranted—few would disagree that a wrong has occurred when a patient dies because of negligence during a medical procedure or when a child is seriously injured by a defective toy, and that the families deserve some compensation—many suits are not. Because of multimillion-dollar judgments, companies are trying to minimize their liability, and sometimes they pass on the costs of the damage awards to their customers in the form of higher prices. Some states have passed laws limiting damage awards and some tort reform is occurring at the federal level. Table A.2 lists the state court systems the U.S. Chamber of Commerce's Institute for Legal Reform has identified as being "friendliest" and "least friendly" to business in terms of juries' fairness, judges' competence and impartiality, and other factors.

The Law of Contracts

Virtually every business transaction is carried out by means of a **contract**, a mutual agreement between two or more parties that can be enforced in a court if one party chooses not

▼ **TABLE A.2** State Court Systems' Reputations for Supporting Business

Most Friendly to Business	Least Friendly to Business
Delaware	Mississippi
Nebraska	West Virginia
Virginia	Alabama
Iowa	Louisiana
Idaho	California
Utah	Texas
New Hampshire	Illinois
Minnesota	Montana
Kansas	Arkansas
Wisconsin	Missouri

Source: U.S. Chamber of Commerce Institute for Legal Reform, in Martin Kasindorf, "Robin Hood Is Alive in Court, Say Those Seeking Lawsuit Limits," *USA Today,* March 8, 2004, p. 4A.

to comply with the terms of the contract. If you rent an apartment or house, for example, your lease is a contract. If you have borrowed money under a student loan program, you have a contractual agreement to repay the money. Many aspects of contract law are covered under the Uniform Commercial Code.

A "handshake deal" is in most cases as fully and completely binding as a written, signed contract agreement. Indeed, many oil-drilling and construction contractors have for years agreed to take on projects on the basis of such handshake deals. However, individual states require that some contracts be in writing to be enforceable. Most states require that at least some of the following contracts be in writing:

- Contracts involving the sale of land or an interest in land.
- Contracts to pay somebody else's debt.
- Contracts that cannot be fulfilled within one year.
- Contracts for the sale of goods that cost more than $500 (required by the Uniform Commercial Code).

Only those contracts that meet certain requirements—called *elements*—are enforceable by the courts. A person or business seeking to enforce a contract must show that it contains the following elements: voluntary agreement, consideration, contractual capacity of the parties, and legality.

For any agreement to be considered a legal contract, all persons involved must agree to be bound by the terms of the contract. *Voluntary agreement* typically comes about when one party makes an offer and the other accepts. If both the offer and the acceptance are freely, voluntarily, and knowingly made, the acceptance forms the basis for the contract. If, however, either the offer or the acceptance are the result of fraud or force, the individual or organization subject to the fraud or force can void, or invalidate, the resulting agreement or receive compensation for damages.

The second requirement for enforcement of a contract is that it must be supported by *consideration*—that is, money or something of value must be given in return for fulfilling a contract. As a general rule, a person cannot be forced to abide by the terms of a promise unless that person receives a consideration. The something-of-value could be money, goods, services, or even a promise to do or not to do something.

Contractual capacity is the legal ability to enter into a contract. As a general rule, a court cannot enforce a contract if either party to the agreement lacks contractual capacity. A person's contractual capacity may be limited or nonexistent if he or she is a minor (under the age of 18), mentally unstable, retarded, insane, or intoxicated.

Legality is the state or condition of being lawful. For an otherwise binding contract to be enforceable, both the purpose of and the consideration for the contract must be legal. A contract in which a bank loans money at a rate of interest prohibited by law, a practice known as usury, would be an illegal contract, for example. The fact that one of the parties may commit an illegal act while performing a contract does not render the contract itself illegal, however.

Breach of contract is the failure or refusal of a party to a contract to live up to his or her promises. In the case of an apartment lease, failure to pay rent would be considered breach of contract. The breaching party—the one who fails to comply—may be liable for monetary damages that he or she causes the other person.

The Law of Agency

An **agency** is a common business relationship created when one person acts on behalf of another and under that person's control. Two parties are involved in an agency relationship: The **principal** is the one who wishes to have a specific task accomplished; the **agent** is the one who acts on behalf of the principal to accomplish the task. Authors, movie stars, and athletes often employ agents to help them obtain the best contract terms.

> An agency is a common business relationship created when one person acts on behalf of another and under that person's control.

An agency relationship is created by the mutual agreement of the principal and the agent. It is usually not necessary that such an agreement be in writing, although putting it in writing is certainly advisable. An agency relationship continues as long as both the principal and the agent so desire. It can be terminated by mutual agreement, by fulfillment of the purpose of the agency, by the refusal of either party to continue in the relationship, or by the death of either the principal or the agent. In most cases, a principal grants authority to the agent through a formal *power of attorney*, which is a legal document authorizing a person to act as someone else's

PATENTS PROVIDE COMPETITIVE ADVANTAGE FOR KODAK

In the fierce world of business competition, patents offer companies a competitive advantage over rivals. It is small wonder then that companies will defend their patents so aggressively. A patent secures an inventor's exclusive rights to an invention for 20 years in the United States. Essentially, the company gets a temporary monopoly on the product, allowing it to reap the profits. Once the patent expires, however, anyone is free to copy the invention. Patenting an invention does not guarantee success, but when one does succeed it can be highly profitable. As Eastman Kodak Co.

struggles to survive a late entrance into digital technology (the company has had only one profitable year since 2004), it relies on patents—its source of intellectual property income—to keep it afloat.

Over the past few years, Kodak has sued a number of companies for patent infringement in order to receive settlement money. For example, the company sued Samsung Electronics Co., claiming that Samsung's camera phone technology infringed on two Kodak patents. Kodak received $550 million. The company also sued LG Electronics for the same reason, netting $400 million. Kodak is currently locked in battle with Apple, each company accusing the other of patent infringement. In addition to lawsuits, the company has negotiated licensing deals regarding its patents. All in all, Kodak's many patents

have raised the money it needs to survive as it restructures.

Although the company's catalog of patents is expansive, some analysts worry that Kodak is running out of opportunities to raise this type of money. Revenue without intellectual property income continues to plummet, and shares keep falling. Can Kodak stretch out its safety net long enough to create profit in other areas of its business?[78]

Discussion Questions

1. Why are companies such as Kodak awarded patents to protect their exclusive use of technology?

2. Why does Kodak have to sue companies that infringe on its patents?

3. What can Kodak do to make a profit if most of its patents expire?

agent. The power of attorney can be used for any agency relationship, and its use is not limited to lawyers. For instance, in real estate transactions, often a lawyer or real estate agent is given power of attorney with the authority to purchase real estate for the buyer. Accounting firms often give employees agency relationships in making financial transactions.

Both officers and directors of corporations are fiduciaries, or people of trust, who use due care and loyalty as an agent in making decisions on behalf of the organization. This relationship creates a duty of care, also called duty of diligence, to make informed decisions. These agents of the corporation are not held responsible for negative outcomes if they are informed and diligent in their decisions. The duty of loyalty means that all decisions should be in the interests of the corporation and its stakeholders. Many people believe that executives at financial firms such as Countrywide Financial, Lehman Brothers, and Merrill Lynch failed to carry out their fiduciary duties. Lawsuits from shareholders called for the officers and directors to pay large sums of money from their own pockets.

The Law of Property

Property law is extremely broad in scope because it covers the ownership and transfer of all kinds of real, personal, and intellectual property. **Real property** consists of real estate and everything permanently attached to it; **personal property** basically is everything else. Personal property can be further subdivided into tangible and intangible property. *Tangible property* refers to items that have a physical existence, such as automobiles, business inventory, and clothing. *Intangible property* consists of rights and duties; its existence may be represented by a document or by some other tangible item. For example, accounts receivable, stock in a corporation, goodwill, and trademarks are all examples of intangible personal property. **Intellectual property** refers to property, such as musical works, artwork, books, and computer software, that is generated by a person's creative activities.

Copyrights, patents, and trademarks provide protection to the owners of property by giving them the exclusive right to use it. *Copyrights* protect the ownership rights on material (often intellectual property) such as books, music, videos, photos, and computer software. The creators of such works, or their heirs, generally have exclusive rights to the published or unpublished works for the creator's lifetime, plus 50 years. *Patents* give inventors exclusive rights to their invention for 20 years. The most intense competition for patents is in the pharmaceutical industry. Most patents take a minimum of 18 months to secure.

A *trademark* is a brand (name, mark, or symbol) that is registered with the U.S. Patent and Trademark Office and is thus legally protected from use by any other firm. Among the symbols that have been so protected are McDonald's golden arches and Coca-Cola's distinctive bottle shape. It is estimated that large multinational firms may have as many as 15,000 conflicts related to trademarks. Companies are diligent about protecting

their trademarks both to avoid confusion in consumers' minds and because a term that becomes part of everyday language can no longer be trademarked. The names *aspirin* and *nylon,* for example, were once the exclusive property of their creators but became so widely used as product names (rather than brand names) that now anyone can use them.

As the trend toward globalization of trade continues, and more and more businesses trade across national boundaries, protecting property rights, particularly intellectual property such as computer software, has become an increasing challenge. While a company may be able to register as a trademark a brand name or symbol in its home country, it may not be able to secure that protection abroad. Some countries have copyright and patent laws that are less strict than those of the United States; some countries will not enforce U.S. laws. China, for example, has often been criticized for permitting U.S. goods to be counterfeited there. Such counterfeiting harms not only the sales of U.S. companies but also their reputations if the knockoffs are of poor quality. Thus, businesses engaging in foreign trade may have to take extra steps to protect their property because local laws may be insufficient to protect them.

The Law of Bankruptcy

Although few businesses and individuals intentionally fail to repay (or default on) their debts, sometimes they cannot fulfill their financial obligations. Individuals may charge goods and services beyond their ability to pay for them. Businesses may take on too much debt in order to finance growth or business events such as an increase in the cost of commodities. An option of last resort in these cases is bankruptcy, or legal insolvency. The recent financial crisis caused a number of well-known companies to declare bankruptcy, including Six Flags, Chrysler, Eddie Bauer, and Circuit City. While some of these companies managed to negotiate deals with their creditors or received a government bailout, the electronics retailer Circuit City had no such luck. The company was forced to liquidate all its U.S. stores.[79]

Individuals or companies may ask a bankruptcy court to declare them unable to pay their debts and thus release them from the obligation of repaying those debts. The debtor's assets may then be sold to pay off as much of the debt as possible. In the case of a personal bankruptcy, although the individual is released from repaying debts and can start over with a clean slate, obtaining credit after bankruptcy proceedings is very difficult. About 2 million households in the United States filed for bankruptcy in 2005, the most ever. However, a new, more restrictive law went into effect in late 2005, allowing fewer consumers to use bankruptcy to eliminate their debts. The law makes it harder for consumers to prove that they should be allowed to clear their debts for what is called a "fresh start" or Chapter 7 bankruptcy. The number of Americans filing personal bankruptcy reached 1.53 million in 2010, up 9 percent from 2009. This is the highest level since the 2005

▼ **TABLE A.3** Types of Bankruptcy

Chapter 7	Requires that the business be dissolved and its assets liquidated, or sold, to pay off the debts. Individuals declaring Chapter 7 retain a limited amount of exempt assets, the amount of which may be determined by state or federal law, at the debtor's option. Although the type and value of exempt assets varies from state to state, most states' laws allow a bankrupt individual to keep an automobile, some household goods, clothing, furnishings, and at least some of the value of the debtor's residence. All nonexempt assets must be sold to pay debts.
Chapter 11	Temporarily frees a business from its financial obligations while it reorganizes and works out a payment plan with its creditors. The indebted company continues to operate its business during bankruptcy proceedings. Often, the business sells off assets and less-profitable subsidiaries to raise cash to pay off its immediate obligations.
Chapter 13	Similar to Chapter 11 but limited to individuals. This proceeding allows an individual to establish a three- to five-year plan for repaying his or her debt. Under this plan, an individual ultimately may repay as little as 10 percent of his or her debt.

law was implemented.[80] Although the person or company in debt usually initiates bankruptcy proceedings, creditors may also initiate them. The subprime mortgage crisis of early 2008 caused a string of bankruptcies among individuals, Chapter 7 and 11 bankruptcies among banks, and other businesses as well. Tougher bankruptcy laws and a slowing economy converged on the subprime crisis to create a situation where bankruptcy filings skyrocketed. Table A.3 describes the various levels of bankruptcy protection a business or individual may seek.

LAWS AFFECTING BUSINESS PRACTICES

One of the government's many roles is to act as a watchdog to ensure that businesses behave in accordance with the wishes of society. Congress has enacted a number of laws that affect business practices; some of the most important of these are summarized in Table A.4. Many state legislatures have enacted similar laws governing business within specific states.

The **Sherman Antitrust Act**, passed in 1890 to prevent businesses from restraining trade and monopolizing markets, condemns "every contract, combination, or conspiracy in restraint of trade." For example, a request that a competitor agree to fix prices or divide markets would, if accepted, result in a violation of the Sherman Act. The search engine Google has faced increased attention from antitrust authorities. In 2009, antitrust authorities were investigating a settlement Google had reached with the Author's Guild and the Association of American Publishers. The $125 million settlement would give Google the ability to scan millions of books into what will be known as the Google Book Search service. The Department of Justice thought this settlement might give Google too much control, particularly over the distribution and pricing of certain books. It began investigating whether Google was breaking any antitrust laws. This was not the first time Google was investigated for antitrust violations. A year earlier, Google had been investigated for a partnership

it was forming with Yahoo!. The deal allowed Google to sell and place advertisements on Yahoo!'s Web pages for a share in the revenue. Authorities felt this would give Google too much power that could enable it to gain monopolistic control over online advertising. Increased pressure caused Google and Yahoo! to delay the alliance.[81] The Sherman Antitrust Act, still highly relevant 100 years after its passage, is being copied throughout the world as the basis for regulating fair competition.

Because the provisions of the Sherman Antitrust Act are rather vague, courts have not always interpreted it as its creators intended. The Clayton Act was passed in 1914 to limit specific activities that can reduce competition. The **Clayton Act** prohibits price discrimination, tying and exclusive agreements, and the acquisition of stock in another corporation where the effect may be to substantially lessen competition or tend to create a monopoly. In addition, the Clayton Act prohibits members of one company's board of directors from holding seats on the boards of competing corporations. The act also exempts farm cooperatives and labor organizations from antitrust laws.

In spite of these laws regulating business practices, there are still many questions about the regulation of business. For instance, it is difficult to determine what constitutes an acceptable degree of competition and whether a monopoly is harmful to a particular market. Many mergers were permitted that resulted in less competition in the banking, publishing, and automobile industries. In some industries, such as utilities, it is not cost-effective to have too many competitors. For this reason, the government permits utility monopolies, although recently, the telephone, electricity, and communications industries have been deregulated. Furthermore, the antitrust laws are often rather vague and require interpretation, which may vary from judge to judge and court to court. Thus, what one judge defines as a monopoly or trust today may be permitted by another judge a few years from now. Businesspeople need to understand what the law says on these issues and try to conduct their affairs within the bounds of these laws.

▼ **TABLE A.4** Major Federal Laws Affecting Business Practices

Act (Date Enacted)	Purpose
Sherman Antitrust Act (1890)	Prohibits contracts, combinations, or conspiracies to restrain trade; establishes as a misdemeanor monopolizing or attempting to monopolize.
Clayton Act (1914)	Prohibits specific practices such as price discrimination, exclusive dealer arrangements, and stock acquisitions in which the effect may notably lessen competition or tend to create a monopoly.
Federal Trade Commission Act (1914)	Created the Federal Trade Commission; also gives the FTC investigatory powers to be used in preventing unfair methods of competition.
Robinson-Patman Act (1936)	Prohibits price discrimination that lessens competition among wholesalers or retailers; prohibits producers from giving disproportionate services of facilities to large buyers.
Wheeler-Lea Act (1938)	Prohibits unfair and deceptive acts and practices regardless of whether competition is injured; places advertising of foods and drugs under the jurisdiction of the FTC.
Lanham Act (1946)	Provides protections and regulation of brand names, brand marks, trade names, and trademarks.
Celler–Kefauver Act (1950)	Prohibits any corporation engaged in commerce from acquiring the whole or any part of the stock or other share of the capital assets of another corporation when the effect substantially lessens competition or tends to create a monopoly.
Fair Packaging and Labeling Act (1966)	Makes illegal the unfair or deceptive packaging or labeling of consumer products.
Magnuson-Moss Warranty (FTC) Act (1975)	Provides for minimum disclosure standards for written consumer product warranties; defines minimum consent standards for written warranties; allows the FTC to prescribe interpretive rules in policy statements regarding unfair or deceptive practices.
Consumer Goods Pricing Act (1975)	Prohibits the use of price maintenance agreements among manufacturers and resellers in interstate commerce.
Antitrust Improvements Act (1976)	Requires large corporations to inform federal regulators of prospective mergers or acquisitions so that they can be studied for any possible violations of the law.
Trademark Counterfeiting Act (1980)	Provides civil and criminal penalties against those who deal in counterfeit consumer goods or any counterfeit goods that can threaten health or safety.
Trademark Law Revision Act (1988)	Amends the Lanham Act to allow brands not yet introduced to be protected through registration with the Patent and Trademark Office.
Nutrition Labeling and Education Act (1990)	Prohibits exaggerated health claims and requires all processed foods to contain labels with nutritional information.
Telephone Consumer Protection Act (1991)	Establishes procedures to avoid unwanted telephone solicitations; prohibits marketers from using automated telephone dialing system or an artificial or prerecorded voice to certain telephone lines.
Federal Trademark Dilution Act (1995)	Provides trademark owners the right to protect trademarks and requires relinquishment of names that match or parallel existing trademarks.
Digital Millennium Copyright Act (1998)	Refined copyright laws to protect digital versions of copyrighted materials, including music and movies.
Children's Online Privacy Protection Act (2000)	Regulates the collection of personally identifiable information (name, address, e-mail address, hobbies, interests, or information collected through cookies) online from children under age 13.
Sarbanes–Oxley Act (2002)	Made securities fraud a criminal offense; stiffened penalties for corporate fraud; created an accounting oversight board; and instituted numerous other provisions designed to increase corporate transparency and compliance.
Do Not Call Implementation Act (2003)	Directs FCC and FTC to coordinate so their rules are consistent regarding telemarketing call practices, including the Do Not Call Registry.
Dodd–Frank Wall Street Reform and Consumer Protection Act (2010)	Increases accountability and transparency in the financial industry, protects consumers from deceptive financial practices, and establishes the Bureau of Consumer Financial Protection.

OUR USE AND DEPENDENCE ON THE INTERNET IS INCREASINGLY CREATING A POTENTIAL LEGAL PROBLEM FOR BUSINESSES.

THE INTERNET: LEGAL AND REGULATORY ISSUES

Our use and dependence on the Internet is increasingly creating a potential legal problem for businesses. With this growing use come questions of maintaining an acceptable level of privacy for consumers and proper competitive use of the medium. Some might consider that tracking individuals who visit or "hit" their website by attaching a "cookie" (identifying you as a website visitor for potential recontact and tracking your movement throughout the site) is an improper use of the Internet for business purposes. Others may find such practices acceptable and similar to the practices of non-Internet retailers who copy information from checks or ask customers for their name, address, or phone number before they will process a transaction. There are few specific laws that regulate business on the Internet, but the standards for acceptable behavior that are reflected in the basic laws and regulations designed for traditional businesses can be applied to business on the Internet as well. One law aimed specifically at advertising on the Internet is the CAN-SPAM Act of 2004. The law restricts unsolicited e-mail advertisements by requiring the consent of the recipient. Furthermore, the CAN-SPAM Act follows the "opt-out" model wherein recipients can elect to not receive further e-mails from a sender simply by clicking on a link.[82]

The central focus for future legislation of business conducted on the Internet is the protection of personal privacy. The present basis of personal privacy protection is the U.S. Constitution, various Supreme Court rulings, and laws such as the 1971 Fair Credit Reporting Act, the 1978 Right to Financial Privacy Act, and the 1974 Privacy Act, which deals with the release of government records. With few regulations on the use of information by businesses, companies legally buy and sell information on customers to gain competitive advantage. Sometimes existing laws are not enough to protect people, and the ease with which information on customers can be obtained becomes a problem. For example, identity theft has increased due to the proliferation of the use of the Internet. In 2009, it was estimated that data and security breaches cost organizations more than $6 million on average each time they occurred. Some of the more common security breaches (and most disturbing) occur at universities, banks, and insurance companies. Another concern is companies that use information from online consumers without the person's knowledge or permission.[83] It has been suggested that the treatment of

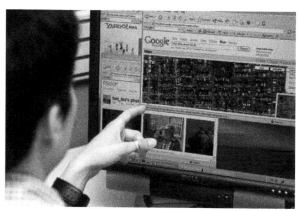

Whether you like it or not, Google, like Yahoo! and AOL, tracks people's Web browsing patterns. By tracking the sites you visit, the companies' advertisers can aim ads targeted closer to your interests.

personal data as property will ensure privacy rights by recognizing that customers have a right to control the use of their personal data.

Internet use is different from traditional interaction with businesses in that it is readily accessible, and most online businesses are able to develop databases of information on customers. Congress has restricted the development of databases on children using the Internet. The Children's Online Privacy Protection Act of 2000 prohibits websites and Internet providers from seeking personal information from children under age 13 without parental consent.

The Internet has also created a copyright dilemma for some organizations that have found that the Web addresses of other online firms either match or are very similar to their company trademark. "Cybersquatters" attempt to sell back the registration of these matching sites to the trademark owner. Companies such as Taco Bell, MTC, and KFC have paid thousands of dollars to gain control of domain names that match or parallel company trademarks. The Federal Trademark Dilution Act of 1995 helps companies address this conflict. The act provides trademark owners the right to protect trademarks, prevents the use of trademark-protected entities, and requires the relinquishment of names that match or closely parallel company trademarks. The reduction of geographic barriers, speed of response, and memory capability of the Internet will continue to create new challenges for the legal and regulatory environment in the future.

LEGAL PRESSURE FOR RESPONSIBLE BUSINESS CONDUCT

To ensure greater compliance with society's desires, both federal and state governments are moving toward increased organizational accountability for misconduct. Before 1991, laws mainly punished those employees directly responsible for an offense. Under new guidelines established by the Federal Sentencing Guidelines for Organizations (FSGO), however, both the responsible employees and the firms that employ them are held accountable for violations of federal law. Thus, the government now places responsibility for controlling and preventing misconduct squarely on the shoulders of top management. The main objectives of the federal guidelines are to train employees, self-monitor and supervise employee conduct, deter unethical acts, and punish those organizational members who engage in illegal acts.

If an organization's culture and policies reward or provide opportunities to engage in misconduct through lack of managerial concern or failure to comply with the seven minimum requirements of the FSGO (provided in Table A.5), then the organization may incur not only penalties but also the loss of customer trust, public confidence, and other intangible assets. For this reason, organizations cannot succeed solely through a legalistic approach to compliance with the sentencing guidelines; top management must cultivate high ethical standards that will serve as barriers to illegal conduct. The organization must want to be a good citizen and recognize the importance of compliance to successful workplace activities and relationships.

The federal guidelines also require businesses to develop programs that can detect—and that will deter employees from engaging in—misconduct. To be considered effective, such compliance programs must include disclosure of any wrongdoing, cooperation with the government, and acceptance of

> "To ensure greater compliance with society's desires, both federal and state governments are moving toward increased organizational accountability for misconduct."

A 2004 amendment to the FSGO requires that a business's governing authority be well informed about its ethics program with respect to content, implementation, and effectiveness. This places the responsibility squarely on the shoulders of the firm's leadership, usually the board of directors. The board must ensure that there is a high-ranking manager accountable for the day-to-day operational oversight of the ethics program. The board must provide for adequate authority, resources, and access to the board or an appropriate subcommittee of the board. The board must ensure that there are confidential mechanisms available so that the organization's employees and agents may report or seek guidance about potential or actual misconduct without fear of retaliation. Finally, the board is required to oversee the discovery of risks and to design, implement, and modify approaches to deal with those risks.

responsibility for the misconduct. Codes of ethics, employee ethics training, hotlines (direct 800 phone numbers), compliance directors, newsletters, brochures, and other communication methods are typical components of a compliance program. The ethics component, discussed in Chapter 2, acts as a buffer, keeping firms away from the thin line that separates unethical and illegal conduct.

Despite the existing legislation, a number of ethics scandals in the early 2000s led Congress to pass—almost unanimously—the **Sarbanes–Oxley Act**, which criminalized securities fraud and strengthened penalties for corporate fraud. It also created an accounting oversight board that requires corporations to establish codes of ethics for financial reporting and to develop greater transparency in financial reports to investors and other

▼ **TABLE A.5** Seven Steps to Compliance

1. Develop standards and procedures to reduce the propensity for criminal conduct.
2. Designate a high-level compliance manager or ethics officer to oversee the compliance program.
3. Avoid delegating authority to people known to have a propensity to engage in misconduct.
4. Communicate standards and procedures to employees, other agents, and independent contractors through training programs and publications.
5. Establish systems to monitor and audit misconduct and to allow employees and agents to report criminal activity.
6. Enforce standards and punishments consistently across all employees in the organization.
7. Respond immediately to misconduct and take reasonable steps to prevent further criminal conduct.

Source: United States Sentencing Commission, *Federal Sentencing Guidelines for Organizations,* 1991.

interested parties. Additionally, the law requires top corporate executives to sign off on their firms' financial reports, and they risk fines and jail sentences if they misrepresent their companies' financial position. Table A.6 summarizes the major provisions of the Sarbanes–Oxley Act.

The Sarbanes–Oxley Act has created a number of concerns and is considered burdensome and expensive to corporations. Large corporations report spending more than $4 million each year to comply with the Act according to Financial Executives International. The Act has caused more than 500 public companies a year to report problems in their accounting systems. Additionally, Sarbanes-Oxley failed to prevent and detect the widespread misconduct of financial institutions that led to the financial crisis. This means that the overwhelming majority of businesses are in compliance with the law.

On the other hand, there are many benefits, including greater accountability of top managers and boards of directors, that improve investor confidence and protect employees, especially their retirement plans. It is believed that the law has more benefits than drawbacks—with the greatest benefit being that boards of directors and top managers are better informed.

> **In spite of the benefits Sarbanes–Oxley offers, it did not prevent widespread corporate corruption from leading to the most recent recession.**

Some companies such as Cisco and Pitney Bowes report improved efficiency and cost savings from better financial information.

In spite of the benefits Sarbanes–Oxley offers, it did not prevent widespread corporate corruption from leading to the most recent recession. The resulting financial crisis prompted the Obama administration to create new regulation to reform Wall Street and the financial industry. In 2010, the Dodd–Frank Wall Street Reform and Consumer Protection Act was passed. In addition to new regulations for financial institutions, the legislation created a Consumer Financial Protection Bureau to protect consumers from complex or deceptive financial products. Table A.7 highlights some of the major provisions of the Dodd–Frank Act.

The Dodd–Frank Act contains 16 titles meant to increase consumer protection, enhance transparency and accountability in the financial sector, and create new financial agencies. In some ways, Dodd–Frank is attempting to improve upon provisions laid out in the Sarbanes–Oxley Act. For instance, Dodd–Frank takes whistleblower protection a step further by offering additional incentives to whistleblowers for reporting misconduct. If whistleblowers report misconduct that results in penalties of

▼ **TABLE A.6** Major Provisions of the Sarbanes-Oxley Act

1. Requires the establishment of a Public Company Accounting Oversight Board in charge of regulations administered by the Securities and Exchange Commission.

2. Requires CEOs and CFOs to certify that their companies' financial statements are true and without misleading statements.

3. Requires that corporate boards of directors' audit committees consist of independent members who have no material interests in the company.

4. Prohibits corporations from making or offering loans to officers and board members.

5. Requires codes of ethics for senior financial officers; code must be registered with the SEC.

6. Prohibits accounting firms from providing both auditing and consulting services to the same client without the approval of the client firm's audit committee.

7. Requires company attorneys to report wrongdoing to top managers and, if necessary, to the board of directors; if managers and directors fail to respond to reports of wrongdoing, the attorney should stop representing the company.

8. Mandates "whistleblower protection" for persons who disclose wrongdoing to authorities.

9. Requires financial securities analysts to certify that their recommendations are based on objective reports.

10. Requires mutual fund managers to disclose how they vote shareholder proxies, giving investors information about how their shares influence decisions.

11. Establishes a 10-year penalty for mail/wire fraud.

12. Prohibits the two senior auditors from working on a corporation's account for more than five years; other auditors are prohibited from working on an account for more than seven years. In other words, accounting firms must rotate individual auditors from one account to another from time to time.

Source: O. C. Ferrell, John Fraedrich, and Linda Ferrell, *Business Ethics: Ethical Decision Making and Cases,* 8th ed. (Mason, OH: South-Western Cengage Learning, 2011), pp. 108–109.

▼ **TABLE A.7** Major Provisions of the Dodd-Frank Wall Street Reform and Consumer Protection Act

1. Enhances stability of the finance industry through the creation of two new financial agencies, the Financial Oversight Stability Council and the Office of Financial Research.

2. Institutes an orderly liquidation procedure for the Federal Deposit Insurance Corporation to liquidate failing companies.

3. Eliminates the Office of Thrift Supervision and transfers its powers to the Comptroller of the Currency.

4. Creates stronger regulation and greater oversight of hedge funds.

5. Establishes the Federal Insurance Agency to gather information and oversee the insurance industry for risks.

6. Requires regulators to have regulations in place for banks. Also prohibits and/or limits proprietary trading, hedge fund sponsorship and private equity funds, and relationships with hedge funds and private equity funds.

7. Regulates derivatives and complex financial instruments by limiting where they can be traded and ensuring that traders have the financial resources to meet their responsibilities.

8. Provides a framework for creating risk-management standards for financial market utilities and the payment, clearing, and settlement activities performed by institutions.

9. Improves investor protection through acts such as creating a whistle-blower bounty program and increasing consumer access to their credit scores.

10. Institutes the Bureau of Consumer Financial Protection to educate consumers and protect them from deceptive financial products.

11. Attempts to reform the Federal Reserve in ways that include limiting the Federal Reserve's lending authority, re-evaluating methods for Federal Reserve regulations and the appointment of Federal Reserve Bank directors, and instituting additional disclosure requirements.

12. Reforms mortgage activities with new provisions that include increasing the lender's responsibility to ensure the borrower can pay back the loan, prohibiting unfair lending practices, requiring additional disclosure in the mortgage loan process, and imposing penalties against those found guilty of noncompliance with the new standards.

Source: *Brief Summary of the Dodd-Frank Wall Street Reform and Consumer Protection Act,* http://banking.senate.gov/public/_files/070110_Dodd_Frank_Wall_Street_Reform_comprehensive_summary_Final.pdf

over $1 million, the whistleblower will be entitled to a percentage of the settlement.[84] Another provision, the Durbin Amendment, limits the swipe fees that debit card issuers are allowed to charge merchants.[85] Additionally, complex financial instruments must now be made more transparent so that consumers will have a better understanding of what these instruments involve.

The Act also created three new agencies: the Consumer Financial Protection Bureau (CFPB), the Office of Financial Research, and the Financial Stability Oversight Council. While the CFPB was passed to protect consumers, the other two agencies work to maintain stability in the financial industry so such a crisis will not reoccur in the future.[86] Although it is too early to tell whether these regulations will serve to create wide-scale positive financial reform, the Dodd-Frank Act is certainly leading to major changes on Wall Street and in the financial sector. ■

chapter two

 in a
nutshell

You must understand the role of ethics and social responsibility in making good business decisions. Learning to recognize business ethics issues, how businesses can improve their ethical behavior, and the impact of how companies respond to these issues is the basis of social responsibility.

The following statements will test your take-away knowledge from this chapter. Do your best to explain each one in the space provided below.

LO.1 Define business ethics and social responsibility and examine their importance.

LO.2 Detect some of the ethical issues that may arise in business.

LO.3 Specify how businesses can promote ethical behavior.

LO.4 Explain the four dimensions of social responsibility.

LO.5 Debate an organization's social responsibilities to owners, employees, consumers, the environment, and the community.

Did your answers include the following important points?

LO.1. Define business ethics and social responsibility and examine their importance.

- The principles and standards that determine acceptable conduct in business organizations are defined as business ethics.
- A business's obligation to maximize its positive impact and minimize its negative impact on society illustrates the concept of social responsibility.
- Business ethics relates to an individual's or a work group's decisions that society evaluates as right or wrong, whereas social responsibility is a broader concept that concerns the impact of the entire business's activities on society.
- Socially responsible businesses win the trust and respect of their employees, customers, and society and increase profits.
- Ethics is important in business because it builds trust and confidence in business relationships.

LO.2. Detect some of the ethical issues that may arise in business.

- An ethical issue is an identifiable problem, situation, or opportunity requiring a person or organization to choose from among several actions that must be evaluated as right or wrong.
- Ethical issues can be categorized in the context of their relation with conflicts of interest, fairness and honesty, communications, and business associations.

LO.3. Specify how businesses can promote ethical behavior.

- Businesses can promote ethical behavior among employees by limiting their opportunity to engage in misconduct.

- Formal codes of ethics, ethical policies, and ethics training programs reduce incidences of unethical behavior by informing employees what is expected of them and providing punishments for those who fail to comply.

LO.4. Explain the four dimensions of social responsibility.

- The four dimensions of social responsibility are economic (being profitable), legal (obeying the law), ethical (doing what is right, just, and fair), and voluntary (being a good corporate citizen).

LO.5. Debate an organization's social responsibilities to owners, employees, consumers, the environment, and the community.

- Businesses must maintain proper accounting procedures, provide all relevant information about the performance of the firm to investors, and protect the owners' rights and investments.
- In relations with employees, businesses are expected to provide a safe workplace, pay employees adequately for their work, and treat them fairly.
- Consumerism refers to the activities undertaken by independent individuals, groups, and organizations to protect their rights as consumers.
- Increasingly, society expects businesses to take greater responsibility for the environment, especially with regard to animal rights, as well as water, air, land, and noise pollution.
- Many businesses engage in activities to make the communities in which they operate better places for everyone to live and work.

Practical Application

LO.1.

- If a very successful professional football team has been ignoring the players' use of illegal muscle-building steroids, the owners should begin focusing on improving the organization's _____.
- A company's obligation to increase its positive impact and decrease its negative impact is its _____.
- The _____ criminalized securities fraud and stiffened penalties for corporate fraud.

LO.2.

- A(n) _____ is the most common ethical issue identified by employees.
- Any payment, gift, or special favor intended to influence the outcome of a decision can be considered a(n) _____.
- If a person takes someone's work and presents it as his or her own without mentioning the source it would be considered an act of

_____.

LO.3.

- _____ occurs when an employee exposes an employer's wrongdoing to outsiders.

- A set of formalized rules and standards that describe what a company expects of its employees is called a(n) _____ .
- According to the text, ethical decisions in an organization are influenced by (1) individual moral standards, (2) the influence of managers and co-workers, and (3) _____.

LO.4.

- Being profitable relates to _____ social responsibility.
- Consumers vote against firms they view as socially irresponsible by not _____.
- Philanthropic contributions made by a business to a charitable organization represent _____ social responsibility.

LO.5.

- Businesses must first be responsible to their _____.
- Many of the laws regulating safety in the workplace are enforced by

_____.
- _____ ensures the fair treatment of consumers who voice complaints about a purchased product.

chapter three

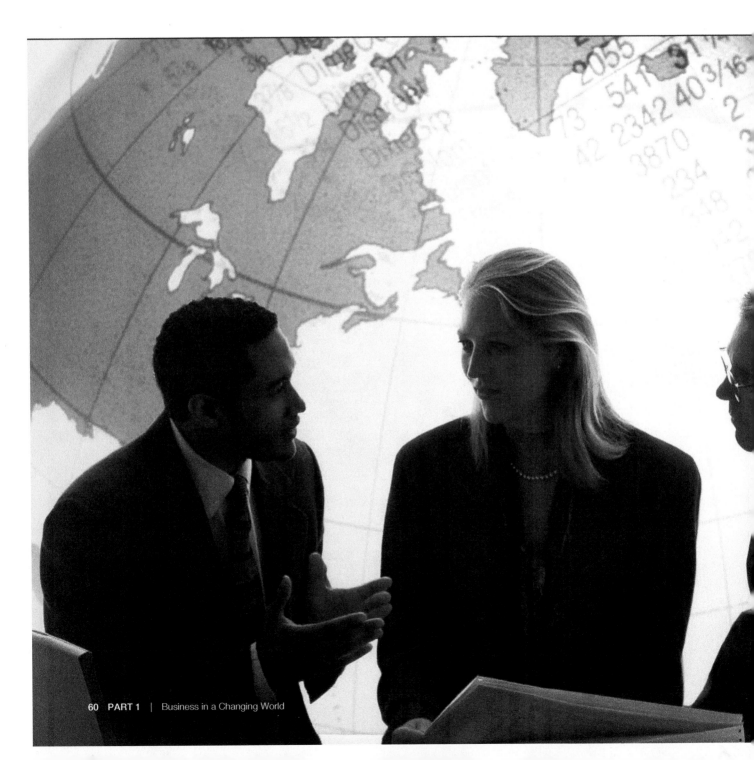

business in a
borderless world

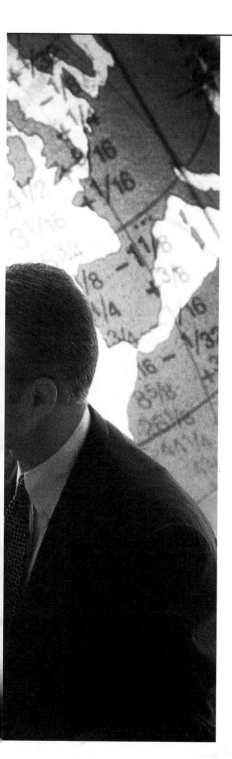

introduction

Consumers around the world can drink Coca-Cola and Pepsi; eat at McDonald's and Pizza Hut; see movies from Mexico, England, France, Australia, and China; and watch CNN and MTV on Samsung and Panasonic televisions. It may surprise you that the Japanese firm Komatsu sells earth-moving equipment to China that is manufactured in Peoria, Illinois.[1] The products you consume today are just as likely to have been made in China, Korea, or Germany as in the United States. Likewise, consumers in other countries buy Western electrical equipment, clothing, rock music, cosmetics, and toiletries, as well as computers, robots, and earth-moving equipment.

Many U.S. firms are finding that international markets provide tremendous opportunities for growth. Accessing these markets can promote innovation, while intensifying global competition spurs companies to market better and less expensive

products. Today, the nearly 7 billion people who inhabit the earth comprise one tremendous marketplace.

In this chapter, we explore business in this exciting global marketplace. First, we look at the nature of international business, including barriers and promoters of trade across international boundaries. Next, we consider the levels of organizational involvement in international business. Finally, we briefly discuss strategies for trading across national borders.

LEARNING OBJECTIVES

L01 Explore some of the factors within the international trade environment that influence business.

L02 Investigate some of the economic, legal-political, social, cultural, and technological barriers to international business.

L03 Specify some of the agreements, alliances, and organizations that may encourage trade across international boundaries.

L04 Summarize the different levels of organizational involvement in international trade.

L05 Contrast two basic strategies used in international business.

international business the buying, selling, and trading of goods and services across national boundaries

absolute advantage a monopoly that exists when a country is the only source of an item, the only producer of an item, or the most efficient producer of an item

comparative advantage the basis of most international trade, when a country specializes in products that it can supply more efficiently or at a lower cost than it can produce other items

outsourcing the transferring of manufacturing or other tasks—such as data processing—to countries where labor and supplies are less expensive

exporting the sale of goods and services to foreign markets

THE ROLE OF INTERNATIONAL BUSINESS

International business refers to the buying, selling, and trading of goods and services across national boundaries. Falling political barriers and new technology are making it possible for more and more companies to sell their products overseas as well as at home. And, as differences among nations continue to narrow, the trend toward the globalization of business is becoming increasingly important. Starbucks, for example, serves 60 million customers a week at 17,000 locations in 55 countries.[3] The Internet provides many companies easier entry to access global markets than opening brick-and-mortar stores.[4] Amazon.com, an online retailer, has distribution centers from

?

DID YOU KNOW?

Subway has surpassed McDonald's as the largest global restaurant chain with over 33,000 units.[2]

brand with the needs of local consumers.[6] To begin our study of international business, we must first consider some economic issues: why nations trade, exporting and importing, and the balance of trade.

Why Nations Trade

Nations and businesses engage in international trade to obtain raw materials and goods that are otherwise unavailable to them or are available elsewhere at a lower price than that at which they themselves can produce. A nation, or individuals and organizations from a nation, sell surplus materials and goods to acquire funds to buy the goods, services, and ideas its people need. Poland and Hungary, for example, want to trade with Western nations so that they can acquire new technology and techniques to revitalize their formerly communist economies. Which goods

> # Falling political barriers and new technology are making it possible for more and more companies to sell their products overseas as well as at home.

Nevada to Germany that fill millions of orders a day and ship them to customers in every corner of the world. Procter & Gamble's Febreze brand passed the $1 billion mark partially due to its strong growth overseas. While U.S. sales of air-fresheners have fallen in recent years, global sales have seen an increase.[5] Indeed, most of the world's population and two-thirds of its total purchasing power are outside the United States.

When McDonald's sells a Big Mac in Moscow, Sony sells a stereo in Detroit, or a small Swiss medical supply company sells a shipment of orthopedic devices to a hospital in Monterrey, Mexico, the sale affects the economies of the countries involved. The U.S. market, with 311 million consumers, makes up only a small part of the nearly 7 billion people elsewhere in the world to whom global companies must consider marketing. Global marketing requires balancing your global

and services a nation sells depends on what resources it has available.

Some nations have a monopoly on the production of a particular resource or product. Such a monopoly, or **absolute advantage**, exists when a country is the only source of an item, the only producer of an item, or the most efficient producer of an item. Because South Africa has the largest deposits of diamonds in the world, one company, De Beers Consolidated Mines Ltd., controls a major portion of the world's diamond trade and uses its control to maintain high prices for gem-quality diamonds. The United States, until recently, held an absolute advantage in oil-drilling equipment. But an absolute advantage not based on the availability of natural resources rarely lasts, and Japan and Russia are now challenging the United States in the production of oil-drilling equipment.

American companies such as KFC have become widely popular in China. Some are making more sales in China than they are in the United States.

Most international trade is based on **comparative advantage**, which occurs when a country specializes in products that it can supply more efficiently or at a lower cost than it can produce other items. The United States has a comparative advantage in producing agricultural commodities such as corn and wheat. The United States at one time had a comparative advantage in

become a controversial practice in the United States because many jobs have moved overseas where those tasks can be accomplished for lower costs. For example, the Philippines has surpassed India as the popular choice for call-center jobs. Call-center jobs are appealing to many Filipinos because the pay is almost as much as the average family income within the

> "Outsourcing has become a controversial practice in the United States because many jobs have moved overseas where those tasks can be accomplished for lower costs."

manufacturing automobiles, heavy machinery, airplanes, and weapons; other countries now hold the comparative advantage for many of these products. Other countries, particularly India and Ireland, are also gaining a comparative advantage over the United States in the provision of some services, such as call-center operations, engineering, and software programming. As a result, U.S. companies are increasingly **outsourcing**, or transferring manufacturing and other tasks to countries where labor and supplies are less expensive. Outsourcing has

country. English is also one of the country's official languages, which makes it easier to communicate with English-speaking customers.[7]

Trade between Countries

To obtain needed goods and services and the funds to pay for them, nations trade by exporting and importing. **Exporting** is the sale of goods and services to foreign markets. The United States exported more than $1.8 trillion in goods and

▼ **TABLE 3.1** U.S. Trade Deficit (in billions of dollars)

	1980	1990	2000	2005	2006	2007	2008	2009	2010*
Exports	$333	$576	$1,133	$1,300	$1,455.7	$1,621.8	$1,826.6	$1,553.1	$1,831.8
Imports	326	632	1,532	2,026	2,204.2	2,333.4	2,522.5	1,933.7	$2,329.7
Trade Surplus/Deficit	7	57	399	726	758.5	711.6	695.9	380.7	497.8

Sources: Department of Commerce and Robert E. Scott and David Ratner, "Trade Picture," The Economic Policy Institute, February 10, 2006, www.epinet.org/content.cfm/webfeatures_econindicators_tradepich20060210 (accessed June 5, 2006); U.S. Census Bureau, Foreign Trade Statistics, www.census.gov/foreign-trade/statistics/highlights/annual.html (accessed April 4, 2008); "Goods and Services Deficit Increases in 2010," U.S. Census Bureau, February 11, 2011, www.census.gov/indicator/www/ustrade.html (accessed March 2, 2011).

services in 2010.[8] In China, General Motors is targeting wealthier customers with the Cadillac, middle management with the Buick Excelle, office workers with the Chevrolet Spark, and rural consumers with the Wuling minivan.[9] U.S. companies that view China as both a growth market for exports and a market for lower cost labor for imports and can strategically integrate these into their operations enjoy significantly higher profits than companies that focus on only one of these opportunities.[10] U.S. businesses export many goods and services, particularly agricultural, entertainment (movies, television shows, etc.), and technological products. **Importing** is the purchase of goods and services from foreign sources. Many of the goods you buy in the United States are likely to be imports or to have some imported components. Sometimes, you may not even realize they are imports. The United States imported more than $2.3 trillion in goods and services in 2010.[11]

Balance of Trade

You have probably read or heard about the fact that the United States has a trade deficit, but what is a trade deficit? A nation's **balance of trade** is the difference in value between its exports and imports. Because the United States (and some other nations as well) imports more products than it exports, it has a negative balance of trade, or **trade deficit.** In 2010 the United States had a trade deficit of $497.8 billion.[12] Table 3.1 shows the U.S. trade deficit. The trade deficit fluctuates according to such factors as the health of the United States and other economies, productivity, perceived quality, and exchange rates. In 2010 the United States had a trade deficit with China of over $273 billion.[13] As Figure 3.1 indicates, U.S. exports to China have been rapidly increasing but not fast enough to offset the imports from China. Trade deficits are harmful because they can mean the failure of businesses, the loss of jobs, and a lowered standard of living.

CHINA STRUGGLES WITH LUXURY BRANDS

Thanks to its rapid economic growth, Chinese demand for luxury items is growing. Some Chinese consumers like luxury products so much that they will make significant sacrifices (such as skipping meals) in order to purchase them. China currently ranks number two among luxury goods markets and is growing faster in this area than any other nation.

Despite a love for high-class products, luxury brands face many difficulties in China. The Administration for Industry and Commerce of Zhejiang province recently took actions against brands such as Tommy Hilfiger for selling goods that did not meet the country's quality standards. Luxury brands can also suffer when they manufacture products in China itself. Giorgio Armani found this out when it manufactured its Emporio Armani line in China. Chinese consumers patronizing Armani wanted to purchase European fashions. After realizing that the items were made in China, they felt deceived. On the other hand, while Chinese consumers enjoy foreign brands, the Chinese government is working to promote brands created within China. These opposing forces (consumer versus government preferences) make it difficult for foreign luxury goods.

In spite of these challenges, companies that can adapt to the Chinese market have done well. Take Italian menswear company Zegna. Zegna owes its success in China, which makes up one-quarter of the company's annual sales, to its willingness to adapt to consumer preferences. For example, Chinese consumers enjoy seeing new inventory on a regular basis. Therefore, Zegna boasts six collections annually compared to four collections common to other companies. These adaptations, in addition to its commitment to quality, have helped Zegna succeed in China. For many luxury brand owners, the success of Zegna and similar brands makes doing business in China well worth the risk.[14]

Discussion Questions

1. Why do you believe that luxury brands are so popular in China?

2. Why is the Chinese government working to discourage consumers from buying foreign luxury brands?

3. Why are Chinese brands not as desired by consumers as foreign luxury brands?

importing the purchase of goods and services from foreign sources	**balance of trade** the difference in value between a nation's exports and its imports	**trade deficit** a nation's negative balance of trade, which exists when that country imports more products than it exports	**balance of payments** the difference between the flow of money into and out of a country

▼FIGURE 3.1
U.S. Exports to China ($ millions of U.S. dollars)

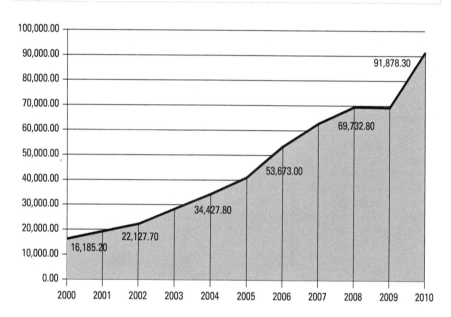

Sources: "Trade in Goods (Imports, Exports and Trade Balance) with China," U.S. Census Bureau: Foreign Trade Statistics, www.census.gov/foreign-trade/balance/c5700.html (accessed March 2, 2011).

▼ **TABLE 3.2** Top Ten Countries with Which United States Has Trade Deficits/Surpluses

Trade Deficit	Trade Surplus
1. China	Hong Kong
2. Mexico	Netherlands
3. Japan	Singapore
4. Federal Republic of Germany	Australia
5. Canada	Belgium
6. Nigeria	United Arab Emirates
7. Saudi Arabia	Turkey
8. Venezuela	Spain
9. Russia	Brazil
10. Angola	Egypt

Sources: "Top Ten Countries with Which the U.S. Has a Trade Deficit," April 2010, www.census.gov/foreign-trade/top/dst/2010/04/deficit.html (accessed March 2, 2011); "Top Ten Countries with Which the U.S. Has a Trade Surplus," December 2010, www.census.gov/foreign-trade/top/dst/current/surplus.html (accessed March 2, 2011).

Of course, when a nation exports more goods than it imports, it has a favorable balance of trade, or trade surplus. Until about 1970, the United States had a trade surplus due to an abundance of natural resources and the relative efficiency of its manufacturing systems. Table 3.2 shows the top 10 countries with which the United States has a trade deficit and a trade surplus.

The difference between the flow of money into and out of a country is called its **balance of payments**. A country's balance of trade, foreign investments, foreign aid, loans, military expenditures, and money spent by tourists comprise its balance of payments. As you might expect, a country with a trade surplus generally has a favorable balance of payments because it is receiving more money from trade with foreign countries than it is paying out. When a country has a trade deficit, more money flows out of the country than into it. If more money flows out of the country than into it from tourism and other sources, the country may experience declining production and higher unemployment, because there is less money available for spending.

INTERNATIONAL TRADE BARRIERS

Completely free trade seldom exists. When a company decides to do business outside its own country, it will encounter a number of barriers to international trade. Any firm considering international business must research the other country's economic, legal, political, social, cultural, and technological background. Such research will help the company choose an appropriate level of involvement and operating strategies, as we will see later in this chapter.

Economic Barriers

When looking at doing business in another country, managers must consider a number of basic economic factors, such as economic development, infrastructure, and exchange rates.

infrastructure the physical facilities that support a country's economic activities, such as railroads, highways, ports, airfields, utilities and power plants, schools, hospitals, communication systems, and commercial distribution systems

exchange rate the ratio at which one nation's currency can be exchanged for another nation's currency

Economic Development

When considering doing business abroad, U.S. businesspeople need to recognize that they cannot take for granted that other countries offer the same things as are found in *industrialized nations*—economically advanced countries such as the United States, Japan, Great Britain, and Canada. Many countries in Africa, Asia, and South America, for example, are in general poorer and less economically advanced than those in North America and Europe; they are often called *less-developed countries* (LDCs). LDCs are characterized by low per-capita income (income generated by the nation's production of goods and services divided by the population), which means that consumers are less likely to purchase nonessential products. Nonetheless, LDCs represent a potentially huge and profitable market for many businesses because they may be buying technology to improve their infrastructures, and much of the population may desire consumer products. For example, pharmaceutical companies offer infant vaccines in LDCs at a fraction of what they cost in developed countries. While the companies make less in profit on these drugs, they build their reputation as good corporate citizens and help many people have better lives. As emerging economies such as China and India have begun to prosper, more citizens are demanding health care. With China now the third-largest vaccine market in the world, pharmaceutical manufacturers like Novartis are partnering with Chinese companies to offer medicines at affordable prices and increase their share in this lucrative industry.[15]

A country's level of development is determined in part by its **infrastructure,** the physical facilities that support its economic activities, such as railroads, highways, ports, airfields, utilities and power plants, schools, hospitals, communication systems, and commercial distribution systems. When doing business in LDCs, for example, a business may need to compensate for rudimentary distribution and communication systems, or even a lack of technology.

Exchange Rates The ratio at which one nation's currency can be exchanged for another nation's currency is the **exchange rate.** Exchange rates vary daily and can be found in newspapers and through many sites on the Internet. Familiarity with exchange rates is important because they affect the cost of imports and exports. When the value of the U.S. dollar declines relative to other currencies, such as the euro, the price of imports becomes relatively expensive for U.S. consumers.

> "Devaluation decreases the value of currency in relation to other currencies."

The infrastructure of countries—their transportation, communication, and other systems—differ around the world. AT&T has used the opportunity to make inroads with consumers who don't want their cell phones to stop working when they go abroad.

On the other hand, U.S. exports become relatively cheap for international markets—in this example, the European Union.

Occasionally, a government may intentionally alter the value of its currency through fiscal policy. Devaluation decreases the value of currency in relation to other currencies. If the U.S. government were to devalue the dollar, it would lower the cost of American goods abroad and make trips to the United States less expensive for foreign tourists. Thus, devaluation encourages the sale of domestic goods and tourism. Mexico has repeatedly devalued the peso for this reason. Revaluation, which increases the value of a currency in relation to other currencies, occurs rarely.

Ethical, Legal, and Political Barriers

A company that decides to enter the international marketplace must contend with potentially complex relationships among the different laws of its own nation, international laws, and the laws of the nation with which it will be trading; various trade restrictions imposed on international trade; changing political climates; and different ethical values. Legal and ethical requirements for successful business are increasing globally. Research in Motion (RIM) ran into legal barriers in Saudi Arabia and the United Arab Emirates. The two countries announced a countrywide ban of the company's Black-Berry devices out of a concern that data on the devices were encrypted and could not be monitored. Additionally, because information on BlackBerrys was routed through RIM's oversea suppliers, the countries felt this could allow outside parties access to personal data. The bans were lifted after RIM agreed to make some changes. As part of the agreement with Saudi Arabia, RIM agreed to use local data servers.[16]

Laws and Regulations

The United States has a number of laws and regulations that govern the activities of U.S. firms engaged in international trade. For example, the Webb-Pomerene Export Trade Act of 1918 exempts American firms from antitrust laws if those firms are acting together to enter international trade. This law allows selected U.S. firms to form monopolies to compete with foreign monopolistic organizations, although they are not allowed to limit free trade and competition within the United States or to use unfair methods of competition in international trade. The United States also has a variety of friendship, commerce, and navigation treaties with other nations. These treaties allow business to be transacted between citizens of the specified countries. For example, Belgium is a gateway to European markets and has lowered its taxes to give U.S. companies greater reason to locate their European operations there. Belgium has the lowest patent income tax and has 0 percent withholding tax on corporate dividends and interest from a U.S. company. This prevents a company from paying both U.S. and Belgian tax, or double taxation.[17]

Once outside U.S. borders, businesspeople are likely to find that the laws of other nations differ from those of the United States. Many of the legal rights that Americans take for granted do not exist in other countries, and a firm doing business abroad must understand and obey the laws of the host country. Some countries have strict laws limiting the amount of local currency that can be taken out of the country and the amount of currency that

can be brought in; others forbid foreigners from owning real property outright. In Mexico, for example, foreigners cannot directly own property in what is known as the "Restricted Zone." The Restricted Zone includes land within 100 kilometers of Mexico's international borders along with land within 50 kilometers of Mexico's oceans and beaches. Foreigners who wish to use property in these areas must obtain a title through a bank title transfer or through a corporation.[18]

> **import tariff** a tax levied by a nation on goods imported into the country

Some countries have copyright and patent laws that are less strict than those of the United States, and some countries fail to honor U.S. laws. Because copying is a tradition in China and Vietnam and laws protecting copyrights and intellectual property are weak and minimally enforced, those countries are flooded with counterfeit videos, movies, CDs, computer software, furniture, and clothing. Companies are angry because the counterfeits harm not only their sales, but also their reputations if the knockoffs are of poor quality. Such counterfeiting is not limited to China or Vietnam. It is estimated that nearly half of all software installed on personal computers worldwide is illegally pirated or copied, amounting to more than $50 billion in global revenue losses annually.[19] In countries where these activities occur, laws against them may not be sufficiently enforced, if counterfeiting is deemed illegal. Thus, businesses engaging in foreign trade may have to take extra steps to protect their products because local laws may be insufficient to do so.

Tariffs and Trade Restrictions

Tariffs and other trade restrictions are part of a country's legal structure but may be established or removed for political reasons. An **import tariff** is a tax levied by a nation on goods imported into the country. A *fixed tariff* is a specific amount of money levied on each unit of a product brought into the country, while an *ad valorem tariff* is based on the value of the item. Most countries allow citizens traveling abroad to bring home a certain amount of merchandise without paying an import tariff. A U.S. citizen may bring $200 worth of merchandise into the United States duty free. After that, U.S. citizens must pay an ad valorem tariff based on the cost of the item and the country of origin. Thus, identical

IS THERE ROOM FOR ENTREPRENEURS IN CUBA?

For the first time in its communist history, the entrepreneur may become part of Cuba's business landscape. However, it will come at a cost. Cuba will lay off over a half million state workers to make way for private-sector jobs.

This marks a major shift in a country traditionally viewed as the enemy of entrepreneurship. Cuban entrepreneurs are subjected to high taxes, advertising bans, no access to bank or foreign credit exchange, hiring restrictions, and more. Creating private-sector job growth will require major economic reforms. According to the Cuban union, the government has announced it will increase the job options available, distribute more licenses to allow citizens

to find work on their own, and lease more land.

These changes seem promising to other countries. A more privatized Cuban economy might enable more foreign investment. There is already talk of extending microloans to Cuba to support small-business growth. However, the willingness of the government to lift restrictions on private enterprise will largely determine whether entrepreneurship in Cuba will take off.[20]

exchange controls regulations that restrict the amount of currency that can be bought or sold

quota a restriction on the number of units of a particular product that can be imported into a country

embargo a prohibition on trade in a particular product

dumping the act of a country or business selling products at less than what it costs to produce them

cartel a group of firms or nations that agree to act as a monopoly and not compete with each other, in order to generate a competitive advantage in world markets

The vegetable cutter in the bottom photo was distributed by the NingHai Well International Trade Co. in China. The dubious honor is given to the "best" product knockoffs by the organization Action Plagiarius in an effort to shame their makers. (The Veggi Cut Revolution, top photo, manufactured by swizzzProzzz AG in Switzerland, is the original item.)

items purchased in different countries might have different tariffs.

Countries sometimes levy tariffs for political reasons, as when they impose sanctions against other countries to protest their actions. However, import tariffs are more commonly imposed to protect domestic products by raising the price of imported ones. Such protective tariffs have become controversial, as Americans become increasingly concerned over the U.S. trade deficit. Protective tariffs allow more expensive domestic goods to compete with foreign ones. For example, the United States has lost a significant number of steelworks over the past few decades to foreign competition in places such as China. Other markets can produce steel more cheaply than the United States. Many people and special interest groups in the United States, such as unions, would like to see tariffs placed on Chinese steel,

which is significantly less expensive, in order to protect remaining U.S. steel production. The United States has also imposed tariffs on imported sugar for almost two centuries. The European Union levies tariffs on many products, including some seafood imports.

Critics of protective tariffs argue that their use inhibits free trade and competition. Supporters of protective tariffs say they insulate domestic industries, particularly new ones, against well-established foreign competitors. Once an industry matures, however, its advocates may be reluctant to let go of the tariff that protected it. Tariffs also help when, because of low labor costs and other advantages, foreign competitors can afford to sell their products at prices lower than those charged by domestic companies. Some Americans argue that tariffs should be used to keep domestic wages high and unemployment low.

Exchange controls restrict the amount of currency that can be bought or sold. Some countries control their foreign trade by forcing businesspeople to buy and sell foreign products through a central bank. If John Deere, for example, receives payments for its tractors in a foreign currency, it may be required to sell the currency to that nation's central bank. When foreign currency is in short supply, as it is in many less-developed countries, the government uses foreign currency to purchase necessities and capital goods and produces other products locally, thus limiting its need for foreign imports.

A **quota** limits the number of units of a particular product that can be imported into a country. A quota may be established by voluntary agreement or by government decree. The United States imposes quotas on certain goods, such as garments produced in Vietnam and China. Quotas are designed to protect the industries and jobs of the country imposing the quota.

An **embargo** prohibits trade in a particular product. Embargoes are generally directed at specific goods or countries and may be established for political, economic, health, or religious reasons. While the United States maintains a trade embargo with Cuba, European hotel chains are engaged in a building boom on the Caribbean island, where tourism is the number-one industry. U.S. hotel chains are eager to build in Cuba but have no opportunity until the embargo is lifted. Even U.S. tourists are forbidden by the U.S. government to vacation in Cuba, although the push to lift the government embargo is growing stronger all the time. If permitted, cruise ships would likely be the first type of U.S. tourism to reach the island since the early 1960s. It may be surprising to know that U.S. farmers export hundreds of millions of dollars worth of commodities to Cuba each year, based on a 2000 law that provided permission for some trade to the embargoed country.[21] Health embargoes prevent the importing of various pharmaceuticals, animals, plants, and agricultural products. Muslim nations forbid the importation of alcoholic beverages on religious grounds.

One common reason for setting quotas or tariffs is to prohibit **dumping**, which occurs when a country or business sells products at less than what it costs to produce them. President Obama, for example, restricted tire imports from China after union workers accused the country of dumping its products into the U.S. markets, which in turn affected domestic tire makers. China retaliated by threatening its own investigations into whether the United States is dumping auto and chicken parts on the Chinese market.[22] A company may dump its products for several reasons. Dumping permits quick entry into a market. Sometimes dumping occurs when the domestic market for a firm's product is too small to support an efficient level of production. In other cases, technologically obsolete products that are no longer salable in the country of origin are dumped overseas. Dumping is relatively difficult to prove, but even the suspicion of dumping can lead to the imposition of quotas or tariffs.

Political Barriers Unlike legal issues, political considerations are seldom written down and often change rapidly. Nations that have been subject to economic sanctions for political reasons in recent years include Cuba, Iran, Syria, and North Korea. While these were dramatic events, political considerations affect international business daily as governments enact tariffs, embargoes, or other types of trade restrictions in response to political events.

Businesses engaged in international trade must consider the relative instability of countries such as Iraq, Haiti, and Venezuela. Political unrest in countries such as Pakistan, Somalia, and the Democratic Republic of the Congo may create a hostile or even dangerous environment for foreign businesses. Natural disasters, like the Haitian or Chilean earthquakes in 2010, can cripple a country's government, making the region even more unstable. Even a developed country such as Japan had its social, economic, and political institutions stressed by the 2011 earthquake and tsunamis. Finally, a sudden change in power can result in a regime that is hostile to foreign investment. Some businesses have been forced out of a country altogether, as when Hugo Chávez conducted a socialist revolution in Venezuela to force out or take over American oil companies. Whether they like it or not, companies are often involved directly or indirectly in international politics.

Political concerns may lead a group of nations to form a **cartel**, a group of firms or nations that agree to act as a monopoly and not compete with each other, to generate a competitive advantage in world markets. Probably the most famous cartel is OPEC, the Organization of Petroleum Exporting Countries, founded in the 1960s to increase the price of petroleum throughout the world and to maintain high prices. By working to ensure stable oil prices, OPEC hopes to enhance the economies of its member nations.

Social and Cultural Barriers

Most businesspeople engaged in international trade underestimate the importance of social and cultural differences; but these differences can derail an important transaction. For example, when Big Boy opened a restaurant in Bangkok, it quickly became popular with European and American tourists, but the local Thais refused to eat there. Instead, they placed gifts of rice and incense at the feet of the Big Boy statue (a chubby boy holding a hamburger) because it reminded them of Buddha. In Japan, customers tiptoed around a logo painted on the floor at the entrance to an Athlete's Foot store because in Japan it is considered taboo to step on a crest.[23] And in Russia, consumers found the American-style energetic happiness of McDonald's employees insincere and offensive when the company opened its first stores there.[24] Unfortunately, cultural norms are rarely written down, and what is written down may well be inaccurate.

Cultural differences include differences in spoken and written language. Although it is certainly possible to translate words from one language to another, the true meaning is sometimes misinterpreted or lost. Consider some translations that went awry in foreign markets:

- Scandinavian vacuum manufacturer Electrolux used the following in an American campaign: "Nothing sucks like an Electrolux."

- The Coca-Cola name in China was first read as "Ke-kou-ke-la," meaning "bite the wax tadpole."

- In Italy, a campaign for Schweppes Tonic Water translated the name into Schweppes Toilet Water.[25]

Translators cannot just translate slogans, advertising campaigns, and website language; they must know the cultural differences that could affect a company's success.

Differences in body language and personal space also affect international trade. Body language is nonverbal, usually unconscious communication through gestures, posture, and facial expressions. Personal space is the distance at which one person feels comfortable talking to another. Americans tend to stand a moderate distance away from the person with whom they are speaking. Arab businessmen tend to stand face-to-face with the object of their conversation. Additionally, gestures vary from culture to culture, and gestures considered acceptable in American society—pointing, for example—may be considered rude in others. Table 3.3 shows some of the behaviors considered rude or unacceptable in other countries. Such cultural differences may generate uncomfortable feelings or misunderstandings when businesspeople of different countries negotiate with each other.

Family roles also influence marketing activities. Many countries do not allow children to be used in advertising, for example. Advertising that features people in nontraditional social roles may or may not be successful either. One airline featured advertisements with beautiful flight attendants serving champagne on a

General Agreement on Tariffs and Trade (GATT) a trade agreement, originally signed by 23 nations in 1947, that provided a forum for tariff negotiations and a place where international trade problems could be discussed and resolved

World Trade Organization (WTO) international organization dealing with the rules of trade between nations

North American Free Trade Agreement (NAFTA) agreement that eliminates most tariffs and trade restrictions on agricultural and manufactured products to encourage trade among Canada, the United States, and Mexico

flight. The ad does not seem unusual in Western markets, but there was a major backlash in the Middle East. Saudi Arabia even considered restricting the airline from flights in that country. Not only is alcohol usage forbidden among Muslims, unveiled women are not allowed to interact with men—especially without their husbands around. Some in Saudi Arabia saw the airline as being insensitive to their religious beliefs and customs.[26]

The people of other nations quite often have a different perception of time as well. Americans value promptness; a business meeting scheduled for a specific time seldom starts more than a few minutes late. In Mexico and Spain, however, it is not unusual for a meeting to be delayed half an hour or more. Such a late start might produce resentment in an American negotiating in Spain for the first time.

Companies engaged in foreign trade must observe the national and religious holidays and local customs of the host country. In many Islamic countries, for example, workers expect to take a break at certain times of the day to observe religious rites. Companies also must monitor their advertising to guard against offending customers. In Thailand and many other countries, public displays of affection between the sexes are unacceptable in advertising messages; in many Middle Eastern nations, it is unacceptable to show the soles of one's feet.[27] In Russia, smiling is considered appropriate only in private settings, not in business.

With the exception of the United States, most nations use the metric system. This lack of uniformity creates problems for both buyers and sellers in the international marketplace. American sellers, for instance, must package goods destined for

foreign markets in liters or meters, and Japanese sellers must convert to the English system if they plan to sell a product in the United States. Tools also must be calibrated in the correct system if they are to function correctly. Hyundai and Honda service technicians need metric tools to make repairs on those cars.

The literature dealing with international business is filled with accounts of sometimes humorous but often costly mistakes that occurred because of a lack of understanding of the social and cultural differences between buyers and sellers. Such problems cannot always be avoided, but they can be minimized through research on the cultural and social differences of the host country.

Technological Barriers

Many countries lack the technological infrastructure found in the United States, and some marketers are viewing such barriers as opportunities. For instance, marketers are targeting many countries such as India and China and some African countries where there are few private phone lines. Citizens of these countries are turning instead to wireless communication through cell phones. Technological advances are creating additional global marketing opportunities. Along with opportunities, changing technologies also create new challenges and competition. The U.S. market share of the personal computer market is dropping as new competitors emerge that are challenging U.S. PC makers. Although Apple is making strides in the tablet industry, its market share in the PC market remains low compared to competitors. In fact, out of the top five global PC companies—Hewlett-Packard, Dell, Acer, Lenovo, and Toshiba—three are from Asian countries.[28]

TRADE AGREEMENTS, ALLIANCES, AND ORGANIZATIONS

Although these economic, political, legal, and sociocultural issues may seem like daunting barriers to international trade, there are also organizations and agreements—such as the General Agreement on Tariffs and Trade, the World Bank, and the International Monetary Fund—that foster international trade and can help companies get involved in and succeed in global markets. Various regional trade agreements, such as the North American Free Trade Agreement and the European Union, also promote trade among member nations by eliminating tariffs and trade restrictions. In this section, we'll look briefly at these agreements and organizations.

General Agreement on Tariffs and Trade

During the Great Depression of the 1930s, nations established so many protective tariffs covering so many products that

▼ **TABLE 3.3** Cultural Behavioral Differences

Region	Gestures Viewed as Rude or Unacceptable
Japan, Hong Kong, Middle East	Summoning with the index finger
Middle and Far East	Pointing with index finger
Thailand, Japan, France	Sitting with soles of shoes showing
Brazil, Germany	Forming a circle with fingers (e.g., the "OK" sign in the United States)
Japan	Winking means "I love you"
Buddhist countries	Patting someone on the head

Source: Adapted from Judie Haynes, "Communicating with Gestures," *EverythingESL* (n.d.), www.everythingesl.net/inservices/body_language.php (accessed March 8, 2010).

international trade became virtually impossible. By the end of World War II, there was considerable international momentum to liberalize trade and minimize the effects of tariffs. The **General Agreement on Tariffs and Trade (GATT)**, originally signed by 23 nations in 1947, provided a forum for tariff negotiations and a place where international trade problems could be discussed and resolved. More than 100 nations abided by its rules. GATT sponsored rounds of negotiations aimed at reducing trade restrictions. The most recent round, the Uruguay Round (1988–1994), further reduced trade barriers for most products and provided new rules to prevent dumping.

The **World Trade Organization (WTO)**, an international organization dealing with the rules of trade between nations, was created in 1995 by the Uruguay Round. Key to the World Trade Organization are the WTO agreements, which are the legal ground rules for international commerce. The agreements were negotiated and signed by most of the world's trading nations and ratified by their parliaments. The goal is to help producers of goods and services and exporters and importers conduct their business. In addition to administering the WTO trade agreements, the WTO presents a forum for trade negotiations, monitors national trade policies, provides technical assistance and training for developing countries, and cooperates with other international organizations. Based in Geneva, Switzerland, the WTO has also adopted a leadership role in negotiating trade disputes among nations.[29] For example, the WTO investigated Chinese accusations of unfair treatment against the European Union after the EU levied tariffs against Chinese-manufactured steel fasteners. The EU claimed that China was dumping its steel fasteners and imposed a tariff of 63 to 87 percent. The WTO ruled in favor of China, claiming that the tariff was discriminating against Chinese exporters.[30]

The North American Free Trade Agreement

The **North American Free Trade Agreement (NAFTA)**, which went into effect on January 1, 1994, effectively merged Canada, the United States, and Mexico into one market of nearly 440 million consumers. NAFTA virtually eliminated all tariffs on goods produced and traded among Canada, Mexico,

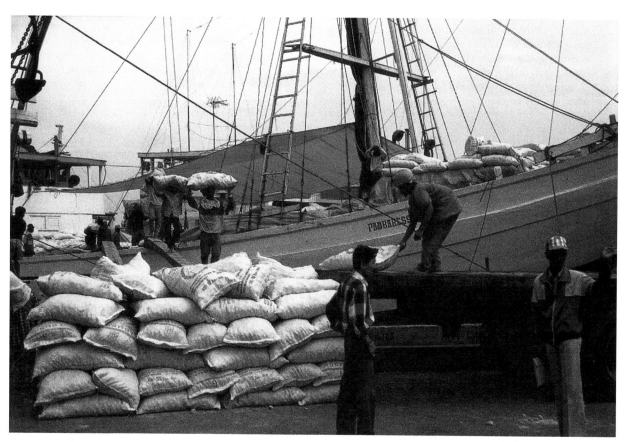

The WTO facilitates trade between nations through the development of trade policies.

"NAFTA makes it easier for U.S. businesses to invest in Mexico and Canada."

and the United States to create a free-trade area. The estimated annual output for this trade alliance is more than $14 trillion. NAFTA makes it easier for U.S. businesses to invest in Mexico and Canada; provides protection for intellectual property (of special interest to high-technology and entertainment industries); expands trade by requiring equal treatment of U.S. firms in both countries; and simplifies country-of-origin rules, hindering Japan's use of Mexico as a staging ground for further penetration into U.S. markets.

Canada's 34 million consumers are relatively affluent, with an estimated GDP per capita of $39,033.693.[31] Trade between the United States and Canada totals approximately $430 billion. About 80 percent of Canada's exports go to the United States, including gold, oil, and uranium.[32] In fact, Canada is the single largest trading partner of the United States.[33]

With an estimated per capita GDP of $14,266, Mexico's 111 million consumers are less affluent than Canadian consumers.[34] However, trade with the United States and Mexico has tripled since NAFTA was initiated.[35] More than 31 million Americans cite their heritage as Mexican, making them the most populous Hispanic group in the country.[36] These individuals often have close ties to relatives in Mexico and assist in Mexican–U.S. economic development and trade. Mexico is on a course of a market economy, rule of law, respect for human rights, and responsible public policies. There is also a commitment to the environment and sustainable human development. Many U.S. companies have taken advantage of Mexico's low labor costs and proximity to the United States to set up production facilities, sometimes called *maquiladoras*. Mexico is also attracting major technological industries, including electronics, software, and aerospace. Mexicali, for example, has attracted such companies as Skyworks Solutions, a maker of cell phone and PDA semiconductors; Gulfstream, a maker of executive jets; and Honeywell, which recently opened a $40 million center in the city. Engineering in Mexicali is booming, with the enrollment of the engineering department at Mexicali's Universidad Autonoma de Baja California doubling within the last five years. Other companies that have an interest in Mexico include Eurocopter and Lenovo, which has a plant in Monterrey.[37] With the maquiladoras and the influx of foreign technological industries, Mexico became the world's 12th-largest economy.[38]

However, there is great disparity within Mexico. The country's southern states cannot seem to catch up with the more affluent northern states on almost any socioeconomic indicator. For example, 47 percent of rural Mexicans in the south are considered extremely poor, compared with just 12 percent in the north. The disparities are growing, as can be seen comparing the south to the northern industrial capital of Monterrey, which is beginning to seem like south Texas.[39] However, drug gang wars threaten the economic stability of Mexico, especially in the northern states close to the U.S. border.

Mexico's membership in NAFTA links the United States and Canada with other Latin American countries, providing additional opportunities to integrate trade among all the nations in the Western Hemisphere. Indeed, efforts to create a free-trade agreement among the 34 nations of North and South America was expected to be completed by 2005. Like NAFTA, the *Free Trade Area of the Americas (FTAA)* will progressively eliminate trade barriers and create the world's largest free-trade zone with 800 million people.[40] However, opposition and demonstrations have hampered efforts to move forward with the proposed plan. Although the deadline was missed and it is not in place yet, there is still a chance for the FTAA to become a reality.

Despite its benefits, NAFTA has been controversial, and disputes continue to arise over the implementation of the trade agreement. For example, a trucking dispute between the United States and Mexico resulted in a ban on Mexican trucks operating within the U.S. border. In retaliation Mexico instituted a punitive tariff on U.S. imports, claiming that the ban violated NAFTA. Americans in support of the ban felt it was necessary to protect the jobs of U.S. truck and warehouse workers. The dispute was eventually resolved, with President Obama agreeing to lift the ban in exchange for tougher standards for Mexican trucks crossing the border.[41] While many Americans feared the agreement would erase jobs in the United States, Mexicans have been disappointed that the agreement failed to create more jobs. Moreover, Mexico's rising standard of living has increased the cost of doing business there; many hundreds of *maquiladoras* have closed their doors and transferred work to China and other nations where labor costs are cheaper. Indeed, China has become the United States' second-largest importer.[42] On the other hand, high transportation costs, intellectual property theft, quality failures, and the difficulty management often incurs in controlling a business so far away and under a communist regime are now causing some manufacturers to reconsider opting for Mexican factories over China, even going so far as to relocate from China back to Mexico.[43]

Although NAFTA has been controversial, it has become a positive factor for U.S. firms wishing to engage in international marketing. Because licensing requirements have been relaxed under the pact, smaller businesses that previously could not afford to invest in Mexico and Canada will be able to do business in those markets without having to locate there. NAFTA's long phase-in period provides ample time for adjustment by those firms affected by reduced tariffs on imports. Furthermore, increased competition should lead to a more efficient market, and the long-term prospects of including most countries in the Western Hemisphere in the alliance promise additional opportunities for U.S. marketers.

The European Union

The **European Union (EU)**, also called the *European Community* or *Common Market,* was established in 1958 to promote trade among its members, which initially included Belgium, France, Italy, West Germany, Luxembourg, and the Netherlands. East and West Germany united in 1991, and by 1995 the United Kingdom, Spain, Denmark, Greece, Portugal, Ireland, Austria, Finland, and Sweden had joined as well. The Czech Republic, Estonia, Hungary, Latvia, Lithuania, Poland, Slovakia, and Slovenia joined in 2004. In 2007, Bulgaria and Romania also became members, and Cyprus and Malta joined in 2008, which brought total membership to 27. Croatia, the Former Yugoslav Republic of Macedonia, Iceland, and Turkey are candidate countries that hope to join the European Union in the near future.[44] Until 1993 each nation functioned as a separate market, but at that time the members officially unified into one of the largest single world markets.[45]

To facilitate free trade among members, the EU is working toward standardization of business regulations and requirements, import duties, and value-added taxes; the elimination of customs checks; and the creation of a standardized currency for use by all members. Many European nations (Austria, Belgium, Finland, France, Germany, Greece, Ireland, Italy, Luxembourg, the Netherlands, Portugal, Spain, and Slovenia) link their exchange rates together to a common currency, the *euro;* however, several EU members have rejected use of the euro in their countries. Although the common currency requires many marketers to modify their pricing strategies and will subject them to increased competition, the use of a single currency frees companies that sell goods among European countries from the nuisance of dealing with complex exchange rates.[46] The long-term goals are to eliminate all trade barriers within the EU, improve the economic efficiency of the EU nations, and stimulate economic growth, thus making the union's economy more competitive in global markets, particularly against Japan and other Pacific Rim nations, and North America. However, several disputes and debates still divide the member nations, and many barriers to completely free trade remain. Consequently, it may take many years before the EU is truly one deregulated market.

The prosperity of the EU has suffered in recent years. EU members experienced a severe economic crisis in 2010 that required steep bailouts from the International Monetary Fund (IMF). The first country to come to the forefront was Greece, which had so much debt that it risked default. With an increase in Greek bond yields and credit risks—along with a severe deficit and other negative economic factors—the country's economy plummeted. Since Greece uses the euro as its currency, the massive

downturn served to decrease the euro's value. This had a profound effect on other countries in the Euro zone (the Euro zone refers collectively to European member countries that have adopted the euro as their form of currency). Ireland, Spain, and Portugal were particularly vulnerable as they had some of the region's largest deficits.[47] Ireland began experiencing problems similar to Greece, including a debt crisis, failing economic health, and rising bond yields.[48] It too required a bailout package from the IMF. Spain's housing bust and a collapse in the construction sector negatively affected its economy as well.[49]

Much as the United States created new agencies to ensure the future stability of U.S. financial markets, the European Union created the European Financial Stability Facility (EFSF) to "safeguard financial stability in the Euro zone." EFSF will be able to raise funds through the issuing of capital such as bonds in order to finance loans for European Union member countries.[50] It is hoped that this organization will maintain stability in the region and prevent such a crisis from reoccurring in the future.

Asia-Pacific Economic Cooperation

The **Asia-Pacific Economic Cooperation (APEC)**, established in 1989, promotes open trade and economic and technical cooperation among member nations, which initially included Australia, Brunei Darussalam, Canada, Indonesia, Japan, Korea, Malaysia, New Zealand, the Philippines, Singapore, Thailand, and the United States. Since then the alliance has grown to include China, Hong Kong, Chinese Taipei, Mexico, Papua New Guinea, Chile, Peru, Russia, and Vietnam. The 21-member alliance represents approximately 41 percent of the world's population, 44 percent of world trade, and 54 percent of world GDP. APEC differs from other international trade alliances in its commitment to facilitating business and its practice of allowing the business/private sector to participate in a wide range of APEC activities.[51]

Companies of the APEC have become increasingly competitive and sophisticated in global business in the last three decades. The Japanese and South Koreans in particular have made tremendous inroads on world markets for automobiles, motorcycles, watches, cameras, and audio and video equipment. Products from Samsung, Sony, Sanyo, Toyota, Daewoo, Mitsubishi, Suzuki, and Toshiba are sold all over the world and have set standards of quality by which other products are often judged. The People's Republic of China, a country of 1.3 billion people, has launched a program of economic reform to stimulate its economy by privatizing many industries, restructuring its banking system, and increasing public spending on

> **European Union (EU)** a union of European nations established in 1958 to promote trade among its members; one of the largest single markets today
>
> **Asia-Pacific Economic Cooperation (APEC)** an international trade alliance that promotes open trade and economic and technical cooperation among member nations

World Bank an organization established by the industrialized nations in 1946 to loan money to underdeveloped and developing countries; formally known as the International Bank for Reconstruction and Development

International Monetary Fund (IMF) organization established in 1947 to promote trade among member nations by eliminating trade barriers and fostering financial cooperation

countertrade agreements foreign trade agreements that involve bartering products for other products instead of for currency

infrastructure (including railways and telecommunications).[52] As a result, China has become a manufacturing powerhouse, with an estimated economic growth rate of 8 to 10 percent a year.[53] China's export market has consistently outpaced its import growth in recent years and its GDP is the world's second-largest behind the United States. As China continues to prosper, working conditions are also beginning to improve. Strikes and calls for unions are increasing among Chinese factory workers, prompting the government to improve wages and labor standards. On the other hand, this rise in labor costs concerns some international companies. Minimum wage increases are estimated to push labor costs up 5 to 15 percent on average, which may be passed onto consumers in the form

of higher prices. This brings up a key ethical concern for consumers and businesses: Would they be willing to accept higher priced items if it means better conditions for workers in different countries?[54]

Increased industrialization has also caused China to become the world's largest emitter of greenhouse gases in 2008. China mainly uses coal-fired power plants; in fact, it builds a new one every 10 days, so it has become the world's largest emitter of carbon dioxide. As companies transfer their manufacturing to China, they increase their CO_2 emissions because China emits 22 percent more than the global average of carbon per kilowatt-hour.[55] On the other hand, China has also begun a quest to become a world leader in green initiatives and renewable energy. This is an increasingly important quest as the country becomes more polluted.

Less visible Pacific Rim regions, such as Thailand, Singapore, Taiwan, Vietnam, and Hong Kong, have also become major manufacturing and financial centers. Vietnam, with one of the world's most open economies, has bypassed its communist

The ship Cosco Ran transports cargo from one side of the globe to the other.

government with private firms moving ahead despite bureaucracy, corruption, and poor infrastructure. In a country of 85 million barely able to feed themselves, Vietnamese firms now compete internationally with an agricultural miracle, making the country one of the world's main providers of farm produce. Coach, Inc. wants to increase its presence in Vietnam, while Guess, Inc. is considering an expansion of its production facilities in Vietnam along with Cambodia and Indonesia.[56]

World Bank

The **World Bank,** more formally known as the International Bank for Reconstruction and Development, was established by

because these countries use private markets as a major source of capital.[58]

GETTING INVOLVED IN INTERNATIONAL BUSINESS

Businesses may get involved in international trade at many levels—from a small Kenyan firm that occasionally exports African crafts to a huge multinational corporation such as Shell Oil that sells products around the globe. The degree of commitment of resources and effort required increases according to the

> "The IMF is the closest thing the world has to an international central bank."

the industrialized nations, including the United States, in 1946 to loan money to underdeveloped and developing countries.

It loans its own funds or borrows funds from member countries to finance projects ranging from road and factory construction to the building of medical and educational facilities. The World Bank and other multilateral development banks (banks with international support that provide loans to developing countries) are the largest source of advice and assistance for developing nations. The International Development Association and the International Finance Corporation are associated with the World Bank and provide loans to private businesses and member countries.

International Monetary Fund

The **International Monetary Fund (IMF)** was established in 1947 to promote trade among member nations by eliminating trade barriers and fostering financial cooperation. It also makes short-term loans to member countries that have balance-of-payment deficits and provides foreign currencies to member nations. The International Monetary Fund tries to avoid financial crises and panics by alerting the international community about countries that will not be able to repay their debts. The IMF's Internet site provides additional information about the organization, including news releases, frequently asked questions, and members.

The IMF is the closest thing the world has to an international central bank. If countries get into financial trouble, they can borrow from the World Bank. However, the global economic crisis created many challenges for the IMF as it was forced to significantly increase its loans to both emerging economies and more developed nations. Ireland accepted a bailout package worth up to £77 billion (120 billion USD) from the IMF and the EU. Similarly, the IMF also loaned 30 billion euros (39 billion USD) to help rescue Greece's struggling economy.[57] The usefulness of the IMF for developed countries is limited

level at which a business involves itself in international trade. This section examines exporting and importing, trading companies, licensing and franchising, contract manufacturing, joint ventures, direct investment, and multinational corporations.

Exporting and Importing

Many companies first get involved in international trade when they import goods from other countries for resale in their own businesses. For example, a grocery store chain may import bananas from Honduras and coffee from Colombia. A business may get involved in exporting when it is called upon to supply a foreign company with a particular product. Such exporting enables enterprises of all sizes to participate in international business. Exporting to other countries becomes a necessity for established countries that seek to grow continually. Products often have higher sales growth potential in foreign countries than they have in the parent country. For example, Heinz exports its ketchup to other countries, including Mexico, Africa, and the Middle East, because there exists much greater potential for growth. Retail sales of packaged food have risen 32 percent in Asian-Pacific countries and 27 percent in Africa, while rising only a mere 4 percent in Europe and declining 1 percent in North America. Mexico in particular has become a crucial part of Heinz's growth strategy because Mexicans consume more ketchup than all but eight other nations.[59] Table 3.4 shows the number of U.S. exporters and the export value by company size, while Figure 3.2 shows some of the world's largest exporting countries.

Exporting sometimes takes place through **countertrade agreements,** which involve bartering products for other products instead of for currency. Such arrangements are fairly common in international trade, especially between Western companies and eastern European nations. An estimated 40 percent or more of all international trade agreements contain countertrade provisions.

Although a company may export its wares overseas directly or import goods directly from its manufacturer, many choose to

trading company a firm that buys goods in one country and sells them to buyers in another country

licensing a trade agreement in which one company—the licensor—allows another company—the licensee—to use its company name, products, patents, brands, trademarks, raw materials, and/or production processes in exchange for a fee or royalty

deal with an intermediary, commonly called an *export agent*. Export agents seldom produce goods themselves; instead, they usually handle international transactions for other firms. Export agents either purchase products outright or take them on consignment. If they purchase them outright, they generally mark up the price they have paid and attempt to sell the product in the international marketplace. They are also responsible for storage and transportation.

An advantage of trading through an agent instead of directly is that the company does not have to deal with foreign currencies or the red tape (paying tariffs and handling paperwork) of international business. A major disadvantage is that, because the export agent must make a profit, either the price of the product must be increased or the domestic company must provide a larger discount than it would in a domestic transaction.

Trading Companies

A **trading company** buys goods in one country and sells them to buyers in another country. Trading companies handle all activities required to move products from one country to another, including consulting, marketing research, advertising, insurance, product research and design, warehousing, and foreign exchange services to companies interested in selling their products in foreign markets. Trading companies are similar to export agents, but their role in international trade is larger. By linking sellers and buyers of goods in different countries, trading companies promote international trade. The best known U.S. trading company is Sears World Trade, which specializes in consumer goods, light industrial items, and processed foods.

Licensing and Franchising

Licensing is a trade arrangement in which one company—the *licensor*—allows another company—the *licensee*—to use its company name, products, patents, brands, trademarks, raw materials, and/or production processes in exchange for a fee or royalty. The Coca-Cola Company and PepsiCo frequently use licensing as a means to market their soft drinks, apparel, and other merchandise in other countries. Licensing is an attractive alternative to direct investment when the political stability of a foreign country is in doubt or when resources are unavailable for direct investment. Licensing is especially advantageous for small manufacturers wanting to launch a well-known brand internationally. Yoplait is a French yogurt that is licensed for production in the United States.

Franchising is a form of licensing in which a company—the *franchiser*—agrees to provide a *franchisee* the name, logo, methods of operation, advertising,

▼ **TABLE 3.4** U.S. Exporters and Value by Company Size

	Number of Exporters	Percentage	Value (millions of dollars)	Percentage
Unknown	101,765	35.2	93,146	8.1
Small (<100 employees)	161,959	56.2	163,505	14.3
Medium (100–499)	17,944	6.2	102,999	9.0
Large (>500)	7,079	2.5	788,019	68.7

Source: "A Profile of U.S. Exporting Companies, 2007–2008," U.S. Census Bureau News, April 13, 2010, www.census.gov/foreign-trade/Press-Release/edb/2008/edbrel.pdf (accessed January 10, 2011).

▼**FIGURE 3.2**
Top Exporting Countries

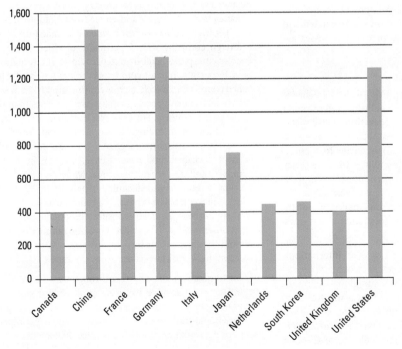

*2010 estimates in billions, calculated on an exchange rate basis.
Source: "Country Comparison: Exports," CIA, *The World Factbook*, https://www.cia.gov/library/publications/the-world-factbook/rankorder/2078rank.html (accessed March 2, 2011).

products, and other elements associated with the franchiser's business, in return for a financial commitment and the agreement to conduct business in accordance with the franchiser's standard of operations. Wendy's, McDonald's, Pizza Hut, and Holiday Inn are well-known franchisers with international visibility. Table 3.5 lists some of the top global franchises.

Licensing and franchising enable a company to enter the international marketplace without spending large sums of money abroad or hiring or transferring personnel to handle overseas affairs. They also minimize problems associated with shipping costs, tariffs, and trade restrictions. And, they allow the firm to establish goodwill for its products in a foreign market, which will help the company if it decides to produce or market its products directly in the foreign country at some future date. However, if the licensee (or franchisee) does not maintain high standards of quality, the product's image may be hurt; therefore, it is important for the licensor to monitor its products overseas and to enforce its quality standards.

franchising a form of licensing in which a company—the franchiser—agrees to provide a franchisee a name, logo, methods of operation, advertising, products, and other elements associated with a franchiser's business, in return for a financial commitment and the agreement to conduct business in accordance with the franchiser's standard of operations

contract manufacturing the hiring of a foreign company to produce a specified volume of the initiating company's product to specification; the final product carries the domestic firm's name

offshoring the relocation of business processes by a company or subsidiary to another country. Offshoring is different than outsourcing because the company retains control of the offshored processes.

Contract Manufacturing

Contract manufacturing occurs when a company hires a foreign company to produce a specified volume of the firm's product to specification; the final product carries the domestic firm's name. Spalding, for example, relies on contract manufacturing for its sports equipment; Reebok uses Korean contract manufacturers to manufacture many of its athletic shoes.

Outsourcing

Earlier, we defined outsourcing as transferring manufacturing or other tasks (such as information technology operations) to companies in countries where labor and supplies are less expensive. Many U.S. firms have outsourced tasks to India, Ireland, Mexico, and the Philippines, where there are many well-educated workers and significantly lower labor costs. Experts estimate that 80 percent of *Fortune* 500 companies have some relationship with an offshore company.[60]

Although outsourcing has become politically controversial in recent years amid concerns over jobs lost to overseas workers, foreign companies transfer tasks and jobs to U.S. companies—sometimes called *insourcing*—far more often than U.S. companies outsource tasks and jobs abroad.[61] However, some firms are bringing their outsourced jobs back after concerns that foreign workers were not adding enough value. For example, some of the bigger banks are now choosing to set up offshore operations themselves rather than outsource. This has to do with increased regulations in foreign countries and concerns over data security. One instance of fraud at the Indian outsourcer Satyam amounted to more than $1 billion.[62]

Offshoring

Offshoring is the relocation of a business process by a company, or a subsidiary, to another country. Offshoring is

different than outsourcing: the company retains control of the process because it is not subcontracting to a different company. Companies may choose to offshore for a number of reasons, ranging from lower wages, skilled labor, or taking

The Canadian frozen yogurt franchise Yogen Fruz has operations on four continents.

▼ **TABLE 3.5** Top Global Franchises

Franchise	Country	Ranking
McDonald's	United States	1
Subway	United States	2
Intercontinental Hotels Group	United Kingdom	6
Yogen Fruz	Canada	15
Kumon	Japan	22
Cartridge World	Australia	33
Engel & Völkers	Germany	38
Pita Pit	Canada	43
Ben & Jerry's	United States	55
Naturhouse	Spain	77

Source: "Top 100 Global Franchises—Ranking," Franchise Direct, www.franchisedirect.com/top100globalfranchises/rankings/ (accessed January 10, 2011).

CHINA'S MONEY AND HOLLYWOOD FILMS MAKE FOR A PARTNERSHIP

China and Hollywood are forging a deepening bond thanks to money and market demand. Hollywood, which relies heavily on investors, has recently discovered the deep pockets of both the Chinese government and individual Chinese investors. At the same time, China, determined to grow its own film industry, is looking toward Hollywood for knowledge and audience expansion.

China's economy is booming, creating a new market heavy on capital and enthusiasm for film. Recent endeavors include government-backed China Film's $5 million investment in *The Karate Kid* remake and

Orange Sky Golden Harvest Entertainment's $25 million investment in Legendary Pictures (known for *The Dark Knight* and other blockbusters) for a 3.3 percent stake in the company. In addition, China's movie audience is growing, up 80 percent from 2009, and the government is driving a large expansion in movie theater construction. With China getting more in-depth knowledge of the moviemaking industry and Hollywood receiving more capital to make its movies, the situation appears to be a win-win for both parties.

However, as with any partnership, there is often a certain degree of conflict. The Chinese government, for instance, prefers to show Chinese-made movies within China and currently permits only 20 foreign films into the country each year. This makes co-producing more ideal as co-produced films do not fall under this ruling and give Chinese filmmakers more international

exposure. Yet with China gaining more expertise in filmmaking, is there a possibility that China could one day become a competitor with Hollywood? Rumor has it that China may be looking into direct investment by purchasing a Hollywood film studio to solidify the partnership. Time will tell whether the increased knowledge that Chinese filmmakers will receive from co-production will one day lead to the creation of China's own Hollywood.[63]

Discussion Questions

1. Why are the Chinese investing in Hollywood films?

2. How is the Chinese government limiting opportunities for the U.S. film industry?

3. Should Hollywood movie companies be concerned about competition from Chinese filmmakers?

---

advantage of time zone differences in order to offer services around the clock. Some banks have chosen not to outsource because of concerns about data security in other countries. These institutions may instead engage in offshoring, which allows a company more control over international operations because the offshore office is an extension of the company. Barclays Bank, for instance, has an international offshore banking unit called Barclays Wealth International. This branch helps the company better serve wealthy clients with international banking needs.[64]

Joint Ventures and Alliances

Many countries, particularly LDCs, do not permit direct investment by foreign companies or individuals. A company may also lack sufficient resources or expertise to operate in another country. In such cases, a company that wants to do business in another country may set up a **joint venture** by finding a local partner (occasionally, the host nation itself) to share the costs and operation of the business. The French hypermarket chain Carrefour, for example, has a joint venture with Majid al Futtaim (MAF), a group of companies that has become a highly successful Middle Eastern business. The venture between Carrefour and MAF resulted in the expansion of MAF–Carrefour hypermarkets in the United Arab Emirates, Qatar, Oman, Saudi Arabia, and Egypt. The partnership has allowed Carrefour to become one of the most popular retailers in Egypt.[65]

In some industries, such as automobiles and computers, strategic alliances are becoming the predominant means of competing. A **strategic alliance** is a partnership formed to

Lenovo chief executive Yang Yuanqing (China) shakes hands with NEC President Nobuhiro Endo (Japan) during an agreement to form a joint venture between the two PC companies.

create competitive advantage on a worldwide basis. In such industries, international competition is so fierce and the costs of competing on a global basis are so high that few firms have the resources to go it alone, so they collaborate with other companies. An example of a strategic alliance is the partnership between Australian airlines Virgin Blue and Skywest.

joint venture the sharing of the costs and operation of a business between a foreign company and a local partner

strategic alliance a partnership formed to create competitive advantage on a worldwide basis

direct investment the ownership of overseas facilities

multinational corporation (MNC) a corporation that operates on a worldwide scale, without significant ties to any one nation or region

multinational strategy a plan, used by international companies, that involves customizing products, promotion, and distribution according to cultural, technological, regional, and national differences

global strategy (globalization) a strategy that involves standardizing products (and, as much as possible, their promotion and distribution) for the whole world, as if it were a single entity

By forming an alliance, the two airlines hope to tap into the increased demand from the mining industry for flights to distant mining sites. As part of the agreement, Skywest can use as many as 18 Virgin Blue turbo-prop aircraft for 10 years. In addition to penetrating a lucrative market, Virgin Blue hopes the alliance will help it extend its influence into regional markets and steal market share from its competitor QantasLink.[66]

Direct Investment

Companies that want more control and are willing to invest considerable resources in international business may consider **direct investment**, the ownership of overseas facilities. Direct investment may involve the development and operation of new facilities—such as when Starbucks opens a new coffee shop in Japan—or the purchase of all or part of an existing operation in a foreign country. India's Tata Motors purchased Jaguar and Land Rover from Ford Motor Company. Tata, a maker of cars and trucks, is attempting to broaden its global presence, including manufacturing these vehicles in the United Kingdom.[67]

The highest level of international business involvement is the **multinational corporation (MNC)**, a corporation, such as IBM or ExxonMobil, that operates on a worldwide scale, without significant ties to any one nation or region. Table 3.6 lists the 10 largest multinational corporations. MNCs are more than simple corporations. They often have greater assets than some of the countries in which they do business. Nestlé, with headquarters in Switzerland, operates more than 300 plants around the world and receives revenues from Europe; North, Central, and South America; Africa; and Asia. The Royal Dutch/Shell Group, one of the world's major oil producers, is another MNC. Its main offices are located in The Hague and London. Other MNCs include BASF, British Petroleum, Matsushita, Mitsubishi, Siemens, Texaco, Toyota, and Unilever. Many MNCs have been targeted by antiglobalization activists at global business forums, and some protests have turned violent. The activists contend that MNCs increase the gap between rich and poor nations, misuse and misallocate scarce resources, exploit the labor markets in LDCs, and harm their natural environments.[68]

INTERNATIONAL BUSINESS STRATEGIES

Planning in a global economy requires businesspeople to understand the economic, legal, political, and sociocultural realities of the countries in which they will operate. These factors will affect the strategy a business chooses to use outside its own borders.

Developing Strategies

Companies doing business internationally have traditionally used a **multinational strategy**, customizing their products, promotion, and distribution according to cultural, technological, regional, and national differences. To succeed in India, for example, McDonald's had to adapt its products to respect religious customs. McDonald's India does not serve beef or pork products and also has vegetarian dishes for its largely vegetarian consumer base. Many soap and detergent manufacturers have adapted their products to local water conditions, washing equipment, and washing habits. For customers in some less-developed countries, Colgate-Palmolive Co. has developed an inexpensive, plastic, hand-powered washing machine for use in households that have no electricity. Even when products are standardized, advertising often has to be modified to adapt to language and cultural differences. Also, celebrities used in advertising in the United States may be unfamiliar to foreign consumers and thus would not be effective in advertising products in other countries.

More and more companies are moving from this customization strategy to a **global strategy (globalization)**, which involves

▼ **TABLE 3.6** Top 10 Largest Corporations

Company	Revenue (in millions)	Country
1. Wal-Mart Stores	$421,849	U.S.
2. Royal Dutch Shell	$378,152	Netherlands
3. Exxon Mobil	$354,674	U.S.
4. BP	$308,928	Britain
5. Sinopec Group	$273,422	China
6. China National Petroleum	$240,294	China
7. State Grid	$226,294	China
8. Toyota Motor	$221,760	Japan
9. Japan Post Holdings	$203,958	Japan
10. Chevron	$196,337	U.S.

Source: "Global 500: Fortune's Annual Ranking of the World's Largest Corporations," *CNNMoney,* http://money.cnn.com/magazines/fortune/global500/2011/full_list/ (accessed July 20, 2011).

SO YOU WANT A JOB // in Global Business /

Have you always dreamt of traveling the world? Whether backpacking your way through Central America or sipping espressos at five-star European restaurants is your style, the increasing globalization of business might just give you your chance to see what the world has to offer. Most new jobs will have at least some global component, even if located within the United States, so being globally aware and keeping an open mind to different cultures is vital in today's business world. Think about the 1.3 billion consumers in China who have already purchased 500 million mobile phones. In the future, some of the largest markets will be in Asia.

Many jobs discussed in chapters throughout this book tend to have strong international components. For example, product management and distribution management are discussed as marketing careers in Chapter 12.

As more and more companies sell products around the globe, their function, design, packaging, and promotions need to be culturally relevant to many different people in many different places. Products very often cross multiple borders before reaching the final consumer, both in their distribution and through the supply chain to produce the products.

Jobs exist in export and import management, product and pricing management, distribution and transportation, and advertising. Many "born global" companies such as Google operate virtually and consider all countries their market. Many companies sell their products through eBay and other Internet sites and never leave the United States Today, communication and transportation facilitates selling and buying products worldwide with delivery in a few days. You

may have sold or purchased a product on eBay outside the United States without thinking about how easy and accessible international markets are to business. If you have, welcome to the world of global business.

To be successful you must have an idea not only of differing regulations from country to country, but of different languages, ethics, and communication styles and varying needs and wants of international markets. From a regulatory side, you may need to be aware of laws related to intellectual property, copyrights, antitrust, advertising, and pricing in every country. Translating is never only about translating the language. Perhaps even more important is ensuring that your message gets through. Whether on a product label or in advertising or promotional materials, the use of images and words varies widely across the globe.

---

standardizing products (and, as much as possible, their promotion and distribution) for the whole world, as if it were a single entity. Examples of globalized products are American clothing, movies, music, and cosmetics. As it has become a global brand, Starbucks has standardized its products and stores. Starbucks was ranked as the world's most engaged brand in terms of online activities, even surpassing Coca-Cola, which is another global brand. Starbucks communicates with fans around the world via Facebook, Twitter, YouTube, and its company website.

Before moving outside their own borders, companies must conduct environmental analyses to evaluate the potential of and problems associated with various markets and to determine what strategy is best for doing business in those markets. Failure to do so may result in losses and even negative publicity. Some companies rely on local managers to gain greater insights and faster response to changes within a country. Astute business-people today "think globally, act locally." That is, while constantly being aware of the total picture, they adjust their firms' strategies to conform to local needs and tastes.

Managing the Challenges of Global Business

As we've pointed out in this chapter, many past political barriers to trade have fallen or been minimized, expanding

TEAM EXERCISE

Visit Transparency International's Country Corruption Index website: www.transparency.org/. Form groups and select two countries. Research some of the economic, ethical, legal, regulatory, and political barriers that would have an impact on international trade. Be sure to pair a fairly ethical country with a fairly unethical country (e.g., Sweden with Myanmar, Ireland with Haiti). Report your findings.

and opening new market opportunities. Managers who can meet the challenges of creating and implementing effective and sensitive business strategies for the global marketplace can help lead their companies to success. For example, the Commercial Service is the global business solutions unit of the U.S. Department of Commerce that offers U.S. firms wide and deep practical knowledge of international markets and industries, a unique global network, inventive use of information technology, and a focus on small and mid-sized businesses. Another example is the benchmarking of best international practices that benefits U.S. firms, which is conducted by the network of CIBERs (Centers for International Business Education and Research) at leading business schools in the United States. These 30 CIBERs are funded by the U.S. government to help U.S. firms become more competitive globally. A major element of the assistance that these governmental organizations can provide firms (especially for small and medium-sized firms) is knowledge of the internationalization process.[69] Small businesses, too, can succeed in foreign markets when their managers have carefully studied those markets and prepared and implemented appropriate strategies. Being globally aware is therefore an important quality for today's managers and will become a critical attribute for managers of the 21st century.

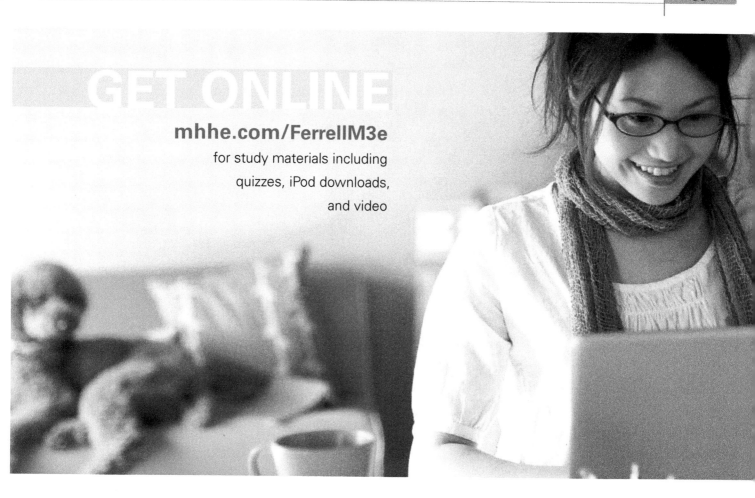

GET ONLINE

mhhe.com/FerrellM3e

for study materials including
quizzes, iPod downloads,
and video

chapter three

active review card
Business in a Borderless World

in a nutshell

To learn about business in a global marketplace, you need to understand the nature of international business, including barriers to and promoters of trade across international boundaries. You must also consider the levels of organizational involvement in international business and the strategies used for trading across national borders.

The following statements will test your take-away knowledge from this chapter. Do your best to explain each one in the space provided below.

LO.1 Explore some of the factors within the international trade environment that influence business.

LO.2 Investigate some of the economic, legal-political, social, cultural, and technological barriers to international business.

LO.3 Specify some of the agreements, alliances, and organizations that may encourage trade across international boundaries.

LO.4 Summarize the different levels of organizational involvement in international trade.

LO.5 Contrast two basic strategies used in international business.

Did your answers include the following important points?

LO.1. Explore some of the factors within the international trade environment that influence business.

- International business is the buying, selling, and trading of goods and services across national boundaries.
- Importing is the purchase of products and raw materials from another nation; exporting is the sale of domestic goods and materials to another nation.
- A nation's balance of trade is the difference in value between its exports and its imports: a negative balance of trade is a trade deficit.
- An absolute or comparative advantage in trade may determine what products a company from a particular nation will export.

LO.2. Investigate some of the economic, legal-political, social, cultural, and technological barriers to international business.

- Companies engaged in international trade must consider the effects of economic, legal, political, social, and cultural differences between nations.
- Wide-ranging legal and political barriers include differing laws (and enforcement), tariffs, exchange controls, quotas, embargoes, political instability, and war.
- Ambiguous cultural and social barriers involve differences in spoken and body language, time, holidays, and other observances and customs.

LO.3. Specify some of the agreements, alliances, and organizations that may encourage trade across international boundaries.

- Among the most important promoters of international business are the General Agreement on Tariffs and Trade, the World Trade Organization, the North American Free Trade Agreement, the European Union, the Asia-Pacific Economic Cooperation, the World Bank, and the International Monetary Fund.

LO.4. Summarize the different levels of organizational involvement in international trade.

- Countertrade agreements occur at the import/export level and involve bartering products for other products, and a trading company links buyers and sellers in different countries to foster trade.
- Licensing and franchising occurs when one company allows a foreign company to use its name, products, patents, brands, trademarks, raw materials, and production process in exchange for a flat fee or royalty.
- Contract manufacturing occurs when a company hires a foreign company to produce a specified volume of the firm's product and allows the final product to carry the domestic firm's name. In a joint venture companies work as a partnership and share the costs and operation of the business.
- Direct investment involves purchasing overseas production and marketing facilities, whereas outsourcing involves transferring manufacturing to countries where labor and supplies are cheap. A multinational corporation is one that operates on a worldwide scale, without ties to any one nation or region.

LO.5. Contrast two basic strategies used in international business.

- A multinational strategy customizes products, promotion, and distribution according to cultural, technological, regional, and national differences, while a global strategy (globalization) standardizes products for the whole world as if it were a single entity.

Practical Application

LO.1.
- South Africa holds a(n) _____ in diamond deposits in the world.
- The difference between the flow of money into and out of a country is called its _____.
- The transfer of manufacturing and other tasks to places where labor and other supplies are less expensive is called _____.

LO.2.
- The United States' prohibition of imported Cuban cigars is an example of a(n) _____.
- A group of nations or companies that band together to act as a monopoly is known as a(n) _____.
- A country/business that wants to gain a quick entry into a new market sometimes engages in _____ its products.

LO.3.
- The _____ makes short-term loans to member countries with trade deficits and provides foreign currencies to member nations.
- The _____ is the largest source of advice and assistance with loans for developing countries.
- Until 1993, each nation of the _____ functioned as a separate market.

LO.4.
- When a company hires a foreign company to produce a specified volume of the firm's product to specification, it is engaging in

    _____.
- PepsiCo allows a Canadian firm to use its name, formula, and brands in return for a royalty. This arrangement is known as

    _____.
- In some industries, _____ allows companies to create competitive advantage on a worldwide basis.

LO.5.
- Standardizing products for the whole world as if it were a single entity is a characteristic of _____ strategy.
- Most companies doing international business have used the _____ strategy; that is, customized their products and distribution to cultural and regional differences.
- The _____ is the global business solutions unit of the U.S. Department of Commerce that offers U.S. firms practical knowledge of international markets and industries, along with a global network.

Starting and Growing a Business

four

options for
organizing business

introduction

The legal form of ownership taken by a business is seldom of great concern to you as a customer. When you eat at a restaurant, you probably don't care whether the restaurant is owned by one person (a sole proprietorship), has two or more owners who share the business (a partnership), or is an entity owned by many stockholders (a corporation); all you want is good food. If you buy a foreign car, you probably don't care whether the company that made it has laws governing its form of organization that are different from those for businesses in the United States. You are buying the car because it is well made, fits your price range, or appeals to your sense of style. Nonetheless, a business's legal form of ownership affects how it operates, how much tax it pays, and how much control its owners have.

continued on p. 84

LEARNING OBJECTIVES

LO1 Define and examine the advantages and disadvantages of the sole proprietorship form of organization.

LO2 Identify two types of partnership, and evaluate the advantages and disadvantages of the partnership form of organization.

LO3 Describe the corporate form of organization, and cite the advantages and disadvantages of corporations.

LO4 Define and debate the advantages and disadvantages of mergers, acquisitions, and leveraged buyouts.

This chapter examines three primary forms of business ownership—sole proprietorship, partnership, and corporation—and weighs the advantages and disadvantages of each. These forms are the most often used whether the business is a traditional brick-and-mortar company, an online-only one, or a combination of both. We also take a look at S corporations, limited liability companies, and cooperatives and discuss some trends in business ownership. You may wish to refer to Table 4.1 to compare the various forms of business ownership mentioned in the chapter.

> Sole proprietorships constitute approximately three-fourths of all businesses in the United States.

SOLE PROPRIETORSHIPS

Sole proprietorships, businesses owned and operated by one individual, are the most common form of business organization in the United States. Common examples include many restaurants, hair salons, flower shops, dog kennels, and independent grocery stores. Many sole proprietors focus on services—small retail stores, financial counseling, appliance repair, child care, and the like—rather than on the manufacture of goods, which often requires large sums of money not available to most small businesses. As you can see in Figure 4.1, proprietorships far outnumber corporations, but they net far fewer sales and less income.

Sole proprietorships are typically small businesses employing fewer than 50 people. (We'll look at small businesses in greater detail in Chapter 5.) Sole proprietorships constitute approximately three-fourths of all businesses in the United States. It is interesting to note that men are twice as likely as women to

▼ **TABLE 4.1** Various Forms of Business Ownership

Structure	Ownership	Taxation	Liability	Use
Sole Proprietorship	1 owner	Individual income taxed	Unlimited	Owned by a single individual and is the easiest way to conduct business
Partnership	2 or more owners	Individual owners' income taxed	Somewhat limited	Easy way for two individuals to conduct business
Corporation	Any number of shareholders	Corporate and shareholder taxed	Limited	A legal entity with shareholders or stockholders
S Corporation	Up to 75 shareholders	Taxed as a partnership	Limited	A legal entity with tax advantages for restricted number of shareholders
Limited Liability Company	Unlimited number of shareholders	Taxed as a partnership	Limited	A way to avoid personal lawsuits

STELLA & DOT: A COMPANY FOR WOMEN BY WOMEN

Stella & Dot, a direct selling jewelry company, puts a fresh spin on the traditional Tupperware and Avon models of personal selling. The company was founded by Jessica Herrin, an entrepreneur who is no stranger to success—at age 24 she launched WeddingChannel.com and later sold it for about $60 million. For a $199 investment, "stylists" interested in selling for Stella & Dot receive a training kit, access to online training materials, and $350 of free jewelry to create a stock of samples. Stylists earn roughly 30 percent commission on trunk shows (home parties) and online sales. The company currently has more than 10,000 stylists.

Stella & Dot was recently selected by a venture capitalist panel as one of the top five companies to watch, as it grew 3,458 percent between 2006 and 2009. The panel's only caution was that a revival in the economy may cause a mass exodus toward traditional jobs and benefits. Herrin, however, firmly believes that this opportunity, designed for women by women, is just beginning to grow.[1]

▼FIGURE 4.1
Comparison of Sole Proprietorships, Partnerships, and Corporations

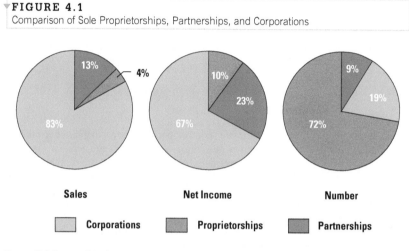

Sales   Net Income   Number

☐ Corporations   ☐ Proprietorships   ☐ Partnerships

Source: U.S. Bureau of the Census, *Statistical Abstract of the United States,* www.census.gov/prod/2009pubs/10statab/business.pdf (accessed March 1, 2010).

start their own business.[2] In many areas, small businesses make up the vast majority of the economy.

Advantages of Sole Proprietorships

Sole proprietorships are generally managed by their owners. Because of this simple management structure, the owner/manager can make decisions quickly. This is just one of many advantages of the sole proprietorship form of business.

Ease and Cost of Formation Forming a sole proprietorship is relatively easy and inexpensive. In some states, creating a sole proprietorship involves merely announcing the new business in the local newspaper. Other proprietorships, such as barber shops and restaurants, may require state and local licenses and permits because of the nature of the business. The cost of these permits may run from $25 to $100. No lawyer is needed to create such enterprises, and the owner can usually take care of the required paperwork without outside assistance.

Of course, an entrepreneur starting a new sole proprietorship must find a suitable site from which to operate the business. Some sole proprietors look no farther than their garage or a spare bedroom when seeking a workshop or office. Among the more famous businesses that sprang to life in their founders' homes are Google, Walt Disney, Dell, eBay, Hewlett-Packard,

Apple Computer, and Mattel.[3] Computers, personal copiers, scanners, and other high-tech gadgets have been a boon for home-based businesses, permitting them to interact quickly with customers, suppliers, and others. Many independent salespersons and contractors can perform their work using a smartphone or tablet computer as they travel. E-mail and social networks have made it possible for many proprietorships to develop in the services area. Internet connections also allow small businesses to establish websites to promote their products and even to make low-cost long-distance phone calls with voice-over Internet protocol (VOIP) technology. One of the most famous services using VOIP is Skype, which allows people to make free calls over the Internet.

Secrecy Sole proprietorships make possible the greatest degree of secrecy. The proprietor, unlike the owners of a partnership or corporation, does not have to discuss publicly his or her operating plans, minimizing the possibility that competitors can obtain trade secrets. Financial reports need not be disclosed, as do the financial reports of publicly owned corporations.

Distribution and Use of Profits All profits from a sole proprietorship belong exclusively to the owner. He or she does not have to share them with any partners or stockholders. The owner decides how to use the funds—for expansion of the business, or salary increases, for travel to purchase additional inventory, or to find new customers.

Flexibility and Control of the Business The sole proprietor has complete control over the business and can make decisions on the spot without anyone else's approval. This control allows the owner to respond quickly to competitive business conditions or to changes in the economy. The ability to quickly change prices or products can provide a competitive advantage for the business.

Government Regulation Sole proprietorships have the most freedom from government regulation. Many government regulations—federal, state, and local—apply only to businesses that have a certain number of employees, and securities laws

Sole proprietorships have the most freedom from government regulation.

IT IS USUALLY DIFFICULT FOR A SMALL SOLE PROPRIETORSHIP TO MATCH THE WAGES AND BENEFITS OFFERED BY A LARGE COMPETING CORPORATION BECAUSE THE PROPRIETORSHIP'S PROFITS MAY NOT BE AS HIGH.

apply only to corporations that issue stock. Nonetheless, sole proprietors must ensure that they follow all laws that do apply to their business. For example, sole proprietorships must be careful to obey employee and consumer protection regulation.

Taxation Profits from sole proprietorships are considered personal income and are taxed at individual tax rates. The owner, therefore, pays one income tax that includes the business and individual income. Another tax benefit is that a sole proprietor is allowed to establish a tax-exempt retirement account or a tax-exempt profit-sharing account. Such accounts are exempt from current income tax, but payments taken after retirement are taxed when they are received.

Closing the Business A sole proprietorship can be dissolved easily. No approval of co-owners or partners is necessary. The only legal condition is that all financial obligations must be paid or resolved.

Disadvantages of Sole Proprietorships

What may be seen as an advantage by one person may turn out to be a disadvantage to another. For profitable businesses managed by capable owners, many of the following factors do not cause problems. On the other hand, proprietors starting out with little management experience and little money are likely to encounter many of the disadvantages.

Unlimited Liability The sole proprietor has unlimited liability in meeting the debts of the business. In other words, if the business cannot pay its creditors, the owner may be forced to use personal, nonbusiness holdings such as a car or a home to pay off the debts. There are only a few states in which houses and homesteads cannot be taken by creditors, even if the proprietor declares bankruptcy. The more wealth an individual has, the greater is the disadvantage of unlimited liability.

Limited Sources of Funds Among the relatively few sources of money available to the sole proprietorship are banks, friends, family, the Small Business Administration, or his or her own funds. The owner's personal financial condition determines his or her credit standing. Additionally, sole proprietorships may have to pay higher interest rates on funds borrowed from banks than do large corporations because they are considered greater risks. Often, the only way a sole proprietor can borrow for business purposes is to pledge a car, a house, other

real estate, or other personal assets to guarantee the loan. If the business fails, the owner may lose the personal assets as well as the business. Publicly owned corporations, in contrast, not only can obtain funds from commercial banks but also can sell stocks and bonds to the public to raise money. If a public company goes out of business, the owners do not lose personal assets.

Limited Skills The sole proprietor must be able to perform many functions and possess skills in diverse fields such as management, marketing, finance, accounting, bookkeeping, and personnel management. Business owners can rely on specialized professionals for advice and services, such as accountants and attorneys. Freelancers, for example, can turn to agents for assistance in obtaining projects and assignments. One firm specializing in this type of assistance for visual effects artists is the Digital Artists Agency, whose clients include David Lombardi, Chris LeDoux, and Academy Award–winner Tim McGovern. The DAA represents artists, many of them freelancers, and connects them to companies.[4] In the end, however, it is up to the business owner to make the final decision in all areas of the business.

Lack of Continuity The life expectancy of a sole proprietorship is directly linked to that of the owner and his or her ability to work. The serious illness of the owner could result in failure of the business if competent help cannot be found.

It is difficult to arrange for the sale of a proprietorship and at the same time assure customers that the business will continue to meet their needs. For instance, how does one sell a veterinary practice? A veterinarian's major asset is patients. If the vet dies suddenly, the equipment can be sold, but the patients will not necessarily remain loyal to the office. On the other hand, a veterinarian who wants to retire could take in a younger partner and sell the practice to the partner over time. One advantage to the partnership is that some of the customers are likely to stay with the business, even if ownership changes.

Lack of Qualified Employees It is usually difficult for a small sole proprietorship to match the wages and benefits offered by a large competing corporation because the proprietorship's profits may not be as high. In addition, there is little room for advancement within a sole proprietorship, so the owner may have difficulty attracting and retaining qualified employees. On the other hand, the trend of large corporations downsizing and outsourcing tasks has created renewed opportunities for small businesses to acquire well-trained employees.

partnership a form of business organization defined by the Uniform Partnership Act as "an association of two or more persons who carry on as co-owners of a business for profit"	general partnership a partnership that involves a complete sharing in both the management and the liability of the business	limited partnership a business organization that has at least one general partner, who assumes unlimited liability, and at least one limited partner, whose liability is limited to his or her investment in the business	articles of partnership legal documents that set forth the basic agreement between partners

Taxation Although we listed taxation as an advantage for sole proprietorships, it can also be a disadvantage, depending on the proprietor's income. Under current tax rates, sole proprietors pay a higher marginal tax rate than do small corporations on income of less than $75,000. However, sole proprietorships avoid the double taxation that occurs with corporations. The tax effect often determines whether a sole proprietor chooses to incorporate his or her business.

PARTNERSHIPS

One way to minimize the disadvantages of a sole proprietorship and maximize its advantages is to have more than one owner. Most states have a model law governing partnerships based on the Uniform Partnership Act. This law defines a **partnership** as "an association of two or more persons who carry on as co-owners of a business for profit." Partnerships are the least used form of business (see Figure 4.1). They are typically larger than sole proprietorships but smaller than corporations.

Partnerships can be a fruitful form of business, as long as you follow some basic keys to success, which are outlined in Table 4.2.

Types of Partnership

There are two basic types of partnership: general partnership and limited partnership. A **general partnership** involves a complete sharing in the management of a business. In a general partnership, each partner has unlimited liability for the debts of the business. For example, Cirque du Soleil grew from a group of Quebec street performers, who acted as partners, into a half-billion-dollar global company. Cirque du Soleil, however, ended its 16-year run as a partnership in the year 2000. Guy Laliberte bought out the other principle partner, Daniel Gauthier. Laliberte maintains a controlling share of the company, and Dubai's state-run private equity firm Istithmar World along with real estate developer Nakheel picked up a 20 percent stake in Cirque du Soleil for more global expansion of permanent show venues.[5] Professionals such as lawyers, accountants, and architects often join together in general partnerships.

A **limited partnership** has at least one general partner, who assumes unlimited liability, and at least one limited partner, whose liability is limited to his or her investment in the business. Limited partnerships exist for risky investment projects where the chance of loss is great. The general partners accept the risk of loss; the limited partners' losses are limited to their initial investment. Limited partners do not participate in the management of the business but share in the profits in accordance with the terms of a partnership agreement. Usually the general partner receives a larger share of the profits after the limited partners have received their initial investment back. Popular examples are oil-drilling partnerships and real estate partnerships.

Articles of Partnership

Articles of partnership are legal documents that set forth the basic agreement between partners. Most states require articles of partnership, but even if they are not required, it makes good sense for partners to draw them up. Articles of partnership usually list the money or assets that each partner has contributed (called *partnership capital*), state each partner's individual management role or duty, specify how the profits and losses of the partnership will be divided among the partners, and describe how a partner may leave the partnership as well as any other restrictions that might apply to the agreement. Table 4.3 lists some of the issues and provisions that should be included in articles of partnership.

▼ **TABLE 4.2** Keys to Success in Business Partnerships

1. Keep profit sharing and ownership at 50/50, or you have an employer/employee relationship.
2. Partners should have different skill sets to complement one another.
3. Honesty is critical.
4. Must maintain face-to-face communication in addition to phone and e-mail.
5. Maintain transparency, sharing more information over time.
6. Be aware of funding constraints, and do not put yourself in a situation where neither you nor your partner can secure additional financial support.
7. To be successful, you need experience.
8. Whereas family should be a priority, be careful to minimize the number of associated problems.
9. Do not become too infatuated with "the idea" as opposed to implementation.
10. Couple optimism with realism in sales and growth expectations and planning.

Source: Abstracted from J. Watananbe, "14 Reasons Why 80% of New Business Partnerships Would Fail Within Their First 5 Years of Existence," http://ezinearticles.com/?14-Reasons-Why-80-Percent-Of-New-Business-Partnerships-Would-Fail-Within-Their-First-5-Years-Of-Exis&id5472498 (accessed March 16, 2010).

WHEN A BUSINESS HAS SEVERAL PARTNERS, IT HAS THE BENEFIT OF A COMBINATION OF TALENTS.

▼ **TABLE 4.3** Issues and Provisions in Articles of Partnership

1. Name, purpose, location
2. Duration of the agreement
3. Authority and responsibility of each partner
4. Character of partners (i.e., general or limited, active or silent)
5. Amount of contribution from each partner
6. Division of profits or losses
7. Salaries of each partner
8. How much each partner is allowed to withdraw
9. Death of partner
10. Sale of partnership interest
11. Arbitration of disputes
12. Required and prohibited actions
13. Absence and disability
14. Restrictive covenants
15. Buying and selling agreements

Source: Adapted from "Partnership Agreement Sample," State of New Jersey, www.state.nj.us/njbusiness/starting/basics/partnership_agreement_sample.shtml (accessed March 15, 2010).

Advantages of Partnerships

Law firms, accounting firms, and investment firms with several hundred partners have partnership agreements that are quite complicated in comparison with the partnership agreement among two or three people owning a computer repair shop. The advantages must be compared with those offered by other forms of business organization, and not all apply to every partnership.

Ease of Organization Starting a partnership requires little more than drawing up articles of partnership. No legal charters have to be granted, but the name of the business should be registered with the state.

Availability of Capital and Credit When a business has several partners, it has the benefit of a combination of talents and skills and pooled financial resources. Partnerships tend to be larger than sole proprietorships and therefore have greater earning power and better credit ratings. Because many limited partnerships have been formed for tax purposes rather than for economic profits, the combined income of all U.S. partnerships is quite low, as shown in Figure 4.1. Nevertheless, the professional partnerships of many lawyers, accountants, and banking firms make quite large profits. For instance, the partners in the international law firm Davis Polk & Wardwell LLP take home an average of approximately $2 million a year.[6]

Combined Knowledge and Skills Partners in the most successful partnerships acknowledge each other's talents and avoid confusion and conflict by specializing in a particular area of expertise such as marketing, production, accounting, or service. The diversity of skills in a partnership makes it possible for the business to be run by a management team of specialists instead of by a generalist sole proprietor. Co-founders Barry Nalebuff and Seth Goldman credit this diversity as being a key component to the success of their company Honest Tea. In less than a decade, Honest Tea went from $250,000 to $13.5 million in sales and attracted the attention of Coca-Cola. Coca-Cola bought a 40 percent stake in the company.[7] Service-oriented partnerships in fields such as law, financial planning, and accounting may attract customers because clients may think that the service offered by a diverse team is of higher quality than that provided by one person. Larger law firms, for example, often have individual partners who specialize in certain areas of the law—such as family, bankruptcy, corporate, entertainment, and criminal law.

In 1996 Stanford students Sergey Brin and Larry Page partnered to form the search engine Google as part of a research project. The company was incorporated in 1998 and is now the world's top search engine.

Decision Making Small partnerships can react more quickly to changes in the business environment than can large partnerships and corporations. Such fast reactions are possible because the partners are involved in day-to-day operations and can make decisions quickly after consultation. Large partnerships with hundreds of partners in many states are not common. In those that do exist, decision making is likely to be slow. However, some partnerships have been successful despite their large size. The accounting firm Baird, Kurtz & Dodson is the 10th largest accounting and advisory firm in the United States with approximately 250 partners and principals and 2,000 personnel. The company has gross revenues of over $400 million. Some have attributed BKD's success to its strong diversification techniques and ability to operate in different market niches.[8]

Regulatory Controls Like a sole proprietorship, a partnership has fewer regulatory controls affecting its activities than does a corporation. A partnership does not have to file public financial statements with government agencies or send out quarterly financial statements to several thousand owners, as do corporations such as Apple and Ford Motor Co. A partnership does, however, have to abide by all laws relevant to the industry or profession in which it operates as well as state and federal laws relating to hiring and firing, food handling, and so on, just as the sole proprietorship does.

Disadvantages of Partnerships

Partnerships have many advantages compared to sole proprietorships and corporations, but they also have some disadvantages.

Limited partners have no voice in the management of the partnership, and they may bear most of the risk of the business while the general partner reaps a larger share of the benefits. There may be a change in the goals and objectives of one partner but not the other, particularly when the partners are multinational organizations. This can cause friction, giving rise to an enterprise that fails to satisfy both parties or even forcing an end to the partnership. Many partnership disputes wind up in court or require outside mediation. A partnership can be jeopardized when two business partners cannot resolve disputes. In *Saunders v. Firtel* (Firtel held a 51 percent stake and Saunders a 49 percent in Adco Medical Supplies Inc.), Saunders was not only a partner, but a paid employee. When the two entered into an unresolvable dispute, Firtel fired Saunders and did not pay wages. Saunders sued under Connecticut law, which states that "when any employer fails to pay an employee's wages . . . the employee may recover, in civil action, twice the full amount of such wages." Saunders won the case because the trial court found the failure to pay wages was willful.[9] In some cases, the ultimate solution may be dissolving the partnership. Major disadvantages of partnerships include the following.

Unlimited Liability In general partnerships, the general partners have unlimited liability for the debts incurred by the business, just as the sole proprietor has unlimited liability for his or her business. Such unlimited liability can be a distinct disadvantage to one partner if his or her personal financial resources are greater than those of the others. A potential partner should check to make sure that all partners have comparable resources to

---

MICROLENDING HELPS SMALL ENTREPRENEURS START BUSINESSES

Sending food and money to disadvantaged communities meets immediate needs, but ending long-term poverty is more difficult. Kiva.org is one business that seeks to tackle this problem head on. Founded by Stanford graduates with an interest in business and technology, Kiva was first designed to lend money to impoverished Ugandan entrepreneurs. It soon expanded its reach to include other developing countries. Kiva is a microfinance business, which means it provides small loans—as little as $25 for equipment, for example—to individuals to start their own businesses.

Kiva partners with microfinance institutions worldwide. These field partners approve entrepreneurs and send their profiles to Kiva. The entrepreneurs' profiles are then posted on Kiva's website, and people who want to lend to an entrepreneur send their donations through the site. Kiva's field partners distribute the loans, work with the entrepreneurs, and collect repayments. Kiva.org does not earn returns on investments for lenders, but it does charge interest rates of between 23 and 48 percent. These interest rates cover loan costs, transaction costs, defaults, and inflation rates—and are much lower than rates charged by informal lenders or predatory lenders who typically supply loans to those who do not qualify for bank loans.

Kiva and over 560,000 lenders have succeeded in providing loans to over half a million entrepreneurs since 2005. The company has given $200 million in worldwide

loans, but Kiva wants to go even further. It has established a five-year plan, aiming to reach $1 billion in global loans, help 2 million entrepreneurs, and achieve organizational sustainability. The buzz about Kiva is positive, and Kiva.org's future looks bright as microlending continues to receive favorable press.[10]

Discussion Questions

1. Kiva.org has been very successful at extending microlending to entrepreneurs in need. What about Kiva.org has helped make it so successful?

2. What is unique about the way Kiva.org is organized that sets it apart from more traditional businesses?

3. Do you think the Kiva.org model of giving loans would work for larger loans, or even for other kinds of businesses?

corporation a legal entity, created by the state, whose assets and liabilities are separate from its owners

stock shares of a corporation that may be bought or sold

help the business in time of trouble. This disadvantage is eliminated for limited partners, who can lose only their initial investment.

Business Responsibility
All partners are responsible for the business actions of all others. Partners may have the ability to commit the partnership to a contract without approval of the other partners. A bad decision by one partner may put the other partners' personal resources in jeopardy. Personal problems such as a divorce can eliminate a significant portion of one partner's financial resources and weaken the financial structure of the whole partnership.

Life of the Partnership
A partnership is terminated when a partner dies or withdraws. In a two-person partnership, if one partner withdraws, the firm's liabilities would be paid

division of the profits does not reflect the work each partner puts into the business. You may have encountered this disadvantage while working on a student group project: You may have felt that you did most of the work and that the other students in the group received grades based on your efforts. Even the perception of an unfair profit-sharing agreement may cause tension between the partners, and unhappy partners can have a negative effect on the profitability of the business.

Limited Sources of Funds
As with a sole proprietorship, the sources of funds available to a partnership are limited. Because no public value is placed on the business (such as the current trading price of a corporation's stock), potential partners do not know what one partnership share is worth. Moreover, because partnership shares cannot be bought and sold easily in public markets, potential owners may not want to tie up their money in assets that cannot be readily sold on short notice. Accumulating enough funds to operate a national business, especially

> "All partners are responsible for the business actions of all others."

off and the assets divided between the partners. Obviously, the partner who wishes to continue in the business would be at a serious disadvantage. The business could be disrupted, financing would be reduced, and the management skills of the departing partner would be lost. The remaining partner would have to find another or reorganize the business as a sole proprietorship. In very large partnerships such as those found in law firms and investment banks, the continuation of the partnership may be provided for in the articles of partnership. The provision may simply state the terms for a new partnership agreement among the remaining partners. In such cases, the disadvantage to the other partners is minimal.

Selling a partnership interest has the same effect as the death or withdrawal of a partner. It is difficult to place a value on a partner's share of the partnership. No public value is placed on the partnership, as there is on publicly owned corporations. What is a law firm worth? What is the local hardware store worth? Coming up with a fair value that all partners can agree to is not easy. Selling a partnership interest is easier if the articles of partnership specify a method of valuation. Even if there is not a procedure for selling one partner's interest, the old partnership must still be dissolved and a new one created. In contrast, in the corporate form of business, the departure of owners has little effect on the financial resources of the business, and the loss of managers does not cause long-term changes in the structure of the organization.

Distribution of Profits
Profits earned by the partnership are distributed to the partners in the proportions specified in the articles of partnership. This may be a disadvantage if the

a business requiring intensive investments in facilities and equipment, can be difficult. Partnerships also may have to pay higher interest rates on funds borrowed from banks than do large corporations because partnerships may be considered greater risks.

Taxation of Partnerships
Partnerships are quasi-taxable organizations. This means that partnerships do not pay taxes when submitting the partnership tax return to the Internal Revenue Service. The tax return simply provides information about the profitability of the organization and the distribution of profits among the partners. Partners must report their share of profits on their individual tax returns and pay taxes at the income tax rate for individuals.

CORPORATIONS
When you think of a business, you probably think of a huge corporation such as General Electric, Procter & Gamble, or Sony because a large portion of your consumer dollars go to such corporations. A **corporation** is a legal entity, created by the state, whose assets and liabilities are separate from its owners. As a legal entity, a corporation has many of the rights, duties, and powers of a person, such as the right to receive, own, and transfer property. Corporations can enter into contracts with individuals or with other legal entities, and they can sue and be sued in court.

Corporations account for the majority of all U.S. sales and income. Thus, most of the dollars you spend as a consumer probably go to incorporated businesses (see Figure 4.1). Most corporations are not mega-companies like General Mills or

Ford Motor Co.; even small businesses can incorporate. As we shall see later in the chapter, many smaller firms elect to incorporate as "S Corporations," which operate under slightly different rules and have greater flexibility than do traditional "C Corporations" like General Mills.

Corporations are typically owned by many individuals and organizations who own shares of the business, called **stock** (thus, corporate owners are often called *shareholders* or *stockholders*). Stockholders can buy, sell, give or receive as gifts, or inherit their shares of stock. As owners, the stockholders are entitled to all profits that are left after all the corporation's other obligations have been paid. These profits may be distributed in the form of cash payments called **dividends**. For example, if a corporation earns $100 million after expenses and taxes and decides to pay the owners $40 million in dividends, the stockholders receive 40 percent of the profits in cash dividends. However, not all after-tax profits are paid to stockholders in dividends. Some corporations may retain profits to expand the business. For example, Berkshire Hathaway has always retained its earnings and reinvested them for the shareholders. This has resulted in an average 20 percent in per share investment over a 40-year period.[11]

Creating a Corporation

A corporation is created, or incorporated, under the laws of the state in which it incorporates. The individuals creating the corporation are known as *incorporators*. Each state has a specific procedure, sometimes called *chartering the corporation,* for incorporating a business. Most states require a minimum of

dividends profits of a corporation that are distributed in the form of cash payments to stockholders

corporate charter a legal document that the state issues to a company based on information the company provides in the articles of incorporation

private corporation a corporation owned by just one or a few people who are closely involved in managing the business

3. Classes of stock (common, preferred, voting, nonvoting) and the number of shares for each class of stock to be issued.

4. Expected life of the corporation (corporations are usually created to last forever).

5. Financial capital required at the time of incorporation.

6. Provisions for transferring shares of stock between owners.

7. Provisions for the regulation of internal corporate affairs.

8. Address of the business office registered with the state of incorporation.

9. Names and addresses of the initial board of directors.

10. Names and addresses of the incorporators.

Based on the information in the articles of incorporation, the state issues a **corporate charter** to the company. After securing this charter, the owners hold an organizational meeting at which they establish the corporation's bylaws and elect a board of directors. The bylaws might set up committees of the board of directors and describe the rules and procedures for their operation.

Types of Corporations

If the corporation does business in the state in which it is chartered, it is known as a *domestic corporation*. In other states where the corporation does business, it is known as a *foreign corporation*. If a corporation does business outside the nation

A corporation may be privately or publicly owned.

three incorporators; thus, many small businesses can be and are incorporated. Another requirement is that the new corporation's name cannot be similar to that of another business. In most states, a corporation's name must end in "company," "corporation," "incorporated," or "limited" to show that the owners have limited liability. (In this text, however, the word *company* means any organization engaged in a commercial enterprise and can refer to a sole proprietorship, a partnership, or a corporation.)

The incorporators must file legal documents generally referred to as *articles of incorporation* with the appropriate state office (often the secretary of state). The articles of incorporation contain basic information about the business. The following 10 items are found in the Model Business Corporation Act, issued by the American Bar Association, which is followed by most states:

1. Name and address of the corporation.

2. Objectives of the corporation.

in which it incorporated, it is called an *alien corporation*. A corporation may be privately or publicly owned.

A **private corporation** is owned by just one or a few people who are closely involved in managing the business. These people, often a family, own all the corporation's stock, and no stock is sold to the public. Many corporations are quite large, yet remain private, including Cargill, a farm products business. It is the nation's largest private corporation with annual revenues of well over $100 billion. Founded at the end of the Civil War, descendants of the original founder have owned equity in the company for more than 140 years.[12] The fifth-largest privately held company in the United States is Mars, founded by Frank C. Mars who spent time in Switzerland learning to create chocolate confectionaries. Mars recently grew significantly through the acquisition of the Wm. Wrigley Jr. Company. Founded in Tacoma, Washington, in 1911, Mars is now the world's leading confectionary company and a leader in pet

public corporation
a corporation whose stock anyone may buy, sell, or trade

initial public offering (IPO) selling a corporation's stock on public markets for the first time

care products with Pedigree and Whiskas.[13] The business was successful early on because it paid employees three times the normal wage for the time. The company remains successful to this day, largely because of its established brands, such as M&Ms, and healthy snack lines for kids, like Generation Max.[14] Other well-known privately held companies include Chrysler, Publix Supermarkets, Dollar General,

A **public corporation** is one whose stock anyone may buy, sell, or trade. Table 4.4 lists the largest U.S. corporations by revenues. Despite their high revenues, Citigroup and American International Group had negative profits in 2010.[15] Thousands of smaller public corporations in the United States have sales under $10 million. In large public corporations such as AT&T, the stockholders are often far removed from the management of the company. In other public corporations, the managers are often the founders and the major shareholders. NASCAR, for example, was founded by William France in 1948, and ever since then his descendants have manned the helm as CEO.

> ## Privately owned corporations are not required to disclose financial information publicly, but they must, of course, pay taxes.

and MGM Entertainment. Privately owned corporations are not required to disclose financial information publicly, but they must, of course, pay taxes.

Grandson Brian France currently fills the post.[16] *Forbes* Global 2000 companies generate around $30 trillion in revenues, $1.4 trillion in profits, and $124 trillion in assets. They are worth $31 trillion in market value. The United States still has the majority of the Global 2000 companies, but other nations are catching up. The rankings of the Global 2000 span across 62 countries.[17] Publicly owned corporations must disclose financial information to the public under specific laws that regulate the trade of stocks and other securities.

▼ **TABLE 4.4** The Largest U.S. Corporations, Arranged by Revenue

Rank	Company	Revenues (in millions of $)
1	Wal-Mart Stores	$421,849.0
2	Exxon Mobil	$354,674.0
3	Chevron	$196,337.0
4	ConocoPhillips	$184,966.0
5	Fannie Mae	$153,825.0
6	General Electric	$151,628.0
7	Berkshire Hathaway	$136,185.0
8	General Motors	$135,592.0
9	Bank of America Corp.	$134,194.0
10	Ford Motor	$128,954.0
11	Hewlett-Packard	$126,033.0
12	AT&T	$124,629.0
13	J.P. Morgan Chase & Co.	$115,475.0
14	Citigroup	$111,055.0
15	McKesson	$108,702.0
16	Verizon Communications	$106,565.0
17	American International Group	$104,417.0
18	International Business Machines	$ 99,870.0
19	Cardinal Health	$ 98,601.9
20	Freddie Mac	98,368.0

Source: "Fortune 500," *CNNMoney,* http://money.cnn.com/magazines/fortune/fortune500/2011/full_list/ (accessed July 20, 2011).

A private corporation that needs more money to expand or to take advantage of opportunities may have to obtain financing by "going public" through an **initial public offering (IPO)**, that is, becoming a public corporation by selling stock so that it can be traded in public markets. In 2010 General Motors launched the world's biggest IPO estimated at about $23.1 billion. This IPO is one step in General Motors' plan to rebound from the massive losses it had incurred in recent years. GM plans to use $11.8 billion of the IPO proceeds to begin paying back the $50 billion bailout it received from the government.[18]

Also, privately owned firms are occasionally forced to go public with stock offerings when a major owner dies and the heirs have large estate taxes to pay. The tax payment may be possible only with the proceeds of the sale of stock. This happened to the brewer Adolph Coors Inc. After Adolph Coors died, the business went public and his family sold shares of stock to the public in order to pay the estate taxes.

On the other hand, public corporations can be "taken private" when one or a few individuals (perhaps the management of the firm) purchase all the firm's stock so that it can no longer be sold publicly. Taking a corporation private may be desirable when new owners want to exert more control over the firm or they want to avoid the necessity of public disclosure of future activities for competitive reasons. For example, RCN Corporation, a broadband provider, was purchased by a private equity group, Abry Partners LLC, for about $535 million in cash. Abry's goal with the purchase is to expand its companies offering broadband and cable service in New York, Boston, and Philadelphia.[19] Taking a corporation private is also one technique for avoiding a takeover by another corporation.

Quasi-public corporations and nonprofits are two types of public corporations. **Quasi-public corporations** are owned and operated by the federal, state, or local government.

quasi-public corporations corporations owned and operated by the federal, state, or local government

nonprofit corporations corporations that focus on providing a service rather than earning a profit but are not owned by a government entity

board of directors a group of individuals, elected by the stockholders to oversee the general operation of the corporation, who set the corporation's long-range objectives

The snack and food company Mars is privately owned by the Mars family. Frank C. Mars founded the firm in 1911, and the company headed by Forest Mars Sr. began selling its most popular candy, M&Ms, in 1941.

> ## "Taking a corporation private is also one technique for avoiding a takeover by another corporation."

The focus of these entities is to provide a service to citizens, such as mail delivery, rather than earning a profit. Indeed, many quasi-public corporations operate at a loss. Examples of quasi-public corporations include the National Aeronautics and Space Administration (NASA) and the U.S. Postal Service.

Like quasi-public corporations, **nonprofit corporations** focus on providing a service rather than earning a profit, but they are not owned by a government entity. Organizations such as the Sesame Workshop, the Elks Clubs, the American Lung Association, the American Red Cross, museums, and private schools provide services without a profit motive. To fund their operations and services, nonprofit organizations solicit donations from individuals and companies and grants from the government and other charitable foundations.

Elements of a Corporation

The Board of Directors
A **board of directors**, elected by the stockholders to oversee the general operation of the corporation, sets the long-range objectives of the corporation. It is the board's responsibility to ensure that the objectives are

achieved on schedule. Board members are legally liable for the mismanagement of the firm or for any misuse of funds. An important duty of the board of directors is to hire corporate officers, such as the president and the chief executive officer

Lionsgate is a diversified entertainment corporation that provides excellent documentation on its corporate governance and financial performance.

preferred stock a special type of stock whose owners, though not generally having a say in running the company, have a claim to profits before other stockholders do

common stock stock whose owners have voting rights in the corporation, yet do not receive preferential treatment regarding dividends

(CEO), who are responsible to the directors for the management and daily operations of the firm. The role and expectations of the board of directors took on greater significance after the accounting scandals of the early 2000s and the passage of the Sarbanes-Oxley Act.[20] As a result, most corporations have restructured how they compensate board directors for their time and expertise.

However, some experts now speculate that Sarbanes-Oxley did little to motivate directors to increase company oversight. One notable case of alleged director misconduct involves a lawsuit filed by the SEC against three directors of DHB Industries. The SEC accused these directors of purposefully ignoring red flags that indicated company misconduct. However, such lawsuits are the exception to the norm. If it cannot be proven that directors did not act in good faith, it is hard for the SEC to develop a case against them.[21] At the same time, the pay rate of directors is rising. In 2009, the median pay for directors at the 200 largest companies was $228,000. At Apple it is even higher at $984,000. Analysts believe that 50 percent of boards could see pay raises as high as 15 percent within the year. Although such pay is meant to attract top-quality directors, concerns exist over whether excessive pay will have unintended consequences. Some believe that pay over $200,000 will cause directors to be more complacent and overlook potential misconduct in order to keep their positions.[22]

Directors can be employees of the company (*inside directors*) or people unaffiliated with the company (*outside directors*). Inside directors are usually the officers responsible for running the company. Outside directors are often top executives from other companies, lawyers, bankers, even professors. Directors today are increasingly chosen for their expertise, competence, and ability to bring diverse perspectives to strategic discussions. Outside directors are also thought to bring more independence to the monitoring function because they are not bound by past allegiances, friendships, a current role in the company, or some other issue that may create a conflict of interest. Many of the corporate scandals uncovered in recent years might have been prevented if each of the companies' boards of directors had been better qualified, more knowledgeable, and more independent.

There is a growing shortage of available and qualified board members. Boards are increasingly telling their own CEOs that they should be focused on serving their company, not serving on outside boards. Because of this, the average CEO sits on less than one outside board. This represents a decline from a decade ago when the average was two. Because many CEOs are turning down outside positions, many companies have taken steps to ensure that boards have experienced directors. They have increased the mandatory retirement age to 72 or older, and some have raised it to 75 or even older. Minimizing the amount of overlap between directors sitting on different boards helps limit conflicts of interest and provides for independence in decision making.

Stock Ownership Corporations issue two types of stock: preferred and common. Owners of **preferred stock** are a special class of owners because, although they generally do not have any say in running the company, they have a claim to profits before any other stockholders do. Other stockholders do not receive any dividends unless the preferred stockholders have already been paid. Dividend payments on preferred stock are usually a fixed percentage of the initial issuing price (set by the board of directors). For example, if a share of preferred stock originally cost $100 and the dividend rate was stated at 7.5 percent, the dividend payment will be $7.50 per share per year. Dividends are usually paid quarterly. Most preferred stock carries a cumulative claim to dividends. This means that if the company does not pay preferred stock dividends in one year because of losses, the dividends accumulate to the next year. Such dividends unpaid from previous years must also be paid to preferred stockholders before other stockholders can receive any dividends.

Although owners of **common stock** do not get such preferential treatment with regard to dividends, they do get some say in the operation of the corporation. Their ownership gives them the right to vote for members of the board of directors and on other important issues. Common stock dividends may vary according to the profitability of the business, and some corporations do not issue dividends at all, but instead plow their profits back into the company to fund expansion.

Common stockholders are the voting owners of a corporation. They are usually entitled to one vote per share of common stock. During an annual stockholders' meeting, common stockholders

Owners of preferred stock have first claim to company profits.

OF ALL THE FORMS OF BUSINESS ORGANIZATION, THE PUBLIC CORPORATION FINDS IT EASIEST TO RAISE MONEY.

elect a board of directors. Some boards find it easier than others to attract high-profile individuals. For example, the board of Procter & Gamble consists of Ernesto Zedillo, former president of Mexico; Kenneth I. Chenault, CEO of the American Express Company; the CEO of Archer Daniels Midland; the CEO of Boeing; and a director of eBay.[23] Because they can choose the board of directors, common stockholders have some say in how the company will operate. Common stockholders may vote by *proxy*, which is a written authorization by which stockholders assign their voting privilege to someone else, who then votes for his or her choice at the stockholders' meeting. It is a normal practice for management to request proxy statements from shareholders who are not planning to attend the annual meeting. Most owners do not attend annual meetings of the very large companies, such as Westinghouse or Boeing, unless they live in the city where the meeting is held.

Common stockholders have another advantage over preferred shareholders. In most states, when the corporation decides to sell new shares of common stock in the marketplace, common stockholders have the first right, called a *preemptive right,* to purchase new shares of the stock from the corporation. A preemptive right is often included in the articles of incorporation. This right is important because it allows stockholders to purchase new shares to maintain their original positions. For example, if a stockholder

DID YOU KNOW?

The first corporation with a net income of more than $1 billion in one year was General Motors, with a net income in 1955 of $1,189,477,082.[24]

held responsible for the firm's debts if it fails. Their liability or potential loss is limited to the amount of their original investment. Although a creditor can sue a corporation for not paying its debts, even forcing the corporation into bankruptcy, it cannot make the stockholders pay the corporation's debts out of their personal assets. Occasionally, the owners of a private corporation may pledge personal assets to secure a loan for the corporation; this would be most unusual for a public corporation.

Ease of Transfer of Ownership Stockholders can sell or trade shares of stock to other people without causing the termination of the corporation, and they can do this without the prior approval of other shareholders. The transfer of ownership (unless it is a majority position) does not affect the daily or long-term operations of the corporation.

Perpetual Life A corporation usually is chartered to last forever unless its articles of incorporation stipulate otherwise. The existence of the corporation is unaffected by the death or withdrawal of any of its stockholders. It survives until the owners sell it or liquidate its assets. However, in some cases, bankruptcy ends a corporation's life. Bankruptcies occur when companies are unable to compete and earn profits. Eventually, uncompetitive businesses must close or seek protection from creditors in bankruptcy court while the business tries to reorganize.

> "Common stockholders are the voting owners of a corporation."

owns 10 percent of a corporation that decides to issue new shares, that stockholder has the right to buy enough of the new shares to retain the 10 percent ownership.

Advantages of Corporations

Because a corporation is a separate legal entity, it has some very specific advantages over other forms of ownership. The biggest advantage may be the limited liability of the owners.

Limited Liability Because the corporation's assets (money and resources) and liabilities (debts and other obligations) are separate from its owners', in most cases the stockholders are not

External Sources of Funds Of all the forms of business organization, the public corporation finds it easiest to raise money. When a corporation needs to raise more money, it can sell more stock shares or issue bonds (corporate "IOUs," which pledge to repay debt), attracting funds from anywhere in the United States and even overseas. The larger a corporation becomes, the more sources of financing are available to it. We take a closer look at some of these in Chapter 15.

Expansion Potential Because large public corporations can find long-term financing readily, they can easily expand into national and international markets. And, as a legal entity, a

BOB'S RED MILL ENCOURAGES LOYALTY THROUGH EMPLOYEE OWNERSHIP

How would you like to get a company as a gift . . . on somebody else's birthday? On February 15, 2010, Bob Moore, founder of Bob's Red Mill Products, gave his employees company ownership through an employee stock ownership plan (ESOP). It was his 81st birthday. Bob's Red Mill was founded over 25 years ago by Bob and Charlee Moore after they stumbled across an old abandoned mill and decided to turn it into a business. Today, Bob's Red Mill offers over 400 whole-grain natural food products, ranging from flour to cereal to baking ingredients. The company boasts sales of over $70 million annually and enjoys consistent growth of 20 to 30 percent per year.

With an ESOP program, Bob's Red Mill has an employee trust fund made up of stock shares. Employees receive shares based on a formula. With seniority comes a greater right to shares, called vesting. At Bob's Red Mill, employees are fully vested after three years of service. With shares often come voting rights, which gives employees a direct say in how the company is run. Upon retirement from the company, employees receive money for their shares. As Bob sees it, he's selling the company to his employees without any money leaving their pockets.

Bob's Red Mill has succeeded thanks to its dedication to high-quality products, excellent customer service, and a reputation for treating employees like family.

Moore regularly receives offers from those looking to purchase Bob's Red Mill for large sums of money, but his dream has always been to reward those who truly made the company what it is today. Although he has no intention of retiring, Moore now believes his company will always be in the hands of those who care deeply about its success.[25]

Discussion Questions

1. Why did Bob Moore give his employees ownership through an employee stock ownership plan (ESOP)?

2. What are the advantages of having employees as owners at Bob's Red Mill Products?

3. Does stock ownership help employees understand the operations and financial success of Bob's Red Mill Products?

---

corporation can enter into contracts without as much difficulty as a partnership.

Disadvantages of Corporations

Corporations have some distinct disadvantages resulting from tax laws and government regulation.

Double Taxation As a legal entity, the corporation must pay taxes on its income just like you do. When after-tax corporate profits are paid out as dividends to the stockholders, the dividends are taxed a second time as part of the individual owner's income. This process creates double taxation for the stockholders of dividend paying corporations. Double taxation does not occur with the other forms of business organization.

Forming a Corporation The formation of a corporation can be costly. A charter must be obtained, and this usually requires the services of an attorney and payment of legal fees. Filing fees ranging from $25 to $150 must be paid to the state that awards the corporate charter, and certain states require that an annual fee be paid to maintain the charter. Today, a number of Internet services such as LegalZoom.com and Business.com make it easier, quicker, and less costly to form a corporation. However, in making it easier for people to form businesses without expert consultation, these services have increased the risk that people will not choose the kind of organizational form that is right for them. Sometimes, one form works better than another. The business's founders may fail to take into account disadvantages, such as double taxation with corporations.

Disclosure of Information Corporations must make information available to their owners, usually through an annual report to shareholders. The annual report contains financial information about the firm's profits, sales, facilities and equipment, and debts, as well as descriptions of the company's operations, products, and plans for the future. Public corporations must also file reports with the Securities and Exchange Commission (SEC), the government regulatory agency that regulates securities such as stocks and bonds. The larger the firm, the more data the SEC requires. Because all reports filed with the SEC are available to the public, competitors can access them. Additionally, complying with securities laws takes time.

With revenues surpassing $380 billion, ExxonMobil is one of the world's largest corporations.

joint venture a partnership established for a specific project or for a limited time

S corporation corporation taxed as though it were a partnership with restrictions on shareholders

limited liability company (LLC) form of ownership that provides limited liability and taxation like a partnership but places fewer restrictions on members

cooperative or co-op an organization composed of individuals or small businesses that have banded together to reap the benefits of belonging to a larger organization

Employee–Owner Separation Many employees are not stockholders of the company for which they work. This separation of owners and employees may cause employees to feel that their work benefits only the owners. Employees without an ownership stake do not always see how they fit into the corporate picture and may not understand the importance of profits to the health of the organization. If managers are part owners but other employees are not, management–labor relations take on a different, sometimes difficult, aspect from those in partnerships and sole proprietorships. However, this situation is changing as more corporations establish employee stock ownership plans (ESOPs), which give shares of the company's stock to its employees. Such plans build a partnership between employee and employer and can boost productivity because they motivate employees to work harder so that they can earn dividends from their hard work as well as from their regular wages.

OTHER TYPES OF OWNERSHIP

In this section we take a brief look at joint ventures, S corporations, limited liability companies, and cooperatives—businesses formed for special purposes.

Joint Ventures

A **joint venture** is a partnership established for a specific project or for a limited time. The partners in a joint venture may be individuals or organizations, as in the case of the international joint ventures discussed in Chapter 3. Control of a joint venture may be shared equally, or one partner may control decision making. Joint ventures are especially popular in situations that call for large investments, such as extraction of natural resources and the development of new products. Dow Jones, owner of *The Wall Street Journal,* formed a joint venture with financial company SBI Holdings in Tokyo to begin an online Japanese version of the *WSJ* site. Dow Jones has a 60 percent stake in the venture. Each company hopes to benefit from the venture, with Dow Jones hoping to increase Web ad sales and SBI Holdings wanting to expand its number of holdings.[26]

S Corporations

An **S corporation** is a form of business ownership that is taxed as though it were a partnership. Net profits or losses of the corporation pass to the owners, thus eliminating double taxation. The benefit of limited liability is retained. Formally known as Subchapter S Corporations, they have become a

popular form of business ownership for entrepreneurs and represent almost half of all corporate filings.[27] Vista Bank Texas is an S Corporation, and the owners get the benefits of tax advantages and limited liability. Advantages of S corporations include the simple method of taxation, the limited liability of shareholders, perpetual life, and the ability to shift income and appreciation to others. Disadvantages include restrictions on the number (75) and types (individuals, estates, and certain trusts) of shareholders and the difficulty of formation and operation.

Limited Liability Companies

A **limited liability company (LLC)** is a form of business ownership that provides limited liability, as in a corporation, but is taxed like a partnership. Although relatively new in the United States, LLCs have existed for many years abroad. Professionals such as lawyers, doctors, and engineers often use the LLC form of ownership. Many consider the LLC a blend of the best characteristics of corporations, partnerships, and sole proprietorships. One of the major reasons for the LLC form of ownership is to protect the members' personal assets in case of lawsuits. LLCs are flexible, simple to run, and do not require the members to hold meetings, keep minutes, or make resolutions, all of which are necessary in corporations. For example, Segway, which markets the Segway Human Transporter, is a limited liability company.

Cooperatives

Another form of organization in business is the **cooperative** or **co-op**, an organization composed of individuals or small businesses that have banded together to reap the benefits of belonging to a larger organization. Oglethorpe Power Corp., for example, is a power cooperative based in the suburbs of Atlanta;[28] Ocean Spray is a cooperative of cranberry farmers. A co-op is set up not to make money as an entity but so that its members can become more profitable or save money. Co-ops are generally expected to operate without profit or to create only enough profit to maintain the co-op organization.

Many cooperatives exist in small farming communities. The co-op stores and markets grain; orders large quantities of fertilizer, seed, and other supplies at discounted prices; and reduces costs and increases efficiency with good management. A co-op can purchase supplies in large quantities and pass the savings on to its members. It also can help distribute the products of its members more efficiently than each could on an individual basis. A cooperative can advertise its members' products and thus generate demand. Ace Hardware, a cooperative of

merger the combination of two companies (usually corporations) to form a new company

acquisition the purchase of one company by another, usually by buying its stock

independent hardware store owners, allows its members to share in the savings that result from buying supplies in large quantities; it also provides advertising, which individual members might not be able to afford on their own.

TRENDS IN BUSINESS OWNERSHIP: MERGERS AND ACQUISITIONS

Companies large and small achieve growth and improve profitability by expanding their operations, often by developing and selling new products or selling current products to new groups of customers in different geographic areas. Such growth, when

When firms that make and sell similar products to the same customers merge, it is known as a *horizontal merger,* as when Martin Marietta and Lockheed, both defense contractors, merged to form Lockheed Martin. Horizontal mergers, however, reduce the number of corporations competing within an industry, and for this reason they are usually reviewed carefully by federal regulators before the merger is allowed to proceed.

When companies operating at different but related levels of an industry merge, it is known as a *vertical merger.* In many instances, a vertical merger results when one corporation merges with one of its customers or suppliers. For example, if Burger King were to purchase a large Idaho potato farm—to ensure a ready supply of potatoes for its french fries—a vertical merger would result.

A *conglomerate merger* results when two firms in unrelated industries merge. For example, the purchase of Sterling Drug, a pharmaceutical firm, by Eastman Kodak, best-known for its

> ## "Companies large and small achieve growth and improve profitability by expanding their operations, often by developing and selling new products or selling current products to new groups of customers in different geographic areas."

carefully planned and controlled, is usually beneficial to the firm and ultimately helps it reach its goal of enhanced profitability. But companies also grow by merging with or purchasing other companies.

A **merger** occurs when two companies (usually corporations) combine to form a new company. An **acquisition** occurs when one company purchases another, generally by buying most of its stock. The acquired company may become a subsidiary of the buyer, or its operations and assets may be merged with those of the buyer. The government sometimes scrutinizes mergers and acquisitions in an attempt to protect customers from monopolistic practices. For example, the decision to authorize Whole Foods' acquisition of Wild Oats was carefully analyzed, as was the merger of Sirius and XM Satellite Radio. In 2010, Novartis took over Alcon, an eye care company owned by Nestlé, for $52 billion. This was the largest merger in Swiss history. By acquiring Alcon, Novartis hopes to tap into the high-growth eye care market, which is expected to have a global growth of 7 percent annually.[29] Acquisitions sometimes involve the purchase of a division or some other part of a company rather than the entire company. The late 1990s saw a merger and acquisition frenzy, which is slowing in the 21st century (see Table 4.5).

films and cameras, represents a conglomerate merger because the two companies are of different industries (Kodak later sold Sterling Drug to a pharmaceutical company).

When a company (or an individual), sometimes called a *corporate raider,* wants to acquire or take over another company, it first offers to buy some or all of the other company's stock at a premium over its current price in a *tender offer.* Most such offers are "friendly," with both groups agreeing to the proposed deal, but some are "hostile," when the second company does not want to be taken over. CKE Restaurants, which operates Carl's Jr. and Hardees fast-food restaurants, adopted a "poison pill" plan to discourage any attempted hostile takeovers. CKE's poison pill is designed to make a hostile takeover more difficult and/or more expensive. The poison pill plan involved giving stockholders the opportunity to receive preferred stock rights in the event of an attempt to buy a minimum of 15 percent of the company's shares.[30]

To head off a hostile takeover attempt, a threatened company's managers may use one or more of several techniques. They may ask stockholders not to sell to the raider; file a lawsuit in an effort to abort the takeover; institute a *poison pill* (in which the firm allows stockholders to buy more shares of stock

After rejecting a leveraged-buyout offer, Sara Lee Corporation decided to split into two separate companies. The corporation spun off its international beverage business from its North American business.

▼ **TABLE 4.5** Major Mergers and Acquisitions Worldwide 2000–2010

Rank	Year	Acquirer*	Target	Transaction Value (in millions of U.S. dollars)
1	2000	America Online Inc. (AOL) (*Merger*)	Time Warner	$164,747
2	2000	Glaxo Wellcome Plc.	SmithKline Beecham Plc.	75,961
3	2004	Royal Dutch Petroleum Co.	Shell Transport & Trading Co.	74,559
4	2006	AT&T Inc.	BellSouth Corporation	72,671
5	2001	Comcast Corporation	AT&T Broadband & Internet Svcs.	72,041
6	2002	Pfizer Inc.	Pharmacia Corporation	59.515
7	2004	JP Morgan Chase & Co.	Bank One Corporation	58,761
8	2010	Kraft	Cadbury	19,500
9	2008	Bank of America	Countrywide	4,000
10	2008	Delta *(Merger)*	Northwest Airlines	2,750
11	2008	JPMorgan Chase & Co.	Bear Stearns Companies Inc.	1,100

*Unless noted, deal was an acquisition.

Sources: Andrew Harris, "Delta Flight Attendants Sue Airline Alleging Discrimination," *Bloomberg Businessweek,* March 2, 2011, www.bloomberg.com/news/2011-03-02/delta-flight-attendants-sue-airline-alleging-discrimination.html (accessed March 18, 2011); Institute of Mergers, Acquisitions and Alliances Research, *Thomson Financial,* www.imaa-institute.org/en/publications+mergers+acquisitions+m&a.php#Reports (accessed March 16, 2010); David Mildenberg, and Guy Beaudin, "Kraft Acquires Cadbury," *Bloomberg Businessweek,* January 3, 2010, www.businessweek.com/managing/content/feb2010/ca2010028_928488.htm (accessed March 1, 2010); "JPMorgan Chase Completes Bear Stearns Acquisition," JPMorganChase News Release, May 31, 2008, www.bearstearns.com/includes/pdfs/PressRelease_BSC_31May08.pdf (accessed March 1, 2010).

leveraged buyout (LBO) a purchase in which a group of investors borrows money from banks and other institutions to acquire a company (or a division of one), using the assets of the purchased company to guarantee repayment of the loan

at prices lower than the current market value) or *shark repellant* (in which management requires a large majority of stockholders to approve the takeover); or seek a *white knight* (a more acceptable firm that is willing to acquire the threatened company). In some cases, management may take the company private or even take on more debt so that the heavy debt obligation will "scare off" the raider.

In a **leveraged buyout (LBO)**, a group of investors borrows money from banks and other institutions to acquire a company (or a division of one), using the assets of the purchased company to guarantee repayment of the loan. In some LBOs, as much

TEAM EXERCISE

Form groups and find examples of mergers and acquisitions. Mergers can be broken down into traditional mergers, horizontal mergers, and conglomerate mergers. When companies are found, note how long the merger or acquisition took, if there were any requirements by the government before approval of the merger or acquisition, and if any failed mergers or acquisitions were found that did not achieve government approval. Report your findings to the class, and explain what the companies hoped to gain from the merger or acquisition.

as 95 percent of the buyout price is paid with borrowed money, which eventually must be repaid.

Because of the explosion of mergers, acquisitions, and leveraged buyouts in the 1980s and 1990s, financial journalists coined the term *merger mania*. Many companies joined the merger mania simply to enhance their own operations by consolidating them with the operations of other firms. Mergers and acquisitions enabled these companies to gain a larger market share in their industries, acquire valuable assets, such as new products or plants and equipment, and lower their costs. Mergers also represent a means of making profits quickly, as was the case during the 1980s when many companies' stock was undervalued. Quite simply, such companies represent a bargain to other companies that can afford to buy them. Additionally, deregulation of some industries has permitted consolidation of

SO YOU'D LIKE TO // Start a Business /

If you have a good idea and want to turn it into a business, you are not alone. Small businesses are popping up all over the United States, and the concept of entrepreneurship is hot. Entrepreneurs seek opportunities and creative ways to make profits. Business emerges in a number of different organizational forms, each with its own advantages and disadvantages. Sole proprietorships are the most common form of business organization in the United States. They tend to be small businesses and can take pretty much any form—anything from a hair salon to a scuba shop, from an organic produce provider to a financial advisor. Proprietorships are everywhere serving consumers' wants and needs. Proprietorships have a big advantage in that they tend to be simple to manage—decisions get made quickly when the owner and the manager are the same person and they are fairly simple and inexpensive to set up. Rules vary by state, but at most all you will need is a license from the state.

Many people have been part of a partnership at some point in their life. Group work in school is an example of a partnership. If you ever worked as a DJ on the weekend with

your friend and split the profits, then you have experienced a partnership. Partnerships can be either general or limited. General partners have unlimited liability and share completely in the management, debts, and profits of the business. Limited partners, on the other hand, consist of at least one general partner and one or more limited partners who do not participate in the management of the company but share in the profits. This form of partnership is used more often in risky investments where the limited partner stands only to lose his or her initial investment. Real estate limited partnerships are an example of how investors can minimize their financial exposure, given the poor performance of the real estate market in recent years. Although it has its advantages, partnership is the least utilized form of business. Part of the reason is that all partners are responsible for the actions and decisions of all other partners, whether or not all of the partners were involved. Usually, partners will have to write up an Articles of Partnership that outlines respective responsibilities in the business. Even in states where it is not required, it is a good idea to draw up this document as a way to cement each partner's

role and hopefully minimize conflict. Unlike a corporation, proprietorships and partnerships both expire upon the death of one or more of those involved.

Corporations tend to be larger businesses, but do not need to be. A corporation can consist of nothing more than a small group of family members. In order to become a corporation you will have to file in the state under which you wish to incorporate. Each state has its own procedure for incorporation, meaning there are no general guidelines to follow. You can make your corporation private or public, meaning the company issues stocks and shareholders are the owners. While incorporating is a popular form of organization because it gives the company an unlimited lifespan and limited liability (meaning that if your business fails you cannot lose personal funds to make up for losses), there is a downside. You will be taxed as a corporation and as an individual resulting in double taxation. No matter what form of organization suits your business idea best, there is a world of options out there for you if you want to be or experiment with being an entrepreneur.

firms within those industries for the first time, as is the case in the banking and airline industries.

Some people view mergers and acquisitions favorably, pointing out that they boost corporations' stock prices and market value, to the benefit of their stockholders. In many instances, mergers enhance a company's ability to meet foreign competition in an increasingly global marketplace. Additionally, companies that are victims of hostile takeovers generally streamline their operations, reduce unnecessary staff, cut costs, and otherwise become more efficient with their operations, which benefits their stockholders whether or not the takeover succeeds.

Critics, however, argue that mergers hurt companies because they force managers to focus their efforts on avoiding takeovers rather than managing effectively and profitably. Some companies have taken on a heavy debt burden to stave off a takeover, later to be forced into bankruptcy when economic downturns left them unable to handle the debt. Mergers and acquisitions also can damage employee morale and productivity, as well as the quality of the companies' products.

Many mergers have been beneficial for all involved; others have had damaging effects for the companies, their employees, and customers. No one can say if mergers will continue to slow, but many experts say the utilities, telecommunications, financial services, natural resources, computer hardware and software, gaming, managed health care, and technology industries are likely targets.

GET ONLINE

mhhe.com/FerrellM3e

for study materials including
quizzes, iPod downloads,
and video

chapter four

active review card
Options for Organizing Business

in a nutshell

Sole proprietorship, partnership, and corporation are three primary forms of business that are used in traditional business, online-only business, or a combination of both. Other forms of business include S corporations, limited liability companies, and cooperatives. In organizing a business, it is helpful to understand the advantages and disadvantages of these forms of business, as well as business trends.

The following statements will test your take-away knowledge from this chapter. Do your best to explain each one in the space provided below.

LO.1 Define and examine the advantages and disadvantages of the sole proprietorship form of organization.

LO.2 Identify two types of partnership, and evaluate the advantages and disadvantages of the partnership form of organization.

LO.3 Describe the corporate form of organization, and cite the advantages and disadvantages of corporations.

LO.4 Define and debate the advantages and disadvantages of mergers, acquisitions, and leveraged buyouts.

Did your answers include the following important points?

LO.1. Define and examine the advantages and disadvantages of the sole proprietorship form of organization.

- The most common form of business is the sole proprietorship. The advantages of this form of business include the fact that it is easy and inexpensive to form, its allows for a high level of secrecy, all profits belong to the owner, the owner has complete control over the business, government regulation is minimal, taxes are paid only once, and the business can be closed easily.

- Disadvantages include the fact that the owner may have to use personal assets to borrow money, sources of external funds are difficult to find, the owner must have many diverse skills, the survival of the business is tied to the life of the owner and his or her ability to work, qualified employees are hard to find, and wealthy sole proprietors pay a higher tax rate than they would under the corporate form of business.

LO.2. Identify two types of partnership, and evaluate the advantages and disadvantages of the partnership form of organization.

- Partnerships may be general or limited and offer the following advantages: they are easy to organize, they may have higher credit ratings because partners may have more combined wealth, partners can specialize, partnerships can make decisions faster than larger businesses, and government regulations are few.

- Disadvantages include the fact that general partners have unlimited liability for the debts of the partnership, partners are responsible for each other's decisions, the death or termination of one partner requires a new partnership agreement, it is difficult to sell a partnership interest at a fair price, the distribution of profits may not correctly reflect the amount of work done by each partner, and partnerships cannot find external sources of funds as easily as large corporations.

LO.3. Describe the corporate form of organization, and cite the advantages and disadvantages of corporations.

- A corporation, which is owned by stockholders, is a legal entity created by the state, whose assets and liabilities are separate from those of its owners. They are chartered by a state through articles of incorporation and have a board of directors made up of corporate officers or people from outside the company.

- Advantages include the fact that owners have limited liability, ownership (stock) can be easily transferred, corporations are long-lasting, raising money is easier, and expansion into new businesses is simpler.

- Disadvantages include the fact that the company is taxed on its income and owners pay a second tax on any profits received as dividends, forming a corporation can be expensive, keeping trade secrets is difficult because so much information must be made available to the public and to government agencies, and owners and managers are not always the same and can have different goals.

LO.4. Define and debate the advantages and disadvantages of mergers, acquisitions, and leveraged buyouts.

- A merger occurs when two companies (usually corporations) combine to form a new company. An acquisition occurs when one company buys most of another company's stock, whereas in a leveraged buyout, a group of investors borrows money to acquire a company, using the assets of the purchased company to guarantee the loan.

- Advantages include the fact that they can help merging firms gain a larger market share in their industries, acquire valuable assets, and lower costs. They can also benefit stockholders by improving companies' market value and stock prices.

- Disadvantages include the fact that they can hurt companies if they force managers to focus on avoiding takeovers at the expense of productivity and profits, they may lead a company to take on too much debt, and they can harm employee morale and productivity.

Practical Application

LO.1.
- One of the most popular and easiest to establish forms of business in the United States is the _____.
- An individual who is the sole owner of a business faces _____ liability in case of debt.

LO.2.
- _____ are the least used form of business organization in the United States.
- The decision-making process in a partnership tends to be faster when the partnership is _____.
- In a partnership owners must share _____, even though a bad decision may have been taken by one of them.

LO.3.
- Another often-used name for stockholder is _____.

- A(n) _____ is one whose stocks anyone may buy, sell, or trade.
- The organizational form that many consider to be a blend of the best characteristics of corporations, partnerships, and sole proprietorships is the _____.

LO.4.
- When two companies combine to form a new company, it is called a(n) _____.
- When companies operating at different, but related, levels of an industry merge, it is known as a(n) _____.
- XYZ, Inc. is attempting to avoid a hostile takeover by a corporate raider by allowing stockholders to buy more shares of stock at prices lower than current market value; the _____ method is being used here to avoid the takeover.

chapter five

small business, entrepreneurship, + franchising

continued on p.104

Although many business students go to work for large corporations upon graduation, others may choose to start their own business or to find employment opportunities in small organizations with 500 or fewer employees. Small businesses employ more than half of all private-sector employees.[1] Each small business represents the vision of its owners to succeed through providing new or better products. Small businesses are the heart of the U.S. economic and social system because they offer opportunities and demonstrate the freedom of people to make their own destinies. Today, the entrepreneurial spirit is growing around the world, from Russia and China to India, Germany, Brazil, and Mexico. For instance, even though China remains a Communist country, private companies employ over 90 percent of the country's workers.[2]

LEARNING OBJECTIVES

LO1 Define entrepreneurship and small business.

LO2 Investigate the importance of small business in the U.S. economy and why certain fields attract small business.

LO3 Specify the advantages of small-business ownership.

LO4 Summarize the disadvantages of small-business ownership, and analyze why many small businesses fail.

LO5 Describe how you go about starting a small business and what resources are needed.

LO6 Evaluate the demographic, technological, and economic trends that are affecting the future of small business.

LO7 Explain why many large businesses are trying to "think small."

enterpreneurship
the process of creating and managing a business to achieve desired objectives

small business
any independently owned and operated business that is not dominant in its competitive area and does not employ more than 500 people

Small Business Administration (SBA) an independent agency of the federal government that offers managerial and financial assistance to small businesses

This chapter surveys the world of entrepreneurship and small business. First, we define entrepreneurship and small business and examine the role of small business in the American economy. Then we explore the advantages and disadvantages of small-business ownership and analyze why small businesses succeed or fail. Next, we discuss how an entrepreneur goes about starting a business and the challenges facing small businesses today. Finally, we look at entrepreneurship in larger organizations.

THE NATURE OF ENTREPRENEURSHIP AND SMALL BUSINESS

In Chapter 1, we defined an entrepreneur as a person who risks his or her wealth, time, and effort to develop for profit an innovative product or way of doing something. **Entrepreneurship** is the process of creating and managing a business to achieve desired objectives. Many large businesses you may recognize (Levi Strauss and Co., Procter & Gamble, McDonald's, Dell Computers, Microsoft, and Google) all began as small businesses based on the visions of their founders. Some entrepreneurs who start small businesses have the ability to see emerging trends; in response, they create a company to provide a product that serves customer needs. For example, rather than inventing a major new technology, an innovative company may take advantage of technology to create new markets, such as Amazon.com. Or it may offer a familiar product that has been improved or placed in a unique retail environment, such as Starbucks and its coffee shops. A company may innovate by focusing on a particular market segment and delivering a combination of features that consumers in that segment could not find anywhere else. For example, Patagonia, a company that uses many organic materials in its clothing, has pledged 1 percent of sales to the preservation and restoration of the natural environment. For example, customers can return their worn-out Capilene® Performance Baselayers for recycling.[3]

Of course, smaller businesses do not have to evolve into such highly visible companies to be successful, but those entrepreneurial efforts that result in rapidly growing businesses gain visibility along with success. Entrepreneurs who have achieved success, like Michael Dell (Dell Computers), Bill Gates (Microsoft), Larry Page and Sergey Brin (Google), and the late Steve Jobs (Apple) are some of the most well known.

The entrepreneurship movement is accelerating, and many new, smaller businesses are emerging. Technology once available only to the largest firms can now be obtained by a small business. Websites, podcasts, online videos, social media, cellular phones, and even expedited delivery services enable small businesses to be more competitive with today's giant corporations. Small businesses can also form alliances with other companies to produce and sell products in domestic and global markets.

What Is a Small Business?

This question is difficult to answer because smallness is relative. In this book, we will define a **small business** as any independently owned and operated business that is not dominant in its competitive area and does not employ more than 500 people. A local Mexican restaurant may be the most patronized Mexican restaurant in your community, but because it does not dominate the restaurant industry as a whole, the restaurant can be considered a small business. This definition is similar to the one used by the **Small Business Administration (SBA)**, an independent agency of the federal government that offers managerial and financial assistance to small businesses. On its website, the SBA outlines the first steps in starting a small business and offers a wealth of information to current and potential small-business owners.

The Role of Small Business in the American Economy

No matter how you define a small business, one fact is clear: They are vital to the American economy. As you can see in Table 5.1, more than 99 percent of all U.S. firms are classified as small businesses, and they employ 50 percent of private workers. Small firms are also important as exporters, representing 97.5 percent of U.S. exporters of goods and contributing 31 percent of the value of exported goods.[4] In addition, small businesses are largely responsible for fueling job creation and innovation. Small businesses also provide opportunities for minorities and women to succeed in business. Women-owned businesses are responsible for more than 23 million American jobs and contribute almost $3 trillion to the national economy. Women own more than 8 million businesses nationwide, with great success in the professional services, retail, communication, and administrative industries.[5] Minority-owned businesses have been growing faster than other classifiable firms as well, representing 21.3 percent of all small businesses. The number of minority-owned businesses is increasing at a rate of 30 percent, even higher than for women-owned firms. Hispanics own the most small businesses (8.3 percent), followed by African Americans (7.1 percent), Asian Americans (5.7 percent), American Indians and Native Alaskans (0.9 percent), and Native Hawaiians and other

Pacific Islanders (0.1 percent).[7] For example, Sacred Power is a Native American–owned power and telecommunications company that generates solar, thermal, and wind energy. As a small business, Sacred Power produces and sells alternative energy to larger power companies for distribution to consumers around the Southwest.

The energy, creativity, and innovative abilities of small-business owners have resulted in jobs for many people. In fact, in the last 15 years, 65 percent of net new jobs annually were created by small businesses.[8] Table 5.2 indicates that 99.7 percent of all businesses employ fewer than 500 people, and businesses employing 19 or fewer people account for 89.4 percent of all businesses.[9]

Many small businesses today are being started because of encouragement from larger ones. Many new jobs are also created by big-company/small-company alliances. Whether through formal joint ventures, supplier relationships, or product or marketing cooperative projects, the rewards of collaborative relationships are creating many jobs for small-business owners and their employees. In India, many small information technology (IT) firms provide IT services to global markets. Because of lower costs, international companies often can find Indian businesses to provide their information processing solutions.[10]

Innovation Perhaps one of the most significant strengths of small businesses is their ability to innovate and to bring significant benefits to customers. Small firms produce over half of all innovations. Among the important 20th-century innovations by U.S. small firms are the airplane, the audio tape recorder, fiber-optic examining equipment, the heart valve, the optical scanner, the pacemaker, the personal computer, soft contact lenses, the Internet, and the zipper. Not all innovations are based on new technology. Consider Oprah Winfrey's success. She developed her own brand image and media production company. She went from having nothing to amassing a fortune

▼ **TABLE 5.1** Importance of Small Businesses to Our Economy

Small firms represent 99.7 percent of all employer firms.

Small firms have generated 65 percent of net new jobs over the past 17 years.

Small firms hire approximately 43 percent of high-tech workers (such as scientists, engineers, computer programmers, and others).

Small firms produce 13 times more patents per employee than large patenting firms.

Small firms employ half of all private sector employees

Small firms pay 44 percent of the total U.S. private payroll.

Source: "FAQs," U.S. Small Business Administration, http://web.sba.gov/faqs/faqindex.cfm?areaID=24 (accessed March 18, 2011).

▼ **TABLE 5.2** Number of Firms by Employment Size

Firm Size	Number of Firms	Percentage of All Firms
0–19 employees	5,410,367	89.4
20–99 employees	532,391	8.8
100–499 employees	88,586	1.5
500 + employees	18,311	0.3

Source: "Statistics of U.S. Businesses (SUSB)" U.S. Census Bureau, Updated December 21, 2010, www.census.gov/econ/susb/ (accessed January 11, 2011).

of $2.3 billion as one of the most recognizable figures in global media. After 26 years on her CBS talk show, she created the Oprah Winfrey Network. Oprah refused to take her company public in order to maintain maximum control, and she protected her brand and media products by refusing to let retailers or other businesses use her name.[11]

The innovation of successful firms take many forms. For instance, small firms make up approximately 52 percent of home-based businesses and 2 percent of franchises. Many of today's largest businesses started off as small firms that used innovation to achieve success.[12] Small businessman Ray Kroc found a new way to sell hamburgers and turned his ideas into one of the most successful fast-food franchises in the world— McDonald's. Small businesses have become an integral part of our lives. James Dyson's name is synonymous with high-quality vacuum cleaners. Today, his $1 billion company produces a bagless vacuum cleaner that commands 25 percent of the U.S.

THE SERVICE SECTOR INCLUDES BUSINESSES THAT DO NOT ACTUALLY PRODUCE TANGIBLE GOODS

market. However, it took a lot of work to achieve such success. Dyson developed 5,127 prototypes before he got the design and function right. He recently created a successful hand dryer and is working to develop other innovative appliances. Entrepreneurs provide fresh ideas and usually have greater flexibility to change than do large companies.

Industries That Attract Small Business

Small businesses are found in nearly every industry, but retailing and wholesaling, services, manufacturing, and high technology are especially attractive to entrepreneurs. These fields are relatively easy to enter and require low initial financing. Small-business owners in these industries also find it easier to focus on specific groups of consumers; new firms in these industries initially suffer less from heavy competition than do established firms.

Retailing and Wholesaling
Retailers acquire goods from producers or wholesalers and sell them to consumers. Main streets and shopping centers and malls are generally lined with independent music stores, sporting-goods stores, dry cleaners,

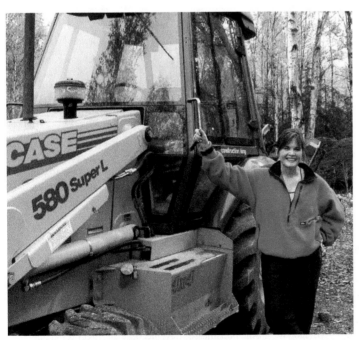

Most of America's new jobs aren't created by big corporations. They are created by small businesses such as Rush Trucking. Rush Trucking was founded in Detroit in the 1980s by Andra Rush after she interned with a transportation company and decided she could do the job better.

boutiques, drugstores, restaurants, caterers, service stations, and hardware stores that sell directly to consumers. Retailing attracts entrepreneurs because gaining experience and exposure in retailing is relatively easy. Additionally, an entrepreneur opening a new retail store does not have to spend the large sums of money for the equipment and distribution systems that a manufacturing business requires. All that a new retailer needs is a lease on store space, merchandise, money to sustain the business, knowledge about prospective customers' needs and desires, and basic management and marketing skills. Some small retailers are also taking their businesses online. For example, Susan Brown invented a donut-shaped pillow with an opening in one side called the "Boppy." The product is sold online and in Babies 'R' Us and Pottery Barn Kids stores. Although approached by Walmart, Brown declined the offer in a desire to keep a more upscale feel. The Boppy has annual sales of around $50 million and was provided startup capital through a microloan of $25,000 from the Colorado Enterprise Fund (a nonprofit, community-development institution).[13] The Boppy was voted the number-one baby product by *American Baby* magazine a record seven times since the award was created in 1998. It remains the industry leader among baby feeding and support pillows.[14]

Wholesalers supply products to industrial, retail, and institutional users for resale or for use in making other products. Wholesaling activities range from planning and negotiating for supplies, promoting, and distributing (warehousing and transporting) to providing management and merchandising assistance to clients. Wholesalers are extremely important for many products, especially consumer goods, because of the marketing activities they perform. Although it is true that wholesalers themselves can be eliminated, their functions must be passed on to some other organization such as the producer, or another intermediary, often a small business. Frequently, small businesses are closer to the final customers and know what it takes to keep them satisfied. Some smaller businesses start out in manufacturing, but find their real niche as a supplier or distributor of larger firms' products.

Services
The service sector includes businesses that do not actually produce tangible goods. The service sector accounts for 80 percent of U.S. jobs, excluding farmworkers.[15] Real estate, insurance and personnel agencies, barbershops, banks, television and computer repair shops, copy centers, dry cleaners, and accounting firms are all service businesses. Similarly, Bikram Choudhury's name is associated with yoga. Bikram Yoga uses a sequence of 26 signature poses, and the business has expanded to training courses, books, CDs, clothing, and numerous franchises. Choudhury is credited with popularizing yoga in the United States and with turning "his particular brand of yoga into the McDonald's of a $3 billion industry."[16] Services also attract individuals—such as beauticians, morticians, jewelers, doctors,

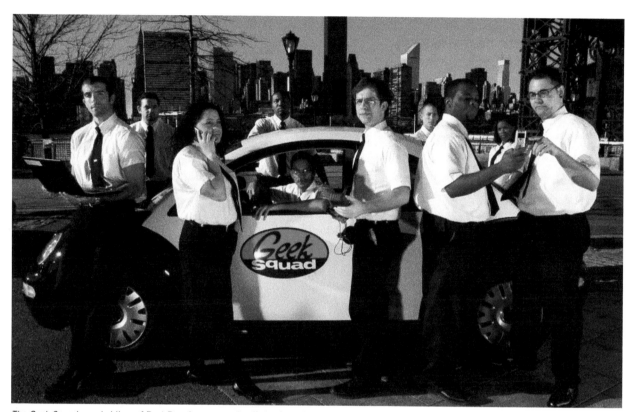

The Geek Squad, a subsidiary of Best Buy, is an example of a business in the service sector. The Geek Squad specializes in technological repair and support services. Its services are available 24/7.

and veterinarians—whose skills are not usually required by large firms. Many of these service providers are retailers who provide their services to ultimate consumers.

Manufacturing Manufacturing goods can provide unique opportunities for small businesses. Started in 1988, the Malcolm Baldrige Award recognizes achievements in quality and performance in businesses of all sizes. It is designed to spur competitive business practices in American industry. In 2010 consulting firm Freese and Nichols Inc. (Fort Worth, Texas), restaurant development firm K&N Management (Austin, Texas), and health care consulting firm Studer Group (Gulf Breeze, Florida) won the award in the small-business category. This is the first case where three small businesses were awarded the Malcolm Baldrige Award at the same time.[17] Small businesses sometimes have an advantage over large firms because they can customize products to meet specific customer needs and wants. Such products include custom artwork, jewelry, clothing, and furniture.

High Technology *High technology* is a broad term used to describe businesses that depend heavily on advanced scientific

DID YOU KNOW?

Small businesses hire 43 percent of high-tech workers in the United States?[18]

and engineering knowledge. People who were able to innovate or identify new markets in the fields of computers, biotechnology, genetic engineering, robotics, and other markets have become today's high-tech giants. Mark Zuckerberg, the CEO of Facebook (a social networking website), for instance, has created a company that is one of the fastest growing dot-coms in history. Facebook has more than 500 million active users, and half of all active users log on to the site on any given day.[19] In general, high-technology businesses require greater capital and have higher initial startup costs than do other small businesses. Many of the biggest, nonetheless, started out in garages, basements, kitchens, and dorm rooms.

ADVANTAGES OF SMALL-BUSINESS OWNERSHIP

There are many advantages to establishing and running a small business. These can be categorized into personal advantages and business advantages. Table 5.3 lists some of the traits that can help entrepreneurs succeed.

▼ **TABLE 5.3** 10 Successful Traits of Young Entrepreneurs

Intuitive	Persistent
Creative	Innovative
Productive	Frugal
Patient	Friendly
Charismatic	Fearless

Source: Yan Susanto, "10 Successful Traits of Young Entrepreneurs," *Retire @ 21,* April 10, 2009, www.retireat21.com/blog/10-successful-traits-of-young-entrepreneurs (accessed March 17, 2011).

Independence

Independence is probably one of the leading reasons that entrepreneurs choose to go into business for themselves. Being a small-business owner means being your own boss. Many people start their own businesses because they believe they will do better for themselves than they could do by remaining with their current employer or by changing jobs. They may feel stuck on the corporate ladder and that no business would take them seriously enough to fund their ideas. Sometimes people who venture forth to start their own small business are those who simply cannot work for someone else. Such people may say that they just do not fit the "corporate mold."

More often, small-business owners just want the freedom to choose whom they work with, the flexibility to pick where and when to work, and the option of working in a family setting. The availability of the computer, copy machine, fax, and Internet has permitted many people to work at home. In the past, most of them would have needed the support that an office provides.

Costs

As already mentioned, small businesses often require less money to start and maintain than do large ones. Obviously, a firm with just 25 people in a small factory spends less money on wages and salaries, rent, utilities, and other expenses than does a firm employing tens of thousands of people in several large facilities. Rather than maintain the expense of keeping separate departments for accounting, advertising, and legal counseling, small businesses often hire other firms (sometimes small businesses themselves) to supply these services as they are needed. Additionally, small-business owners can sometimes rely on friends and family members to help them save money by volunteering to work on a difficult project.

Flexibility

With small size comes the flexibility to adapt to changing market demands. Small businesses usually have only one layer of management—the owners. Decisions therefore can be made and executed quickly. In larger firms, decisions about even routine matters can take weeks because they must pass through multiple levels of management before action is authorized. When Taco Bell introduces a new product, for example, it must

first research what consumers want, then develop the product and test it before introducing it nationwide—a process that sometimes takes years. An independent snack shop, however, can develop and introduce a new product (perhaps to meet a customer's request) in a much shorter time.

Focus

Small firms can focus their efforts on a precisely defined market niche—that is, a specific group of customers. Many large corporations must compete in the mass market or for large market segments. Smaller firms can develop products for particular groups of customers or to satisfy a need that other companies have not addressed. For example, Fatheadz, based in Indianapolis, Indiana, focuses on producing sunglasses for people with big heads. To be an official "fathead" you need a ball cap size of at least 7⅝ and a head circumference above the ear of at least 23.5 inches. The idea arose when Rico Elmore was walking down the Las Vegas strip with his brother and realized that he had lost his sunglasses. He went to a nearby sunglass shop, and out of 300 pairs of glasses, he could not find one that fit. He decided to start a company addressing this need, and Fatheadz now distributes its designs in Walmart optical stores throughout the country.[20] By targeting small niches or product needs, small businesses can sometimes avoid competition from larger firms, helping them grow into stronger companies.

Reputation

Small firms, because of their capacity to focus on narrow niches, can develop enviable reputations for quality and service. A good example of a small business with a formidable reputation is W. Atlee Burpee and Co., which has the country's premier bulb and seed catalog. Burpee has an unqualified returns policy (complete satisfaction or your money back) that demonstrates a strong commitment to customer satisfaction.

DISADVANTAGES OF SMALL-BUSINESS OWNERSHIP

The rewards associated with running a small business are so enticing that it's no wonder many people dream of it. However, as with any undertaking, small-business ownership has its disadvantages.

High Stress Level

A small business is likely to provide a living for its owner, but not much more (although there are exceptions as some examples in this chapter have shown). There are ongoing worries about competition, employee problems, new equipment, expanding inventory, rent increases, or changing market demand. In addition to other stresses, small-business owners tend to be victims of physical and psychological stress. The small-business person is often the owner, manager, sales force,

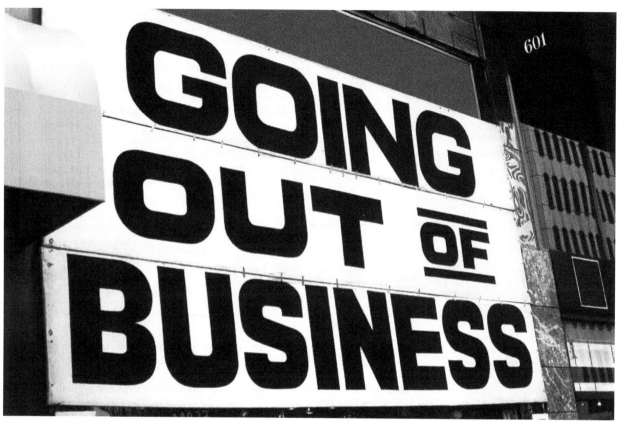

Entrepreneurs experience a great deal of independence but also a great deal of stress. Many fail.

shipping and receiving clerk, bookkeeper, and custodian. Having to multitask can result in long hours for most small-business owners. Many creative persons fail, not because of their business concepts, but rather because of difficulties in managing their business.

High Failure Rate

Despite the importance of small businesses to our economy, there is no guarantee of success. Half of all new employer firms fail within the first five years.[21] Restaurants are a case in point. Look around your own neighborhood, and you can probably spot the locations of several restaurants that are no longer in business.

Small businesses fail for many reasons (see Table 5.4). A poor business concept—such as insecticides for garbage cans (research found that consumers are not concerned with insects in their garbage)—will produce disaster nearly every time. Expanding a hobby into a business may work if a genuine market niche exists, but all too

often people start such a business without identifying a real need for the goods or services. Other notable causes of small-business failure include the burdens imposed by government regulation, insufficient funds to withstand slow sales, and vulnerability to competition from larger companies. However, three major causes of small-business failure deserve a close

▼ **TABLE 5.4** 10 Common Mistakes That Startup and Small Companies Make

1. Overestimating the enthusiasm for their product or service.
2. Not validating demand and interest in the product.
3. Starting to work with customers only when the product is ready for sale.
4. Underestimating the difficulty in penetrating the market.
5. Overestimating the product's uniqueness and underestimating the competition.
6. Underestimating the effort needed to build the product.
7. Hiring "big-company types" who are used to having a support staff.
8. Not focusing on the main product and being tempted by side projects.
9. Under- or overpricing the product.
10. Not having a vision for long-term growth.

Source: David Lavenda, "10 Common Mistakes That Startup and Small Companies Make," FC Expert Blog (*Fast Company*), September 8, 2009, www.fastcompany.com/blog/david-lavenda/whatever-it-takes/10-common-mistakes-startupsmall-companies-make (accessed March 17, 2011).

ANOTHER TYPE OF ENTREPRENEURSHIP

Entrepreneurs do not just operate in business. The entrepreneurial spirit can also be found in the social sector. A social entrepreneur is someone who is driven to create social change by identifying and implementing solutions to social problems. An emphasis is being placed on the social entrepreneur as a necessary component for future economic growth. One of the most famous social entrepreneurs is Muhammad Yunus, founder of microfinance bank Grameen. Another example is Mimi Silbert, founder of the Delancey Street Foundation. Silbert provides residency and life-work skills education to former felons, substance abusers, the homeless, and more.

Although social entrepreneurship has long been privately funded, both the American and British governments are recognizing its importance. The Obama administration has formed the Social Innovation Fund (SIF), with $50 million in public money matched by philanthropic donations, to be distributed among nonprofits. The SIF seeks to unite social entrepreneurs, private capital, the government, and the public to create solutions for positive social change. The administration also founded the Office of Social Innovation and Civic Participation (OSICP). In Britain, the government has launched the Big Society Bank, which is similar to the SIF. Both governments aim to unite the private and public sectors to encourage social innovation, which they see as both doing good and providing jobs to those in need. To motivate innovation, the OSICP is hoping to offer monetary rewards to social innovators.

Despite noble missions, those running SIF and the Big Society Bank are likely to be met with resistance, primarily political. For this reason, social entrepreneurs may need to develop new skills enabling them to break through bureaucracy. It is hopeful that uniting the public and private funding sectors will empower more social entrepreneurs to bring their ideas to life.[22]

Discussion Questions

1. What are the potential benefits of social entrepreneurship in our society?
2. Given that the primary resistance to social entrepreneurship is political, how can our government minimize resistance and create incentives for investment?
3. What social areas do you feel social entrepreneurs should invest in?

---

look: undercapitalization, managerial inexperience or incompetence, and inability to cope with growth.

Undercapitalization The shortest path to failure in business is **undercapitalization**, the lack of funds to operate a business normally. Too many entrepreneurs think that all they need is enough money to get started and that the business can survive on cash generated from sales soon thereafter. But almost all businesses suffer from seasonal variations in sales, which make cash tight, and few businesses make money from the start. Many small rural operations cannot obtain financing within their own communities because small rural banks often lack the necessary financing expertise or assets sizable enough to counter the risks involved with small-business loans. Without sufficient funds, the best small-business idea in the world will fail.

Managerial Inexperience or Incompetence Poor management is the cause of many business failures. Just because an entrepreneur has a brilliant vision for a small business does not mean he or she has the knowledge or experience to manage a growing business effectively. A person who is good at creating great product ideas and marketing them may lack the skills and experience to make good management decisions in hiring, negotiating, finance, and control. Moreover, entrepreneurs may neglect those areas of management they know little about or find tedious, at the expense of the business's success.

Inability to Cope with Growth Sometimes, the very factors that are advantages for a small business turn into serious disadvantages when the time comes to grow. Growth often requires the owner to give up a certain amount of direct authority, and it is frequently hard for someone who has called all the shots to give up control. It has often been said that the greatest impediment to the success of a business is the entrepreneur. Similarly, growth requires specialized management skills in areas such as credit analysis and promotion—skills that the founder may lack or not have time to apply. The founders of many small businesses, including Dell Computers, found that they needed to bring in more experienced managers to help manage their companies through growing pains.

Poorly managed growth probably affects a company's reputation more than anything else, at least initially. And products that do not arrive on time or goods that are poorly made can quickly reverse a success. The principle immediate threats to small and mid-sized businesses include rising inflation, energy and other supply shortages or cost escalations, and excessive household and/or corporate debt.

STARTING A SMALL BUSINESS

We've told you how important small businesses are, and why they succeed and fail, but *how do you go about* starting your own business in the first place? To start any business, large or small, you must have some kind of general idea. Sam Walton, founder of Walmart stores, had a vision of a discount retailing enterprise that spawned the world's largest retailing empire and changed the way companies look at business. Next, you need to devise a strategy to guide planning and development in the business. Finally, you must make decisions about form of ownership, the financial resources needed, and whether to acquire an existing business, start a new one, or buy a franchise.

The Business Plan

A key element of business success is a **business plan**—a precise statement of the rationale for the business and a step-by-step explanation of how it will achieve its goals. The business plan should include an explanation of the business, an analysis of the competition, estimates of income and expenses, and other information. It should also establish a strategy for acquiring sufficient funds to keep the business going. Many financial institutions decide whether to loan a small business money based on its business plan. A good business plan should act as a guide and reference document—not a shackle that limits the business's flexibility and decision-making ability. The business plan must be revised periodically to ensure that the firm's goals and strategies adapt to changes in the environment. Business plans allow companies to assess market potential, determine price and manufacturing requirements, identify optimal distribution channels, and refine product selection. Ben and Matthew Freund, who grew up on their father's dairy farm in Connecticut, developed an innovative way to deal with their abundance of cow manure. They created a digestion and dehydration process to eliminate the odor and to form the product into CowPots, which can be buried in the ground to fertilize plants. Cow-Pots will last for months above ground but begin to degrade when planted.[23] Business plans allow for companies such as Ben and Matthew's to assess market potential, determine price, identify manufacturing possibilities and requirements, identify optimal distribution channels, and brand the products. The Small Business Administration website provides an overview of a plan for small businesses to use to gain financing.

Forms of Business Ownership

After developing a business plan, the entrepreneur has to decide on an appropriate legal form of business ownership—whether it is best to operate as a sole proprietorship, partnership, or corporation—and to examine the many factors that affect that decision, which we explored in Chapter 4.

Financial Resources

The expression "it takes money to make money" holds especially true in developing a business enterprise. To make money from a small business, the owner must first provide or obtain money (capital) to get started and to keep it running smoothly. Even a small retail store will probably need at least $50,000 in initial financing to rent space, purchase or lease necessary equipment and furnishings, buy the initial inventory, and provide working capital. Often, the small-business owner has to put up a significant percentage of the necessary capital. Few new business owners have a large amount of their own capital and must look to other sources for additional financing.

The most important source of funds for any new business is the owner.

Equity Financing The most important source of funds for any new business is the owner. Many owners include among their personal resources ownership of a home, the accumulated value in a life-insurance policy, or a savings account. A new business owner may sell or borrow against the value of such assets to obtain funds to operate a business. Additionally, the owner may bring useful personal assets—such as a computer, desks and other furniture, a car or truck—as part of his or her ownership interest in the firm. Such financing is referred to as *equity financing* because the owner uses real personal assets rather than borrowing funds from outside sources to get started in a new business. The owner can also provide working capital by reinvesting profits into the business or simply by not drawing a full salary.

Small businesses can also obtain equity financing by finding investors for their operations. They may sell stock in the business to family members, friends, employees, or other investors. For instance, Petra Cooper was the 41-year-old president of McGraw-Hill Ryerson Publishing in Toronto when she decided to make a dramatic career change. After researching small-business opportunities, she decided to start a creamery, Fifth Town Artisan Cheese. Before quitting McGraw-Hill, she took two years of vacation time to study cheese making and constructed a model, energy-efficient dairy on 20 acres in Prince Edward Island, Canada. Cooper exceeded her initial $500,000 budget, but found an investor and obtained a bridge loan from a bank. By the end of her first year, Cooper already had $1 million in revenues and nearly broke even on the investment.[24] **Venture capitalists** are persons or organizations that agree to provide some funds for a new business in exchange for an ownership interest or stock. Venture capitalists hope to purchase the stock of a small business at a low price and then sell the stock for a profit after the business has grown successful. The renewable energy industry has recently become a popular investment option among venture capitalists, who have invested over $20 billion in "cleantech," or renewable energy technology, since 2005.[25] Although these forms of equity financing have helped many small businesses, they require that the small-business owner share the profits of the business—and sometimes control, as well—with the investors.

Debt Financing New businesses sometimes borrow more than half of their financial resources. Banks are the main suppliers of external financing to small businesses. On the federal level, the Small Business Administration offers financial assistance to

undercapitalization the lack of funds to operate a business normally

business plan a precise statement of the rationale for a business and a step-by-step explanation of how it will achieve its goals

venture capitalists persons or organizations that agree to provide some funds for a new business in exchange for an ownership interest or stock

franchise a license to sell another's products or to use another's name in business, or both

franchiser the company that sells a franchise

franchisee the purchaser of a franchise

1-800-GOT-JUNK? will haul away what your garbage collector won't. The company has more than 175 franchises, throughout Canada, the United States, and Australia.

qualifying businesses. They can also look to family and friends as sources for long-term loans or other assets, such as computers or an automobile, that are exchanged for an ownership interest in a business. In such cases, the business owner can usually structure a favorable repayment schedule and sometimes negotiate an interest rate below current bank rates. If the business goes bad, however, the emotional losses for all concerned may greatly exceed the money involved. Anyone lending a friend or family member money for a venture should state the agreement clearly in writing before any money changes hands.

The amount a bank or other institution is willing to loan depends on its assessment of the venture's likelihood of success and of the entrepreneur's ability to repay the loan. The bank will often require the entrepreneur to put up *collateral*, a financial interest in the property or fixtures of the business, to guarantee payment of the debt. Additionally, the small-business owner may have to

Banks and other financial institutions can also grant a small business a *line of credit*—an agreement by which a financial institution promises to lend a business a predetermined sum on demand. A line of credit permits an entrepreneur to take quick advantage of opportunities that require external funding. Small businesses may obtain funding from their suppliers in the form of a *trade credit*—that is, suppliers allow the business to take possession of the needed goods and services and pay for them at a later date or in installments. Occasionally, small businesses engage in *bartering*—trading their own products for the goods and services offered by other businesses. For example, an accountant may offer accounting services to an office supply firm in exchange for office supplies and equipment.

Additionally, some community groups sponsor loan funds to encourage the development of particular types of businesses. State and local agencies may guarantee loans, especially to minority business people or for development in certain areas.

Approaches to Starting a Small Business

Starting from Scratch versus Buying an Existing Business

Although entrepreneurs often start new small businesses from scratch much the way we have discussed in this section, they may elect instead to buy an existing business. This has the advantage of providing a built-in network of customers, suppliers, and distributors and reducing some of the guesswork inherent in starting a new business from the ground up. However, an entrepreneur who buys an existing business also takes on any problems the business already has.

Franchising

Many small-business owners find entry into the business world through franchising. A license to sell another's products or to use another's name in business, or both, is a **franchise**. The company that sells a franchise is the **franchiser**. Dunkin' Donuts, Subway, and Jiffy Lube are well-known franchisers with national visibility. The purchaser of a franchise is called a **franchisee**.

The franchisee acquires the rights to a name, logo, methods of operation, national advertising, products, and other elements

Many small-business owners find entry into the business world through franchising.

provide personal property as collateral, such as his or her home, in which case the loan is called a *mortgage*. If the small business fails to repay the loan, the lending institution may eventually claim and sell the collateral or mortgage to recover its loss.

associated with the franchiser's business in return for a financial commitment and the agreement to conduct business in accordance with the franchiser's standard of operations. The initial fee to join a franchise varies greatly. In addition, franchisees buy equipment, pay for training, and obtain a mortgage or lease. The franchisee also pays the franchiser a monthly or annual fee based on a percentage of sales or profits. In return, the franchisee often receives building specifications and designs, site recommendations, management and accounting support, and perhaps most importantly, immediate name recognition. Visit the website of the International Franchise Association to learn more on this topic.

The practice of franchising first began in the United States in the 19th century when Singer used it to sell sewing machines. The method of goods distribution soon became commonplace in the automobile, gasoline, soft drink, and hotel industries. The concept of franchising grew especially rapidly during the 1960s, when it expanded to diverse industries. Table 5.5 shows the 10 fastest growing franchises and the top 10 new franchises.

The entrepreneur will find that franchising has both advantages and disadvantages. Franchising allows a franchisee the opportunity to set up a small business relatively quickly, and because of its association with an established brand, a franchise outlet often reaches the breakeven point faster than an independent business would. Franchisees commonly report the following advantages:

- Management training and support.
- Brand-name appeal.
- Standardized quality of goods and services.
- National and local advertising programs.
- Financial assistance.
- Proven products and business formats.
- Centralized buying power.
- Site selection and territorial protection.
- Greater chance for success.[26]

However, the franchisee must sacrifice some freedom to the franchiser. Some shortcomings experienced by franchisees include:

- Franchise fees and profit sharing with the franchiser.
- Strict adherence to standardized operations.
- Restrictions on purchasing.
- Limited product line.
- Possible market saturation.
- Less freedom in business decisions.[27]

Strict uniformity is the rule rather than the exception. Entrepreneurs who want to be their own bosses are often frustrated with the restrictions of a franchise.

Help for Small-Business Managers

Because of the crucial role that small business and entrepreneurs play in the U.S. economy, a number of organizations offer programs to improve the small-business owner's ability to compete. These include entrepreneurial training programs and programs sponsored by the Small Business Administration. Such programs provide small-business owners with invaluable assistance in managing their businesses, often at little or no cost to the owner.

Entrepreneurs can learn critical marketing, management, and finance skills in seminars and college courses. In addition, knowledge, experience, and judgment are necessary for success in a new business. While knowledge can be communicated and some experiences can be simulated in the classroom, good judgment must be developed by the entrepreneur. Local chambers of commerce and the U.S. Department of Commerce offer information and assistance helpful in operating a small business. National publications such as *Inc.* and *Entrepreneur* share statistics, advice, tips, and success/failure stories. Additionally, most urban areas have weekly business journals/newspapers that provide stories on local businesses as well as on business techniques that a manager or small business can use.

The Small Business Administration offers many types of management assistance to small businesses, including counseling for firms in difficulty, consulting on improving operations, and training for owners/managers and their employees. Among its many programs, the SBA funds Small Business Development Centers (SBDCs). These are business clinics, usually located on college campuses, that provide counseling at no charge and training at only a nominal charge. SBDCs are often the SBA's principal means of providing direct management assistance.

The Service Corps of Retired Executives (SCORE) and the Active Corps of Executives (ACE) are volunteer agencies funded by the SBA to provide advice for owners of small firms. Both are staffed by experienced managers whose talents and experience the small firms could not ordinarily afford. SCORE has 12,400 volunteers at nearly 400 locations in the United States and has served more than 8.5 million small businesses.[28] The SBA also has organized Small Business Institutes (SBIs) on almost 500 university and college campuses in the United States. Seniors,

▼ **TABLE 5.5** Fastest Growing and Hottest New Franchises

Top 10 Fastest Growing Franchises	Top 10 New Franchises
Stratus Building Solutions	HealthSource Chiropractic and Progressive Rehab
Jan-Pro Franchising International Inc.	Oreck Clean Home Center
Subway	Oxi Fresh Franchising Co.
CleanNet USA Inc.	Always Best Care Senior Services
Anago Cleaning Systems	The Senior's Choice Inc.
Pizza Hut Inc.	Accessible Home Health Care
Liberty Tax Service	Caring Transitions
Vanguard Cleaning Systems	Yogurtland Franchising Inc.
Bonus Building Care	Murphy Business & Financial Corp.
System4	Retro Fitness LLC

Sources: "2011 Fastest-Growing Franchises," *Entrepreneur,* www.entrepreneur.com/franchises/fastestgrowing/index.html (accessed January 11, 2011).

graduate students, and faculty at each SBI provide on-site management counseling.

Finally, the small-business owner can obtain advice from other small-business owners, suppliers, and even customers. A customer may approach a small business it frequents with a request for a new product, for example, or a supplier may offer suggestions for improving a manufacturing process. Networking—building relationships and sharing information with colleagues—is vital for any businessperson, whether you work for a huge corporation or run your own small business. Communicating with other business owners is a great way to find ideas for dealing with employees and government regulation, improving processes, or solving problems. New technology is making it easier to network. For example, some states are establishing social networking sites for the use of their businesses to network and share ideas.

THE FUTURE FOR SMALL BUSINESS[29]

Although small businesses are crucial to the economy, their size and limited resources can make them more vulnerable to turbulence and change in the marketplace than large businesses. Next, we take a brief look at the demographic, technological, and economic trends that will have the most impact on small business in the future.

Demographic Trends

America's baby boom started in 1946 and ended in 1964. Many boomers are over 50, and in the next few years, millions more will pass that mark. The baby boomer generation represents 26.1 percent of Americans and includes about 78 million people.[30] This segment of the population is wealthy, but many small businesses do not actively pursue it. Some exceptions, however, include Gold Violin, which sells designer canes and other products online and through a catalog, and LifeSpring, which delivers nutritional meals and snacks directly to the customer. Industries such as travel, financial planning, and health care will continue to grow as boomers age. Many experts believe that the boomer demographic is the market of the future.

Another market with huge potential for small business is the echo boomers, also called millennials or Generation Y. Millennials number around 75 million and possess a number of unique characteristics. Born between 1977 and 1994, this cohort is not solely concerned about money. Those who fall into this group are also concerned with advancement, recognition, and improved capabilities. They need direct, timely feedback and frequent encouragement and recognition. Millennials do well when training sessions combine entertainment with learning. Working remotely is more acceptable to this group than previous generations, and virtual communication may become as important as face-to-face meetings.[31]

Yet another trend is the growing number of immigrants living in the United States, who now represent about one-eighth, or 12 percent, of the population. If this trend continues, by 2050 nearly one in five Americans will be classified as immigrants. The Latino population, the nation's largest minority group, is expected to triple in size by 2050.[32]

This vast group provides still another greatly untapped market for small businesses. Retailers who specialize in ethnic

---

GUITAR SYNDICATE, INC. LEARNS TO SELL ON FACEBOOK

Facebook fan pages have become a popular way for companies to connect with consumers. Yet some small businesses are taking the Facebook phenomenon a step further: they are using the site to sell actual products. One of these early adopters is Guitar Syndicate, Inc., a brick-and-mortar music business based in Kansas City. The company has been gathering Facebook fans through weekly contests and giveaways since 2009. Recently, it joined forces with Core Commerce and discovered Facebook's online store. Guitar Syndicate now uploads inventory right onto its Facebook page. Should a "fan" purchase a Guitar Syndicate product via Facebook, Core Commerce software takes the customer directly to Guitar Syndicate's website to complete payment. Guitar Syndicate sales have grown by almost 20 percent since its Facebook store was added.

Having a Facebook fan page has created many advantages for Guitar Syndicate. Fan pages are inexpensive and easy to produce, making them accessible to both small businesses and large corporations. On the other hand, having an effective Facebook fan page requires commitment. Facebook friends want to feel like an important part of the company. This requires a company like Guitar Syndicate to be dedicated in responding to fan posts. Facebook pages also carry risks. It is easy for dissatisfied customers to post negative comments on Facebook, which can easily become viral and create negative publicity for the company.

Despite these risks, Facebook has helped generate business for Guitar Syndicate on a more consistent basis. With the average user spending over an hour a day on Facebook, the social networking site offers a significant opportunity for newer companies like Guitar Syndicate to get their names out there.[33]

Discussion Questions

1. How has Facebook increased awareness of Guitar Syndicate, Inc. as well as sales?

2. How would you critique the cost of "Facebook marketing"?

3. What do you think are the keys of success for small businesses like Guitar Syndicate to become profitable through social media like Facebook?

COMMUNICATING WITH OTHER BUSINESS OWNERS IS A GREAT WAY TO FIND IDEAS FOR DEALING WITH EMPLOYEES AND GOVERNMENT REGULATION, IMPROVING PROCESSES, OR SOLVING PROBLEMS.

products, and service providers who offer bi- or multilingual employees, will find a large amount of business potential in this market. Table 5.6 ranks top cities in the United States for small businesses and startups.

Technological and Economic Trends

Advances in technology have opened up many new markets to small businesses. Undoubtedly, the Internet will continue to provide new opportunities for small businesses. Arianna Huffington launched the popular *Huffington Post,* a news and blogging website, in 2005. The site has broken a number of important news stories. Partly because of its accessible format and the way it agglomerates news stories from many sites, HuffPo attracts approximately 25 million views a month. In 2011, AOL agreed to acquire the Huffington Post for $315 million.[34]

Technological advances and an increase in service exports have created new opportunities for small companies to expand their operations abroad. Changes in communications and technology can allow small companies to customize their services quickly for international customers. Also, free-trade agreements and trade alliances are helping create an environment in which small businesses have fewer regulatory and legal barriers.

In recent years, economic turbulence has provided both opportunities and threats for small businesses. As large information technology companies such as Cisco, Oracle, and Sun Microsystems had to recover from an economic slowdown and an oversupply of Internet infrastructure products, some smaller firms found new niche markets. Smaller companies can react

quickly to change and can stay close to their customers. While well-funded dot-coms were failing, many small businesses were learning how to use the Internet to promote themselves and sell products online. For example, arts and crafts dealers

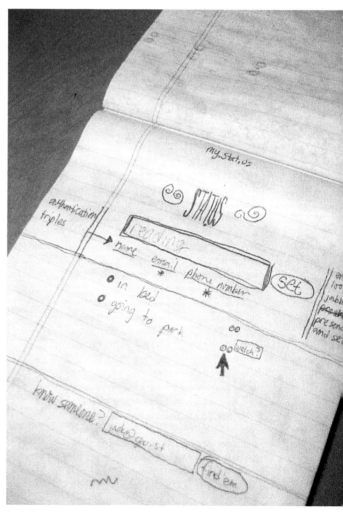

Jack Dorsey founded the idea for Twitter on a sketchpad. Dorsey says the idea was based on how dispatched vehicles, such as cabs, communicate with one another. Via radio, they are constantly squawking to each other about where they are and what they are doing.

▼ **TABLE 5.6** Top Cities to Launch a Small Business

1.	Pittsburgh, PA
2.	Miami, FL
3.	Menlo Park, CA
4.	Arlington, VA
5.	Chattanooga, TN
6.	Littleton, CO
7.	Ventura, CA
8.	Gahanna, OH

Source: "8 great cities to start a business," *CNNMoney,* http://money.cnn.com/smallbusiness/best places launch/2010/ (accessed March 21, 2011).

intrapreneurs
individuals in large firms who take responsibility for the development of innovations within the organizations

and makers of specialty products found they could sell their wares on existing websites, such as eBay. Service providers related to tourism, real estate, and construction also found they could reach customers through their own or existing websites.

Deregulation of the energy market and interest in alternative fuels and in fuel conservation have spawned many small businesses. Southwest Windpower Inc. manufactures and markets small wind turbines for producing electric power for homes, sailboats, and telecommunications. Solar Attic Inc. has developed a process to recover heat from home attics to use in heating water or swimming pools. As entrepreneurs begin to realize that worldwide energy markets are valued in the hundreds of billions of dollars, the number of innovative companies entering this market will increase.

In addition, many small businesses have the desire and employee commitment to purchase such environmentally friendly products. New Belgium Brewing Company received the U.S. Environmental Protection Agency and Department of Energy Award for leadership in conservation for making a 10-year commitment to purchase wind energy. The company's employees unanimously agreed to cover the increased costs of wind-generated electricity from the employee profit-sharing program.

The future for small business remains promising. The opportunities to apply creativity and entrepreneurship to serve customers are unlimited. While large organizations such as Walmart, which has more than 2.1 million employees, typically must adapt to change slowly, a small business can adapt immediately to customer and community needs and changing trends. This flexibility provides small businesses with a definite advantage over large companies.

SO YOU WANT TO BE // An Entrepreneur or Small-Business Owner /

In times when jobs are scarce, many people turn to entrepreneurship as a way to find employment. As long as there are unfulfilled needs from consumers, there will be a demand for entrepreneurs and small businesses. Entrepreneurs and small-business owners have been, and will continue to be, a vital part of the U.S. economy, whether in retailing, wholesaling, manufacturing, technology, or services. Creating a business around your idea has a lot of advantages. For many people, independence is the biggest advantage of forming their own small business, especially for those who do not work well in a corporate setting and like to call their own shots. Smaller businesses are also cheaper to start up than large ones in terms of salaries, infrastructure, and equipment. Smallness also provides a lot of flexibility to change with the times. If consumers suddenly start demanding new and different products or services, a small business is more likely to deliver quickly.

Starting your own business is not easy, especially in slow economic times. Even in a good economy, taking an idea and turning it into a business has a very high failure rate. The possibility of failure can increase even more when

money is tight. Reduced revenues and expensive materials can hurt a small business more than a large one because small businesses have fewer resources. When people are feeling the pinch from rising food and fuel prices, they tend to cut back on other expenditures—which could potentially harm your small business. The increased cost of materials will also affect your bottom line. However, several techniques can help your company survive:

• Set clear payment schedules for all clients. Small businesses tend to be worse about collecting payments than large ones, especially if the clients are acquaintances. However, you need to keep cash flowing into the company in order to keep business going.

• Take the time to learn about tax breaks. A lot of people do not realize all of the deductions they can claim on items such as equipment and health insurance.

• Focus on your current customers, and don't spend a lot of time looking for new ones. It is far less expensive for a company to keep its existing customers happy.

• Although entrepreneurs and small-business owners are more likely to be friends with

their customers, do not let this be a temptation to give things away for free. Make it clear to your customers what the basic price is for what you are selling and charge for extra features, extra services, etc.

• Make sure the office has the conveniences employees need—like a good coffee maker and other drinks and snacks. This will not only make your employees happy, but it will also help maintain productivity up by keeping employees closer to their desks.

• Use your actions to set an example. If money is tight, show your commitment to cutting costs and making the business work by doing simple things like taking the bus to work or bringing a sack lunch every day.

• Don't forget to increase productivity in addition to cutting costs. Try not to focus so much attention on cost cutting that you don't try to increase sales.

In unsure economic times, these measures should help new entrepreneurs and small-business owners sustain their businesses. Learning how to run a business on a shoestring is a great opportunity to cut the fat and to establish lean, efficient operations.[35]

MAKING BIG BUSINESSES ACT "SMALL"

The continuing success and competitiveness of small businesses through rapidly changing conditions in the business world have led many large corporations to take a closer look at what makes their smaller rivals tick. More and more firms are emulating small businesses in an effort to improve their own bottom line. Beginning in the 1980s and continuing through the present, the buzzword in business has been to *downsize* or *right-size* to reduce management layers, corporate staff, and work tasks in order to make the firm more flexible, resourceful, and innovative. Many well-known U.S. companies, including IBM, Ford, Apple Inc., General Electric, Xerox, and 3M, have downsized to improve their

TEAM EXERCISE

Explore successful global franchises. Go to the companies' websites and find the requirements for applying for three franchises. The chapter provides examples of successful franchises. What do the companies provide, and what is expected to be provided by the franchiser? Compare and contrast each group's findings for the franchises researched. For example, at Subway, the franchisee is responsible for the initial franchise fee, finding locations, leasehold improvements and equipment, hiring employees and operating restaurants, and paying an 8 percent royalty to the company and a fee into the advertising fund. The company provides access to formulas and operational systems, store design and equipment ordering guidance, a training program, an operations manual, a representative on-site during opening, periodic evaluations and ongoing support, and informative publications.

competitiveness, as have German, British, and Japanese firms. Other firms have sought to make their businesses "smaller" by making their operating units function more like independent small businesses, each responsible for its profits, losses, and resources. Of course, some large corporations, such as Southwest Airlines, have acted like small businesses from their inception, with great success.

Trying to capitalize on small-business success in introducing innovative new products, more and more companies are attempting to instill a spirit of entrepreneurship into even the largest firms. In major corporations, **intrapreneurs**, like entrepreneurs, take responsibility for, or "champion," the development of innovations of any kind *within* the larger organization.[36] Often, they use company resources and time to develop a new product for the company. ■

GET ONLINE

mhhe.com/FerrellM3e

for study materials including quizzes, iPod downloads, and video

chapter five

active review card
Small Business, Entrepreneurship,
and Franchising

in a
nutshell

A successful entrepreneur or small-business owner understands the advantages and disadvantages of owning a small business, challenges facing small businesses today, and why small businesses succeed or fail.

The following statements will test your take-away knowledge from this chapter. Do your best to explain each one in the space provided below.

LO.1 Define entrepreneurship and small business.

LO.2 Investigate the importance of small business in the U.S. economy and why certain fields attract small business.

LO.3 Specify the advantages of small-business ownership.

LO.4 Summarize the disadvantages of small-business ownership, and analyze why many small businesses fail.

LO.5 Describe how you go about starting a small business and what resources are needed.

LO.6 Evaluate the demographic, technological, and economic trends that are affecting the future of small business.

LO.7 Explain why many large businesses are trying to "think small."

Did your answers include the following important points?

LO.1. Define entrepreneurship and small business.

- An entrepreneur is a person who creates a business or product and manages his or her resources and takes risks to gain a profit; entrepreneurship is the process of creating and managing a business to achieve desired objectives.
- A small business is one that is not dominant in its competitive area and does not employ more than 500 people.

LO.2. Investigate the importance of small business in the U.S. economy and why certain fields attract small business.

- Small businesses are vital to the American economy because they provide products, jobs, innovation, and opportunities.
- Retailing, wholesaling, services, manufacturing, and high technology attract small businesses because these industries are relatively easy to enter, require relatively low initial financing, and may experience less heavy competition.

LO.3. Specify the advantages of small-business ownership.

- Small-business ownership offers some personal advantages, including independence, freedom of choice, and the option of working at home.
- Business advantages include flexibility, the ability to focus on a few key customers, and the chance to develop a reputation for quality and service.

LO.4. Summarize the disadvantages of small-business ownership, and analyze why many small businesses fail.

- Small businesses have many disadvantages for their owners, such as expense, physical and psychological stress, and a high failure rate.
- Small businesses fail for many reasons: undercapitalization, management inexperience or incompetence, neglect,

disproportionate burdens imposed by government regulation, and vulnerability to competition from larger companies.

LO.5. Describe how you go about starting a small business and what resources are needed.

- Have an idea for developing a small business and devise a business plan to guide the development of the business. Then you must decide what form of business ownership to use and provide funds, either your own or funds provided by friends, families, banks, investors, or other organizations.
- You must also decide whether to start a new business from scratch, buy an existing one, or buy a franchise operation.

LO.6. Evaluate the demographic, technological, and economic trends that are affecting the future of small business.

- Changing demographic trends include more elderly people as baby boomers age; a large gain in the 11- to 28-year-old age range known as echo boomers, millennials, or Generation Y; and an increasing number of immigrants to the United States.
- Technological advances and an increase in service exports have created new opportunities for small companies to expand their operations abroad, while trade agreements and alliances have created an environment in which small business has fewer regulatory and legal barriers.
- Economic turbulence presents both opportunities for and threats to the survival of small businesses.

LO.7. Explain why many large businesses are trying to "think small."

- Large companies are copying small businesses in an effort to make their firms more flexible, resourceful, and innovative, and improve the bottom line.
- This involves downsizing and intrapreneurship, where an employee takes responsibility for developing innovations within the larger organization.

Practical Application

LO.1.

- Small businesses provide opportunities for _____ and _____ to succeed in business.
- The Small Business Administration was established to provide _____ assistance to small businesses.
- Small business refers to an owner-managed business that employs not more than _____ people.

LO.2.

- Small businesses generated _____ of all new jobs created in the United States in recent years.
- _____ attracts entrepreneurs because gaining experience and exposure is relatively easy.
- The fastest growing sector of the U.S. economy is represented by _____.

LO.3.

- When market conditions change rapidly, a small business usually has fewer layers of management to work through in making decisions; this advantage of a small business is called _____.
- _____ is one of the leading reasons that entrepreneurs choose to go into business for themselves.
- Unlike many large corporations, small businesses can focus on developing products and services for a defined _____, that is, specific customers.

LO.4.

- Many people turn a hobby into a business without identifying a(n) _____ for that product; this leads to failure.

- _____ is one of the leading reasons for business failure as most businesses suffer from seasonal variations in sales.
- Initially, the factor that probably affects a company's reputation more than anything else is poorly managed _____.

LO.5.

- Since Rachel Hollings decided to purchase the rights to own and operate a McDonald's fast-food restaurant rather than start her own operation, she is probably a(n) _____.
- A mortgage is an example of _____.
- _____ are persons or organizations that agree to provide some funds for a new business in exchange for an ownership interest or stock.

LO.6.

- The _____ segment of the population is probably the wealthiest in the United States.
- The _____ population, the nation's largest minority group, is a vast untapped market for small businesses.
- Deregulation of the _____ market and an interest in fuel conservation has spawned many small businesses.

LO.7.

- Reducing management layers, corporate staff, and work tasks to make a firm more flexible, resourceful, and innovative is known as _____.
- Individuals who take responsibility for the development of innovations of any kind within larger organizations are called _____.

Managing for Quality and Competitiveness

the nature of
management

six

For any organization—small or large, for profit or nonprofit—to achieve its objectives, it must have equipment and raw materials to turn into products to market, employees to make and sell the products, and financial resources to purchase additional goods and services, pay employees, and generally operate the business. To accomplish this, it must also have one or more managers to plan, organize, staff, direct, and control the work that goes on.

This chapter introduces the field of management. It examines and surveys the various functions, levels, and areas of management in business. The skills that managers need for success and the steps that lead to effective decision making are also discussed.

LEARNING OBJECTIVES

LO1 Define management, and explain its role in the achievement of organizational objectives.

LO2 Describe the major functions of management.

LO3 Distinguish among three levels of management and the concerns of managers at each level.

LO4 Specify the skills managers need in order to be successful.

LO5 Summarize the systematic approach to decision making used by many business managers.

management a process designed to achieve an organization's objectives by using its resources effectively and efficiently in a changing environment

managers those individuals in organizations who make decisions about the use of resources and who are concerned with planning, organizing, staffing, directing, and controlling the organization's activities to reach its objectives

planning the process of determining the organization's objectives and deciding how to accomplish them; the first function of management

THE IMPORTANCE OF MANAGEMENT

Management is a process designed to achieve an organization's objectives by using its resources effectively and efficiently in a changing environment. *Effectively* means having the intended result; *efficiently* means accomplishing the objectives with a minimum of resources. **Managers** make decisions about the use of the organization's resources and are concerned with planning, organizing, staffing, directing, and controlling the organization's activities so as to reach its objectives. The decision to introduce new products in order to reach objectives is often a key management duty. After several years of decline in the automobile industry, Ford management introduced the Ford Fiesta from Europe into the United States. The car provides good driving dynamics, European styling, a low price, and up to 38 mpg. The car fits well with Ford's existing product mix in the United States.[1] Management is universal. It takes place not only in business, but also in government, the military, labor unions, hospitals, schools, and religious groups—any organization requiring the coordination of resources.

Every organization must acquire resources (people, raw materials and equipment, money, and information) to effectively pursue its objectives and coordinate their use to turn out a final good or service. Employees are one of the most important resources in helping a business attain its objectives. Successful companies recruit, train, compensate, and provide benefits (such as shares of stock and health insurance) to foster employee loyalty. Acquiring suppliers is another important part of managing resources and in ensuring that products are made available to customers. As

firms reach global markets, companies such as Walmart, Union Pacific, and Cargill enlist hundreds of diverse suppliers that provide goods and services to support operations. A good supplier maximizes efficiencies and provides creative solutions to help the company reduce expenses and reach its objectives. Finally, the manager needs adequate financial resources to pay for essential activities: Primary funding comes from owners and shareholders, as well as banks and other financial institutions. All these resources and activities must be coordinated and controlled if the company is to earn a profit. Organizations must also have adequate supplies of resources of all types, and managers must carefully coordinate their use if they are to achieve the organization's objectives.

MANAGEMENT FUNCTIONS

To harmonize the use of resources so that the business can develop, produce, and sell products, managers engage in a series of activities: planning, organizing, staffing, directing, and controlling (Figure 6.1). Although this book discusses each of the five functions separately, they are interrelated; managers may perform two or more of them at the same time.

Planning

Planning, the process of determining the organization's objectives and deciding how to accomplish them, is the first function of management. Planning is a crucial activity, for it designs the map that lays the groundwork for the other functions. It involves forecasting events and determining the best course of action from a set of options or choices. The plan itself specifies what should be done, by whom, where, when, and how. For example, General Electric implemented a plan to improve its reputation for sustainability and to reduce costs resulting from inefficiencies. Its planning resulted in a program called "Ecomagination," which addresses sustainability through calling attention to GE's solar energy programs, hybrid locomotives,

ENTREPRENEUR'S LEADERSHIP GUIDES COMPANY TOWARD EXCEPTIONAL CUSTOMER SERVICE

While customer satisfaction is important for all industries, Gentle Giant Movers lives by it. Founder

Larry O'Toole's message to his employees is to give 100 percent, regardless of the situation. The company nurtures its customers—even the more difficult ones—by giving advice on topics such as how to prepare children for a move and offering money-back satisfaction guarantees. O'Toole also loves and solicits feedback, positive or negative, and uses the information to constantly improve service. To his credit, customers love Gentle

Giant, and many of his former employees are highly successful. Ninety-five percent of those employees still with the company now hold management positions. Today, Gentle Giant Movers is a $27 million company with its own foundation focused upon youth leadership and homeless prevention. Gentle Giant's goal is to win lifelong customers, and O'Toole has created an empowering environment in which he and his employees can do just that.[2]

mission the statement of an organization's fundamental purpose and basic philosophy

fuel cell development, lower-emissions aircraft, and development of lighter and stronger materials, among many other projects. Ecomagination is part of GE's specific plans to produce products with an emphasis on clean technology and renewable energy.[3] All businesses—from the smallest restaurant to the largest multinational corporation—need to develop plans for achieving success. But before an organization can plan a course of action, it must first determine what it wants to achieve.

Mission

A **mission**, or mission statement, is a declaration of an organization's fundamental purpose and basic philosophy. It seeks to answer the question: "What business are we in?" Good mission statements are clear and concise statements that explain the organization's reason for existence. A well-developed mission statement, no matter what the industry or size of business, will answer five basic questions:

1. Who are we?
2. Who are our customers?
3. What is our operating philosophy (basic beliefs, values, ethics, etc.)?
4. What are our core competencies and competitive advantages?
5. What are our responsibilities with respect to being a good steward of environmental, financial, and human resources?

A mission statement that delivers a clear answer to these questions provides the foundation for the development of a strong organizational culture, a good marketing plan, and a coherent business strategy. The tea company Celestial Seasonings states that its mission is to provide "the highest quality, most environmentally responsible product possible" and to "be an active participant in making the world a better place."[4]

Goals

A goal is the result that a firm wishes to achieve. A company almost always has multiple goals, which illustrates the complex nature of business. A goal has three key components: an attribute sought, such as profits, customer satisfaction, or product quality; a target to be achieved, such as the volume of sales or extent of management training to be achieved; and a time frame, which is the time period in which the goal is to be achieved. Walmart, for example, under its former CEO Lee Scott, set goals of improving its reputation as an environmentally friendly company. Some of its goals involve reducing greenhouse gas emissions, increasing the fuel efficiency of its fleet, and requiring its suppliers to use less packaging. To be successful, company goals should be specific. Walmart plans to improve the fuel efficiency of its truck fleet by 25 percent within a specified time frame. It also has systems in place to measure its progress toward these goals. To be successful at achieving goals, it is necessary to know what is to be achieved, how much, when, and how succeeding at a goal is to be determined.

> Objectives [are] the ends or results desired by an organization.

Objectives

Objectives, the ends or results desired by an organization, derive from the organization's mission. A business's objectives may be elaborate or simple. Common objectives relate to profit, competitive advantage, efficiency, and growth. The principal difference between goals and objectives is that objectives are generally stated in such a way that they are measurable. Organizations with profit as an objective want to have money and assets left over after paying off business expenses. Objectives regarding competitive advantage are generally stated in terms of percentage of sales increase and market share, with the goal of increasing those figures. Efficiency objectives involved making the best use of the organization's resources. Dalhousie University has developed energy calculators for small and medium-sized businesses to help them become more aware of their energy usage and to reduce their energy expenditure.

Growth objectives relate to an organization's ability to adapt and to get new products to the marketplace in a timely fashion. Other organizational objectives include service and social responsibility goals. AT&T, Campbell Soup Company, Intel Corporation, and Old National Bank received the 2010 Corporate Engagement Award of Excellence from Points of Light Institute for their commitment to employee volunteerism, which helps the community, improves stakeholder relations, and motivates employees.[5] Recognition such as this helps show achievement of social responsibility objectives. Objectives provide direction for all

▼FIGURE 6.1
The Functions of Management

Managers

| Planning activities to achieve the organization's objectives | Organizing resources and activities to achieve the organization's objectives | Staffing the organization with qualified people | Directing employees' activities toward achievement of objectives | Controlling the organization's activities to keep it on course |

strategic plans those plans that establish the long-range objectives and overall strategy or course of action by which a firm fulfills its mission

tactical plans short-range plans designed to implement the activities and objectives specified in the strategic plan

operational plans very short-term plans that specify what actions individuals, work groups, or departments need to accomplish in order to achieve the tactical plan and ultimately the strategic plan

crisis management or contingency planning an element in planning that deals with potential disasters such as product tampering, oil spills, fire, earthquake, computer virus, or airplane crash

organizing the structuring of resources and activities to accomplish objectives in an efficient and effective manner

Southwest Airlines acquired AirTran as a part of its strategic plan to expand operations.

managerial decisions; additionally, they establish criteria by which performance can be evaluated.

Plans There are three general types of plans for meeting objectives—strategic, tactical, and operational. A firm's highest managers develop its **strategic plans**, which establish the long-range objectives and overall strategy or course of action by which the firm fulfills its mission. Strategic plans generally cover periods ranging from 2 to 10 years or even longer. They include plans to add products, purchase companies, sell unprofitable segments of the business, issue stock, and move into international markets. Faced with stiff competition, rising costs, and slowing sales, some companies are closing U.S. plants and moving production to factories abroad. For example, Converse Inc. (tennis shoes), Lionel LLC (model trains), and Zebco (fishing reels) all stopped U.S. production in favor of Asian factories. Strategic plans must take into account the organization's capabilities and resources, the changing business environment, and organizational objectives. Plans should be market-driven, matching customers' desire for value with operational capabilities, processes, and human resources.[6]

Tactical plans are short range and designed to implement the activities and objectives specified in the strategic plan. These plans, which usually cover a period of one year or less, help keep the organization on the course established in the strategic plan. Because tactical plans allow the organization to react to changes in the environment while continuing to focus on the company's overall strategy, management must periodically review and update them. Declining performance or failure to meet objectives set out in tactical plans may be one reason for revising them. When public concern emerged over Americans' high level of plastic bag consumption, which stands at more than 110 billion bags a year, the grocery chain Whole Foods

stopped offering plastic bags altogether. Walmart and Kroger also began to offer reusable canvas and nylon bags in response to this problem.[7] A fast-paced and ever-changing market requires companies to develop short-run or tactical plans to deal with stakeholder concerns.

A retailing organization with a five-year strategic plan to invest $5 billion in 500 new retail stores may develop five tactical plans (each covering one year) specifying how much to spend to set up each new store, where to locate, and when to open each new store. Tactical plans are designed to execute the overall strategic plan. Because of their short-term nature, they are easier to adjust or abandon if changes in the environment or the company's performance so warrant.

Operational plans are very short term and specify what actions specific individuals, work groups, or departments need to accomplish in order to achieve the tactical plan and ultimately the strategic plan. They may apply to just one month, week, or even day. For example, a work group may be assigned a weekly production quota to ensure there are sufficient products available to elevate market share (tactical goal) and ultimately help the firm be number one in its product category (strategic goal). Returning to our retail store example, operational plans may specify the schedule for opening one new store, hiring and training new employees, obtaining merchandise, and opening for actual business.

Another element of planning is **crisis management or contingency planning**, which deals with potential disasters such as product tampering, oil spills, fire, earthquake, computer viruses, or even a reputation crisis due to unethical or illegal conduct by one or more employees. After the *Deepwater Horizon* oil rig exploded in 2010, BP PLC demonstrated the weaknesses of its contingency plan. It was soon found that the 582-page response plan that BP had adopted in case of a Gulf spill was outdated and contained numerous errors, including the listing of a wildlife expert as an emergency responder who had been dead since 2005. As part of its contingency plan, BP had claimed the company could recover approximately 500,000 barrels of oil a day should a spill occur. The leak released far below that rate into the Gulf, but despite the company's claims it took months for BP to contain it. BP is an example of a company that had an ineffective and out-of-date contingency plan.[8] Businesses that have contingency plans tend to respond more effectively when problems occur than do businesses that lack such planning, hopefully avoiding a BP–level disaster.

Many companies, including Ashland Oil, H. J. Heinz, and Johnson & Johnson (J&J), have crisis management teams to deal specifically with problems, permitting other managers to continue to focus on their regular duties. Some companies even hold periodic disaster drills to ensure that their employees know how to respond when a crisis does occur. After the horrific earthquake in Japan, many companies in U.S. earthquake zones reevaluated their crisis management plans. Crisis management plans generally cover maintaining business operations throughout a crisis and communicating with the public, employees, and officials about the nature of and the company's response to the problem. Communication is especially important to minimize panic and damaging rumors; it also demonstrates that the company is aware of the problem and plans to respond. Johnson & Johnson failed to respond adequately when it was forced to issue a massive number of recalls due to manufacturing errors at its McNeil Laboratories plants. Contamination was found in over 40 types of children's medications; recalled products included Tylenol, Benadryl, and Sudafed, among others. Not only did J&J receive criticism for its defective products, it was also criticized by the government for not acting quickly enough to recall the products. Even after the recalls took place, McNeil was found to be in violation of several federal laws. J&J signed an agreement to fix the deficiencies. The crisis cost the company over $900 million in sales.[9] Incidents such as this highlight the importance of tactical planning for crises and the need to respond publicly and quickly when a disaster occurs.

Organizing

Rarely are individuals in an organization able to achieve common goals without some form of structure. **Organizing** is the structuring of resources and activities to accomplish objectives in an efficient and effective manner. Managers organize by reviewing plans and determining what activities are necessary to implement them; then, they divide the work into small units and assign it to specific individuals, groups, or departments. As companies reorganize for greater efficiency, more often than not, they are organizing work into teams to handle core processes such as new product development instead of organizing around traditional departments such as marketing and production.

Organizing is important for several reasons. It helps create synergy, whereby the effect of a whole system equals more than that of its parts. It also establishes lines of authority, improves communication, helps avoid duplication of resources, and can improve competitiveness by speeding up decision making. When media company Thompson, a business information giant, purchased Reuters Group, a news agency and financial data group, a new organizational structure was needed in order to merge core services for customers. The new organization resulted in four customer divisions: financial data and trading, legal and tax, scientific and health care, and media.[10] Because organizing is so important, we'll take a closer look at it in Chapter 7.

Staffing

Once managers have determined what work is to be done and how it is to be organized, they must ensure that the organization has enough employees with appropriate skills to do the work. Hiring people to carry out the work of the organization is known as **staffing**. Beyond recruiting people for positions within the firm, managers must determine what skills are needed for specific jobs, how to motivate and train employees, how much to pay, what benefits to provide, and how to prepare employees for higher-level jobs in the firm at a later date. These elements of staffing will be explored in detail in Chapters 9 and 10.

Another aspect of staffing is **downsizing**, the elimination of significant numbers of employees from an organization, which has been a pervasive and much-talked-about trend. Staffing can be outsourced to companies that focus on hiring

staffing the hiring of people to carry out the work of the organization

downsizing the elimination of a significant number of employees from an organization

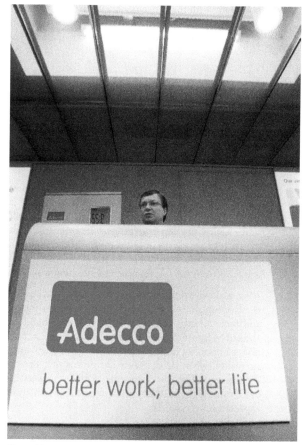

Downsizing workers and outsourcing their jobs isn't a popular move by companies. But it can help a firm rapidly reduce its costs and stay in business. Adecco is one of many companies that outsources part of its operations.

directing motivating and leading employees to achieve organizational objectives

controlling the process of evaluating and correcting activities to keep the organization on course

and managing employees. For instance, the Bartech Group provides search and staffing services, workforce solutions, business processes outsourcing, and consulting services. The Bartech Group bills and manages $1 billion for customers such as General Motors and Eaton.[11] Many firms downsize by outsourcing production, sales, and technical positions to companies in other countries with lower labor costs. Downsizing has helped numerous firms reduce costs quickly and become more profitable (or become profitable after lengthy losses) in a short period of time. Whether it is called downsizing, rightsizing, trimming the fat, or the new reality in business, the implications of downsizing have been dramatic. During the recent economic recession, many companies laid off workers to cut costs, and the nationwide unemployment rate climbed above 10 percent.[12]

Downsizing and outsourcing, however, have painful consequences. Obviously, the biggest casualty is those who lose their jobs, along with their incomes, insurance, and pensions. Some find new jobs quickly; others do not. Another victim is the morale of the remaining employees at downsized firms. Those

the implementation of deadlines, and then encouraging them to do their work. For example, as a sales manager you would need to learn how to motivate salespersons; provide leadership; teach sales teams to be responsive to customer needs; manage organizational issues; as well as evaluate sales results. Finally, directing also involves determining and administering appropriate rewards and recognition. All managers are involved in directing, but it is especially important for lower-level managers who interact daily with the employees operating the organization. For example, an assembly-line supervisor for Frito-Lay must ensure that her workers know how to use their equipment properly and have the resources needed to carry out their jobs safely and efficiently, and she must motivate her workers to achieve their expected output of packaged snacks.

Managers may motivate employees by providing incentives—such as the promise of a raise or promotion—for them to do a good job. But most workers want more than money from their jobs: They need to know that their employer values their ideas and input. Smart managers, therefore, ask workers to contribute ideas for reducing costs, making equipment more efficient, improving customer service, or even developing new products. This participation makes workers feel important, and the company benefits. Recognition and

> ["Participation makes workers feel important, and the company benefits."]

left behind often feel insecure, angry, and sad, and their productivity may decline as a result, the opposite of the effect sought. Managers can expect that 70 to 80 percent of those surviving a downsize will take a "wait-and-see" attitude and will require active leadership. Ten to 15 percent will be openly hostile or try to sabotage change in order to return to the way things were before. The remaining 10 to 15 percent will be the leaders who will try proactively to help make the situation work.[13]

After a downsizing situation, an effective manager will promote optimism and positive thinking and minimize criticism and fault-finding. Management should also build teamwork and encourage positive group discussions. Honest communication is important during a time of change and will lead to trust. In reality, when departments are downsized, the remaining employees end up working harder to fill the gaps left by layoffs. Truthfulness about what has happened and also about future expectations is essential.

Directing

Once the organization has been staffed, management must direct the employees. **Directing** is motivating and leading employees to achieve organizational objectives. Good directing involves telling employees what to do and when to do it through

appreciation are often the best motivators. Employees who understand more about their effect on the financial success of the company may be induced to work harder for that success, and managers who understand the needs and desires of workers can encourage their employees to work harder and more productively. The motivation of employees is discussed in detail in Chapter 9.

Controlling

Planning, organizing, staffing, and directing are all important to the success of an organization, whether its objective is earning a profit or something else. But what happens when a firm fails to reach its goals despite a strong planning effort? **Controlling** is the process of evaluating and correcting activities to keep the organization on course. Control involves five activities: (1) measuring performance, (2) comparing present performance with standards or objectives, (3) identifying deviations from the standards, (4) investigating the causes of deviations, and (5) taking corrective action when necessary.

Controlling and planning are closely linked. Planning establishes goals and standards. By monitoring performance and comparing it with standards, managers can determine whether performance is on target. When performance is substandard, management must determine why and take appropriate actions to get the firm back on course. In short, the control function helps managers assess the success of their plans. You might relate this to your performance in this class. If you did not perform as well on early projects or exams, you must take corrective action such as increasing studying or using website resources to achieve your overall objective of getting an A or B in the course. When the outcomes of plans do not meet expectations, the control process facilitates revision of the plans. Control can take many forms such as visual inspections, testing, and statistical modeling processes. The basic idea is to ensure that operations meet requirements and are satisfactory to reach objectives.

The control process also helps managers deal with problems arising outside the firm. For example, if a firm is the subject of negative publicity, management should use the control process to determine why and to guide the firm's response.

TYPES OF MANAGEMENT

All managers—whether the sole proprietor of a restaurant or the hundreds of managers of a large company such as Paramount Pictures—perform the five functions just discussed. In the case of the restaurant, the owner handles all the functions, but in a large company with more than one manager, responsibilities must be divided and delegated. This division of responsibility is generally achieved by establishing levels of management and areas of specialization—finance, marketing, and so on.

Levels of Management

As we have hinted, many organizations have multiple levels of management—top management, middle management, and first-line, or supervisory management. These levels form a pyramid, as shown in Figure 6.2. As the pyramid shape implies, there are generally more middle managers than top managers, and still more first-line managers. Very small organizations may have only one manager (typically, the owner), who assumes the responsibilities of all three

levels. Large businesses have many managers at each level to coordinate the use of the organization's resources. Managers at all three levels perform all five management functions, but the amount of time they spend on each function varies, as we shall see (Figure 6.3).

▼**FIGURE 6.2**
Levels of Management

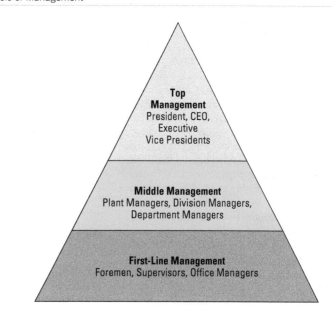

▼**FIGURE 6.3**
Importance of Management Functions to Managers in Each Level

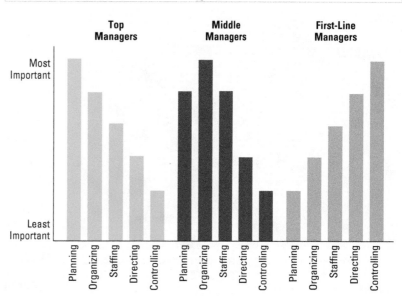

top managers the president and other top executives of a business, such as the chief executive officer (CEO), chief financial officer (CFO), and chief operations officer (COO), who have overall responsibility for the organization

middle managers those members of an organization responsible for the tactical planning that implements the general guidelines established by top management

first-line managers those who supervise both workers and the daily operations of an organization

Top Management In businesses, **top managers** include the president and other top executives, such as the chief executive officer (CEO), chief financial officer (CFO), and chief operations officer (COO), who have overall responsibility for the organization. For example, Mark Zuckerberg, CEO and founder of Facebook, manages every aspect of the company, from finance and advertising to product design and corporate strategy. Under Zuckerberg's direction, Facebook revolutionized the social media industry. Less than a decade after it was founded, the company has achieved a value of approximately $60 billion, has a user base of over 500 million, and expects its advertising revenue to double to $4.05 billion annually. Facebook is also in talks to hold an IPO to generate additional revenue.[14] In public corporations, even chief executive officers have a boss—the firm's board of directors. With technological advances accelerating and privacy concerns increasing, some companies are adding a new top management position—chief privacy

?

DID YOU KNOW?

Only 3 percent of *Fortune* 500 CEOs are women.[16]

officer (CPO). The position of privacy officer has grown so widespread that the International Association of Privacy Professionals boasts 7,700 members in 52 countries.[15] In government, top management refers to the president, a governor, or a mayor or city manager; in education, a chancellor of a university or a superintendent of education.

Top-level managers spend most of their time planning. They make the organization's strategic decisions, decisions that focus on an overall scheme or key idea for using resources to take advantage of opportunities. They decide whether to add products, acquire companies, sell unprofitable business segments, and move into foreign markets. For instance, top managers at PAI Partners and Sodiaal made the choice to sell a 51 percent interest in Yoplait SAS to General Mills. For its acquisition of 51 percent of the company, General Mills has agreed to pay over $1.13 billion.[17] Top managers also represent their company to the public and to government regulators.

Given the importance and range of top management's decisions, top managers generally have many years of varied experience and command top salaries. In addition to salaries, top managers' compensation packages typically include bonuses, long-term incentive awards, stock, and stock options. Table 6.1 lists the 10 highest paid CEOs including bonuses, stock options, and other compensation. Top management may also get perks and special treatment that is criticized by stakeholders.

Compensation committees are increasingly working with boards of directors and CEOs to attempt to keep pay in line with performance in order to benefit stockholders and key stakeholders. The majority of major companies cite their concern about attracting capable leadership for the CEO and other top executive positions in their organizations. Sixty-seven percent are concerned about their ability to attract and retain the most competent leadership. Many companies are attempting to curb high CEO pay by connecting compensation and job performance. James P. Gorman, CEO of Morgan Stanley, received a compensation package based on a variety of stocks and options. The total package could be worth almost $9 million. Many of the units are tied to his performance, such as meeting financial and corporate goals and remaining at Morgan Stanley for the length of his contract.[18] Successful management translates into happy stockholders who are willing to compensate their top executives fairly and in line with performance.

Workforce diversity is an important issue in today's corporations for top managers. Effective managers at enlightened corporations have found that diversity is good for workers and for

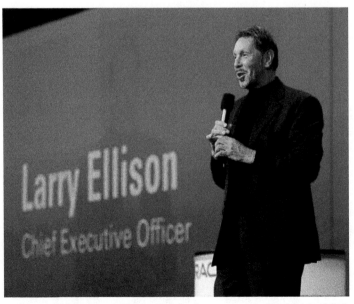

High compensation for CEOs is often necessary to attract the top talent. Larry Ellison, chief executive officer of Oracle, is the second-highest paid CEO.

the bottom line. Putting together different kinds of people to solve problems often results in better solutions. Betsy Holden, a former CEO of Kraft Foods, said, "When we look at the composition of teams within our company, we have found that those with a variety of perspectives are simply the most creative."[19] A diverse workforce is better at making decisions regarding issues related to consumer diversity. W. Garrison Jackson runs a multicultural public relations and advertising agency that helps corporate America reach black, Hispanic, Asian, and other minority consumers. These fast growing demographic groups are key target markets for many companies including Colgate-Palmolive, General Mills, and IBM.[20] Managers from companies devoted to workforce diversity devised five rules that make diversity recruiting work (see Table 6.2). Diversity is explored in greater detail in Chapter 10.

Middle Management Rather than making strategic decisions about the whole organization, **middle managers** are responsible for tactical planning that will implement the general guidelines established by top management. Thus, their responsibility is more narrowly focused than that of top managers. Middle managers are involved in the specific operations of the organization and spend more time organizing than other managers. In business, plant managers, division managers, and department managers make up middle management. The product manager for laundry detergent at a consumer products manufacturer, the department chairperson

▼ **TABLE 6.1** The Highest Paid CEOs

Rank	CEO	Company	Pay ($ in millions)
1.	H Lawrence Culp Jr	Danaher	141.36
2.	Lawrence J. Ellison	Oracle	130.23
3.	Aubrey K McClendon	Chesapeake Energy	114.29[1]
4.	Ray R. Irani	Occidental Petroleum	103.07
5.	David C Novak	Yum Brands	76.49
6.	John C Martin	Gilead Sciences	60.40
7.	Sol J Barer	Celgene	59.31[1]
8.	Keith A Hutton	XTO Energy	54.78[1, 2]
9.	Richard C Adkerson	Freeport Copper	48.75[1]
10.	Jen-Hsun Huang	Nvidia	31.40

[1]Prior-year data.

[2]New CEO; compensation may be for another executive office.

Source: "CEO Compensation," *Forbes*, April 28, 2010, www.forbes.com/lists/2010/12/boss-10 CEO-Compensation Rank.html (accessed January 12, 2011).

Most people get their first managerial experience as first-line managers.

in a university, and the head of a state public health department are all middle managers. The ranks of middle managers have been shrinking as more and more companies downsize to be more productive.

First-Line Management Most people get their first managerial experience as **first-line managers**, those who supervise workers and the daily operations of the organization. They are responsible for implementing the plans established by middle management and directing workers' daily performance on the job. They spend most of their time directing and controlling. Common titles for first-line managers are foreman, supervisor, and office manager.

▼ **TABLE 6.2** Five Rules of Successful Diversity Recruiting

Rule	Action
1. Get everyone involved.	Educate all employees on the tangible benefits of diversity recruiting to garner support and enthusiasm for those initiatives.
2. Showcase your diversity.	Prospective employees are not likely to become excited about joining your company just because you say that your company is diversity-friendly; they need to see it.
3. Work with diversity groups within your community.	By supporting community-based diversity organizations, your company will generate the priceless word-of-mouth publicity that will lead qualified diversity candidates to your company.
4. Spend money.	If you are serious about diversity recruiting, you will need to spend some money getting your message out to the right places.
5. Sell, sell, sell—and measure your return on investment.	Employers need to sell their company to prospective diversity employees and present them with a convincing case as to why their company is a good fit for the diversity candidate.

Source: Adapted from Juan Rodriguez, "The Five Rules of Successful Diversity Recruiting," *Diversityjobs.com*, www.diversityjobs.com/Rules-of-Successful-Diversity-Recruiting (accessed February 25, 2010).

financial managers those who focus on obtaining needed funds for the successful operation of an organization and using those funds to further organizational goals

production and operations managers those who develop and administer the activities involved in transforming resources into goods, services, and ideas ready for the marketplace

human resources managers those who handle the staffing function and deal with employees in a formalized manner

marketing managers those who are responsible for planning, pricing, and promoting products and making them available to customers

information technology (IT) managers those who are responsible for implementing, maintaining, and controlling technology applications in business, such as computer networks

Areas of Management

At each level, there are managers who specialize in the basic functional areas of business: finance, production and operations, human resources (personnel), marketing, and administration.

Financial Management **Financial managers** focus on obtaining the money needed for the successful operation of the organization and using that money in accordance with organizational goals. Among the responsibilities of financial managers are projecting income and expenses over a specified period, determining short- and long-term financing needs and finding sources of financing to fill those needs, identifying and selecting appropriate ways to invest extra funds, monitoring the flow of financial resources, and protecting the financial resources of the organization. A financial manager at Ford, for example, may be asked to analyze the costs and revenues of a car model to determine its contribution to Ford's profitability. All organizations must have adequate financial resources to acquire the physical and human resources that are necessary to create goods and services. Consequently, financial resource management is of the utmost importance.

Production and Operations Management **Production and operations managers** develop and administer the activities involved in transforming resources into goods, services, and ideas ready for the marketplace. Production and operations managers are typically involved in planning and designing production facilities, purchasing raw materials and supplies, managing inventory, scheduling processes to meet demand, and ensuring that products meet quality standards. Because no business can exist without the production of goods and services, production and operations managers are vital to an organization's success. Production can be a complicated process because companies, no matter what the size, must balance different considerations such as cost, performance, extra features, and styling. For example, the Tesla Roadster Sport is faster than the Porsche Boxter Spyder, but it does not handle as well. Both companies face the challenges inherent in producing products that balance high performance and maintaining quality standards in order to gain competitive advantage from their designs, production, and operations excellence. An additional challenge to small companies is to do all these things while remaining profitable.[21]

Human Resources Management **Human resources managers** handle the staffing function and deal with employees in a formalized manner. Once known as personnel managers, they determine an organization's human resource needs; recruit and hire new employees; develop and administer employee benefits, training, and performance appraisal

programs; and deal with government regulations concerning employment practices. For example, some companies recognize that their employees' health affects their costs. Therefore, more progressive companies provide health care facilities and outside health club memberships, encourage proper nutrition, and discourage smoking in an effort to improve employee health and lower the costs of providing health care benefits.

Marketing Management **Marketing managers** are responsible for planning, pricing, and promoting products and making them available to customers through distribution. The marketing manager who oversees Samsung televisions, for example, must make decisions regarding a new television's size, features, name, price, and packaging, as well as plan what type of stores to distribute the television through and the advertising campaign that will introduce the new television to consumers. General Motors must determine a way to make the vehicles that consumers want to buy while still turning a profit. This will require top management to get rank-and-file employees to understand and support a fleet of green, eco-friendly cars, including the Volt, a plug-in hybrid.[22] Within the realm of marketing, there are several areas of specialization: product development and management, pricing, promotion, and distribution. Specific jobs are found in areas such as marketing research, advertising, personal selling, retailing, telemarketing, and Internet marketing.

Information Technology (IT) Management **Information technology (IT) managers** are responsible for implementing, maintaining, and controlling technology applications in business, such as computer networks. Google, the world's largest online search engine, employs more than 10,000 employees, many of whom are IT managers. Google searches for IT managers and employees who are enthusiastic about their field and Google's products. To keep their engineers motivated, Google allows them to spend up to 20 percent of their time working on personal projects.[23] One major task in IT management is securing computer systems from unauthorized users while making the system easy to use for employees, suppliers, and others who have legitimate reasons to access the system. Another crucial task is protecting the systems' data, even during a disaster such as a fire. IT managers are also responsible for teaching and helping employees use technology resources efficiently through training and support. At many companies, some aspects of IT management are outsourced to third-party firms that can perform this function expertly and efficiently.

Administrative Management **Administrative managers** are not specialists; rather they manage an entire business or a major segment of a business. Such managers coordinate the activities of specialized managers, which would include marketing managers, production managers, and financial managers. Because of the broad nature of their responsibilities, administrative managers are often called general managers. However, this does not mean that administrative managers lack expertise in any particular area. Many top executives have risen through the ranks of financial management, production and operations management, or marketing management; but most top managers are actually administrative managers, employing skills in all areas of management.

skills, analytical skills, and human relations skills. Table 6.3 describes some of the roles managers may fulfill.

Leadership

Leadership is the ability to influence employees to work toward organizational goals. Strong lead-

administrative managers those who manage an entire business or a major segment of a business; they are not specialists but coordinate the activities of specialized managers

leadership the ability to influence employees to work toward organizational goals

> " Strong leaders manage and pay attention to the culture of their organizations and the needs of their customers. "

SKILLS NEEDED BY MANAGERS

Managers are typically evaluated using the metrics of how effective and efficient they are. Managing effectively and efficiently requires certain skills—leadership, technical expertise, conceptual

ers manage and pay attention to the culture of their organizations and the needs of their customers. Table 6.4 offers some tips for successful leadership, while Table 6.5 on page 131 lists America's 10 most admired companies and their CEOs. The list is compiled annually for *Fortune* magazine by executives and analysts who grade companies according to nine attributes, including quality of management.

▼ **TABLE 6.3** Managerial Roles

Type of Role	Specific Role	Examples of Role Activities
Decisional	Entrepreneur	Commit organizational resources to develop innovative goods and services; decide to expand internationally to obtain new customers for the organization's products.
	Disturbance handler	Move quickly to take corrective action to deal with unexpected problems facing the organization from the external environment, such as a crisis like an oil spill, or from the internal environment, such as producing faulty goods or services.
	Resource allocator	Allocate organizational resources among different functions and departments of the organization; set budgets and salaries of middle and first-level managers.
	Negotiator	Work with suppliers, distributors, and labor unions to reach agreements about the quality and price of input, technical, and human resources; work with other organizations to establish agreements to pool resources to work on joint projects.
Informational	Monitor	Evaluate the performance of managers in different functions and take corrective action to improve their performance; watch for changes occurring in the external and internal environment that may affect the organization in the future.
	Disseminator	Inform employees about changes taking place in the external and internal environment that will affect them and the organization; communicate to employees the organization's vision and purpose.
	Spokesperson	Launch a national advertising campaign to promote new goods and services; give a speech to inform the local community about the organization's future intentions.
Interpersonal	Figurehead	Outline future organizational goals to employees at company meetings; open a new corporate headquarters building; state the organization's ethical guidelines and the principles of behavior employees are to follow in their dealings with customers and suppliers.
	Leader	Provide an example for employees to follow; give direct commands and orders to subordinates; make decisions concerning the use of human and technical resources; mobilize employee support for specific organizational goals.
	Liaison	Coordinate the work of managers in different departments; establish alliances between different organizations to share resources to produce new goods and services.

Source: Gareth R. Jones and Jennifer M. George, *Essentials of Contemporary Management*, 3rd ed. (Burr Ridge, IL: McGraw-Hill/Irwin, 2007), p. 14.

technical expertise the specialized knowledge and training needed to perform jobs that are related to particular areas of management

conceptual skills the ability to think in abstract terms and to see how parts fit together to form the whole

analytical skills the ability to identify relevant issues, recognize their importance, understand the relationships between them, and perceive the underlying causes of a situation

▼ **TABLE 6.4** Seven Tips for Successful Leadership

- Build effective and responsive interpersonal relationships.
- Communicate effectively—in person, print, e-mail, etc.
- Build the team and enable employees to collaborate effectively.
- Understand the financial aspects of the business.
- Know how to create an environment in which people experience positive morale and recognition.
- Lead by example.
- Help people grow and develop.

Source: Susan M. Heathfield, "Seven Tips About Successful Management," *About.com*, http://humanresources.about.com/cs/managementissues/qt/mgmtsuccess.htm (accessed February 25, 2010).

Managers often can be classified into three types based on their leadership style. *Autocratic leaders* make all the decisions and then tell employees what must be done and how to do it. They generally use their authority and economic rewards to get employees to comply with their directions. *Democratic leaders* involve their employees in decisions. The manager presents a situation and encourages his or her subordinates to express opinions and contribute ideas. The manager then considers the employees' points of view and makes the decision. *Free-rein leaders* let their employees work without much interference. The manager sets performance standards and allows employees to find their own ways to meet them. For this style to be effective, employees must know what the standards are, and they must be motivated to attain them. The free-rein style of leadership can be a powerful motivator because it demonstrates a great deal of trust and confidence in the employee.

The effectiveness of the autocratic, democratic, and free-rein styles depends on several factors. One consideration is the type of employees. An autocratic style of leadership is generally best for stimulating unskilled, unmotivated employees; highly skilled, trained, and motivated employees may respond better to democratic or free-rein leadership styles. Employees who have been involved in decision making generally require less supervision than those not similarly involved. Other considerations are the manager's abilities and the situation itself. When a situation requires quick decisions, an autocratic style of leadership may be best because the manager does not have to consider input from a

NICK'S PIZZA & PUB SUCCEEDS ON "TRUST AND TRACK" SYSTEM OF MANAGEMENT

At Nick's Pizza & Pub, working with pizza is fun, rewarding, and challenging. Much of the company's success can be attributed to the strong management techniques of founder Nick Sarillo. When Sarillo started Nick's Pizza & Pub in 1995, he knew from the beginning that he wanted to create an environment with a dedicated workforce and a culture defined by honesty, loyalty, and excellent customer service. Sarillo rejected the traditional "command and control" management style in favor of creating a company culture in which he could trust his employees to work hard and behave ethically. The result is termed a "trust and track" management style.

Although Sarillo continually tracks what is going on inside the restaurant, he gives his employees responsibility over certain managerial functions. New hires at Nick's Pizza & Pub attend a two-day orientation, where they learn about the company's culture and are certified for particular jobs. Employees are expected to take responsibility for tasks that might traditionally be part of the supervisor's job. Sarillo wants his employees to feel like they are actively involved in the company's success and treats his mostly teenage workforce with respect. Nick's Pizza & Pub also cares for its customers. During the recession when unemployment was high, the restaurant gave customers half off on pizzas on Mondays and Tuesdays.

The result of the "trust and track" style is happier workers who choose to stick with the company. Whereas turnover is roughly 200 percent for the industry, Nick's Pizza & Pub experiences 20 percent. The annual operating profit rate is also high at 14 percent, compared to the 6.6 percent experienced by competitors. Sarillo's unusual but effective management style has created a corporate culture that translates into dedicated employees, satisfied customers, and over $7 million in annual sales.[24]

Discussion Questions

1. Why is Nick Sarillo a good manager?
2. Of the basic functions in recruiting and staffing a pizza restaurant, which of the following do you think is most important and why: hiring, training, evaluating, or compensating?
3. How would you defend Nick Sarillo's management approach from a financial point of view?

EMPLOYEES WHO HAVE BEEN INVOLVED IN DECISION MAKING GENERALLY REQUIRE LESS SUPERVISION THAN THOSE NOT SIMILARLY INVOLVED.

▼ **TABLE 6.5** America's Most Admired Companies and Their CEOs

Company	Chief Executive Officer
Apple	Steve Jobs/Tim Cook*
Google	Eric Schmidt
Berkshire Hathaway	Warren Buffett
Johnson & Johnson	William Weldon
Amazon.com	Jeff Bezos
Procter & Gamble	Robert McDonald
Toyota Motor	Akio Toyoda
Goldman Sachs	Lloyd Blankfein
Walmart	Mike Duke
Coca-Cola	Muhtar Kent

*Steve Jobs resigned as CEO of Apple in 2011 and passed away in October 2011. Tim Cook has taken his place.

Source: Adapted from "America's Most Admired Companies 2010," *Fortune,* http://money.cnn.com/magazines/fortune/mostadmired/2010/index.html (accessed January 12, 2011).

lot of people. If a special task force must be set up to solve a quality-control problem, a normally democratic manager may give free rein to the task force. Many managers, however, are unable to use more than one style of leadership. Some are incapable of allowing their subordinates to participate in decision making, let alone make any decisions. Thus, what leadership style is "best" depends on specific circumstances, and effective managers will strive to adapt their leadership style as circumstances warrant. Many organizations offer programs to develop goal leadership skills. When plans fail, very often leaders are held responsible for what goes wrong. For example, banking giant Citigroup's CFO Charles Prince resigned after the subprime credit meltdown forced Citigroup to write down billions of dollars. While at Citigroup, Prince had focused on improving ethics. He also supported a corporate creed that leaders should "accept accountability for our failures."[25]

Technical Expertise

Managers need **technical expertise**, the specialized knowledge and training required to perform jobs related to their area of management. Accounting managers need to be able to perform accounting jobs, and production managers need to be able to perform production jobs. Although a production manager may not actually perform a job, he or she needs technical expertise to train employees, answer questions, provide guidance, and solve problems. Technical skills are most needed by first-line managers and least critical to top-level managers.

Today, most organizations rely on computers to perform routine data processing, simplify complex calculations, organize and maintain vast amounts of information to communicate, and help managers make sound decisions. For this reason, most managers have found computer expertise to be an essential skill in doing their jobs well.

Conceptual Skills

Conceptual skills, the ability to think in abstract terms, and to see how parts fit together to form the whole, are needed by all managers, but particularly top-level managers. Top management must be able to evaluate continually where the company will be in the future. Conceptual skills also involve the ability to think creatively. Recent scientific research has revealed that creative thinking, which is behind the development of many innovative products and ideas, including fiber optics and compact disks, can be learned. As a result, IBM, AT&T, GE, Hewlett-Packard, Intel, and other top U.S. firms hire creative consultants to teach their managers how to think creatively.

Analytical Skills

Analytical skills refer to the ability to identify relevant issues and recognize their importance, understand the relationships between them, and perceive the underlying causes of a situation. When managers have identified critical factors and causes, they can take appropriate action. All managers need to think logically, but this skill is probably most important to the success of top-level managers. To be analytical, it is necessary to think about a broad range of issues and to weigh different options before taking action. Because analytical skills are so important, questions that require analytical skills are often a part of job interviews. Questions such as "How would you resolve a problem at work if you had access to a large amount of data?" may be part of the interview process. The answer would require the interviewee to try to explain how to sort data to find relevant facts that could resolve the issue. Analytical thinking is required in complex or difficult situations where the solution is often not clear. Resolving ethical issues often requires analytical skills.

human relations
skills the ability to deal
with people, both inside and
outside the organization

Human Relations Skills

People skills, or **human relations skills,** are the ability to deal with people, both inside and outside the organization. Those who can relate to others, communicate well with others, understand the needs of others, and show a true appreciation for others are generally more successful than managers who lack such skills. People skills are especially important in hospitals, airline companies, banks, and other organizations that provide services. For example, at Southwest Airlines, every new employee attends "You,

WHERE DO MANAGERS COME FROM?

Good managers are not born; they are made. An organization acquires managers in three ways: promoting employees from within, hiring managers from other organizations, and hiring managers straight out of universities.

Promoting people within the organization into management positions tends to increase motivation by showing employees that those who work hard and are competent can advance in the

> "Promoting people within the organization into management positions tends to increase motivation by showing employees that those who work hard and are competent can advance in the company."

Southwest and Success," a day-long class designed to teach employees about the airline and its reputation for impeccable customer service. All employees in management positions at Southwest take mandatory leadership classes that address skills related to listening, staying in touch with employees, and handling change without compromising values.

company. Internal promotion also provides managers who are already familiar with the company's goals and problems. Procter & Gamble prefers to promote managers from within, which creates managers who are familiar with the company's products, policies, and culture and builds company loyalty. Promoting from within, however, can lead to problems: It may limit innovation. The new manager may continue the practices and policies of previous managers. Thus it is vital for companies—even companies committed to promotion from within—to hire outside people from time to time to bring fresh ideas to the table.

Finding managers with the skills, knowledge, and experience required to run an organization or department can be difficult. Specialized executive employment agencies—sometimes called headhunters, recruiting managers, or executive search firms—can help locate candidates from other companies. The downside is that even though outside people can bring fresh ideas to

Flight attendant David Holmes became a YouTube sensation by rapping passenger instructions on Southwest Airlines flights. Southwest Airlines' managers and employees are well known for their excellent human relations skills and for making the workplace fun.

General Electric's excellent managerial training programs are renowned around the world. The company knows good managers aren't born. They are made.

WALMART GOES SMALLER

With thousands of Walmart stores across the United States, it is hard to imagine any region without the familiar big-box retailer. However, there is one market where Walmart is notably absent: urban areas. Cities like Chicago, New York City, and Detroit have been against the idea of Walmart Supercenters within their limits. This is becoming a problem for Walmart, as it has recently lost 2 percent of U.S. same-store sales while its competitor Target has gained. With suburbs and smaller towns becoming increasingly saturated, Walmart is looking toward urban areas. In order to do so, Walmart is planning to open up stores on a smaller scale.

Smaller formats are not new to Walmart. The company runs 152 Neighborhood Markets (at roughly 42,000 square feet) and four Marketside groceries in the United States, along with many smaller formats in Mexico. Yet in areas where space is a significant issue and sentiments for small businesses are high, Walmart is being forced to adapt its strategy and go smaller. These moves are starting to pay off. After six years of trying to break into Chicago, the city's zoning committee recently approved plans for a Walmart on its south side. The desperate need for jobs and Walmart's agreement to raise entry-level pay to 50 cents above minimum wage seem to have made this possible. To succeed in the city, Walmart will have to abandon the look and feel of the big box. Management says it will scale down these urban stores to 8,000 square feet.

The focus will be on groceries, although consumers will be able to order other items online and pick them up at the store. Whether Walmart is successful in Chicago will likely pave the way for the company's future plans for stores in the big city.[26]

Discussion Questions

1. Why do you think there has been so much resistance to Walmart's expansion in urban areas?

2. How has Walmart's management changed its tactics and objectives to begin to win the approval of zoning commissions and committees?

3. From an operations management point-of-view, what challenges will Walmart face running significantly smaller stores, and how could this impact the consumer?

---

a company, hiring them may cause resentment among existing employees as well as involve greater expense in relocating an individual to another city or state.

Schools and universities provide a large pool of potential managers, and entry-level applicants can be screened for their developmental potential. People with specialized management skills such as those with an MBA (master's of business administration) degree may be good candidates. Business students in the 21st century must remain flexible during their job searches. Before applying for a job, graduates should understand the company, the people, and the company's core values to ascertain whether they would be a good fit. Students may not have the exact skills for which the company is searching, but if they fit well with the culture, they can be trained. On-the-job training and socialization can help new recruits achieve success in their position and can help them reach their objectives. Finding employees who are trainable and a good fit with corporate culture means that organizations have a workforce staffed with potential future managers. Businesses that are recovering from the most recent economic recession should be willing to embrace new ideas and new employees willing to undergo change.

DECISION MAKING

Managers make many different kinds of decisions, such as the hours in a workday, which employees to hire, what products to introduce, and what price to charge for a product. Decision making is important in all management functions and at all levels, whether the decisions are on a strategic, tactical, or operational level. A systematic approach using the following six steps usually leads to more effective decision making: (1) recognizing and defining the decision situation, (2) developing options to resolve the situation, (3) analyzing the options, (4) selecting the best option, (5) implementing the decision, and (6) monitoring the consequences of the decision (Figure 6.4).

Recognizing and Defining the Decision Situation

The first step in decision making is recognizing and defining the situation. The situation may be negative—for example, huge losses on a particular product—or positive—for example, an opportunity to increase sales.

▼**FIGURE 6.4**
Steps in the Decision-Making Process

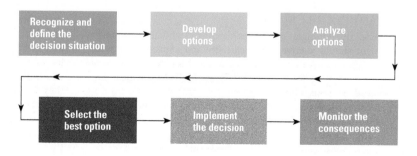

AFTER DEVELOPING A LIST OF POSSIBLE COURSES OF ACTION, MANAGEMENT SHOULD ANALYZE THE PRACTICALITY AND APPROPRIATENESS OF EACH OPTION.

Situations calling for small-scale decisions often occur without warning. Situations requiring large-scale decisions, however, generally occur after some warning signs. Effective managers pay attention to such signals. Declining profits, small-scale losses in previous years, inventory buildup, and retailers' unwillingness to stock a product are signals that may foreshadow huge losses to come. If managers pay attention to such signals, problems can be contained.

Once a situation has been recognized, management must define it. Losses reveal a problem—for example, a failing product. One manager may define the situation as a product quality problem; another may define it as a change in consumer preference. These two viewpoints may lead to vastly different solutions. The first manager, for example, may seek new sources of raw materials of better quality. The second manager may believe that the product has reached the end of its lifespan and decide to discontinue it. This example emphasizes the importance of carefully defining the problem rather than jumping to conclusions.

Developing Options

Once the decision situation has been recognized and defined, the next step is to develop a list of possible courses of action. The best lists include both standard and creative plans. As a general rule, more time and expertise are devoted to the development stage of decision making when the decision is of major importance. When the decision is of lesser importance, less time and expertise will be spent on this stage. Options may be developed individually, by teams, or through analysis of similar situations in comparable organizations. Creativity is a very important part of selecting the most viable option. Creativity depends on new and useful ideas, regardless of where they originate or the method used to create them. The best option can range from a required solution to an identified problem or volunteered solution, to an observed problem by an outside work group member.[27]

Analyzing Options

After developing a list of possible courses of action, management should analyze the practicality and appropriateness of each option. An option may be deemed impractical because of a lack of financial resources, legal restrictions, ethical and social responsibility considerations, authority constraints, technological constraints, economic limitations, or simply a lack of information and expertise. For example, a small computer manufacturer may recognize an opportunity to introduce a new type of computer but lack the financial resources to do so.

Other options may be more practical for the computer company: It may consider selling its technology to another computer company that has adequate resources, or it may allow itself to be purchased by a larger company that can introduce the new technology.

When assessing appropriateness, the decision maker should consider whether the proposed option adequately addresses the situation. When analyzing the consequences of an option, managers should consider its impact on the situation and on the organization as a whole. For example, when considering a price cut to boost sales, management must think about the consequences of the action on the organization's cash flow and consumers' reaction to the price change.

Selecting the Best Option

When all courses of action have been analyzed, management must select the best one. Selection is often a subjective procedure because many situations do not lend themselves to quantitative analysis. Of course, it is not always necessary to select only one option and reject all others; it may be possible to select and use a combination of several options. William Wrigley Jr. made a decision to sell his firm to Mars for $23 billion. The firm was founded by his great-grandfather in 1891, but hard times forced Wrigley to take what was considered to be the best option. This option was to create the Mars-Wrigley firm, currently the world's largest confectionary company with a distribution network in 180 countries.[28] A different set of choices would have been available to the company had it been able to purchase Hershey for $12 billion a few years earlier.

Implementing the Decision

To deal with the situation at hand, the selected option or options must be put into action. Implementation can be fairly simple or very complex, depending on the nature of the decision. Effective implementation of a decision to abandon a product, close a plant, purchase a new business, or something similar requires planning. For example, when a product is dropped, managers must decide how to handle distributors and customers and what to do with the idle production facility. Additionally, they should anticipate resistance from people within the organization (people tend to resist change because they fear the unknown). Finally, management should be ready to deal with the unexpected consequences. No matter how well planned implementation is, unforeseen problems will arise. Management must be ready to address these situations when they occur.

Monitoring the Consequences

After managers have implemented the decision, they must determine whether it has accomplished the desired result. Without proper monitoring, the consequences of decisions may not be known quickly enough to make efficient changes. If the desired result is achieved, management can reasonably conclude that it made a good choice. If the desired result is not achieved, further analysis is warranted. Was the decision simply wrong, or did the situation change? Should some other option have been implemented?

If the desired result is not achieved, management may discover that the situation was incorrectly defined from the beginning. That may require starting the decisionmaking process all over again. Finally, management may determine that the decision was good even though the desired results have not yet shown

they discuss anything and everything remotely connected with their business.

Managers spend a lot of time establishing and updating an agenda of goals and plans for carrying out their responsibilities. An **agenda** contains both specific and vague items, covering short-term goals and long-term objectives. Like a calendar, an agenda helps the manager figure out what must be done and how to get it done to meet the objectives set by the organization. Technology tools such as smart phones can help managers manage their agendas, contacts, communications, and time.

agenda a calendar, containing both specific and vague items, that covers short-term goals and long-term objectives

networking the building of relationships and sharing of information with colleagues who can help managers achieve the items on their agendas

> Managers also spend a lot of time networking—building relationships and sharing information with colleagues who can help them achieve the items on their agendas.

up, or it may determine a flaw in the decision's implementation. In the latter case, management would not change the decision but would change the way in which it is implemented.

THE REALITY OF MANAGEMENT

Management is not a cut-and-dried process. There is no mathematical formula for managing an organization and achieving organizational goals, although many managers passionately wish for one! Managers plan, organize, staff, direct, and control, but management expert John P. Kotter says even these functions can be boiled down to two basic activities:

1. Figuring out what to do despite uncertainty, great diversity, and an enormous amount of potentially relevant information, and

2. Getting things done through a large and diverse set of people despite having little direct control over most of them.[29]

Managers spend as much as 75 percent of their time working with others—not only with subordinates but with bosses, people outside their hierarchy at work, and people outside the organization itself. In these interactions

TEAM EXERCISE

Form groups and assign the responsibility of locating examples of crisis management implementation for companies dealing with natural disasters (explosions, fires, earthquakes, etc), technology disasters (viruses, plane crashes, compromised customer data, etc), or ethical or legal disasters. How did these companies communicate with key stakeholders? What measures did the company take to provide support to those involved in the crisis? Report your findings to the class.

Managers also spend a lot of time **networking**—building relationships and sharing information with colleagues who can help them achieve the items on their agendas. Managers spend much of their time communicating with a variety of people and participating in activities that on the surface do not seem to have much to do with the goals of their organization. Nevertheless, these activities are crucial to getting the job done. Networks are not limited to immediate subordinates and bosses; they include other people in the company as well as customers, suppliers, and friends. These contacts provide managers with information and advice on diverse topics. Managers ask, persuade, and even intimidate members of their network in order to get information and to get things done. Networking helps managers carry out their responsibilities. Andrea Nierenberg, independent business consultant and founder of Nierenberg Group Inc., has been called a "networking success story" by *The Wall Street Journal*. She writes three notes a day: one to a client, one to a friend, and one to a prospective client. She maintains a database of 3,000 contacts. However, she believes that it isn't how many people you know, but how many you have helped and who know you well enough to recommend you that really count. Opportunity can knock almost anywhere with such extensive networking. Grateful for numerous referrals to her

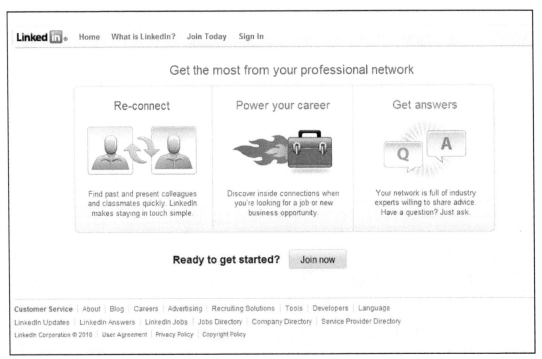

Websites like LinkedIn are helping managers and employees network with one another to achieve their professional goals.

friends, Nierenberg's dentist introduced her to a Wall Street executive who happened to be in the dentist's office at the same time as Nierenberg. She followed up on the meeting and later landed four consulting projects at the executive's firm.[30] Her clients include Citigroup, Time Inc., TIAA-CREF, Food Network, Coach, and Tiffany.[31]

Finally, managers spend a great deal of time confronting the complex and difficult challenges of the business world today. Some of these challenges relate to rapidly changing technology (especially in production and information processing), increased scrutiny of individual and corporate ethics and social responsibility, the impact of social media, the changing nature of the workforce, new laws and regulations, increased global competition and more challenging foreign markets, declining educational standards (which may limit the skills and knowledge of the future labor and customer pool), and time itself—that is, making the best use of it. But such diverse issues cannot simply be plugged into a computer program that supplies correct, easy-to-apply solutions. It is only through creativity and imagination that managers can make effective decisions that benefit their organizations. ■

SO YOU WANT TO BE A MANAGER // What Kind of Manager Do You Want to Be?/

Managers are needed in a wide variety of organizations. Experts suggest that employment will increase by millions of jobs by 2016. But the requirements for the jobs become more demanding with every passing year—with the speed of technology and communication increasing by the day, and the stress of global commerce increasing pressures to perform. However, if you like a challenge and if you have the right kind of personality, management remains a viable field. Even as companies are forced to restructure, management remains a vital role in business. In fact, the Bureau of Labor Statistics predicts that management positions in public relations, marketing, and advertising are set to increase around 12 percent overall between 2006 and 2016. Financial managers will be in even more demand, with jobs increasing 13 percent in the same time period. Computer and IT managers will continue to be in strong demand, with the number of jobs increasing 16 percent between 2006 and 2016.[32]

Salaries for managerial positions remain strong overall. While pay can vary significantly depending on your level of experience, the firm where you work, and the region of the country where you live, below is a list of the nationwide average incomes for a variety of different managers:

Chief Executives: $151,370

Computer and Information Systems Managers: $113, 880

Financial Managers: $106,200

Marketing Managers: $113,400

Human Resources Managers: $99,810

Operations Managers: $103,780

Medical/Health Services Managers: $84,980

Administrative Managers: $76,370

Sales Managers: $106,790[33]

In short, if you want to be a manager, there are opportunities in almost every field. There may be fewer middle-management positions available in firms, but managers remain a vital part of most industries and will continue to be long into the future—especially as navigating global business becomes ever more complex.

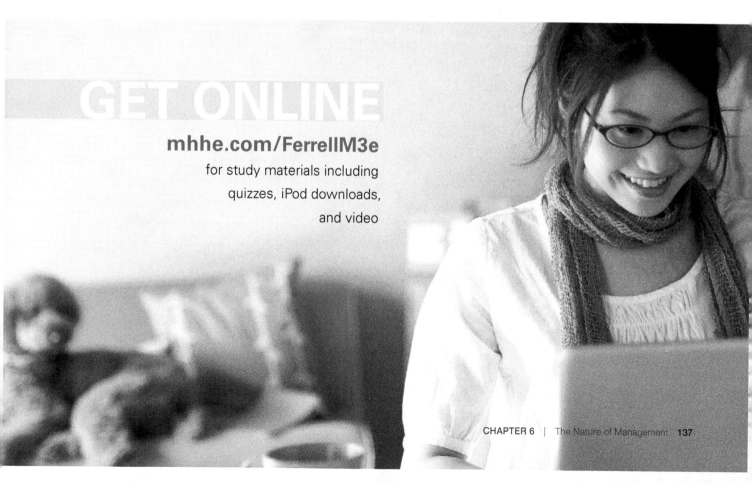

GET ONLINE

mhhe.com/FerrellM3e

for study materials including quizzes, iPod downloads, and video

chapter SIX

active review card
The Nature of Management

in a nutshell

A successful manager needs to possess certain skills and follow steps for effective decision making. In doing so, managers accomplish various functions and participate in differing levels and areas of management.

The following statements will test your take-away knowledge from this chapter. Do your best to explain each one in the space provided below.

LO.1 Define management, and explain its role in the achievement of organizational objectives.

LO.2 Describe the major functions of management.

LO.3 Distinguish among three levels of management and the concerns of managers at each level.

LO.4 Specify the skills managers need in order to be successful.

LO.5 Summarize the systematic approach to decision making used by many business managers.

Did your answers include the following important points?

LO.1. Define management, and explain its role in the achievement of organizational objectives.

- Management is a process designed to achieve an organization's objectives by using its resources effectively and efficiently in a changing environment.
- Managers make decisions about the use of the organization's resources and are concerned with planning, organizing, staffing, directing, and controlling the organization's activities to reach its objectives.

LO.2. Describe the major functions of management.

- Planning is the process of determining the organization's objectives and deciding how to accomplish them. Organizing is the structuring of resources and activities to accomplish those objectives efficiently and effectively.
- Staffing obtains people with the necessary skills to carry out the work of the company.
- Directing is motivating and leading employees to achieve organizational objectives and controlling the process of evaluating and correcting activities to keep the organization on course.

LO.3. Distinguish among three levels of management and the concerns of managers at each level.

- Top management is responsible for the whole organization and focuses primarily on strategic planning. Middle management develops plans for specific operating areas and carries out the general guidelines set by top management.
- First-line, or supervisory, management supervises the workers and day-to-day operations.
- Managers can also be categorized as to their area of responsibility: finance, production and operations, human resources, marketing, or administration.

LO.4. Specify the skills managers need in order to be successful.

- Managers need leadership skills, technical expertise, conceptual skills, analytical skills, and human relations skills.

LO.5. Summarize the systematic approach to decision making used by many business managers.

- A systematic approach to decision making follows these steps: recognizing and defining the situation, developing options, analyzing options, selecting the best option, implementing the decision, and monitoring the consequences.

Practical Application

LO.1.

- If a manager is concerned about doing work with the least cost and waste, her primary managerial concern is _____.
- _____ make decisions about the use of an organization's resources and are concerned with planning, organizing, leading, and controlling the organization's activities.
- Managers need to make efficient use of the company's _____ to reach organizational objectives.

LO.2.

- The type of planning conducted on a long-range basis by top managers is usually called _____.
- Dividing work into small units and assigning it to individuals are tasks related to _____.
- Hiring people to carry out the work of the organization is known as _____.

LO.3.

- _____ are responsible for tactical planning that will implement the general guidelines established by the top management.
- Decisions regarding adding new products, acquiring companies, and moving into foreign markets would most typically be made by the _____.

- Most people get their first managerial experience as _____ supervising workers and daily operations.

LO.4.

- Joe met with department heads to listen to their opinions about buying a new machine. Although they all thought it was a good idea, Joe did not buy the machine. Joe's leadership style is _____.
- To train employees, answer questions, and provide guidance in doing a task, managers need _____.
- Those managers who can communicate well, understand the needs of others, and are able to deal effectively with people inside and outside the organization are said to have good _____ skills.

LO.5.

- When analyzing options in the decision-making process, managers must consider the appropriateness and _____ of each option.
- Effective implementation of a major decision requires _____.
- Managers need to spend a lot of time in _____ with those who can help in the realization of organizational objectives.

chapter seven

organization, **teamwork**, + communication

introduction

An organization's structure determines how well it makes decisions and responds to problems, and it influences employees' attitudes toward their work. A suitable structure can minimize a business's costs and maximize its efficiency. Even companies that operate within the same industry may utilize different organizational structures. For example, in the medical device industry, 3M is organized by line of business (health care products, office products, security tools), whereas Medtronic has similar business groups, but it also has top-level, functional units that focus on legal issues, strategy, and human resources operating above each of the lines of business.[1]

Because a business's structure can so profoundly affect its success, this chapter will examine organizational structure in detail. First, we discuss how an organization's culture affects its operations. Then we consider the development of structure, including how tasks and responsibilities are organized through specialization and departmentalization. Next, we explore some of the forms organizational structure may take. Finally, we consider communications within business.

LEARNING OBJECTIVES

LO1 Define organizational structure, and relate how organizational structures develop.

LO2 Describe how specialization and departmentalization help an organization achieve its goals.

LO3 Distinguish between groups and teams, and identify the types of groups that exist in organizations.

LO4 Determine how organizations assign responsibility for tasks and delegate authority.

LO5 Compare and contrast some common forms of organizational structure.

LO6 Describe how communication occurs in organizations.

ORGANIZATIONAL CULTURE

One of the most important aspects of organizing a business is determining its **organizational culture**, a firm's shared values, beliefs, traditions, philosophies, rules, and role models for behavior. Also called corporate culture, an organizational culture exists in every organization, regardless of size, organizational type, product, or profit objective. Sometimes behaviors, programs, and policies enhance and support the organizational culture. For example, when U.S. unemployment hit 10 percent during the last recession, Pfizer implemented a program whereby customers who had lost their jobs and did not have prescription coverage could get 70 of its brand name drugs (Lipitor, Celebrex, Zoloft, Lyrica, etc.) for free for one year. According to Pfizer CEO Jeffrey Kindler, "We did it because we thought it was the right thing to do. But, it was motivational for our employees and got a great response from customers. In the long run it will help our business."[2] A firm's culture may be expressed formally through its mission statement, codes of ethics, memos, manuals, and ceremonies, but it is more commonly expressed informally. Examples of informal expressions of culture include dress codes (or the lack thereof), work habits, extracurricular activities, and stories. Employees often learn the accepted standards through discussions with co-workers.

TOMS Shoes' organizational culture is determined by the founder's desire to provide as many shoes as possible to children in developing countries (where shoeless children walk for miles to get water, food, and medical care). Blake Mycoskie gives hundreds of thousands of shoes to children around the world each year, creating a strong organizational culture of giving back and corporate social responsibility. His company operates with a program that for every shoe purchased, a shoe will be donated to children in need.[3] Disneyland/DisneyWorld and McDonald's have organizational cultures focused on cleanliness, value, and service. At M5 Networks, a $32 million company that sells VoIP phone systems, employees are encouraged to learn how to play musical instruments as part of their company culture. The organization hires music instructors to come to the office in the afternoons. CEO Dan Hoffman believes that company bands will bring together workers from different areas of the firm who normally would not interact. He also sees this as a way to encourage his employees to learn new things, which he feels is essential for company growth.[4] When such values and philosophies are shared by all members of an organization, they will be expressed in its relationships with stakeholders. However, organizational cultures that lack such positive values may result in employees who are unproductive and indifferent and have poor attitudes, which will be reflected externally to customers. The corporate culture may have contributed to the misconduct at a number of well-known companies. For example, a survey found that executives in financial and technology companies are mostly cutthroat in collecting intelligence about competition, leading to unethical acts.[5]

Organizational culture helps ensure that all members of a company share values and suggests rules for how to behave and deal with problems within the organization. Table 7.1 confirms that executives in this study believe that corporate culture has a

CHANGING THE ORGANIZATIONAL CULTURE BY REACHING POTENTIAL EMPLOYEES

With corporate social responsibility becoming a hot topic in the business world, companies are looking for talented individuals to create a positive impact on society. As this focus has grown, corporations have begun working with universities to incorporate social responsibility and sustainability into curriculum as a way to train potential employees before they leave campus. Some, such as Campbell Soup Co., are partnering with universities to offer students real-world projects involving these issues. Others, such as Dow Chemical Co. and Intel Corp., are sending their social responsibility and sustainability experts to lecture on university campuses. These experiences offer students perspectives that go beyond academic theory, focusing instead on real-world situations. This involvement has the potential to change organizational cultures by changing values about social responsibility.

Taking this movement one step further, IBM and Columbia University have joined forces through Smarter Students for a Smarter Planet, an initiative aimed at training students to one day enter positions within the green sector. IBM will donate the technology needed to train such students. Graduate students will have opportunities to work side-by-side with IBM researchers and other professionals in their chosen fields. With the green tech industry growing, corporate responsibility as a whole is generating new opportunities for business majors.

Despite these partnerships, specialization in social responsibility and sustainability is rarely featured in many traditional recruiting interviews, causing some to question the point of such educational initiatives. On the other hand, some of the world's most ethical and socially responsible companies are the most profitable. Training individuals to think and act more responsibly will likely yield positive results in corporate America. Many students involved in these programs are looking to utilize what they learn to make business, and the world, a better place.[6]

Discussion Questions

1. How does training future employees before they leave campus have the potential to influence an organization's culture?

2. How do real-world social responsibility projects help students prepare for their business careers?

3. Is there a conflict of interest between using resources to improve the social responsibility culture and making profits?

significant impact on organizational performance and the ability to retain good employees. The key to success in any organization is satisfying stakeholders, especially customers. Establishing a positive organizational culture sets the tone for all other decisions, including building an efficient organizational structure.

DEVELOPING ORGANIZATIONAL STRUCTURE

Structure is the arrangement or relationship of positions within an organization. Rarely is an organization, or any group of individuals working together, able to achieve common objectives without some form of structure, whether that structure is explicitly defined or only implied. A professional baseball team such as the Colorado Rockies is a business organization with an explicit formal structure that guides the team's activities so that it can increase game attendance, win games, and sell souvenirs such as t-shirts. But even an informal group playing softball for fun has an organization that specifies who will pitch, catch, bat, coach, and so on.

organizational culture a firm's shared values, beliefs, traditions, philosophies, rules, and role models for behavior

structure the arrangement or relationship of positions within an organization

▼ **TABLE 7.1** Impact of Corporate Culture on Business Performance

Culture has a strong or very strong impact on an organization's performance	82%
My corporate culture has a strong impact on the ability to retain top talent	68
My organization's culture drives sales and increases revenue	61
My organization's culture creates a sense of belonging	57
My organization's culture lowers turnover	53

Source: "Ten Most Admired Corporate Cultures," February 10, 2010, http://cthrc.ca/en/member_area/member_news/ten_most_admired_corporate_cultures.aspx (accessed March 1, 2010).

The organizational structure at TOMS Shoes consists of two parts. The for-profit component of the company manages overall operations. Its nonprofit component, Friends of TOMS, is responsible for volunteer activities and shoe donations.

GROWTH REQUIRES ORGANIZING—THE STRUCTURING OF HUMAN, PHYSICAL, AND FINANCIAL RESOURCES TO ACHIEVE OBJECTIVES IN AN EFFECTIVE AND EFFICIENT MANNER.

Governments and nonprofit organizations also have formal organizational structures to facilitate the achievement of their objectives. Getting people to work together efficiently and coordinating the skills of diverse individuals require careful planning. Developing appropriate organizational structures is therefore a major challenge for managers in both large and small organizations.

An organization's structure develops when managers assign work tasks and activities to specific individuals or work groups and coordinate the diverse activities required to reach the firm's objectives. When Macy's, for example, has a sale, the store manager must work with the advertising department to make the public aware of the sale, with department managers to ensure that extra salespeople are scheduled to handle the increased customer traffic, and with merchandise buyers to ensure that enough sale merchandise is available to meet expected consumer demand. All the people occupying these positions must work together to achieve the store's objectives.

The best way to begin to understand how organizational structure develops is to consider the evolution of a new business such as a clothing store. At first, the business is a sole proprietorship in which the owner does everything—buys, prices, and displays the merchandise; does the accounting and tax records; and assists customers. As the business grows, the owner hires a salesperson and perhaps a merchandise buyer to help run the store. As the business continues to grow, the owner hires more salespeople. The growth and success of the business now require the owner to be away from the store frequently, meeting with suppliers, engaging in public relations, and attending trade shows. Thus,

the owner must designate someone to manage the salespeople and maintain the accounting, payroll, and tax functions. If the owner decides to expand by opening more stores, still more managers will be needed. Figure 7.1 shows these stages of growth with three **organizational charts** (visual displays of organizational structure, chain of command, and other relationships).

Growth requires organizing—the structuring of human, physical, and financial resources to achieve objectives in an effective and efficient manner. Growth necessitates hiring people who have specialized skills. With more people and greater specialization, the organization needs to develop a formal structure to function efficiently. Imagine the organizational changes that Nathan's Famous hot dogs underwent from 1916 when it operated a single Coney Island hot dog shop to a company that now operates an international chain of fast-food restaurants as well as selling food products through supermarkets. The company sells more than 425 million hot dogs a year and generates nearly $51 million in revenue.[7] As we shall see, structuring an organization requires that management assign work tasks to specific individuals and departments and assign responsibility for the achievement of specific organizational objectives.

ASSIGNING TASKS

For a business to earn profits from the sale of its products, its managers must first determine what activities are required to achieve its objectives. At Celestial Seasonings, for example,

▼**FIGURE 7.1**
The Evolution of a Clothing Store, Phases 1, 2, and 3

employees must purchase herbs from suppliers, dry the herbs and place them in tea bags, package and label the tea, and then ship the packages to grocery stores around the country. Other necessary activities include negotiating with supermarkets and other retailers for display space, developing new products, planning advertising, managing finances, and managing employees. All these activities must be coordinated, assigned to work groups, and controlled. Two important aspects of assigning these work activities are specialization and departmentalization.

Specialization

After identifying all activities that must be accomplished, managers then break down these activities into specific tasks that can be handled by individual employees. This division of labor into small, specific tasks and the assignment of employees to do a single task is called **specialization**.

---

organizational chart a visual display of the organizational structure, lines of authority (chain of command), staff relationships, permanent committee arrangements, and lines of communication

specialization the division of labor into small, specific tasks and the assignment of employees to do a single task

departmentalization the grouping of jobs into working units usually called departments, units, groups, or divisions

---

dissatisfied and leave. Although some degree of specialization is necessary for efficiency, because of differences in skills, abilities, and interests, all people are not equally suited for all jobs. We examine some strategies to overcome these issues in Chapter 9.

Departmentalization

After assigning specialized tasks to individuals, managers next organize workers doing similar jobs into groups to make them easier to manage. **Departmentalization** is the grouping of jobs into working units usually called departments, units, groups, or divisions. As we shall see, departments are

---

> *Specialization means workers do not waste time shifting from one job to another, and training is easier.*

The rationale for specialization is efficiency. People can perform more efficiently if they master just one task rather than all tasks. In *The Wealth of Nations*, 18th-century economist Adam Smith discussed specialization, using the manufacture of straight pins as an example. Individually, workers could produce 20 pins a day when each employee produced complete pins. Thus, 10 employees working independently of each other could produce 200 pins a day. However, when one worker drew the wire, another straightened it, a third cut it, and a fourth ground the point, 10 workers could produce 48,000 pins per day.[8] To save money and achieve the benefits of specialization, some companies outsource and hire temporary workers to provide key skills. Many highly skilled, diverse, experienced workers are available through temp agencies.

Specialization means workers do not waste time shifting from one job to another, and training is easier. However, efficiency is not the only motivation for specialization. Specialization also occurs when the activities that must be performed within an organization are too numerous for one person to handle. Recall the example of the clothing store. When the business was young and small, the owner could do everything; but when the business grew, the owner needed help waiting on customers, keeping the books, and managing other business activities.

Overspecialization can have negative consequences. Employees may become bored and dissatisfied with their jobs, and the result of their unhappiness is likely to be poor quality work, more injuries, and high employee turnover. This is why some manufacturing firms allow job rotation so that employees do not become

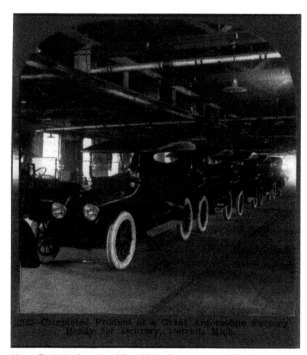

Henry Ford, the founder of Ford Motor Company, revolutionized manufacturing by creating assembly lines like this one to specialize the tasks his workers performed.

CHAPTER 7 | Organization, Teamwork, and Communication **143** commonly organized by function, product, geographic region, or customer (Figure 7.2). Most companies use more than one departmentalization plan to enhance productivity. For instance, many consumer goods manufacturers have departments for specific product lines (beverages, frozen dinners, canned goods, and so on) as well as departments dealing with legal, purchasing, finance, human resources, and other business functions. For smaller companies, accounting can be set up online, almost as an automated department. Accounting software can handle electronic transfers so you never have to worry about a late bill. Many city governments also have departments for specific services (e.g., police, fire, waste disposal) as well as departments for legal, human resources, and other business functions. Figure 7.3

depicts the organizational chart for the city of Corpus Christi, Texas, showing these departments.

Functional Departmentalization Functional departmentalization groups jobs that perform similar functional activities, such as finance, manufacturing, marketing, and human resources. Each of these functions is managed by an expert in the work done by the department—an engineer supervises the production department; a financial executive supervises the finance department. This approach is common in small organizations. A weakness of functional departmentalization is that, because it tends to emphasize departmental units rather than the organization as a whole, decision making that involves more than one department

▼**FIGURE 7.2**
Departmentalization

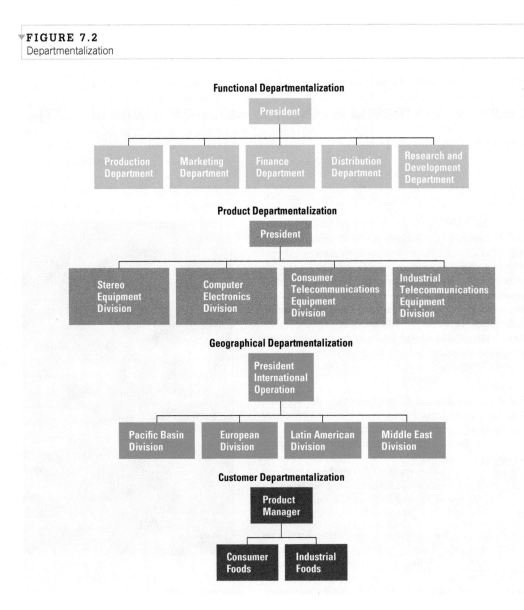

may be slow, and it requires greater coordination. Thus, as businesses grow, they tend to adopt other approaches to organizing jobs.

Product Departmentalization

Product departmentalization, as you might guess, organizes jobs around the products of the firm. Procter & Gamble has global units, such as laundry and cleaning products, paper products, and health care products. Each division develops and implements its own product plans, monitors the results, and takes corrective action as necessary. Functional activities—production, finance, marketing, and others—are located within each product division. Consequently, organizing by products duplicates functions and resources and emphasizes the product rather than achievement of the organization's overall objectives. However, it simplifies decision making and helps coordinate all activities related to a product or product group. Campbell Soup Company is organized into four segments: (1) U.S. Soup, Sauces and Beverages, which includes Campbell's soups, Swanson broth, Prego pasta sauce, V8 juice and juice drinks, Campbell's tomato juice, and related products; (2) Baking and Snacking, which includes Pepperidge Farm cookies, crackers,

> **functional departmentalization** the grouping of jobs that perform similar functional activities, such as finance, manufacturing, marketing, and human resources
>
> **product departmentalization** the organization of jobs in relation to the products of the firm

FIGURE 7.3
An Organizational Chart for the City of Corpus Christi

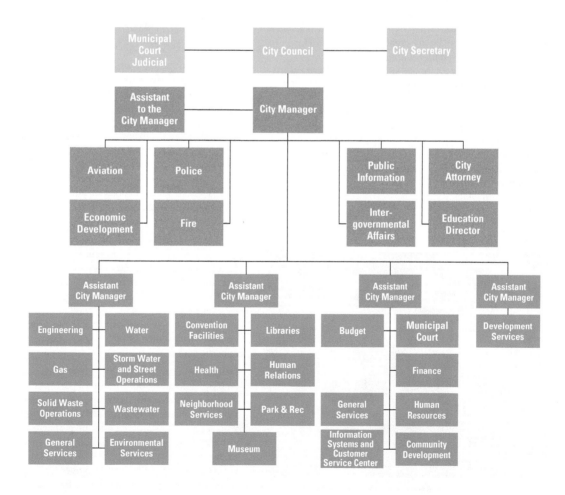

Source: "City of Corpus Christi Organizational Chart," City of Corpus Christi www.cctexas.com/files/g5/cityorgchart.pdf (accessed February 11, 2010).

geographical departmentalization the grouping of jobs according to geographic location, such as state, region, country, or continent

customer departmentalization the arrangement of jobs around the needs of various types of customers

delegation of authority giving employees not only tasks, but also the power to make commitments, use resources, and take whatever actions are necessary to carry out those tasks

responsibility the obligation, placed on employees through delegation, to perform assigned tasks satisfactorily and be held accountable for the proper execution of work

accountability the principle that employees who accept an assignment and the authority to carry it out are answerable to a superior for the outcome

bakery and frozen products, and Arnott's biscuits and salty snacks; (3) International Soup, Sauces and Beverages, which includes soup, sauces, and beverages sold outside the United States, and (4) North America Foodservice, which includes prepared food operations.[9]

Geographical Departmentalization
Geographical departmentalization groups jobs according to geographic location, such as a state, region, country, or continent. Frito-Lay, for example, is organized into four regional divisions, allowing the company to get closer to its customers and respond more quickly and efficiently to regional competitors. Multinational corporations often use a geographical approach because of vast differences between different regions. Coca-Cola, General Motors, and Caterpillar are organized by region. However, organizing by region requires a large administrative staff and control system to coordinate operations, and tasks are duplicated among the different regions.

Customer Departmentalization
Customer departmentalization arranges jobs around the needs of various types of customers. Banks, for example, typically have separate departments for commercial banking activities and for consumer or retail banking. This permits the bank to address the unique requirements of each group. Airlines, such as British Airways and Delta, provide prices and services customized

for either business/frequent travelers or infrequent/vacationing customers. Customer departmentalization, like geographical departmentalization, does not focus on the organization as a whole and therefore requires a large administrative staff to coordinate the operations of the various groups.

ASSIGNING RESPONSIBILITY

After all workers and work groups have been assigned their tasks, they must be given the responsibility to carry them out. Management must determine to what extent it will delegate responsibility throughout the organization and how many employees will report to each manager.

Delegation of Authority

Delegation of authority means not only giving tasks to employees but also empowering them to make commitments, use resources, and take whatever actions are necessary to carry out those tasks. Let's say a marketing manager at Nestlé has assigned an employee to design a new package that is less wasteful (more environmentally responsible) than the current package for one of the company's frozen dinner lines. To carry out the assignment, the employee needs access to information and the authority to make certain decisions on packaging materials, costs, and so on. Without the authority to carry out the assigned task, the employee would have to get the approval of others for every decision and every request for materials.

As a business grows, so do the number and complexity of decisions that must be made; no one manager can handle them all. Hotels such as Westin Hotels and Resorts and the Ritz-Carlton give authority to service providers, including front desk personnel, to make service decisions such as moving a guest to another room or providing a discount to guests who experience a problem at the hotel. Delegation of authority frees a manager to concentrate on larger issues, such as planning or dealing with problems and opportunities.

Delegation also gives a **responsibility**, or obligation, to employees to carry out assigned tasks satisfactorily and holds them accountable for the proper execution of their assigned work. The principle of **accountability** means that employees who accept an assignment and the authority to carry it out are answerable to a superior for the outcome. Returning to the Nestlé example, if the packaging design prepared by the employee is unacceptable or late, the employee must accept the blame. If the new design is innovative, attractive, and cost-efficient, as well as environmentally responsible, or is completed ahead of schedule, the employee will accept the credit.

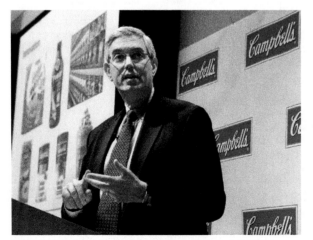

The Campbell Soup Company uses product departmentalization to organize its company. However, the firm also engages in a type of geographical departmentalization for various regions.

The process of delegating authority establishes a pattern of relationships and accountability between a superior and his or her subordinates. The president of a firm delegates responsibility for all marketing activities to the vice president of marketing. The vice president accepts this responsibility and has the authority to obtain all relevant information, make certain decisions, and delegate any or all activities to his or her subordinates. The vice president, in turn, delegates all advertising activities to the advertising manager, all sales activities to the sales manager, and so on. These managers then delegate specific tasks to their subordinates. However, the act of delegating authority to a subordinate does not relieve the superior of accountability for the delegated job. Even though the vice president of marketing delegates work to subordinates, he or she is still ultimately accountable to the president for all marketing activities.

Degree of Centralization

The extent to which authority is delegated throughout an organization determines its degree of centralization.

Centralized Organizations

In a **centralized organization**, authority is concentrated at the top, and very little decision-making authority is delegated to lower levels. Although decision-making authority in centralized organizations rests with top levels of management, a vast amount of responsibility for carrying out daily and routine procedures is delegated to even the lowest levels of the organization. Many government organizations, including the U.S. Army, the U.S. Postal Service, and the IRS, are centralized.

Businesses tend to be more centralized when the decisions to be made are risky and when low-level managers are not highly skilled in decision making. In the banking industry, for example, authority to make routine car loans is given to all loan managers, while the authority to make high-risk loans, such as for a large residential development, may be restricted to upper-level loan officers.

Overcentralization can cause serious problems for a company, in part because it may take longer for the organization as a whole to implement decisions and to respond to changes and problems on a regional scale. McDonald's, for example, was one of the last chains to introduce a chicken sandwich because of the amount of research, development, test marketing, and layers of approval the product had to go through.

centralized organization a structure in which authority is concentrated at the top, and very little decision-making authority is delegated to lower levels

decentralized organization an organization in which decision-making authority is delegated as far down the chain of command as possible

Decentralized Organizations

A **decentralized organization** is one in which decision-making authority is delegated as far down the chain of command as possible. Decentralization is characteristic of organizations that operate in complex, unpredictable environments. Businesses that face intense competition often decentralize to improve responsiveness and enhance creativity. Lower-level managers who interact with the external environment often develop a good understanding of it and thus are able to react quickly to changes.

Delegating authority to lower levels of managers may increase the organization's productivity. Decentralization requires that lower-level managers have strong decision-making skills. In recent years the trend has been toward more decentralized organizations, and some of the largest and most successful companies, including GE, IBM, Google, Nike, and JCPenney, have decentralized decision-making authority. McDonald's, realizing most of its growth outside the United States, is becoming increasingly decentralized and "glo-cal," varying products in specific markets to better meet consumer demands. This change in organizational structure for McDonald's is fostering greater innovation and local market success. McDonald's, which was long known for the homogeneity of its products, has embraced local cuisine on a limited scale. In Italy, McDonald's introduced the McItaly, a burger made with only Italian products. The

FAMILY TEAM MAKES JOHNNY CUPCAKES A BUSINESS SUCCESS

It might sound like a bakery, but Johnny Cupcakes is actually the name of a successful apparel retailer. Founded in 2001 by John Earle, Johnny Cupcakes sells limited edition clothing and accessories—all featuring cupcake designs. John began selling his first t-shirts out of the trunk of his car and the suitcase he used while touring with his band. As business accelerated, John's mother and sister began helping him fill orders. His parent's house became his warehouse. Along the road to success, John turned down distribution offers from Nordstrom, Urban Outfitters, and more. Instead, he opened up his own stores in Hull, Massachusetts (his hometown), Los Angeles, and Boston. Customers often camp outside to score new designs and attend special events. Through it all, John has been supported by his family and friends, who are also his co-workers. His mother serves as his chief financial officer, his sister runs human resources and customer service, his sister's best friend is training as bookkeeper, and his father assists with various aspects of the business. Although the creative inspiration rests with John, Johnny Cupcakes is truly a family affair.[10]

span of management
the number of subordinates who report to a particular manager

organizational layers
the levels of management in an organization

line structure the simplest organizational structure in which direct lines of authority extend from the top manager to the lowest level of the organization

line-and-staff structure
a structure having a traditional line relationship between superiors and subordinates and also specialized managers—called staff managers—who are available to assist line managers

burger is designed with the red and green Italian flag in mind; customers can choose from artichoke spread and Asiago cheese or onion, lettuce, and pancetta.[11] Diversity and decentralization seem to be McDonald's keys to being better, not just bigger. Nonprofit organizations benefit from decentralization as well.

Span of Management

How many subordinates should a manager manage? There is no simple answer. Experts generally agree, however, that top managers should not directly supervise more than four to eight people, while lower-level managers who supervise routine tasks are capable of managing a much larger number of subordinates. For example, the manager of the finance department may supervise 25 employees, whereas the vice president of finance may supervise only five managers. **Span of management** refers to the number of subordinates who report to a particular manager. A *wide span of management* exists when a manager directly supervises a very large number of employees. A *narrow span of management* exists when a manager directly supervises only a few subordinates (Figure 7.4). At Whole Foods, the best employees

one another, the manager has few responsibilities other than supervision, the level of interaction between superiors and subordinates is low, few problems arise, subordinates are highly competent, and a set of specific operating procedures governs the activities of managers and their subordinates, a wide span of management will be more appropriate. Narrow spans of management are typical in centralized organizations, while wide spans of management are more common in decentralized firms.

Organizational Layers

Complementing the concept of span of management is **organizational layers**, the levels of management in an organization.

A company with many layers of managers is considered tall; in a tall organization, the span of management is narrow (see Figure 7.4). Because each manager supervises only a few subordinates, many layers of management are necessary to carry out the operations of the business. McDonald's, for example, has a tall organization with many layers, including store managers, district managers, regional managers, and functional managers (finance, marketing, and so on), as well as a chief executive officer and many vice presidents. Because there are more managers in tall organizations than in flat

A COMPANY WITH MANY LAYERS OF MANAGERS IS CONSIDERED TALL.

are recruited and placed in small teams in one of eight departments. Employees are empowered to discount, give away, and sample products, as well as to assist in creating a respectful workplace where goals are achieved, individual employees succeed, and customers are core in business decisions. This approach allows Whole Foods to offer unique and "local market" experiences in each of its stores. This level of customization is in contrast to more centralized national supermarket chains such as Kroger, Safeway, and Publix.[12]

Should the span of management be wide or narrow? To answer this question, several factors need to be considered. A narrow span of management is appropriate when superiors and subordinates are not in close proximity, the manager has many responsibilities in addition to the supervision, the interaction between superiors and subordinates is frequent, and problems are common. However, when superiors and subordinates are located close to

organizations, administrative costs are usually higher. Communication is slower because information must pass through many layers.

Organizations with few layers are flat and have wide spans of management. When managers supervise a large number of employees, fewer management layers are needed to conduct

FIGURE 7.4
Span of Management: Wide Span and Narrow Span

Wide Span: Flat Organization   Narrow Span: Tall Organization

▼FIGURE 7.5
Line Structure

Convenience Store

Owner — Manager — Assistant Manager — Hourly Employee

the organization's activities. Managers in flat organizations typically perform more administrative duties than managers in tall organizations because there are fewer of them. They also spend more time supervising and working with subordinates.

Many of the companies that have decentralized also flattened their structures and widened their spans of management, often by eliminating layers of middle management. Many corporations, including Avon, AT&T, and Ford Motor Company, did so to reduce costs, speed up decision making, and boost overall productivity.

FORMS OF ORGANIZATIONAL STRUCTURE

Along with assigning tasks and the responsibility for carrying them out, managers must consider how to structure their authority relationships—that is, what structure the organization itself will have and how it will appear on the organizational chart. Common forms of organization include line structure, line-and-staff structure, multidivisional structure, and matrix structure.

Line Structure

The simplest organizational structure, **line structure**, has direct lines of authority that extend from the top manager to employees at the lowest level of the organization. For example, a convenience store employee may report to an assistant manager, who reports to the store manager, who reports to a regional manager, or, in an independent store, directly to the owner (Figure 7.5). This structure has a clear chain of command, which enables managers to make decisions quickly. A mid-level manager facing a decision must consult only one person, his or her

immediate supervisor. However, this structure requires that managers possess a wide range of knowledge and skills. They are responsible for a variety of activities and must be knowledgeable about them all. Line structures are most common in small businesses.

Line-and-Staff Structure

The **line-and-staff structure** has a traditional line relationship between superiors and subordinates, and specialized managers—called staff managers—are available to assist line managers (Figure 7.6). Line managers can focus on their area of expertise in the operation of the business, while staff managers provide advice and support to line departments on specialized matters such as finance, engineering, human resources, and the law. In

▼FIGURE 7.6
Line-and-Staff Structure

——— Line relationship
- - - - Staff relationship

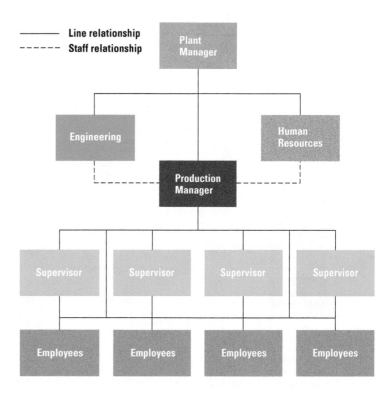

multidivisional structure a structure that organizes departments into larger groups called divisions

matrix structure a structure that sets up teams from different departments, thereby creating two or more intersecting lines of authority; also called a project-management structure

group two or more individuals who communicate with one another, share a common identity, and have a common goal

team a small group whose members have complementary skills; have a common purpose, goals, and approach; and hold themselves mutually accountable

the city of Corpus Christi (refer back to Figure 7.3), for example, assistant city managers are line managers who oversee groups of related departments. However, the city attorney, police chief, and fire chief are effectively staff managers who report directly to the city manager (the city equivalent of a business chief executive officer). Staff managers do not have direct authority over line managers or over the line manager's subordinates, but they do have direct authority over subordinates in their own departments. However, line-and-staff organizations may experience problems with overstaffing and ambiguous lines of communication. Additionally, employees may become frustrated because they lack the authority to carry out certain decisions.

Multidivisional Structure

As companies grow and diversify, traditional line structures become difficult to coordinate, making communication difficult and decision making slow. When the weaknesses of the structure—the "turf wars," miscommunication, and working at cross-purposes—exceed the benefits, growing firms tend to restructure, often into the divisionalized form. A **multidivisional structure** organizes departments into larger groups called divisions. Just as departments might be formed on

the basis of geography, customer, product, or a combination of these, so too divisions can be formed based on any of these methods of organizing. Within each of these divisions, departments may be organized by product, geographic region, function, or some combination of all three. Indra Nooyi, CEO of PepsiCo, rearranged the company's organizational structure. Prior to her tenure, PepsiCo was organized geographically. She created new units—PepsiCo Americas Foods (PAF), PepsiCo Americas Beverages (PAB), PepsiCo Europe, and PepsiCo Asia, Middle East & Africa—that span international boundaries and make it easier for employees in different geographic regions to share business practices.[13]

Multidivisional structures permit delegation of decision-making authority, allowing divisional and department managers to specialize. They allow those closest to the action to make the decisions that will affect them. Delegation of authority and divisionalized work also mean that better decisions are made faster, and they tend to be more innovative. Most importantly, by focusing each division on a common region, product, or customer, each is more likely to provide products that meet the needs of its particular customers. However, the divisional structure inevitably creates work duplication, which makes it more difficult to realize the economies of scale that result from grouping functions together.

Matrix Structure

Another structure that attempts to address issues that arise with growth, diversification, productivity, and competitiveness, is the matrix. A **matrix structure**, also called a project management structure, sets up teams from different departments, thereby creating two or more intersecting lines of authority (Figure 7.7). The matrix structure superimposes project-based departments on the more traditional, function-based departments. Project teams bring together specialists from a variety of areas to work together on a single project, such as developing a new fighter jet. In this arrangement, employees are responsible to two managers—functional managers and project managers. Matrix structures are usually temporary: Team members typically go back to their functional or line department after a project is finished. However, more firms are becoming permanent matrix structures, creating and dissolving project teams as needed to meet customer needs. The aerospace industry

▼**FIGURE 7.7**
Matrix Structure

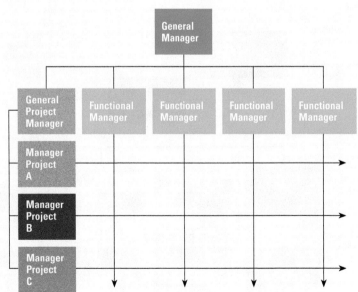

was one of the first to apply the matrix structure, but today it is used by universities and schools, accounting firms, banks, and organizations in other industries.

Matrix structures provide flexibility, enhanced cooperation, and creativity, and they enable the company to respond quickly to changes in the environment by giving special attention to specific projects or problems. However, they are generally expensive and quite complex, and employees may be confused as to whose authority has priority—the project manager's or the immediate supervisor's.

THE ROLE OF GROUPS AND TEAMS IN ORGANIZATIONS

Regardless of how they are organized, most of the essential work of business occurs in individual work groups and teams, so we'll take a closer look at them now. Although some experts do not make a distinction between groups and teams, in recent years there has been a gradual shift toward an emphasis on teams and managing them to enhance individual and organizational success. Some experts now believe that highest productivity results only when groups become teams.[14]

Traditionally, a **group** has been defined as two or more individuals who communicate with one another, share a common identity, and have a common goal. A **team** is a small group whose members have complementary skills; have a common purpose, goals, and approach; and hold themselves mutually accountable.[15] All teams are groups, but not all groups are

teams. Table 7.2 points out some important differences between them. Work groups emphasize individual work products, individual accountability, and even individual leadership. Salespeople working independently for the same company could be a work group. In contrast, work teams share leadership roles, have both individual and mutual accountability, and create collective work products. In other words, a work group's performance depends on what its members do as individuals, while a team's performance is based on creating a knowledge center and a competency to work together to accomplish a goal. When CEO Joe Albanese had to leave his CEO position at Commodore Builders for active duty in the Army, his team rebalanced his workload and continued its projects. Albanese had established teams that focused on collaboration. A core team was prepared to lead the company in his absence. Albanese simply unplugged himself, leaving the team to perform his duties, including day-to-day leadership. During Albanese's 10-month deployment to the Middle East, the company grew by 40 percent.[16]

The type of groups an organization establishes depends on the tasks it needs to accomplish and the situation it faces. Some specific kinds of groups and teams include committees, task forces, project teams, product-development teams, quality-assurance teams, and self-directed work teams. All of these can be *virtual teams*—employees in different locations who rely on e-mail, audio conferencing, fax, Internet, videoconferencing, or other technological tools to accomplish their goals. With more than 84 percent of American employees working in a different location than their supervisors, virtual teams are becoming a part of everyday business.[17]

FORD DEVELOPS ALL-WOMEN TEAM TO GREEN ITS VEHICLES

Ford is going green with its formation of its all-women renewable materials research team—also known as Ford's Green Team. Debbie Mielewski and her five female colleagues are all engineers looking to make Ford cars more eco-friendly. The idea for the team started when Mielewski was asked to reshape Ford's plastics department. She brought her own green concerns to the job and began researching how to make Ford's cars more sustainable. To date, Mielewski and her team have been awarded ten prize patents for innovations such as soy-filled seats and the blending of traditional plastics with wheat fibers. The

group also focuses on reusing damaged materials, rather than throwing them away.

In an industry dominated by men—only one-fourth of auto employees and one-tenth of auto executives are women—Ford's green team feels that it has unique skills and insights to contribute. Many members of the team have children, and they bring a passion to protect the environment for future generations to their work. In addition, the six members find that they are able to collaborate well. They tend to divide into teams, rather than working solo, in order to have constant support and feedback. The team emphasizes communication and collective decision making, which they feel has been an important factor in their achievements.

The green team has already made an impact on the company. A recent press

release states that in one year the company has kept almost 30 million pounds of plastic out of landfills and saved $4.5 million by utilizing recycled materials. Ford plans to replace fiberglass and plastics with sustainable, eco-friendly alternatives, which will lead to a smaller carbon footprint and a reduced use of petroleum. It looks like the Green Team has a winning strategy.[18]

Discussion Questions

1. Why did Ford form an all-women renewable materials research team to make cars more eco-friendly?

2. Why is collective decision making a benefit to Ford's Green Team?

3. Will Ford's Green Team contribute to consumer loyalty and success?

committee a permanent, formal group that performs a specific task

task force a temporary group of employees responsible for bringing about a particular change

project teams groups similar to task forces that normally run their operation and have total control of a specific work project

product-development teams a specific type of project team formed to devise, design, and implement a new product

quality-assurance teams (or quality circles) small groups of workers brought together from throughout the organization to solve specific quality, productivity, or service problems

self-directed work team (SDWT) a group of employees responsible for an entire work process or segment that delivers a product to an internal or external customer

▼ **TABLE 7.2** Differences between Groups and Teams

Working Group	Team
Has strong, clearly focused leader	Has shared leadership roles
Has individual accountability	Has individual and group accountability
Has the same purpose as the broader organizational mission	Has a specific purpose that the team itself delivers
Creates individual work products	Creates collective work products
Runs efficient meetings	Encourages open-ended discussion and active problem-solving meetings
Measures its effectiveness indirectly by its effects on others (e.g., financial performance of the business)	Measures performance directly by assessing collective work products
Discusses, decides, and delegates	Discusses, decides, and does real work together

Source: Robert Gatewood, Robert Taylor, and O. C. Ferrell, *Management: Comprehension Analysis and Application,* 1995, p. 427. Copyright © 1995 Richard D. Irwin, a Times Mirror Higher Education Group, Inc., company. Reproduced with permission of the McGraw-Hill Companies.

be formed from individuals outside a company. When Toyota experienced a major product recall, the president, Akio Toyoda, formed and led a Global Quality Task Force to conduct quality improvements throughout the worldwide operations of the company. With massive recalls looming, the company focused on (1) improving the quality inspection process, (2) enhancing customer research, (3) establishing an automotive center of quality excellence, (4) utilizing external industry experts, (5) increasing the frequency of communication with regional authorities, and (6) improving regional autonomy.[19]

Teams

Teams are becoming far more common in the U.S. workplace as businesses strive to enhance productivity and global competitiveness. In general, teams have the benefit of being able to pool members' knowledge and skills and make greater use of them than can individuals working alone. Team building is becoming increasingly popular in organizations, with around half of executives indicating their companies had team-building training. Teams require harmony, cooperation, synchronized effort, and flexibility to maximize their contribution.[20] Teams can also create more solutions to problems

> Teams are becoming far more common in the U.S. workplace as businesses strive to enhance productivity and global competitiveness.

Committees

A **committee** is usually a permanent, formal group that does some specific task. For example, many firms have a compensation or finance committee to examine the effectiveness of these areas of operation as well as the need for possible changes. Ethics committees are formed to develop and revise codes of ethics, suggest methods for implementing ethical standards, and review specific issues and concerns.

Task Forces

A **task force** is a temporary group of employees responsible for bringing about a particular change. They typically come from across all departments and levels of an organization. Task force membership is usually based on expertise rather than organizational position. Occasionally, a task force may

than can individuals. Furthermore, team participation enhances employee acceptance of, understanding of, and commitment to team goals. Teams motivate workers by providing internal rewards in the form of an enhanced sense of accomplishment for employees as they achieve more, and external rewards in the form of praise and certain perks. Consequently, they can help get workers more involved. They can help companies be more innovative, and they can boost productivity and cut costs.

According to psychologist Ivan Steiner, team productivity peaks at about five team members. People become less motivated, and group coordination becomes more difficult after this size. Jeff Bezos, Amazon.com CEO, says that he has a "two-pizza rule": If a team cannot be fed by two pizzas, it is too large. Keep teams small enough where everyone gets a piece of the action.[21]

Project Teams

Project teams are similar to task forces, but normally they run their operation and have total control of a specific work project. Like task forces, their membership is likely to cut across the firm's hierarchy and be composed of people from different functional areas. They are almost always temporary, although a large project, such as designing and building a new airplane at Boeing Corporation, may last for years.

Product-development teams are a special type of project team formed to devise, design, and implement a new product. Sometimes product-development teams exist within a functional area—research and development—but now they more frequently include people from numerous functional areas and may even include customers to help ensure that the end product meets the customers' needs. Washington State University's School of Food Science has several student product-development teams. Students develop innovative new food products and present them annually at the Institute of Food Technologists Student Association competition. WSU student projects include Tu Mazi, a mango-flavored probiotic milk powder created for consumers in developing nations, and Erupt-a-Cake, a ready-to-bake dessert featuring gummy dinosaurs.[22]

Quality-Assurance Teams

Quality-assurance teams, sometimes called quality circles, are fairly small groups of workers brought together from throughout the organization to solve specific quality, productivity, or service problems. Although the *quality circle* term is not as popular as it once was, the concern about quality is stronger than ever. The use of teams to address quality issues will no doubt continue to increase throughout the business world.

Self-Directed Work Teams

A **self-directed work team (SDWT)** is a group of employees responsible for an entire work process or segment that delivers a product to an internal or external customer.[23] SDWTs permit the flexibility to change rapidly to meet the competition or respond to customer needs. The defining characteristic of an SDWT is the extent to which it is empowered or given authority to make and implement work decisions. Thus, SDWTs are designed to give employees a feeling of "ownership" of a whole job. With shared team responsibility for work outcomes, team members often have broader job assignments and cross-train to master other jobs, thus permitting greater team flexibility.

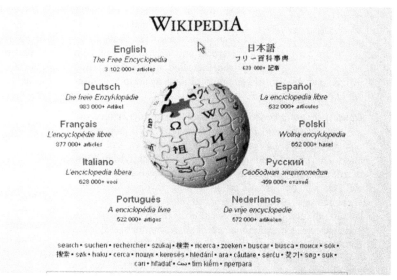

Online sites such as wikis are allowing employee teams to share information and work collaboratively on documents. The most well-known wiki is the online encyclopedia Wikipedia.

COMMUNICATING IN ORGANIZATIONS

Communication within an organization can flow in a variety of directions and from a number of sources, each using both oral and written forms of communication. The success of communication systems within the organization has a tremendous effect on the overall success of the firm. Communication mistakes can lower productivity and morale.

?

Alternatives to face-to face communications—such as meetings—are growing thanks to technology such as voice-mail, e-mail, and online newsletters. Many companies use internal networks called intranets to share information with employees. Intranets increase communication across different departments and levels of management and help with the flow of everyday business activities. Companies can even integrate aspects of social media into their intranets, allowing employees to post comments and pictures, participate in polls, and create group calendars. However, increased access to the Internet at work has also created many problems, including employee abuse of company mail and Internet access.[25]

Formal Communication

Formal channels of communication are intentionally defined and designed by the organization. They represent the flow of communication within the formal organizational structure, as

grapevine an informal channel of communication, separate from management's formal, official communication channels

shown on organizational charts. Traditionally, formal communication patterns were classified as vertical and horizontal, but with the increased use of teams and matrix structures, formal communication may occur in a number of patterns (Figure 7.8).

Upward communication flows from lower to higher levels of the organization and includes information such as progress reports, suggestions for improvement, inquiries, and grievances. *Downward communication* refers to the traditional flow of information from upper organizational levels to lower levels. This type of communication typically involves directions, the assignment of tasks and responsibilities, performance feedback, and certain details about the organization's strategies and goals. Speeches, policy and procedures manuals, employee handbooks, company leaflets, telecommunications, and job descriptions are examples of downward communication.

Horizontal communication involves the exchange of information among colleagues and peers on the same organizational level, such as across or within departments. Horizontal information informs, supports, and coordinates activities both within the department and with other departments. At times, the business will formally require horizontal communication among particular organizational members, as is the case with task forces or project teams.

TEAM EXERCISE

Assign the responsibility of providing the organizational structure for a company one of your team members has worked for. Was your organization centralized or decentralized in terms of decision making? Would you consider the span of control to be wide or narrow? Were there any types of teams, committees, or task forces utilized in the organization? Report your work to the class.

With more and more companies downsizing and increasing the use of self-managed work teams, many workers are being required to communicate with others in different departments and on different levels to solve problems and coordinate work. When these individuals from different units and organizational levels communicate, it is *diagonal communication*. One benefit of companies doing more with fewer employees is that productivity (output per work hour) increased by 9.5 percent in one year. Increased productivity allows companies to increase wages and leads to increased standards of living.[26]

Informal Communication Channels

Along with the formal channels of communication shown on an organizational chart, all firms communicate informally as well. Communication between friends, for instance, cuts across department, division, and even management-subordinate boundaries. Such friendships and other nonwork social relationships comprise the *informal organization* of a firm, and their impact can be great.

The most significant informal communication occurs through the **grapevine**, an informal channel of communication, separate from management's formal, official communication channels. Grapevines exist in all organizations. Information passed along the grapevine may relate to the job or organization, or it may be gossip and rumors unrelated to either. The accuracy of grapevine information has been of great concern to managers.

▼**FIGURE 7.8**
The Flow of Communication in an Organizational Hierarchy

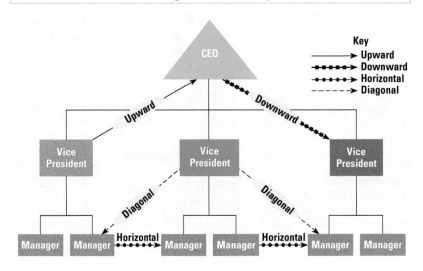

Additionally, managers can turn the grapevine to their advantage. Using it as a "sounding device" for possible new policies is one example. Managers can obtain valuable information from the grapevine that could improve decision making. Some organizations use the grapevine to their advantage by floating ideas, soliciting feedback, and reacting accordingly. People love to gossip, and managers need to be aware that grapevines exist in every organization. Managers who understand how the grapevine works also can use it to their advantage by feeding it facts to squelch rumors and incorrect information.

Monitoring Communications

Technological advances and the increased use of electronic communication in the workplace have made monitoring its use necessary for most companies. Failing to monitor employee's use of e-mail and the Internet can be costly. Many companies require that employees sign and follow a policy on appropriate Internet use. These agreements often require that employees will use corporate computers only for work-related activities. Additionally, several companies use software programs to monitor employee computer usage.[27] Instituting practices that show respect for employee privacy but do not abdicate employer responsibility are increasingly necessary in today's workplace. Several websites provide model policies and detailed guidelines for conducting electronic monitoring, including the Model Electronic Privacy Act on the American Civil Liberties Union site.

SO YOU WANT A JOB // Managing Organizational Culture, Teamwork, and Communication /

Jobs dealing with organizational culture and structure are usually at the top of the organization. If you want to be a CEO or high-level manager, you will help shape these areas of business. On the other hand, if you are an entrepreneur or small-business person, you will need to make decisions about assigning tasks, departmentalization, and assigning responsibility. Even managers in small organizations have to make decisions about decentralization, span of management, and forms of organizational structure. While these decisions may be part of your job, there are usually no job titles dealing with these specific areas. Specific jobs that attempt to improve organizational culture could include ethics and compliance positions as well as those who are in charge of communicating memos, manuals, and policies that help establish the culture. These positions will be in communications, human resources, and positions that assist top organizational managers.

Teams are becoming more common in the workplace, and it is possible to become a member of a product-development group or quality-assurance team. There are also human resources positions that encourage teamwork through training activities. The area of corporate communications provides lots of opportunities for specific jobs that facilitate communication systems. Thanks to technology, there are job positions to help disseminate information through online newsletters, intranets, or internal computer networks to share information to increase collaboration. In addition to the many advances using electronic communications, there are technology concerns that create new job opportunities. Monitoring workplace communications such as the use of e-mail and the Internet have created new industries. There have to be internal controls in the organization to make sure that the organization does not engage in any copyright infringement. If this is an area of interest, there are specific jobs that provide an opportunity to use your technological skills to assist in maintaining appropriate standards in communicating and using technology.

If you go to work for a large company with many divisions, you can expect a number of positions dealing with the tasks discussed here. If you go to work for a small company, you will probably engage in most of these tasks as a part of your position. Organizational flexibility requires individual flexibility, and those employees willing to take on new domains and challenges will be the employees who survive and prosper in the future.

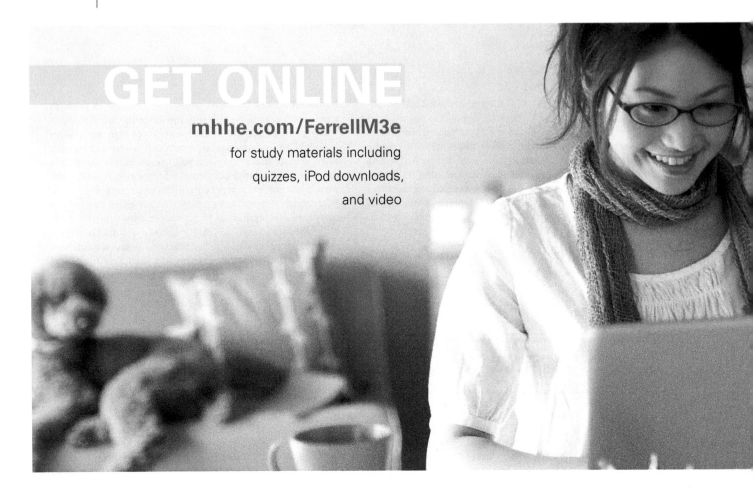

GET ONLINE

mhhe.com/FerrellM3e

for study materials including
quizzes, iPod downloads,
and video

chapter seven

active review card
Organization, Teamwork, and Communication

nutshell
in a

An organization's culture affects its operations. It is important in organizing a business to understand the development of structure, including how tasks and responsibilities are organized through specialization and departmentalization, as well as the different forms organizational structure may take.

The following statements will test your take-away knowledge from this chapter. Do your best to explain each one in the space provided below.

LO.1 Define organizational structure, and relate how organizational structures develop.

LO.2 Describe how specialization and departmentalization help an organization achieve its goals.

LO.3 Distinguish between groups and teams, and identify the types of groups that exist in organizations.

LO.4 Determine how organizations assign responsibility for tasks and delegate authority.

LO.5 Compare and contrast some common forms of organizational structure.

LO.6 Describe how communication occurs in organizations.

Did your answers include the following important points?

LO.1. Define organizational structure, and relate how organizational structures develop.

- Structure is the arrangement or relationship of positions within an organization; it develops when managers assign work activities to work groups and specific individuals and coordinate the diverse activities required to attain organizational objectives.
- Organizational structure evolves to accommodate growth, which requires people with specialized skills.

LO.2. Describe how specialization and departmentalization help an organization achieve its goals.

- Structuring an organization requires that management assign work tasks to specific individuals and groups. Under specialization, managers break labor into small, specialized tasks and assign employees to do a single task, fostering efficiency.
- Departmentalization is the grouping of jobs into working units.
- Businesses may departmentalize by function, product, geographic region, or customer, or they may combine two or more of these.

LO.3. Distinguish between groups and teams and identify the types of groups that exist in organizations.

- A group is two or more persons who communicate, have a common identity, and have a common goal, whereas a team is a small group whose members have complementary skills, a common purpose, goals, and approach, and who hold themselves mutually accountable.
- The major distinction is that individual performance is most important in groups, while collective work group performance counts most in teams.

- Special kinds of groups include task forces, committees, project teams, product-development teams, quality-assurance teams, and self-directed work teams.

LO.4. Determine how organizations assign responsibility for tasks and delegate authority.

- Delegation of authority means assigning tasks to employees and giving them the power to make commitments, use resources, and take whatever actions are necessary to accomplish the tasks.
- The extent to which authority is delegated throughout an organization determines its degree of centralization.

LO.5. Compare and contrast some common forms of organizational structure.

- Line structures have direct lines of authority that extend from the top manager to employees at the lowest level of the organization.
- A multidivisional structure gathers departments into larger groups called divisions. A matrix or project-management structure sets up teams from different departments, thereby creating two or more intersecting lines of authority.

LO.6. Describe how communication occurs in organizations.

- Communication occurs both formally and informally in organizations. Formal communication may be downward, upward, horizontal, and even diagonal.
- Informal communication takes place through friendships and the grapevine.

Practical Application

LO.1.
- The arrangement or relationship of positions within an organization is called _____.
- Work philosophies, values, dress codes, work habits, extracurricular activities, and stories make up _____.

LO.2.
- _____ departmentalization arranges jobs around the needs of various types of customers.
- General Motors is organized into these groups: GMC Trucks, Chevrolet, Buick, and Cadillac. This is called _____ departmentalization.
- Adam Smith illustrated improvements in efficiency through the application of _____.

LO.3.
- A temporary group of employees responsible for bringing about a particular change is a(n) _____.
- A special type of project team formed to devise, design, and implement a new product is a(n) _____.
- A(n) _____ is a group of employees responsible for an entire work process or segment that delivers a product to an internal or external customer.

LO.4.
- An organization with many layers of managers is considered to be _____.

- An organization operating in a complex and unpredictable environment is likely to be _____.
- When the decisions of a company are very risky and low-level managers lack decision-making skills, the company will tend to _____.

LO.5.
- The _____ of organization allows managers to specialize in their area of expertise.
- The _____ organizational form is likely to be complex and expensive.
- _____ permit delegation of decision-making authority, and ensure that better divisions are made faster.

LO.6.
- When managers recognize that a(n) _____ exists, they should use it to their advantage.
- Progress reports and complaints are part of _____ communication.
- When individuals from different organizational units and levels communicate with each other it is called _____ communication.

chapter eight

managing service +
manufacturing options

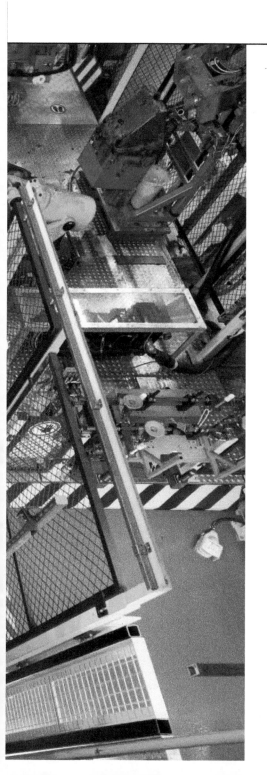

All organizations create products—goods, services, or ideas—for customers. Thus, organizations as diverse as Toyota, Campbell Soup, UPS, and a public hospital share a number of similarities relating to how they transform resources into the products we consume. Most hospitals use similar admission procedures, while online social media companies, like Facebook and Twitter, use their technology and operating systems to create social networking opportunities and sell advertising. Such similarities are to be expected. But even organizations in unrelated industries take similar steps in creating goods or services. The check-in procedures of hotels and commercial airlines are comparable, for example. The way Subway assembles a sandwich and the way GMC assembles a truck are similar (both use automation and an assembly line). These similarities are the result of operations management, the focus of this chapter.

Here, we discuss the role of production or operations management in acquiring and managing the resources necessary to create goods and services. Production and operations management involves planning and designing the processes that will transform those resources into finished products, managing the movement of those resources through the transformation process, and ensuring that the products are of the quality expected by customers.

operations management (OM) the development and administration of the activities involved in transforming resources into goods and services

manufacturing the activities and processes used in making tangible products; also called production

production the activities and processes used in making tangible products; also called manufacturing

operations the activities and processes used in making both tangible and intangible products

inputs the resources—such as labor, money, materials, and energy—that are converted into outputs

outputs the goods, services, and ideas that result from the conversion of inputs

THE NATURE OF OPERATIONS MANAGEMENT

Operations management (OM), the development and administration of the activities involved in transforming resources into goods and services, is of critical importance. Operations managers oversee the transformation process and the planning and designing of operations systems, managing logistics, quality, and productivity. Quality and productivity have become fundamental aspects of operations management because a company that cannot make products of the quality desired by consumers, using resources efficiently and effectively, will not be able to remain in business. OM is the "core" of most organizations because it is responsible for the creation of the organization's goods or services.

Historically, operations management has been called "production" or "manufacturing" primarily because of the view that it was limited to the manufacture of physical goods. Its focus was on methods and techniques required to operate a factory efficiently. The change from "production" to "operations" recognizes the increasing importance of organizations that provide services and ideas. Additionally, the term *operations* represents an interest in viewing the operations function as a whole rather than simply as an analysis of inputs and outputs.

Today, OM includes a wide range of organizational activities and situations outside of manufacturing, such as health care, food service, banking, entertainment, education, transportation, and charity. Thus, we use the terms **manufacturing** and **production** interchangeably to represent the activities and processes used in making *tangible* products, whereas we use the broader term **operations** to describe those processes used in the making of *both tangible and intangible products*. Manufacturing provides tangible products such as Hewlett-Packard's latest printer, and operations provides intangibles such as a stay at Wyndham Hotels and Resorts.

The Transformation Process

At the heart of operations management is the transformation process through which **inputs** (resources such as labor, money, materials, and energy) are converted into **outputs** (goods, services, and ideas). The transformation process combines inputs in predetermined ways using different equipment, administrative procedures, and technology to create a product (Figure 8.1). To ensure that this process generates quality products efficiently, operations managers control the process by taking measurements (feedback) at various points in the transformation process and comparing them to previously established standards. If there is any deviation between the actual and desired outputs, the manager may take some sort of corrective action. All adjustments made to create a satisfying product are a part of the transformation process.

Transformation may take place through one or more processes. In a business that manufactures oak furniture, for example, inputs pass through several processes before being turned into the final outputs—furniture that has been designed to meet the desires of customers (Figure 8.2). The furniture maker must first strip the oak trees of their bark and saw them into appropriate sizes—one step in the transformation process. Next, the firm dries the strips of oak lumber, a second form of transformation. Third, the dried wood is routed into its appropriate shape and made smooth. Fourth, workers assemble and treat the wood pieces, then stain or varnish the piece of assembled furniture. Finally, the completed piece of furniture is stored until it can be shipped

▼**FIGURE 8.1**
The Transformation Process of Operations Management

to customers at the appropriate time. Of course, many businesses choose to eliminate some of these stages by purchasing already processed materials—lumber, for example—or outsourcing some tasks to third-party firms with greater expertise.

Operations Management in Service Businesses

Different types of transformation processes take place in organizations that provide services, such as airlines, colleges, and most nonprofit organizations. An airline transforms inputs such as employees, time, money, and equipment through processes such as booking flights, flying airplanes, maintaining equipment, and training crews. The output of these processes is flying passengers and/or packages to their destinations. In a nonprofit organization like Habitat for Humanity, inputs such as money, materials, information, and volunteer time and labor are used to transform raw materials into homes for needy families. In this setting, transformation processes include fund-raising and promoting the cause in order to gain new volunteers and donations of supplies, as well as pouring concrete, raising walls, and setting roofs. Transformation processes occur in all organizations, regardless of what they produce or

▼**FIGURE 8.2**
Inputs, Outputs, and Transformation Processes in the Manufacture of Oak Furniture

Inputs	Transformation	Outputs
oak trees	cutting or	oak furniture
labor	sawing	
information/	routing	
knowledge	measuring	
stain or varnish	assembling	
router/saw	staining/varnishing	
warehouse space/	storing	
time		

their objectives. For most organizations, the ultimate objective is for the produced outputs to be worth more than the combined costs of the inputs.

Unlike tangible goods, services are effectively actions or performances that must be directed toward the consumers who use them. Thus, there is a significant customer-contact component to most services. Examples of high-contact services include health care, real estate, tax preparation, and food service. At the Inn at Little Washington in Washington, Virginia, for example, food servers are critical to delivering the perfect dining experience expected by the most discriminating diners. Wait staff are expected not only to be courteous, but

SHELL USES NEW REFINERY TO SUPPORT SUSTAINABILITY

Royal Dutch Shell PLC has partnered with Qatar (a country in the Middle East) to create a $19 billion refinery that may bring the company to the forefront of sustainability. The plant, Pearl GTL (gas-to-liquids), is designed to transform natural gas into odor-free, pollutant-free fuel. The venture, which is the largest GTL project to date, has the potential for high returns in a flooded natural gas market. More importantly, the development of a new transformation process has the potential to create a new natural gas.

Shell has been working with GTL for almost four decades and believes it can

succeed with Pearl. Lower natural gas prices will likely spur demand, particularly as GTL fuel is roughly half the cost of crude oil. GTL fuel is also purer than traditional crude, appealing to more environmentally conscious consumers and businesses.

Yet despite the benefits of GTL fuel, some have criticized the process. For instance, the GTL process is extremely expensive. Critics feel that alternative procedures are more cost-effective. In addition, the GTL process consumes a great deal of energy, calling into question the effectiveness of its environmental sustainability. Others argue that GTL is profitable only when oil prices are high and that Shell has an equal chance of winning or losing on the venture.

However, Shell is optimistic. Not only does it feel that Pearl will pay itself off in five years, but it also has the added bonus

of experience. Shell has operated a smaller GTL plant in Malaysia since 1993 and has already worked through many of the glitches in the GTL process. Finally, Qatar is rich in labor and energy reserves; if this partnership proves fruitful, Shell may have access to more profitable relationships in the future. Creating a more sustainable future for energy products can be a significant contribution to society.[1]

Discussion Questions

1. Why is the development of the new transformation process GTL (gas-to-liquids) so important?

2. What are some of the production or operational barriers that Shell must overcome in order to make GTL successful?

3. Should Shell continue the GTL project if it fails to pay off in five years?

THE ACTUAL PERFORMANCE OF THE SERVICE TYPICALLY OCCURS AT THE POINT OF CONSUMPTION.

also to demonstrate a detailed knowledge of the restaurant's offerings, and even to assess the mood of guests in order to respond to diners appropriately.[2] Low-contact services, such as online auction services like eBay, often have a strong high-tech component.

Regardless of the level of customer contact, service businesses strive to provide a standardized process, and technology offers an interface that creates an automatic and structured response. The ideal service provider will be high-tech and high-touch. JetBlue, for example, strives to maintain an excellent website; friendly, helpful customer contact; and satellite TV service at every seat on each plane. Thus, service organizations must build their operations around good execution, which comes from hiring and training excellent employees, developing flexible systems, customizing services, and maintaining adjustable capacity to deal with fluctuating demand.[3]

Another challenge related to service operations is that the output is generally intangible and even perishable. Few services can be saved, stored, resold, or returned.[4] A seat on an airline or a table in a restaurant, for example, cannot be sold or used at a later date. Because of the perishability of services, it can be extremely difficult for service providers to accurately estimate the demand in order to match the right supply of a service. If an airline overestimates demand, for example, it will still have to fly each plane even with empty seats. The flight costs the same regardless of whether it is 50 percent full or 100 percent full, but the former will result in much higher costs per passenger. If the airline underestimates demand, the result can be long lines of annoyed customers or even the necessity of bumping some customers off an overbooked flight.

Businesses that manufacture tangible goods and those that provide services or ideas are similar yet different. For example,

Although service organizations tend to vary depending on the service provider, businesses strive to standardize operations to ensure a high level of quality. The wait staff at this hotel wear uniforms and are trained to behave a certain way when interacting with customers.

both types of organizations must make design and operating decisions. Most goods are manufactured prior to purchase, but most services are performed after purchase. Flight attendants at Southwest Airlines, hotel service personnel, and even the New Orleans Saints football team engage in performances that are a part of the total product. Though manufacturers and service providers often perform similar activities, they also differ in several respects. We can classify these differences in five basic ways.

Nature and Consumption of Output

First, manufacturers and service providers differ in the nature and consumption of their output. For example, the term *manufacturer* implies a firm that makes tangible products. A service provider, on the other hand, produces more intangible outputs such as U.S. Postal Service delivery of priority mail or a business stay in a Hyatt hotel. As mentioned earlier, the very nature of the service provider's product requires a higher degree of customer contact. Moreover, the actual performance of the service typically occurs at the point of consumption. At the Hyatt, the business traveler may evaluate in-room communications and the restaurant. Automakers, on the other hand, can separate the production of a car from its actual use. Manufacturing, then, can occur in an isolated environment, away from the customer. On the other hand, service providers, because of their need for customer contact, are often more limited than manufacturers in selecting work methods, assigning jobs, scheduling work, and exercising control over operations. At FedEx, the Quality Improvement Process (QIP) includes sayings such as "Do it right the first time," and "Make the first time you do it the only time anyone has to do it." The quality of the service experience is often controlled by a service contact employee. However, some hospitals are studying the manufacturing processes and quality control mechanisms applied in the automotive industry in an effort to improve their service quality. By analyzing work processes to find unnecessary steps to eliminate and using teams to identify and address problems as soon as they occur, these hospitals are slashing patient waiting times, decreasing inventories of wheelchairs, readying operating rooms sooner, and generally moving patients through their hospital visit more quickly, with fewer errors, and at a lower cost.[5]

Uniformity of Inputs

A second way to classify differences between manufacturers and service providers has to do with the uniformity of inputs. Manufacturers typically have more control over the amount of variability of the resources they use than do service providers. For example, each customer calling Fidelity Investments is likely to require different services due to differing needs, whereas many of the tasks required to manufacture a Ford Focus are the same across each unit of output. Consequently, the products of service organizations tend to be more "customized" than those of their manufacturing counterparts. Consider, for example, a haircut versus a bottle of shampoo. The haircut is much more

Subway's inputs are sandwich components such as bread, tomatoes, and lettuce, while its outputs are customized sandwiches.

likely to incorporate your specific desires (customization) than is the bottle of shampoo.

Uniformity of Output

Manufacturers and service providers also differ in the uniformity of their output, the final product. Because of the human element inherent in providing services, each service tends to be performed differently. Not all grocery checkers, for example, wait on customers in the same way. If a barber or stylist performs 15 haircuts in a day, it is unlikely that any two of them will be exactly the same. Consequently, human and technological elements associated with a service can result in a different day-to-day or even hour-to-hour performance of that service. The service experience can even vary at McDonald's or Burger King despite the fact that the two chains employ very similar procedures and processes. Moreover, no two customers are exactly alike in their perception of the service experience. Health care offers another excellent example of this challenge. Every diagnosis, treatment, and surgery varies because every individual is different. In manufacturing, the high degree of automation available allows manufacturers to generate uniform outputs and, thus, the operations are more effective and efficient. For example, we would expect every Movado or Rolex watch to maintain very high standards of quality and performance.

Labor Required A fourth point of difference is the amount of labor required to produce an output. Service providers are generally more labor-intensive (require more labor) because of the high level of customer contact, perishability of the output (must be consumed immediately), and high degree of variation of inputs and outputs (customization). For example, Adecco provides temporary support personnel. Each temporary worker's performance determines Adecco's product quality. A manufacturer, on the other hand, is likely to be more capital-intensive because of the machinery and technology used in the mass production of highly similar goods. For instance, it would take a considerable investment for Nokia to make a digital phone that has a battery with longer life.

Measurement of Productivity The final distinction between service providers and manufacturers involves the measurement of productivity for each output produced. For manufacturers, measuring productivity is fairly straightforward because of the tangibility of the output and its high degree of uniformity. For the service provider, variations in demand (for example, higher demand for air travel in some seasons than in others), variations in service requirements from job to job, and the intangibility of the product make productivity measurement more difficult. Consider, for example, how much easier it is to measure the productivity of employees involved in the production of Intel computer processors as opposed to serving the needs of Prudential Securities' clients.

It is convenient and simple to think of organizations as being either manufacturers or service providers as in the preceding discussion. In reality, however, most organizations are a combination of the two, with both tangible and intangible qualities embodied in what they produce. For example, Porsche provides customer services such as toll-free hotlines and warranty protection, while banks may sell checks and other tangible products that complement their primarily intangible product offering. Thus, we consider "products" to include both tangible physical goods as well as intangible service offerings. It is the level of tangibility of its principal product that tends to classify a company as either a manufacturer or a service provider. From an OM standpoint, this level of tangibility greatly influences the nature of the company's operational processes and procedures.

PLANNING AND DESIGNING OPERATIONS SYSTEMS

Before a company can produce any product, it must first decide what it will produce and for what group of customers. It must then determine what processes it will use to make these products as well as the facilities it needs to produce them. These decisions comprise operations planning. Although planning was once the sole realm of the production and operations department, today's successful companies involve all departments within an organization, particularly marketing and research and development, in these decisions.

Planning the Product

Before making any product, a company first must determine what consumers want and then design a product to satisfy that want. Most companies use marketing research (discussed in Chapter 11) to determine the kinds of goods and services to provide and the features they must possess. Twitter and Facebook provide new opportunities for businesses to discover what consumers want, then design the product accordingly. Cordarounds.com, a clothing company based in San Francisco, found that many people in California bike to work. Based on information gathered on Twitter, the company developed a line of bike-ready clothing lined with reflective material. When bike commuters roll up their pant legs to ride home, the reflective material helps them stay safe even when they are riding home after dark. Cordarounds also uses Google's AdWords, another digital media source, to advertise affordably. Cordarounds began as a small company and is growing rapidly as more people become concerned about the environment and choose biking over driving.[6] Marketing research can also help gauge the demand for a product and how much consumers are willing to pay for it. But when a market's environment changes, firms have to be flexible.

Developing a product can be a lengthy, expensive process. For example, in the automobile industry, developing the new technology for night vision, bumper-mounted sonar systems that make parking easier, and a satellite service that locates and analyzes car problems has been a lengthy, expensive process. Most companies work to reduce development time and costs. For example, through Web collaboration, faucet manufacturer Moen reduced the time required to take an idea to a finished product in stores to just 16 months, a drop of 33 percent.[7] Once management has developed an idea for a product that customers will buy, it must then plan how to produce the product.

Within a company, the engineering or research and development department is charged with turning a product idea into a workable design that can be produced economically. In smaller companies, a single individual (perhaps the owner) may be solely responsible for this crucial activity. Regardless of who is responsible for product design, planning does not stop with a blueprint for a product or a description of a service; it must

standardization the making of identical interchangeable components or products	**modular design** the creation of an item in self-contained units, or modules, that can be combined or interchanged to create different products	**customization** making products to meet a particular customer's needs or wants	**capacity** the maximum load that an organizational unit can carry or operate

also work out efficient production of the product to ensure that enough is available to satisfy consumer demand. How does a lawn mower company transform steel, aluminum, and other materials into a mower design that satisfies consumer and environmental requirements? Operations managers must plan for the types and quantities of materials needed to produce the product, the skills and quantity of people needed to make the product, and the actual processes through which the inputs must pass in their transformation to outputs.

Designing the Operations Processes

Before a firm can begin production, it must first determine the appropriate method of transforming resources into the desired product. Often, consumers' specific needs and desires dictate a process. Customer needs, for example, require that all 3/4-inch bolts have the same basic thread size, function, and quality; if they did not, engineers and builders could not rely on 3/4-inch bolts in their construction projects. A bolt manufacturer, then, will likely use a standardized process so that every 3/4-inch bolt produced is like every other one. On the other hand, a bridge often must be customized so that it is appropriate for the site and expected load; furthermore, the bridge must be constructed on site rather than in a factory. Typically, products are designed to be manufactured by one of three processes: standardization, modular design, or customization.

Standardization Most firms that manufacture products in large quantities for many customers have found that they can make them cheaper and faster by standardizing designs. **Standardization** is making identical, interchangeable components or even complete products. With standardization, a customer may not get exactly what he or she wants, but the product generally costs less than a custom-designed product. Television sets, ballpoint pens, and tortilla chips are standardized products; most are manufactured on an assembly line. Standardization speeds up production and quality control and reduces production costs. And, as in the example of the 3/4-inch bolts, standardization provides consistency so that customers who need certain products to function uniformly all the time will get a product that meets their expectations. As a result of its entry into the World Trade Organization, China promoted the standardization of agricultural production across the country, resulting in increased agricultural production.

Modular Design **Modular design** involves building an item in self-contained units, or modules, that can be combined or interchanged to create different products. Personal computers, for example, are generally composed of a number of components—CPU case, motherboard, chips, hard drives, graphics card, and so on—that can be installed in different configurations to meet the customer's needs. Because many modular components are produced as integrated units, the failure of any portion of a modular component usually means replacing the entire component. Modular design allows products to be repaired quickly, thus reducing the cost of labor, but the component itself is expensive, raising the cost of repair materials. Many automobile manufacturers use modular design in the production process. Manufactured homes are built on a modular design and often cost about one-fourth the cost of a conventionally built house.

Customization **Customization** is making products to meet a particular customer's needs or wants. Products produced in this way are generally unique. Such products include repair services, photocopy services, custom artwork, jewelry, and furniture, as well as large-scale products such as bridges, ships, and computer software. Custom designs are used in communications and service products. A Web-based design service, myemma.com, creates a custom template using a company's logo and colors to create a unique page for a website. It also provides tools for interacting with customers and tracking deliveries.[8] Ship design is another industry that uses customization. Builders generally design and build each ship to meet the needs of the customer who will use it. Delta Marine Industries, for example, custom-builds each luxury yacht to the customer's exact specifications and preferences for things like helicopter garages, golf courses, and swimming pools. Mass customization relates to making products that meet the needs or wants of a large number of individual customers. The customer can select the model, size, color, style, or design of the product. Dell can customize a computer with the exact configuration that fits a customer's needs. Services such as fitness programs and travel packages can also be custom designed for a large number of individual customers. For both goods and services, customers get to make choices and have options to determine the final product.

Planning Capacity

Planning the operational processes for the organization involves two important areas: capacity planning and facilities planning. The term **capacity** basically refers to the maximum load that an organizational unit can carry or operate. The unit of measurement may be a worker or machine, a department, a branch, or even an entire plant. Maximum capacity can be stated in terms of the inputs or outputs provided. For example, an electric plant might state plant capacity in terms of the maximum number of kilowatt-hours that can be produced without

fixed-position layout a layout that brings all resources required to create the product to a central location

project organization a company using a fixed-position layout because it is typically involved in large, complex projects such as construction or exploration

process layout a layout that organizes the transformation process into departments that group related processes

intermittent organizations organizations that deal with products of a lesser magnitude than do project organizations; their products are not necessarily unique but possess a significant number of differences

product layout a layout requiring that production be broken down into relatively simple tasks assigned to workers, who are usually positioned along an assembly line

causing a power outage, while a restaurant might state capacity in terms of the maximum number of customers who can be effectively—comfortably and courteously—served at any one particular time.

Efficiently planning the organization's capacity needs is an important process for the operations manager. Capacity levels that fall short can result in unmet demand, and consequently, lost customers. On the other hand, when there is more capacity available than needed, operating costs are driven up needlessly due to unused and often expensive resources. To avoid such situations, organizations must accurately forecast demand and then plan capacity based on these forecasts. Another reason for the importance of efficient capacity planning has to do with long-term commitment of resources. Often, once a capacity decision—such as factory size—has been implemented, it is very difficult to change the decision without incurring substantial costs. Large utilities companies have come to realize that although change can be expensive, not adjusting to future demand and

?

DID YOU KNOW?

Hershey's has the production capacity to make more than 80 million chocolate kisses per day.[9]

stakeholder desires will be more expensive in the long run. For this reason, utilities companies like PNM in New Mexico have made a commitment to including more renewable energy in their supply mix, complying with ISO 14001 emissions guidelines for power plants, and taking a pro-cap-and-trade stance.[10]

Planning Facilities

Once a company knows what process it will use to create its products, it then can design and build an appropriate facility in which to make them. Many products are manufactured in factories, but others are produced in stores, at home, or where the product ultimately will be used. Companies must decide where to locate their operations facilities, what layout is best for producing their particular product, and even what technology to apply to the transformation process.

Many firms are developing both a traditional organization for customer contact as well as a virtual organization. Charles Schwab Corporation, a securities brokerage and investment company, maintains traditional offices and has developed complete telephone and Internet services for customers. Through its website, investors can obtain personal investment information and trade securities over the Internet without leaving their home or office.

Apple stores are designed to make the most efficient use of space. The layout of the stores allows customers to test its products before purchasing.

Facility Location Where to locate a firm's facilities is a significant question because, once the decision has been made and implemented, the firm must live with it due to the high costs involved. When a company decides to relocate or open a facility at a new location, it must pay careful attention to factors such as proximity to market, availability of raw materials, availability of transportation, availability of power, climatic influences, availability of labor, community characteristics (quality of life), and taxes and inducements. Inducements and tax reductions have become an increasingly important criterion in recent years. To increase production and to provide incentives for small startups, many states are offering tax inducements for solar companies. State governments are willing to forego some tax revenue in exchange for job growth, getting in on a burgeoning industry as well as the good publicity generated by the company. In a very solar-friendly state like Colorado, companies may get tax reductions for starting production, and consumers receive additional rebates for installing solar systems in their homes and businesses.[11] The facility-location decision is complex because it involves the evaluation of many factors, some of which cannot be measured with precision. Because of the long-term impact of the decision, however, it is one that cannot be taken lightly.

Facility Layout Arranging the physical layout of a facility is a complex, highly technical task. Some industrial architects specialize in the design and layout of certain types of businesses. There are three basic layouts: fixed-position, process, and product.

A company using a **fixed-position layout** brings all resources required to create the product to a central location. The product—perhaps an office building, house, hydroelectric plant, or bridge—does not move. A company using a fixed-position layout may be called a **project organization** because it is typically involved in large, complex projects such as construction or exploration. Project organizations generally make a unique product, rely on highly skilled labor, produce very few units, and have high production costs per unit.

Firms that use a **process layout** organize the transformation process into departments that group related processes. A metal fabrication plant, for example, may have a cutting department, a drilling department, and a polishing department. A hospital

products produced on assembly lines are automobiles, television sets, vacuum cleaners, toothpaste, and meals from a cafeteria. Continuous manufacturing organizations using a product layout are characterized by the standardized products they produce, the large number of units produced, and the relatively low unit cost of production.

Many companies actually use a combination of layout designs. For example, an automobile manufacturer may rely on an assembly line (product layout) but may also use a process layout to manufacture parts.

Technology Every industry has a basic, underlying technology that dictates the nature of its transformation process. The steel industry continually tries to improve steelmaking techniques. The health care industry performs research into medical technologies and pharmaceuticals to improve the quality of health care service. Two developments

continuous manufacturing organizations companies that use continuously running assembly lines, creating products with many similar characteristics

computer-assisted design (CAD) the design of components, products, and processes on computers instead of on paper

computer-assisted manufacturing (CAM) manufacturing that employs specialized computer systems to actually guide and control the transformation processes

> Every industry has a basic, underlying technology that dictates the nature of its transformation process.

may have an X-ray unit, an obstetrics unit, and so on. These types of organizations are sometimes called **intermittent organizations**, which deal with products of a lesser magnitude than do project organizations, and their products are not necessarily unique but possess a significant number of differences. Doctors, makers of custom-made cabinets, commercial printers, and advertising agencies are intermittent organizations because they tend to create products to customers' specifications and produce relatively few units of each product. Because of the low level of output, the cost per unit of product is generally high.

The **product layout** requires that production be broken down into relatively simple tasks assigned to workers, who are usually positioned along an assembly line. Workers remain in one location, and the product moves from one worker to another. Each person in turn performs his or her required tasks or activities. Companies that use assembly lines are usually known as **continuous manufacturing organizations**, so named because once they are set up, they run continuously, creating products with many similar characteristics. Examples of

that have strongly influenced the operations of many businesses are computers and robotics.

Computers have been used for decades and on a relatively large scale since IBM introduced its 650 series in the late 1950s. The operations function makes great use of computers in all phases of the transformation process. **Computer-assisted design (CAD)**, for example, helps engineers design components, products, and processes on the computer instead of on paper. **Computer-assisted manufacturing (CAM)** goes a step further, employing specialized computer systems to actually guide and control the transformation processes. Such systems can monitor the transformation process, gathering information about the equipment used to produce the products and about the product itself as it goes from one stage of the transformation process to the next. The computer provides information to an operator who may, if necessary, take corrective action. In some highly automated systems, the computer itself can take corrective action. At Dell's OptiPlex Plant, electronic instructions are sent to double-decker conveyor belts that speed computer components to assembly stations. Two-member teams

flexible manufacturing the direction of machinery by computers to adapt to different versions of similar operations

computer-integrated manufacturing (CIM) a complete system that designs products, manages machines and materials, and controls the operations function

are told by computers which PC or server to build, with initial assembly taking only three to four minutes. Then more electronic commands move the products (more than 20,000 machines on a typical day) to a finishing area to be customized, boxed, and sent to waiting delivery trucks.

Using **flexible manufacturing**, computers can direct machinery to adapt to different versions of similar operations. For example, with instructions from a computer, one machine can be programmed to carry out its function for several different versions of an engine without shutting down the production line for refitting.

Robots are also becoming increasingly useful in the transformation process. These "steel-collar" workers have become particularly important in industries such as nuclear power, hazardous-waste disposal, ocean research, and space construction and maintenance, in which human lives would otherwise be at risk. Robots are used in numerous applications by companies around the world. Many assembly operations—cars, television sets, telephones, stereo equipment, and numerous other products—depend on industrial robots. The Robotic Industries Association estimates that about 196,000 robots are now at work in U.S. factories, making the United States one of the two largest users of robotics, second only to Japan.[12] Researchers continue to make more sophisticated robots, and

some speculate that in the future robots will not be limited to space programs and production and operations, but will also be able to engage in farming, laboratory research, and even household activities. Moreover, robotics are increasingly being used in the medical field. There are an estimated 1 million robots being used in manufacturing around the world, most of them in high-tech industries. They now help doctors perform an estimated 86 percent of prostate cancer surgeries in the United States.[13]

When all these technologies—CAD/CAM, flexible manufacturing, robotics, computer systems, and more—are integrated, the result is **computer-integrated manufacturing (CIM)**, a complete system that designs products, manages machines and materials, and controls the operations function. Companies adopt CIM to boost productivity and quality and reduce costs. Such technology, and computers in particular, will continue to make strong inroads into operations on two fronts—one dealing with the technology involved in manufacturing and one dealing with the administrative functions and processes used by operations managers. The operations manager must be willing to work with computers and other forms of technology and to develop a high degree of computer literacy.

Sustainability and Manufacturing

Manufacturing and operations systems are moving quickly to establish environmental sustainability and minimize negative impact on the natural environment. Sustainability deals with reducing the consumption of resources and the long-term well-being of the planet, including natural entities and the interactions of individuals, organizations, and businesses. Sustainability issues are becoming increasingly important to stakeholders and consumers, as they pertain to the future health of the planet. Some sustainability issues include pollution of the land, air, and water, climate change, waste management, deforestation, urban sprawl, protection of biodiversity, and genetically modified foods.

For example, Walmart is working to make its stores and products more environmentally friendly. Walmart has created a series of broad environmental goals, striving to eventually create zero waste, to run entirely on renewable energy, and to sell sustainable products. The company works with suppliers to reduce cardboard and plastic packaging. Walmart already increased the efficiency of its truck fleet by 38 percent and intends to double its efficiency by October 2015. Walmart is also changing its lighting and other electrical use for maximum efficiency. All of these initiatives relate to making operations greener, contributing to environmental sustainability, providing savings, and being a role model for other businesses.[14]

While Walmart illustrates green initiatives in operations, New Belgium Brewing illustrates green initiatives in operations and manufacturing. New Belgium was the first brewery

The outdoor clothing company Patagonia is always looking for a greener way to design, produce, and recycle its products. The company's mission statement: Build the best product, cause no unnecessary harm, and use business to inspire and implement solutions to the environmental crisis.

to adopt 100 percent wind-powered electricity, reducing carbon emissions by 1,800 metric tons a year. It uses a steam condenser to capture hot water to be reused for boiling the next batch of barley and hops. Then the steam is redirected to heat the floor tiles and de-ice the loading docks in cold Colorado weather. Used barley and hops are given to local farmers to feed cattle. The company is moving to aluminum cans because they can be recycled an infinite number of times, and recycling one can saves enough electricity to run a television for three hours. The company has won an award from the Environmental Protection Agency and is a role model for other businesses.

Walmart and New Belgium Brewing demonstrate that reducing waste, recycling, conserving, and using renewable energy not only protect the environment, but can also gain the support of stakeholders. Green operations and manufacturing can improve a firm's reputation along with customer and employee loyalty, leading to improved profits.

Much of the movement to green manufacturing and operations is the belief that global warming and climate change must decline. The McKinsey Global Institute (MGI) says that just by investing in existing technologies, the world's

MANAGING THE SUPPLY CHAIN

A major function of operations is **supply chain management**, which refers to connecting and integrating all parties or members of the distribution system in order to satisfy customers.[18] Also called logistics, supply chain management includes all the activities involved in obtaining and managing raw materials and component parts, managing finished products, packaging them, and getting them to customers. Sunny Delight had to quickly recreate its supply chain after spinning off from Procter & Gamble. This means it had to develop ordering, shipping, and billing, as well as warehouse management systems and transportation, so it could focus on growing and managing the Sunny Delight brand.[19] The supply chain integrates firms such as raw material suppliers, manufacturers, retailers, and ultimate consumers into a seamless flow of information and products.[20] Some aspects of logistics (warehousing, packaging, distributing) are so closely linked

supply chain management connecting and integrating all parties or members of the distribution system in order to satisfy customers

purchasing the buying of all the materials needed by the organization; also called procurement

> "A major function of operations is supply chain management, which refers to connecting and integrating all parties or members of the distribution system in order to satisfy customers."

energy use could be reduced by 50 percent by the year 2020. Just creating green buildings and higher mileage cars could yield $900 billion in savings per year by 2020.[15] Companies like General Motors are adapting to stakeholder demands for greater sustainability by producing smaller and more fuel-efficient cars. For example, the Chevy Volt can run for up to 40 miles on one overnight charge before switching to a gas-powered generator. The Volt is also a FlexFuel vehicle, which means that it can use either traditional gasoline or E85 ethanol, which some people believe is better for the environment.[16] Green products produced through green operations and manufacturing are our future. A report authored by the Center for American Progress cites ways that cities and local governments can play a role. For example, Los Angeles plans to save the city utility costs by retrofitting hundreds of city buildings while creating a green careers training program for low-income residents. Newark, New Jersey, and Richmond, California, also have green jobs training programs. Albuquerque, New Mexico, was the first city to sign on to a pledge to build a green economy as part of its efforts to create green jobs to stimulate the city's economy.[17] Government initiatives provide space for businesses to innovate their green operations and manufacturing.

with marketing that we will discuss them in Chapter 12. In this section, we look at purchasing, managing inventory, outsourcing, and scheduling, which are vital tasks in the transformation of raw materials into finished goods. To illustrate logistics, consider a hypothetical small business—we'll call it Rushing Water Canoes Inc.—that manufactures aluminum canoes, which it sells primarily to sporting goods stores and river-rafting expeditions. Our company also makes paddles and helmets, but the focus of the following discussion is the manufacture of the company's quality canoes as they proceed through the logistics process.

Purchasing

Purchasing, also known as procurement, is the buying of all the materials needed by the organization. The purchasing department aims to obtain items of the desired quality in the right quantities at the lowest possible cost. Rushing Water Canoes, for example, must procure not only aluminum and other raw materials, and various canoe parts and components, but also machines and equipment, manufacturing supplies (oil, electricity, and so on), and office supplies in order to make its canoes. People in the purchasing department locate and evaluate suppliers of these items. They must constantly be on the lookout for new materials or parts that will do a better job or

inventory all raw materials, components, completed or partially completed products, and pieces of equipment a firm uses

inventory control the process of determining how many supplies and goods are needed and keeping track of quantities on hand, where each item is, and who is responsible for it

economic order quantity (EOQ) model a model that identifies the optimum number of items to order to minimize the costs of managing (ordering, storing, and using) them

just-in-time (JIT) inventory management a technique using smaller quantities of materials that arrive "just in time" for use in the transformation process and therefore require less storage space and other inventory management expense

cost less than those currently being used. The purchasing function can be quite complex and is one area made much easier and more efficient by technological advances.

Not all companies purchase all of the materials needed to create their products. Oftentimes, they can make some components more economically and efficiently than can an outside supplier. Coors, for example, manufactures its own cans at a subsidiary plant. On the other hand, firms sometimes find that it is uneconomical to make or purchase an item, and instead arrange to lease it from another organization. Some airlines, for example, lease airplanes rather than buy them. Whether to purchase, make, or lease a needed item generally depends on cost, as well as on product availability and supplier reliability.

Managing Inventory

Once the items needed to create a product have been procured, some provision has to be made for storing them until they are needed. Every raw material, component, completed or partially completed product, and piece of equipment a firm uses—its **inventory**—must be accounted for, or controlled. There are three basic types of inventory. *Finished-goods inventory* includes those products that are ready for sale, such as a fully assembled automobile ready to ship to a dealer. *Work-in-process inventory* consists of those products that are partly completed or are in some stage of the transformation process. At McDonald's, a cooking hamburger represents work-in-process inventory because it must go through several more stages before it can be sold to a customer. *Raw materials inventory* includes all the materials that have been purchased to be used as inputs for making other products. Nuts and bolts are raw materials for an automobile manufacturer, while hamburger patties, vegetables, and buns are raw materials for the fast-food restaurant. Our fictional Rushing Water Canoes has an inventory of materials for making canoes, paddles, and helmets, as well as its inventory of finished products for sale to consumers. **Inventory control** is the process of determining how many supplies and goods are needed and keeping track of quantities on hand, where each item is, and who is responsible for it.

Operations management must be closely coordinated with inventory control. The production of televisions, for example, cannot be planned without some knowledge of the availability of all the necessary materials—the chassis, picture tubes, color guns, and so forth. Also, each item held in inventory—any

We won't let your chicken go bad.

Once a chicken goes bad, there's no turning back. So, if you ship or receive fish, chicken, beef, or virtually any food product, you need to know FAC.

Food service logistics is our business... our only business.

We're so good at serving the food industry, that we not only save our customers millions of

FAC Food Service Logistics

800.285.7004
www.faclogistics.com

dollars every year, we also save the day. Fish never tastes like tires. Beef never travels second class. Best of all, good chicken never goes bad.

Call us today for a review that will demonstrate all the benefits of dealing with a food service logistics specialist. Call customer service at 800.285.7004.

FAC Food Service Logistics helps manage the supply chain and inventory of food companies in the United States so their products—chicken included—arrive on time and unspoiled.

type of inventory—carries with it a cost. For example, storing fully assembled televisions in a warehouse to sell to a dealer at a future date requires not only the use of space, but also the purchase of insurance to cover any losses that might occur due to fire or other unforeseen events.

Inventory managers spend a great deal of time trying to determine the proper inventory level for each item. The answer to the question of how many units to hold in inventory depends on variables such as the usage rate of the item, the cost of maintaining the item in inventory, future costs of inventory and other procedures associated with ordering or making the item, and the cost of the item itself. For example, the price of copper has fluctuated between $1.50 and $4 a pound over the last five years. Firms using copper wiring for construction, copper pipes for plumbing, and other industries requiring copper have to analyze the trade-offs between inventory costs and expected changes in the price of copper. Several approaches may be used to determine how many units of a given item should be procured at one time and when that procurement should take place.

The Economic Order Quantity Model To control the number of items maintained in inventory, managers need to determine how much of any given item they should order. One popular approach is the **economic order quantity (EOQ) model**, which identifies the optimum number of items to order to minimize the costs of managing (ordering, storing, and using) them.

Just-in-Time Inventory Management An increasingly popular technique is **just-in-time (JIT) inventory**

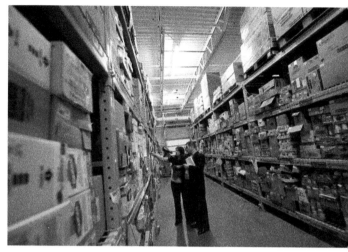

Managing inventory involves finding the right balance between excess inventory and not enough inventory. While too much inventory will increase storage costs, companies that have an inventory shortage miss out on additional sales.

management, which eliminates waste by using smaller quantities of materials that arrive "just in time" for use in the transformation process and therefore require less storage space and other inventory management expense. JIT minimizes inventory by providing an almost continuous flow of items from suppliers to the production facility. Many U.S. companies, including Hewlett-Packard, IBM, and Harley-Davidson, have adopted JIT to reduce costs and boost efficiency.

TRADER JOE'S: SECRETS OF SUCCESS

First founded in 1967 in California, Trader Joe's is composed of 344 stores in 25 states plus the District of Columbia. Despite its large reach, Trader Joe's exudes the same neighborhood store atmosphere that it did back in 1967. Trader Joe's excellent operations and customer service has generated a loyal customer following that has made it a success.

One of Trader Joe's biggest assets is uniqueness. In addition to maintaining a neighborhood store feel, Trader Joe's maintains smaller facilities and product lines than comparable stores—a deliberate operational move to create its specialty image. Trader Joe's stocks about 4,000 items compared to the 50,000 stocked by

the typical grocery store. Inventory control has been a key advantage to reducing costs and focusing on a limited number of quality products. While many markets sell as many as 50 selections of one food item, Trader Joe's sells only a few. With sales of roughly $8 billion, Trader Joe's also sets itself apart with its private label products. Today, 80 percent of company sales come from private label items.

Additionally, Trader Joe's excels at quality and supplier relationships. It employs four product developers who travel the world in search of best product/price combinations. Suppliers covet contracts with Trader Joe's, which charges less in fees and is known for on-time payments. Trader Joe's has vowed to sell only sustainable seafood by 2012 and refuses to carry products containing genetically modified ingredients. Its responsible measures make it a

regular on the *Ethisphere* "World's Most Ethical Companies" list. Trader Joe's has also crafted its distribution process to create efficiency and reduce costs. It expands only into areas that can support this streamlined distribution system. With its popularity continuing to rise, customers seem impressed by the way Trader Joe's is redefining the grocery shopping experience.[21]

Discussion Questions

1. How does inventory control contribute to Trader Joe's success?

2. Why do supplier relationships and a focus on price/quality relations help create loyal Trader Joe's customers?

3. How does being rated as one of the world's most ethical companies contribute to Trader Joe's success?

material-requirements planning (MRP) a planning system that schedules the precise quantity of materials needed to make the product

routing the sequence of operations through which the product must pass

scheduling the assignment of required tasks to departments or even specific machines, workers, or teams

Let's say that Rushing Water Canoes uses 20 units of aluminum from a supplier per day. Traditionally, its inventory manager might order enough for one month at a time: 440 units per order (20 units per day times 22 workdays per month). The expense of such a large inventory could be considerable because of the cost of insurance coverage, recordkeeping, rented storage space, and so on. The just-in-time approach would reduce these costs because aluminum would be purchased in smaller quantities, perhaps in lot sizes of 20, which the supplier would deliver once a day. Of course, for such an approach to be effective, the supplier must be extremely reliable and relatively close to the production facility.

Material-Requirements Planning Another inventory management technique is **material-requirements planning (MRP)**, a planning system that schedules the precise quantity

or other tasks to independent companies, often overseas. Many companies elect to outsource some aspects of their operations to companies that can provide these products more efficiently, at a lower cost, and with greater customer satisfaction. Globalization has put pressure on supply chain managers to improve speed and balance resources against competitive pressures. Companies outsourcing to China, in particular, face heavy regulation, high transportation costs, inadequate facilities, and unpredictable supply chain execution. Therefore, suppliers need to provide useful, timely, and accurate information about every aspect of the quality requirements, schedules, and solutions to dealing with problems. For example, Chinese suppliers took responsibility for the lead paint on children's toys crisis in the United States, but it was an overall management and supply chain system failure that permitted these toxic toys to be sold in U.S. stores.[22]

Many high-tech firms have outsourced the production of chips, computers, and telecom equipment to Asian companies. The hourly labor costs in countries such as China, India, and Vietnam are far less than in the United States, Europe, or even Mexico. These developing countries have improved their manufacturing capabilities, infrastructure, and technical and business skills, making them more attractive regions for global sourcing. On the other hand, the cost of outsourcing halfway around the world

> ## Many executives view outsourcing as an innovative way to boost productivity and remain competitive against low-wage offshore factories.

of materials needed to make the product. The basic components of MRP are a master production schedule, a bill of materials, and an inventory status file. At Rushing Water Canoes, for example, the inventory-control manager will look at the production schedule to determine how many canoes the company plans to make. He or she will then prepare a bill of materials—a list of all the materials needed to make that quantity of canoes. Next, the manager will determine the quantity of these items that RWC already holds in inventory (to avoid ordering excess materials) and then develop a schedule for ordering and accepting delivery of the right quantity of materials to satisfy the firm's needs. Because of the large number of parts and materials that go into a typical production process, MRP must be done on a computer. It can be, and often is, used in conjunction with just-in-time inventory management.

Outsourcing

Increasingly, outsourcing has become a component of supply chain management in operations. As we mentioned in Chapter 3, outsourcing refers to the contracting of manufacturing

must be considered in decisions. While information technology is often outsourced today, transportation, human resources, services, and even marketing functions can be outsourced. Our hypothetical Rushing Water Canoes might contract with a local janitorial service to clean its offices and with a local accountant to handle routine bookkeeping and tax-preparation functions.

Outsourcing, once used primarily as a cost-cutting tactic, has increasingly been linked with the development of competitive advantage through improved product quality, speeding up the time it takes products to get to the customer, and overall supply chain efficiencies. Table 8.1 provides the world's top five outsourcing providers that assist mainly in information technology. Outsourcing allows companies to free up time and resources to focus on what they do best and to create better opportunities to focus on customer satisfaction. Many executives view outsourcing as an innovative way to boost productivity and remain competitive against low-wage offshore factories. However, outsourcing may create conflict with labor and negative public opinion when it results in U.S. workers being replaced by lower-cost workers in other countries.

Many athletic shoe manufacturers such as Nike outsource production to China and Vietnam to take advantage of lower labor costs.

▼ **TABLE 8.1** The World's Top Five Outsourcing Providers

Company	Services*
Accenture	Human resource management; information and communication technology management; financial management
Infosys Technologies	Information technology consulting; product engineering; software development; IT solutions
Sodexo	Real estate and asset management; facility services; service vouchers and cards
Wipro Technologies	Information technology management; business and process solutions
IBM	Customer relationship management; human resource management; information technology; strategic consulting

*The services section was provided by the authors.

Sources: "IAOP Announces 2010 Rankings for The World's Best Outsourcing Providers and Advisors," International Association of Outsourcing Professionals, https://www.iaop.org/content/23/196/2043/, (accessed January 12, 2011); "About Us," Infosys, www.infosys.com/about/what-we-do/pages/index.aspx (accessed January 12, 2011).

Routing and Scheduling

After all materials have been procured and their use determined, managers must then consider the **routing**, or sequence of operations through which the product must pass. For example, before employees at Rushing Water Canoes can form aluminum sheets into a canoe, the aluminum must be cut to size. Likewise, the canoe's flotation material must be installed before workers can secure the wood seats. The sequence depends on the product specifications developed by the engineering department of the company.

Once management knows the routing, the actual work can be scheduled. **Scheduling** assigns the tasks to be done to departments or even specific machines, workers, or teams. At Rushing Water, cutting aluminum for the company's canoes might be scheduled to be done by the "cutting and finishing" department on machines designed especially for that purpose.

Many approaches to scheduling have been developed, ranging from simple trial and error to highly sophisticated computer programs. One popular method is the *Program Evaluation and Review Technique (PERT)*, which identifies all the major activities or events required to complete a project, arranges them in a sequence or path, determines the critical path, and estimates the time required for each event. Producing a McDonald's Big Mac, for example, involves removing meat, cheese, sauce, and vegetables from the refrigerator; grilling the hamburger patties; assembling the ingredients; placing the completed Big Mac in its package; and serving it to the customer (Figure 8.3). The cheese, pickles, onions, and sauce cannot be put on before the hamburger patty is completely grilled and placed on the bun. The path that requires the longest time from start to finish is called the *critical path* because it determines the minimum amount of time in which the process can be completed. If any of the activities on the critical path for production of the Big Mac fall behind schedule, the sandwich will not be completed on time, causing customers to wait longer than they usually would.

MANAGING QUALITY

Quality, like cost and efficiency, is a critical element of operations management, for defective products can quickly ruin a firm. Quality reflects the degree to which a good or service meets the demands and requirements of customers. Customers are increasingly dissatisfied with the quality of service provided by many airlines. Table 8.2 gives the rankings of U.S. airlines in certain operational areas. Smaller carriers are considered to have

better operational efficiency than larger airlines such as Delta or American.[23] Determining quality can be difficult because it depends on customers' perceptions of how well the product meets or exceeds their expectations. For example, customer satisfaction on airlines can vary wildly depending on individual customers' perspectives. However, the airline industry is notorious for its dissatisfied customers. Flight delays are a common complaint from airline passengers; 20 percent of all flights arrive more than 15 minutes late. However, most passengers do not select an airline based on how often flights arrive on time.[24]

The fuel economy of an automobile or its reliability (defined in terms of frequency of repairs) can be measured with some degree of precision. Although automakers rely on their own measures of vehicle quality, they also look to independent sources such as the J.D. Power and Associates annual initial quality survey for confirmation of their quality assessment as well as consumer perceptions of quality for the industry, as indicated in Figure 8.4.

It is especially difficult to measure quality characteristics when the product is a service. A company has to decide exactly which quality characteristics it considers important and then define those characteristics in terms that can be measured. The inseparability of production and consumption and the level of customer contact influence the selection of characteristics of the service that are most important. Employees in high-contact services such as hairstyling, education, legal services, and even the barista at Starbucks are an important part of the product.

The Malcolm Baldrige National Quality Award is given each year to companies that meet rigorous standards of quality. The Baldrige criteria are (1) leadership, (2) information and

FIGURE 8.3
A Hypothetical PERT Diagram for a McDonald's Big Mac

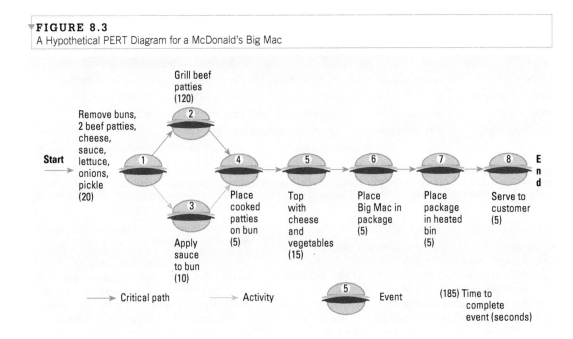

quality control the processes an organization uses to maintain its established quality standards

analysis, (3) strategic planning, (4) human resource development and management, (5) process management, (6) business results, and (7) customer focus and satisfaction. The criteria have become a worldwide framework for driving business improvement. Seven companies won the award in 2010, representing four different categories: MEDRAD (manufacturing), Nestlé Purina PetCare Co. (manufacturing), Freese and Nichols Inc. (small business), K&N Management (small business), Studer Group (small business), Advocate Good Samaritan Hospital (health care), and Montgomery Country Public Schools (education).[25]

Quality is so important that we need to examine it in the context of operations management. **Quality control** refers to the processes an organization uses to maintain its established quality standards. Best Buy's Geek Squad helps reduce returns of PCs by 40 percent when they deliver and set up a computer. This demonstrates that measuring perceived quality relates to more than just technical defects of a product, but also to other characteristics.[26] Quality has become a major concern in many organizations, particularly in light of intense foreign competition and increasingly demanding

▼ **TABLE 8.2** Rankings of Major U.S. Airlines, Best to Worst

	On-Time	Cancelled Flights	Baggage Handling	Bumping Passengers	Customer Complaints
1	Alaska	Alaska	Air Tran	JetBlue	Southwest
2	United	Southwest	JetBlue	AirTran	Alaska
3	AirTran	Continental	US Airways	Delta	AirTran
4	US Airways	AirTran	Continental	American	JetBlue
5	Continental	US Airways	Alaska	Alaska	American
6	Southwest	United	Southwest	United	Continental
7	American	American	United	Southwest	US Airways
8	Delta	JetBlue	Delta	US Airways	United
9	JetBlue	Delta	American	Continental	Delta

Source: FlightStats.com for full-year on-time cancellations; DOT Air Travel Consumer Report for 11 months of mishandled bags and complaint data plus nine months of overbooking data. Information obtained from Scott McCartney, "The Big Guys Finish Last in 2010 Airline Rankings," *USA Today,* January 13, 2011, pp. D1, D4.

▼**FIGURE 8.4**
J.D. Power and Associates Initial Automobile Quality Study

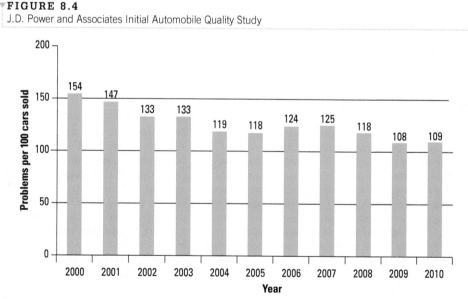

Sources: J.D. Power and Associates 2009 Initial Quality Study, http://businesscenter.jdpower.com/news/pressrelease.aspx?ID=2009108 (accessed February 16, 2010); J.D. Power and Associates 2010 Initial Quality Study, June 17, 2010, http://businesscenter.jdpower.com/news/pressrelease.aspx?ID=2010099 (accessed January 12, 2011).

total quality management (TQM) a philosophy that uniform commitment to quality in all areas of an organization will promote a culture that meets customers' perceptions of quality

statistical process control a system in which management collects and analyzes information about the production process to pinpoint quality problems in the production system

ISO 9000 a series of quality-assurance standards designed by the International Organization for Standardization (ISO) to ensure consistent product quality under many conditions

ISO 14000 a comprehensive set of environmental standards that encourages companies to conduct business in a cleaner, safer, and less wasteful way. ISO 14000 provides a uniform set of standards globally.

STELLA & CHEWY'S: THE FOOD DOGS LOVE

After being told that her dog Chewy was deathly ill, Marie Moody's only chance of saving him was to change his diet. She began purchasing organic meat and vegetables to create her own dog food. Almost immediately, Chewy's health improved.

Moody began feeding her other dog, Stella, the same mixture and noticed positive results in her as well. Stella & Chewy's dog food, consisting of fresh meats and organic produce, was born.

Moody began in her apartment kitchen and later moved to Wisconsin to expand manufacturing. She developed partnerships with organic and antibiotic-free meat producers and hired animal scientists to help create technology to keep the food pathogen-free. Today, Stella & Chewy's uses hydrostatic high pressure to pasteurize without removing nutrients and taste. The company has a third party test each batch of food. Maintaining quality is critical to a raw food diet and for building a product that consumers trust. Stella & Chewy's has flourished, becoming the dog food of choice for many pet lovers.[27]

---

customers. To regain a competitive edge, a number of firms have adopted a total quality management approach. **Total quality management (TQM)** is a philosophy that uniform commitment to quality in all areas of the organization will promote a culture that meets customers' perceptions of quality. It involves coordinating efforts to improve customer satisfaction, increasing employee participation, forming and strengthening supplier partnerships, and facilitating an organizational culture of continuous quality improvement. TQM requires constant improvements in all areas of the company as well as employee empowerment.

Continuous improvement of an organization's goods and services is built around the notion that quality is free; by contrast, *not* having high-quality goods and services can be very expensive, especially in terms of dissatisfied customers.[28] A primary tool of the continuous improvement process is *benchmarking*, the measuring and evaluating of the quality of the organization's goods, services, or processes as compared with the quality produced by the best-performing companies in the industry.[29] Benchmarking lets the organization know where it stands competitively in its industry, thus giving it a goal to aim for over time. Now that online digital media are becoming more important in businesses, companies such as Compuware Gomez offer benchmarking tools so companies can monitor and compare the success of their websites. Such tools allow companies to track traffic to the site versus competitors' sites. Studies have shown a direct link between website performance and online sales, meaning this type of benchmarking is important.[30]

Companies employing total quality management (TQM) programs know that quality control should be incorporated throughout the transformation process, from the initial plans to the development of a specific product through the product and production-facility design processes to the actual manufacture of the product. In other words, they view quality control as an element of the product itself, rather than as simply a function of the operations process. When a company makes the product correctly from the outset, it eliminates the need to rework defective products, expedites the transformation process itself, and allows employees to make better use of their time and materials. One method through which many companies have tried to improve quality is **statistical process control**, a system in which management collects and analyzes information about the production process to pinpoint quality problems in the production system.

International Organization for Standardization (ISO)

Regardless of whether a company has a TQM program for quality control, it must first determine what standard of quality it desires and then assess whether its products meet that standard. Product specifications and quality standards must be set so the company can create a product that will compete in the marketplace. Rushing Water Canoes, for example, may specify that each of its canoes has aluminum walls of a specified uniform thickness, that the front and back be reinforced with a specified level of steel, and that each contain a specified amount of flotation material for safety. Production facilities must be designed that can produce products with the desired specifications.

Quality standards can be incorporated into service businesses as well. A hamburger chain, for example, may establish standards relating to how long it takes to cook an order and serve it to customers, how many fries are in each order, how thick the burgers are, or how many customer complaints might be acceptable. Once the desired quality characteristics, specifications, and standards have been stated in measurable terms, the next step is inspection.

The International Organization for Standardization (ISO) has created a series of quality management standards—**ISO 9000**—designed to ensure that customer's quality standards are met. The standards provide a framework for documenting how a certified business keeps records, trains employees, tests products, and fixes defects. To obtain ISO 9000 certification, an independent auditor must verify that a business's factory, laboratory, or office meets the quality standards spelled out by the International Organization for Standardization. The certification process can require significant investment, but for many companies, the process is essential to being able to compete. Thousands of U.S. firms have been certified, and many more are working to meet the standards. Certification has become a virtual necessity for doing business in Europe in some high-technology businesses. ISO 9002 certification was established for service providers. **ISO 14000** is a comprehensive set of environmental standards that encourages a cleaner and safer world. ISO 14000 is a valuable standard because currently considerable variation exists between the regulations in different nations, and even regions within a nation. These variations make it difficult for organizations committed to sustainability to find acceptable global solutions to problems. The goal of the ISO 14000 standards is to promote a more uniform approach to environmental management and to help companies attain and measure improvements in their environmental performance.

Inspection

Inspection reveals whether a product meets quality standards. Some product characteristics may be discerned by fairly simple inspection techniques—weighing the contents of cereal boxes or measuring the time it takes for a customer to receive his or her hamburger. As part of the ongoing quality-assurance program at Hershey Foods, all wrapped Hershey Kisses are checked, and all imperfectly wrapped kisses are rejected. Other inspection techniques are more elaborate. Automobile manufacturers use automated machines to open and close car doors to test the durability of latches and hinges. The food-processing and pharmaceutical industries use various chemical tests to determine the quality of their output. Rushing Water Canoes might use a special device that can precisely measure the thickness of each canoe wall to ensure that it meets the company's specifications.

Organizations normally inspect purchased items, work-in-process, and finished items. The inspection of purchased items and finished items takes place after the fact;

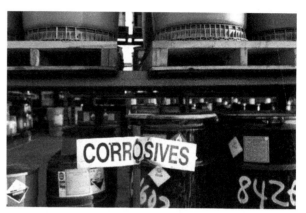

The ISO 9000 standards are international standards that relate to quality management. ISO14000 standards relate to environmental management—managing businesses to minimize harmful effects to the environment.

the inspection of work-in-process is preventive. In other words, the purpose of inspection of purchased items and finished items is to determine what the quality level is. For items that are being worked on—an automobile moving down the assembly line or a canoe being assembled—the purpose of the inspection is to find defects before the product is completed so that necessary corrections can be made.

Sampling

An important question relating to inspection is how many items should be inspected. Should all canoes produced by Rushing Water be inspected or just some of them? Whether to inspect 100 percent of the output or only part of it is related to the cost of the inspection process, the destructiveness of the inspection process (some tests last until the product fails), and the potential cost of product flaws in terms of human lives and safety.

Some inspection procedures are quite expensive, use elaborate testing equipment, destroy products, and/or require a significant number of hours to complete. In such cases, it is usually desirable to test only a sample of the output. If the sample passes inspection, the inspector may assume that all the items in the lot from which the sample was drawn would also pass inspection. By using principles of statistical inference, management can employ sampling techniques that ensure a relatively high probability of reaching the right conclusion—that is, rejecting a lot that does not meet standards and accepting a lot that does. Nevertheless, there will always be a risk of making an incorrect conclusion—accepting a population that *does not* meet standards (because the sample was satisfactory) or rejecting a population that *does* meet standards (because the sample contained too many defective items).

TEAM EXERCISE

Form groups and assign the responsibility of finding companies that outsource their production to other countries. What are the key advantages of this outsourcing decision? Do you see any drawbacks or weaknesses in this approach? Why would a company not outsource when such a tactic can be undertaken to cut manufacturing costs? Report your findings to the class.

SO YOU WANT A JOB // in Operations Management /

While you might not have been familiar with terms such as *supply chain* or *logistics* or *total quality management* before taking this course, careers abound in the operations management field. You will find these careers in a wide variety of organizations—manufacturers, retailers, transportation companies, third-party logistics firms, government agencies, and service firms. Approximately $1.3 trillion is spent on transportation, inventory, and related logistics activities, and logistics alone accounts for more than 9.5 percent of U.S. gross domestic product.[31] Closely managing how a company's inputs and outputs flow from raw materials to the end consumer is vital to a firm's success. Successful companies also need to ensure that quality is measured and actively managed at each step.

Supply chain managers have a tremendous impact on the success of an organization. These managers are engaged in every facet of the business process, including planning, purchasing, production, transportation, storage and distribution, customer service, and more. Their performance helps organizations control expenses, boost sales, and maximize profits.

Warehouse managers are a vital part of manufacturing operations. A typical warehouse manager's duties include overseeing and recording deliveries and pickups, maintaining inventory records and the product tracking system, and adjusting inventory levels to reflect receipts and disbursements. Warehouse managers also have to keep in mind customer service and employee issues. Warehouse managers can earn up to $60,000 in some cases.

Operations management is also required in service businesses. With more than 80 percent of the U.S. economy in services, jobs exist for services operations. Many service contact operations require standardized processes that often use technology to provide an interface that provides an automatic quality performance. Consider jobs in health care, the travel industry, fast food, and entertainment. Think of any job or task that is a part of the final product in these industries. Even an online retailer such as Amazon.com has a transformation process that includes information technology and human activities that facilitate a transaction. These services have a standardized process and can be evaluated based on their level of achieved service quality.

Total quality management is becoming a key attribute for companies to ensure that quality pervades all aspects of the organization. Quality-assurance managers may make salaries in the $55,000 to $65,000 range. These managers monitor and advise on how a company's quality management system is performing and publish data and reports regarding company performance in both manufacturing and service industries.

Sampling is likely to be used when inspection tests are destructive. Determining the life expectancy of lightbulbs by turning them on and recording how long they last would be foolish: There is no market for burned-out lightbulbs. Instead, a generalization based on the quality of a sample would be applied to the entire population of lightbulbs from which the sample was drawn. However, human life and safety often depend on the proper functioning of specific items, such as the navigational systems installed in commercial airliners. For such items, even though the inspection process is costly, the potential cost of flawed systems—in human lives and safety—is too great not to inspect 100 percent of the output. ▪

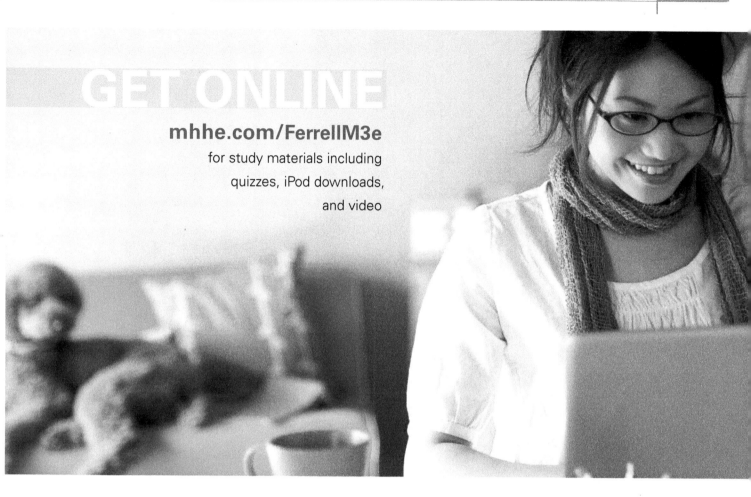

GET ONLINE

mhhe.com/FerrellM3e

for study materials including
quizzes, iPod downloads,
and video

chapter eight

active review card
Managing Service and Manufacturing Operations

in a nutshell

Production and operations management involves planning and designing the processes that will transform resources into finished products, managing the movement of resources through the transformation process, and ensuring that the products are of the quality expected by customers.

The following statements will test your take-away knowledge from this chapter. Do your best to explain each one in the space provided below.

LO.1 Define operations management, and differentiate between operations and manufacturing.

LO.2 Explain how operations management differs in manufacturing and service firms.

LO.3 Describe the elements involved in planning and designing an operations system.

LO.4 Specify some techniques managers may use to manage the logistics of transforming inputs into finished products.

LO.5 Assess the importance of quality in operations management.

Did your answers include the following important points?

LO.1. Define operations management, and differentiate between operations and manufacturing.

- Operations management (OM) is the development and administration of the activities involved in transforming resources into goods and services.
- The terms *manufacturing* and *production* are used interchangeably to describe the activities and processes used in making tangible products, whereas *operations* is a broader term used to describe the process of making both tangible and intangible products.

LO.2. Explain how operations management differs in manufacturing and service firms.

- Manufacturers and service firms both transform inputs and outputs, but service providers differ from manufacturers in several ways: They have greater customer contact because the service occurs at the point of consumption; their inputs and outputs are more variable than those of manufacturers; because of the human element, service providers are generally more labor intensive and their productivity measurement is more complex.

LO.3. Describe the elements involved in planning and designing an operations system.

- Operations planning relates to decisions about what products to make, for whom, and what processes and facilities are needed to produce them.
- Common facility layouts include fixed-position layouts, process layouts, and product layouts.
- Where to locate operations facilities is a crucial decision that depends on proximity to market, availability of raw materials,

availability of transportation, availability of power, climatic influences, availability of labor, and community characteristics.

- Technology is also vital to operations, particularly computer-assisted design, computer-assisted manufacturing, flexible manufacturing, robotics, and computer-integrated manufacturing.

LO.4. Specify some techniques managers may use to manage the logistics of transforming inputs into finished products.

- Logistics, or supply chain management, includes all the activities involved in obtaining and managing raw materials and component parts, managing finished products, packaging them, and getting them to customers.
- Common approaches to inventory control include the economic order quantity (EOQ) model, the just-in-time (JIT) inventory concept, and material-requirements planning (MRP).
- Logistics also includes routing and scheduling processes and activities to complete products.

LO.5. Assess the importance of quality in operations management.

- Quality is a critical element of operations management because low-quality products can hurt people and harm business.
- Quality control refers to the processes an organization uses to maintain its established quality standards.
- To control quality, a company must establish what standard of quality is desired and determine whether its products meet that standard through inspection.

Practical Application

LO.1.
- Viewed from the perspective of operations, the money used to purchase a carpenter's tools and the electricity used to run his power saw are _____.
- If an employee is involved with transforming resources into goods and services, then she is in _____.
- From an operations perspective, food sold at a restaurant and services provided by a plumbing company are _____.

LO.2.
- Due to the high degree of automation, products in the manufacturing industry are more _____ than those in the service industry.
- Most goods are manufactured _____ purchase while most services are performed _____ purchase.
- The service industry is _____ intensive while the manufacturing industry is _____ intensive.

LO.3.
- Television sets, ballpoint pens, and tortilla chips are _____ products as they are produced on an assembly line.

- If ABC Computer Company is trying to determine the demand for its future products and how much consumers are willing to pay, the company will probably rely on _____.
- When a customer goes to a print shop to order business cards, the manufacturing process used would most likely be _____.

LO.4.
- A company that requires all its resources to be brought to a central location is using a(n) _____.
- Materials that have been purchased to be used as inputs in making other products are included in _____.
- _____ helps engineers design components, products, and processes on the computer instead of on paper.

LO.5.
- Determining how many items are to be inspected is called _____.
- The degree to which a good or service meets the demands and requirements of customers is called _____.
- _____ is a philosophy that a uniform commitment to quality in all areas of an organization will promote a culture that meets customers' perceptions of quality.

Creating the Human Resource Advantage

chapter nine

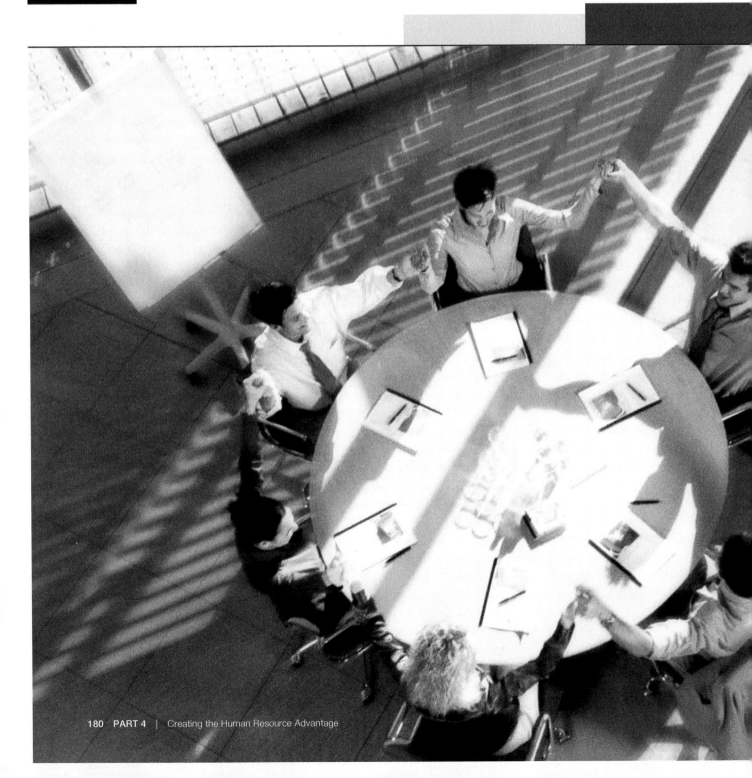

motivating
the workforce

introduction

Because employees do the actual work of the business and influence whether the firm achieves its objectives, most top managers agree that employees are an organization's most valuable resource. To achieve organizational objectives, employees must have the motivation, ability (appropriate knowledge and skills), and tools (proper training and equipment) to perform their jobs. Chapter 10 covers topics related to managing human resources, such as those listed earlier. This chapter focuses on how to motivate employees.

We examine employees' needs and motivation, managers' views of workers, and several strategies for motivating employees. Managers who understand the needs of their employees can help them reach higher levels of productivity and thus contribute to the achievement of organizational goals.

LEARNING OBJECTIVES

L01 Define human relations, and determine why its study is important.

L02 Summarize early studies that laid the groundwork for understanding employee motivation.

L03 Compare and contrast the human-relations theories of Abraham Maslow and Frederick Herzberg.

L04 Investigate various theories of motivation, including theories X, Y, and Z; equity theory; and expectancy theory.

L05 Describe some of the strategies that managers use to motivate employees.

human relations the study of the behavior of individuals and groups in organizational settings

motivation an inner drive that directs a person's behavior toward goals

NATURE OF HUMAN RELATIONS

What motivates employees to perform on the job is the focus of **human relations**, the study of the behavior of individuals and groups in organizational settings. In business, human relations involves motivating employees to achieve organizational objectives efficiently and effectively. The field of human relations has become increasingly important over the years as businesses strive to understand how to boost workplace morale, maximize employees' productivity and creativity, and motivate their ever more diverse employees to be more effective.

Motivation is an inner drive that directs a person's behavior toward goals. A goal is the satisfaction of some need, and a need is the difference between a desired state and an actual state. Both needs and goals can be motivating. Motivation explains why people behave as they do; similarly, a lack of motivation explains, at times, why people avoid doing what they should do. Motivating employees to do the wrong things or for the wrong reasons can be problematic, however. Encouraging employees to take excessive risks through high compensation, for example, is not a good idea and can lead to ethical misconduct disasters for a corporation. The most recent financial crisis resulted from firms allowing or encouraging excessive risk taking in order to achieve financial rewards. A person who recognizes or feels a need is motivated to take action to satisfy the need and achieve a goal (Figure 9.1). Consider a person who takes a job as a salesperson. If his or her performance is far below other salespeople's, he or she will likely recognize a need to increase sales. To satisfy that need and achieve success, the person may try to acquire new insights from successful salespeople or obtain additional training to improve sales skills. In addition, a sales manager might try different means to motivate the salesperson to work harder and improve his or her skills. Human relations is concerned with the needs of employees, their goals and how they try to achieve them, and the impact of those needs and goals on job performance.

Effectively motivating employees helps keep them engaged in their work. Engagement involves emotional involvement and commitment. Being engaged results in carrying out the expectations and obligations of employment. Many employees are actively engaged in their jobs, while others are not. Some employees do the minimum amount of work required to get by, and some employees are completely disengaged. Motivating

▼**FIGURE 9.1**
The Motivation Process

FULL YIELD SEEKS TO REVOLUTIONIZE EMPLOYEE HEALTH

How do businesses lower employee health care costs while supporting healthier, motivated employees? Entrepreneur Zoe Finch Totten feels she has the answer. Her company, The Full Yield, plans to revolutionize the health care industry by teaching employees how to improve their health with wiser food choices. It seems simple enough. Research shows that many diseases that contribute to high health care costs stem from poor diet. Better employee health, therefore, translates into lower health insurance costs. Big businesses are taking note, with 60 percent promoting employee wellness via benefits. The Full Yield is there to help.

The program costs $750 per person annually for education and support on shifting to a whole food diet. Insurance company Harvard Pilgrim Health has already signed up 350 of its employees for the program, and Finch Totten has the support of major organizations like Danone and the City of Boston. Although the road ahead will be challenging, the success of Full Yield could contribute to healthier, happier employees—and businesses as well![1]

employees to stay engaged is a key responsibility of management. For example, to test if his onsite production managers were fully engaged in their jobs, former Van Halen frontman David Lee Roth placed a line in the band's rider asking for a bowl of M&Ms with the brown ones removed. It was a means for the band to test local stage production crews' attention to detail. Because their shows were highly technical, Lee Roth would demand a complete recheck of everything if he found brown M&Ms in the bowl.[2]

One prominent aspect of human relations is **morale**—an employee's attitude toward his or her job, employer, and colleagues. High morale contributes to high levels of productivity, high returns to stakeholders, and employee loyalty. Conversely, low morale may cause high rates of absenteeism and turnover (when employees quit or are fired and must be replaced by new employees). Google recognizes the value of happy, committed employees and strives to engage in practices that will minimize turnover. Employees have the opportunity to have a massage every other week; onsite laundry service; free all-you-can-eat

gourmet meals and snacks; and the "20% a week" rule, which allows engineers to work on whatever project they want for one day each week.[3]

Employees are motivated by their perceptions of extrinsic and intrinsic rewards. An **intrinsic reward** is the personal satisfaction and enjoyment that you feel from attaining a goal. For example, in this class you may feel personal enjoyment in learning how business works and aspire to have a career in business or to operate your own business one day. **Extrinsic rewards** are benefits and/or recognition that you receive from someone else. In this class, your grade is extrinsic recognition of your efforts and success in the class. In business, praise and recognition, pay increases, and bonuses are extrinsic rewards. If you believe that

morale an employee's attitude toward his or her job, employer, and colleagues

intrinsic rewards the personal satisfaction and enjoyment that you feel after attaining a goal

extrinsic rewards benefits and/or recognition received from someone else

Many companies offer onsite day care as a benefit for employees who have children. Company benefits such as these tend to increase employee satisfaction and motivation.

classical theory of motivation theory suggesting that money is the sole motivator for workers

your job provides an opportunity to contribute to society or the environment, then that aspect would represent an intrinsic reward. Both intrinsic and extrinsic rewards contribute to motivation that stimulates employees to do their best in contributing to business goals.

Respect, involvement, appreciation, adequate compensation, promotions, a pleasant work environment, and a positive organizational culture are all morale boosters. Table 9.1 lists some ways to retain good employees. Nike seeks to provide a comprehensive compensation and benefits package, which includes traditional elements such as medical, dental, vision, life and disability insurance, paid holidays and time off, sabbaticals, and team as well as individual compensation plans.

?

DID YOU KNOW?

Absenteeism can cost a company as much as 36 percent of payroll.[4]

More comprehensive benefits include employee discounts on Nike products, scholarships for children of employees, employee assistance plans, tuition assistance, group legal plans, and matching gift programs. At the Beaverton, Oregon, world headquarters, Nike employees may take advantage of onsite day care and fitness centers, onsite cafés and restaurants, an onsite hair and nail salon, discounted annual TriMet transit passes ($25 annual fee versus $600), and several other work-life resources.[5] Many companies offer a diverse array of benefits designed to improve the quality of employees' lives and increase their morale and satisfaction. Some of the best companies to work for offer onsite day care, concierge services (e.g., dry cleaning, shoe repair, prescription renewal), domestic partner benefits to same-sex couples, and fully paid sabbaticals. Table 9.2 offers suggestions as to how leaders can motivate employees on a daily basis.

HISTORICAL PERSPECTIVES ON EMPLOYEE MOTIVATION

Throughout the 20th century, researchers have conducted numerous studies to try to identify ways to motivate workers and increase productivity. From these studies have come theories that have been applied to workers with varying degrees of success. A brief discussion of two of these theories—the classical theory of motivation and the Hawthorne studies—provides a background for understanding the present state of human relations.

Classical Theory of Motivation

The birth of the study of human relations can be traced to time and motion studies conducted at the turn of the century by Frederick W. Taylor and Frank and Lillian Gilbreth. Their studies analyzed how workers perform specific work tasks in an

Even small symbols of recognition, such as an "Employee of the Month" parking space, can serve as strong motivators for employees.

▼ **TABLE 9.1** Top 10 Ways to Retain Great Employees

1. Satisfied employees know clearly what is expected from them every day at work.
2. The quality of the supervision an employee receives is critical to employee retention.
3. The ability of the employee to speak his or her mind freely within the organization is another key factor in employee retention.
4. Talent and skill utilization is another environmental factor your key employees seek in your workplace.
5. The perception of fairness and equitable treatment is important in employee retention.
6. Employees must have the tools, time, and training necessary to do their jobs well—or they will move to an employer who provides them.
7. The best employees, those employees you want to retain, seek frequent opportunities to learn and grow in their careers, knowledge, and skill.
8. Take time to meet with new employees to learn about their talents, abilities, and skills. Meet with each employee periodically.
9. No matter the circumstances, never, never, ever threaten an employee's job or income.
10. Staff members must feel rewarded, recognized, and appreciated.

Source: Susan M. Heathfield, "Top Ten Ways to Retain Your Great Employees," *About.com*, http://humanresources.about.com/od/retention/a/more_retention.htm (accessed February 18, 2010).

▼ **TABLE 9.2** You Can Make Their Day: Tips for the Leader about Employee Motivation

1. Use simple, powerful words.
2. Make sure people know what you expect.
3. Provide regular feedback.
4. People need positive and not so positive consequences.
5. It's about discipline, not magic.
6. Continue learning and trying out new ideas for employee motivation.
7. Make time for people.
8. Focus on the development of people.
9. Share the goals and the context: communicate.

Source: Susan M. Heathfield, "You Can Make Their Day: Ten Tips for the Leader About Employee Motivation," *About.com*, http://humanresources.about.com/od/motivationsucces3/a/lead_motivation.htm (accessed February 18, 2010).

Working conditions are important. However, the Hawthorne studies, which were carried out at the electric company shown here beginning in the 1920s, found that the workers became more productive because of the attention they received—regardless of their working conditions.

effort to improve the employees' productivity. These efforts led to the application of scientific principles to management.

According to the **classical theory of motivation**, money is the sole motivator for workers. Taylor suggested that workers who were paid more would produce more, an idea that would benefit both companies and workers. To improve productivity, Taylor thought that managers should break down each job into its component tasks (specialization), determine the best way to perform each task, and specify the output to be achieved by a worker performing the task. Taylor also believed that incentives would motivate employees to be more productive. Thus, he suggested that managers link workers' pay directly to their output. He developed the piece-rate system, under which employees were paid a certain amount for each unit they produced; those who exceeded their quota were paid a higher rate per unit for all the units they produced.

We can still see Taylor's ideas in practice today in the use of financial incentives for productivity. Moreover, companies are increasingly striving to relate pay to performance at both the hourly and managerial level. Incentive planners choose an individual incentive to motivate and reward their employees. In contrast, team incentives are used to generate partnership and collaboration to accomplish organizational goals. Boeing develops sales teams for most of its products, including commercial airplanes. The team dedicated to each product shares in the sales incentive program.

More and more corporations are tying pay to performance in order to motivate—even up to the CEO level. The topic of executive pay has become controversial in recent years, and many

corporate boards of directors have taken steps to link executive compensation more closely to corporate performance. Despite these changes, many top executives still receive large compensation packages. H. Lawrence Culp, Jr., CEO of Danaher Corporation, is the highest paid executive, with a total compensation of $141.36 million.[6]

Like most managers of the early 20th century, Taylor believed that satisfactory pay and job security would motivate employees to work hard. However, later studies showed that other factors are also important in motivating workers.

The Hawthorne Studies

Elton Mayo and a team of researchers from Harvard University wanted to determine what physical conditions in the workplace—such as light and noise levels—would stimulate employees to be most productive. From 1924 to 1932, they studied a group of workers at the Hawthorne Works Plant of the Western Electric Company and measured their productivity under various physical conditions.

What the researchers discovered was quite unexpected and very puzzling: Productivity increased regardless of the physical conditions. This phenomenon has been labeled the Hawthorne effect. When questioned about their behavior, the employees expressed satisfaction because their co-workers in

"Taylor believed that satisfactory pay and job security would motivate employees to work hard. However, later studies showed that other factors are also important in motivating workers."

Maslow's hierarchy a theory that arranges the five basic needs of people—physiological, security, social, esteem, and self-actualization—into the order in which people strive to satisfy them

physiological needs the most basic human needs to be satisfied—water, food, shelter, and clothing

security needs the need to protect oneself from physical and economic harm

social needs the need for love, companionship, and friendship—the desire for acceptance by others

esteem needs the need for respect—both self-respect and respect from others

the experiments were friendly and, more importantly, because their supervisors had asked for their help and cooperation in the study. In other words, they were responding to the attention they received, not the changing physical work conditions. The researchers concluded that social and psychological factors could significantly affect productivity and morale. Medtronic, often called the "Microsoft of the medical-device industry," has a built-in psychological factor that influences employee morale. The company makes life-saving medical devices, such as pacemakers, neurostimulators, and stents. New hires at Medtronic receive medallions inscribed with a portion of the firm's mission statement, "alleviate pain, restore health, and extend life." There is an annual party where people whose bodies function thanks to Medtronic devices give testimonials. Obviously, Medtronic employees feel a sense of satisfaction in their jobs. Figure 9.2 indicates what executives consider to be most valuable in maintaining an effective work-life balance.

The Hawthorne experiments marked the beginning of a concern for human relations in the workplace. They revealed that human factors do influence workers' behavior and that managers who understand the needs, beliefs, and expectations of people have the greatest success in motivating their workers.

▼**FIGURE 9.2**
Value of Employer Work-Life Concessions

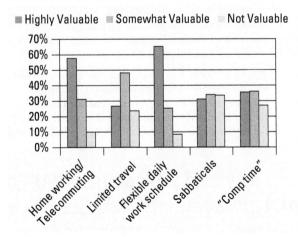

Source: "BlueSteps 2010 Executive Work-Life Balance Survey," http://viewswire. eiu.com/report_dl.asp?mode=fi&fi=757215260.PDF (accessed January 13, 2011).

THEORIES OF EMPLOYEE MOTIVATION

The research of Taylor, Mayo, and many others has led to the development of a number of theories that attempt to describe what motivates employees to perform. In this section, we will discuss some of the most important of these theories. The successful implementation of ideas based on these theories will vary, of course, depending on the company, its management, and its employees. It should be noted, too, that what worked in the past may no longer work today. Good managers must have the ability to adapt their ideas to an ever-changing, diverse group of employees.

Maslow's Hierarchy of Needs

Psychologist Abraham Maslow theorized that people have five basic needs: physiological, security, social, esteem, and self-actualization. **Maslow's hierarchy** arranges these needs into the order in which people strive to satisfy them (Figure 9.3).

Physiological needs, the most basic and first needs to be satisfied, are the essentials for living—water, food, shelter, and clothing. According to Maslow, humans devote all their efforts to satisfying physiological needs until they are met. Only when these needs are met can people focus their attention on satisfying the next level of needs—security.

Security needs relate to protecting yourself from physical and economic harm. Actions that may be taken to achieve security include reporting a dangerous workplace condition to management, maintaining safety equipment, and purchasing insurance with income protection in the event you become unable to work. Once security needs have been satisfied, people may strive for social goals.

Social needs are the need for love, companionship, and friendship—the desire for acceptance by others. To fulfill social needs, a person may try many things: making friends with a co-worker, joining a group, volunteering at a hospital, throwing a party. Once their social needs have been satisfied, people attempt to satisfy their need for esteem.

Esteem needs relate to respect—both self-respect and respect from others. One aspect of esteem needs is competition—the need to feel that you can do something better than anyone else. Competition often motivates people to increase their productivity. Esteem needs are not as easily satisfied as the needs at lower levels in Maslow's hierarchy because they do not always provide tangible evidence of success. However, these needs can

self-actualization needs the need to be the best one can be; at the top of Maslow's hierarchy

be realized through rewards and increased involvement in organizational activities. Until esteem needs are met, people focus their attention on achieving respect. When they feel they have achieved some measure of respect, self-actualization becomes the major goal of life.

Self-actualization needs, at the top of Maslow's hierarchy, mean being the best you can be. Self-actualization involves maximizing your potential. A self-actualized person feels that she or he is living life to its fullest in every way. For Stephen King, self-actualization might mean being praised as the best fiction writer in the world; for actress Halle Berry, it might mean winning an Oscar.

Maslow's theory maintains that the more basic needs at the bottom of the hierarchy must be satisfied before higher-level goals can be pursued. Thus, people who are hungry and homeless are not concerned with obtaining respect from their colleagues. Only when physiological, security, and social needs have been more or less satisfied do people seek esteem. Maslow's theory also suggests that if a low-level need is suddenly reactivated, the individual will try to satisfy that need rather than higher-level needs. Many laid off workers probably shift their focus from high-level esteem needs to the need for security. When U.S. unemployment reached 10 percent during the last recession and the job market appeared increasingly insecure, many employees, particularly those in manufacturing, banking, and finance, felt they had to shift their focus back to security needs. Managers should learn from Maslow's hierarchy that employees will be motivated to contribute to organizational goals only if they are able to first satisfy their physiological, security, and social needs through their work.

Herzberg's Two-Factor Theory

In the 1950s psychologist Frederick Herzberg proposed a theory of motivation that focuses on the job and on the environment where work is done. Herzberg studied various factors relating to the job and their relation to employee motivation and concluded that they can be divided into hygiene factors and motivational factors (Table 9.3).

▼**FIGURE 9.3**
Maslow's Hierarchy of Needs

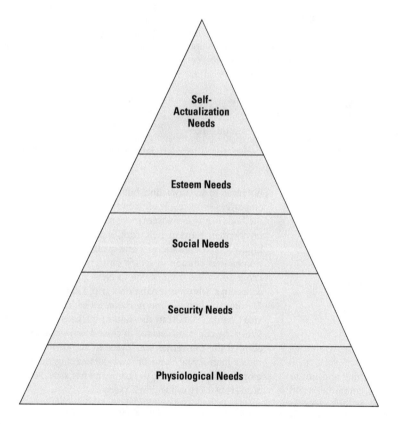

- Self-Actualization Needs
- Esteem Needs
- Social Needs
- Security Needs
- Physiological Needs

Source: Adapted from Abraham H. Maslow, "A Theory of Human Motivation," *Psychology Review* 50 (1943), pp. 370–396. American Psychology Association.

> **Maslow's theory maintains that the more basic needs at the bottom of the hierarchy must be satisfied before higher-level goals can be pursued.**

REWARDING PERFORMERS WITH TIME OFF

During the most recent recession, several organizations decided to decrease employee incentives (perks) due to the difficult financial environment. Although incentives are rising again, there are still fewer employee perks than there were pre-recession. However, some employers are taking an unusual approach by offering more time off as a reward—even for part-time workers. Indeed, a survey of companies in the Washington, DC/Baltimore area revealed that 73 percent of surveyed employers now offer paid time off to part-time workers rather than creating full-time positions, which come with their own share of costs.

Three companies that reward employees with extra time off include Travelzoo (a global travel deal website), Bluewolf, Inc. (an IT consulting firm), and Patagonia. At Bluewolf, emphasis is placed on outcome rather than time spent at a desk, enabling its 175 employees to take unlimited time off to travel, volunteer, and more. Travelzoo offers its employees of more than one year an annual $1,500–$32,000 with three extra vacation days and the chance to snatch up a deal listed on its site. In return, employees are merely required to submit pictures and brief write-ups to the company's subscriber newsletter. After one year of employment, Patagonia covers up to 60 days' worth of an employee's salary to allow the employee to volunteer with a grassroots organization. Like those at Travelzoo, employees are asked to report back about their experiences.

Studies have suggested that these types of incentives boost bottom-line profits and enhance employee retention. Points of Light Foundation claims that over 80 percent of companies feel that volunteering raises profits. This may be due to the fact that consumers are increasingly doing business with socially responsible companies. Employees also become committed to companies that give back to communities and appreciate their efforts.[7]

Discussion Questions

1. Do you think providing time off is an incentive that will increase employee performance?

2. Could giving employees additional time off diminish the performance of other employees who do not get the reward?

3. Would you rather have time off as a reward for good performance or a financial reward?

▼ **TABLE 9.3** Herzberg's Hygiene and Motivational Factors

Hygiene Factors	Motivational Factors
Company policies	Achievement
Supervision	Recognition
Working conditions	Work itself
Relationships with peers, supervisors, and subordinates	Responsibility
Salary	Advancement
Security	Personal growth

Hygiene factors, which relate to the work setting and not to the content of the work, include adequate wages, comfortable and safe working conditions, fair company policies, and job security. These factors do not necessarily motivate employees to excel, but their absence may be a potential source of dissatisfaction and high turnover. Employee safety and comfort are clearly hygiene factors.

Many people feel that a good salary is one of the most important job factors, even more important than job security and the chance to use one's mind and abilities. Salary and security, two of the hygiene factors identified by Herzberg, make it possible for employees to satisfy the physiological and security needs identified by Maslow. However, the presence of hygiene factors is unlikely to motivate employees to work harder.

Motivational factors, which relate to the content of the work itself, include achievement, recognition, involvement, responsibility, and advancement. The absence of motivational factors may not result in dissatisfaction, but their presence is likely to motivate employees to excel. Many companies are beginning to employ methods to give employees more responsibility and control and to involve them more in their work, which serves to motivate them to higher levels of productivity and quality. L.L.Bean employees have tremendous latitude to satisfy customer's needs. One employee drove 500 miles from Maine to New York to deliver a canoe to a customer who was leaving on a trip. L.L.Bean is one of the top 25 companies on *Bloomberg Businessweek's* list of "Customer Service Champs." L.L.Bean also ranks high in employee satisfaction. When the company decided to close down a call center, L.L.Bean allowed the call-center employees to act as home-based agents rather than laying them off and outsourcing the work. Besides empowering employees, the company has strict service training, answering every call within 20 seconds.[8]

Herzberg's motivational factors and Maslow's esteem and self-actualization needs are similar. Workers' low-level needs (physiological and security) have largely been satisfied by minimum-wage laws and occupational-safety standards set by various government agencies and are therefore not motivators. Consequently, to improve productivity, management should focus on satisfying workers' higher-level needs (motivational factors) by providing opportunities for achievement, involvement, and advancement and by recognizing good performance.

McGregor's Theory X and Theory Y

In *The Human Side of Enterprise*, Douglas McGregor related Maslow's ideas about personal needs to management. McGregor contrasted two views of management—the

hygiene factors
aspects of Herzberg's theory of motivation that focus on the work setting and not the content of the work; these aspects include adequate wages, comfortable and safe working conditions, fair company policies, and job security

motivational factors aspects of Herzberg's theory of motivation that focus on the content of the work itself; these aspects include achievement, recognition, involvement, responsibility, and advancement

Theory X McGregor's traditional view of management whereby it is assumed that workers generally dislike work and must be forced to do their jobs

Theory Y McGregor's humanistic view of management whereby it is assumed that workers like to work and that under proper conditions employees will seek out responsibility in an attempt to satisfy their social, esteem, and self-actualization needs

The Dirty Jobs *television series recognizes individuals who take on society's undesirable, but essential, jobs.*

traditional view, which he called Theory X, and a humanistic view, which he called Theory Y.

According to McGregor, managers adopting **Theory X** assume that workers generally dislike work and must be forced to do their jobs. They believe that the following statements are true of workers:

1. The average person naturally dislikes work and will avoid it when possible.

2. Most workers must be coerced, controlled, directed, or threatened with punishment to get them to work toward the achievement of organizational objectives.

3. The average worker prefers to be directed and to avoid responsibility, has relatively little ambition, and wants security.[9]

Managers who subscribe to the Theory X view maintain tight control over workers, provide almost constant supervision, try to motivate through fear, and make decisions in an autocratic fashion, eliciting little or no input from their subordinates. The Theory X style of management focuses on physiological and security needs and virtually ignores the higher needs discussed by Maslow.

The Theory X view of management does not take into account people's needs for companionship, esteem, and personal growth, whereas Theory Y, the contrasting view of management, does. Managers subscribing to the **Theory Y** view assume that workers like to work and that under proper conditions employees will seek out responsibility in an attempt to satisfy their

Theory Z a management philosophy that stresses employee participation in all aspects of company decision making

social, esteem, and self-actualization needs. McGregor describes the assumptions behind Theory Y in the following way:

1. The expenditure of physical and mental effort in work is as natural as play or rest.

2. People will exercise self-direction and self-control to achieve objectives to which they are committed.

3. People will commit to objectives when they realize that the achievement of those goals will bring them personal reward.

4. The average person will accept and seek responsibility.

5. Imagination, ingenuity, and creativity can help solve organizational problems, but most organizations do not make adequate use of these characteristics in their employees.

6. Organizations today do not make full use of workers' intellectual potential.[10]

Obviously, managers subscribing to the Theory Y philosophy have a management style very different from managers subscribing to the Theory X philosophy. Theory Y managers maintain less control and supervision, do not use fear as the primary motivator, and are more democratic in decision making, allowing subordinates to participate in the process. Theory Y managers address the high-level needs in Maslow's hierarchy as well as physiological and security needs. Today, Theory Y enjoys widespread support and may have displaced Theory X.

Theory Z

Theory Z is a management philosophy that stresses employee participation in all aspects of company decision making. It was first described by William Ouchi in his book *Theory Z—How American Business Can Meet the Japanese Challenge*. Theory Z incorporates many elements associated with the Japanese approach to management, such as trust and intimacy, but Japanese ideas have been adapted for use in the United States. In a Theory Z organization, managers and workers share responsibilities; the management style is participative; and employment is long term and often lifelong. Japan has faced a significant period of slowing economic progress and competition from China and other Asian nations. This has led to experts questioning Theory Z, particularly at firms such as Sony and Toyota. Theory Z results in employees feeling organizational ownership. Research has found that such feelings of ownership may produce positive attitudinal and behavioral effects for employees.[11] In a Theory Y organization, managers focus on assumptions about the nature of the worker. The two theories can be seen as complementary. Table 9.4 compares the traditional

> "Theory Y managers maintain less control and supervision, do not use fear as the primary motivator, and are more democratic in decision making."

▼ **TABLE 9.4** Comparison of American, Japanese, and Theory Z Management Styles

	American	Japanese	Theory Z
Duration of employment	Relatively short term; workers subject to layoffs when business slows	Lifelong; no layoffs	Long term; layoffs rare
Rate of promotion	Rapid	Slow	Slow
Amount of specialization	Considerable; worker develops expertise in one area only	Minimal; worker develops expertise in all aspects of the organization	Moderate; worker learns all aspects of the organization
Decision making	Individual	Consensual; input from all concerned parties is considered	Consensual; emphasis on quality
Responsibility	Assigned to the individual	Shared by the group	Assigned to the individual
Control	Explicit and formal	Less explicit and less formal	Informal but with explicit performance measures
Concern for workers	Focus is on work only	Focus extends to worker's whole life	Focus includes worker's life and family

Source: Adapted from William Ouchi, *Theory Z—How American Business Can Meet the Japanese Challenge*, p. 58. © 1981 by Addison-Wesley Publishing Company, Inc. Reprinted by permission of Perseus Books Publishers, a member of Perseus Books, L.L.C.

American management style, the Japanese management style, and Theory Z (the modified Japanese management style).

Variations on Theory Z

Theory Z has been adapted and modified for use in a number of U.S. companies. One adaptation involves workers in decisions through quality circles. Quality circles (also called quality-assurance teams) are small, usually having five to eight members who discuss ways to reduce waste, eliminate problems, and improve quality, communication, and work satisfaction. Such quality teams are a common technique for harnessing the knowledge and creativity of hourly employees to solve problems in companies. As Theory Z has questioned the use of quality circles, their prevalence has declined. Quality circles have been replaced with quality methods.

Quality circles are often modified and operate under names such as *participative management, employee involvement,* or *self-directed work teams.* Regardless of the term used to describe such programs, they strive to give employees more control over their jobs while making them more responsible for the outcome of their efforts. Such programs often organize employees into work teams of 5 to 15 members who are responsible for producing an entire product item. Team members are cross-trained and can therefore move from job to job within the team. Each team essentially manages itself and is responsible for its quality, scheduling, ordering and use of materials, and problem solving. Many firms have successfully employed work teams to boost morale, productivity, quality, and competitiveness.

Equity Theory

According to **equity theory**, how much people are willing to contribute to an organization depends on their assessment of the fairness, or equity, of the rewards they will receive in exchange. In a fair situation, a person receives rewards proportional to the contribution he or she makes to the organization. However, in practice, equity is a subjective notion. Each worker regularly develops a personal input-output ratio by taking stock of his or her contribution (inputs) to the organization in time, effort, skills, and experience and assessing the rewards (outputs) offered by the organization in pay, benefits, recognition, and promotions. The worker compares his or her ratio to the input-output ratio of some other person—a "comparison other," who may be a co-worker, a friend working in another organization, or an "average" of several people working in the organization. If the two ratios are close, the individual will feel that he or she is being treated equitably.

Let's say you have a high-school education and earn $25,000 a year. When you compare your input-output ratio with that of a co-worker who has a college degree and makes $35,000 a year, you will probably feel that you are being paid fairly. However, if you perceive that your personal input-output ratio is lower than that of your college-educated co-worker, you may

feel that you are being treated unfairly and be motivated to seek change. Or if you learn that your co-worker who makes $35,000 has only a high-school diploma, you may feel cheated by your employer. To achieve equity, you could try to increase your outputs by asking for a raise or promotion. You could also try to have your co-worker's inputs increased or his or her outputs decreased. Failing to achieve equity, you may be motivated to look for a job at a different company.

equity theory an assumption that how much people are willing to contribute to an organization depends on their assessment of the fairness, or equity, of the rewards they will receive in exchange

expectancy theory the assumption that motivation depends not only on how much a person wants something but also on how likely he or she is to get it

Because almost all the issues involved in equity theory are subjective, they can be problematic. Author David Callahan has argued that feelings of inequity may underlie some unethical or illegal behavior in business. For example, due to employee theft and shoplifting, Walmart experiences billions in inventory losses every year. Some employees may take company resources to restore what they perceive to be equity. Theft of company resources is the number one ethical issue, based on a survey by the Ethics Resource Center.[12] Callahan believes that employees who do not feel they are being treated equitably may be motivated to equalize the situation by lying, cheating, or otherwise "improving" their pay, perhaps by stealing.[13] Managers should try to avoid equity problems by ensuring that rewards are distributed on the basis of performance and that all employees clearly understand the basis for their pay and benefits.

Expectancy Theory

Psychologist Victor Vroom described **expectancy theory**, which states that motivation depends not only on how much a person wants something but also on the person's perception of how likely he or she is to get it. A person who wants something and has reason to be optimistic will be strongly motivated. For example, say you really want a promotion. And let's say because you have taken some night classes to improve your skills, and moreover, have just made a large, significant sale, you feel confident that you are qualified and able to handle the new position. Therefore, you are motivated to try to get the promotion. In contrast, if you do not believe you are likely to get what you want, you may not be motivated to try to get it, even though you really want it.

STRATEGIES FOR MOTIVATING EMPLOYEES

Based on the various theories that attempt to explain what motivates employees, businesses have developed several strategies for motivating their employees and boosting

behavior modification
changing behavior and encouraging appropriate actions by relating the consequences of behavior to the behavior itself

job rotation
movement of employees from one job to another in an effort to relieve the boredom often associated with job specialization

job enlargement the addition of more tasks to a job instead of treating each task as separate

job enrichment the incorporation of motivational factors, such as opportunity for achievement, recognition, responsibility, and advancement, into a job

morale and productivity. Some of these techniques include behavior modification and job design, as well as the already described employee involvement programs and work teams.

Behavior Modification

Behavior modification involves changing behavior and encouraging appropriate actions by relating the consequences of behavior to the behavior itself. The concept of behavior modification was developed by psychologist B. F. Skinner, who showed that there are two types of consequences that can modify behavior—reward and punishment. Skinner found that behavior that is rewarded will tend to be repeated, while behavior that is punished will tend to be eliminated. For example, employees who know that they will receive a bonus such as an expensive restaurant meal for making a sale over $2,000 may be more motivated to make sales. Workers who know they will be punished for being tardy are likely to make a greater effort to get to work on time.

However, the two strategies may not be equally effective. Punishing unacceptable behavior may provide quick results but may lead to undesirable long-term side effects, such as employee dissatisfaction and increased turnover. In general, rewarding appropriate behavior is a more effective way to modify behavior.

Job Design

Herzberg identified the job itself as a motivational factor. Managers have several strategies that they can use to design jobs to help improve employee motivation. These include job rotation, job enlargement, job enrichment, and flexible scheduling strategies.

Job Rotation

Job rotation allows employees to move from one job to another in an effort to relieve the boredom that is often associated with job specialization. Businesses often turn to specialization in hopes of increasing productivity, but there is a negative side effect to this type of job design: Employees become bored and dissatisfied, and productivity declines. Job rotation reduces this boredom by allowing workers to undertake a greater variety of tasks and by giving them the opportunity to learn new skills. With job rotation, an employee spends a specified amount of time performing one job and then moves on to another, different job. The worker eventually returns to the initial job and begins the cycle again.

Job rotation is a good idea, but it has one major drawback. Because employees may eventually become bored with all the jobs in the cycle, job rotation does not totally eliminate the

URSULA BURNS MOTIVATES EMPLOYEES

In 2009 Ursula Burns became the first black female CEO of a *Fortune* 500 corporation when she took over the top position at Xerox. Burns credits her rise from intern to CEO to hard work. While she admits that Xerox's support of diversity probably helped her at the beginning of her career, Burns's straightforward style and strong work ethic helped her rise to the top.

Raised in poverty by a single mother who worked hard so that her children could attend private school, Burns learned the value of hard work at an early age. She first went to work at Xerox as an intern in 1980 and never left the company. Burns was quickly

promoted, finally becoming president in 2007. Thanks to her no-nonsense management style, Burns helped Xerox find success by improving efficiency and customer service.

According to her peers, Burns has all the skills necessary to successfully lead Xerox as the company's top manager: technical expertise and conceptual, analytical, and human relations skills. Burns will need these skills in coming years. During the last economic recession, Xerox faced losses as customers purchased less and product prices fell. People and businesses are also beginning to use less paper as they move from copies to e-mail to share information. However, Burns has a strong history of innovation and is making plans to expand Xerox's capabilities.

One of her strategies is to adjust the company's corporate culture. She hopes

to use the downturn as a time to encourage her employees worldwide to become more independent and self-managing. Her goal is to establish trust between herself and her workers, empowering them to make the right decisions on their own. Burns's shared commitment to both employees and innovation may be just what Xerox needs to point the company in a new direction.[14]

Discussion Questions

1. Why do you think Ursula Burns is so successful?

2. What kind of skills do you think are most useful to Ursula Burns as CEO of Xerox?

3. How do you think Ursula Burns's early life prepared her for her current position at Xerox?

problem of boredom. Job rotation is extremely useful, however, in situations where a person is being trained for a position that requires an understanding of various units in an organization. Eli Lilly is a strong believer in the benefits of job rotation. The company leaves employees in their current jobs and asks them to take on short-term assignments outside their field of expertise or interest. The results of the process have been positive, and Nokia is trying the same process with similar outcomes.[15] Many executive training programs require trainees to spend time learning a variety of specialized jobs. Job rotation is also used to cross-train today's self-directed work teams.

Job Enlargement

Job enlargement adds more tasks to a job instead of treating each task as separate. Like job rotation, job enlargement was developed to overcome the boredom associated with specialization. The rationale behind this strategy is that jobs are more satisfying as the number of tasks performed by an individual increases. Employees sometimes enlarge, or craft, their jobs by noticing what needs to be done and then changing tasks and relationship boundaries to adjust. Individual orientation and motivation shape opportunities to craft new jobs and job relationships. Job enlargement strategies have been more successful in increasing job satisfaction than have job rotation strategies. IBM, AT&T, and Maytag are among the many companies that have used job enlargement to motivate employees.

Job Enrichment

Job enrichment incorporates motivational factors such as opportunity for achievement, recognition, responsibility, and advancement into a job. It gives workers not only more tasks within the job, but more control and authority over the job. Job enrichment programs enhance a worker's feeling of responsibility and provide opportunities for growth and advancement when the worker is able to take on the more challenging tasks. Hyatt Hotels Corporation and General Foods use job enrichment to improve the quality of work life for their employees. The potential benefits of job enrichment are great, but it requires careful planning and execution.

Flexible Scheduling Strategies

Many U.S. workers work a traditional 40-hour workweek consisting of five 8-hour days with fixed starting and ending times. Facing problems of poor morale and high absenteeism as well as a diverse workforce with changing needs, many managers have turned to flexible scheduling strategies such as flextime, compressed workweeks, job sharing, part-time work, and telecommuting. A survey by CareerBuilder.com showed that 40 percent of working fathers were offered flexible work schedules versus 53 percent of working mothers.[16]

Flextime is a program that allows employees to choose their starting and ending times, as long as they are at work during a specified core period (Figure 9.4). It does not reduce the total number of hours that employees work; instead, it gives employees more flexibility in choosing which hours they work. A firm may specify that employees must be present from 10:00 a.m. to 3:00 p.m. One employee may choose to come in at 7:00 a.m. and leave at the end of the core time, perhaps to attend classes at a nearby college after work. Another employee, a mother who lives in the suburbs, may come in at 9:00 a.m. in order to have time to drop off her children at a day-care center and commute by public transportation to her job. Flextime provides many benefits, including improved ability to recruit and retain workers who wish to balance work and home life. Customers can be better served by allowing more coverage of customers over longer hours, workstations and facilities can be better utilized by staggering employee use, and rush hour traffic may be reduced. In addition, flexible schedules have been associated with an increase in healthy behaviors on the part of employees. More flexible schedules are associated with healthier lifestyle choices such as increased physical activity and healthier sleep habits.[17]

Related to flextime are the scheduling strategies of the compressed workweek and job

> ## Flextime provides many benefits, including improved ability to recruit and retain workers who wish to balance work and home life.

flextime a program that allows employees to choose their starting and ending times, provided that they are at work during a specified core period

▼**FIGURE 9.4**
Flextime, Showing Core and Flexible Hours

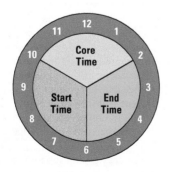

compressed workweek a four-day (or shorter) period during which an employee works 40 hours

job sharing performance of one full-time job by two people on part-time hours

sharing. The **compressed work-week** is a four-day (or shorter) period in which an employee works 40 hours. Under such a plan, employees typically work 10 hours per day for four days and have a three-day weekend. The compressed workweek reduces the company's operating expenses because its actual hours of operation are reduced. It is also sometimes used by parents who want to have more days off to spend with their families. The U.S. Bureau of Labor Statistics notes that the following career options provide greater flexibility in scheduling: medical transcriptionist, financial manager, nurse, database administrator, accountant, software developer, physical therapist assistant, paralegal, graphic designer, and private investigator.[18]

Job sharing occurs when two people do one job. One person may work from 8:00 a.m. to 12:30 p.m.; the second person comes in at 12:30 p.m. and works until 5:00 p.m. Job sharing gives both people the opportunity to work as well as time to fulfill other obligations, such as parenting or school. With job sharing, the company has the benefit of the skills of two people for one job, often at a lower total cost for salaries and benefits than one person working eight hours a day would be paid.

Two other flexible scheduling strategies attaining wider use include allowing full-time workers to work part time for a certain period and allowing workers to work at home either full or part time. Employees at some firms may be permitted to work part time for several months in order to care for a new baby or an elderly parent or just to slow down for a little while to "recharge

TEAM EXERCISE

Form groups and outline a compensation package that you would consider ideal in motivating an employee, recognizing performance, and assisting the company in attaining its cost-to-performance objectives. Think about the impact of intrinsic and extrinsic motivation and recognition. How can flexible scheduling strategies be used effectively to motivate employees? Report your compensation package to the class.

their batteries." When the employees return to full-time work, they are usually given a position comparable to their original full-time position. Other firms are allowing employees to telecommute or telework (work at home a few days of the week), staying connected via computers, modems, and telephones. Today, 33.7 million Americans are teleworkers, working most often from home, a customer's business, or from their cars.[19]

Although many employees ask for the option of working at home to ease the responsibilities of caring for family members, some have discovered that they are more productive at home without the distractions of the workplace. An assessment of 12 company telecommuting programs, including Apple, AT&T, and the state of California, found that positive productivity changes occurred. Traveler's Insurance Company reports its telecommuters to be 20 percent more productive than its traditional employees.[20] Other employees, however, have discovered that they are not suited for working at home. Many chief financial officers, for example, believe that telecommuting is not conducive to their jobs. A survey of finance executives revealed that only 18.3 percent of finance departments allow their employees to work from home on a regular basis as part of their flexible working arrangements.[21] Still, work-at-home programs do help reduce overhead costs for businesses. For example, some companies used to maintain a surplus of office space but have reduced the surplus through employee telecommuting, "hoteling" (being assigned to a desk through a reservation system), and "hot-desking" (several people using the same desk but at different times).

Companies are turning to flexible work schedules to provide more options to employees who are trying to juggle their work duties with other responsibilities and needs. Preliminary results indicate that flexible scheduling plans increase job satisfaction, which, in turn, leads to increases in productivity. Some recent research, however, has indicated there are potential problems with telecommuting. Some managers are reluctant to adopt the practice because the pace of change in today's workplace is faster than ever, and telecommuters may be left behind or actually cause managers more work in helping them stay abreast of changes. Some employers also worry that telecommuting workers create a security risk by creating more opportunities for computer hackers or equipment thieves. Some employees have found that working outside the office may hurt career advancement opportunities, and some report that instead of helping them balance work and family responsibilities, telecommuting increases the strain by blurring the barriers between the office and home. Co-workers call at all hours, and telecommuters are apt to continue to work when they are not supposed to (after regular business hours or during vacation time).

REI, the outdoor-sporting company, encourages its workers to have a healthy work-life balance. Among other benefits, employees get paid to take a sabbatical after a number of years of service.

Businesses have come up with different ways to motivate employees, including rewards such as trophies and plaques to show the company's appreciation.

Importance of Motivational Strategies

Motivation is more than a tool that managers can use to foster employee loyalty and boost productivity. It is a process that affects all the relationships within an organization and influences many areas such as pay, promotion, job design, training opportunities, and reporting relationships. Employees are motivated by the nature of the relationships they have with their supervisors, by the nature of their jobs, and by characteristics of the organization. Table 9.5 shows the top 10 companies in the *Fortune* 100 Best Companies to Work For, along with the types of strategies they use to motivate employees. Even the economic environment can change an employee's motivation. In a slow growth or recession economy, sales can flatten or decrease and morale can drop because of the need to cut jobs. In the most recent recession, many workers feared

---

SO YOU THINK // You May Be Good at Motivating a Workforce /

If you are good at mediation, can smooth over conflict, and have a good understanding of motivation and human relations theories, then you might be a good leader, human resource manager, or training expert. Most organizations, especially as they grow, will need to implement human relations programs. These are necessary to teach employees about sensitivity to other cultures, religions, and beliefs, as well as for teaching the workforce about the organization so that they understand how they fit in the larger picture. Employees need to appreciate the benefits of working together to make the firm run smoothly, and they also need to understand how their contributions help the firm. To stay motivated, most employees need to feel like what they do each day contributes something of value to the firm. Disclosing information and including employees in decision-making processes will also help employees feel valuable and wanted within the firm.

There are many different ways employers can reward and encourage employees. However, employers must be careful when considering what kinds of incentives to use. Different cultures value different kinds of incentives more highly than others. For example, a Japanese worker would probably not like it if she were singled out from the group and given a large cash bonus as reward for her work. Japanese workers tend to be more group oriented, and therefore anything that singles out individuals would not be an effective way of rewarding and motivating. American workers, on the other hand, are very individualistic, and a raise and public praise might be more effective. However, what might motivate a younger employee (bonuses, raises, and perks) may not be the same as what motivates a more seasoned, experienced, and financially successful employee (recognition, opportunity for greater influence, and increased training). Motivation is not an easy thing to understand, especially as firms become more global and more diverse.

Another important part of motivation is enjoying where you work and your career opportunities. Here is a list of the best places to do business and start careers in the United States, according to *Forbes* magazine. Chances are, workers who live in these places have encountered fewer frustrations than those places at the bottom of the list and, therefore, would probably be more content with where they work. [22]

▼ Best Places for Business and Careers

Rank	Metro Area	Job Growth Projected Rank	Metro Area Population (in thousands)
1.	Des Moines, IA	10	563
2.	Provo, UT	29	556
3.	Raleigh, NC	14	1,126
4.	Fort Collins, CO	21	298
5.	Lincoln, NE	72	298
6.	Denver, CO	49	2,552
7.	Omaha, NE	54	850
8.	Huntsville, AL	2	406
9.	Lexington, KY	32	471
10.	Austin, TX	12	1,705

Source: Kurt Badenhausen, "The Best Places for Business and Careers," *Forbes*, April 14, 2010, www.forbes.com/2010/04/13/best-places-for-business=beltway-business-places-10_lander.html, accessed April 13, 2011.

▼ **TABLE 9.5** Best Companies to Work For

Rank	Companies	Motivational Strategies
1.	SAS	Employee benefits such as on-site health care, kids summer camp, and salon
2.	Boston Consulting Group	Good pay, dedication to social work
3.	Wegmans Food Markets	Emphasizes employee well-being through exercise and healthy eating
4.	Google	10 percent pay hike, ability to award one another "spot bonuses"
5.	Netapp	Generous pay and bonuses
6.	Zappos.com	Fun corporate culture, free lunches, a life coach on hand
7.	Camden Property Trust	Allows employees to rent furnished apartments for personal vacations at $20 a night
8.	Nugget Market	Holds employee rallies where awards are delivered and employees are given a chance to win bonuses
9.	Recreational Equipment (REI)	Four-week sabbaticals after 15 years of service, steep discounts on clothes
10.	Dreamworks Animation SKG	Movie screenings, afternoon yoga, art classes, monthly parties

Source: "The 100 Best Companies to Work For," *Fortune,* February 7, 2011, pp. 91–101.

losing their jobs and increased the amount they were saving. The firm may have to work harder to keep good employees and to motivate all employees to work to overcome obstacles. In good economic times, employees may be more demanding and be on the lookout for better opportunities. New rewards or incentives may help motivate workers in such economies.

Motivation tools, then, must be varied as well. Managers can further nurture motivation by being honest, supportive, empathetic, accessible, fair, and open. Motivating employees to increase satisfaction and productivity is an important concern for organizations seeking to remain competitive in the global marketplace. ■

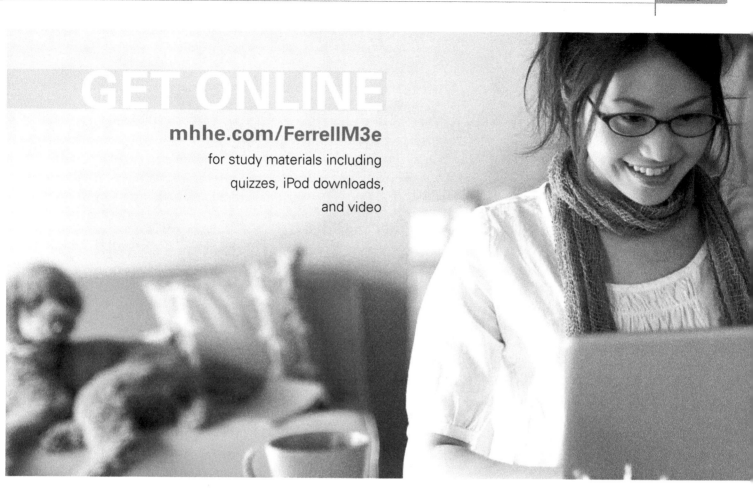

GET ONLINE

mhhe.com/FerrellM3e

for study materials including
quizzes, iPod downloads,
and video

chapter nine

active review card
Motivating the Workforce

in a
nutshell

Managers who understand the needs and motivations of workers and strategies for motivating them can help workers reach higher levels of productivity, subsequently contributing to the achievement of organizational goals.

The following statements will test your take-away knowledge from this chapter. Do your best to explain each one in the space provided below.

LO.1 Define human relations, and determine why its study is important.

LO.2 Summarize early studies that laid the groundwork for understanding employee motivation.

LO.3 Compare and contrast the human-relations theories of Abraham Maslow and Frederick Herzberg.

LO.4 Investigate various theories of motivation, including Theories X, Y, and Z; equity theory; and expectancy theory.

LO.5 Describe some of the strategies that managers use to motivate employees.

Did your answers include the following important points?

LO.1. Define human relations, and determine why its study is important.

- Human relations is the study of the behavior of individuals and groups in organizational settings. Its focus is what motivates employees to perform on the job.
- Human relations is important because businesses need to understand how to motivate their employees to be more effective, boost workplace morale, and maximize employees' productivity and creativity.

LO.2. Summarize early studies that laid the groundwork for understanding employee motivation.

- Time and motion studies by Frederick Taylor and others helped them analyze how employees perform specific work tasks in an effort to improve their productivity.
- Taylor and the early practitioners of the classical theory of motivation felt that money and job security were the primary motivations of employees; however, the Hawthorne Studies revealed that human factors also influence workers' behavior.

LO.3. Compare and contrast the human-relations theories of Abraham Maslow and Frederick Herzberg.

- Abraham Maslow defined five basic needs of all people and arranged them in the order in which they must be satisfied: physiological, security, social, esteem, and self-actualization.
- Frederick Herzberg divided the characteristics of jobs into hygiene factors and motivational factors.

- Herzberg's hygiene factors can be compared to Maslow's physiological and security needs; motivational factors may include Maslow's social, esteem, and self-actualization needs.

LO.4. Investigate various theories of motivation, including Theories X, Y, and Z; equity theory; and expectancy theory.

- Douglas McGregor contrasted two views of management: Theory X suggests workers dislike work, while Theory Y suggests that workers not only like work, but seek out responsibility to satisfy their higher-order needs.
- Theory Z stresses employee participation in all aspects of company decision making, while the equity theory indicates that how much people are willing to contribute to an organization depends on their assessment of the fairness, or equity, of the rewards they will receive in exchange.
- The expectancy theory states that motivation depends not only on how much a person wants something, but also on the person's perception of how likely he or she is to get it.

LO.5. Describe some of the strategies that managers use to motivate employees.

- Strategies for motivating workers include behavior modification and job design. Among the job design strategies businesses use are job rotations, job enlargement, job enrichment, and flexible scheduling strategies.

Practical Application

LO.1.
- An inner drive that directs behavior toward objectives is called _____.
- Good morale in an employee is likely to result in _____.
- A(n) _____ is the personal satisfaction that we feel from achieving a goal.

LO.2.
- Prior to the Hawthorne Studies, management theorists believed that the primary motivators of employees were job security and _____.
- The birth of the study of human relations can be traced to _____ and _____ studies.

LO.3.
- According to Maslow, living life to the fullest is most closely associated with fulfilling one's _____ need.
- According to Frederick Herzberg, the aspects that relate to the work setting form the _____ factors.

LO.4.
- Jim has learned that his company is offering a Hawaiian vacation to its best salesperson. He almost won last year and really wants the trip. He is working very hard because he thinks he has a good chance to win. This exemplifies the _____ theory.
- Jack believes that he can get some extra work completed before the deadline by withholding his workers' vacation schedules until the job is completed. Jack is a manager who follows _____.
- The approach that suggests that imagination, ingenuity, and creativity can help solve organizational problems is _____.

LO.5.
- A work system that allows employees to choose their starting and ending times as long as they are at work during a specified core period is called _____.
- _____ adds tasks to a job instead of treating each task as a separate job.
- When Kelly reprimands Sarah each time Sarah is late for work, Kelly is applying _____.

ten

managing
human resources

If a business is to achieve success, it must have sufficient numbers of employees who are qualified and motivated to perform the required duties. Thus, managing the quantity (from hiring to firing) and quality (through training, compensating, and so on) of employees is an important business function. Meeting the challenge of managing increasingly diverse human resources effectively can give a company a competitive edge in a global marketplace.

This chapter focuses on the quantity and quality of human resources. First we look at how human resources managers plan for, recruit, and select qualified employees. Next we look at training, appraising, and compensating employees, aspects of human resources management designed to retain valued employees. Along the way, we'll also consider the challenges of managing unionized employees and workplace diversity.

LEARNING OBJECTIVES

LO1 Define human resources management, and explain its significance.

LO2 Summarize the processes of recruiting and selecting human resources for a company.

LO3 Discuss how workers are trained and their performance appraised.

LO4 Identify the types of turnover companies may experience, and explain why turnover is an important issue.

LO5 Specify the various ways a worker may be compensated.

LO6 Discuss some of the issues associated with unionized employees, including collective bargaining and dispute resolution.

LO7 Describe the importance of diversity in the workforce.

THE NATURE OF HUMAN RESOURCES MANAGEMENT

Chapter 1 defined human resources as labor, the physical and mental abilities that people use to produce goods and services. **Human resources management (HRM)** refers to all the activities involved in determining an organization's human resources needs, as well as acquiring, training, and compensating people to fill those needs. Human resources managers are concerned with maximizing the satisfaction of employees and motivating them to meet organizational objectives productively. In some companies, this function is called personnel management.

HRM has increased in importance over the last few decades, in part because managers have developed a better understanding of human relations through the work of Maslow, Herzberg, and others. Moreover, the human resources themselves are changing. Employees today are concerned not only about how much a job pays; they are concerned also with job satisfaction, personal performance, recreation, benefits, the work environment, and their opportunities for advancement. Once dominated by white men, today's workforce includes significantly more women, African Americans, Hispanics, and other minorities, as well as

Today's organizations are more diverse, with a greater range of women, minorities, and older workers.

older workers and workers with disabilities. Human resources managers must be aware of these changes and leverage them to increase the productivity of their employees. Every manager practices some of the functions of human resources management at all times.

PLANNING FOR HUMAN RESOURCES NEEDS

When planning and developing strategies for reaching the organization's overall objectives, a company must consider whether it will have the human resources necessary to carry out its plans. After determining how many employees and what skills are needed to satisfy the overall plans, the human resources department (which may range from the owner in a small business to hundreds of people in a large corporation) ascertains how many employees the company currently has and how many will be retiring or otherwise leaving the organization during the planning period. With this information, the human resources manager can then forecast how many more employees the company will need to hire and what qualifications they must have, or determine if layoffs are required to meet demand more efficiently. HRM planning also requires forecasting the availability of people in the workforce who will have the necessary qualifications to meet the organization's future needs. The human resources manager then develops a strategy for satisfying the organization's human resources needs. As organizations strive to increase efficiency through outsourcing, automation, or learning to effectively use temporary workers, hiring needs can change dramatically.

Next, managers analyze the jobs within the organization so that they can match the human resources to the available assignments. **Job analysis** determines, through observation and study, pertinent information about a job—the specific tasks that comprise it; the knowledge, skills, and abilities necessary to perform it; and the environment in which it will be performed. Managers use the information obtained through a job analysis to develop job descriptions and job specifications.

A **job description** is a formal, written explanation of a specific job that usually includes job title, tasks to be performed (for instance, waiting on customers), relationship with other jobs, physical and mental skills required (such as lifting heavy boxes or calculating data), duties, responsibilities, and working conditions. A **job specification** describes the qualifications necessary for a specific job, in terms of education (some jobs

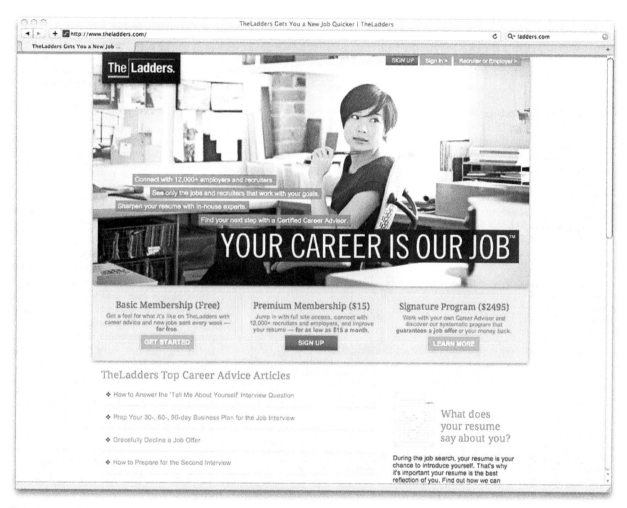

TheLadders.com is a website that targets job seekers looking for jobs with an annual pay of $100,000 or more.

require a college degree), experience, personal characteristics (ads frequently request outgoing, hardworking persons), and physical characteristics. Both the job description and job specification are used to develop recruiting materials such as newspapers, trade publications, and online advertisements.

RECRUITING AND SELECTING NEW EMPLOYEES

After forecasting the firm's human resources needs and comparing them to existing human resources, the human resources manager should have a general idea of how many new employees the firm needs to hire. With the aid of job analyses, management can then recruit and select employees who are qualified to fill specific job openings.

Recruiting

Recruiting means forming a pool of qualified applicants from which management can select employees. There are two sources from which to develop this pool of applicants—internal and external.

Internal sources of applicants include the organization's current employees. Many firms have a policy of giving first consideration to their own employees—or promoting from within. The cost of hiring current employees to fill job openings is inexpensive when compared with the cost of hiring from external sources, and it is good for employee morale. However, hiring from within creates another job vacancy to be filled.

External sources consist of advertisements in newspapers and professional journals, employment agencies, colleges, vocational schools, recommendations from current employees, competing firms, unsolicited applications, and online services. Internships are also a good way to solicit for potential employees. Many

ABILITY AND PERFORMANCE TESTS ARE USED TO DETERMINE WHETHER AN APPLICANT HAS THE SKILLS NECESSARY FOR THE JOB.

companies hire college students or recent graduates to low-paying internships that give them the opportunity to get hands-on experience on the job. If the intern proves to be a good fit, an organization may then hire the intern as a full-time worker. Figure 10.1 illustrates some of the top benefits of becoming an intern. There are also hundreds of websites where employers can post job openings and job seekers can post their résumés, including Monster.com and CareerBuilder.com. TheLadders.com is a website that focuses on jobs starting at $100,000 a year. It seeks higher educated and more experienced individuals for high-paying positions. Employers looking for employees for specialized jobs can use more focused sites such as computerwork.com. Increasingly, companies can turn to their own websites for potential candidates: Nearly all of the *Fortune* 500 firms provide career websites where they recruit, provide employment information, and take applications. Employers can also use social networking sites such as LinkedIn to post jobs and search for candidates. Figure 10.2 indicates that many consumers believe social networking sites may eventually supplant traditional résumés. Using external sources of applicants is generally more expensive than hiring from within, but it may be necessary if there are no current employees who meet the job specifications or there are better-qualified people outside of the organization. Recruiting for entry-level managerial and professional positions is often carried out on college and university campuses. For managerial or professional positions above the entry level, companies sometimes depend on employment agencies or executive search firms, sometimes called *headhunters*, which specialize in luring qualified people away from other companies.

▼FIGURE 10.1
Benefits of an Internship

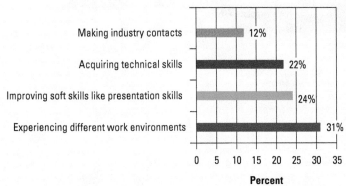

Making industry contacts — 12%
Acquiring technical skills — 22%
Improving soft skills like presentation skills — 24%
Experiencing different work environments — 31%

Percent

Source: Creative Group Survey of 125 Advertising Executives and 125 Senior Marketing Executives, "'What I did this summer . . . ',", April 15, 2009, http://creativegroup.mediaroom.com/index.php?s=43&item=91 (accessed October 11, 2011).

▼FIGURE 10.2
Will profiles on networking sites replace traditional résumés?

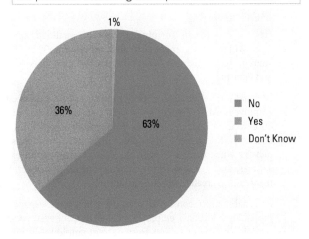

1%
36%
63%

■ No
■ Yes
■ Don't Know

Source: OfficeTeam survey of 500 human resources managers. Reprinted in *USA Today,* March 16, 2011.

Selection

Selection is the process of collecting information about applicants and using that information to decide which ones to hire. It includes the application itself, as well as interviewing, testing, and reference checking. This process can be quite lengthy and expensive. Procter & Gamble, for example, offers online applications for jobs in 80 countries. The first round of evaluations involves assessment, and if this stage goes well, the candidate interviews in the region or country to which the applicant applied.[1] Such rigorous scrutiny is necessary to find those applicants who can do the work expected and fit into the firm's structure and culture. If an organization finds the "right" employees through its recruiting and selection process, it will not have to spend as much money later in recruiting, selecting, and training replacement employees.

The Application In the first stage of the selection process, the individual fills out an application form and perhaps has a brief interview. The application form asks for the applicant's name, address, telephone number, education, and previous work experience. The goal of this stage of the selection process is to get acquainted with the applicants and to weed out those who are obviously not qualified for the job. For employees with work experience, most companies ask for the following information before contacting a potential candidate: current salary, reason for seeking a new job, years of experience, availability, and level of interest in the position. In addition to identifying obvious qualifications, the application can provide subtle clues about whether a person is appropriate for a particular job. For instance, an applicant who gives unusually creative answers may be perfect for a position at an advertising agency; a person who turns in a sloppy, hurriedly scrawled application probably would not be appropriate for a technical job requiring precise adjustments. Many companies now accept online applications. The online application for Target is designed not only to collect biographical data on the applicant, but also to create a picture of the applicant and how that person might contribute to the company. The completion of the survey takes about 45 minutes, depending on the position. To get a better view of the fit between the applicant and the company, the online application contains a questionnaire that asks applicants more specific questions, from how they might react in a certain situation to personality attributes like self-esteem or ability to interact with people.

The Interview

The next phase of the selection process involves interviewing applicants. Table 10.1 provides some insights on finding the right work environment. Interviews allow management to obtain detailed information about the applicant's experience and skills, reasons for changing jobs, attitudes toward the job, and an idea of whether the person would fit in with the company. Table 10.2 lists some of the most common questions asked by interviewers, while Table 10.3 reveals some common mistakes candidates make in interviewing. Furthermore, the interviewer can answer the applicant's questions about the requirements for the job, compensation, working conditions, company policies, organizational culture, and so on. A potential employee's questions may be just as revealing as his or her answers.

Testing

Another step in the selection process is testing. Ability and performance tests are used to determine whether an applicant has the skills necessary for the job. Aptitude, IQ, or personality tests may be used to assess an applicant's potential for a certain kind of work and his or her ability to fit into the organization's culture. One of the most commonly used tests is the Myers-Briggs Type Indicator. Myers-Briggs Type Indicator Test is used

▼ **TABLE 10.1** Interviewing Tips

1. Evaluate the work environment. Do employees seem to get along and work well in teams?
2. Evaluate the attitude of employees. Are employees happy, tense, or overworked?
3. Are employees enthusiastic and excited about their work?
4. What is the organizational culture, and would you feel comfortable working there?

Source: Adapted from "What to Look for During Office Visits," http://careercenter.tamu.edu/guides/interviews/lookforinoffice.cfm?sn=parents (accessed April 13, 2011).

▼ **TABLE 10.2** Most Common Questions Asked during the Interview

1. Tell me about yourself.
2. Why should I hire you?
3. Please tell me about your future objectives.
4. Has your education prepared you for your career?
5. Have you been a team player?
6. Did you encounter any conflict with your previous professors or employer? What are the steps that you have taken to resolve this issue?
7. What is your biggest weakness?
8. How would your professors describe you?
9. What are the qualities that a manager should possess?
10. If you could turn back time, what would you change?

Source: "Job Interview Skills Training: Top Ten Interview Questions for College Graduates," February 17, 2010, www.articlesbase.com/business-articles/job-interview-skills-training-top-ten-interview-questions-for-college-graduates-1871741.html (accessed April 13, 2011).

BURGERVILLE: FAST FOOD THAT EMPLOYEES CAN LOVE

If you're looking for a unique spin on fast food and a business committed to corporate social responsibility, check out Burgerville. Founded in 1961 by George Propstra, there are currently 39 locations found throughout Washington and Oregon. The company is dedicated to fresh, local, and sustainable concepts, so much so that it began offering compostable cups, straws, and lids. However, what really makes this chain unique is its employee health care plan. Burgerville pays 90 percent of premiums for employees working at least 20 hours weekly—a rarity in fast food. An employee survey revealed health care as a primary issue, and Burgerville responded. Today, the company sees less turnover and higher productivity. Burgerville has received the Com-Psych Corporation "Health at Work Award" Silver Award for committing to affordable health care and the YMCA "Spirit of Health Award" for employee health care benefits and its commitment to sustainable business practices. The company motto is "serve with love," and this is certainly easier to do when your company loves you back![2]

Some jobs require potential hires to undergo physical examinations such as drug tests.

Background checks are important for detecting past misconduct or criminal activities committed by job applicants.

TABLE 10.3 Mistakes Made in Interviewing

1. Not taking the interview seriously.
2. Not dressing appropriately (dressing down).
3. Not appropriately discussing experience, abilities, and education.
4. Being too modest about your accomplishments.
5. Talking too much.
6. Too much concern about compensation.
7. Speaking negatively of a former employer.
8. Not asking enough or appropriate questions.
9. Not showing the proper enthusiasm level.
10. Not engaging in appropriate follow-up to the interview.

Source: "Avoid the Top 10 Job Interview Mistakes," All Business, www.allbusiness.com/human-resources/careers-job-interview/1611-1.html (April 13, 2011).

worldwide by millions of people each year. Although polygraph ("lie detector") tests were once a common technique for evaluating the honesty of applicants, in 1988 their use was restricted to specific government jobs and those involving security or access to drugs. Applicants may also undergo physical examinations to determine their suitability for some jobs, and many companies require applicants to be screened for illegal drug use. Illegal drug use and alcoholism can be particularly damaging to businesses. There are more than 11 million heavy drinkers and 16 million illegal drug users in the United States. Of this group, 75 percent are employed full time and around half work for small businesses. On average in small businesses, 1 out of 10 employees are either alcohol or drug abusers. Small businesses may have a higher percentage of these employees because they do not engage in systematic drug testing. If you employ a drug or alcohol abuser, you can expect a 33 percent loss in productivity from this employee, which costs employers roughly $7,000 annually. Overall, substance abuse costs American employers $160 billion each year through high employee turnover and absenteeism, workplace accidents, higher workers' compensation costs, higher medical costs, and workplace theft and violence.[3]

Because computer knowledge is a requirement for many jobs today, certain companies also require an applicant to take a typing test or tests to determine their knowledge of MS Word, Excel, PowerPoint, and/or other necessary programs. Like the application form and the interview, testing serves to eliminate those who do not meet the job specifications.

Reference Checking Before making a job offer, the company should always check an applicant's references. Reference checking usually involves verifying educational background and previous work experience. Background checking is important because applicants may misrepresent themselves on their applications or résumés. The star of *Dinner: Impossible* on the Food Network fabricated portions of his résumé, including the claim that he cooked for Britain's royal family. The Food Network, upon learning of these errors, did not renew Robert

Title VII of the Civil Rights Act prohibits discrimination in employment and created the Equal Employment Opportunity Commission

▼ **TABLE 10.4** Top 10 Résumé Lies

1. Stretching dates of employment

2. Inflating past accomplishments and skills

3. Enhancing job titles and responsibilities

4. Education exaggeration and fabricating degrees

5. Unexplained gaps and periods of "self employment"

6. Omitting past employment

7. Faking credentials

8. Fabricating reasons for leaving previous job

9. Providing fraudulent references

10. Misrepresenting military record

Source: Christopher T. Marquet and Lisa J. B. Peterson, "Résumé Fraud: The Top 10 Lies," www.marquetinternational.com/pdf/Resume%20Fraud-Top%20 Ten%20Lies.pdf (accessed April 13, 2011).

Irvine's contract, indicating that viewers place trust in the network and the accuracy of information that it provides and that Irvine "challenged that trust."[4] Irvine had to work for months to apologize and set the record straight about his chef credentials. Food Network ultimately did rehire him to host *Dinner: Impossible.* As Table 10.4 illustrates, some of the most common types of résumé lies include the faking of credentials, overstatements of skills or accomplishments, lies concerning education/ degrees, omissions of past employment, and the falsification of references.[5] Reference checking is a vital, albeit often overlooked, stage in the selection process. Managers charged with hiring should be aware, however, that many organizations will confirm only that an applicant is a former employee, perhaps with beginning and ending work dates, and will not release details about the quality of the employee's work.

Legal Issues in Recruiting and Selecting

Legal constraints and regulations are present in almost every phase of the recruitment and selection process, and a violation of these regulations can result in lawsuits and fines. Therefore, managers should be aware of these restrictions to avoid legal problems. Some of the laws affecting human resources management are discussed below.

Because one law pervades all areas of human resources management, we'll take a quick look at it now. **Title VII of the Civil Rights Act** of 1964 prohibits discrimination in employment. It also created the Equal Employment Opportunity Commission (EEOC), a federal agency dedicated to increasing job opportunities for women and minorities and eliminating job discrimination based on race, religion, color, sex, national origin, or disability. As a result of Title VII, employers must not impose sex distinctions in job specifications, job descriptions, or newspaper advertisements. In 2010 workplace discrimination charges filed with the EEOC totaled 99,922. Monetary compensation for victims reached more than $404 million. Race discrimination charges made up 36 percent of the total, while sexual discrimination charges consisted of 29 percent.[6] The Civil Rights Act of 1964 also outlaws the use of discriminatory tests for applicants. Aptitude tests and other indirect tests must be validated; in other words, employers must be able to demonstrate that scores on such tests are related to job performance, so that no one race has an advantage in taking the tests or is alternatively discriminated against. Although many hope for improvements in organizational diversity, in a survey of 357 global senior executives, 76 percent have one or no minorities among their top executives. Minorities make up 17 percent of the U.S. workforce, and that number should hit 20 percent by 2016. In spite of a lack of diversity, many of these companies indicate an initiative to support workplace diversity.[7]

Other laws affecting HRM include the Americans with Disabilities Act (ADA), which prevents discrimination against persons with disabilities. It also classifies people with AIDS as disabled and, consequently, prohibits using a positive AIDS test as reason to deny an applicant employment. The Age Discrimination in Employment Act specifically outlaws discrimination based on age. Its focus is banning hiring practices that discriminate against people between the ages of 40 and 69, but it also outlaws policies that require employees to retire before the age of 70. Generally, when companies need employees, recruiters head to college campuses, and when downsizing is necessary, many older workers are offered early retirement. For instance, roughly 9 percent of retirees said they were forced to retire.[8] However, the last few years have seen a new trend of older people working more. Approximately 28 million people 55 or older held jobs in 2010, the highest level yet for this age range. Conversely, the number of people in the workforce between the ages of 16 and 24 hit its lowest level during the same period.[9] Figure 10.3 shows the changes within these two age groups. Indeed there are many benefits that companies are realizing in hiring older workers. Some of these benefits include the fact that they are more dedicated, punctual, honest, and detail-oriented; are good listeners; take pride in their work; exhibit good organizational skills; are efficient and confident; are mature; can be seen as role models; have good communication skills; and offer an opportunity for a reduced labor cost because of already having insurance plans.[10]

The Equal Pay Act mandates that men and women who do equal work must receive the same wage. Wage differences are acceptable only if they are attributed to seniority, performance, or qualifications. In the United States, the typical full-time female employee earns 19 percent less than the average full-time male employee. In a study by PayScale, some of the biggest gender pay gaps can be found in positions such as chief executive (women earn 71 percent of what men earn), hospital administrator (women earn 77 percent of what men earn), and chief operating officer (women earn 80 percent of what men earn). Performance quality in these jobs is relatively subjective. Jobs like engineers, actuaries, or electricians, where the performance evaluation is

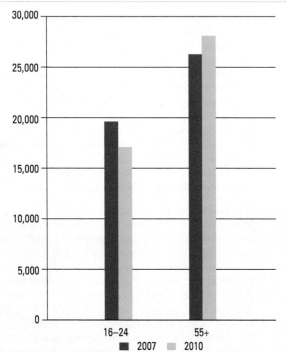

FIGURE 10.3
U.S. Population Employed within Two Age Groups (in Thousands)

2007   2010

Source: U.S. Department of Labor, Bureau of Labor Statistics, labor force statistics from the *Current Population Survey,* http://data.bls.gov:8080/PDQ/outside.jsp?survey=ln (accessed January 31, 2011).

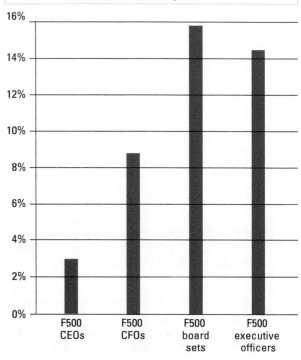

FIGURE 10.4
Women Leaders at *Fortune* 500 Companies

Sources: "U.S. Women in Business," *Catalyst,* December 2010, www.catalyst.org/publication/132/us-women-in-business; Alix Stuart, "Women CFOs Holding Steady," July 14, 2010, www.cfo.com/article.cfm/14510069/c_14511151?f=home_todayinfinance; "Women CEOs," CNNMoney.com, http://money.cnn.com/magazines/fortune/fortune500/2010/womenceos/ (accessed January 13, 2011).

more objective, result in greater salary parity between men and women.[11] However, despite the wage inequalities that still exist, women in the workplace are becoming increasingly accepted among both genders. The working mother is no longer a novelty; in fact, many working mothers seek the same amount of achievement as working men and women who are not mothers. One survey revealed that 69 percent of young working mothers reported that they want to move up in their careers compared to 48 percent in 2002. Also, more and more men believe that a woman can be a good mother and still maintain a successful career. About 67 percent of the male respondents believe that working women can still be good mothers compared to 49 percent in 1977. Figure 10.4 shows the percentage of women who hold some of the country's top leadership positions.[12]

DEVELOPING THE WORKFORCE

Once the most qualified applicants have been selected, have been offered positions, and have accepted their offers, they must be formally introduced to the organization and trained

so they can begin to be productive members of the workforce. **Orientation** familiarizes the newly hired employees with fellow workers, company procedures, and the physical properties of the company. It generally includes a tour of the building; introductions to supervisors, co-workers, and subordinates; and the distribution of organizational manuals describing the organization's policy on vacations, absenteeism, lunch breaks, company benefits, and so on. Orientation also involves socializing the new employee into the ethics and culture of the new company. Many larger companies now show videotapes of procedures, facilities, and key personnel in the organization to help speed the adjustment process.

Training and Development

Although recruiting and selection are designed to find employees who have the knowledge, skills, and abilities the company needs, new employees still must undergo **training** to learn how to do their specific job tasks. *On-the-job training* allows workers to learn by actually performing the tasks of the job, while *classroom training* teaches employees with lectures, conferences, videotapes, case studies, and Web-based training. For instance, McDonald's trains those interested in company operations and leadership development at the Fred L. Turner Training Center, otherwise known as Hamburger University. Hamburger University employs full-time professors to train students in a variety of topics, including crew development, restaurant management, middle management, and executive development. Training includes classroom instruction, hands-on instruction, and computer e-learning, with instruction available in 28 different languages.[13] **Development** is training that augments the skills and knowledge of managers and professionals. Training and development are also used to improve the skills of employees in their present positions and to prepare them for increased responsibility and job promotions. Training is therefore a vital function of human resources management. Companies are engaging in more experiential and involvement-oriented training exercises for employees. Use of role-plays, simulations, and online training methods are becoming increasingly popular in employee training.

Assessing Performance

Assessing an employee's performance—his or her strengths and weaknesses on the job—is one of the most difficult tasks for managers. However, performance appraisal is crucial because it gives employees feedback on how they are doing and what they need to do to improve. It also provides a basis for determining how to compensate and reward employees, and it generates information about the quality of the firm's selection, training, and development activities. Table 10.5 identifies 16 characteristics that may be assessed in a performance review.

Performance appraisals may be objective or subjective. An objective assessment is quantifiable. For example, a Westinghouse employee might be judged by how many circuit boards

he typically produces in one day or by how many of his boards have defects. A Century 21 real estate agent might be judged by the number of houses she has shown or the number of sales she has closed. A company can also use tests as an objective method of assessment. Whatever method they use, managers must take into account the work environment when they appraise performance objectively.

When jobs do not lend themselves to objective appraisal, the manager must relate the employee's performance to some other standard. One popular tool used in subjective assessment is the ranking system, which lists various performance factors on which the manager ranks employees against each other. Although used by many large companies, ranking systems are unpopular with many employees. Qualitative criteria, such as teamwork and communication skills, used to evaluate employees are generally hard to gauge. Such grading systems have triggered employee lawsuits that allege discrimination in grade/ranking assignments. For example, one manager may grade a company's employees one way, while another manager grades a group more harshly depending on the managers' grading style. If layoffs occur, then employees graded by the second manager may be more likely to lose their jobs. Other criticisms of grading systems include unclear wording or inappropriate words that a manager may unintentionally write in a performance evaluation, like *young* or

> **orientation** familiarizing newly hired employees with fellow workers, company procedures, and the physical properties of the company

> **training** teaching employees to do specific job tasks through either classroom development or on-the-job experience

> **development** training that augments the skills and knowledge of managers and professionals

▼ **TABLE 10.5** Performance Characteristics

- **Productivity**—rate at which work is regularly produced
- **Quality**—accuracy, professionalism, and deliverability of produced work
- **Job knowledge**—understanding of the objectives, practices, and standards of work
- **Problem solving**—ability to identify and correct problems effectively
- **Communication**—effectiveness in written and verbal exchanges
- **Initiative**—willingness to identify and address opportunities for improvement
- **Adaptability**—ability to become comfortable with change
- **Planning and organization skills**—reflected through the ability to schedule projects, set goals, and maintain organizational systems
- **Teamwork and cooperation**—effectiveness of collaborations with co-workers
- **Judgment**—ability to determine appropriate actions in a timely manner
- **Dependability**—responsiveness, reliability, and conscientiousness demonstrated on the job
- **Creativity**—extent to which resourceful ideas, solutions, and methods for task completion are proposed
- **Sales**—demonstrated through success in selling products, services, yourself, and your company
- **Customer service**—ability to communicate effectively with customers, address problems, and offer solutions that meet or exceed their expectations
- **Leadership**—tendency and ability to serve as a doer, guide, decision maker, and role model
- **Financial management**—appropriateness of cost controls and financial planning within the scope defined by the position

Source: "Performance Characteristics," Performance Review from www.salary.com/Careerresources/docs/related_performance_review_part2_popup.html (accessed June 12, 2001). Used with permission.

For multinational corporations such as McDonald's, employee training and performance assessments might need to be slightly adapted for different cultures.

pretty to describe an employee's appearance. These liabilities can all be fodder for lawsuits should employees allege that they were treated unfairly. It is therefore crucial that managers use clear language in performance evaluations and be consistent with all employees. Several employee grading computer packages have been developed to make performance evaluations easier for managers and clearer for employees.[14]

Another performance appraisal method used by many companies is the 360-degree feedback system, which provides feedback

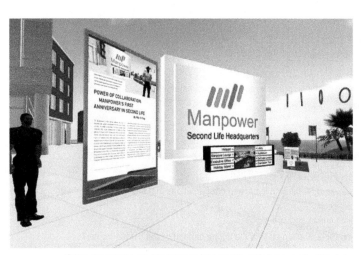

Some companies are choosing to incorporate training opportunities into virtual worlds such as Second Life.

from a panel that typically includes superiors, peers, and subordinates. Because of the tensions it may cause, peer appraisal appears to be difficult for many. However, companies that have success with 360-degree feedback tend to be open to learning and willing to experiment and are led by executives who are direct about the expected benefits as well as the challenges.[15] Managers and leaders with a high emotional intelligence (sensitivity to their own as well as others' emotions) assess and reflect upon their interactions with colleagues on a daily basis. In addition, they conduct follow-up analysis on their projects, asking the right questions and listening carefully to responses without getting defensive of their actions.[16]

Whether the assessment is objective or subjective, it is vital that the manager discuss the results with the employee, so that the employee knows how well he or she is doing the job. The results of a performance appraisal become useful only when they are communicated, tactfully, to the employee and presented as a tool to allow the employee to grow and improve in his or her position and beyond. Performance appraisals are also used to determine whether an employee should be promoted, transferred, or terminated from the organization.

Turnover

Turnover, which occurs when employees quit or are fired and must be replaced by new employees, results in lost productivity from the vacancy, costs to recruit replacement employees, and management time devoted to interviewing, training, and socialization expenses for new employees. Clarkston Consulting in Durham, North Carolina, was going through a phase where employees were dissatisfied. They were working more than the industry norm of 56 hours per week (not including travel), and turnover was increasing. The company engaged in intense training to improve skills and understand competitive and best practices, and it introduced a truncated travel schedule. The travel program allowed employees to leave home on Monday, stay in a hotel and work at the client's site for four days, and return to work at home on Friday. Removing large amounts of travel from evenings and weekends significantly improved morale, productivity, and satisfaction.[17] Part of the reason for turnover may be overworked employees as a result of downsizing and a lack of training and advancement opportunities.[18] Of course, turnover is not always an unhappy occasion when its takes the form of a promotion or transfer.

A **promotion** is an advancement to a higher-level job with increased authority, responsibility, and pay. In some companies and most labor unions, seniority—the length of time a person has been with the company or at a particular job classification—

should be carefully explained to all employees and should be set forth in employee handbooks. Table 10.6 illustrates what *not* to do when you are terminated.

Many companies have downsized in recent years, laying off tens of thousands of employees in their effort to become more productive and competitive. Chrysler underwent a restructuring plan that cut 3,000 jobs and three models, including the PT Cruiser, Dodge Durango, and Chrysler Aspen. The company also rejected hundreds of car dealership agreements, resulting in significant job losses.[19]

> **turnover** occurs when employees quit or are fired and must be replaced by new employees

> **promotion** an advancement to a higher-level job with increased authority, responsibility, and pay

> **transfer** a move to another job within the company at essentially the same level and wage

> **separations** employment changes involving resignation, retirement, termination, or layoff

> ## The results of a performance appraisal become useful only when they are communicated, tactfully, to the employee and presented as a tool to allow the employee to grow and improve in his or her position and beyond.

is the key issue in determining who should be promoted. Most managers base promotions on seniority only when they have candidates with equal qualifications: Managers prefer to base promotions on merit.

A **transfer** is a move to another job within the company at essentially the same level and wage. Transfers allow workers to obtain new skills or to find a new position within an organization when their old position has been eliminated because of automation or downsizing.

Separations occur when employees resign, retire, are terminated, or are laid off. Employees may be terminated, or fired, for poor performance, violation of work rules, absenteeism, and so on. Businesses have traditionally been able to fire employees *at will*, that is, for any reason other than for race, religion, sex, or age, or because an employee is a union organizer. However, recent legislation and court decisions now require that companies fire employees fairly, for just cause only. Managers must take care, then, to warn employees when their performance is unacceptable and may lead to dismissal, elevating the importance of performance evaluations. They should also document all problems and warnings in employees' work records. To avoid the possibility of lawsuits from individuals who may feel they have been fired unfairly, employers should provide clear, business-related reasons for any firing, supported by written documentation if possible. Employee disciplinary procedures

Layoffs are sometimes temporary; employees may be brought back when business conditions improve. For instance, after the most recent recession Chrysler began to rehire some of the workers it had been forced to lay off.[20] When layoffs are to be permanent, employers often help employees find other jobs and may extend benefits while the employees search for new employment. Such actions help lessen the trauma of the layoffs. Fortunately, there are several business areas that are choosing not to downsize. Table 10.7 shows some industries that are planning to hire in the near future.

▼ **TABLE 10.6** What You Should Not Do When You Are Terminated

1. Do not tell off your boss and co-workers, even if you think they deserve it.
2. Do not damage company property or steal something.
3. Do not forget to ask for a reference.
4. Do not badmouth your employer or any of your co-workers to your replacement.
5. Do not badmouth your employer to a prospective employer when you go on a job interview.

Source: Dawn Rosenberg McKay, "Five Things Not to Do When You Leave Your Job," http://careerplanning.about.com/od/jobseparation/a/leave_ mistakes.htm (accessed April 13, 2011).

that a high turnover rate in a company may signal problems either with the selection and training process, the compensation program, or even the type of company. To help reduce turnover, companies have tried a number of strategies, including giving employees more interesting job responsibilities (job enrichment), allowing for increased job flexibility, and providing more employee benefits.

A well-organized human resources department strives to minimize losses due to separations and transfers because recruiting and training new employees is very expensive. Note

▼ **TABLE 10.7** Job Areas for Which Employers Plan to Hire Recent Graduates

	All Job Areas	Entry Level	Middle Level	Senior Level	Executive Level	Total
Accounting	24%	64%	65%	22%	15%	100%
Consulting	27	51	72	20	12	100
Business development	31	47	73	28	16	100
Investment banking	16	57	66	22	15	100
Finance other than investment banking	42	55	71	20	11	100
General management	29	48	72	32	19	100
HR or organization management	17	58	71	29	19	100
Information technology or MIS	15	61	75	26	17	100
Marketing or sales	45	50	70	22	11	100
Operations and logistics	25	53	73	27	13	100
Other job areas	17	56	69	25	13	100

Source: "Corporate Recruiters Survey: 2010 General Data Report," Graduate Management Admission Council®, www.gmac.com/NR/rdonlyres/8C83F765-646D-44AC-AF8C-D76687593C7B/0/2010CRS_GeneralDataReport.pdf (accessed January 13, 2011).

KING ARTHUR FLOUR: AN EMPLOYEE-CENTERED CORPORATE CULTURE

You might think flour is boring, but at King Arthur Flour employees love the stuff! The company was founded in 1790—the year after George Washington was elected president. It has grown slowly from five employees in 1990 to over 160 today. What makes these employees so passionate about flour? They own the business. Although King Arthur Flour operated as a family-owned business for five decades, it is now 100 percent employee owned. Therefore, employees control their fate and have a true stake in their flour.

In 1990 King Arthur was essentially a mail-order business. Today it sells to

bakeries and grocery stores, runs a retail store in Vermont, and excels in public relations and marketing. Employees throughout the business are honored as valuable members of a team. All employees are offered training and development opportunities such as baking/cooking workshops, along with free products and store discounts. The company has won awards based on its structure: number six on Best Places to Work in Vermont and part of *The Wall Street Journal's* Top Small Workplaces.

Employees at King Arthur are also dedicated to sustainability and the environment. The company advocates sustainable living by recycling, composting, decreasing energy consumption, and reducing its use of toxic products. King Arthur does not use chemical additives in its flour, nor does it use genetically modified wheat. The company is a member of the Vermont Business Environmental Partnership (promoting

improved environmental and economic performance) and Green Up Day, and it is a certified Founding B Corporation (meaning it has met rigorous social and environmental performance standards).

Overall, King Arthur appears to be a fun place to work—where those who love cooking, baking, and sustainability can come together in partnership to run their own company.[21]

Discussion Questions

1. King Arthur Flour is 100 percent employee owned. How does this change how the business operates, and how is it run versus other organizational models?

2. What are some of the perks of working at King Arthur Flour?

3. Why is King Arthur Flour such a great place to work? Would you like to work there?

COMPENSATING THE WORKFORCE

People generally don't work for free, and how much they are paid for their work is a complicated issue. Also, designing a fair compensation plan is an important task because pay and benefits represent a substantial portion of an organization's expenses. Wages that are too high may result in the company's products being priced too high, making them uncompetitive in the market. Wages that are too low may damage employee morale and result in costly turnover. Remember that compensation is one of the hygiene factors identified by Herzberg.

Designing a fair compensation plan is a difficult task because it involves evaluating the relative worth of all jobs within the business while allowing for individual efforts. Compensation for a specific job is typically determined through a **wage/salary survey**, which tells the company how much compensation comparable firms are paying for specific jobs that the firms have in common. Compensation for individuals within a specific job category depends on both the compensation for that job and the individual's productivity. Therefore, two employees with identical jobs may not receive exactly the same pay because of individual differences in performance.

Financial Compensation

Financial compensation falls into two general categories—wages and salaries. **Wages** are financial rewards based on the number of hours the employee works or the level of output achieved. Wages based on the number of hours worked are called time wages. The federal minimum wage increased to $7.25

per hour in 2009 for covered nonexempt workers.[22] Many states also mandate minimum wages; in the case where the two wages are in conflict, the higher of the two wages prevails. There may even be differences between city and state minimum wages. In New Mexico, the minimum wage is $7.50, whereas in the state capital of Santa Fe, the minimum wage is $9.85, due to a higher cost of living.[23] Table 10.8 compares wage and other information for Costco and Walmart, two well-known discount chains. Time wages are appropriate when employees are continually interrupted and when quality is more important than quantity. Assembly-line workers, clerks, and maintenance personnel are commonly paid on a time-wage basis. The advantage of time wages is the ease of computation. The disadvantage is that time wages provide no incentive to increase productivity. In fact, time wages may encourage employees to be less productive.

To overcome these disadvantages, many companies pay on an incentive system, using piece wages or commissions. Piece wages are based on the level of output achieved. A major advantage of piece wages is that they motivate employees to supervise their own activities and to increase output. Skilled craftworkers are often paid on a piece-wage basis.

The other incentive system, **commission**, pays a fixed amount or a percentage of the employee's sales. Kele & Co Jewelers in Plainfield, Illinois, makes sterling silver jewelry and offers semiprecious stones and gemstones at affordable prices. Its handcrafted jewelry is sold through the Internet (www.keleonline.com) and through independent sales representatives (ISRs) all over the country. The unique aspect of Kele's sales process is its innovative sales and commission structure. ISRs have no minimum sales quotas, sales are shared among team members during training and after being promoted, and there is no requirement to purchase inventory as jewelry is shipped from Kele headquarters. ISRs receive a 30 percent commission on sales. Kele also pays for the design, development, and maintenance of a website to support ISRs. The goal is to increase the profit margin and earning potential of the salespeople. The company's goal is to become the largest direct sales company in the industry.[24] This method motivates employees to sell as

▼ **TABLE 10.8** Costco versus Walmart

	Costco	Walmart
Number of employees	147,000	2,100,000+
Revenues	$71.4 billion	$405 billion
Average hourly wage	$19	$11.75 full time
World's most admired ranking	21	9
Strengths	Management quality; financial soundness; people management	Management quality; financial soundness; global competitiveness

Sources: "Fortune Global 500," *CNN Money.com*, http://money.cnn.com/magazines/fortune/global500/2010/full_list/; "World's Most Admired Companies," *CNNMoney.com*, http://money.cnn.com/magazines/fortune/mostadmired/2010/full_list/; Edward Teach, "Because It's the Right Thing to Do," *CFO Magazine*, March 1, 2010, www.cfo.com/article.cfm/14476783/1/c_14477052?f=insidecfo; "Walmart," updated May 8, 2010, nyjobsource.com, http://nyjobsource.com/walmart.html (accessed January 14, 2011).

salary a financial reward calculated on a weekly, monthly, or annual basis

bonuses monetary rewards offered by companies for exceptional performance as incentives to further increase productivity

profit sharing a form of compensation whereby a percentage of company profits is distributed to the employees whose work helped generate them

benefits nonfinancial forms of compensation provided to employees, such as pension plans, health insurance, paid vacation and holidays, and the like

CHALLENGES OF WORKING AT HOME

Working from home may sound like a dream. Yet when that dream comes true, employees find some downsides that they did not expect. Perhaps the greatest challenge is the balancing of work and home life. In a traditional job setting, work occurs in the office while leisure occurs at home. However, those who work at home lack this clear boundary. Lack of office space, family distractions, and sticking to set schedules are additional challenges work-at-home employees face.

These challenges are not going away anytime soon. According to Interactive Data Corporation, over 18.4 million U.S. workers set up home-based businesses. Interactive Data predicts this number will grow annually by roughly 350,000 for the next few years. The situation has led experts to recommend methods to help work-at-home employees.

First, employees working at home should have a clear work space, even if it is only a desk on which work materials reside. Maintaining a schedule of strict hours devoted to work and then communicating these hours to family and friends is important. Additionally, for some workers who crave socialization, working alone might be difficult. However, thanks to technology, employees can often work in social settings like coffee shops or libraries.

Those who can't get past these challenges have pursued other creative alternatives. Some freelancers and entrepreneurs have begun renting office space at work areas designed to accommodate the self-employed. These spaces have a more relaxed atmosphere than a normal work environment; one of these "work spaces," for instance, is located in a Victorian home in Brooklyn. Other work-at-home entrepreneurs opt to form weekly work gatherings, where individuals can work on their laptops while being able to socialize with others. For many self-motivated individuals, the rewards of working away from the office overcome the sacrifices.[25]

Discussion Questions

1. Why is working at home a challenge to many employees?

2. How does one create a boundary between work and home life when working at home?

3. Would you be more productive working at home or renting space at an out-of-home work area?

> The most common counseling services offered include drug- and alcohol-abuse treatment programs, fitness programs, smoking cessation clinics, stress-management clinics, financial counseling, family counseling, and career counseling.

much as they can. Some companies also combine payment based on commission with time wages or salaries.

A **salary** is a financial reward calculated on a weekly, monthly, or annual basis. Salaries are associated with white-collar workers such as office personnel, executives, and professional employees. Although a salary provides a stable stream of income, salaried workers may be required to work beyond usual hours without additional financial compensation.

In addition to the basic wages or salaries paid to employees, a company may offer **bonuses** for exceptional performance as an incentive to increase productivity further. Many workers receive a bonus as a "thank you" for good work and an incentive to continue working hard. Many owners and managers are recognizing that simple bonuses and perks foster happier employees and reduce turnover.

Another form of compensation is **profit sharing**, which distributes a percentage of company profits to the employees whose work helped generate those profits. Some profit-sharing plans involve distributing shares of company stock to employees. Usually referred to as *ESOPs*—employee stock ownership plans—they have been gaining popularity in recent years. One reason for the popularity of ESOPs is the sense of partnership that they create between the organization and employees. Profit sharing can also motivate employees to work hard, because increased productivity and sales mean that the profits or the stock dividends will increase. Many organizations offer employees a stake in the company through stock purchase plans, ESOPs, or stock investments through 401(k) plans. Employees below senior management levels rarely received stock options, until recently. Companies are adopting broad-based stock option plans to build a stronger link between employees' interests and the organization's interests. ESOPs have met with enormous success over the years, and employee-owned stock has even outperformed the stock market during certain periods. Many businesses have found employee stock options a great way to boost productivity and increase morale. As a result, approximately 12,000 companies have adopted ESOPs within the United States.[26]

Benefits

Benefits are nonfinancial forms of compensation provided to employees, such as pension plans for retirement; health, disability, and life insurance; holidays and paid days off for vacation or illness; credit union membership; health programs; child care; elder care; assistance with adoption; and more. According to the Bureau of Labor Statistics, employer costs for employee compensation for civilian workers in the United States average $27.42 per hour worked. Wages and salaries account for approximately 70.8 percent of those costs, while benefits account for 29.2 percent of the cost. Legally required benefits (Social Security, Medicare, federal and state employment insurance, and workers' compensation) account for 7.7 percent of total compensation.[27] Such benefits increase employee security and, to a certain extent, their morale and motivation.

Table 10.9 lists some of the benefits Internet search engine Google offers its employees. Although health insurance is a common benefit for full-time employees, rising health care costs have forced a growing number of employers to trim this benefit. Even government workers, whose wages and benefits used to be virtually guaranteed safe, have seen reductions in health care and other benefits. For example, the City Council of Pensacola, Florida, voted to sharply reduce city workers' benefits and wages in order to deal with a budget shortfall after the most recent recession left the city struggling financially.[28]

A benefit increasingly offered is the employee assistance program (EAP). Each company's EAP is different, but most offer counseling for and assistance with those employees' personal problems that might hurt their job performance if not addressed. The most common counseling services offered include drug- and alcohol-abuse treatment programs, fitness programs, smoking cessation clinics, stress-management clinics, financial counseling, family counseling, and career

▼ **TABLE 10.9** Google's Employee Benefits

- Health insurance:
  - Employee medical insurance (spouse and domestic-partner insurance also available)
  - Dental insurance
  - Vision insurance
- Vacation (15 days per year for one–three years' employment; 20 days off for four–five years' employment; 25 days for more than six years' employment)
- Twelve paid holidays/year
- Savings plans
  - 401(k) retirement plan, matched by Google
  - Flexible spending accounts
- Disability and life insurance
- Employee Assistance Program
- Free lunches and snacks
- Massages, gym membership, hair stylist, fitness class, and bike repair
- Weekly activities
- Maternity leave
- Adoption assistance
- Tuition reimbursement
- Employee referral plan
- On-site doctor
- Backup child care
- Holiday parties, health fair, credit union, roller hockey, outdoor volleyball court, discounts for local attractions

Source: "Google Benefits," www.google.com/intl/en/jobs/lifeatgoogle/benefits (accessed April 13, 2011).

Larger companies such as Google will sometimes offer onsite gyms or workout facilities as an employee benefit.

labor unions employee organizations formed to deal with employers for achieving better pay, hours, and working conditions

collective bargaining the negotiation process through which management and unions reach an agreement about compensation, working hours, and working conditions for the bargaining unit

labor contract the formal, written document that spells out the relationship between the union and management for a specified period of time—usually two or three years

MANAGING UNIONIZED EMPLOYEES

Employees who are dissatisfied with their working conditions or compensation have to negotiate with management to bring about change. Dealing with management on an individual basis is not always effective, however, so employees may organize themselves into **labor unions** to deal with employers and to achieve better pay, hours, and working conditions. Organized employees are backed by the power of a large group that can hire specialists to represent the entire union in its dealings with management. Union workers make significantly more than nonunion employees. The United States has a roughly 13.6 percent unionization rate. Figure 10.5 displays unionization rates by state. On average, unionized workers have 15 percent higher hourly wages than nonunionized employees in similar positions.[29]

counseling. EAPs help reduce costs associated with poor productivity, absenteeism, and other workplace issues by helping employees deal with personal problems that contribute to these issues. For example, exercise and fitness programs reduce health insurance costs by helping employees stay healthy. Family counseling may help workers trying to cope with a divorce or other personal problems to better focus on their jobs.

Companies try to provide the benefits they believe their employees want, but diverse people may want different things. In recent years, some single workers have felt that co-workers with spouses and children seem to get "special breaks" and extra time off to deal with family issues. Some companies use flexible benefit programs to allow employees to choose the benefits they would like, up to a specified amount.

Fringe benefits include sick leave, vacation pay, pension plans, health plans, and any other extra compensation. Soft benefits include perks that help balance life and work. They include onsite child care, spas, food service, and even laundry services and hair salons. These soft benefits motivate employees and give them more time to focus on their jobs.

Cafeteria benefit plans provide a financial amount to employees so that they can select the specific benefits that fit their needs. The key is making benefits flexible, rather than giving employees identical benefits. As firms go global, the need for cafeteria or flexible benefit plans becomes even more important. For some employees, benefits are a greater motivator and differentiator in jobs than wages. For many Starbucks employees who receive health insurance when working part time, this benefit could be the most important compensation.

Over the last two decades, the list of fringe benefits has grown dramatically, and new benefits are being added every year.

▼**FIGURE 10.5**

Union Membership Rates by State

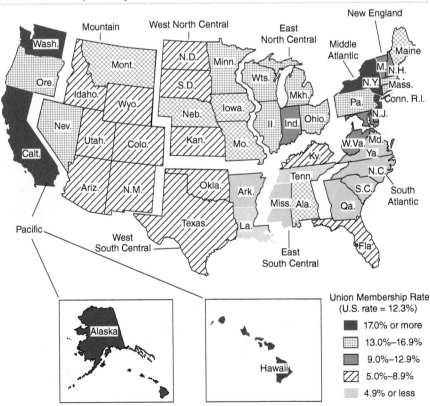

Source: U.S. Department of Labor, *Bureau of Labor Statistics,* January 21, 2011.

However, union growth has slowed in recent years, and prospects for growth do not look good. One reason is that most blue-collar workers, the traditional members of unions, have already been organized. Factories have become more automated and need fewer blue-collar workers. The United States has shifted from a manufacturing to a service economy, further reducing the demand for blue-collar workers. Moreover, in response to foreign competition, U.S. companies are scrambling to find ways to become more productive and cost efficient. Job enrichment programs and participative management have blurred the line between management and workers. Because workers' say in the way plants are run is increasing, their need for union protection is decreasing.

Nonetheless, labor unions have been successful in organizing blue-collar manufacturing, government, and health care workers, as well as smaller percentages of employees in other industries. Consequently, significant aspects of HRM, particularly compensation, are dictated to a large degree by union contracts at many companies. Therefore, we'll take a brief look at collective bargaining and dispute resolution in this section.

Collective Bargaining

Collective bargaining is the negotiation process through which management and unions reach an agreement about compensation, working hours, and working conditions for the bargaining unit (Figure 10.6). The objective of negotiations is to reach agreement about a **labor contract**, the formal, written document that spells out the relationship between the union and management for a specified period of time, usually two or three years.

In collective bargaining, each side tries to negotiate an agreement that meets its demands; compromise is frequently necessary. Management tries to negotiate a labor contract that permits the company to retain control over things like work schedules; the hiring and firing of workers; production standards; promotions, transfers, and separations; the span of management in each department; and discipline. Unions tend to focus on contract issues such as magnitude of wages; better pay rates for overtime, holidays, and undesirable shifts; scheduling of pay increases; and benefits. These issues will be spelled out in the labor contract, which union members will vote to either accept (and abide by) or reject.

Many labor contracts contain a *cost-of-living escalator* (or *adjustment*) *(COLA) clause,* which calls for automatic wage increases during periods of inflation to protect the "real" income of the employees. During tough economic times, unions may be forced to accept *givebacks*—wage and benefit concessions made to employers to allow them to remain competitive or, in some cases, to survive and continue to provide jobs for union workers.

Resolving Disputes

Sometimes, management and labor simply cannot agree on a contract. Most labor disputes are handled through collective bargaining or through grievance procedures. When these processes break down, however, either side may resort to more drastic measures to achieve its objectives.

FIGURE 10.6
The Collective Bargaining Process

picketing a public protest against management practices that involves union members marching and carrying antimanagement signs at the employer's plant or work site

strikes employee walkouts; one of the most effective weapons of labor unions

boycott an attempt to keep people from purchasing the products of a company

lockout management's version of a strike, wherein a work site is closed so that employees cannot go to work

strikebreakers people hired by management to replace striking employees; called "scabs" by striking union members

Labor Tactics Picketing is a public protest against management practices and involves union members marching (often waving antimanagement signs and placards) at the employer's plant or work site. Picketing workers hope that their signs will arouse sympathy for their demands from the public and from other unions. Picketing may occur as a protest or in conjunction with a strike.

Strikes (employee walkouts) are one of the most effective weapons labor has. By striking, a union makes carrying out the normal operations of a business difficult at best and impossible at worst. Strikes receive widespread publicity, but they remain a weapon of last resort. For example, after the French government announced plans to overhaul pensions and raise the retirement age from 60 to 62, citizens engaged in a nationwide strike to protest the changes. The strikes shut down schools and delayed rail and flight services.[30] The threat of a strike is often enough to get management to back down. In fact, the number of worker-days actually lost to strikes is less than the amount lost to the common cold.

A boycott is an attempt to keep people from purchasing the products of a company. In a boycott, union members are asked not to do business with the boycotted organization. Some unions may even impose fines on members who ignore the boycott. To gain further support for their objectives, a union involved in a boycott may also ask the public—through picketing and advertising—not to purchase the products of the picketed firm.

Management Tactics Management's version of a strike is the lockout; management actually closes a work site so that

Workers at a GE Aircraft Engines facility went on strike to protest the company's decision to outsource jobs overseas.

employees cannot go to work. Lockouts are used, as a general rule, only when a union strike has partially shut down a plant and it seems less expensive for the plant to close completely. For instance, National Football League team owners locked out players after a dispute over revenues and a failure to accept a new collective bargaining agreement. The lockout placed the 2011 NFL season in jeopardy as neither side seemed willing to capitulate.[31]

Strikebreakers, called "scabs" by striking union members, are people hired by management to replace striking employees. Managers hire strikebreakers to continue operations and reduce the losses associated with strikes—and to show the unions that they will not bow to their demands. Strikebreaking is generally a last-resort measure for management because it does great damage to the relationship between management and labor.

Outside Resolution Management and union members normally reach mutually agreeable decisions without outside assistance. Sometimes though, even after lengthy negotiations, strikes, lockouts, and other tactics, management and labor still cannot resolve a contract dispute. In such cases, they have three choices: conciliation, mediation, and arbitration. Conciliation brings in a neutral third party to keep labor and management talking. The conciliator has no formal power over union representatives or over management. The conciliator's goal is to get both parties to focus on the issues and to prevent negotiations from breaking down. Like conciliation, mediation involves bringing in a neutral third party, but the mediator's role is to suggest or propose a solution to the problem. Mediators have no formal power over either labor or management. With arbitration, a neutral third party is brought in to settle the dispute, but the arbitrator's solution is legally binding and enforceable. Generally, arbitration takes place on a voluntary basis—management and labor must agree to it, and they usually split the cost (the arbitrator's fee and expenses) between them. Occasionally, management and labor submit to *compulsory arbitration,* in which an outside party (usually the federal government) requests arbitration as a means of eliminating a prolonged strike that threatens to disrupt the economy.

THE IMPORTANCE OF WORKFORCE DIVERSITY

Customers, employees, suppliers—all the participants in the world of business—come in different ages, genders, races, ethnicities, nationalities, and abilities, a truth that business has

conciliation a method of outside resolution of labor and management differences in which a third party is brought in to keep the two sides talking

mediation a method of outside resolution of labor and management differences in which the third party's role is to suggest or propose a solution to the problem

arbitration settlement of a labor/management dispute by a third party whose solution is legally binding and enforceable

diversity the participation of different ages, genders, races, ethnicities, nationalities, and abilities in the workplace

come to label **diversity**. Understanding this diversity means recognizing and accepting differences as well as valuing the unique perspectives such differences can bring to the workplace.

The Characteristics of Diversity

When managers speak of diverse workforces, they typically mean differences in gender and race. While gender and race are important characteristics of diversity, others are also important. We can divide these differences into primary and secondary characteristics of diversity. In the lower segment of Figure 10.7, age, gender, race, ethnicity, abilities, and sexual orientation represent *primary characteristics* of diversity which are inborn and cannot be changed. In the upper section of Figure 10.7 are eight *secondary characteristics* of diversity—work background, income, marital status, military experience, religious beliefs, geographic location, parental status, and education—which *can* be changed. We acquire, change, and discard them as we progress through our lives.

FIGURE 10.7
Characteristics of Diversity

Source: Marilyn Loden and Judy B. Rosener, *Workforce America! Managing Employee Diversity as a Vital Resource,* 1991, p. 20. Used with permission. Copyright © 1991 The McGraw-Hill Companies.

Defining characteristics of diversity as either primary or secondary enhances our understanding, but we must remember that each person is defined by the interrelation of all characteristics. In dealing with diversity in the workforce, managers must consider the complete person—not one or a few of a person's differences.

Why Is Diversity Important?

The U.S. workforce is becoming increasingly diverse. Once dominated by white men, today's workforce includes significantly more women, African Americans, Hispanics, and other minorities, as well as older workers and workers with

> Once dominated by white men, today's workforce includes significantly more women, African Americans, Hispanics, and other minorities, as well as older workers and workers with disabilities.

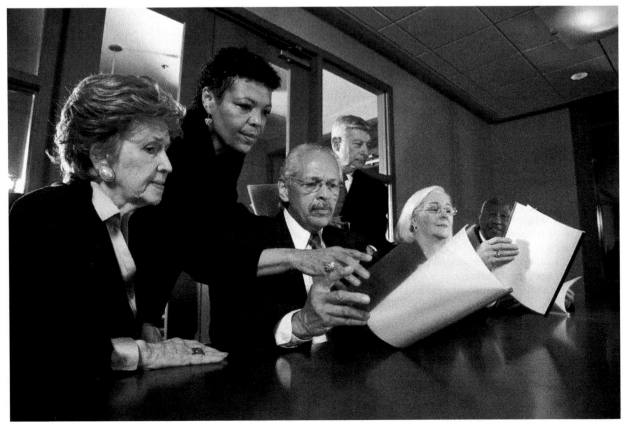

Some of the major benefits of diversity include a wider range of employee perspectives, greater innovation and creativity, and the ability to target a diverse customer base more effectively.

▼ **TABLE 10.10** Population by Race

Ethnic Group	Percentage	Total ($ millions)
Total population	100%	$308.7
White	72%	223.6
Black	13%	38.9
Asian	5%	14.7
American Indian or Alaska Native	0.9%	2.9
Hawaiian or Pacific Islander	0.2%	0.5
Other race	6%	19.1
Two or more races	3%	9.0
Hispanic	16%	50.5

*The U.S. Census Bureau does not include a separate listing for Hispanic origin. The 16 percent who are classified as Hispanic are included in the given segments (they may be classified as white, black, etc., depending on origins). This is why the percentages will come out greater than 100 percent.

Source: "2010 Census Shows America's Diversity," U.S. Census Bureau, March 24, 2011, www.census.gov/newsroom/releases/archives/2010 census/cbll -cn 125.html (accessed April 13, 2011).

disabilities. Table 10.10 presents some of the population data from the Census Bureau. It is estimated that within the next 50 years, Hispanics will represent 24 percent of the population, while African Americans and Asians/Pacific Islanders will comprise 15 percent and 9 percent, respectively.[32] These groups have traditionally faced discrimination and higher unemployment rates and have been denied opportunities to assume leadership roles in corporate America. Consequently, more and more companies are trying to improve HRM programs to recruit, develop, and retain more diverse employees to better serve their diverse customers. Some firms are providing special programs such as sponsored affinity groups, mentoring programs, and special career development opportunities. Sodexo has implemented a diversity scorecard index that uses both quantitative and qualitative measurements to measure the company's progress in the recruitment, retaining, and promotion of women and minority employees. Sodexo held managers responsible for diversity by creating a link between scorecard results and management bonuses. The result was a 23 percent increase of minority employees in the company since the implementation of the scorecard and an 11 percent increase in female employees.[33] Table 10.11 shows the top 20 companies for minorities according to a study by *Diversity, Inc.* Effectively managing diversity in the workforce involves cultivating and valuing its benefits and minimizing its problems.

The Benefits of Workforce Diversity

There are a number of benefits to fostering and valuing workforce diversity, including the following:

1. More productive use of a company's human resources.

2. Reduced conflict among employees of different ethnicities, races, religions, and sexual orientations as they learn to respect each other's differences.

3. More productive working relationships among diverse employees as they learn more about and accept each other.

4. Increased commitment to and sharing of organizational goals among diverse employees at all organizational levels.

5. Increased innovation and creativity as diverse employees bring new, unique perspectives to decision-making and problem-solving tasks.

6. Increased ability to serve the needs of an increasingly diverse customer base.[34]

Companies that do not value their diverse employees are likely to experience greater conflict, as well as prejudice and discrimination. Among individual employees, for example, racial slurs and gestures, sexist comments, and other behaviors by co-workers harm the individuals at whom such behavior is directed. The victims of such behavior may feel hurt, depressed, or even threatened and suffer from lowered self-esteem, all of which harm their productivity and morale. In such cases, women and minority employees may simply leave the firm, wasting the time, money, and other resources spent on hiring and training them. When discrimination comes from a supervisor, employees may also fear for their jobs. A discriminatory atmosphere not only can harm productivity and increase turnover, but it may also subject a firm to costly lawsuits and negative publicity.

Astute businesses recognize that they need to modify their human resources management programs to target the needs of

affirmative action programs legally mandated plans that try to increase job opportunities for minority groups by analyzing the current pool of workers, identifying areas where women and minorities are underrepresented, and establishing specific hiring and promotion goals, with target dates, for addressing the discrepancy

▼ **TABLE 10.11** The *DiversityInc* Top 50 Companies for Diversity

1. Sodexo	26. Cummins
2. Johnson & Johnson	27. HSBC–North America
3. AT&T	28. Monsanto Co.
4. Kaiser Permanente	29. General Mills
5. Ernst & Young	30. Aetna
6. PricewaterhouseCoopers	31. Capital One
7. Marriot International	32. Prudential Financial
8. IBM Corp.	33. The Walt Disney Co.
9. Bank of America	34. JPMorgan Chase
10. Abbott	35. Kraft Foods
11. Verizon Communications	36. Toyota Motor North America
12. American Express Co.	37. Cisco Systems
13. Merck & Co.	38. Blue Cross Blue Shield of Florida
14. Colgate-Palmolive	39. Time Warner
15. KPMG	40. Target Corp.
16. Novartis Pharmaceuticals Corp	41. SC Johnson
17. The Coca-Cola Co.	42. MetLife
18. Procter & Gamble	43. Wells Fargo & Co.
19. Starwood Hotels & Resorts Worldwide	44. Ford Motor Co.
20. Health Care Service Corp.	45. Comerica
21. Cox Communications	46. JCPenney
22. Accenture	47. Northrop Grumman Corp.
23. Time Warner Cable	48. Xerox Corp.
24. MGM Mirage	49. Automatic Data Processing
25. Deloitte	50. WellPoint

Source: "The 2010 DiversityInc Top 50 List," *DiversityInc*, April 5, 2010, www.diversityincbestpractices.com/content/1934/article/7378/ (accessed January 14, 2011).

all their diverse employees as well as the needs of the firm itself. They realize that the benefits of diversity are long term in nature and come only to those organizations willing to make the commitment. Most importantly, as workforce diversity becomes a valued organizational asset, companies spend less time managing conflict and more time accomplishing tasks and satisfying customers, which is, after all, the purpose of business.

Affirmative Action

Many companies strive to improve their working environment through **affirmative action programs**, legally mandated plans that try to increase job opportunities for minority groups by analyzing the current pool of workers, identifying areas where women and minorities are underrepresented, and establishing specific hiring and promotion goals along with target dates for meeting those goals to resolve

TEAM EXERCISE

Form groups and go to monster.com and look up job descriptions for positions in business (account executive in advertising, marketing manager, human resources director, production supervisor, financial analyst, bank teller, etc). What are the key requirements for the position that you have been assigned (education, work experience, language/computer skills, etc.)? Does the position announcement provide a thorough understanding of the job? Was any key information that you would have expected omitted? Report your findings to the class.

the discrepancy. Affirmative action began in 1965 as Lyndon B. Johnson issued the first of a series of presidential directives. It was designed to make up for past hiring and promotion prejudices, to overcome workplace discrimination, and to provide equal employment opportunities for blacks and whites. Since then, minorities have made solid gains.

Legislation passed in 1991 reinforces affirmative action but prohibits organizations from setting hiring quotas that might result in reverse discrimination. Reverse discrimination occurs when a company's policies force it to consider only minorities or women instead of concentrating on hiring the person who is best qualified. More companies are arguing that affirmative action stifles their ability to hire the best employees, regardless of their minority status. Because of these problems, affirmative action became politically questionable. ▪

SO YOU WANT TO WORK // in Human Resources /

Managing human resources is a challenging and creative facet of a business. It is the department that handles the recruiting, hiring, training, and firing of employees. Because of the diligence and detail required in hiring and the sensitivity required in firing, human resources managers have a broad skill set. Human resources, therefore, is vital to the overall functioning of the business because without the right staff a firm will not be able to effectively carry out its plans. Like in basketball, a team is only as strong as its individual players, and those players must be able to work together and to enhance strengths and downplay weaknesses. In addition, a good human resources manager can anticipate upcoming needs and changes in the business, hiring in line with the dynamics of the market and organization.

Once a good workforce is in place, human resources managers must ensure that employees are properly trained and oriented and that they clearly understand some elements of what the organization expects. Hiring new people is expensive, time-consuming,

and turbulent; thus, it is imperative that all employees are carefully selected, trained, and motivated so that they will remain committed and loyal to the company. This is not an easy task, but it is one of the responsibilities of the human resources manager. Because even with references, a résumé, background checks, and an interview, it can be hard to tell how a person will fit in the organization—the HR manager needs to have skills to be able to anticipate how every individual will "fit in." Human resources jobs include compensation, labor relations, benefits, training, ethics, and compliance managers. All of the tasks associated with the interface with hiring, developing, and maintaining employee motivation come into play in human resources management. Jobs are diverse and salaries will depend on responsibilities, education, and experience.

One of the major considerations for an HR manager is workforce diversity. A multicultural, multiethnic workforce consisting of men and women will help bring a variety of viewpoints and improve the quality and creativity of organizational decision making.

Diversity is an asset and can help a company from having blindspots or harmony in thought, background, and perspective, which stifles good team decisions. However, a diverse workforce can present some management challenges. Human resources management is often responsible for managing diversity training and compliance to make sure employees do not violate the ethical culture of the organization or break the law. Different people have different goals, motivations, and ways of thinking about issues that are informed by their culture, religion, and the people closest to them. No one way of thinking is more right or more wrong than others, and they are all valuable. A human resources manager's job can become very complicated, however, because of diversity. To be good at human resources, you should be aware of the value of differences, strive to be culturally sensitive, and ideally should have a strong understanding and appreciation of different cultures and religions. Human resources managers' ability to manage diversity and those differences will affect their overall career success.

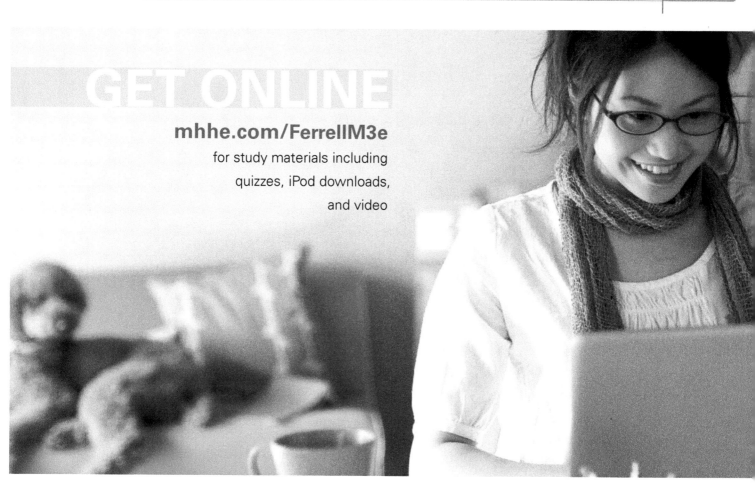

GET ONLINE

mhhe.com/FerrellM3e

for study materials including
quizzes, iPod downloads,
and video

chapter ten

active review card
Managing Human Resources

in a nutshell

Human resources managers need to plan for, recruit, and select qualified employees. Yet another aspect of the human resources manager's job is to train, appraise, compensate, and retain valued employees, which can present an added challenge among unionized and diverse employees.

The following statements will test your take-away knowledge from this chapter. Do your best to explain each one in the space provided below.

LO.1 Define human resources management, and explain its significance.

LO.2 Summarize the processes of recruiting and selecting human resources for a company.

LO.3 Discuss how workers are trained and their performance appraised.

LO.4 Identify the types of turnover companies may experience, and explain why turnover is an important issue.

LO.5 Specify the various ways a worker may be compensated.

LO.6 Discuss some of the issues associated with unionized employees, including collective bargaining and dispute resolution.

LO.7 Describe the importance of diversity in the workforce.

Did your answers include the following important points?

LO.1. Define human resources management, and explain its significance.

- Human resources management refers to all the activities involved in determining an organization's human resources needs and acquiring, training, and compensating people to fill those needs.
- It is concerned with maximizing the satisfaction of employees and improving their efficiency to meet organizational objectives.

LO.2. Summarize the processes of recruiting and selecting human resources for a company.

- Human resources managers must determine the firm's human resources needs, develop a strategy to meet those needs, and recruit qualified applicants from whom management will select the employees.
- Selection is the process of collecting information about applicants, using that information to decide which to hire, and putting potential hires through the process of application, interview, testing, and reference checking.

LO.3. Discuss how workers are trained and their performance is appraised.

- Training teaches employees how to do their job tasks, while development is training that augments the skills and knowledge of managers and professionals as well as current employees.
- Appraising performance involves identifying an employee's strengths and weaknesses on the job. Performance appraisals may be subjective or objective.

LO.4. Identify the types of turnover companies may experience, and explain why turnover is an important issue.

- A promotion is an advancement to a higher-level job with increased authority, responsibility, and pay. A transfer is a move to another job within the company, typically at the same level and wage.

- Separations occur when employees resign, retire, are terminated, or are laid off. Turnovers due to separation are expensive because of the time, money, and effort required to select, train, and manage new employees.

LO.5. Specify the various ways a worker may be compensated.

- Wages are financial compensation based on the number of hours worked or the number of units produced, while commissions are a fixed amount or percentage of a sale paid as compensation.
- Salaries are compensation calculated on a weekly, monthly, or annual basis, regardless of the number of hours worked or the number of items produced.
- Bonuses and profit sharing are types of financial incentives, while benefits are nonfinancial forms of compensation, such as vacation, insurance, and sick leave.

LO.6. Discuss some of the issues associated with unionized employees, including collective bargaining and dispute resolution.

- Collective bargaining is the negotiation process through which management and unions reach an agreement on a labor contract.
- If labor and management cannot agree on a contract, labor union members may picket, strike, or boycott the firm, while management may lock out striking employees, hire strikebreakers, or form employers' associations.
- In a deadlock, labor disputes may be resolved by a third party.

LO.7. Describe the importance of diversity in the workforce.

- Companies with diverse workforces experience more productive use of human resources, reduced conflict, better work relationships among workers, increased commitment to and sharing of organizational goals, increased innovation and creativity, and enhanced ability to serve diverse customers.

Practical Application

LO.1.
- In some companies, the department that handles the human resources management function is still called _____.
- The observation and study of information about a job is called _____.
- The qualifications required for a job are spelled out in a job _____.

LO.2.
- _____ tests are restricted to specific government jobs and those involving security or access to drugs.
- Professionals who specialize in luring qualified people away from other companies are known as _____.
- Recruiting for entry-level managerial and professional positions is often carried out on _____.

LO.3.
- The _____ includes a panel consisting of the employee's peers, superiors, and subordinates.
- If Greta received training by watching videotapes and discussing case studies, she received _____ training.
- Joseph has worked at his position for years. He is currently participating in management seminars at company expense. This is an example of _____.

LO.4.
- Sandy Smith moved to a new job that involved more responsibility and an increase in compensation. She received a(n) _____.

- Susan was terminated from her job by her employer because she was repeatedly late to work. She was _____.
- A(n) _____ rate signifies problems with the selection and training program.

LO.5.
- To motivate employees such as car salespersons to sell as much as they can, they are paid _____.
- June works at McDonald's part-time as a grill operator. She will probably be paid with the _____ compensation method.
- An employee stock ownership plan is an example of _____.

LO.6.
- Workers seeking to improve pay and working conditions may join together to form a(n) _____.
- _____ make carrying out normal business operations difficult, if not impossible.
- A(n) _____ might be brought in as a neutral third party to keep union and management representatives talking.

LO.7.
- Age, gender, and race are _____ characteristics of diversity.
- Secondary characteristics of diversity _____.
- Having a diverse workforce has many benefits. One benefit is the _____ use of a company's human resources.

Marketing: Developing Relationships

chapter eleven

Marketing involves planning and executing the development, pricing, promotion, and distribution of ideas, goods, and services to create exchanges that satisfy individual and organizational goals. These activities ensure that the products consumers want to buy are available at a price they are willing to pay and that consumers are provided with information about product features and availability. Organizations of all sizes and objectives engage in these activities.

In this chapter, we focus on the basic principles of marketing. First we define and examine the nature of marketing. Then we look at how marketers develop marketing strategies to satisfy the needs and wants of their customers. Next we discuss buying behavior and how marketers use research to determine what consumers want to buy and why. Finally, we explore the impact of the environment on marketing activities.

customer-driven **marketing**

LEARNING OBJECTIVES

LO1 Define marketing, and describe the exchange process.

LO2 Specify the functions of marketing.

LO3 Explain the marketing concept and its implications for developing marketing strategies.

LO4 Examine the development of a marketing strategy, including market segmentation and marketing mix.

LO5 Investigate how marketers conduct marketing research and study buying behavior.

LO6 Summarize the environmental forces that influence marketing decisions.

marketing a group of activities designed to expedite transactions by creating, distributing, pricing, and promoting goods, services, and ideas

exchange the act of giving up one thing (money, credit, labor, goods) in return for something else (goods, services, or ideas)

NATURE OF MARKETING

A vital part of any business undertaking, **marketing** is a group of activities designed to expedite transactions by creating, distributing, pricing, and promoting goods, services, and ideas. These activities create value by allowing individuals and organizations to obtain what they need and want. A business cannot achieve its objectives unless it provides something that customers value. But just creating an innovative product that meets many users' needs isn't sufficient in today's volatile global marketplace. Products must be conveniently available, competitively priced, and uniquely promoted.

Marketing is an important part of a firm's overall strategy. Other functional areas of the business—such as operations, finance, and all areas of management—must be coordinated with marketing decisions. Businesses try to respond to consumer wants and needs and to anticipate changes in the environment. Unfortunately, it is difficult to understand and predict what consumers want: Motives are often unclear; few principles can be applied consistently; and markets tend to fragment, each desiring customized products, new value, or better service.

It is important to note what marketing is not: It is not manipulating consumers to get them to buy products they do not want. It is not just selling and advertising; it is a systematic approach to satisfying consumers. Marketing focuses on the many activities—planning, pricing, promoting, and distributing products—that foster exchanges.

> A business cannot achieve its objectives unless it provides something that customers value.

The Exchange Relationship

At the heart of all business is the **exchange**, the act of giving up one thing (money, credit, labor, goods) in return for something else (goods, services, or ideas). Businesses exchange their goods, services, or ideas for money or credit supplied by customers in a voluntary *exchange relationship,* illustrated in Figure 11.1. The buyer must feel good about the purchase, or the exchange will not continue. If your cell phone service works everywhere, you will probably feel good about using its services. But if you have a lot of dropped calls, you will probably use another phone service next time.

For an exchange to occur, certain conditions are required. As indicated by the arrows in Figure 11.1, buyers and sellers must be able to communicate about the "something of value" available to each. An exchange does not necessarily take place just because buyers and sellers have something of value to exchange. Each participant must be willing to give up his or her respective "something of value" to receive the "something" held by the other. You are willing to exchange your "something of value"—your money or credit—for soft drinks, football tickets, or new shoes because you consider those products more valuable or more important than holding on to your cash or credit potential.

When you think of marketing products, you may think of tangible things—cars, MP3 players, or books, for example. What most consumers want, however, is a way to get a job done, solve a problem, or gain some enjoyment. You may purchase a Hoover vacuum cleaner not because you want a vacuum cleaner but because you want clean carpets. Starbucks serves coffee drinks at a premium price, providing convenience, quality, and an inviting environment. Therefore, the tangible product itself may not be as important as the image or the benefits associated with the product. This intangible "something of value" may be capability gained from using a product or the image evoked by it, or even the brand name. Good examples of brand names that are easy to remember include Avon's Skin So Soft, Tide detergent, and the Ford Mustang. The label or brand name may also offer the added bonus of being a conversation piece in a social environment, such as Dancing Bull or Smoking Loon wine.

Functions of Marketing

Marketing focuses on a complex set of activities that must be performed to accomplish objectives and generate exchanges. These activities include buying, selling, transporting, storing, grading, financing, marketing research, and risk taking.

Buying Everyone who shops for products (consumers, stores, businesses, governments) decides whether and what to buy. A marketer

▼**FIGURE 11.1** The Exchange Process: Giving Up One Thing in Return for Another

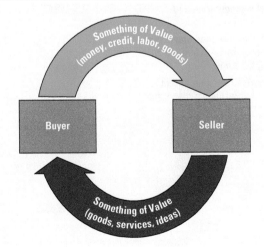

value a customer's subjective assessment of benefits relative to costs in determining the worth of a product

Many companies use celebrities to promote their products, as Nikon does with actor Ashton Kutcher. Companies hope that celebrity promotion will create additional value for consumers by extending their positive perceptions of the celebrity to the products.

must understand buyers' needs and desires to determine what products to make available.

Selling The exchange process is expedited through selling. Marketers usually view selling as a persuasive activity that is accomplished through promotion (advertising, personal selling, sales promotion, publicity, and packaging).

Transporting Transporting is the process of moving products from the seller to the buyer. Marketers focus on transportation costs and services.

Storing Like transporting, storing is part of the physical distribution of products and includes warehousing goods. Warehouses hold some products for lengthy periods in order to create time utility. Time utility has to do with being able to satisfy demand in a timely manner. This especially pertains to a seasonal good such as orange juice. Fresh oranges are available only for a few months annually, but consumers demand juice throughout the entire year. Sellers must arrange for cold storage of orange juice concentrate so that they can maintain a steady supply all of the time.

Grading Grading refers to standardizing products by dividing them into subgroups and displaying and labeling them so that consumers clearly understand their nature and quality. Many products, such as meat, steel, and fruit, are graded according to a set of standards that often are established by the state or federal government.

Financing For many products, especially large items such as automobiles, refrigerators, and new homes, the marketer arranges credit to expedite the purchase.

Marketing Research Through research, marketers ascertain the need for new goods and services. By gathering information regularly, marketers can detect new trends and changes in consumer tastes.

Risk Taking Risk is the chance of loss associated with marketing decisions. Developing a new product creates a chance of loss if consumers do not like it enough to buy it. Spending money to hire a sales force or to conduct marketing research also involves risk. The implication of risk is that most marketing decisions result in either success or failure.

Creating Value with Marketing[1]

Value is an important element of managing long-term customer relationships and implementing the marking concept. We view **value** as a customer's subjective assessment of benefits relative to costs in determining the worth of a product (customer value = customer benefits − customer costs).

Customer benefits include anything a buyer receives in an exchange. Hotels and motels, for example, basically provide a room with a bed and bathroom, but each firm provides a different level of service, amenities, and atmosphere to satisfy its guests. Hampton Inn offers the minimum services necessary to maintain a quality, efficient, low-price overnight accommodation. In contrast, the Ritz-Carlton provides every imaginable service a guest might desire and strives to ensure that all service is of the highest quality. Customers judge which type of accommodation offers them the best value according to the benefits they desire and their willingness and ability to pay for the costs associated with the benefits.

Customer costs include anything a buyer must give up to obtain the benefits the product provides. The most obvious cost is the monetary price of the product, but nonmonetary costs can be equally important in a customer's determination of value. Two nonmonetary costs are the time and effort customers expend to find and purchase desired products. To reduce time and effort, a company can increase product availability, thereby making it more convenient for buyers to purchase the firm's products. Another nonmonetary cost is risk, which can be reduced by offering basic warranties for an additional charge. Another risk-reduction strategy is increasingly popular in today's catalog/telephone/Internet shopping environment. L.L.Bean, for example, uses a guarantee to reduce the risk involved in ordering merchandise from its catalogs.

In developing marketing activities, it is important to recognize that customers receive benefits based on their experiences. For

marketing concept
the idea that an organization should try to satisfy customers' needs through coordinated activities that also allow it to achieve its own goals

example, many computer buyers consider services such as fast delivery, ease of installation, technical advice, and training assistance to be important elements of the product. Customers also derive benefits from the act of shopping and selecting products. These benefits can be affected by the atmosphere or environment of a store, such as Red Lobster's nautical/seafood theme.

The Marketing Concept

A basic philosophy that guides all marketing activities is the **marketing concept**, the idea that an organization should try to satisfy customers' needs through coordinated activities that also allow it to achieve its own goals. According to the marketing concept, a business must find out what consumers desire and then develop the good, service, or idea that fulfills their needs or wants. The business must then get the product to the customer. In addition, the business must continually alter, adapt, and develop products to keep pace with changing consumer needs and wants. For instance, there has been increasing pressure on the snack food industry to provide healthier snacks. In response to this growing health trend, Frito-Lay is reengineering its snack food recipes to replace artificial

Although demand for bananas is high, the competitive nature of the market makes it unlikely that any one seller will gain market share. The marketing of bananas would therefore be quite different from marketing more differentiated goods.

ingredients with natural ones such as canola oil and rosemary. Frito-Lay's goal is to create more natural snack foods while retaining the taste of the originals.[2] To remain competitive, the company must be prepared to add to or adapt its product line to satisfy customers' desires for new fads or changes in eating habits. Each business must determine how best to implement the marketing concept, given its own goals and resources.

Trying to determine customers' true needs is increasingly difficult because no one fully understands what motivates people to buy things. However, Estée Lauder, founder of her namesake cosmetics company, had a pretty good idea. When a prestigious store in Paris rejected her perfume in the 1960s, she "accidentally" dropped a bottle on the floor where nearby customers could get a whiff of it. So many asked about the scent that Galeries Lafayette was obliged to place an order. Lauder ultimately built an empire using then-unheard-of tactics like free samples and gifts with purchases to market her "jars of hope."[3]

Although customer satisfaction is the goal of the marketing concept, a business must also achieve its own objectives, such as boosting productivity, reducing costs, or achieving a percentage of a specific market. If it does not, it will not survive. For example, Dell could sell computers for $50 and give customers a lifetime guarantee, which would be great for customers but not so great for Dell. Obviously, the company must strike a balance between achieving organizational objectives and satisfying customers.

To implement the marketing concept, a firm must have good information about what consumers want, adopt a consumer orientation, and coordinate its efforts throughout the entire organization; otherwise, it may be awash with goods, services, and ideas that consumers do not want or need. Successfully implementing the marketing concept requires that a business view the customer's perception of value as the ultimate measure of work performance and improving value, and the rate at which this is done, as the measure of success.[4] Everyone in the organization who interacts with customers—*all* customer-contact employees—must know what customers want. They are selling ideas, benefits, philosophies, and experiences—not just goods and services.

Someone once said that if you build a better mousetrap, the world will beat a path to your door. Suppose you do build a better mousetrap. What will happen? Actually, consumers are not likely to beat a path to your door because the market is so competitive. A coordinated effort by everyone involved with the mousetrap is needed to sell the product. Your company must

> According to the marketing concept, a business must find out what consumers desire and then develop the good, service, or idea that fulfills their needs or wants.

market orientation
an approach requiring organizations to gather information about customer needs, share that information throughout the firm, and use that information to help build long-term relationships with customers

reach out to customers and tell them about your mousetrap, especially how your mousetrap works better than those offered by competitors. If you do not make the benefits of your product widely known, in most cases, it will not be successful. Consider Apple's 323 national and international retail stores, which market computers and electronics in a way unlike any other computer manufacturer or retail establishments. The upscale stores, located in high-rent shopping districts, show off Apple's products in airy, stylish settings to encourage consumers to try new things—like making a movie on a computer. The stores also offer special events like concerts and classes to give customers ideas on how to maximize their use of Apple's products.[5] You must also find—or create—stores willing to sell your mousetrap to consumers. You must implement the marketing concept by making a product with satisfying benefits and making it available and visible.

Orville Wright said that an airplane is "a group of separate parts flying in close formation." This is what most companies are trying to accomplish: They are striving for a team effort to deliver the right good or service to customers. A breakdown at any point in the organization—whether it be in production, purchasing, sales, distribution, or advertising—can result in lost sales, lost revenue, and dissatisfied customers.

Evolution of the Marketing Concept

The marketing concept may seem like the obvious approach to running a business and building relationships with customers. However, businesspeople are not always focused on customers when they create and operate businesses. Many companies fail to grasp the importance of customer relationships and fail to implement customer strategies. A firm's marketing department needs to share information about customers and their desires with the entire organization. Our society and economic system have changed over time, and marketing has become more important as markets have become more competitive.

The Production Orientation
During the second half of the 19th century, the Industrial Revolution was well under way in the United States. New technologies, such as electricity, railroads, internal combustion engines, and mass-production techniques, made it possible to manufacture goods with ever increasing efficiency. Together with new management ideas and ways of using labor, products poured into the marketplace, where demand for manufactured goods was strong.

The Sales Orientation
By the early part of the 20th century, supply caught up with and then exceeded demand, and

businesspeople began to realize they would have to "sell" products to buyers. During the first half of the 20th century, businesspeople viewed sales as the primary means of increasing profits in what has become known as a sales orientation. Those who adopted the sales orientation perspective believed the most important marketing activities were personal selling and advertising. Today some people still inaccurately equate marketing with a sales orientation.

The Market Orientation
By the 1950s, some businesspeople began to recognize that even efficient production and extensive promotion did not guarantee sales. These businesses, and many others since, found that they must first determine what customers want and then produce it, rather than making the products first and then trying to persuade customers that they need them. Managers at General Electric first suggested that the marketing concept was a companywide philosophy of doing business. As more organizations realized the importance of satisfying customers' needs, U.S. businesses entered the marketing era, one of market orientation.

A **market orientation** requires organizations to gather information about customer needs, share that information throughout the entire firm, and use it to help build long-term relationships with customers. Top executives, marketing managers, nonmarketing managers (those in production, finance, human resources, and so on), and customers all become mutually dependent and cooperate in developing and carrying out a market orientation. Nonmarketing managers must communicate with marketing managers to share information important to understanding the customer. Consider the 120-year history of Wrigley's gum. In 1891 the gum was given away to promote sales of baking powder (the company's original product). The gum was launched as its own product in 1893, and after four generations of Wrigley family CEOs, the company continues to reinvent itself and focus on consumers. In 2008, the family made the decision to sell the company to Mars. Wrigley now functions as a stand-alone subsidiary of Mars. The deal combined such popular brands as Wrigley's gums and Life Savers with Mars' M&Ms, Snickers, and Skittles to form the world's largest confectionary company.

Trying to assess what customers want, which is difficult to begin with, is further complicated by the rate at which trends, fashions, and tastes can change. Businesses today want to satisfy customers and build meaningful long-term relationships with them. It is more efficient and less expensive for the company to retain

"Our society and economic system have changed over time, and marketing has become more important as markets have become more competitive."

The Nissan Leaf is marketed as an eco-friendly vehicle for consumers who care about the environment.

The Jonas brothers promote Marquis Jet to create added value among its target market. Marquis Jet targets more of the business market through its Marquis Jet Card, which allows card holders to purchase flight time as needed rather than having to maintain their own fleet.

existing customers and even increase the amount of business each customer provides the organization than to find new customers. Most companies' success depends on increasing the amount of repeat business; therefore, relationship building between company and customer is key. Many companies are turning to technologies associated with customer relationship management to help build relationships and boost business with existing customers.

Communication remains a major element of any strategy to develop and manage long-term customer relationships. By providing multiple points of interactions with customers—that

is, websites, telephone, fax, e-mail, and personal contact—companies can personalize customer relationships.[6] Like many online retailers, Amazon.com stores and analyzes purchase data in an attempt to understand each customer's interests. This information helps the retailer improve its ability to satisfy individual customers and thereby increase sales of books, music, movies, and other products to each customer. The ability to identify individual customers allows marketers to shift their focus from targeting groups of similar customers to increasing their share of an individual customer's purchases. Regardless of

P&G MAKES INROADS IN INDIA

Four billion global customers may seem like a lot, but for Procter & Gamble CEO Bob McDonald it's just the beginning. McDonald intends to raise this number to 5 billion by 2015. The key to this growth is through targeting emerging economies like India and the Philippines. The company must therefore adapt its products to meet consumer needs in these countries. While P&G has built its profits on offering premium products in developed markets, economies in which income is as low as $1 per day require P&G to adapt its marketing strategy. To work within this constraint, P&G has begun offering single-serving, no frills packages to low-income global consumers.

Of the countries targeted by P&G, McDonald sees India as a major opportunity for expansion. Currently, P&G counts one-third of India's 1.2 billion consumers as customers. The company aims to expand this number by 500 million with an emphasis on needs-based innovation and new product introduction. For example, P&G introduced the world's lowest-cost disposable diaper—at 12 cents each—in the hopes that its convenience and affordability will convince Indian mothers to switch from cloth to disposable diapers.

The second challenge for P&G is finding a way to get its innovative products onto shelves. With few large retailers in India, small stores with limited space can easily stock P&G items like razors and toothbrushes.

Disposable diapers, however, take up more room. Competition is another problem. In India, P&G must fight against major competitors like Unilever and Colgate-Palmolive. P&G's Indian sales have been growing steadily, but it lags behind Unilever with sales of $800 million versus $3.8 billion. The trick for P&G will be to balance its products with the needs of its Indian customers—both retailers and end users.[7]

Discussion Questions

1. What are the marketing challenges of a large developing country with low consumer income?

2. How is Procter & Gamble adapting products for the market in India?

3. Why is it hard to get products available to consumers in India?

marketing strategy a plan of action for developing, pricing, distributing, and promoting products that meet the needs of specific customers

market a group of people who have a need, purchasing power, and the desire and authority to spend money on goods, services, and ideas

target market a specific group of consumers on whose needs and wants a company focuses its marketing efforts

total-market approach an approach whereby a firm tries to appeal to everyone and assumes that all buyers have similar needs

market segmentation a strategy whereby a firm divides the total market into groups of people who have relatively similar product needs

market segment a collection of individuals, groups, or organizations who share one or more characteristics and thus have relatively similar product needs and desires

the medium through which communication occurs, customers should ultimately be the drivers of marketing strategy because they understand what they want. Customer relationship management systems should ensure that marketers listen to customers in order to respond to their needs and concerns and build long-term relationships.

DEVELOPING A MARKETING STRATEGY

To implement the marketing concept and customer relationship management, a business needs to develop and maintain a **marketing strategy**, a plan of action for developing, pricing,

distributing, and promoting products that meet the needs of specific customers. This definition has two major components: selecting a target market and developing an appropriate marketing mix to satisfy that target market.

Selecting a Target Market

A **market** is a group of people who have a need, purchasing power, and the desire and authority to spend money on goods, services, and ideas. A **target market** is a more specific group of consumers on whose needs and wants a company focuses its marketing efforts. For example, Crayola targets girls aged 9 to 12 with its Pop Art Pixies craft line. After conducting focus groups, Crayola realized that many children stopped using their products once they reached the tween years. In response, the company began issuing craft kits that would appeal to the creative side of the tween market. The kits include materials that enable girls to build their own unique creations, such as eco-friendly water bottles, sun catchers, and wind chimes.[8]

Marketing managers may define a target market as a relatively small number of people within a larger market, or they may define it as the total market (Figure 11.2). Rolls-Royce, for example, targets its products at a very exclusive, high-income market—people who want the ultimate in prestige in an automobile. On the other hand, Ford Motor Company manufactures a variety of vehicles including Lincolns, Mercurys, and Ford Trucks in order to appeal to varied tastes, needs, and desires.

Some firms use a **total-market approach**, in which they try to appeal to everyone and assume that all buyers have similar needs and wants. Sellers of salt, sugar, and many agricultural products use a total-market approach because everyone is a potential consumer of these products. Most firms, though, use **market segmentation** and divide the total market into groups of people. A **market segment** is a collection of individuals, groups, or organizations who share one or more characteristics and thus have relatively similar product needs and desires. Women are the largest market segment, with 51 percent of the U.S. population. Approximately 12.8 million firms in the United States are owned by women.[9] At the household level, segmentation can identify each woman's social attributes, culture, and stages in life to determine preferences and needs.

▼**FIGURE 11.2** Target Market Strategies

concentration approach a market segmentation approach whereby a company develops one marketing strategy for a single market segment

multisegment approach a market segmentation approach whereby the marketer aims its efforts at two or more segments, developing a marketing strategy for each

Another market segment on which many marketers are focusing is the growing Hispanic population. Olive Garden launched a campaign to make Italian food more appealing to Hispanic diners. The restaurant chain created a Spanish version of its website, provided all locations with menus in Spanish, and even sponsored several segments on Univision television shows.[10] One of the challenges for marketers in the future will be to effectively address an increasingly racially diverse United States. The minority population of the United States is about 107.2 million (35 percent of the total population).[11] In future decades, the purchasing power of minority market segments is set to grow by leaps and bounds. Table 11.1 shows the buying power and market share percentages of different market segments. Companies will have to learn how to most effectively reach these growing segments. Companies use market segmentation to focus their efforts and resources on specific target markets so that they can develop a productive marketing strategy. Two common approaches to segmenting markets are the concentration approach and the multisegment approach.

▼ **TABLE 11.1** U.S. Buying Power Statistics by Race

	1990	2000	2009	2014
Total	4,270.5	7,187.6	10,717.8	13,097.1
White	3,816.2	6,231.2	9,125.2	11,032.7
Black	318.1	590.2	910.4	1,136.8
American Indian	19.7	39.1	64.7	82.7
Asian	116.5	268.7	508.6	696.5
Multiracial	N/A	58.4	108.9	148.3

Source: Jeffrey M. Humphreys, "The Multicultural Economy 2009," *GBEC* 69 (3rd Quarter, 2009), p. 3, www.terry.uga.edu/selig/docs/GBEC0903q.pdf (accessed March 30, 2010).

Market Segmentation Approaches In the **concentration approach**, a company develops one marketing strategy for a single market segment. The concentration approach allows a firm to specialize, focusing all its efforts on the one market segment. Porsche, for example, directs all its marketing efforts toward high-income individuals who want to own high-performance vehicles. A firm can generate a large sales volume by penetrating a single market segment deeply. The concentration approach may be especially effective when a firm can identify and develop products for a segment ignored by other companies in the industry.

> ## A firm can generate a large sales volume by penetrating a single market segment deeply.

Procter & Gamble uses a multisegment marketing strategy around the globe. In China, it offers an advanced laundry detergent formula for the high end of the market, a mid-priced brand for the medium end of the market, and a basic inexpensive product for the low end of the market.

In the **multisegment approach**, the marketer aims its marketing efforts at two or more segments, developing a marketing strategy for each. Many firms use a multisegment approach that includes different advertising messages for different segments. Companies also develop product variations to appeal to different market segments. The U.S. Post Office, for example, offers personalized stamps; Mars Inc. sells personalized M&M's through mymms.com; various on-demand television services ensure that consumers watch only what they want to watch; and LEGO toy company offers a service through its website wherein children can design their own sets. Companies also develop product variations to appeal to different market segments. For example, Samsung has widened its range of smartphones to appeal to the high-end and lower-end consumer. The company offers models for those who want a smartphone with the maximum capabilities. However, Samsung has also developed an ultra-cheap model targeted at consumers in developing countries, where consumers have not traditionally been able to afford smartphones.[12] Many other firms also attempt to use a multisegment approach to market segmentation, such as the manufacturer of Raleigh bicycles, which has designed separate marketing strategies for racers, tourers, commuters, and children.

Niche marketing is a narrow market segment focus when efforts are on one small, well-defined group that has a unique, specific set of needs. Many airlines cater to first-class flyers, who comprise only 10 percent of international air travelers. To meet the needs of these elite customers, airlines include special perks along with the spacious seats. Continental offers business passengers traveling overseas an in-flight menu featuring broiled beef tenderloin and seafood-filled pastry blossoms, and Delta is installing flat-bed seats on dozens of airplanes.[13]

For a firm to successfully use a concentration or multisegment approach to market segmentation, several requirements must be met:

1. Consumers' needs for the product must be heterogeneous.

2. The segments must be identifiable and divisible.

3. The total market must be divided in a way that allows estimated sales potential, cost, and profits of the segments to be compared.

4. At least one segment must have enough profit potential to justify developing and maintaining a special marketing strategy.

5. The firm must be able to reach the chosen market segment with a particular market strategy.

Bases for Segmenting Markets
Companies segment markets on the basis of several variables:

1. *Demographic*—age, sex, race, ethnicity, income, education, occupation, family size, religion, social class. These characteristics are often closely related to customers' product needs and purchasing behavior, and they can be readily measured. For example, deodorants are often segmented by sex: Secret and Soft n' Dri for women; Old Spice and Mennen for men.

2. *Geographic*—climate, terrain, natural resources, population density, subcultural values. These influence consumers' needs and product usage. Climate, for example, influences consumers' purchases of clothing, automobiles, heating and air conditioning equipment, and leisure activity equipment.

3. *Psychographic*—personality characteristics, motives, lifestyles. Soft-drink marketers provide their products in several types of packaging, including two-liter bottles and cases of cans, to satisfy different lifestyles and motives.

4. *Behavioristic*—some characteristic of the consumer's behavior toward the product. These characteristics commonly involve some aspect of product use.

marketing mix the four marketing activities—product, price, promotion, and distribution—that the firm can control to achieve specific goals within a dynamic marketing environment

Developing a Marketing Mix

The second step in developing a marketing strategy is to create and maintain a satisfying marketing mix. The **marketing mix** refers to four marketing activities—product, price, distribution, and promotion—that the firm can control to achieve specific goals within a dynamic marketing environment (Figure 11.3). The buyer or the target market is the central focus of all marketing activities.

Product A product—whether a good, a service, an idea, or some combination—is a complex mix of tangible and intangible attributes that provide satisfaction and benefits. A *good* is a physical entity you can touch. A Porsche Cayenne, a Hewlett-Packard printer, and a kitten available for adoption at an animal shelter are examples of goods. A *service* is the application of human and mechanical efforts to people or objects to provide intangible benefits to customers. Air travel, dry cleaning, haircuts, banking, insurance, medical care, and day care are examples of services. *Ideas* include concepts, philosophies, images, and issues. For instance, an attorney, for a fee, may advise you about what rights you have in the event that the IRS decides to audit your tax return. Other marketers of ideas include political parties, churches, and schools.

A product has emotional and psychological, as well as physical characteristics, that include everything that the buyer receives from an exchange. This definition includes supporting services such as installation, guarantees, product information, and promises of repair. Products usually have both favorable and unfavorable attributes; therefore, almost every purchase or exchange involves trade-offs as consumers try to maximize their benefits and satisfaction and minimize unfavorable attributes.

▼**FIGURE 11.3** The Marketing Mix: Product, Price, Promotion, and Distribution

Marketing Environment

TWITTER TREASURE HUNT GETS CONSUMERS TO HUNT WHILE THEY PLAY

Jason Sutherland's Peninsula Shops have become a friend to small businesses in the California Bay Area. For an annual fee of $180, Sutherland promotes a local company on Twitter, Facebook, and the Peninsula site. One of Sutherland's tactics is the Twitter Treasure Hunt. First, Sutherland tweets trivia questions about a local company. Participants who correctly answer the questions can win a prize. For example, Sutherland challenged participants to identify the business located at 325 Sharon Park Drive in Menlo Park. The answer was Martha's Pastries, and the winner received a $10 gift certificate. While the winners are pleased, local business owners are also thrilled with increased store traffic. One business's website traffic jumped 400 percent for the day, while Martha's Pastries' sales rose 7 percent for the quarter. Overall, Sutherland says the Twitter Treasure Hunt surpasses traditional click-through e-mail marketing advertisements with a response rate of up to 26 percent versus 5 percent. With his innovative way to reward consumers and help businesses, Sutherland creates a profitable situation for both.[14]

Products are among a firm's most visible contacts with consumers. If they do not meet consumer needs and expectations, sales will be difficult, and product life spans will be brief. The product is an important variable—often the central focus—of the marketing mix; the other variables (price, promotion, and distribution) must be coordinated with product decisions.

Price Almost anything can be assessed by a **price**, a value placed on an object exchanged between a buyer and a seller. Although the seller usually establishes the price, it may be negotiated between buyer and seller. The buyer usually exchanges purchasing power—income, credit, wealth—for the satisfaction or utility associated with a product. Because financial price is the measure of value commonly used in an exchange, it quantifies value and is the basis of most market exchanges.

Marketers view price as much more than a way of assessing value, however. It is a key element of the marketing mix because it relates directly to the generation of revenue and profits. Prices can also be changed quickly to stimulate demand or respond to competitors' actions. The sudden increase in the cost of commodities such as oil can create price increases or a drop in consumer demand for a product. When gas prices rise, consumers purchase more fuel-efficient cars; when prices fall, consumers return to larger vehicles with a smaller price tag.[16]

Distribution **Distribution** (sometimes referred to as "place" because it helps to remember the marketing mix as the "4 Ps") is making products available to customers in the quantities desired. For example, consumers can rent DVDs and videogames from a physical store, a vending machine, or an online service. Intermediaries, usually wholesalers and retailers, perform many of the activities required to move products efficiently from producers to consumers or industrial buyers. These activities involve transporting, warehousing, materials handling, and inventory control, as well as packaging and communication.

Critics who suggest that eliminating wholesalers and other middlemen would result in lower prices for consumers do not recognize that eliminating intermediaries would not do away with the need for their services. Other institutions would have to perform those services, and consumers would still have to pay for them. In addition, in the absence of wholesalers, all producers would have to deal directly with retailers or customers, keeping voluminous records and hiring extra people to deal with customers.

Promotion **Promotion** is a persuasive form of communication that attempts to expedite a marketing exchange by influencing individuals, groups, and organizations to accept goods, services, and ideas. Promotion includes advertising, personal selling, publicity, and sales promotion, all of which we will look at more closely in Chapter 12.

The aim of promotion is to communicate directly or indirectly with individuals, groups, and organizations to facilitate exchanges. When marketers use advertising and other forms of promotion, they must effectively manage their promotional resources and understand product and target-market characteristics to ensure that these promotional activities contribute to the firm's objectives.

Most major companies have set up websites on the Internet to promote themselves and their products. The home page for Betty Crocker, for example, offers recipes; meal planning; blogs and message boards; the company's history; descriptions for its

DID YOU KNOW?

During its first year of operation, sales of Coca-Cola averaged just nine drinks per day for total first-year sales of $50. Today, Coca-Cola products are consumed at the rate of 1.7 billion drinks per day.[15]

Redbox departed from the more traditional brick-and-mortar rental stores by choosing to distribute its DVD rentals through vending machines.

products; online shopping for complementary items such as dinnerware, linens, and gifts; and the ability to print a shopping list based on recipes chosen or ingredients on hand in the consumer's kitchen. The websites for The Gap and Old Navy provide consumers with the opportunity to purchase clothing and other items from the convenience of their homes or offices. Some sites, however, simply promote a company's products but do not offer them for sale online.

at least 1.5 percent each year for the next 5 to 10 years. This shift in consumer preferences is already changing the way companies produce and market bottled beverages.[17] Marketing research is vital because the marketing concept cannot be implemented without information about customers.

A marketing information system is a framework for accessing information about customers from sources both inside and outside the organization. Inside the organization, there is a continuous flow of information about prices, sales, and expenses. Outside the organization, data are readily available through private or public reports and census statistics, as well as from many other sources. Computer networking technology provides a framework for companies to connect to useful databases and customers with instantaneous information about product acceptance, sales performance, and buying behavior. This information is important to planning and marketing strategy development.

price a value placed on an object exchanged between a buyer and a seller

distribution making products available to customers in the quantities desired

promotion a persuasive form of communication that attempts to expedite a marketing exchange by influencing individuals, groups, and organizations to accept goods, services, and ideas

marketing research a systematic, objective process of getting information about potential customers to guide marketing decisions

primary data marketing information that is observed, recorded, or collected directly from respondents

> "The aim of promotion is to communicate directly or indirectly with individuals, groups, and organizations to facilitate exchanges."

MARKETING RESEARCH AND INFORMATION SYSTEMS

Before marketers can develop a marketing mix, they must collect in-depth, up-to-date information about customer needs. **Marketing research** is a systematic, objective process of getting information about potential customers to guide marketing decisions. Such information might include data about the age, income, ethnicity, gender, and educational level of people in the target market, their preferences for product features, their attitudes toward competitors' products, and the frequency with which they use the product. For example, demand for most carbonated beverages has been declining for several years as consumers turn away from high-calorie bottled beverages. Experts predict that soft-drink sales will continue to fall

Two types of data are usually available to decision makers. **Primary data** are observed, recorded, or collected directly from respondents. If you've ever participated in a telephone survey about a product, recorded your TV viewing habits for ACNielsen or Arbitron, or even responded to a political opinion poll, you provided the researcher with primary data. Primary data must be gathered by researchers who develop a method to observe phenomena or research respondents. Many companies use "mystery shoppers" to visit their retail establishments and report on whether the stores were adhering to the companies' standards of service. These undercover customers document their observations of store appearance, employee effectiveness, and customer treatment. This $1.5 billion industry provides valuable information that helps companies improve their organizations and refine their marketing strategies.[18] Table 11.2 provides the results of an online mystery shopping study of several retailers. Companies also use surveys and focus groups to gauge customer opinion. A weakness of

secondary data
information that is compiled inside or outside an organization for some purpose other than changing the current situation

surveys is that respondents are sometimes untruthful in order to avoid seeming foolish or ignorant.

Some methods for marketing research use passive observation of consumer behavior and open-ended questioning techniques. Called ethnographic or observational research, the approach can help marketers determine what consumers really think about their products and how different ethnic or demographic groups react to them.

Secondary data are compiled inside or outside the organization for some purpose other than changing the current situation. Marketers typically use information compiled by the U.S. Census Bureau and other government agencies, databases created by marketing research firms, as well as sales and other internal reports, to gain information about customers.

Online Marketing Research

The marketing of products and collecting of data about buying behavior—information on what people actually buy and

how they buy it—represents marketing research of the future. New information technologies are changing the way businesses learn about their customers and market their products. Interactive multimedia research, or *virtual testing,* combines sight, sound, and animation to facilitate the testing of concepts as well as packaging and design features for consumer products. The evolving development of telecommunications and computer technologies is allowing marketing researchers quick and easy access to a growing number of online services and a vast database of potential respondents.

Marketing research can use digital media and social networking sites to gather useful information for marketing decisions. Sites such as Twitter, Facebook, Myspace, and LinkedIn can be good substitutes for focus groups. Online surveys can serve as an alternative to mail, telephone, or personal interviews.

Social networks are a great way to obtain information from consumers who are willing to share their experiences about products and companies. In a way, this process identifies those consumers who develop an identity or passion for certain products, as well as those consumers who have concerns about quality or performance. It is possible for firms to tap into existing

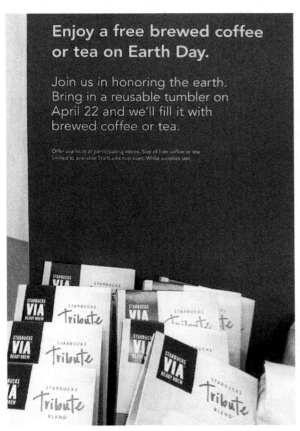

Starbucks conducts research to understand buyer behavior and provides motivational incentives to encourage consumers to patronize its stores.

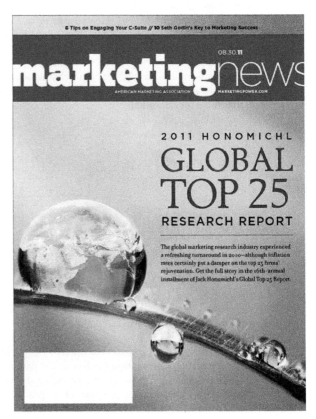

Marketers can go to Marketing News *to learn more about new approaches being developed for research and to learn about top marketing research firms in the world.*

buying behavior
the decision processes
and actions of people who
purchase and use products

perception the process
by which a person selects,
organizes, and interprets
information received from
his or her senses

motivation inner drive
that directs a person's
behavior toward goals

learning changes in a
person's behavior based on
information and experience

attitude knowledge and
positive or negative feelings
about something

personality the
organization of an
individual's distinguishing
character traits, attitudes,
or habits

▼ **TABLE 11.2** Online Mystery Shopping Study: Customer Service Leaders

	Number of Hours for E-mail Response	Customer Service Rep Knowledge[a]	Number of Clicks from Product Selection through Checkout	Number of Business Days for Delivery
Blue Nile	0.22	2.0	5.0	3.0
Brooks Brothers	3.07	3.0	5.0	3.0
Coach	2.48	2.0	4.0	3.0
Crutchfield	1.27	3.0	5.0	3.0
Green Mountain	19.73	3.0	5.0	3.0
Museum of Modern Art	20.48	2.0	4.0	4.0
Lands' End	6.52	2.5	4.0	3.0
REI	0.37	2.0	5.0	3.0
Saks Fifth Avenue	0.88	3.0	5.0	4.0
Zappos	0.98	3.0	3.0	1.0
Average of 100 retailers	20.69	2.24	5.42	4.05

[a]Based on a scale of 1 to 3, with 3 being the most knowledgeable.

Source: "E-retailers Reach Out to Engage Shoppers," *Internet Retailer,* April 2010, www.internetretailer.com/article.asp?id=34189 (accessed April 1, 2010).

online social networks and simply "listen" to what consumers have on their mind. Firms can also encourage consumers to join a community or group so that they can share their opinions with the business.

A good outcome from using social networks is the opportunity to reach new voices and gain varied perspectives on the creative process of developing new products and promotions. For example, websites such as 99designs.com assist with product design. To some extent, social networking is democratizing design by welcoming consumers to join in the development process for new products.[19]

BUYING BEHAVIOR

Carrying out the marketing concept is impossible unless marketers know what, where, when, and how consumers buy; conducting marketing research into the factors that influence buying behavior helps marketers develop effective marketing strategies. **Buying behavior** refers to the decision processes and actions of people who purchase and use products. It includes the behavior of both consumers purchasing products for personal or household use as well as organizations buying products for business use. Marketers analyze buying behavior because a firm's marketing strategy should be guided by an understanding of buyers. People view pets as part of their families, and they want their pets to have the best of everything. Iams, which markets the Iams and Eukanuba pet food brands, recognized this trend and shifted its focus. Today, it markets high-quality pet food, fancy pet treats, sauces, and other items. Both psychological and social variables are important to an understanding of buying behavior.

Psychological Variables of Buying Behavior

Psychological factors include the following:

- **Perception** is the process by which a person selects, organizes, and interprets information received from his or her senses, as when hearing an advertisement on the radio or touching a product to better understand it.

- **Motivation,** as we said in Chapter 9, is an inner drive that directs a person's behavior toward goals. A customer's behavior is influenced by a set of motives rather than by a single motive. A buyer of a home computer, for example, may be motivated by ease of use, ability to communicate with the office, and price.

- **Learning** brings about changes in a person's behavior based on information and experience. If a person's actions result in a reward, he or she is likely to behave the same way in similar situations. If a person's actions bring about a negative result, however—such as feeling ill after eating at a certain restaurant—he or she will probably not repeat that action.

- **Attitude** is knowledge and positive or negative feelings about something. For example, a person who feels strongly about protecting the environment may refuse to buy products that harm the earth and its inhabitants.

- **Personality** refers to the organization of an individual's distinguishing character traits, attitudes, or habits. Although market research on the relationship between personality and buying behavior has been inconclusive, some marketers believe that the type of car or clothing a person buys reflects his or her personality.

social roles a set of expectations for individuals based on some position they occupy

reference groups groups with whom buyers identify and whose values or attitudes they adopt

social classes a ranking of people into higher or lower positions of respect

Social Variables of Buying Behavior

Social factors include **social roles**, which are a set of expectations for individuals based on some position they occupy. A person may have many roles: mother, wife, student, executive. Each of these roles can influence buying behavior. Consider a woman choosing an automobile. Her father advises her to buy a safe, gasoline-efficient car, such as a Volvo. Her teenaged daughter wants her to buy a cool car, such as a Ford Mustang; her young son wants her to buy a Ford Explorer to take on camping trips. Some of her colleagues at work say she should buy a hybrid Prius to help the environment. Thus, in choosing which car to buy, the woman's buying behavior may be affected by the opinions and experiences of her family and friends and by her roles as mother, daughter, and employee.

Other social factors include reference groups, social classes, and culture.

- **Reference groups** include families, professional groups, civic organizations, and other groups with whom buyers identify and whose values or attitudes they adopt. A person may use a reference group as a point of comparison or a source of information. A person new to a community may ask other group members to recommend a family doctor, for example.

- **Social classes** are determined by ranking people into higher or lower positions of respect. Criteria vary from one

People's cultures have a big impact on what they buy. The food-seller Goya Foods sells more than three dozen types of beans to U.S. supermarkets because people with different cultural roots demand different types of beans. Which products are delivered to certain stores depends on the heritage of those living in each area.

YELP: WHERE CONSUMERS HOLD THE POWER

If you want recommendations on a business, Yelp may be just what you need. Founded by Jeremy Stoppelman and Russel Simmons, Yelp is a site on which consumers can rate and review businesses. Approximately 30 million users visit the site monthly. Yet while consumers may love Yelp, the site has a love-hate relationship with many business owners.

On the one hand, businesses with loyal customers who post positive reviews on Yelp appreciate the viral nature of the site. A positive review can influence a range of potential customers. On the other hand, Yelp makes it easy for consumers to post

negative reviews. All a business owner can do is respond either publicly on the site or privately via e-mail to a reviewer. Yelp also runs an algorithm that filters certain reviews, claiming that this helps weed out false reviews.

Yelp earns money by selling ad space on the site to represented businesses, but according to Stoppelman, this does not allow business owners any greater freedom to control review content. What it does give them is the ability to eliminate advertisements of other companies on their pages, the possibility for their ads to appear on other pages, and the opportunity to post photo and video content.

Despite Stoppelman's assurances, businesses have accused Yelp of manipulating reviews either to gain more advertising customers or to punish companies that

refuse to advertise through Yelp's paid system. To combat complaints, Yelp has made filtered reviews visible, although they are clearly marked as filtered. Stoppelman continues to support the company's algorithm and claims that Yelp is striving for greater transparency. Whether or not Yelp's actions serve to pacify its detractors, companies are increasingly realizing that the power structure between business and consumer is changing—often in the consumer's favor.[20]

Discussion Questions

1. What is the benefit of Yelp to consumers?
2. What challenges face businesses that are evaluated on Yelp?
3. How does Yelp contribute to improving competition and the quality of products?

society to another. People within a particular social class may develop common patterns of behavior. People in the upper-middle class, for example, might buy a Lexus or a Cadillac as a symbol of their social class.

- **Culture** is the integrated, accepted pattern of human behavior, including thought, speech, beliefs, actions, and artifacts. Culture determines what people wear and eat and where they live and travel. Many Hispanic Texans and New Mexicans, for example, buy *masa trigo,* the dough used to prepare flour tortillas, which are basic to southwestern and Mexican cuisine.

Understanding Buying Behavior

Although marketers try to understand buying behavior, it is extremely difficult to explain exactly why a buyer purchases a particular product. The tools and techniques for analyzing consumers are not exact. Marketers may not be able to determine accurately what is highly satisfying to buyers, but they know that trying to understand consumer wants and needs is the best way to satisfy them. During the last economic recession

> **culture** the integrated, accepted pattern of human behavior, including thought, speech, beliefs, actions, and artifacts

consumer behavior shifted from conspicuous consumption to more responsible purchasing. Consumers became more price conscious and increased their use of coupons and other promotions. Bargain stores like Dollar Tree Inc. and Family Dollar, for instance, received many new customers who opted to "trade down" from more prestigious retailers. Even after the recession ended, several consumers indicated that they would continue to shop at these bargain stores for certain items.[21] Retailers must adjust to meet these new needs of consumers.[22]

THE MARKETING ENVIRONMENT

A number of external forces directly or indirectly influence the development of marketing strategies; the following political, legal, regulatory, social, competitive, economic, and technological forces comprise the marketing environment.

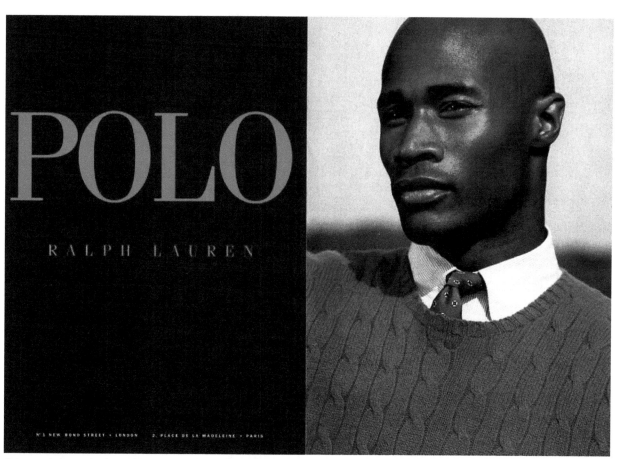

Polo appeals to people who want to express social roles or identify with a reference group.

- *Political, legal, and regulatory forces*—laws and regulators' interpretation of laws; law enforcement and regulatory activities; regulatory bodies; legislators and legislation; and political actions of interest groups. Specific laws, for example, require that advertisements be truthful and that all health claims be documented.

- *Social forces*—the public's opinions and attitudes toward issues such as living standards, ethics, the environment, lifestyles, and quality of life. For example, social concerns have led marketers to design and market safer toys for children.

- *Competitive and economic forces*—competitive relationships, unemployment, purchasing power, and general economic conditions (prosperity, recession, depression, recovery, product shortages, and inflation).

- *Technological forces*—computers and other technological advances that improve distribution, promotion, and new-product development.

Marketing requires creativity and consumer focus because environmental forces can change quickly and dramatically. Changes can arise from social concerns and economic forces such as price increases, product shortages, and altering levels of demand for commodities. Recently, climate change, global warming, and the impact of carbon emissions on our environment have become social concerns and are causing businesses to rethink marketing strategies. Possibly the most important concern is to make businesses, consumers, and governments consider carbon emissions and how their purchases affect the environment. Escalating fossil fuel use in economies such as China and India has placed strong upward pressure on oil prices. China's fast development has made it the

planet's largest contributor to greenhouse gases. For example, 80 percent of electricity generation in China is derived from coal, while coal generates only 45 percent of the total electricity in the United States. China's pollution will create an environmental catastrophe unless there is increased pressure to utilize alternate energy sources.[23]

The average American generates about five tons of greenhouse gases annually. Many people are disturbed by this statistic and have resolved to take actions that reduce their energy usage and their impact on the environment through the use of carpooling, driving hybrid cars, using Energy Star products, and even washing their clothes in cold water instead of hot. In addition to fueling the demand for low-energy products, these developments are also accelerating the development of renewable energy such as solar and wind.[24] If there is a cap on carbon emissions in the United States, the prices would rise for fossil fuels such as coal, oil, and gas. More expensive renewable energy sources such as solar, wind, and biofuels would have a better chance for growth. For example, if turbine wind farms and transmission lines were built in Montana and the Dakotas, the region would have enough wind to provide 886 million megawatt hours a year, which would generate billions of dollars in revenue and improve prosperity.[25]

Because such environmental forces are interconnected, changes in one may cause changes in others. Consider that because of evidence linking children's consumption of soft drinks and fast foods to health issues such as obesity, diabetes, and osteoporosis, marketers of such products have experienced negative publicity and calls for legislation regulating the sale of soft drinks in public schools.

Although the forces in the marketing environment are sometimes called uncontrollables, they are not totally so. A marketing manager can influence some environmental variables. For example, businesses can lobby legislators to dissuade them from passing unfavorable legislation. Figure 11.4 shows the variables in the marketing environment that affect the marketing mix and the buyer. ■

> **TEAM EXERCISE**
>
> Form groups and assign the responsibility of finding examples of companies that excel in one dimension of the marketing mix (price, product, promotion, and distribution). Provide several company and product examples, and defend why this would be an exemplary case. Present your research to the class.

▼FIGURE 11.4 The Marketing Mix and the Marketing Environment

SO YOU WANT A JOB // in Marketing /

You probably did not think as a child how great it would be to grow up and become a marketer. That's because often marketing is associated with sales jobs, but opportunities in marketing, public relations, product management, advertising, e-marketing, and customer relationship management and beyond represent almost one-third of all jobs in today's business world. To enter any job in the marketing field, you must balance an awareness of customer needs with business knowledge while mixing in creativity and the ability to obtain useful information to make smart business decisions.

Marketing starts with understanding the customer. Marketing research is a vital aspect in marketing decision making and presents many job opportunities. Market researchers survey customers to determine their habits, preferences, and aspirations. Activities include concept testing, product testing, package testing, test-market research, and new-product research. Salaries vary, depending on the nature and level of the position as well as the type, size, and location of the firm. An entry-level market analyst may make between $24,000 and $50,000, while a market research director may earn from $75,000 to $200,000 or more.

One of the most dynamic areas in marketing is direct marketing, where a seller solicits a response from a consumer using direct communications methods such as telephone, online communication, direct mail, or catalogs. Jobs in direct marketing include buyers, catalog managers, research/mail-list managers, or order fulfillment managers. Most positions in direct marketing involve planning and market analysis. Some require the use of databases to sort and analyze customer information and sales history.

Use of the Internet for retail sales is growing, and the Internet continues to be very useful for business-to-business sales. E-marketing offers many career opportunities, including customer relationship management (CRM). CRM helps companies market to customers through relationships, maintaining customer loyalty. Information technology plays a huge role in such marketing jobs, as you need to combine technical skills and marketing knowledge to effectively communicate with customers. Job titles include e-marketing manager, customer relationship manager, and e-services manager. A CRM customer service manager may receive a salary in the $40,000 to $45,000 range, and experienced individuals in charge of online product offerings may earn up to $100,000.

A job in any of these marketing fields will require a strong sense of the current trends in business and marketing. Customer service is vital to many aspects of marketing, so the ability to work with customers and to communicate their needs and wants is important. Marketing is everywhere, from the corner grocery or local nonprofit organization to the largest multinational corporation, making it a shrewd choice for an ambitious and creative person. We will provide additional job opportunities in marketing in Chapter 12.

GET ONLINE

mhhe.com/FerrellM3e

for study materials including
quizzes, iPod downloads,
and video

chapter eleven

active review card
Customer-Driven Marketing

in a nutshell

Marketers develop marketing strategies to satisfy the needs and wants of their customers; they also need to consider buying behavior and use research to determine what consumers want to buy and why. Marketers also need to consider the impact of the environment on marketing activities.

The following statements will test your take-away knowledge from this chapter. Do your best to explain each one in the space provided below.

LO.1 Define marketing, and describe the exchange process.

LO.2 Specify the functions of marketing.

LO.3 Explain the marketing concept and its implications for developing marketing strategies.

LO.4 Examine the development of a marketing strategy, including market segmentation and marketing mix.

LO.5 Investigate how marketers conduct marketing research and study buying behavior.

LO.6 Summarize the environmental forces that influence marketing decisions.

Did your answers include the following important points?

LO.1. Define marketing, and describe the exchange process.

- Marketing is a group of activities designed to expedite transactions by creating, distributing, pricing, and promoting goods, services, and ideas.
- Marketing facilitates exchange, the act of giving up one thing in return for something else. The central focus is to satisfy needs.

LO.2. Specify the functions of marketing.

- Marketing includes many varied and interrelated activities: buying, selling, transporting, storing, grading, financing, marketing research, and risk taking.

LO.3. Explain the marketing concept and its implications for developing marketing strategies.

- The marketing concept is the idea that an organization should try to satisfy customers' needs through coordinated activities that also allow it to achieve its goals.
- If a company does not implement the marketing concept by providing products that consumers need and want while achieving its own objectives, it will not survive.

LO.4. Examine the development of a marketing strategy, including market segmentation and marketing mix.

- A marketing strategy is a plan of action for creating a marketing mix for a specific target market. Some firms use a total-market approach, designating everyone as the target market.

- Most firms divide the total market into segments of people who have relatively similar product needs.
- A company using a concentration approach develops one marketing strategy for a single market segment, whereas a multisegment approach aims marketing efforts at two or more segments, developing a different marketing strategy for each segment.

LO.5. Investigate how marketers conduct marketing research and study buying behavior.

- Carrying out the marketing concept is impossible unless marketers know what, where, when, and how consumers buy; marketing research into the factors that influence buying behavior helps marketers develop effective marketing strategies.
- Marketing research is a systematic, objective process of getting information about potential customers to guide marketing decisions.
- Buying behavior is the decision processes and actions of people who purchase and use products.

LO.6. Summarize the environmental forces that influence marketing decisions.

- There are several forces that influence marketing activities: political, legal, regulatory, social, competitive, economic, and technological.

Practical Application

LO.1.

- James Johnson has developed a new product, found a store willing to sell it, and agreed to help promote the product's sale. He is engaging in _____.
- When a customer hands the cashier $1 and receives a loaf of bread, a(n) _____ has occurred.

LO.2.

- When a storeowner spends a lot of money for new products that have yet to be proved sales items, the owner is engaging in the marketing function of _____.
- Richard has acquired a supply of canned fruits and vegetables. He does not yet have a buyer for them, but he's using promotion and other activities to find a buyer. He is performing the marketing function of _____.

LO.3.

- The goal of the marketing concept is _____.
- _____ remains a major element of any strategy to develop and manage long-term customer relationships.
- During the Industrial Revolution, new technologies fueled strong _____.

LO.4.

- A plan of action for developing, pricing, distributing, and promoting products that meets the needs of a specific customer is a(n) _____.
- People visiting a ski resort would be viewed by a ski equipment storeowner as the business's _____.
- The aim of _____ is to communicate directly or indirectly with individuals, groups, and organizations to facilitate exchanges.

LO.5.

- _____ is a systematic and objective process of getting information on potential customers.
- _____ is a psychological variable of buyer behavior.
- _____ are the least expensive data to collect.

LO.6.

- Purchasing power, recession, and inflation are associated with _____ forces.
- The public's opinions and attitudes toward living standards, ethics, and the environment are considered _____ forces.

chapter

twelve

dimensions of
marketing strategy

The key to developing a marketing strategy is selecting a target market and maintaining a marketing mix that creates long-term relationships with customers.

Getting just the right mix of product, price, promotion, and distribution is critical if a business is to satisfy its target customers and achieve its own objectives (implement the marketing concept).

In Chapter 11, we introduced the concept of marketing and the various activities important in developing a marketing strategy. In this chapter, we'll take a closer look at the four dimensions of the marketing mix—product, price, distribution, and promotion—used to develop the marketing strategy. The focus of these marketing mix elements is a marketing strategy that builds customer relationships and satisfaction.

LEARNING OBJECTIVES

LO1 Describe the role of product in the marketing mix, including how products are developed, classified, and identified.

LO2 Define price, and discuss its importance in the marketing mix, including various pricing strategies a firm might employ.

LO3 Identify factors affecting distribution decisions, such as marketing channels and intensity of market coverage.

LO4 Specify the activities involved in promotion, as well as promotional strategies and promotional positioning.

THE MARKETING MIX

The marketing mix is the part of marketing strategy that involves decisions regarding controllable variables. To develop meaningful customer relationships, marketers have to develop and manage the dimensions of the marketing mix to give their firm an advantage over competitors. Successful companies offer at least one dimension of value that surpasses all competitors in the marketplace in meeting customer expectations. However, this does not mean that a company can ignore the other dimensions of the marketing mix; it must maintain acceptable, and if possible distinguishable, differences in the other dimensions as well.

Walmart, for example, emphasizes price ("Save money, live better"). Procter & Gamble is well known for its promotion of top consumer brands such as Tide, Cheer, Crest, Ivory, and Head & Shoulders. Dell Computers' efficient distribution

?

DID YOU KNOW?

Less than 10 percent of new products succeed in the marketplace, and 90 percent of successes come from a handful of companies.[1]

and customization processes explain why it has secured such a large share of the computer industry.[2]

PRODUCT STRATEGY

As mentioned previously, the term *product* refers to goods, services, and ideas. Because the product is often the most visible of the marketing mix dimensions, managing product decisions is crucial. In this section, we'll consider product development, classification, mix, life cycle, and identification.

Developing New Products

Each year thousands of products are introduced, but few of them succeed. For instance, The Coca-Cola Company spent two years developing Coke Blāk, a Coca-Cola coffee drink aimed at an older audience. The product failed to take off in the United States and was discontinued less than two years after its launch.[3] Figure 12.1

While attending Yale in 1966, FedEx founder Fred Smith studied a mathematical discipline called topology, which inspired his vision for creating the company. Realizing the potential efficiencies of connecting all points on a network through a central hub, Smith used what he learned to get FedEx off the ground.

shows the different steps in the product development process. Before introducing a new product, a business must follow a multistep process: idea development, the screening of new ideas, business analysis, product development, test marketing, and commercialization. A firm can take considerable time to get a product ready for the market: It took more than 20 years for the first photocopier, for example. Although the Nissan Leaf was officially unveiled in 2009, it was not released until late 2010. This did not stop the Nissan Leaf from winning the Green Car Vision Award in 2010, several months before its release.[4]

Idea Development New ideas can come from marketing research, engineers, and outside sources such as advertising agencies and management consultants. Microsoft has a separate division—Microsoft Research—where scientists devise technology of the future. The division has more than 800 researchers who work in a university-like research atmosphere.

Research teams then present their ideas to Microsoft engineers who are developing specific products. As we said in Chapter 11, ideas sometimes come from customers, too. Other sources are brainstorming and intracompany incentives or rewards for good ideas. New ideas can even create a company. Las Vegas–based Shuffle Master, for example, grew out of entrepreneur John Breeding's idea for a card-shuffling machine. The Shuffle Master now has more than 22,000 shuffling units installed around the world.[5]

New Idea Screening The next step in developing a new product is idea screening. In this phase, a marketing manager should look at the organization's resources and objectives and assess the firm's ability to produce and market the product. Important aspects to be considered at this stage are consumer desires, the competition, technological changes, social trends, and political, economic, and environmental considerations.

> ## Each year thousands of products are introduced, but few of them succeed.

FIGURE 12.1
Product Development Process

Basically, there are two reasons new products succeed: They are able to meet a need or solve a problem better than products already available or they add variety to the product selection currently on the market. Bringing together a team of knowledgeable people including designers, engineers, marketers, and customers is a great way to screen ideas. Using the Internet to encourage collaboration represents a rich opportunity for marketers to screen ideas. Most new product ideas are rejected during screening because they seem inappropriate or impractical for the organization.

Business Analysis Business analysis is a basic assessment of a product's compatibility in the marketplace and its potential profitability. Both the size of the market and competing products are often studied at this point. The most important question relates to market demand: How will the product affect the firm's sales, costs, and profits?

Product Development If a product survives the first three steps, it is developed into a prototype that should reveal the intangible attributes it possesses as perceived by the consumer. Product development is often expensive, and few product ideas make it to this stage. New product research and development costs vary. Adding a new color to an existing item may cost $100,000 to $200,000, but launching a completely new product can cost millions of dollars. The Coca-Cola Co. reduced the time and cost of product development research by 50 percent when it created an online panel of 100 teenagers and asked them how to remake its Powerade sports drink.[6]

test marketing
a trial minilaunch of a product in limited areas that represent the potential market

commercialization
the full introduction of a complete marketing strategy and the launch of the product for commercial success

consumer products products intended for household or family use

business products
products that are used directly or indirectly in the operation or manufacturing processes of businesses

During product development, various elements of the marketing mix must be developed for testing. Copyrights, tentative advertising copy, packaging, labeling, and descriptions of a target market are integrated to develop an overall marketing strategy.

▼**FIGURE 12.2**
ACNielsen Market Decisions

**Market Decisions
Test Market Locations**

◆ **Permanent Test Markets
("Data Markets")**

★ **Additional "Custom" Test Markets**

Source: "Test Marketing," ACNielsen (n.d.), www.acnielsen.com/services/testing/test1.htm (accessed June 5, 2004). Reprinted with permission of ACNielsen Market Decisions.

Test Marketing Test marketing is a trial minilaunch of a product in limited areas that represent the potential market. It allows a complete test of the marketing strategy in a natural environment, giving the organization an opportunity to discover weaknesses and eliminate them before the product is fully launched. Consider Tide Basic, a product released by Procter & Gamble to appeal to money-conscious consumers during the most recent recession. Tide Basic was a stripped-down version of the company's Tide laundry detergent that cost 20 percent less. It was meant to appeal to consumers who needed to save money but still wanted the same basic benefits that Tide had to offer. P&G started out by testing it in limited markets and then initially introduced the new product into only 100 stores in the South. However, the product was not on the market for long before Procter & Gamble discontinued it. Tide Basic demonstrates that even at the test marketing stage, products have a high chance of being discarded.[7] Because test marketing requires significant resources and expertise, market research companies like ACNielsen can assist firms in test marketing their products. Figure 12.2 shows the permanent sites as well as custom locations for test marketing.

Commercialization Commercialization is the full introduction of a complete marketing strategy and the launch of the product for commercial success. During commercialization, the firm gears up for full-scale production, distribution, and promotion. To compete more effectively against coffee chains like Starbucks, McDonald's introduced its first American McCafé in Chicago in 2001. In 2007, the company introduced iced coffee to its menu and began testing its new line of espresso-based beverages. However, it took two more years before McDonald's implemented nationwide commercialization of its McCafés. The launch was McDonald's largest in 30 years.[8]

Classifying Products

Products are usually classified as either consumer products or industrial products. **Consumer products** are for household or family use; they are not intended for any purpose other than

When consumers are shopping for specialty products such as rare antiques, they go to great lengths to get what they want and often aren't willing to accept substitutes.

daily living. They can be further classified as convenience products, shopping products, and specialty products on the basis of consumers' buying behavior and intentions.

- *Convenience products,* such as eggs, milk, bread, and newspapers, are bought frequently, without a lengthy search, and often for immediate consumption. Consumers spend virtually no time planning where to purchase these products and usually accept whatever brand is available.

- *Shopping products,* such as furniture, audio equipment, clothing, and sporting goods, are purchased after the consumer has compared competitive products and "shopped around." Price, product features, quality, style, service, and image all influence the decision to buy.

- *Specialty products,* such as ethnic foods, designer clothing and shoes, art, and antiques, require even greater research and shopping effort. Consumers know what they want and go out of their way to find it; they are not willing to accept a substitute.

Business products are used directly or indirectly in the operation or manufacturing processes of businesses. They are usually purchased for the operation of an organization or the production of other products; thus, their purchase is tied to specific goals and objectives. They too can be further classified:

- *Raw materials* are natural products taken from the earth, oceans, and recycled solid waste. Iron ore, bauxite, lumber, cotton, and fruits and vegetables are examples.

- *Major equipment* covers large, expensive items used in production. Examples include earth-moving equipment, stamping machines, and robotic equipment used on auto assembly lines.

- *Accessory equipment* includes items used for production, office, or management purposes, which usually do not become part of the final product. Computers, fax machines, calculators, and hand tools are examples.

- *Component parts* are finished items, ready to be assembled into the company's final products. Tires, window glass, batteries, and spark plugs are component parts of automobiles.

- *Processed materials* are things used directly in production or management operations but are not readily identifiable as component parts. Varnish, for example, is a processed material for a furniture manufacturer.

- *Supplies* include materials that make production, management, and other operations possible,

such as paper, pencils, paint, cleaning supplies, and so on.

- *Industrial services* include financial, legal, marketing research, security, janitorial, and exterminating services. Purchasers decide whether to provide these services internally or to acquire them from an outside supplier.

Product Line and Product Mix

Product relationships within an organization are of key importance. A **product line** is a group of closely related products that are treated as a unit because of a similar marketing strategy. At Colgate-Palmolive, for example, the oral-care product line includes Colgate toothpaste, toothbrushes, and dental floss. A **product mix** is all the products offered by an organization. Figure 12.3 displays a sampling of the product mix and product lines of the Colgate-Palmolive Company.

Product Life Cycle

Like people, products are born, grow, mature, and eventually die. Some products have very long lives. Ivory Soap was introduced in 1879 and is still popular. In contrast, a new computer chip is usually outdated within a year because of technological breakthroughs and rapid changes in the computer industry. There are four stages in the life cycle of a product: introduction, growth, maturity, and decline (Figure 12.4). The stage a product is in helps determine marketing strategy. While pickup trucks have historically sold very well in the United States, sales have reached the maturity stage, declining after a peak in 2004. The percentage of new vehicles sold reveals more car sales than truck sales. As oil prices continue to fluctuate and carbon outputs become more of a concern, consumers are looking for better gas mileage, and the demand for fuel-efficient cars is on

▼FIGURE 12.3
Colgate-Palmolive's Product Mix and Product Lines

◄──────── **Product Mix** ──────────►			
Oral Care	*Personal Care*	*Household Care*	*Pet Nutrition*
Colgate Total Toothpaste	Softsoap Liquid Soaps	Palmolive Dishwashing Liquids	Hill's Science Diet
Colgate MaxFresh Toothpaste	Softsoap Foam Works for Kids	Murphy Oil Soap	Hill's Prescription Diet
		Ajax Powder Cleanser	
Colgate 360° Toothbrush	Irish Spring bar soaps	Suavitel Liquid Fabric Conditioners	
Colgate Wave	Speed Stick	Suavital Dryer Sheets	
	Lady Speed Stick		
Colgate 2in1 Kids	Afta Aftershave		
Colgate Dora the Explorer	Skin Bracer Aftershave		

(left vertical label: Product Lines)

Source: "Colgate World of Care," Colgate-Palmolive Company, 2008, www.colgate.com/app/Colgate/US/HomePage.cvsp (accessed April 8, 2010).

SILLY BANDZ: A FLASH IN THE PAN, OR HERE TO STAY?

The title for toy fad in 2010 went to Silly Bandz, the company credited with beginning the U.S. craze for stretchy bracelets. Yet for all of its popularity, it is uncertain whether Silly Bandz is a fad (something that quickly ascends in popularity and just as quickly vanishes) or a trend (something with lasting relevance). Silly Bandz founder Robert Croak is determined to make Silly Bandz last through multiple product lines, licensing deals, and more.

Silly Bandz was born when Croak visited a Chinese trade show and discovered rubber bands shaped like animals. He decided to make a sturdier version into a bracelet. Croak believed that kids would be drawn to collecting and trading these bands. In terms of marketing, Croak claims that everything was done virally via social media sites like Facebook, YouTube, and the Silly Bandz website. Although Croak has no publicist or marketing plan, this hasn't seemed to deter the product's success. In 2009 the company sold 100 packages per week. One year later, it was selling roughly one million packages weekly.

The question is whether this item has a future. Retailers have begun cutting back on Silly Bandz, with 7-Eleven reporting a 97 percent drop in sales since its peak. Croak wants to extend the product's life by introducing related products and improving existing ones. He has signed deals with Marvel Comics and Justin Bieber to represent Marvel's characters and Bieber's likeness in Silly Bandz form. The company has introduced Silly Necklaces, Silly Ringz, and Silly Caribinerz. Croak is also in talks with Zoo Games to develop a videogame. Will these efforts be enough to extend the brand for years to come? Or will Silly Bandz soon become a product beloved only by collectors?[9]

Discussion Questions

1. Do you think Silly Bandz are a fad or a trend?

2. Why do you think children are drawn to Silly Bandz?

3. Can you think of ways to extend the Silly Bandz brand?

FIGURE 12.4
The Life Cycle of a Product

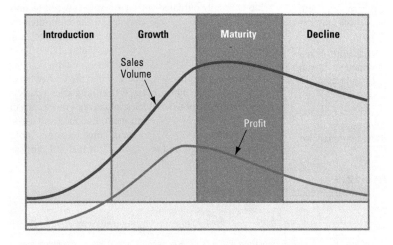

the rise. Electric vehicles are in the introductory stage but with continued demand will quickly pass into the growth stage.[10]

In the *introductory stage,* consumer awareness and acceptance of the product are limited, sales are zero, and profits are negative. Profits are negative because the firm has spent money on research, development, and marketing to launch the product. During the introductory stage, marketers focus on making consumers aware of the product and its benefits. When former restaurant owner Sean O'Connor introduced Batter Blaster, a canned organic pancake and waffle batter mix with a point-and-shoot nozzle, the company started a major media campaign to spread awareness of the product and its benefits. By using a combination of word-of-mouth advertising, social networking sites, and large publicity stunts like forming a team to cook more than 76,000 pancakes in a record eight hours, the company has gotten Batter Blaster into 15,000 U.S. outlets and realized annual revenues of $19.5 million.[11] Figure 12.5 shows some familiar products at different stages of the product life cycle. Sales accelerate as the product enters the growth stage of the life cycle.

In the *growth stage,* sales increase rapidly and profits peak, then start to decline. One reason profits start to decline during the growth stage is that new companies enter the market, driving prices down and increasing marketing expenses. Consider Apple's iPod, the most popular digital music player with more than 70 percent of the music player market. Since its launch, 275 million iPods have been sold and over 10 billion songs sold. To maintain its high growth, Apple has also introduced the iTunes 10, the iPod Classic, and the iPod Touch.[12] During the growth stage, the firm tries to strengthen its position in the market by emphasizing the product's benefits and identifying market segments that want these benefits.

Sales continue to increase at the beginning of the *maturity stage,* but then the sales curve peaks and starts to decline while profits continue to decline. This stage is characterized by severe competition and heavy expenditures. In the highly competitive snack food industry, Quaker is converting mature products

branding
the process of naming and identifying products

trademark
a brand that is registered with the U.S. Patent and Trademark Office and is thus legally protected from use by any other firm

▼**FIGURE 12.5**
Products at Different Stages of the Life Cycle

Introduction	Growth	Maturity	Decline
3D television	DVRs	Flat-screen televisions	AM/FM radios
YouTube movies	Netflix	Laptop computers	VCRs
Electric cars	Tablet computers	Netbook computers	Desktop computers

to single-serve lower-calorie treats. Because 100-calorie packs were a smash success for Quaker and competitor Kraft, rivals across the industry are introducing 90-, 80-, even 60-calorie versions of mature products in hopes of maintaining sales.[13]

During the *decline stage,* sales continue to fall rapidly. Profits also decline and may even become losses as prices are cut and necessary marketing expenditures are made. As profits drop, firms may eliminate certain models or items. To reduce expenses and squeeze out any remaining profits, marketing expenditures may be cut back, even though such cutbacks accelerate the sales decline. Finally, plans must be made for phasing out the product and introducing new ones to take its place. In 2010, General Motors sold its final Hummer SUVs at steeply reduced prices. The company discontinued the brand because of its poor fuel economy, negative public opinion, and plummeting sales. GM also phased out its Saturn and Pontiac brands.

At the same time, it should be noted that product stages do not always go one way. Some products that have moved to the maturity stage or to the decline stage can still rebound through redesign or new uses for the product. One prime example is baking soda. Originally, baking soda was used only for cooking, which meant it reached the maturity stage very quickly. However, once it was discovered that baking soda could be used as a deodorizer, sales shot up and bumped baking soda back into the growth stage.[14] Similarly, Mattel is trying to make a comeback with Barbie by releasing new lines of redesigned dolls. For example, their "fashionista" dolls have 12 movable joints and wear clothes similar to what is found on the runway. Mattel also released So in Style, its first line of black dolls.[15]

Identifying Products

Branding, packaging, and labeling can be used to identify or distinguish one product from others. As a result, they are key marketing

> During the *decline stage,* sales continue to fall rapidly. Profits also decline and may even become losses as prices are cut and necessary marketing expenditures are made.

activities that help position a product appropriately for its target market.

Branding Branding is the process of naming and identifying products. A *brand* is a name, term, symbol, design, or combination that identifies a product and distinguishes it from other products. Consider that Google, iPod, and TiVo are brand names that are used to identify entire product categories, much like Xerox has become synonymous with photocopying and Kleenex with tissues. Protecting a brand name is important in maintaining a brand identity. The world's 10 most valuable brands are shown in Table 12.1. The brand name is the part of the brand that can be spoken and consists of letters, words, and numbers—such as WD-40 lubricant. A *brand mark* is the part of the brand that is a distinctive design, such as the silver star on the hood of a Mercedes or McDonald's golden arches logo. A **trademark** is a brand that is registered with the U.S. Patent and Trademark Office and is thus legally protected from use by any other firm.

▼ **TABLE 12.1** The 10 Most Valuable Brands in the World

Rank	Brand	Brand Value 2011 ($M)	% Brand Value Change 2011 vs. 2010
1	Apple	$153,285	84%
2	Google	111,498	−2
3	IBM	100,849	17
4	McDonald's	81,016	23
5	Microsoft	78,243	2
6	Coca-Cola	73,752	8
7	AT&T	69,916	N/A
8	Marlboro	67,522	18
9	China Mobile	57,326	9
10	GE	50,318	12

Source: "Brandz Top 100 Most Valuable Global Brands 2011," Millward Brown Optimor, www.millwardbrown.com/libraries/optimor_brandz_files/2011_brandz_top100_chart.sflb.ashx (accessed August 11, 2011).

manufacturer brands brands initiated and owned by the manufacturer to identify products from the point of production to the point of purchase

private distributor brands brands, which may cost less than manufacturer brands, that are owned and controlled by a wholesaler or retailer

generic products products with no brand name that often come in simple packages and carry only their generic name

packaging the external container that holds and describes the product

Another type of brand that has developed is **generic products**—products with no brand name at all. They often come in plain simple packages that carry only the generic name of the product—peanut butter, tomato juice, aspirin, dog food, and so on. They appeal to consumers who may be willing to sacrifice quality or product consistency to get a lower price.

Companies use two basic approaches to branding multiple products. In one, a company gives each product within its complete product mix its own brand name. Warner-Lambert, for example, sells many well-known consumer products—Dentyne, Chiclets, Listerine, Halls, Rolaids, and Trident—each individually branded. This branding policy ensures that the name of one product does not affect the names of others, and different brands can be targeted at different segments of the same market, increasing the company's market share (its percentage of the sales for the total market for a product). Another approach to branding is to develop a family of brands with each of the firm's products carrying the same name or at least part of the name. Gillette, Sara Lee, and IBM use this approach. Finally, consumers may react differently to domestic versus foreign brands, Table 12.2 provides a snapshot of the most popular car brands with the majority from different countries.

This phone with no brand name would appear to be a generic product and does not provide a signal to the consumer as to product quality.

Packaging The **packaging**, or external container that holds and describes the product, influences consumers' attitudes and their buying decisions. In a Harris Interactive Panel, three-fourths of respondents replied they would be willing to pay more money for certain packaging attributes. Some of the more important attributes cited included reusability, "staying

Two major categories of brands are manufacturer brands and private distributor brands. **Manufacturer brands** are brands initiated and owned by the manufacturer to identify products from the point of production to the point of purchase. Kellogg's, Sony, and Texaco are examples. **Private distributor brands**, which may be less expensive than manufacturer brands, are owned and controlled by a wholesaler or retailer, such as Kenmore appliances (Sears) and Sam's grocery products (Walmart and Sam's Wholesale Club). The names of private brands do not usually identify their manufacturer. While private-label brands were once considered cheaper and of poor quality, such as Walmart's Ol'Roy dog food, many private-label brands are increasing in quality and image and are competing with national brands. For instance, several companies are hiring professional designers to design their private-label brands, replacing the traditional two-color packaging schemes often associated with private-label products. In fact, the grocery retailer Tesco has several types of private-label brands, and its branding strategy has performed so effectively that consumers may end up paying more for Tesco's own products than for branded goods.[16] Manufacturer brands are fighting hard against private distributor brands.

▼ **TABLE 12.2**   Best-Selling Vehicle Brands

Ranking	Car Model	Country of Origin
1	Ford F-Series Pickup	United States
2	Chevrolet Silverado	United States
3	Toyota Camry	Japan
4	Honda Accord	Japan
5	Toyota Corolla	Japan
6	Nissan Altima	Japan
7	Honda Civic	Japan
8	Ford Fusion	United States
9	Chevrolet Malibu	United States
10	Hyundai Sonata	South Korea

Source: Joann Muller, "The Year's Bestselling Cars," ABC News, November 10, 2010, http://abcnews.go.com/Business/forbes-years-bestselling-cars/story?id=12069787 (accessed January 14, 2011).

fresh longer," and stating that the product is "made in the United States."[17] It is estimated that consumers' eyes linger only 2.5 seconds on each product on an average shopping trip; therefore, product packaging should be designed to attract and hold consumers' attention.

A package can perform several functions including protection, economy, convenience, and promotion. Beverage manufacturers have been redesigning their bottles to make them more convenient for consumers and to promote them to certain markets. Scientists videotaped people drinking from different types of bottles and made plaster casts of their hands. They found that the average gulp is around 1 ounce and that half the population would rather suck liquid through a pop-up top than sip it. Since the early 1990s, soft drinks in 20-ounce plastic bottles revitalized U.S. sales for Coca-Cola and PepsiCo by getting Americans to drink larger servings. Recent concerns about health and the desire for lower-priced options have led both companies to test a variety of smaller container sizes to win back lost customers.[18]

Labeling Labeling, the presentation of important information on the package, is closely associated with packaging. The content of labeling, often required by law, may include ingredients or content, nutrition facts (calories, fat, etc.), care instructions, suggestions for use (such as recipes), the manufacturer's address and toll-free number, website, and other useful information. This information can have a strong impact on sales. The labels of many products, particularly food and drugs, must carry warnings, instructions, certifications, or manufacturers' identifications.

Product Quality Quality reflects the degree to which a good, service, or idea meets the demands and requirements of customers. Quality products are often referred to as reliable, durable, easily maintained, easily used, a good value, or a trusted brand name. The level of quality is the amount of quality that a product possesses, and the consistency of quality depends on the product maintaining the same level of quality over time.

Quality of service is difficult to gauge because it depends on customers' perceptions of how well the service meets or exceeds their expectations. In other words, service quality is judged by consumers, not the service providers. A bank may define service quality as employing friendly and knowledgeable employees, but the bank's customers may be more concerned with waiting time, ATM access, security, and statement accuracy. Similarly, an airline traveler considers on-time arrival, on-board food service, and satisfaction with the ticketing and boarding process. The American Customer Satisfaction Index produces customer satisfaction scores for 10 economic sectors, 44 industries, and more than 200 companies. The latest results show that overall customer satisfaction was 75.7 (out of a possible 100), with increases in some industries balancing drops in others. Customer satisfaction with the banking industry has started to recover, while satisfaction with health insurance went down 2.7 percent.[19] Table 12.3 shows the rankings of nine U.S. airline carriers. Southwest Airlines had the least customer complaints, whereas Delta had the highest customer complaint rate.[20]

The quality of services provided by businesses on the Internet can be gauged by consumers on such sites as ConsumerReports.org and BBBOnline. The subscription service offered by ConsumerReports.org provides consumers with a view of e-commerce sites' business, security, and privacy policies, while BBBOnline is dedicated to promoting responsibility online. As consumers join in by posting business and product reviews on the Internet on sites such as Yelp, the public can often get a

labeling the presentation of important information on a package

quality the degree to which a good, service, or idea meets the demands and requirements of customers

The labels on these Clorox Green Works cleaning supplies inform consumers that the chemicals are derived from natural sources.

▼ **TABLE 12.3** Airline Rankings According to Customer Complaints (From Least to Greatest)

Rank	Airline
1	Southwest
2	Alaska
3	AirTran
4	JetBlue
5	American
6	Continental
7	US Airways
8	United
9	Delta

Source: Scott McCartney, "The Big Guys Finish Last in 2010 Airline Rankings," *The Wall Street Journal*, January 13, 2011, p. D1.

Google built a high-quality search engine that soon dominated the industry and made it one of the most valuable brands worldwide.

▼FIGURE 12.6
Calculating the Value of Your Product

Step 1:	Step 2:	Step 3:	Step 4:
Identity target customers.	Identity their best alternative.	Determine your product's difference.	Calculate value based on its differentiation.

Source: Rafi Mohammed, "Use Price to Profit and Grow," *Forbes.com,* March 25, 2010, www.forbes.com/2010/03/25/ profit-gain-value-mckinsey-sears-whirlpool-cmo-network-rafi-mohammed.html (accessed March 31, 2010).

---

much better idea of the quality of certain goods and services. Quality can also be associated with where the product is made. For example, "Made in U.S.A." labeling can be perceived as having a different value and quality. There are differences in the perception of quality and value between the U.S. consumers and Europeans when comparing products made in the United States, Japan, Korea, and China.[21]

PRICING STRATEGY

Previously, we defined price as the value placed on an object exchanged between a buyer and a seller. Buyers' interest in price stems from their expectations about the usefulness of a product or the satisfaction they may derive from it. Because buyers have limited resources, they must allocate those resources to obtain the

price skimming
charging the highest possible price that buyers who want the product will pay

penetration price
a low price designed to help a product enter the market and gain market share rapidly

products they most desire. They must decide whether the benefits gained in an exchange are worth the buying power sacrificed. Almost anything of value can be assessed by a price. Many factors may influence the evaluation of value, including time constraints, price levels, perceived quality, and motivations to use available information about prices.[22] Figure 12.6 illustrates a method for calculating the value of your product. Indeed, consumers vary in their response to price: Some focus solely on the lowest price, while others consider quality or the prestige associated with a product and its price. Some types of consumers are increasingly "trading up" to more status-conscious products, such as automobiles, home appliances, restaurants, and even pet food, yet remain price-conscious for other products such as cleaning and grocery goods. In setting prices, marketers must consider not just a company's cost to produce a product or service, but the perceived value of that item in the marketplace. Products' perceived value has benefited marketers at Starbucks, Sub-Zero, BMW, and Petco—which can charge premium prices for high-quality, prestige products—as well as Sam's Clubs and Costco—which offer basic household products at everyday low prices.

Price is a key element in the marketing mix because it relates directly to the generation of revenue and profits. In large part, the ability to set a price depends on the supply of and demand for a product. For most products, the quantity demanded goes up as the price goes down, and as the price goes up, the quantity demanded goes down. Changes in buyers' needs, variations in the effectiveness of other marketing mix variables, the presence of substitutes, and dynamic environmental factors can influence demand. New demand has greatly increased prices for industrial-grade diamonds as jewelers have turned to the impure gems, typically used for drill bits and saws, as a fashion statement. Even diamond giant De Beers has turned to the fashion, with its

In a highly competitive industry, CenturyLink has developed a pricing objective of boosting market share with its $14.95 discounted Internet service.

Talisman collection of rough-cut and uncut diamond jewelry capitalizing on ancient beliefs of the power and allure of uncut diamonds.[23]

Price is probably the most flexible variable in the marketing mix. Although it may take years to develop a product, establish channels of distribution, and design and implement promotion, a product's price may be set and changed in a few minutes. Under certain circumstances, of course, the price may not be so flexible, especially if government regulations prevent dealers from controlling prices. Of course, price also depends on the cost to manufacture a good or provide a service or idea. A firm may temporarily sell products below cost to match competition, to generate cash flow, or even to increase market share, but in the long run it cannot survive by selling its products below cost.

Pricing Objectives

Pricing objectives specify the role of price in an organization's marketing mix and strategy. They usually are influenced not only by marketing mix decisions but also by finance, accounting, and production factors. Maximizing profits and sales, boosting market share, maintaining the status quo, and survival are four common pricing objectives.

Specific Pricing Strategies

Pricing strategies provide guidelines for achieving the company's pricing objectives and overall marketing strategy. They specify how price will be used as a variable in the marketing mix. Significant pricing strategies relate to the pricing of new products, psychological pricing, and price discounting.

Pricing New Products Setting the price for a new product is critical: The right price leads to profitability; the wrong price may kill the product. In general, there are two basic strategies to setting the base price for a new product. **Price skimming** is charging the highest possible price that buyers who want the product will pay. Starbucks' new Via coffee, for example, sells at a price of $2.95 for a trio of single-serve packets and $9.95 for 12 packets. Per serving, Via is priced four times higher than market leader Nestlé.[24] This strategy allows the company to generate much-needed revenue to help offset the costs of research and development. Conversely, a **penetration price** is a low price designed to help a product enter the market and gain market share rapidly. For example, when Industrias Añaños introduced Kola Real to capitalize on limited penetration of Coca-Cola and Pepsi Cola in Peru, it set an ultralow penetration price to appeal to the poor who predominate in the region. Kola Real quickly secured one-fifth of the Peruvian market and has since made significant gains in Ecuador, Venezuela, and Mexico, forcing larger soft-drink marketers to cut prices.[25] Penetration pricing is less flexible than price skimming; it is more difficult to raise a penetration price than to lower a skimming price. Penetration

The pricing strategy of an independently owned ice cream business can have a premium price objective because of the quality of the product and the unique atmosphere.

pricing is used most often when marketers suspect that competitors will enter the market shortly after the product has been introduced.

Psychological Pricing

Psychological pricing encourages purchases based on emotional rather than rational responses to the price. For example, the assumption behind *even/odd pricing* is that people will buy more of a product for $9.99 than $10 because it seems to be a bargain at the odd price. The assumption behind *symbolic/prestige pricing* is that high prices connote high quality. Thus the prices of certain fragrances are set artificially high to give the impression of superior quality. Some over-the-counter drugs are priced high because consumers associate a drug's price with potency.

Price Discounting

Temporary price reductions, or **discounts**, are often employed to boost sales. Although there

> **Today, there are too many stores competing for too few customers, and, as a result, competition between similar retailers has never been more intense.**

are many types, quantity, seasonal, and promotional discounts are among the most widely used. Quantity discounts reflect the economies of purchasing in large volume. Seasonal discounts to buyers who purchase goods or services out of season help even out production capacity. Promotional discounts attempt to improve sales by advertising price reductions on selected products to increase customer interest. Often promotional pricing is geared toward increased profits. Taco Bell, with its reputation for value, has been labeled the "best-positioned U.S. brand" to do well in a recession economy as consumers look for cheaper fast-food options. Taco Bell offers a Why Pay More? menu with selections priced at 79¢, 89¢, and 99¢. KFC, Wendy's, and McDonald's all offer Value Menus as well, with items priced around $1.

DISTRIBUTION STRATEGY

The best products in the world will not be successful unless companies make them available where and when customers want to buy them. In this section, we will explore dimensions of distribution strategy, including the channels through which products are distributed, the intensity of market coverage, and the physical handling of products during distribution.

Marketing Channels

A **marketing channel**, or channel of distribution, is a group of organizations that move products from their producer to customers. Marketing channels make products available to buyers when and where they desire to purchase them. Organizations that bridge the gap between a product's manufacturer and the ultimate consumer are called *middlemen*, or intermediaries. They create time, place, and ownership utility. Two intermediary organizations are retailers and wholesalers.

Retailers buy products from manufacturers (or other intermediaries) and sell them to consumers for home and household use rather than for resale or for use in producing other products. Toys 'Я' Us, for example, buys products from Mattel and other manufacturers and resells them to consumers. Retailing usually occurs in a store, but the Internet, vending machines, mail-order catalogs, and entertainment, such as going to a Chicago Bulls basketball game, also provide opportunities for retailing. By bringing together an assortment of products from competing producers, retailers create utility. Retailers arrange for products to be moved from producers to a convenient retail establishment (place utility). They maintain hours of operation for their retail stores to make merchandise

psychological pricing encouraging purchases based on emotional rather than rational responses to the price

discounts temporary price reductions, often employed to boost sales

marketing channel a group of organizations that move products from their producer to customers; also called a channel of distribution

retailers intermediaries who buy products from manufacturers (or other intermediaries) and sell them to consumers for home and household use rather than for resale or for use in producing other products

wholesalers intermediaries who buy from producers or from other wholesalers and sell to retailers

available when consumers want it (time utility). They also assume the risk of ownership of inventories (ownership utility). Table 12.4 describes various types of general merchandise retailers.

Today, there are too many stores competing for too few customers, and, as a result, competition between similar retailers has never been more intense. In addition, retailers face challenges such as shoplifting, as indicated in Table 12.5. Further, competition between different types of stores is changing the nature of retailing. Supermarkets compete with specialty food stores, wholesale clubs, and discount stores. Department stores compete with nearly every other type of store including specialty stores, off-price chains, category killers, discount stores, and online retailers. Many traditional retailers, such as Walmart and Macy's, have created online shopping sites to retain customers and compete with online-only retailers. One of the best-known online-only, or cyber, merchants is Amazon.com. Amazon offers millions of products from which to choose, all from the privacy and convenience of the purchaser's home. In some cases, Web merchants offer wide selections, ultra-convenience, superior service, knowledge, and the best products.

Wholesalers are intermediaries who buy from producers or from other wholesalers and sell to retailers. They usually do not sell in significant quantities to ultimate consumers. Wholesalers perform the functions listed in Table 12.6.

▼ **TABLE 12.4**   General Merchandise Retailers

Type of Retailer	Description	Examples
Department store	Large organization offering wide product mix and organized into separate departments	Macy's, JCPenney, Sears
Discount store	Self-service, general merchandise store offering brand name and private brand products at low prices	Walmart, Target
Supermarket	Self-service store offering complete line of food products and some nonfood products	Kroger, Albertson's, Winn-Dixie
Superstore	Giant outlet offering all food and nonfood products found in supermarkets, as well as most routinely purchased products	Walmart Supercenters
Hypermarket	Combination supermarket and discount store, larger than a superstore	Carrefour
Warehouse club	Large-scale, members-only establishments combining cash-and-carry wholesaling with discount retailing	Sam's Club, Costco
Warehouse showroom	Facility in a large, low-cost building with large on-premises inventories and minimum service	Ikea
Catalog showroom	Type of warehouse showroom where consumers shop from a catalog and products are stored out of buyers' reach and provided in manufacturer's carton	Service Merchandise

Source: William M. Pride and O. C. Ferrell, *Marketing: Concepts and Strategies,* 2008, p. 428. Copyright 2008 by Houghton Mifflin Company. Reprinted with permission.

▼ **TABLE 12.5**   Statistics on Shoplifting in the United States

Number of shoplifters in the United States	27 million (1 in 11 people)
Amount retailers lose per year	More than $13 billion (more than $35 million per day)
Percentage of shoplifters who are adults	75%
Percentage of adult shoplifters who started in their teens	55%
Average frequency of habitual shoplifters	About 1.6 times per week

Source: "Shoplifting Statistics," National Association for Shoplifting Prevention, www.shopliftingprevention.org/WhatNASPOffers/NRC/PublicEducStats.htm (accessed March 31, 2010).

▼ **TABLE 12.6**   Major Wholesaling Functions

Supply chain management	Creating long-term partnerships among channel members
Promotion	Providing a sales force, advertising, sales promotion, and publicity
Warehousing, shipping, and product handling	Receiving, storing, and stockkeeping
	Packaging
	Shipping outgoing orders
	Materials handling
	Arranging and making local and long-distance shipments
Inventory control and data processing	Processing orders
	Controlling physical inventory
	Recording transactions
	Tracking sales data for financial analysis
Risk taking	Assuming responsibility for theft, product obsolescence, and excess inventories
Financing and budgeting	Extending credit
	Making capital investments
	Forecasting cash flow
Marketing research and information systems	Providing information about market
	Conducting research studies
	Managing computer networks to facilitate exchanges and relationships

Source: William M. Pride and O. C. Ferrell, *Marketing: Concepts and Strategies,* 2008, p. 389. Copyright 2008 by Houghton Mifflin Company. Reprinted with permission.

Wholesalers are extremely important because of the marketing activities they perform, particularly for consumer products. Although it is true that wholesalers can be eliminated, their functions must be passed on to some other entity, such as the producer, another intermediary, or even the customer. Wholesalers help consumers and retailers by buying in large quantities, then selling to retailers in smaller quantities. By stocking an assortment of products, wholesalers match products to demand.

Supply Chain Management

In an effort to improve distribution channel relationships among manufacturers and other channel intermediaries, supply chain management creates alliances between channel members. In Chapter 8, we defined supply chain management as connecting and integrating all parties or members of the distribution system in order to satisfy customers. It involves long-term partnerships among marketing channel members working together to reduce costs, waste, and unnecessary movement in the entire marketing channel in order to satisfy customers. It goes beyond traditional channel members (producers, wholesalers, retailers, customers) to include *all* organizations involved in moving products from the producer to the ultimate customer. In a survey of business managers, a disruption in the supply chain was viewed as the number-one crisis that could decrease revenue.[26]

The focus shifts from one of selling to the next level in the channel to one of selling products *through* the channel to a satisfied ultimate customer. Information, once provided on a guarded, "as needed" basis, is now open, honest, and ongoing. Perhaps most importantly, the points of contact in the relationship expand from one-on-one at the salesperson–buyer level to multiple interfaces at all levels and in all functional areas of the various organizations.

Channels for Consumer Products

Typical marketing channels for consumer products are shown in Figure 12.7. In Channel A, the product moves from the producer directly to the consumer. Farmers who sell their fruit and vegetables to consumers at roadside stands use a direct-from-producer-to-consumer marketing channel.

In Channel B, the product goes from producer to retailer to consumer. This type of channel is used for products such as college textbooks, automobiles, and appliances. In Channel C, the product is handled by a wholesaler and a retailer before it reaches the consumer. Producer-to-wholesaler-to-retailer-to-consumer marketing channels distribute a wide range of products including refrigerators, televisions, soft drinks, cigarettes, clocks, watches, and office products. In Channel D, the product goes to an agent, a wholesaler, and a retailer before going to the consumer. This long channel of distribution is especially useful for convenience products. Candy and some produce are often sold by agents who bring buyers and sellers together.

Services are usually distributed through direct marketing channels because they are generally produced *and* consumed simultaneously. For example, you cannot take a haircut home for later use. Many services require the customer's presence and participation: The sick patient must visit the physician to receive treatment; the child must be at the day care center to receive care; the tourist must be present to sightsee and consume tourism services.

Channels for Business Products

In contrast to consumer goods, more than half of all business products, especially expensive equipment or technically complex products, are sold through direct marketing channels. Business customers like to communicate directly with producers of such products to gain the technical assistance and personal assurances that only the producer can offer. For this reason, business buyers prefer to purchase expensive and highly complex mainframe computers directly from IBM, Cray, and other mainframe producers. Other business products may be distributed through channels employing wholesaling intermediaries such as industrial distributors and/or manufacturer's agents.

Intensity of Market Coverage

▼**FIGURE 12.7**
Marketing Channels for Consumer Products

A major distribution decision is how widely to distribute a product—that is, how many and what type of outlets should carry it. The intensity of market coverage depends on buyer behavior, as well as the nature of the target market and the competition. Wholesalers and retailers provide various intensities of market coverage and must be selected carefully to ensure success. Market coverage may be intensive, selective, or exclusive.

Intensive distribution makes a product available in as many outlets as possible. Because availability is important to purchasers of convenience products such as bread, milk, gasoline, soft drinks, and chewing gum, a nearby location with a minimum of time spent searching and waiting in line is most important to the consumer. To saturate markets intensively, wholesalers and many varied retailers try to make the product available at every location where a consumer might desire to purchase it. Zoom

WILL BABY CARROTS BECOME THE NEW SNACK FOOD?

Bolthouse Farms and similar companies are challenging the $18 billion salty snack food industry by making baby carrots just as fun as junk food. The baby carrot industry has launched a $25 million marketing campaign to promotionally position baby carrots as a healthier, hip snack food in the minds of consumers. As part of the campaign, baby carrot sellers are switching to chiplike packaging and edgy slogans. The website babycarrots.com was also launched to promote this new image, featuring a baby carrots iPhone game app, fun videos, and more. In addition, Bolthouse is working to intensively distribute its revamped products into schools through the installation of carrot vending machines. The machines have already met with some success. At one school, students began purchasing baby carrots—at 50 cents a pack—soon after the machine was installed. If Bolthouse and its compatriots are correct, kids are just as open to healthy snacks as they are to junk food. The marketing campaigns simply have to resonate with them.[27]

Railroads are one of the least expensive transportation modes for shipping products. However, they lack the flexibility that trucks have.

Systems provides robotic vending machines for products beyond candy and drinks. Zoom has more than a thousand machines in airports and hotels across the United States, some selling items such as Apple iPods, Neutrogena hair and skin products, and Sony products. The vending machines accept credit cards and allow sales to occur in places where storefronts would be impossible.[28] Through partnering with different companies, today's ZoomShops sell a variety of brands including products from Sephora, Best Buy, Macy's, and Rosetta Stone.[29]

Actress Vanessa Hudgens endorses the junior fashion brand Candie's. Candie's is exclusively sold through Kohl's Department Stores.

Selective distribution uses only a small number of all available outlets to expose products. It is used most often for products that consumers buy only after shopping and comparing price, quality, and style. Many products sold on a selective basis require salesperson assistance, technical advice, warranties, or repair service to maintain consumer satisfaction. Typical products include automobiles, major appliances, clothes, and furniture.

Exclusive distribution exists when a manufacturer gives an intermediary the sole right to sell a product in a defined geographic territory. Such exclusivity provides an incentive for a dealer to handle a product that has a limited market. Exclusive distribution is the opposite of intensive distribution in that products are purchased and consumed over a long period of time, and service or information is required to develop a satisfactory sales relationship. Products distributed on an exclusive basis include high-quality musical instruments, yachts, airplanes, and high-fashion leather goods.

Physical Distribution

Physical distribution includes all the activities necessary to move products from producers to customers—inventory control, transportation, warehousing, and materials handling. Physical distribution creates time and place utility by making products available when they are wanted, with adequate service and at minimum cost. Both goods and services require physical distribution. Many physical distribution activities are part of supply chain management, which we discussed in Chapter 8; we'll take a brief look at a few more now.

Transportation **Transportation**, the shipment of products to buyers, creates time and place utility for products, and thus is a key element in the flow of goods and services from producer to consumer. The five major modes of transportation used to move products between cities in the United States are railways, motor vehicles, inland waterways, pipelines, and airways.

Railroads offer the least expensive transportation for many products. Heavy commodities, foodstuffs, raw materials, and coal are examples of products carried by railroads. Trucks have greater flexibility than railroads because they can reach more locations. Trucks handle freight quickly and economically, offer door-to-door service, and are more flexible in their packaging requirements than are ships or airplanes. Air transport offers speed and a high degree of dependability but is the most expensive means of transportation; shipping is the least expensive and slowest form. Pipelines are used to transport petroleum, natural gas, semiliquid coal, wood chips, and certain chemicals. Many products can be moved most efficiently by using more than one mode of transportation.

Factors affecting the selection of a mode of transportation include cost, capability to handle the product, reliability, and availability, and, as suggested, selecting transportation modes requires trade-offs. Unique characteristics of the product and consumer desires often determine the mode selected.

Warehousing Warehousing is the design and operation of facilities to receive, store, and ship products. A warehouse facility receives, identifies, sorts, and dispatches goods to storage; stores them; recalls, selects, or picks goods; assembles the shipment; and finally, dispatches the shipment.

Companies often own and operate their own private warehouses that store, handle, and move their own products. They can also rent storage and related physical distribution services from public warehouses. Regardless of whether a private or a public warehouse is used, warehousing is important because it makes products available for shipment to match demand at different geographic locations.

Materials Handling Materials handling is the physical handling and movement of products in warehousing and transportation. Handling processes may vary significantly due to product characteristics. Efficient materials-handling procedures

increase a warehouse's useful capacity and improve customer service. Well-coordinated loading and movement systems increase efficiency and reduce costs.

Importance of Distribution in a Marketing Strategy

Distribution decisions are among the least flexible marketing mix decisions. Products can be changed over time; prices can be changed quickly; and promotion is usually changed regularly. But distribution decisions often commit resources and establish contractual relationships that are difficult if not impossible to change. As a company attempts to expand into new markets, it may require a complete change in distribution. Moreover, if a firm does not manage its marketing channel in the most efficient manner and provide the best service, then a new competitor will evolve to create a more effective distribution system.

PROMOTION STRATEGY

The role of promotion is to communicate with individuals, groups, and organizations to facilitate an exchange directly or indirectly. It encourages marketing exchanges by attempting to

warehousing
the design and operation of facilities to receive, store, and ship products

materials handling
the physical handling and movement of products in warehousing and transportation

FINDING THE REAL GREEN PRODUCTS

What makes a green product green? This question is actually quite complicated. The growing popularity of eco-friendly products is encouraging businesses to create and sell more green items. However, some businesses are cutting corners by touting their products as green when they really aren't—a form of misconduct known as greenwashing. Greenwashers make unjustifiable "green" claims about their products to appeal to the eco-friendly consumer. As a result, 40 percent of consumers claim that they don't know how to ensure that a company is really eco-friendly.

One common way that companies engage in greenwashing is by sustainably sourcing one product ingredient while the

other ingredients remain unsustainable. This might be akin to a company claiming that its product is green since one of the ingredients is organic cotton, while simultaneously glossing over the fact that the product also consists of nonrecyclable plastics or chemicals. Unfortunately, the subjective nature of greenwashing makes it harder to detect, as consumers themselves differ on what is green and what is greenwashing. For instance, some consumers feel misled by Cascade Farm's logo of a small idyllic farm when they discover that the brand is actually owned by General Mills. Others are unconcerned as long as the brand's organic claims are true.

The topic of greenwashing has become so pervasive that it is prompting government intervention. The Federal Trade Commission is releasing guidelines to define what is acceptable in green advertising. The FTC has also begun cracking down

on companies making false claims. For now consumers must investigate green claims for themselves. Such an investigation could include looking for third-party certification of a product's "greenness," paying attention to ingredient lists, and looking for information at trustworthy websites. However, until more stringent guidelines are created, the term *green* is likely to remain steeped in subjectivity.[30]

🔖 Discussion Questions

1. How do you tell if a product is really green?

2. Are you concerned that Cascade Farms, owned by General Mills, is making valid organic claims?

3. What will happen to companies and their products if consumers find their green claims are false?

integrated marketing communications	advertising	advertising campaign
coordinating the promotion mix elements and synchronizing promotion as a unified effort	a paid form of nonpersonal communication transmitted through a mass medium, such as television commercials or magazine advertisements	designing a series of advertisements and placing them in various media to reach a particular target market

persuade individuals, groups, and organizations to accept goods, services, and ideas. Promotion is used not only to sell products but also to influence opinions and attitudes toward an organization, person, or cause. The state of Texas, for example, has successfully used promotion to educate people about the costs of highway litter, which has thereby reduced littering. Most people probably equate promotion with advertising, but it also includes personal selling, publicity, and sales promotion. The role that these elements play in a marketing strategy is extremely important.

The Promotion Mix

Advertising, personal selling, publicity, and sales promotion are collectively known as the promotion mix because a strong promotion program results from the careful selection and blending of these elements. The process of coordinating the promotion mix elements and synchronizing promotion as a unified effort is called **integrated marketing communications**. When planning promotional activities, an integrated marketing communications approach results in the desired message for customers. Different elements of the promotion mix are coordinated to play their appropriate roles in delivery of the message on a consistent basis.

Advertising Perhaps the best-known form of promotion, **advertising** is a paid form of nonpersonal communication transmitted through a mass medium, such as television commercials, magazine advertisements or online ads. Even Google, one of the most powerful brands in the world, advertises. Google has turned to outdoor advertising on buses, trains, and ballparks in San Francisco and Chicago to promote its Google Maps feature.[31] Commercials featuring celebrities, customers, or unique creations (the Energizer Bunny, for example) serve to grab viewers' attention and pique their interest in a product. Table 12.7 shows companies that spent more than $1 billion on ads in the United States in one year.

An **advertising campaign** involves designing a series of advertisements and placing them in various media to reach a particular target audience. The basic content and form of an advertising campaign are a function of several factors. A product's features, uses, and benefits affect the content of the campaign message and individual ads. Characteristics of the people in the target audience—gender, age, education, race, income, occupation, lifestyle, and other attributes—influence both content and form. When Procter & Gamble promotes Crest toothpaste to children, the company emphasizes daily brushing and cavity control, whereas it promotes tartar control and whiter teeth when marketing to adults. To communicate effectively, advertisers use words, symbols, and illustrations

ADVERTISING MEDIA ARE THE VEHICLES OR FORMS OF COMMUNICATION USED TO REACH A DESIRED AUDIENCE.

▼ **TABLE 12.7**   Top 10 Leading National Advertisers

Organization	Advertising Expenditures (in millions)
1. Procter & Gamble	$4,188.9
2. Verizon Communications	3,020.0
3. AT&T	2,797.0
4. General Motors Co.	2,214.9
5. Johnson & Johnson	2,060.9
6. Pfizer	2,097.0
7. Walt Disney Company	2,003.8
8. Time Warner	1,848.1
9. L'Oreal	1,833.6
10. Kraft Foods	1,748.4

Source: "Marketer Trees 2010," *Ad Age Data Center,* December 20, 2010, http://adage.com/datacenter/marketertrees2010update#225 (accessed April 7, 2011).

that are meaningful, familiar, and attractive to people in the target audience.

An advertising campaign's objectives and platform also affect the content and form of its messages. If a firm's advertising objectives involve large sales increases, the message may include hard-hitting, high-impact language and symbols. When campaign objectives aim at increasing brand awareness, the message may use much repetition of the brand name and words and illustrations associated with it. Thus, the advertising platform is the foundation on which campaign messages are built.

Advertising media are the vehicles or forms of communication used to reach a desired audience. Print media include newspapers, magazines, direct mail, and billboards, while electronic media include television, radio, and cyber ads. Newspapers, television, and direct mail are the most widely used advertising media.

This advertisement for Perrier water promotes a message of hope and relief. While many advertisers are informative in nature, this particular ad focuses more on making an emotional impact.

Choice of media obviously influences the content and form of the message. Effective outdoor displays and short broadcast spot announcements require concise, simple messages. Magazine and newspaper advertisements can include considerable detail and long explanations. Because several kinds of media offer geographic selectivity, a precise message can be tailored to a particular geographic section of the target audience. For example, a company advertising in *Time* might decide to use one message in the New England region and another in the rest of the nation. A company may also choose to advertise in only one region. Such geographic selectivity lets a firm use the same message in different regions at different times.

The use of online advertising is increasing. However, advertisers are demanding more for their ad dollars and proof that they are working. Certain types of ads are more popular than pop-up ads and banner ads that consumers find annoying. One

technique is to blur the lines between television and online advertising. TV commercials may point viewers to a website for more information, where short "advertainment" films continue the marketing message. For instance, Super Bowl advertisers are beginning to use social media sites to complement their television advertisements. Mercedes-Benz and Audi both created social media contests to offer rewards to consumers who were willing to promote the brands through these sites in unconventional ways. The contests were held before the 2011 Super Bowl. The companies hoped to create longer lasting relationships with consumers than they would have done if they had simply used a 30-second television slot during the Super Bowl.[32]

Infomercials—typically 30-minute blocks of radio or television air time featuring a celebrity or upbeat host talking about and demonstrating a product—have evolved as an advertising

personal selling
direct, two-way communication
with buyers and potential buyers

publicity
nonpersonal communication
transmitted through the mass
media but not paid for directly by
the firm

method. Toll-free numbers and website addresses are usually provided so consumers can conveniently purchase the product or obtain additional information. Although many consumers and companies have negative feelings about infomercials, apparently they get results.

Personal Selling
Personal selling is direct, two-way communication with buyers and potential buyers. For many products—especially large, expensive ones with specialized uses, such as cars, appliances, and houses—interaction between a salesperson and the customer is probably the most important promotional tool.

Personal selling is the most flexible of the promotional methods because it gives marketers the greatest opportunity to communicate specific information that might trigger a purchase. Only personal selling can zero in on a prospect and attempt to persuade that person to make a purchase. Although personal selling has a lot of advantages, it is one of the most costly forms of promotion. A sales call on an industrial customer can cost as much as $200 or $300.

There are three distinct categories of salespersons: order takers (for example, retail sales clerks and route salespeople), creative salespersons (for example, automobile, furniture, and insurance salespeople), and support salespersons (for example, customer educators and goodwill builders who usually do not take orders). For most of these salespeople, personal selling is a six-step process:

1. *Prospecting:* Identifying potential buyers of the product.

2. *Approaching:* Using a referral or calling on a customer without prior notice to determine interest in the product.

Many Internet companies, such as Google, offer advertising services to companies who want to target consumers through digital media.

3. *Presenting:* Getting the prospect's attention with a product demonstration.

4. *Handling objections:* Countering reasons for not buying the product.

5. *Closing:* Asking the prospect to buy the product.

6. *Following up:* Checking customer satisfaction with the purchased product.

Publicity
Publicity is nonpersonal communication transmitted through the mass media but not paid for directly by the firm. A firm does not pay the media cost for publicity and is not identified as the originator of the message; instead, the message is presented in news story form. Obviously, a company can benefit from publicity by releasing to news sources newsworthy messages about the firm and its involvement with the public. Many companies have *public relations* departments to try to gain favorable publicity and minimize negative publicity for the firm.

Although advertising and publicity are both carried by the mass media, they differ in several major ways. Advertising messages tend to be informative, persuasive, or both; publicity is mainly informative. Advertising is often designed to have an immediate impact or to provide specific information to persuade a person to act; publicity describes what a firm is doing, what products it is launching, or other newsworthy information, but seldom calls for action. When advertising is used, the organization must pay for media time and select the media that will best reach target audiences. The mass media willingly carry publicity because they believe it has general public interest. Advertising can be repeated a number of times; most publicity appears in the mass media once and is not repeated.

Advertising, personal selling, and sales promotion are especially useful for influencing an exchange directly. Publicity is extremely important when communication focuses on a company's activities and products and is directed at interest groups, current and potential investors, regulatory agencies, and society in general.

A variation of traditional advertising is buzz marketing, in which marketers attempt to create a trend or acceptance of a product. Companies seek out trendsetters in communities and get them to "talk up" a brand to their friends, family, co-workers, and others. For example, to create buzz around the newest season of the television show *Mad Men,* the AMC network and partnering sponsors hold a "New York's Gone Mad" event in Manhattan's Time Square. The event features a live screening of the premiere, a 1960s costume contest, trivia contest, and cocktail party. Digital media is also heavily utilized to publicize the event.[33] Other marketers using the buzz technique include Hebrew National ("mom squads" grilled the company's hot dogs), and Chrysler (its retro PT Cruiser was planted in rental fleets). The idea behind buzz marketing is that

sales promotion
direct inducements offering added value or some other incentive for buyers to enter into an exchange

push strategy
an attempt to motivate intermediaries to push the product down to their customers

pull strategy
the use of promotion to create consumer demand for a product so that consumers exert pressure on marketing channel members to make it available

an accepted member of a particular social group will be more credible than any form of paid communication.[34] The concept works best as part of an integrated marketing communication program that also includes traditional advertising, personal selling, sales promotion, and publicity.

A related concept is viral marketing, which describes the concept of getting Internet users to pass on ads and promotions to others. For example, the restaurant Kogi, which operates Korean taco trucks that traverse the Los Angeles area, was dubbed by *Newsweek* as "America's First Viral Restaurant" after it began using Twitter and the Web to announce the whereabouts of its taco trucks.[35]

Sales Promotion

Sales promotion involves direct inducements offering added value or some other incentive for buyers to enter into an exchange. Sales promotions are generally easier to measure and less expensive than advertising. The major tools of sales promotion are store displays, premiums, samples and demonstrations, coupons, contests and sweepstakes, refunds, and trade shows. Coupon-clipping in particular has become more common during the recent recession. While coupons in the past decade traditionally had a fairly low redemption rate, with about 2 percent being redeemed, the recent recession caused an upsurge in coupon usage. In one marketing research study, 60 percent of respondents under the age of 35 reported using coupons during a six-month period. The website "Coupon Mom" also saw a significant rise in membership, from a membership of 100,000 per month to 1.5 million per month one year later.[36] While coupons can be a valuable tool in sales promotion, they cannot be relied upon to stand, but should be part of an overall promotion mix. Sales promotion stimulates customer purchasing and increases dealer effectiveness in selling products. It is used to enhance and supplement other forms of promotion. Test drives allow salespersons to demonstrate vehicles, which can help purchase decisions. Sampling a product may also encourage consumers to buy. PepsiCo, for example, used sampling to promote its Sierra Mist soft drink to reach more than 5 million potential consumers at well-traveled sites such as Times Square and Penn Station.[37] In a given year, almost three-fourths of consumer product companies may use sampling.

Promotion Strategies: To Push or To Pull

In developing a promotion mix, organizations must decide whether to fashion a mix that pushes or pulls the product (Figure 12.8). A **push strategy** attempts to motivate intermediaries to push the product down to their customers. When a push strategy is used, the company attempts to motivate wholesalers and retailers to make the product available to their customers. Sales personnel may be used to persuade intermediaries to offer the product, distribute promotional materials, and offer special promotional incentives for those who agree to carry the product. For example, Kimberly-Clark has begun partnering with its retailers to create a "win–win situation" for both types of companies. By sharing point-of-sales data with retailers and running more effective promotions, Kimberly-Clark hopes to create favorable relationships with its intermediaries to push its products through the system.[38] A **pull strategy** uses promotion to create consumer demand for a product so that consumers exert pressure on marketing channel members to make it available. For example, Anheuser-Busch launched the "Budweiser Happy Hour"—a nationwide event where consumers 21 years and older could receive free Budweiser samples—in order to generate interest among younger beer drinkers. Although beer demand is high for consumers between the ages of 21 and 30, younger beer drinkers have largely ignored the Budweiser brand. Anheuser-Busch is thereby using a pull strategy in an attempt to create demand among this age group.[39] Such sampling prior to a product roll-out encourages consumers to request the product from their favorite retailer.

A company can use either strategy, or it can use a variation or combination of the two. The exclusive use of advertising indicates a pull strategy. Personal selling to marketing channel members indicates a push strategy. The allocation of

Companies use a pull strategy by offering coupons through the RetailMeNot website in the hopes of convincing customers to visit their stores.

promotional positioning
the use of promotion to create and maintain an image of a product in buyers' minds

promotional resources to various marketing mix elements probably determines which strategy a marketer uses.

Objectives of Promotion

The marketing mix a company uses depends on its objectives. It is important to recognize that promotion is only one element of the marketing strategy and must be tied carefully to the goals of the firm, its overall marketing objectives, and the other elements of the marketing strategy. Firms use promotion for many reasons, but typical objectives are to stimulate demand, to stabilize sales, and to inform, remind, and reinforce customers.

Increasing demand for a product is probably the most typical promotional objective. Stimulating demand, often through advertising and sales promotion, is particularly important when a firm is using a pull strategy.

Another goal of promotion is to stabilize sales by maintaining the status quo—that is, the current sales level of the product. During periods of slack or decreasing sales, contests, prizes, vacations, and other sales promotions are sometimes offered to customers to maintain sales goals. Advertising is often used to stabilize sales by making customers aware of slack use periods.

TEAM EXERCISE

Form groups and search for examples of convenience products, shopping products, specialty products, and business products. How are these products marketed? Provide examples of any ads that you can find to show examples of the promotional strategies for these products. Report your findings to the class.

For example, auto manufacturers often provide rebates, free options, or lower-than-market interest rates to stabilize sales and thereby keep production lines moving during temporary slowdowns. A stable sales pattern allows the firm to run efficiently by maintaining a consistent level of production and storage and utilizing all its functions so that it is ready when sales increase.

An important role of any promotional program is to inform potential buyers about the organization and its products. A major portion of advertising in the United States, particularly in daily newspapers, is informational. Providing information about the availability, price, technology, and features of a product is very important in encouraging a buyer to move toward a purchase decision. Nearly all forms of promotion involve an attempt to help consumers learn more about a product and a company.

Promotion is also used to remind consumers that an established organization is still around and sells certain products that have uses and benefits. Often advertising reminds customers that they may need to use a product more frequently or in certain situations. Pennzoil, for example, has run television commercials reminding car owners that they need to change their oil every 3,000 miles to ensure proper performance of their cars.

▼**FIGURE 12.8**
Push and Pull Strategies

SO YOU WANT TO BE // a Marketing Manager /

Many jobs in marketing are closely tied to the marketing mix functions: distribution, product, promotion, and price. Often the job titles could be sales manager, distribution or supply chain manager, advertising account executive, or store manager.

A distribution manager arranges for transportation of goods within firms and through marketing channels. Transportation can be costly, and time is always an important factor, so minimizing their effects is vital to the success of a firm. Distribution managers must choose one or a combination of transportation modes from a vast array of options, taking into account local, federal, and international regulations for different freight classifications; the weight, size, and fragility of products to be shipped; time schedules; and loss and damage ratios. Manufacturing firms are the largest employers of distribution managers.

A product manager is responsible for the success or failure of a product line. This requires a general knowledge of advertising, transportation modes, inventory control, selling and sales management, promotion, marketing research, packaging, and pricing. Frequently, several years of selling and sales management experience are prerequisites for such a position as well as college training in business administration. Being a product manager can be rewarding both financially and psychologically.

Some of the most creative roles in the business world are in the area of advertising. Advertising pervades our daily lives, as businesses and other organizations try to grab our attention and tell us about what they have to offer. Copywriters, artists, and account executives in advertising must have creativity, imagination, artistic talent, and expertise in expression and persuasion. Advertising is an area of business in which a wide variety of educational backgrounds may be useful, from degrees in advertising itself, to journalism or liberal arts degrees. Common entry-level positions in an advertising agency are found in the traffic department, account service (account coordinator), or the media department (media assistant). Advertising jobs are also available in many manufacturing or retail firms, nonprofit organizations, banks, professional associations, utility companies, and other arenas outside of an advertising agency.

Although a career in retailing may begin in sales, there is much more to retailing than simply selling. Many retail personnel occupy management positions, focusing on selecting and ordering merchandise, promotional activities, inventory control, customer credit operations, accounting, personnel, and store security. Many specific examples of retailing jobs can be found in large department stores. A section manager coordinates inventory and promotions and interacts with buyers, salespeople, and consumers. The buyer's job is fast-paced, often involving much travel and pressure. Buyers must be open-minded and foresighted in their hunt for new, potentially successful items. Regional managers coordinate the activities of several retail stores within a specific geographic area, usually monitoring and supporting sales, promotions, and general procedures. Retail management can be exciting and challenging. Growth in retailing is expected to accompany the growth in population and is likely to create substantial opportunities in the coming years.

While a career in marketing can be very rewarding, marketers today agree that the job is getting tougher. Many advertising and marketing executives say the job has gotten much more demanding in the past 10 years, viewing their number-one challenge as balancing work and personal obligations. Other challenges include staying current on industry trends or technologies, keeping motivated/inspired on the job, and measuring success. If you are up to the challenge, you may find that a career in marketing is just right for you to utilize your business knowledge while exercising your creative side as well.

Reinforcement promotion attempts to assure current users of the product that they have made the right choice and tells them how to get the most satisfaction from the product. Also, a company could release publicity statements through the news media about a new use for a product. Additionally, firms can have salespeople communicate with current and potential customers about the proper use and maintenance of a product—all in the hope of developing a repeat customer.

Promotional Positioning

Promotional positioning uses promotion to create and maintain an image of a product in buyers' minds. It is a natural result of market segmentation. In both promotional positioning and market segmentation, the firm targets a given product or brand at a portion of the total market. A promotional strategy helps differentiate the product and makes it appeal to a particular market segment. For example, to appeal to safety-conscious consumers, Volvo heavily promotes the safety and crashworthiness of Volvo automobiles in its advertising. Volkswagen has done the same thing with its edgy ads showing car crashes. Promotion can be used to change or reinforce an image. Effective promotion influences customers and persuades them to buy. ∎

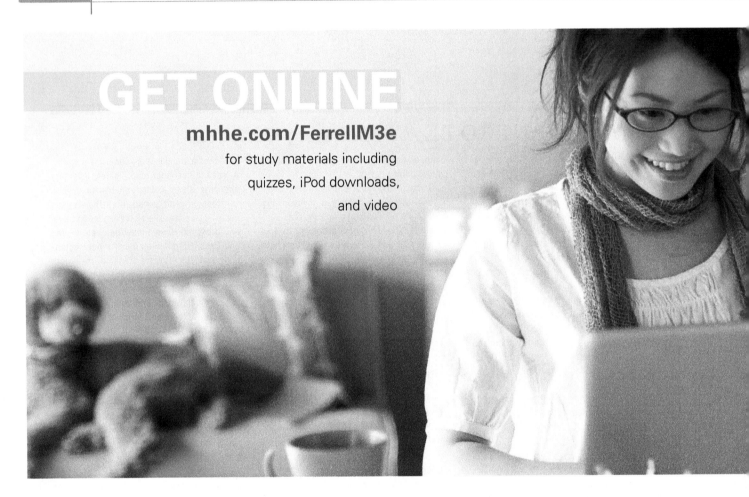

GET ONLINE

mhhe.com/FerrellM3e

for study materials including
quizzes, iPod downloads,
and video

chapter twelve

active review card
Dimensions of Marketing
Strategy

nutshell

There are four dimensions of marketing—product, price, distribution, and promotion.
These elements are used to develop a marketing strategy that builds customer
relationships and satisfaction.

The following statements will test your take-away knowledge from this chapter. Do your
best to explain each one in the space provided below.

LO.1 Describe the role of product in the marketing mix, including how products are developed,
classified, and identified.

LO.2 Define price, and discuss its importance in the marketing mix, including various pricing
strategies a firm might employ.

LO.3 Identify factors affecting distribution decisions, such as marketing channels and intensity of
market coverage.

LO.4 Specify the activities involved in promotion, as well as promotional strategies and promotional positioning.

Did your answers include the following important points?

LO.1. Describe the role of product in the marketing mix, including how products are developed, classified, and identified.

- Products are among a firm's most visible contacts with consumers and must meet consumers' needs to be successful. New-product development is a multistep process including idea development, the screening of new ideas, business analysis, product development, test marketing, and commercialization.
- Products are classified as either consumer or business products. Consumer products can be further classified as convenience, shopping, or specialty products.
- The business product classifications are raw materials, major equipment, component parts, processed materials, supplies, and industrial services.
- Products can also be classified by the stage of the product life cycle. Identifying products includes branding, packaging, and labeling.

LO.2. Define price, and discuss its importance in the marketing mix, including various pricing strategies a firm might employ.

- Price is the value placed on an object exchanged between a buyer and a seller. Pricing objectives include survival, maximization of profits and sales volume, and maintenance of the status quo.
- A firm may use price skimming or penetration pricing when introducing a new product. Psychological pricing and price discounting are other strategies.

LO.3. Identify factors affecting distribution decisions, such as marketing channels and intensity of market coverage.

- Making products available to customers is facilitated by middlemen or intermediaries, who bridge the gap between the producer of the product and its ultimate user.
- A marketing channel is a group of marketing organizations that directs the flow of products from producers to consumers.
- Market coverage relates to the number and variety of outlets that make products available to customers; it may be intensive, selective, or exclusive.

LO.4. Specify the activities involved in promotion, as well as promotional strategies and promotional positioning.

- Promotion encourages marketing exchanges by persuading individuals, groups, and organizations to accept goods, services, and ideas. The promotion mix includes advertising, personal selling, publicity, and sales promotion.
- A push strategy attempts to motivate intermediaries to push the product down to the customers, whereas a pull strategy tries to create consumer demand for a product so that the consumers exert pressure on marketing channel members to make the product available.
- Typical promotion objectives are to stimulate demand, stabilize sales, and inform, remind, and reinforce customers. Promotional positioning is the use of promotion to create and maintain an image of the product in the mind of the buyer.

Practical Application

LO.1.

- _____ allows a company to discover the strengths and weaknesses of a product before it is fully launched in the market.
- _____ are less expensive than manufacturer brands and are owned and controlled by a wholesaler or retailer.
- _____ generally appeal to those consumers who are willing to sacrifice quality and product consistency for the sake of lower prices.

LO.2.

- The pricing policy that allows a company to cover the product's development cost most quickly is _____.
- _____ enables a product to enter the market and rapidly gain market share.
- A cosmetics company believes that it makes more sense to sell its eye shadow at $11.99 rather than $12.00; it is using _____.

LO.3.

- _____ buy products from manufacturers and sell them to consumers for home and household use.
- When a product is to be made available in as many outlets as possible, wholesalers and retailers engage in _____.

LO.4.

- When Ford pays a television network to air its commercial, it is using _____.
- When Chiquita uses newspaper ads to introduce its new fruit drink to consumers before introducing it to supermarkets, it is using the _____.
- The mass media willingly carry _____ for a company or product believing it has general public interest.

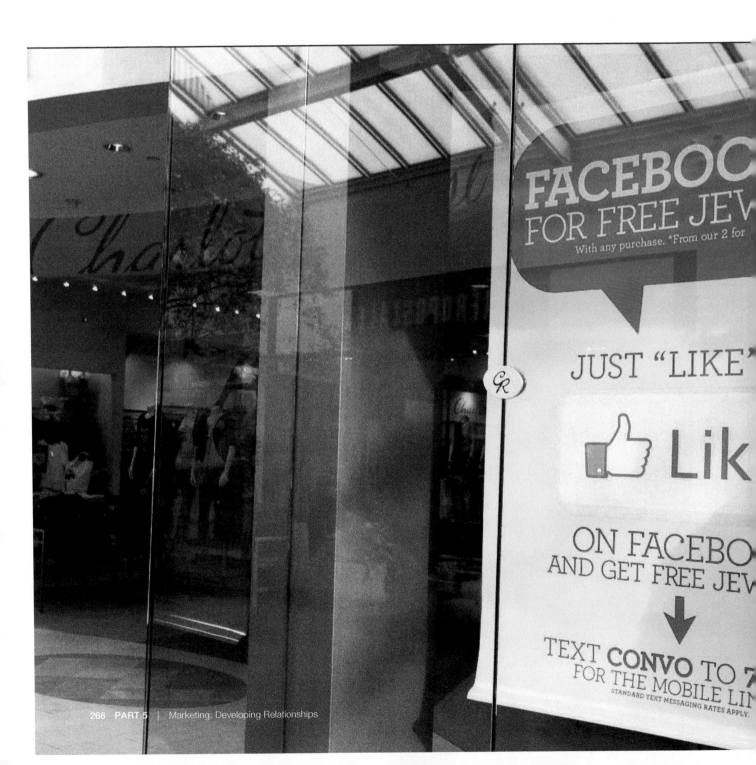

chapter thirteen

digital marketing
+ social networking

introduction[1]

The Internet and information technology have dramatically changed the environment for business. Marketers' new ability to convert all types of communications into digital media has created efficient, inexpensive ways of connecting businesses and consumers and has improved the flow and the usefulness of information. Businesses have the information they need to make more informed decisions, and consumers have access to a greater variety of products and more information about choices and quality.

The defining characteristic of information technology in the 21st century is accelerating change. New systems and applications advance so rapidly that it is almost impossible to keep up with the latest developments. Startup companies emerge that quickly overtake existing approaches to digital media. When Google first arrived on the scene, a number of search engines were fighting for dominance, including Excite, Infoseek, Lycos, and Webcrawler. With its fast, easy-to-use search engine, Google became number one and is now challenging many industries, including advertising, newspapers, mobile phones, and book publishing. Despite its victory, Google is constantly being challenged itself by competitors like Yahoo and Baidu. The Chinese search engine Baidu represents a particular threat

continued on p. 268

LEARNING OBJECTIVES

LO1 Define digital media and digital marketing and recognize their increasing value in strategic planning.

LO2 Understand the characteristics of digital media and how they differentiate these methods from traditional marketing activities.

LO3 Demonstrate the role of digital marketing and social networking in today's business environment.

LO4 Show how digital media affect the marketing mix.

LO5 Define social networking and illustrate how businesses can use different types of social networking media.

LO6 Identify legal and ethical considerations in digital media.

e-business
carrying out the goals of business through utilization of the Internet

digital media
electronic media that function using digital codes via computers, cellular phones, smartphones, and other digital devices that have been released in recent years

digital marketing
uses all digital media, including the Internet and mobile and interactive channels, to develop communication and exchanges with customers

addressability
the ability of a business to identify customers before they make purchases

continued from p. 267

as it is the fifth-largest "pure-play" Internet company (after Google, Amazon.com, Tencent, and eBay) and has the majority of the Chinese Internet market. Google is also being challenged by social networks, which most observers believe will dominate digital communication in the future.[2] Today, people spend more time on social networking sites, such as Facebook, than they spend on e-mail.

In this chapter we first provide some key definitions related to digital marketing and social networking. Next we discuss using digital media in business and marketing. We look at marketing mix considerations when using digital media and pay special attention to social networking. Then we focus on digital marketing strategies—particularly new communication channels like social networks—and consider how consumers are changing their information searches and consumption behavior to fit emerging technologies and trends. Finally, we examine the legal and social issues associated with information technology, digital media, and e-business.

WHAT IS DIGITAL MARKETING?

Let's start with a clear understanding of our focus in this chapter. First, we can distinguish **e-business** from tradi-

tional business by noting that conducting e-business means carrying out the goals of business through the use of the Internet. **Digital media** are electronic media that function using

digital codes—when we refer to digital media, we mean media available via computers and other digital devices, including mobile and wireless ones like cell phones and smartphones.

Digital marketing uses all digital media, including the Internet and mobile and interactive channels, to develop communication and exchanges with customers. *Digital marketing* is a term we will use often because we are interested in all types of digital communications, regardless of the electronic channel that transmits the data.

GROWTH AND BENEFITS OF DIGITAL COMMUNICATION

The Internet has created tremendous opportunities for businesses to forge relationships with consumers and business customers, target markets more precisely, and even reach previously inaccessible markets at home and around the world. The Internet also facilitates business transactions, allowing companies to network with manufacturers, wholesalers, retailers, suppliers, and outsource firms to serve customers more quickly and more efficiently. The telecommunication opportunities created by the Internet have set the stage for digital marketing's development and growth.

Digital communication offers a completely new dimension in connecting with others. Some of the characteristics that distinguish digital from traditional communication are addressability, interactivity, accessibility, connectivity, and control. Let's look at what these mean and how they enhance marketing.

The ability of a business to identify customers before they make a purchase is **addressability**. Digital media make it possible for visitors on a website like Amazon.com to provide information about their needs and wants before they buy. A social

> "Digital communication offers a completely new dimension in connecting with others."

network such as Facebook lets users create a profile to keep in touch or to build a network of identified contacts including friends, colleagues, and businesses. Companies such as Procter

interactivity
allows customers to express their needs and wants directly to the firm in response to its communications

accessibility
allows consumers to find information about competing products, prices, and reviews and become more informed about a firm and the relative value of its products

connectivity
the use of digital networks to provide linkages between information providers and users

control
consumers' ability to regulate the information they receive via the Internet, and the rate and sequence of their exposure to that information

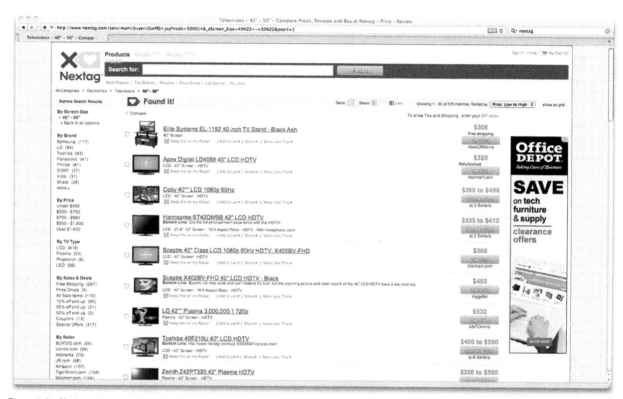

The website Nextag puts power in the hands of consumers by allowing them to compare prices of products at different stores before buying.

& Gamble create social network accounts to share information with consumers and find out their opinions about products and reactions to new ideas.

Interactivity allows customers to express their needs and wants directly to the firm in response to its communications. In traditional one-way forms of communications, such as television advertising, the customer must contact the company by phone or other means. Interactivity relies on digital media that can make a conversation between the firm and the customer happen without any delay; thus, real relationships become possible. Digital media such as blogs and social networks allow marketers to engage with customers, shape their expectations and perceptions, and benefit from broader market reach at lower cost.

Accessibility allows consumers to find information about competing products, prices, and reviews and become more informed about a firm and the relative value of its products. Mobile devices—including smartphones, mobile computing devices like the iPad, and PDAs—allow customers to leave their desktops and access digital networks from anywhere. Thanks to the popularity of the iPhone and BlackBerry, businesses and their

customers can stay in constant touch. Benjamin Moore & Co. has an iPhone app (application) that allows customers to match anything, such as their own home-decorating color samples and photographs, with shades of Benjamin Moore® paint. Many companies are adopting a digital media philosophy of open communication with customers; for example, a firm can go to a site such as GeniusRocket.com, a marketing firm that provides customized services linking businesses with customers, to request ideas for new products.

Connectivity keeps customers, employees, and businesses connected with each other. It involves the use of digital networks to provide linkages between information providers and users. Social networking is a key form of connectivity made easier on a global scale by Facebook, Myspace, LinkedIn, Twitter, and other networking sites. Facebook has a larger audience than any television network that has ever existed. Firms can also target precise markets through local social networking sites such as Orkut, a Google-owned service operating in India and Brazil.

Control refers to consumers' ability to regulate the information they receive via the Internet, and the rate and sequence of their exposure to that information. Consumers choose the websites they view, the blogs they follow, and the social networking sites to which they belong. This trend toward a consumer-controlled market requires marketers to approach their jobs in a different way than they did in traditional marketing.

USING DIGITAL MEDIA IN BUSINESS

The phenomenal growth of digital media has provided new ways of conducting business. Given almost instant communication with precisely defined consumer groups, firms can use real-time exchanges to stimulate interactive communication, forge closer relationships, and learn more accurately about consumer and supplier needs. Consider that Amazon.com, one of the most successful e-businesses, ranked number 100 on the *Fortune* 500 list of America's largest corporations.[3] Amazon is a true global e-business, and was one of the early success stories in the industry, getting 50 percent of its revenue from international sales.[4] Many of you may not remember a world before Amazon because it has completely transformed how many people shop. Previously, consumers had to travel store to store in order to find goods and compare prices.

Because it is fast and inexpensive, digital communication is making it easier for businesses to conduct marketing research, provide and obtain price and product information, and advertise, as well as to fulfill their business goals by selling goods and services online. Even the U.S. government engages in digital marketing activities—marketing everything from Treasury bonds and other financial instruments to oil-drilling leases and wild horses. Procter & Gamble uses the Internet as a fast, cost-effective means for marketing research, judging consumer demand for potential new products by inviting online consumers to sample new-product prototypes and provide feedback. If a product gets rave reviews from the samplers, the company might decide to introduce it. By testing concepts online, companies can save significant time and money in getting new products to market.

New businesses and even industries are evolving that would not exist without digital media. Hulu is a video website that lets consumers watch a broad collection of premium videos from more than 260 content companies, anytime and from anywhere. The company has partnered with several companies to advertise on their sites, including Johnson & Johnson and Best Buy. In fact, Hulu's growing popularity is allowing it to compete with YouTube.[5]

The reality, however, is that Internet markets are more similar to traditional markets than they are different. Thus, successful e-business strategies, like traditional business strategies, focus on creating products that customers need or want, not merely developing a brand name or reducing the costs associated with online transactions. Instead of changing all industries, e-business has had much more impact in certain industries where the cost of business and customer transactions has been very high. For example, investment trading is less expensive online because customers can buy and sell investments, such as stocks and mutual funds, on their own. Firms such as Charles Schwab Corp., the biggest online brokerage firm, have been innovators in promoting online trading. Traditional brokers such as Merrill Lynch have had to follow with online trading for their customers.

Because the Internet lowers the cost of communication, it can contribute significantly to any industry or activity that depends on the flow of digital information such as entertainment, health care, government services, education, and computer services like software development. The publishing industry is transitioning away from print newspapers, magazines, and books as more consumers purchase e-readers, like the Kindle or iPad, or read the news online. Even your textbook is available electronically. Because publishers save money on paper, ink, and shipping, many times electronic versions of books are cheaper than their paper counterparts.

Need paint? Benjamin Moore & Co. has an app that can help you pick out the perfect color on your iPhone.

NEW BUSINESSES AND EVEN INDUSTRIES ARE EVOLVING THAT WOULD NOT EXIST WITHOUT DIGITAL MEDIA.

Digital media can also improve communication within and between businesses. In the future, most significant gains will come from productivity improvements within businesses. Communication is a key business function, and improving the speed and clarity of communication can help businesses save time and improve employee problem-solving abilities. Digital media can be a communications backbone that helps to store knowledge, information, and records in management information systems so co-workers can access it when faced with a problem to solve. A well-designed management information system that utilizes digital technology can, therefore, help reduce confusion, improve organization and efficiency, and facilitate clear communications. Given the crucial role of communication and information in business, the long-term impact of digital media on economic growth is substantial, and it will inevitably grow over time.

Firms also need to control access to their digital communication systems to ensure worker productivity. This can be a challenge. For example, in companies across the United States, employees are surfing the Internet for as much as an hour during each workday. Many firms are trying to curb this practice by limiting employees' access to instant messaging services, streaming music, and websites with adult content.[6]

DIGITAL MEDIA AND THE MARKETING MIX

While digital marketing shares some similarities with conventional marketing techniques, a few valuable differences stand out. First, digital media make customer communications faster and interactive. Second, digital media help companies reach new target markets more easily, affordably, and quickly than ever before. Finally, digital media help marketers utilize new resources in seeking out and communicating with customers. One of the most important benefits of digital marketing is the ability of marketers and customers to easily share information. Through websites, social networks, and other digital media, consumers can learn about everything they consume and use in their lives, ask questions, voice complaints, indicate preferences, and otherwise communicate about their needs and desires. Many marketers use e-mail, mobile phones, social networking, wikis, video sharing, podcasts, blogs, videoconferencing, and other technologies to coordinate activities and communicate with employees, customers, and suppliers. Twitter, considered both a social network and a micro blog, illustrates how these digital technologies can combine to create new communication opportunities.

Nielsen Marketing Research revealed that consumers now spend more time on social networking sites than they do on e-mail, and social network use is still growing. The most avid online social networkers are Australians, followed by British, Italians, and Americans.[7] With digital media, even small businesses can reach new markets through these inexpensive communication channels. Brick-and-mortar companies like Walmart utilize online catalogs and company websites and blogs to supplement their retail stores. Internet companies like Amazon.com and Zappos.com that lack physical stores let customers post reviews of their purchases on their websites, creating company-sponsored communities.

One aspect of marketing that has not changed with digital media is the importance of achieving the right marketing mix. Product, distribution, promotion, and pricing are as important as ever for successful online marketing strategies. More than one-fourth of the world's population now uses the Internet.[8] That means it is essential for businesses large and small to use digital media effectively, not only to grab or maintain market share but also to streamline their organizations and offer customers entirely new benefits and convenience. Let's look at how businesses are using digital media to create effective marketing strategies on the Web.

Product Considerations Like traditional marketers, digital marketers must anticipate consumer needs and preferences, tailor their products and services to meet these needs, and continually upgrade them to remain competitive. The connectivity created by digital media provide the opportunity for adding services and can enhance product benefits. Some products, such as online games, applications and virtual worlds, are only available via digital media. Netflix offers a much wider array of movies and games than the average movie rental stores, along with a two-week free trial, quick delivery and easy returns, online video streaming of some movies, and no late fees. Netflix also prides itself on its recommendation engine, which recommends movies for users based on their previous rental history and how they rate movies they have seen. As Netflix demonstrates, the Internet can make it much easier to anticipate consumer needs. However, fierce competition makes quality product and service offerings more important than ever.[9]

Distribution Considerations The Internet is a new distribution channel for making products available at the right time, at the right place, and in the right quantities. Marketers' ability to process orders electronically and increase the speed of communications via the Internet reduces inefficiencies, costs, and redundancies while increasing speed throughout the marketing channel. Shipping times and costs have become an important consideration in attracting customers, prompting many companies to offer consumers low shipping costs or next-day delivery. For example, Walmart is attempting to take market share away from e-marketers like Amazon.com by reducing delivery time and creating a "site to store" system that eliminates shipping

Walmart is experimenting with a new distribution system to compete against online retailers. The company is eliminating shipping costs for consumers who order products online and then pick them up at the store. The company hopes to capture market share away from competitors that charge shipping costs.

NESTLÉ EXPERIENCES THE DARK SIDE OF SOCIAL MEDIA

Social media can have an ugly side, as Nestlé found out firsthand after an attack launched by environmental organization Greenpeace. It started after Greenpeace discovered that Nestlé was sourcing a portion of its palm oil (an ingredient used in its chocolate bars) nonsustainably. The problem from Greenpeace's perspective is that many palm oil producers destroy rain forests in order to grow the plants from which the oil is harvested; it is argued that this action increases global warming and threatens orangutan populations.

Greenpeace began its attack by releasing a report, protesting outside Nestlé's headquarters, and launching a video on YouTube. Greenpeace altered Nestlé's Kit-Kat logo to read Killer. Although Nestlé forced Greenpeace to pull the video, thousands of protesters had already shared it via their Facebook and Twitter accounts. The commentary on Nestlé's Facebook page and Twitter feed was scathing. Worse yet, the news had gone viral, making it nearly impossible for Nestlé to contain.

Nestlé responded by severing ties with the company in question and promised to do a thorough audit of all third-party suppliers. It made a commitment to source 50 percent of sustainable palm oil by 2011 and 100 percent by 2015. Nestlé also partnered with The Forest Trust to create responsible sourcing guidelines. Despite its response, Nestlé continued to get hammered in the press for its initial handling of protesters.

As this situation demonstrates, the relative newness of social media has left many companies with their guard down. In the future, Nestlé and other businesses should consider using social media not as a way to quench negative publicity, but as a method to address consumer concerns.[10]

Discussion Questions

1. Do you think consumers of Nestlé's Kit-Kat bar would not buy the product if they knew about the palm oil source?

2. Did Nestlé handle the protests appropriately?

3. What should Nestlé do in the future to avoid negative social media publicity?

costs for consumers who pick up their deliveries in the store. This offer has the increased benefit of getting customers into the store, where they might make add-on purchases. Walmart has even tested a new distribution concept to complement store pickups: a drive-through window that allows customers to pick up the products they ordered through Walmart's website. Through even more sophisticated distribution systems, Walmart hopes to overtake online retailers to become the biggest online merchant.[11]

free samples to generate consumer demand for their products.

Social Networking

A **social network** is "a web-based meeting place for friends, family, co-workers and peers that lets users create a profile and connect with other users for the

social network
a Web-based meeting place for friends, family, co-workers, and peers that lets users create a profile and connect with other users for a wide range of purposes

> ## Social networks are a valued part of marketing because they are changing the way consumers communicate with each other and with firms.

Promotion Considerations Perhaps one of the best ways businesses can utilize digital media is for promotion purposes—whether they are increasing brand awareness, connecting with consumers, or taking advantage of social networks or virtual worlds (discussed later) to form relationships and generate positive publicity or "buzz" about their products. Thanks to online promotion, consumers can be more informed than ever, including reading customer-generated content before making purchasing decisions. Consumer consumption patterns are radically changing, and marketers must adapt their promotional efforts to meet them.

These effects are not limited to the Western world. In a revolutionary shift in China, where online shopping had not been widely adopted by consumers, businesses are now realizing the benefits of marketing online. One of the first adopters of Internet selling was the Chinese company Taobao, a consumer auction site that also features sections for Chinese brands and retailers. Taobao provides online promotion of retailers and products featured on its site. The majority of online sales in China take place on Taobao.[12] Consumer trends like these demonstrate that the shift to digital media promotion is well under way worldwide.

Pricing Considerations Price is the most flexible element of the marketing mix. Digital marketing can enhance the value of products by providing extra benefits such as service, information, and convenience. Through digital media, discounts and other promotions can be quickly communicated. As consumers have become better informed about their options, the demand for low-priced products has grown, leading to the creation of deal sites where consumers can directly compare prices. Expedia.com, for instance, provides consumers with a wealth of travel information about everything from flights to hotels that lets them compare benefits and prices. Many marketers offer buying incentives like online coupons or

purposes that range from getting acquainted, to keeping in touch, to building a work related network."[13] Social networks are a valued part of marketing because they are changing the way consumers communicate with each other and with firms. Sites such as Facebook, Myspace, Twitter, and LinkedIn have emerged as opportunities for marketers to build communities, provide product information, and learn about consumer needs. By the time you read this, it is possible there will be new social network sites that continue to advance digital communication and opportunities for marketers.

You might be surprised to know that social networks have existed in some form or other for 40 years. The precursors of today's social networks began in the 1970s as online bulletin boards that allowed users with common interests to interact with one another. The first modern social network was Six Degrees.com,

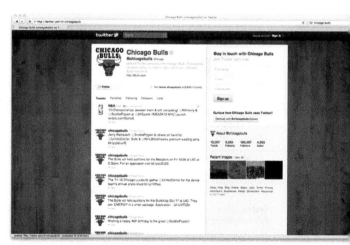

Twitter allows the Chicago Bulls to post event updates and interact with loyal fans.

blog
a Web-based journal in which a writer can editorialize and interact with other Internet users

wiki
software that creates an interface that enables users to add or edit the content of some types of websites

viral marketing
a marketing tool that uses the Internet, particularly social networking and video sharing sites, to spread a message and create brand awareness.

launched in 1997. This system permitted users to create a profile and connect with friends—the core attributes of today's networks.[14] Although Six Degrees eventually shut down for lack of interest, the seed of networking had been planted.[15] Other social networks followed, with each new generation becoming increasingly sophisticated. Today's sites offer a multitude of consumer benefits, including the ability to download music, games, and applications; upload photos and videos; join groups; find and chat with friends; comment on friends' posts; and post and update status messages. Table 13.1 lists some popular social networks in different countries.

As the number of social network users increases, interactive marketers are finding opportunities to reach out to consumers in new target markets. MyYearBook.com is a social networking site that offers teenagers a forum in which to write about particular subjects important to them, including sensitive topics facing today's younger generation. Its popularity with teenagers is rising; the site's traffic has increased 36 percent annually, with most users coming from the United States. For advertisers, the site is an opportunity to connect with teens and young adults, a demographic that is difficult to reach with traditional marketing. Advertisers from Nikon and Paramount Pictures have both made deals to advertise through MyYearBook.com.[16]

▼ **TABLE 13.1** Popular Social Networking Sites in Different Countries

South Korea	Cyworld
Netherlands	Hyves
Japan	Mixi
Brazil	Orkut
China	QZone
France	SkyRock
Germany	StudiVZ
Spain	Tuenti
Russia	Vkontakte
United Kingdom	Bebo
United States	Facebook

Source: "Nine Extremely Successful Non-English Social Networking Sites," Pingdom, September 9, 2009, http://royal.pingdom.com/2009/09/09/nine-extremely-successful-non-english-social-networking-sites/ (accessed March 25, 2010); Sorav Jain, "40 Most Popular Social Networking Sites of the World," Social Media Today, http://socialmediatoday.com/index.php?q=soravjain/195917/40-most-popular-social-networking-sites-world (accessed January 17, 2011).

We'll have more to say about how marketers utilize social networks later in this chapter.

An important question relates to how social media sites are adding value to the economy. Marketers at companies like Ford and Zappos, for instance, are using social media to promote products and build consumer relationships. Most corporations are supporting Facebook pages and Yammer accounts for employees to communicate across departments and divisions. Professionals such as professors, doctors, and engineers also share ideas on a regular basis. Even staffing organizations use social media, bypassing traditional e-mail and telephone channels. While billions of dollars in investments are being funneled into social media, it may be too early to assess the exact economic contribution of social media to the entire economy.[17]

TYPES OF CONSUMER-GENERATED MARKETING AND DIGITAL MEDIA

While digital marketing has generated exciting opportunities for companies to interact with their customers, digital media are also more consumer-driven than traditional media. Internet users are creating and reading consumer-generated content as never before and are having a profound effect on marketing in the process.

Two factors have sparked the rise of consumer-generated information:

1. The increased tendency of consumers to publish their own thoughts, opinions, reviews, and product discussions through blogs or digital media.

2. Consumers' tendencies to trust other consumers over corporations. Consumers often rely on the recommendations of friends, family, and fellow consumers when making purchasing decisions.

Marketers who know where online users are likely to express their thoughts and opinions can use these forums to interact with them, address problems, and promote their companies. Types of digital media in which Internet users are likely to participate include blogs, wikis, video sharing sites, podcasts, social networking sites, virtual reality sites, and mobile applications. Let's look a little more closely at each.

Blogs and Wikis

Today's marketers must recognize that the impact of consumer-generated material like blogs and wikis and their significance to online consumers have increased a great deal. **Blogs** (short for web logs) are Web-based journals in which writers can editorialize and interact with other Internet users. Two-thirds of Internet users read blogs, and more than half of bloggers say they blog about topics and brands about which they feel strongly.[18]

The blogging phenomenon is not limited to North America. In South Korea, for example, more than two-thirds of the online population creates blogs or similar material.[19]

Blogs give consumers power, sometimes more than companies would like. Bloggers can post whatever they like about a company or its products, whether their opinions are positive or negative, true or false. When a Korean Dunkin' Donuts worker created a blog alleging that a company factory had unsanitary conditions, the company forced him to delete the blog. However, readers had already created copies of it and spread it across the Internet after the original's removal.[21] In other cases, a positive review of a product or service posted on a popular blog can result in large increases in sales. Thus, blogs can represent a potent threat or opportunity to marketers.

Rather than trying to eliminate blogs that cast their companies in a negative light, some firms are using their own blogs, or employee blogs, to answer consumer concerns or defend their corporate reputations. Boeing operates a corporate blog to highlight company news and to post correspondence from Boeing enthusiasts from all over the world.[22] As blogging changes the face of media, smart companies are using it to build enthusiasm for their products and create relationships with consumers.

Wikis are websites where users can add to or edit the content of posted articles. One of the best known is Wikipedia, an online encyclopedia with over 17 million entries in over 250 languages on nearly every subject imaginable (Encyclopedia Britannica only has 120,000 entries).[23] Wikipedia is one of the 10 most popular sites on the Web, and because much of its content can be edited by anyone, it is easy for online consumers to add detail and supporting evidence and to correct inaccuracies in content. Wikipedia used to be completely open to editing, but in order to stop vandalism, the site had to make some topics off-limits that are now editable only by a small group of experts.

Like all digital media, wikis have advantages and disadvantages for companies. Wikis about controversial companies like Walmart and Nike often contain negative publicity, such as about workers' rights violations. However, monitoring relevant wikis can provide companies with a better idea of how consumers feel about the company or brand. Some companies have also begun to use wikis as internal tools for teams working on projects that require a great deal of documentation.[24]

There is too much at stake financially for marketers to ignore wikis and blogs. Despite this fact, less than one-fifth of *Fortune* 500 companies have a blog.[25] Marketers who want to form better customer relationships and promote their company's products must not underestimate the power of these two media outlets.

?

DID YOU KNOW?

Searching is the most popular online activity, while social networking and blogging are fourth.[20]

Video Sharing

Video sharing sites allow virtually anybody to upload videos, from professional marketers at *Fortune* 500 corporations to the average Internet user. Some of the most popular video sharing sites include YouTube, Video, Yahoo.com, Metacafe.com, and Hulu.

Video sharing sites give companies the opportunity to upload ads and informational videos about their products. A few videos become viral at any given time, and although many of these gain popularity because they embarrass the subject in some way, others reach viral status because people find them entertaining. **Viral marketing** occurs when a message gets sent from person to person to person. It can be an extremely effective tool for marketers—particularly on the Internet, where one click can send a message to dozens or hundreds of people simultaneously. However, viral marketing often requires marketers to develop an offbeat sense of humor and creativity in order to catch the viewer's attention—something with which some marketers may not be comfortable. For instance, IBM created a series of six videos called "The Art of the Sale," which presents three attributes of the company's mainframe computer in a humorous format reminiscent of episodes of *The Office*. Though some wrote off the video as a forced attempt at humorous marketing, it received hundreds of thousands of hits on YouTube.[26]

Businesses have also begun to utilize consumer-generated video content, saving money they would have spent on hiring advertising firms to develop professional advertising campaigns. Unilever is one of many companies incorporating consumer-generated content into its marketing strategies. Its Consumer Creative Challenge encourages consumers to

Procter & Gamble launched a successful campaign on Twitter featuring the Old Spice Man (former NFL receiver Isaiah Mustafa). Fans were invited to interact with Mustafa through Twitter posts. The number of Old Spice fans significantly increased after the campaign.

podcast
an audio or video file that can be downloaded from the Internet with a subscription that automatically delivers new content to listening devices or personal computers

send in their amateur videos for Unilever brands such as Ben & Jerry's, Vaseline, and Axe. The 2010 grand-prize winner received £7,000 (more than $11,000) and had her Vaseline video aired at the London Film Festival. Unilever announced that it would integrate the video into future marketing campaigns.[27] Marketers believe consumer videos appear more authentic and create enthusiasm for the product among consumer participants.

Google is so confident that video sharing sites will revolutionize online marketing that it purchased YouTube for $1.65 billion in 2006.[28] If Google is correct in its predictions, then online videos clips—both corporate-sponsored and consumer-generated—are likely to revolutionize the marketing industry.

Photo Sharing

Photo sharing sites allow users to upload and share their photos and short videos with the world. Well-known photo sharing sites include SmugMug, Webshots, Photobucket, and Flickr. Flickr is owned by Yahoo and is the most popular photo sharing site on the Internet. A Flickr user can upload images, edit them, classify the images, create photo albums, and share photos with friends without having to e-mail bulky image files or send photos through the mail. Flickr is so popular that the site experiences thousands of new image uploads every minute.

NPR supplements its radio station with podcasts downloadable through the iTunes site.

One of Flickr's rivals is Picasa Web Albums, a Google photo sharing site that developed out of Google's photo-editing program Picasa. The program has grown rapidly and is growing in popularity, as it provides more features than Flickr and other major photo sharing websites. Picasa Web Albums is free, and generates revenues through ads shown on the site. If users want to use more than 1 GB of storage space, they can rent additional space up to 16 TBs.

As one Web marketer puts it, companies that use photo sharing "add a personal touch to their businesses."[33] Although it is too early to gauge the effects of marketing through photo shar-

> "Podcasting offers the benefit of convenience, giving users the ability to listen to or view content when and where they choose."

Most users have free accounts that allow them to upload two videos and 100 MB of photos per month, but for around $25 a year, users can open an unlimited Pro account.[29] Photo sharing represents an opportunity for companies to market themselves visually by displaying snapshots of company events, company staff, and/or company products. Companies can direct viewers to their photostreams (their sets of photographs) by marking their pictures with the appropriate keywords, or tags.[30] Tags are essential for marketing on Flickr as they help direct traffic to the corporate photostreams.

Many businesses with pictures on Flickr have a link connecting their Flickr photostreams to their corporate websites.[31] General Motors, for example, uses Flickr not only to showcase its cars and important events, but also to provide links that connect users to GM's blog.[32] In addition to the White House's stream of photos by official White House photographers, President Obama has his own Flickr photostream, which he used to post images that relate directly to his legislative bills.

ing sites, more and more marketers will likely use the site as an inexpensive way to reach their audience.

Podcasting

Podcasts are audio or video files that can be downloaded from the Internet via a subscription that automatically delivers new content to listening devices or personal computers. Podcasting offers the benefit of convenience, giving users the ability to listen to or view content when and where they choose.

Podcasting is rapidly gaining in popularity. Dozens of online programs, such as Apple's iPodderX and Podcast Studio or Android's dPod, offer podcasting services. Other companies, such as Yodio, combine podcasting with photos to create customized online greeting card–style messages. It is estimated that by 2013, more than 37 million U.S. consumers will be downloading podcasts every month. Most current podcast users are between 18 and 29 years of age, making podcasts a good marketing tool for reaching this demographic.[34] The

Student Loan Network offers a free weekly Financial Aid Podcast to college-age students. It gives advice on affordable college education, credit cards, and other financial subjects important to young people. Listeners also have the added benefit of making comments and offering feedback on the podcasts.[35]

As podcasting continues to catch on, radio stations and television networks like CBC Radio, NPR, MSNBC, and PBS are creating podcasts of their shows to profit from this growing trend. Many companies hope to use podcasts to create brand awareness, promote their products, and encourage customer loyalty.

Social Networks

It is estimated that two-thirds of consumers in the United States have visited social networks or blogs.[36] One in three South Korean and one in five Japanese Internet users participate in social networks.[37] As social networks evolve, both marketers and the owners of social networking sites are realizing the opportunities such networks offer—an influx of advertising dollars for site owners and a large reach for the advertiser. As a result, marketers have begun investigating and experimenting with promotion on social networks. Four of the most prominent sites are Myspace, Facebook, LinkedIn, and Twitter.

Myspace Myspace offers users the chance to create a profile and connect with other Myspace members across the world. Users can invite people to be their friends, watch videos, listen to and promote music, instant message their friends, write on various topics (called forums), network with friends and colleagues, and play games. Since 2006, Myspace has been accessible in a variety of languages, including Swedish, Chinese, Spanish, Portuguese, and Turkish. Alternate versions also exist depending on the locality.[38]

Businesses have come up with unique ways to utilize Myspace to interact with consumers. Before it retired him, Burger King had created a fictional profile for its mascot, The King, on Myspace to appeal to a younger age group. By allowing consumers to become "friends," businesses can provide updates to everyone in their network and permit users to post comments. Companies also advertise through Myspace. For instance, Google renewed its contract to sell ads through Myspace, and the social media site became a part of Google's DoubleClick Ad Exchange that allows publishers to sell display advertising in an auction.[39] Additionally, Myspace offers aspiring artists a chance to showcase their talent and has become the largest artist community on the Web. Emerging musicians are using Myspace to record and share their music, and users can create social playlists of music from brand name artists.[40] Myspace can be a creative means of marketing through the use of profiles, advertising, music, videos, and other forms of media.

Facebook In April 2008, the social networking site Facebook surpassed Myspace in its number of members, becoming the most popular social networking site in the world.[41] It is estimated that nearly a third of Internet users have visited

FACEBOOK AND TWITTER OFFER BUSINESSES BOTH OPPORTUNITIES AND CHALLENGES

To advertise on social media sites, or not to advertise? It depends on who you ask. Users of social media are increasingly coming upon advertisements on their pages, and some are unhappy about it. They feel that social media sites are a place to have fun, not to be subjected to yet more marketing. Marketers, on the other hand, love the added exposure they receive; with over 400 million Facebook users and 100 million Twitter users, these sites offer businesses access to many market segments at once. However, businesses soon learn that marketing their brands on social media sites is not so easy.

One challenge is frequent monitoring of Facebook and Twitter pages. Simply posting ads or creating Facebook fan pages is not enough. As consumers are frequently turning to these social media sites to post complaints or concerns, companies must be vigilant to respond. Additionally, although it contains several features to support company advertisements, Facebook cannot always enforce appropriate ad content. It counts on users to complain when inappropriate ads are posted. This can be a problem for both consumers, who might be exposed to ads they feel are inappropriate, and businesses, who could unintentionally alienate their target market. (Facebook is currently updating its rules and restrictions.)

Businesses must also face the fact that their social media marketing activities can still bomb. Fox found this out the hard way when it began broadcasting live Twitter overlays over reruns of *Fringe* and *Glee*. Viewers found the overlays intrusive and distracting. The campaign was a failure. Other companies have accounts on both Facebook and Twitter, but they simply haven't done anything to make them exciting. These setbacks show that although social media offers exciting new marketing opportunities, campaigns must be carefully thought out and implemented to be successful.[42]

Discussion Questions

1. Do you think consumers would be willing to pay for the use of social media sites if there were no marketing activities?

2. Why do some marketers post what are considered by some as inappropriate advertisements?

3. What do marketers need to do to make advertising on social media sites acceptable to consumers?

MANY MARKETERS ARE TURNING TO FACEBOOK TO MARKET PRODUCTS, INTERACT WITH CONSUMERS, AND GAIN PUBLICITY.

the site.[43] Facebook users create profiles, which they can make public or private, and then search the network for people with whom to connect. Users must be a "friend" of the person whose profile they are trying to view before they can see that user's personal information. Many believe Facebook appeals to a broader demographic than does Myspace, attracting parents and grandparents as well as teens and college students.[44] In fact, the fastest-growing group on Facebook is women 55 and over.[45]

For this reason, many marketers are turning to Facebook to market products, interact with consumers, and gain publicity. It is possible for a consumer to become a "fan" of a major company like Starbucks by clicking on the "Like" icon on the coffee retailer's Facebook page. Companies are also using Facebook to generate awareness about their companies and encourage repeat visits. Allstate held a contest on Facebook that encouraged fans to revisit the company's Facebook page. Each day during the contest, Allstate would post a picture on its page and invite fans to "tag" themselves into the picture. The first "taggers" would be eligible to win a Ford Fusion Hybrid. Everyone else who tagged themselves would be eligible to win one of 440 Visa gift cards.[46]

Social networking sites are also useful for small businesses. Hansen Cakes in Beverly Hills uses interactive marketing on a social networking outlet to drum up more business.[47] One of the bakery's cake decorators provides updates on her current projects and offers free cake samples to local Facebook users. Facebook lets companies better engage in relationship marketing, or the creation of relationships that mutually benefit the marketing business and the customer. Other companies that have utilized relationship marketing to help consumers feel more connected to their products are Pepsi and Walt Disney Co. The Pepsi Refresh project invites consumers to suggest local charities that are making a positive impact. Consumers vote for their favorites, and Pepsi donates money to the winning causes. The company utilized Facebook, Twitter, and blogging to spread the word about the Refresh Project.[48] The Walt Disney Co. has created many different Facebook pages, which have succeeded in generating over 100 million Facebook fans. Some of its success is attributed to the Disney Pages promotion tab on its main Disney Facebook page. The tab allows users to access promotional content without having to navigate away from Facebook. In many ways, Facebook is becoming an e-commerce platform whereby companies can sell products through the site. DigiSynd, Disney's social media agency, was able to use a platform on Facebook called Disney Tickets Together that allowed fans to purchase tickets

for movies like *Toy Story 3*. These new opportunities for businesses demonstrate the evolution of Facebook into a marketing destination.[49]

LinkedIn   LinkedIn is a social networking site geared toward professionals from all over the world. With 120 million professional members, including executives from all the *Fortune* 500 companies, it is the fourth-largest social networking site and logs several million visitors a month.[50]

A LinkedIn profile resembles a résumé. It contains information about past and current job experiences, qualifications, goals, and educational background. Like all social networking sites, it lets users locate and connect with other members and join groups, which are often professional organizations. LinkedIn facilitates job searches and allows companies to search the network for potential employees with the necessary skills. Microsoft, Target, eBay, and Netflix have all used the LinkedIn network to recruit new employees.[51] Employers are also using LinkedIn to search for potential employers. Approximately 28 percent of college students have indicated that they plan to use LinkedIn to search for employment opportunities.[52]

Although a professional networking site like LinkedIn seems more like a recruiting site than a marketing tool, companies do use it to familiarize users with their business. In addition to listing job openings, Target's LinkedIn page also offers stock information, a link to the company website, some background on the business, and links to news updates on company activities and products. Procter & Gamble has a LinkedIn page that allows users to locate professionals, research careers, and get updates about the company. LinkedIn Groups—a feature on the site that highlights particular industries—is a useful tool for companies that want to describe their expertise and activities. Organizations can also build a group on LinkedIn based around their company or industry for no charge.[53] Smart marketers can use LinkedIn to reach professionals not only for recruiting purposes, but also to spread information about and interest in the company.

Twitter   Twitter is a hybrid of a social networking site and a micro-blogging site that asks users one simple question: "What are you doing?" Members can post answers of up to 140 characters, which are then available for their registered "followers" to read. It sounds simple enough, but Twitter's effect on digital media has been immense. The site quickly progressed from a novelty to a social networking staple, attracting millions of viewers each month.[54] About 11 percent of Internet users have used a micro-blogging site like Twitter.[55]

The thrill of Twitter is that users get to tell the world about their daily lives in short messages, known as "tweets." These tweets can be mundane, such as "I'm eating a sandwich," to interesting. President Obama used Twitter to announce "We just made history" when he won the 2008 presidential election. Halfway across the world, Russian president Dmitry Medvedev actually had to rebuke one of his regional governors for tweeting during a government session on educational policy.[56] Twitter has quickly transformed from novelty to serious marketing tool, with the company announcing plans to generate revenue through sponsored tweets and working to make the service more user-friendly.[57]

Although 140 characters may not seem like enough for companies to send an effective message, some have become experts at using Twitter in their marketing strategies. JetBlue and KFC have both used Twitter in marketing campaigns. JetBlue rewarded 1,000 tickets to followers for its 10th anniversary. KFC agreed to award $20,000 in tuition fees for the best tweet it received from high schoolers. These efforts are having an impact; approximately 23 percent of users report that they follow businesses on Twitter.[58]

Like other social networking tools, Twitter is also being used to build customer relationships. For example, Toyota recruited social media influencers to use Twitter to create buzz about one of its Lexus products. These tweets are more personalized than other types of media. To avoid deceiving consumers about the nature of these messages, the FTC recently created guidelines requiring influencers who are receiving pay for company tweets to disclose this fact to viewers.[59]

Finally, companies are using Twitter to gain a competitive advantage. Microsoft's search engine Bing developed a partnership with Twitter in which Bing sorts the millions of tweets by relevance and the popularity of the person tweeting. By doing a Bing-Twitter search, Twitter fans can get the most important tweets in real time.[60] Firms also have a chance to utilize promoted tweets, promoted accounts, and promoted trends offered on the site. Marketers can pay Twitter to highlight advertisements or company brands to a wider array of users while they search for specific terms or topics.[61] The race is on among companies that want to use Twitter to gain a competitive edge.

Virtual Worlds

Games and programs allowing viewers to develop avatars that exist in an online virtual world have exploded in popularity in the 21st century. Second Life is a social network with a twist. It is a virtual, three-dimensional game world created by users that features its own economy, its own lands, and residents of every shape and size. Internet users who participate in Second Life choose a fictional persona, called an *avatar,* to communicate

with one another, purchase goods with virtual Linden dollars (convertible to real dollars at a rate of around 250 Linden dollars per $1), and even own virtual businesses. For entertainment purposes, residents can shop, attend concerts, or travel to virtual environments—all while spending real money. Farmville provides a similar virtual world experience, except it is limited to life on a farm.

Second Life has the most potential for marketers, given that avatars can purchase property, goods, and services. While the businesses in Second Life are virtual ones, real-world marketers and organizations have been eager to capitalize on the site's popularity. Second Life allows businesses to reach consumers in ways that are creative and fun. For instance, to connect with consumers and build brand loyalty, car companies like Toyota and General Motors began selling virtual cars to Second Life residents.[62] Other businesses are looking toward Second Life to familiarize consumers with their products and services. For instance, large corporations like Best Buy and H&R Block offer support services on Second Life.

Second Life has become so popular that even professors are using it as a way to connect with their students. Ulrike Schultz is a business professor at Southern Methodist University. Students can choose to attend her real-world class, the virtual one, or both. Schultz sees virtual worlds as the next step in communications and feels that it is a great way to connect with young people who are accustomed to being wired for most of their waking hours.[63] Schultz sees opportunities for businesses in virtual environments, not only to promote and sell products, but also to engage in virtual teamwork

Second Life residents can purchase Linden dollars, the currency of Second Life, to buy virtual products.

between physically distant employees and in role-playing exercises. Prestigious universities like the University of Texas, Harvard Law School, Bowling Green State University, and the University of California at Davis all have virtual classrooms in Second Life.

Companies are also using Second Life to encourage residents to participate in company activities. CNN created a virtual news hub and began encouraging residents to submit stories that occur in this virtual world.[64] Such firms are not only creating brand loyalty by connecting with Second Life residents, they are also using consumer knowledge and money to earn virtual and real-world profits. Although the presence of real-world companies in virtual worlds is still in the experimental stages, virtual worlds like Second Life offer a novel way for marketers to interact with consumers.

Mobile Marketing

As digital marketing becomes increasingly sophisticated, consumers are beginning to utilize mobile devices like smartphones as a highly functional communication method. The iPhone and BlackBerry have changed the way consumers communicate, and a growing number of travelers are using their smartphones to find online maps, travel guides, and taxis. In industries such as hotels, airlines, and car rental agencies, mobile phones have become a primary method for booking reservations and communicating about services. They can act as airline boarding passes, GPS devices, and even hotel room keys. Travel companies are collecting personal information so they can send consumers relevant updates about travel opportunities. FARELOGIX, a travel software company, is working with a number of airlines to introduce features that allow airlines to sell services such as priority boarding. While airlines already make these services available on their websites, they also want to communicate with travelers who experience unexpected changes on their trips. Other marketing uses of mobile phones include sending shoppers timely messages related to discounts and shopping opportunities.[65]

Yowza!!, a mobile phone app, uses the GPS devices in cell phones to locate consumers and send them coupons from retailers in that area.

Marketing over mobile devices has been made possible largely by mobile applications or apps—programs that can be loaded onto certain mobile devices to allow users to perform a variety of functions, from playing games to comparing product prices from different stores. The latter is becoming particularly useful for consumers. The smartphone's ability to find retailers and entertainment and to organize an itinerary is changing the nature of consumer and business relationships. Large hotels, such as Hilton Hotels, are increasingly using iPhone apps that allow guests to check in early, order room service so food is waiting for them when they arrive, and even specify bed and pillow types.

The most important feature of apps is the convenience and cost savings they offer the consumer. To remain competitive, companies are beginning to use mobile marketing to offer additional customer incentives, with some success. Jiffy Lube offered coupons for one of its franchises over mobile devices. The company estimated that 50 percent of the new customers who came to the franchise did so as a result of its mobile marketing.[66]

Another application that marketers are finding useful is the QR scanning app. You might have noticed that black-and-white squares have begun appearing on magazines, posters, storefront displays, and more. These are QR codes, and they contain messages not visible to the naked eye. To read these messages, smartphone users must download the QR scanning application. When coming across a QR code, they simply open their smartphones and scan the black-and-white square. The QR scanning app will recognize the code and open up the link, video, or image on the phone's screen. Marketers are using QR codes to market their companies and offer consumer discounts. As more people adopt smartphones, these apps are likely to add a whole new layer to digital marketing.[67]

USING DIGITAL MEDIA TO REACH CONSUMERS

We've seen that customer-generated communications and digital media connect consumers. These connections let consumers share information and experiences without company interference so they get more of the "real story" on a product or company feature. In many ways, these media take some of the professional marketer's power to control and dispense information and place it in the hands of the consumer.

However, this shift does not have to spell doom for marketers, who can choose to utilize the power of the consumer and Internet technology to their advantage. While consumers use digital media to access more product information, marketers can use the same sites to get better and more targeted information about the consumer—often more than they could gather through traditional marketing venues. Marketers increasingly use consumer-generated content to aid their own marketing efforts, even going so far as to incorporate Internet bloggers in their publicity campaigns. Finally, marketers are also beginning to use the Internet to track the success of their online marketing campaigns, creating an entirely new way of gathering marketing research.

The challenge for digital media marketers is to constantly adapt to new technologies and changing consumer patterns. Unfortunately, the attrition rate for digital media channels is very high, with some dying off each year as new ones emerge. Social networks are no exception: the earliest ones, like Six Degrees, disappeared when they failed to catch on with the general public, and Friendster, though still active, has been far surpassed by newer networks. As time passes, digital media are becoming more sophisticated so as to reach consumers in more effective ways. Those that are not able to adapt and change eventually fail.

Mastering digital media presents a daunting task for businesses, particularly those used to more traditional means of marketing. For this reason, it is essential that marketers focus on the changing social behaviors of consumers, the ways in which they gather and use information, and the way the Internet is enabling them to get involved in the marketing process.

Charlene Li and Josh Bernoff of Forrester Research, a technology and market research company, emphasize the need for marketers to understand these changing relationships in the online media world. By grouping consumers into different segments based on how they utilize digital media, marketers can gain a better understanding of the online market and how best to proceed.[68]

Table 13.2 shows six ways to group consumers based on their Internet activity (or lack thereof). The categories are not mutually exclusive; online consumers can participate in more than one at a time.

Creators are consumers who create their own media outlets, such as blogs, podcasts, consumer-generated videos, and

▼ **TABLE 13.2** Social Technographics

Creators	• Publish a blog
	• Publish your own Web pages
	• Upload video you created
	• Upload audio/music you created
	• Write articles or stories and post them
Critics	• Post ratings/reviews of products or services
	• Comment on someone else's blog
	• Contribute to online forums
	• Contribute to/edit articles in a wiki
Collectors	• Use RSS feeds
	• Add tags to Web pages or photos
	• "Vote" for websites online
Joiners	• Maintain profile on a social networking site
	• Visit social networking sites
Spectators	• Read blogs
	• Watch video from other users
	• Listen to podcasts
	• Read online forums
	• Read customer ratings/reviews
Inactives	• None of the activities

Source: Charlene Li and Josh Bernoff, *Groundswell* (Boston: Harvard Business Press, 2008), p. 43.

or site that catches the eye of a collector is likely to be posted, discussed on collector sites, and made available to other online users looking for information.

Joiners include all who become users of Myspace, Twitter, Facebook, or other social networking sites. It is not unusual

"The challenge for digital media marketers is to constantly adapt to new technologies and changing consumer patterns."

wikis.[69] Consumer-generated media are increasingly important to online marketers as a conduit for addressing consumers directly. The second category, *critics,* consists of people who comment on blogs or post ratings and reviews. Because many online shoppers read ratings and reviews to aid their purchasing decisions, critics should be a primary component in a company's digital marketing strategy. *Collectors* are the most recently recognized category. They collect information and organize content generated by critics and creators.[70] Because collectors are active members of the online community, a company story

for consumers to be members of several social networking sites at once. Joiners use these sites to connect and network with other users, but as we've seen, marketers too can take significant advantage of these sites to connect with consumers and form customer relationships.[71] The last two segments are Spectators and Inactives. *Spectators,* who read online information but do not join groups or post anywhere, are the largest group in most countries. *Inactives* are online users who do not participate in any digital online media, but their numbers are dwindling.

VIEWPOINTS NETWORK HELPS COMPANIES MANAGE BRANDS ONLINE

As more companies turn toward social media to promote their products, Viewpoints Network is there to help. Founded by entrepreneur Matt Moog in 2006, Viewpoints Network consists of a product review website (the second largest) and a software suite to help companies use social media to create effective marketing campaigns. Clients include such well-known companies as Procter & Gamble, Sears, and Kraft.

Viewpoints Network utilizes the power of viral marketing with over a million members registered on its website. When a company hires Viewpoints Network to promote a brand, Viewpoints Network invites members, specifically opinion leaders, to try the product. Members then write product reviews and share them with their friends on sites like Twitter and Facebook. This represents a growing trend where consumers use the feedback of other consumers—many that they've never met—in their purchasing decisions. According to founder Matt Moog, this will require a significant change in marketing: the incorporation of the consumer into the marketing mix.[72]

Marketers who want to capitalize on social and digital media marketing need to consider what proportion of online consumers are creating, rating, collecting, joining, or simply reading online materials. As in traditional marketing efforts, they need to know their target market. For instance, where spectators make up the majority of the online population, companies should post their own corporate messages through blogs and websites promoting their organizations.

USING DIGITAL MEDIA TO LEARN ABOUT CONSUMERS

Marketing research and information systems can use digital media and social networking sites to gather useful information about consumers and their preferences. Sites such as Twitter, Facebook, Myspace, and LinkedIn can be good substitutes for focus groups. Online surveys can serve as an alternative to mail, telephone, or personal interviews.

Crowdsourcing describes how marketers use digital media to find out the opinions or needs of the crowd (or potential markets). Communities of interested consumers join sites like threadless.com, which designs t-shirts, or crowdspring.com, which creates logos and print and Web designs. These companies give interested consumers opportunities to contribute and give feedback on product ideas. Crowdsourcing lets companies gather and utilize consumers' ideas in an interactive way when creating new products. There are even sites that crowdsource entire advertising campaigns, like victorandspoils.com. Mobile phone brand LG offered the public more than $80,000 for ideas about what the mobile phone should look like in two, five, or ten years. Barilla, the Italian pasta brand, gets consumers involved in designing new pasta for little expense—far less than the cost of banner ads on websites.

There is no end to the opportunities to gain information, insights, and new-product ideas from consumers. For instance, Rupert Barksfield developed the Multi-Pet Feeder to end pet feeding-time frenzy when one greedy pet eats the other pet's food. Barksfield paid $99 to post a concept and some drawings at quirky.com, and 30,000 people passed judgment on his idea.[73]

Consumer feedback is an important part of the digital media equation. Some of the oldest forms of digital media are online forums, where participants post and respond to messages and discuss specific topics. About one-fifth of U.S. and Japanese Internet users participate in discussion forums, whose topics can range from consumer products to movies. Ratings and reviews have become exceptionally popular; 25 percent of the U.S. online population reads this type of consumer-generated feedback.[74] Retailers such as Amazon, Netflix, and Priceline allow consumers to post comments on their sites about the books, movies, and travel arrangements they sell. Today, most online shoppers search the Internet for ratings and reviews before making major purchase decisions.

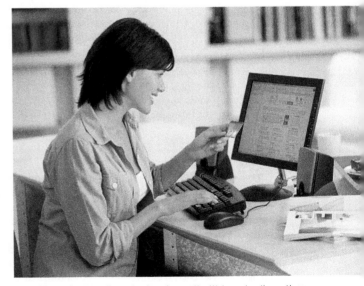

About three-quarters of people shopping on the Web read online ratings and reviews before making a purchasing decision.

While consumer-generated content about a firm can be either positive or negative, digital media forums do allow businesses to closely monitor what their customers are saying. In the case of negative feedback, businesses can communicate with consumers to address problems or complaints much more easily than through traditional communication channels. Hotels and resorts, for example, have begun monitoring social media sites to see what their guests are saying about them. In some cases, guests who have complained about their rooms using digital media have found themselves upgraded to better rooms that very night.[75] Yet despite the ease and obvious importance of online feedback, many companies do not yet take full advantage of the digital tools at their disposal.

LEGAL AND SOCIAL ISSUES IN INTERNET MARKETING

The extraordinary growth of information technology, the Internet, and e-business has generated many legal and social issues for consumers and businesses. These issues include privacy concerns, the risk of identity theft and online fraud, and the need to protect intellectual property. The U.S. Federal Trade Commission (FTC) compiles an annual list of consumer complaints related to the Internet and digital media. Figure 13.1 outlines the major sources of complaints. We discuss each of these in this section, as well as steps that individuals, companies, and the government have taken to address them.

Privacy

Businesses have long tracked consumers' shopping habits with little controversy. However, observing the contents of a consumer's shopping cart or the process a consumer goes through when choosing a box of cereal generally does not result in the collection of specific, personally identifying data. Although by using credit cards, shopping cards, and coupons forces consumers to give up a certain degree of anonymity in the traditional shopping process, they can still choose to remain anonymous by paying cash. Shopping on the Internet, however, allows businesses to track them on a far more personal level, from the contents of their online purchases to the websites they favor. Current technology has made it possible for marketers to amass vast quantities of personal information, often without consumers' knowledge, and to share and sell this information to interested third parties.

How is personal information collected on the Web? Many sites follow users online by storing a "cookie," or an identifying string of text, on users' computers. Cookies permit website operators to track how often a user visits the site, what he or she looks at while there, and in what sequence. They also allow website visitors to customize services, such as virtual shopping carts, as well as the particular content they see when they log onto a Web page. Users have the option of turning off cookies on their machines, but nevertheless the potential for misuse has left many consumers uncomfortable with this technology. The European Union even passed a law that requires companies to get users' consent before using cookies to track their information. Because of this law Yahoo Inc. now allows Internet users in the United Kingdom to choose whether to opt out of having their Internet habits tracked.[76]

Even information that consumers willingly post can be used improperly. Facebook in particular has been criticized over the last few years of mishandling user information. In 2010 an online security consultant collected public user information from over 100 million Facebook users and placed them in a file for companies to download. This type of "scraping"—where companies offer to collect personal information from social networking sites and other online forums—is becoming increasingly common. Since Internet privacy issues have become such a problem, regulators are proposing bills to address the issue. One proposed bill, called the "do not track"

FIGURE 13.1
Consumer Complaints to Government Agencies by Type

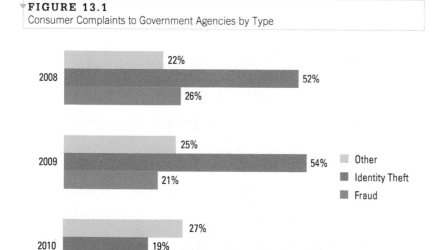

Source: Federal Trade Commission, *Consumer Sentinel Network Data Book,* March 2011, www.ftc.gov/sentinel/reports/sentinel-annual-reports/sentinel-cy2010.pdf (accessed April 11, 2011).

bill, has been supported by several legislators. The "do not track" bill would be an online equivalent of the "do not call" bill for telephones, allowing users to opt out of having their information tracked. A social networkers' bill of rights for users is also an option. Table 13.3 outlines some laws already in place to protect Internet privacy.[77]

Federal regulation could pose a significant threat to Web advertisers, who use consumer information to better target advertisements. Such regulations could harm search engines and social networking sites as well. According to Facebook, 80 percent of the world's 100 largest advertisers are on Facebook. As a result of this threat, Google, Facebook, and other Web-based companies are increasing their lobbying efforts to ward off regulation that may be potentially damaging. In one year, Google spent approximately $4 million on lobbying efforts. Self-regulation is another option some Web advertisers are pursuing.[78]

On the other hand, certain advertising agencies, networks, and industry trade groups have made the decision to work with Internet-browser makers to create a "do-not-track" system. This represents a major shift for these advertising groups, which until recently have largely opposed such a system. However, although Microsoft and Mozilla have both integrated "do-not-track" features into their browsers, advertisers have a choice as to whether they will respect users' do-not-track requests.[79]

Several nonprofit organizations have stepped in to help companies develop privacy policies. Among the best known are TRUSTe and the Better Business Bureau Online. TRUSTe is a nonprofit organization devoted to promoting global trust in Internet technology. Companies that agree to abide by TRUSTe's privacy standards may display a "trustmark" on their websites; thousands of websites currently do so.[80] The BBBOnLine program provides verification, monitoring and review, consumer dispute resolution, a compliance seal, enforcement mechanisms, and an educational component. It is managed by the Council of Better Business Bureaus, an organization with considerable experience in conducting self-regulation and dispute-resolution programs, and it employs guidelines and requirements outlined by the FTC and the U.S. Department of Commerce.[81] The hope among online marketers is that widespread adoption of these privacy policies may prevent regulation that could make it more difficult to advertise effectively online.

Identity Theft

Identity theft occurs when criminals obtain personal information that allows them to impersonate someone else in order to use the person's credit to access financial accounts and make purchases. Many of these breaches occur at banks, universities, and other businesses that contain sensitive consumer information.[82]

▼ **TABLE 13.3** A Timeline of Internet-Related Privacy Policies

Year	Legislation	Major Provisions
1986	Electronic Communications Privacy Act	Extended laws on wiretaps to electronic transmissions.
1987	Computer Security Act	Improved the regulation of public information by making the National Institute of Standards and Technology (NIST) responsible for the standardization of communication protocols, data structures, and interfaces in telecommunications and computer systems.
1988	Computer Matching and Privacy Protection Act	Amended the 1986 Privacy Act by regulating the use of computer matching, the computerized comparison of individual information for purposes of determining eligibility for federal benefits programs.
1996	Digital Millenium Copyright Act	Refined copyright laws to protect digital versions of copyrighted materials, including music and movies.
1998	European Union Directive	Required companies to explain how the personal information they collect will be used and to obtain the individual's permission.
1999	Anti-Cyber Squatting Consumer Protection Act	Made it illegal to register others' trademarks as domain names in order to profit from the sale or transfer of the domain name, tarnish the trademark owner's reputation, or mislead consumers.
1999	Uniform Electronic Transactions Act	Set guidelines for electronic transactions, including the retention of records, electronic contracts, and electronic signatures.
2000	Children's Online Privacy and Protection Act (COPPA)	Regulated the online collection of personally identifiable information (name, address, e-mail address, hobbies, interests, or information collected through cookies) from children under 13.
2003	Controlling the Assault of Non-Solicited Pornography and Marketing Act (CAN-SPAM)	Banned fraudulent or deceptive unsolicited commercial e-mail and required senders to provide information about how recipients can opt out of receiving additional messages.

Sources: "Federal Statutes Relevant in the Information Sharing Environment (ISE)," Justice Information Sharing: U.S. Department of Justice, Office of Justice Programs, February 27, 2009, www.it.ojp.gov/default.aspx?area=privacy&page=1285 (accessed February 18, 2010); Report to Congress: The Anticybersquatting Consumer Protection Act of 1999, section 3006 concerning the abusive registration of domain names, www.uspto.gov/web/offices/dcom/olia/tmcybpiracy/repcongress.pdf (accessed February 18, 2010).

This requires organizations to implement increased security measures to prevent database theft. As you can see in Figure 13.2, the most common complaints relate to credit card fraud, followed by utility fraud, bank fraud, employment-related fraud, government document fraud, and loan fraud.

The Internet's relative anonymity and speed make possible both legal and illegal access to databases storing Social Security numbers, driver's license numbers, dates of birth, mothers' maiden names, and other information that can be used to establish a credit card or bank account in another person's name in order to make fraudulent transactions. One growing scam used to initiate identity theft fraud is the practice of *phishing,* whereby con artists counterfeit a well-known website and send out e-mails directing victims to it. There visitors find instructions to reveal sensitive information such as their credit card numbers. Phishing scams have faked websites for PayPal, AOL, and the Federal Deposit Insurance Corporation.

Some identity theft problems are resolved quickly, while other cases take weeks and hundreds of dollars before a victim's bank balances and credit standings are restored. To deter identity theft, the National Fraud Center wants financial institutions to implement new technologies such as digital certificates, digital signatures, and biometrics—the use of fingerprinting or retina scanning.

Online Fraud

Online fraud includes any attempt to conduct fraudulent activities online, such as by deceiving consumers into releasing personal information. It is becoming a major source of frustration among users of social networking sites, because cybercriminals are finding new ways to use sites like Facebook and Twitter to commit fraudulent activities. For instance, they will create profiles under a company's name to either damage the company's reputation (particularly larger, more controversial companies) or lure that company's customers into releasing personal information the perpetrators can use for monetary gain.

> **identity theft**
> when criminals obtain personal information that allows them to impersonate someone else in order to use their credit to access financial accounts and make purchases
>
> **online fraud**
> any attempt to conduct fraudulent activities online

Another tactic is to copy a blog entry from a reputable company and repost it with a link that connects the user to the criminal's own fraudulent site, where he or she attempts to sell the user goods (under the reputable company's name) or collect personal information. For instance, a fraudster may repost a blog written by a professional sport organization with a fraudulent link that connects users to a site that sells unlicensed sporting goods.[83] Criminals may also use social networking sites to pose as charitable institutions. After the 2010 earthquake in Haiti, fraudsters set up fake accounts to scam Facebook users into donating money for the fraudsters' own financial gain.[84]

Despite any number of safeguards, the best protection for consumers is to be careful when they divulge information online. The surest way to stay out of trouble is never to give out personal information, like a Social Security or credit card number, unless it is a site you trust and that you know is legitimate.

Intellectual Property

In addition to protecting personal privacy, Internet users and others want to protect their rights to property they may create, including songs, movies, books, and software. Such intellectual property consists of the ideas and creative materials developed to solve problems, carry out applications, and educate and entertain others.

Although intellectual property is generally protected by patents and copyrights, each year losses from the illegal copying of computer programs, music, movies, compact discs, and books reaches billions of dollars in the United States alone. This has become a particular problem with digital media sites. Chinese search engine Baidu has been accused of offering a MP3 service that allows users to download proprietary songs for free. The

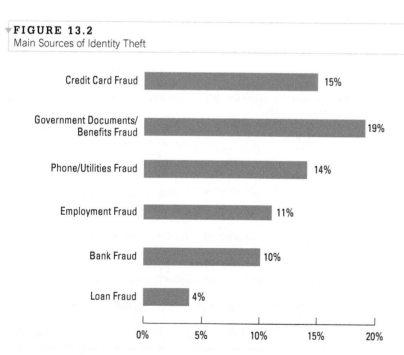

▼FIGURE 13.2
Main Sources of Identity Theft

- Credit Card Fraud — 15%
- Government Documents/Benefits Fraud — 19%
- Phone/Utilities Fraud — 14%
- Employment Fraud — 11%
- Bank Fraud — 10%
- Loan Fraud — 4%

(0% 5% 10% 15% 20%)

Source: Federal Trade Commission, *Consumer Sentinel Network Data Book,* March 2011, www.ftc.gov/sentinel/reports/sentinel-annual-reports/sentinel-cy2010.pdf (accessed April 11, 2011).

DEVELOPING A STRATEGIC UNDERSTANDING OF HOW DIGITAL MARKETING CAN MAKE BUSINESS MORE EFFICIENT AND PRODUCTIVE IS INCREASINGLY NECESSARY.

The file-sharing protocol BitTorrent allows users to share and download files. The U.S. Copyright Group recently obtained the IP addresses of users who downloaded specific movies using BitTorrent technology and are taking action against thousands of BitTorrent users for illegally downloading protected content.

recording industry sued Baidu in 2005 for Internet piracy, but the Chinese government sided with Baidu.[85] Another example is YouTube, which has faced lawsuits over its users' possible infringement of other companies' copyrights. In one case, Viacom Inc. sued YouTube's owner, Google, claiming Google had violated its copyrights by allowing users to post protected film clips on YouTube.[86] Although YouTube is responsible for the video content shown on its sites, it can be difficult for Google to monitor and remove all the videos that may contain copyrighted content, given the many millions of clips that are loaded onto YouTube daily.

Illegal sharing of content is another major intellectual property problem. Consumers rationalize the pirating of software, videogames, movies, and music for a number of reasons. First, many feel they just don't have the money to pay for what they want. Second, because their friends engage in piracy and swap digital content, some users feel influenced to engage in this activity. Others enjoy the thrill of getting away with something with a low risk of consequences. And finally, some people feel being tech-savvy allows them to take advantage of the opportunity to pirate content.[87]

The software industry loses over $50 billion globally each year due to theft and illegal use of software products, according to

the Business Software Alliance.[88] About 90 percent of illegal software copying is actually done by businesses. For example, a firm may obtain a license to install a specific application on 100 of its computers but actually installs it on 300. In some cases, software is illegally made available through the Internet by companies that have taken the software from the producer and set up their own distribution system.

DIGITAL MEDIA'S IMPACT ON MARKETING

To be successful in business, you need to know much more than how to use a social networking site to communicate with friends. Developing a strategic understanding of how digital marketing can make business more efficient and productive is increasingly necessary. If you are thinking of becoming an entrepreneur, then the digital world can open doors to new resources and customers. Smart phones, mobile broadband, and Webcams are among the tools that can make the most of the online business world, creating greater efficiency at less cost. For example, rather than using traditional phone lines, Skype helps people make and receive calls via the Internet and provides free video calling and text messaging for about 10 percent of the cost of a land line.[89] It is up to businesses and entrepreneurs to develop strategies that achieve business success using existing and future technology, software, and networking opportunities.

Traditional businesses accustomed to using print media can find the transition to digital challenging. New media may require employees with new skills or additional training for current employees. There is often a gap between technical knowledge of how to develop sites and how to develop effective digital marketing strategies to enhance business success. Determining the correct blend of traditional and new media requires careful consideration; the mix will vary depending on the business, its size, and its target market. Future career opportunities will require skills in both traditional and digital media areas so that marketers properly understand and implement marketing strategies that help businesses achieve a competitive advantage. ■

TEAM EXERCISE

Develop a digital marketing promotion for a local sports team. Use Twitter, Facebook, and other social networking media to promote ticket sales for next season's schedule. In your plan, provide specific details and ideas for the content you would use on the sites. Also, describe how you would encourage fans and potential fans to go to your site. How would you use digital media to motivate sports fans to purchase tickets and merchandise and attend games?

SO YOU WANT TO BE // a Digital Marketer /

The business world has grown increasingly dependent on digital marketing to maintain communication with stakeholders. Reaching customers is often a major concern, but digital marketing can also be used to communicate with suppliers, concerned community members, and special interest groups about issues related to sustainability, safety practices, and philanthropic activities. Many types of jobs exist: account executive directors of social media and director of marketing for digital products, as well as digital advertisers, online marketers, global digital marketers, and brand managers are prominently listed on career opportunity websites.

Entrepreneurs are taking advantage of the low cost of digital marketing, building social networking sites to help market their products. In fact, some small businesses such as specialty publishing, personal health and beauty, and other specialty products can use digital marketing as the primary channel for reaching consumers. Many small businesses are posting signs outside their stores with statements such as "Follow us on Twitter" or "Check out our Facebook page."

To utilize digital marketing, especially social networking, requires more than information technology skills related to constructing websites, graphics, videos, podcasts, and so on. Most importantly, one must be able to determine how digital media can be used in implementing a marketing strategy. All marketing starts with identifying a target market and developing a marketing mix to satisfy customers. Digital marketing is just another way to reach customers, provide information, and develop relationships. Therefore, your opportunity for a career in this field is greatly based on understanding the messages, desired level of interactivity, and connectivity that helps achieve marketing objectives.

As social media use skyrockets, digital marketing professionals will be in demand. The experience of many businesses and research indicate digital marketing is a powerful way to increase brand exposure and generate traffic. In fact, a study conducted on Social Media Examiner found that 85 percent of marketers surveyed believe generating exposure for their business is their number-one advantage in Internet marketing. As consumers use social networking for their personal communication, they will be more open to obtaining information about products through this channel. Digital marketing could be the fastest-growing opportunity in business.

To prepare yourself for a digital marketing career, learn not only the technical aspects, but also how social media can be used to maximize marketing performance. A glance at careerbuilder.com indicates that management positions such as account manager, digital marketing manager, and digital product manager can pay from $60,000 to $170,000 or more per year.

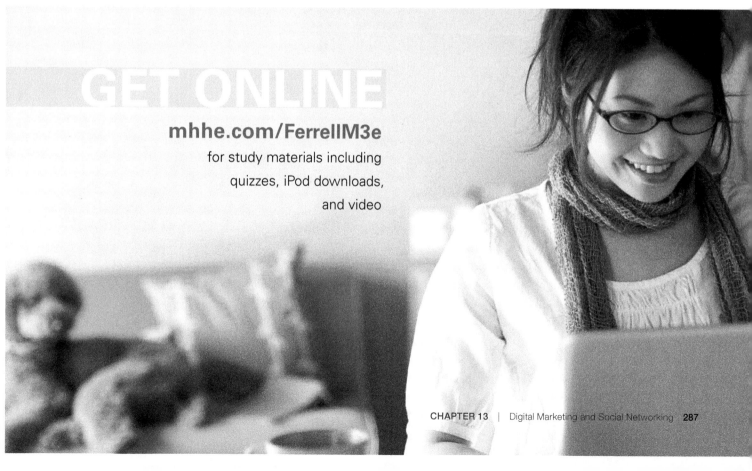

GET ONLINE

mhhe.com/FerrellM3e

for study materials including
quizzes, iPod downloads,
and video

CHAPTER 13 | Digital Marketing and Social Networking **287**

chapter thirteen

active review card
Digital Marketing and Social Networking

in a nutshell

You must understand the concepts of digital media and digital marketing and how they have become extremely important in strategic planning. The Internet and social networking are becoming increasingly important in people's lives, so you need to understand their impact on business today.

The following statements will test your take-away knowledge from this chapter. Do your best to explain each one in the space provided below.

LO.1 Define digital media and digital marketing and recognize their increasing value in strategic planning.

LO.2 Understand the characteristics of digital media and how they differentiate these methods from traditional marketing activities.

LO.3 Demonstrate the role of digital marketing and social networking in today's business environment.

LO.4 Show how digital media affect the marketing mix.

LO.5 Define social networking and illustrate how businesses can use different types of social networking media.

LO.6 Identify legal and ethical considerations in digital media.

Did your answers include the following important points?

LO.1. Define digital media and digital marketing and recognize their increasing value in strategic planning.

- Digital media are electronic media that function using digital codes—available via computers and other digital services like cell phones and smartphones.
- Digital marketing uses digital media to create communications and exchanges with customers.

LO.2. Understand the characteristics of digital media and how they differentiate these methods from traditional marketing activities.

- The Internet facilitates business transactions, allowing companies to network with manufacturers, wholesalers, retailers, suppliers, and outsource firms to serve customers quickly and efficiently.
- Digital communication offers a completely new dimension in connecting with others through better addressability, interactivity, accessibility, connectivity, and control.

LO.3. Demonstrate the role of digital marketing and social networking in today's business environment.

- Firms can use real-time exchanges to stimulate interactive communication, forge closer relationships, and learn more accurately about consumer and supplier needs.
- Digital communication is making it easier for businesses to conduct marketing research, provide price and product information, and advertise.

LO.4. Show how digital media affect the marketing mix.

- The connectivity created by digital media provides the opportunity for adding services and product benefits.

- The Internet is a new distribution channel making products available at the right time, at the right place, and in the right quantities.
- Online promotions are creating well-informed consumers.
- Digital media enhance the value of products by providing extra benefits such as service, information, and convenience.

LO.5. Define social networking and illustrate how businesses can use different types of social networking media.

- A social network is a Web-based meeting place for friends, family, co-workers, and peers that lets users create a profile and connect with other users for different purposes.
- Internet users participate in blogs, wikis, video sharing sites, podcasts, social networking sites, virtual reality sites, and mobile applications.
- Marketers have begun investigating and experimenting with promotion on social networks.
- Companies are using the virtual world to gather information about consumer tastes and preferences, as well as feedback on products.
- Mobile phones are also being used for getting across to consumers and conducting business, especially in the service industry.

LO.6. Identify legal and ethical considerations in digital media.

- The Internet and e-business have raised concerns such as privacy concerns, the risk of identity theft, online fraud, and intellectual property rights.

Practical Application

LO.1.

- _____ uses digital media to develop communication and exchanges with customers.
- _____ means carrying out the goals of business through the use of the Internet.

LO.2.

- The ability of a business to identify customers before they make purchases is called _____.
- _____ allows customers to find out more information about products, prices, and reviews and become better informed about a company.

LO.3.

- The Internet _____ the cost of communication and is therefore significant in industries like entertainment, health care, and education.
- Digital media can be a(n) _____ backbone that helps store knowledge, information, and records in management information systems for the employees of a company.

LO.4.

- The Internet has become a new _____ to make products available for people.

- A recent market research study reveals that people today spend more time on _____ than they do on _____.
- The aspect of marketing that still remains unchanged by the digital media is the importance of achieving the _____.

LO.5.

- Some companies have started using _____ as internal tools for projects that require a lot of documentation.
- Marketers generally engage in _____ of their products on social networking sites.
- _____ only read online information and are the largest group in most countries.

LO.6.

- The BBBOnline program is managed by the _____, which follows guidelines on self-regulation and monitoring established by the U.S. Department of Commerce.
- _____ is a method of initiating identity theft fraud that is growing rapidly.
- _____ of content is a major intellectual property problem especially in the areas of software, music, movies, and videogames.

Financing the Enterprise

introduction

Accounting, the financial "language" that organizations use to record, measure, and interpret all of their financial transactions and records, is very important in business. All businesses—from a small family farm to a giant corporation—use the language of accounting to make sure they use their money wisely and to plan for the future. Nonbusiness organizations such as charities and governments also use accounting to demonstrate to donors and taxpayers how well they are using their funds and meeting their stated objectives.

This chapter explores the role of accounting in business and its importance in making business decisions. First, we discuss the uses of accounting information and the accounting

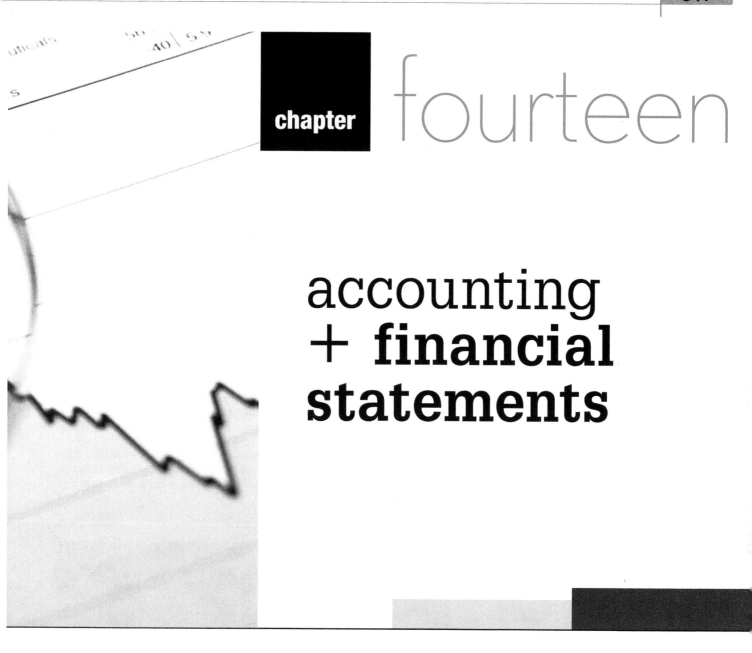

chapter fourteen

accounting
+ financial
statements

process. Then, we briefly look at some simple financial statements and accounting tools that are useful in analyzing organizations worldwide.

LEARNING OBJECTIVES

LO1 Define accounting, and describe the different uses of accounting information.

LO2 Demonstrate the accounting process.

LO3 Examine the various components of an income statement in order to evaluate a firm's "bottom line."

LO4 Interpret a company's balance sheet to determine its current financial position.

LO5 Analyze the statement of cash flows to evaluate the increase and decrease in a company's cash balance.

accounting
the recording, measurement, and interpretation of financial information

certified public accountant (CPA) an individual who has been state certified to provide accounting services ranging from the preparation of financial records and the filing of tax returns to complex audits of corporate financial records

THE NATURE OF ACCOUNTING

Simply stated, **accounting** is the recording, measurement, and interpretation of financial information. Large numbers of people and institutions, both within and outside businesses, use accounting tools to evaluate organizational operations. The Financial Accounting Standards Board has been setting the principles standards of financial accounting and reporting in the private sector since 1973. Its mission is to establish and improve standards of financial accounting and reporting for the guidance and education of the public, including issuers, auditors, and users of financial information. However, the accounting scandals at the turn of the last century resulted when many accounting firms and businesses failed to abide by generally accepted accounting principles, or GAAP. Consequently, the federal government has taken a greater role in making rules, requirements, and policies for accounting firms and businesses through the Securities and Exchange Commission's (SEC) Public Company Accounting Oversight Board. For example, Ernst & Young, a leading accounting firm, was barred from undertaking new audit clients for six months as a penalty for abusing the agency's auditor-independence rules.[1]

To better understand the importance of accounting, we must first understand who prepares accounting information and how it is used.

Accountants

Many of the functions of accounting are carried out by public or private accountants.

Public Accountants
Individuals and businesses can hire a **certified public accountant (CPA)**, an individual who has been certified by the state in which he or she practices to provide accounting services ranging from the preparation of financial records and the filing of tax returns to complex audits of corporate financial records. Certification gives a public accountant the right to express, officially, an unbiased opinion regarding the accuracy of the client's financial statements. Most public accountants are either self-employed or members of large public accounting firms such as Ernst & Young, KPMG, Deloitte Touche Tohmatsu, and PricewaterhouseCoopers, together referred to as "the Big Four." In addition, many CPAs work for one of the second-tier accounting firms that are much smaller than the Big Four firms, as illustrated in Table 14.1.

KPMG is part of the "Big Four," or the four largest international accounting firms. The other three are PricewaterhouseCoopers, Ernst & Young, and Deloitte Touche Tomatsu.

▼ **TABLE 14.1** Leading Accounting Firms

Company	2010 U.S. Revenues ($ Millions)	2010 Partners
"Top Seven Firms"		
Deloitte Touche	$10,722	2,968
Ernst & Young	$7,620	2,500
PricewaterhouseCoopers	$7,369	2,235
KPMG	$5,076	1,847
RSM/McGladrey & Pullen	$1,460	751
Grant Thornton	$1,147	535
BDO	$620	273

Source: Accounting Today, *Top 100 Firms, 2010,* special supplement to *Accounting Today,* p. 18. Published by SourceMedia, www.hawcpa.com/pdf/actodaytop100_2010-dl%5B1%5D.pdf.

While there will always be companies and individual money managers who can successfully hide illegal or misleading accounting practices for a while, eventually they are exposed. After the accounting scandals of Enron and Worldcom in the early 2000s, Congress passed the Sarbanes-Oxley Act, which required firms to be more rigorous in their accounting and reporting practices. Sarbanes-Oxley made accounting firms separate their consulting and auditing businesses and punished corporate executives with potential jail sentences for inaccurate, misleading, or illegal accounting statements. This seemed to reduce the accounting errors among non-financial companies, but declining housing prices exposed some of the questionable practices by banks and mortgage companies. In 2008–2009, the world experienced a financial crisis—part of which was due to excessive risk taking and inappropriate accounting practices. Many banks failed to understand the true state of their financial health. Other banks hid risks from the public through a practice known as "window-dressing," which occurs when banks "temporarily" get rid of debt before reporting their financial information to the public. Citigroup Inc. engaged in this by listing short-term debt as sales when it should have been labeled as borrowings.[2]

Banks also developed questionable lending practices and investments based on subprime mortgages made to individuals who had poor credit. When housing prices declined and people suddenly found that they owed more on their mortgages than their homes were worth, they began to default. To prevent a depression, the government intervened and bailed out some of the United States' largest banks. Congress is continuing to work on legislation that will strengthen the oversight of financial institutions. Most likely this legislation will limit the types of assets commercial banks can buy;

the amount of capital they must maintain; and the use of derivative instruments such as options, futures, and structured investment products.

A growing area for public accountants is *forensic accounting,* which is accounting that is fit for legal review. It involves analyzing financial documents in search of fraudulent entries or financial misconduct. Functioning as much like detectives as accountants, forensic accountants have been used since the 1930s. In the wake of the accounting scandals of the early 2000s, many auditing firms are rapidly adding or expanding forensic or fraud-detection services. Additionally, many forensic accountants root out evidence of "cooked books" for federal agencies like the Federal Bureau of Investigation or the Internal Revenue Service. The Association of Certified Fraud Examiners, which certifies accounting professionals as *certified fraud examiners (CFEs),* has grown to more than 45,000 members.[4]

Private Accountants Large corporations, government agencies, and other organizations may employ their own **private accountants** to prepare and analyze their financial statements. With titles such as controller, tax accountant, or internal auditor, private accountants are deeply involved in many of the most important financial decisions of the organizations for which they work. Private accountants can be CPAs and may become **certified management accountants (CMAs)** by passing a rigorous examination by the Institute of Management Accountants.

Accounting or Bookkeeping?

The terms *accounting* and *bookkeeping* are often mistakenly used interchangeably. Much narrower and far more mechanical than accounting, bookkeeping is typically limited to the routine, day-to-day recording of business transactions. Bookkeepers are responsible for obtaining and recording the information that accountants require to analyze a firm's financial position. They generally require less training than accountants. Accountants, on the other hand, usually complete course work beyond their basic four- or five-year college accounting degrees. This additional training allows accountants not only to record financial information, but to understand, interpret, and even develop the sophisticated accounting systems necessary to classify and analyze complex financial information.

?

DID YOU KNOW?

Corporate fraud costs are estimated at $2.9 trillion annually.[3]

private accountants accountants employed by large corporations, government agencies, and other organizations to prepare and analyze their financial statements

certified management accountants (CMAs) private accountants who, after rigorous examination, are certified by the National Association of Accountants and who have some managerial responsibility

managerial accounting the internal use of accounting statements by managers in planning and directing the organization's activities

cash flow the movement of money through an organization over a daily, weekly, monthly, or yearly basis

budget an internal financial plan that forecasts expenses and income over a set period of time

The Uses of Accounting Information

Accountants summarize the information from a firm's business transactions in various financial statements (which we'll look at in a later section of this chapter) for a variety of stakeholders, including managers, investors, creditors, and government agencies. Many business failures may be directly linked to ignorance of the information "hidden" inside these financial statements. Likewise, most business successes can be traced to informed managers who understand the consequences of their decisions. While maintaining and even increasing short-run profits is desirable, the failure to plan sufficiently for the future can easily lead an otherwise successful company to insolvency and bankruptcy court.

Basically, managers and owners use financial statements (1) to aid in internal planning and control and (2) for external purposes such as reporting to the Internal Revenue Service, stockholders, creditors, customers, employees, and other interested parties. Figure 14.1 shows some of the users of the accounting information generated by a typical corporation.

Internal Uses Managerial accounting refers to the internal use of accounting statements by managers in planning and directing the organization's activities. Perhaps management's greatest single concern is **cash flow**, the movement of money through an organization over a daily, weekly, monthly, or yearly basis. Obviously, for any business to succeed, it needs to generate enough cash to pay its bills as they fall due. However, it is not at all unusual for highly successful and rapidly growing companies to struggle to make payments to employees, suppliers, and lenders because of an inadequate cash flow. One common reason for a so-called cash crunch, or shortfall, is poor managerial planning.

Managerial accountants also help prepare an organization's **budget**, an internal financial plan that forecasts expenses and income over a set period of time. It is not unusual for an organization to prepare separate daily, weekly, monthly, and yearly budgets. Think of a budget as a financial map, showing how the company expects to move from Point A to Point B over a specific period of time. While most companies prepare *master budgets* for the entire firm, many also prepare budgets for smaller segments of the organization such as divisions, departments, product lines, or projects. "Top-down" master budgets begin at the upper management level and filter down to the individual department level, while "bottom-up" budgets start at the department or project level and are combined at the

---

RECESSION ENCOURAGED UNITED PARCEL SERVICE (UPS) TO RETHINK THE BUDGETING PROCESS

Finance managers became key players as the recent recession forced many companies to alter how they budget. With plummeting revenues, the recessionary business climate seemed to offer few positives. For example, for the United Parcel Service (UPS), the recession removed the company's ability to predict the path its finances would take. Management no longer had concrete information with which to make such predictions.

However, instead of seeing this as a liability, UPS Chief Financial Officer Kurt

Kuehn and several others saw this as an opportunity to improve the financial function of budgeting. According to Keuhn, UPS was forced to adapt to focus on bare bones costs. Instead of focusing so extensively on absolute targets and measures, managers began to examine the minute details of budgeting. As a result, they created a system allowing them to match spending to changing revenue. This new philosophy was applied to every department. Focus on growth was replaced with an emphasis on balancing gains and losses in revenue with the company's spending costs. A good portion of this focus was turned toward identifying and trimming unnecessary spending. For UPS, this resulted in a more flexible budget that received periodic reviews. The company is now making a comeback; recent quarterly numbers beat analyst predictions.

Financial consultants have long advocated for this shift and continue to urge CFOs to increase budget revisions. For

example, rather than having a budget with set forecasts, managers should continually review the budget and make changes when needed. In addition, consultants are advising companies to plan for a variety of scenarios. Having strategies in place can potentially save a company, and periodic reviews of the budget can help companies identify changing scenarios and develop appropriate strategies. The effects of the recession might just change how finance departments view budgeting—for the better![5]

Discussion Questions

1. Why did UPS change its budgeting process?

2. What changes did UPS make in its budgeting?

3. Do you think that UPS's new budgeting process would work well during a more prosperous economic period?

annual report
summary of a firm's financial information, products, and growth plans for owners and potential investors

▼**FIGURE 14.1**
The Users of Accounting Information

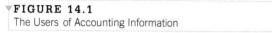

Source: Belverd E. Needles, Henry R. Anderson, and James C. Caldwell, *Principles of Accounting,* 4th edition. Copyright © 1990 by Houghton Mifflin Company. Reprinted with permission.

Financial statements evaluate the return on stockholders' investment and the overall quality of the firm's management team. As a result, poor performance, as documented in the financial statements, often results in changes in top management. Potential investors study the financial statements in a firm's annual report to determine whether the company meets their investment requirements and whether the returns from a given firm are likely to compare favorably with other similar companies.

Banks and other lenders look at financial statements to determine a company's ability to meet current and future debt obligations if a loan or credit is granted. To determine this ability, a short-term lender examines a firm's cash flow to assess its ability to repay a loan quickly with cash generated from sales. A long-term lender is more interested in the company's profitability and indebtedness to other lenders.

chief executive's office. Generally, the larger and more rapidly growing an organization, the greater will be the likelihood that it will build its master budget from the ground up.

Regardless of focus, the principal value of a budget lies in its breakdown of cash inflows and outflows. Expected operating expenses (cash outflows such as wages, materials costs, and taxes) and operating revenues (cash inflows in the form of payments from customers) over a set period of time are carefully forecast and subsequently compared with actual results. Deviations between the two serve as a "trip wire" or "feedback loop" to launch more detailed financial analyses in an effort to pinpoint trouble spots and opportunities.

External Uses Managers also use accounting statements to report the business's financial performance to outsiders. Such statements are used for filing income taxes, obtaining credit from lenders, and reporting results to the firm's stockholders. They become the basis for the information provided in the official corporate **annual report**, a summary of the firm's financial information, products, and growth plans for owners and potential investors. While frequently presented between slick, glossy covers prepared by major advertising firms, the single most important component of an annual report is the signature of a certified public accountant attesting that the required financial statements are an accurate reflection of the underlying financial condition of the firm. Financial statements meeting these conditions are termed *audited*. The primary external users of audited accounting information are government agencies, stockholders and potential investors, and lenders, suppliers, and employees.

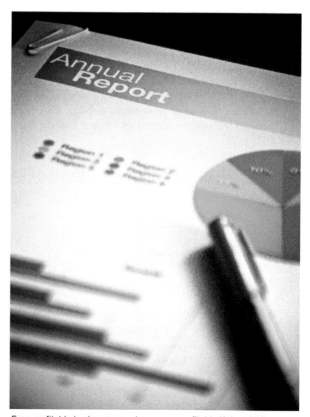

Even profitable businesses can become unprofitable if they don't manage their cash flows right.

As one of the biggest banks in the United States, Wells Fargo specializes in banking, mortgage, and financial services. The data it provides can be used in financial statements.

Labor unions and employees use financial statements to establish reasonable expectations for salary and other benefit requests. Just as firms experiencing record profits are likely to face added pressure to increase employee wages, so too are employees unlikely to grant employers wage and benefit concessions without considerable evidence of financial distress.

THE ACCOUNTING PROCESS

Many view accounting as a primary business language. It is of little use, however, unless you know how to "speak" it. Fortunately, the fundamentals—the accounting equation and the double-entry bookkeeping system—are not difficult to learn.

"Many view accounting as a primary business language."

BLOOM ENERGY SERVERS CUT COSTS, INCREASE SUSTAINABILITY

Bloom Energy has been flying under the radar for years, but now it is ready for the spotlight. With the help of $400 million from venture capitalists, the company has developed Energy Servers (power generators) that utilize new fuel cell technology to produce clean economical power on-site. These servers are designed to reduce electricity costs as well as greenhouse gas emissions. The commercial version now runs $700,000 to $800,000, and Bloom is working on a version for the private home. Fuel cell technology is nothing new, but Bloom CEO KR Sridhar says the company's proprietary technology utilizes low-cost materials—making it a more accessible option than those offered by rival companies. *Fortune* 500 companies have started purchasing Bloom's Energy Servers. Among users is Adobe Systems, which has installed the largest installation of Bloom Energy Servers to date, and eBay, which claims that its devices saved $100,000 on its power bill. Bloom's venture capital backers see the company as an important component in the overall quest toward clean but affordable electricity.[6]

assets
a firm's economic resources, or items of value that it owns, such as cash, inventory, land, equipment, buildings, and other tangible and intangible things

liabilities
debts that a firm owes to others

owners' equity
equals assets minus liabilities and reflects historical values

accounting equation
assets equal liabilities plus owners' equity

double-entry bookkeeping a system of recording and classifying business transactions that maintains the balance of the accounting equation

These two concepts serve as the starting point for all currently accepted accounting principles.

The Accounting Equation

Accountants are concerned with reporting an organization's assets, liabilities, and owners' equity. To help illustrate these concepts, consider a hypothetical floral shop called Anna's Flowers, owned by Anna Rodriguez. A firm's economic resources, or items of value that it owns, represent its **assets**—cash, inventory, land, equipment, buildings, and other tangible and intangible things. The assets of Anna's Flowers include counters, refrigerated display cases, flowers, decorations, vases, cards, and other gifts, as well as something known as "goodwill," which in this case is Anna's reputation for preparing and delivering beautiful floral arrangements on a timely basis. **Liabilities**, on the other hand, are debts the firm owes to others. Among the liabilities of Anna's Flowers are a loan from the Small Business Administration and money owed to flower suppliers and other creditors for items purchased. The **owners' equity** category contains all of the money that has ever been contributed to the company that never has to be paid back. The funds can come from investors who have given money or assets to the company, or it can come from past profitable operations. In the case of Anna's Flowers, if Anna were to sell off, or liquidate, her business, any money left over after selling all the shop's assets and paying off its liabilities would comprise her owners' equity. The relationship between assets, liabilities, and owners' equity is

a fundamental concept in accounting and is known as the **accounting equation**:

$$\text{Assets} = \text{Liabilities} + \text{Owners' equity}$$

Double-Entry Bookkeeping

Double-entry bookkeeping is a system of recording and classifying business transactions in separate accounts in order to maintain the balance of the accounting equation. Returning to Anna's Flowers, suppose Anna buys $325 worth of roses on credit from the Antique Rose Emporium to fill a wedding order. When she records this transaction, she will list the $325 as a liability or a debt to a supplier. At the same time, however, she will also record $325 worth of roses as an asset in an account known as "inventory." Because the assets and liabilities are on different sides of the accounting equation, Anna's accounts increase in total size (by $325) but remain in balance:

$$\text{Assets} = \text{Liabilities} + \text{Owners' equity}$$
$$\$325 = \$325$$

Thus, to keep the accounting equation in balance, each business transaction must be recorded in two separate accounts.

In the final analysis, all business transactions are classified as either assets, liabilities, or owners' equity. However, most organizations further break down these three accounts to provide more specific information about a transaction. For example, assets may be broken down into specific categories such as cash, inventory, and equipment, while liabilities may include bank loans, supplier credit, and other debts.

Figure 14.2 shows how Anna used the double-entry bookkeeping system to account for all of the transactions that took place in her first month of business. These transactions include her initial investment of $2,500, the loan from the Small Business Administration, purchases of equipment and inventory, and the purchase of roses on credit. In her first month of business, Anna generated revenues of $2,000 by selling $1,500 worth of inventory. Thus, she deducts, or (in accounting notation that is appropriate for assets) *credits,* $1,500 from inventory and adds, or *debits,* $2,000 to the cash account. The difference between Anna's $2,000 cash inflow and her $1,500 outflow is represented by a credit to owners' equity, because it is money that belongs to her as the owner of the flower shop.

A firm's assets include tangible items, as in the case of this restaurant's service tables, equipment, and even the atmosphere created by the wall's artwork.

accounting cycle
the four-step procedure of an
accounting system: examining
source documents, recording
transactions in an accounting
journal, posting recorded
transactions, and preparing
financial statements

journal a time-ordered list of
account transactions

ledger a book or computer file
with separate sections for each
account

The Accounting Cycle

In any accounting system, financial data typically pass through a four-step procedure sometimes called the **accounting cycle**. The steps include examining source documents, recording transactions in an accounting journal, posting recorded transactions, and preparing financial statements. Figure 14.3 shows how Anna works through them. Traditionally, all of these steps were performed using paper, pencils, and erasers (lots of erasers!), but today the process is often fully computerized.

Step One: Examine Source Documents Like all good managers, Anna Rodriguez begins the accounting cycle by gathering and examining source documents—checks, credit card receipts, sales slips, and other related evidence concerning specific transactions.

Step Two: Record Transactions Next, Anna records each financial transaction in a **journal**, which is basically just a time-ordered list of account transactions. While most businesses keep a general journal in which all transactions are recorded, some classify transactions into specialized journals for specific types of transaction accounts.

Step Three: Post Transactions Anna next transfers the information from her journal into a **ledger**, a book or computer program with separate files for each account. This process is known as *posting*. At the end of the accounting period (usually yearly, but occasionally quarterly or monthly), Anna prepares a *trial balance*, a summary of the balances of all the accounts in the general ledger. If, upon totaling, the trial balance doesn't balance (that is, the accounting equation is not in balance), Anna or her accountant must look for mistakes (typically an error in one or more of the ledger entries) and correct them. If the trial balance is correct, the accountant can then begin to prepare the financial statements.

Step Four: Prepare Financial Statements The information from the trial balance is also used to prepare the company's financial statements. In the case of public corporations and certain other organizations, a CPA must *attest,* or certify, that the organization followed generally accepted accounting principles in preparing the financial statements. When these statements have been completed, the organization's books are "closed," and the accounting cycle begins anew for the next accounting period.

FINANCIAL STATEMENTS

The end result of the accounting process is a series of financial statements. The income statement, the balance sheet, and the statement of cash flows are the best-known examples of financial statements. They are provided to stockholders and potential investors in a firm's annual report as well as to other relevant outsiders such as creditors, government agencies, and the Internal Revenue Service.

▼**FIGURE 14.2**

The Accounting Equation and Double-Entry Bookkeeping for Anna's Flowers

	Assets			= Liabilities	+	Owners' Equity
	Cash	Equipment	Inventory	Debts to suppliers	Loans	Equity
Cash invested by Anna	$2,500.00					$2,500.00
Loan from SBA	$5,000.00				$5,000.00	
Purchase of furnishings	–$3,000.00	$3,000.00				
Purchase of inventory	–$2,000.00		$2,000.00			
Purchase of roses			$325.00	$325.00		
First month sales	$2,000.00		–$1,500.00			$500.00
Totals	$4,500.00	$3,000.00	$825.00	$325.00	$5,000.00	$3,000.00
	$8,325			= $5,325	+	$3,000
	$8,325 Assets			= $8,325 (Liabilities + Owners' Equity)		

▼FIGURE 14.3
The Accounting Process for Anna's Flowers

Step 1:
Source documents
show that a
transaction
took place.

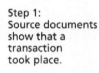

Receipt
Anna's Flowers

| July 7 | Wedding floral arrangements | $500.00 |
| | Consultation services | 250.00 |

Step 2:
The transaction
is recorded
in the journal.

Assets

Cash

| July 7 Brown wedding | $750.00 |

Step 3:
The transaction
is posted to the
general ledger
under the
appropriate
account (asset,
liability, or some
further breakdown
of these main
accounts).

Date		Explanation	PR	Debit	Credit	Balance Debit	Balance Credit
2011							
July	1		1	2,000		2,000	
	3		1		1,250		1,250
	4		1				
	7	Brown wedding	1		750		750
	14		1				

Step 4: At the end
of the accounting
period, the ledger
is used to prepare
the firm's financial
statements.

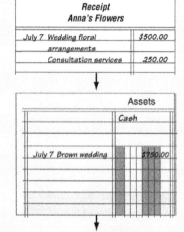

Anna's Flowers
Income Statement
December 31, 2011

Revenues:		
Net sales		$123,850
Consulting		73,850
Total revenues		$197,700
Expenses:		
Cost of goods sold	$72,600	
Selling expenses	37,700	
General and admin.	18,400	
Other expenses	5,600	
Total expenses		134,300
Net income		$ 63,400

Anna's Flowers
Balance Sheet
December 31, 2011

Assets
Current assets:

Cash	$17,850	
Accounts receivable	10,200	
Merch. Inventory	8,750	
Tot. assets		$36,800

Property and Equipment

Equipment	11,050	
Office building	73,850	
Tot. prop. & equip.		84,900
Total assets		$121,700

Liabilities and Owner's Equity
Current liabilities

Accounts payable	$12,600	
Tot. cur. liabilities		12,600

Long-term liabilities

Mortgage payable		23,600
Total liabilities		36,200

Owner's equity:

Anna Rodriguez, capital		$ 85,500
Tot. liabilities and owners' equity		$ 121,700

Anna's Flowers
Annual Budget
for 2011

	Sales	Consulting	Total
January	10,500	4,500	15,000
February	10,000	5,500	15,500
March	10,800	5,700	16,500
April	10,100	6,050	16,150
May	12,000	6,000	18,000
June	12,100	6,250	18,350
July	13,000	6,600	19,600
August	9,950	6,000	15,950
September	9,700	6,200	15,900
October	9,900	7,000	16,900
November	8,500	7,150	15,650
December	7,300	6,900	14,200
Annual	$123,850	$73,850	$197,700

income statement a financial report that shows an organization's profitability over a period of time— month, quarter, or year	**revenue** the total amount of money received from the sale of goods or services, as well as from related business activities	**cost of goods sold** the amount of money a firm spent to buy or produce the products it sold during the period to which the income statement applies	**gross income (or profit)** revenues minus the cost of goods sold required to generate the revenues	**expenses** the costs incurred in the day-to-day operations of an organization	**depreciation** the process of spreading the costs of long-lived assets such as buildings and equipment over the total number of accounting periods in which they are expected to be used	**net income** the total profit (or loss) after all expenses, including taxes, have been deducted from revenue; also called net earnings

It is important to recognize that not all financial statements follow precisely the same format. The fact that different organizations generate income in different ways suggests that when it comes to financial statements, one size definitely does not fit all. Manufacturing firms, service providers, and nonprofit organizations each use a different set of accounting principles or rules upon which the public accounting profession has agreed. As we have already mentioned, these are sometimes referred to as *generally accepted accounting principles (GAAP)*. Each country has a different set of rules that the businesses within that country are required to use for their accounting process and financial statements. Moreover, as is the case in many other disciplines, certain concepts have more than one name. For example, *sales* and *revenues* are often interchanged, as are *profits, income,* and *earnings.* Table 14.2 lists a few common equivalent terms that should help you decipher their meaning in accounting statements.

The Income Statement

The question, "What's the bottom line?" derives from the income statement, where the bottom line shows the overall profit or loss of the company after taxes. Thus, the **income statement** is a financial report that shows an organization's profitability over a period of time, be that a month, quarter, or year. By its very design, the income statement offers one of the clearest possible pictures of the company's overall revenues and the costs incurred in generating those revenues. Other names for the income statement include profit and loss (P&L) statement or operating statement. A sample income statement with line-by-line explanations is presented in Table 14.3, while Table 14.4 presents the income statement of Starbucks. The income statement indicates the firm's profitability or income (the bottom line), which is derived by subtracting the firm's expenses from its revenues.

Revenue **Revenue** is the total amount of money received (or promised) from the sale of goods or services, as well as from other business activities such as the rental of property and investments. Nonbusiness entities typically obtain revenues through donations from individuals and/or grants from governments and private foundations. Starbucks' income statement (see Table 14.4) shows three sources of revenue: retail sales, licensing, and food service.

For most manufacturing and retail concerns, the next major item included in the income statement is the **cost of goods sold,** the amount of money the firm spent (or promised to spend) to buy and/or produce the products it sold during the accounting period. This figure may be calculated as follows:

$$\text{Cost of goods sold} = \text{Beginning inventory} + \text{Interim purchases} - \text{Ending inventory}$$

Let's say that Anna's Flowers began an accounting period with an inventory of goods for which it paid $5,000. During the period, Anna bought another $4,000 worth of goods, giving the shop a total inventory available for sale of $9,000. If, at the end of the accounting period, Anna's inventory was worth $5,500, the cost of goods sold during the period would have been $3,500 ($5,000 + $4,000 − $5,500 = $3,500). If Anna had total revenues of $10,000 over the same period of time, subtracting the cost of goods sold ($3,500) from the total revenues of $10,000 yields the store's **gross income or profit** (revenues minus the cost of goods sold required to generate the revenues): $6,500. As indicated in Table 14.4, the cost of goods sold was just over $4.458 billion in 2010. Notice that Starbucks calls it cost of sales, rather than cost of goods sold. This is because Starbucks buys raw materials and supplies and produces drinks.

Expenses **Expenses** are the costs incurred in the day-to-day operations of an organization. Three common expense accounts shown on income statements are (1) selling, general,

▼ **TABLE 14.2** Equivalent Terms in Accounting

Term	Equivalent Term
Revenues	Sales
	Goods or services sold
Gross profit	Gross income
	Gross earnings
Operating income	Operating profit
	Earnings before interest and taxes (EBIT)
	Income before interest and taxes (IBIT)
Income before taxes (IBT)	Earnings before taxes (EBT)
	Profit before taxes (PBT)
Net income (NI)	Earnings after taxes (EAT)
	Profit after taxes (PAT)
Income available to common stockholders	Earnings available to common stockholders

▼ TABLE 14.3 Sample Income Statement

The following exhibit presents a sample income statement with all the terms defined and explained.

Company Name for the Year Ended December 31	
Revenues (sales)	Total dollar amount of products sold (includes income from other business services such as rental-lease income and interest income).
Less: Cost of goods sold	The cost of producing the goods and services, including the cost of labor and raw materials as well as other expenses associated with production.
Gross profit	The income available after paying all expenses of production.
Less: Selling and administrative expense	The cost of promoting, advertising, and selling products as well as the overhead costs of managing the company. This includes the cost of management and corporate staff. One non-cash expense included in this category is depreciation, which approximates the decline in the value of plant and equipment assets due to use over time. In most accounting statements, depreciation is not separated from selling and administrative expenses. However, financial analysts usually create statements that include this expense.
Income before interest and taxes (operating income or EBIT)	This line represents all income left over after operating expenses have been deducted. This is sometimes referred to as operating income since it represents all income after the expenses of operations have been accounted for. Occasionally, this is referred to as EBIT, or earnings before interest and taxes.
Less: Interest expense	Interest expense arises as a cost of borrowing money. This is a financial expense rather than an operating expense and is listed separately. As the amount of debt and the cost of debt increase, so will the interest expense. This covers the cost of both short-term and long-term borrowing.
Income before taxes (earnings before taxes—EBT)	The firm will pay a tax on this amount. This is what is left of revenues after subtracting all operating costs, depreciation costs, and interest costs.
Less: Taxes	The tax rate is specified in the federal tax code.
Net income	This is the amount of income left after taxes. The firm may decide to retain all or a portion of the income for reinvestment in new assets. Whatever it decides not to keep it will usually pay out in dividends to its stockholders.
Less: Preferred dividends	If the company has preferred stockholders, they are first in line for dividends. That is one reason why their stock is called "preferred."
Income to common stockholders	This is the income left for the common stockholders. If the company has a good year, there may be a lot of income available for dividends. If the company has a bad year, income could be negative. The common stockholders are the ultimate owners and risk takers. They have the potential for very high or very poor returns since they get whatever is left after all other expenses.
Earnings per share	Earnings per share is found by taking the income available to the common stockholders and dividing by the number of shares of common stock outstanding. This is income generated by the company for each share of common stock.

and administrative expenses; (2) research, development, and engineering expenses; and (3) interest expenses (remember that the costs directly attributable to selling goods or services are included in the cost of goods sold). Selling expenses include advertising and sales salaries. General and administrative expenses include salaries of executives and their staff and the costs of owning and maintaining the general office. Research and development costs include scientific, engineering, and marketing personnel and the equipment and information used to design and build prototypes and samples. Interest expenses include the direct costs of borrowing money.

The number and type of expense accounts vary from organization to organization. Included in the general and administrative category is a special type of expense known as **depreciation**, the process of spreading the costs of long-lived assets such as buildings and equipment over the total number of accounting periods in which they are expected to be used. Consider a manufacturer that purchases a $100,000 machine expected to last about 10 years. Rather than showing an expense of $100,000 in the first year and no expense for that equipment over the next nine years, the manufacturer is allowed to report depreciation expenses of $10,000 per year in each of the next 10 years because that better matches the cost of the machine to the years the machine is used. Each time this depreciation is "written off" as an expense, the book value of the machine is also reduced by $10,000. The fact that the equipment has a zero value on the firm's balance sheet when it is fully depreciated (in this case, after 10 years) does not necessarily mean that it can no longer be used or is economically worthless. Indeed, in some industries, machines used every day have been reported as having no book value whatsoever for more than 30 years.

Net Income **Net income** (or net earnings) is the total profit (or loss) after all expenses including taxes have been deducted from revenue. Generally, accountants divide profits

▼ **TABLE 14.4** Starbucks Corporation Consolidated Statements of Earnings (in millions, except earnings per share)

Report Date	10/03/2010	09/27/2009	09/28/2008
Net Revenues:			
Company-operated retail revenue	$ 8,963.5	$ 8,180.1	$ 8,771.9
Specialty:			
Licensing	1,340.9	1,222.3	1,171.6
Foodservice and other	403.0	372.2	439.5
Total specialty	1,743.9	1,594.5	1,611.1
Total net revenues	10,707.4	9,774.6	10,383
Cost of sales including occupancy costs	4,458.6	4,324.9	4,645.3
Store operating expenses	3,551.4	3,425.1	3,745.1
Other operating expenses	293.2	264.4	330.1
Depreciation and amortization expenses	510.4	534.7	549.3
General and administrative expenses	569.5	453.0	456.0
Restructuring charges	53.0	332.4	266.9
Total operating expenses	9,436.1	9,334.5	9,992.7
Income from equity investees	148.1	121.9	113.6
Operating income	1,419.4	562.0	503.9
Interest income and other income, net	50.3	37.0	9.0
Interest expense	(32.7)	(39.1)	(53.4)
Earnings before income taxes	1,437.0	559.9	455.7
Income taxes	488.7	168.4	144.0
Net earnings (attributable to Starbucks Corporation)	945.6	390.8	$ 315.5
Per common shares:			
Net earnings—basic	$ 1.27	$ 0.53	$ 0.43
Net earnings—diluted	$ 1.24	$ 0.52	$ 0.43
Weighted average shares outstanding:			
Basic	744.4	738.7	731.5
Diluted	764.2	745.9	741.7
Cash dividends per share	$0.36	$0	$0

Source: *Starbucks 2010 Annual Report,* page 39.

into individual sections such as operating income and earnings before interest and taxes. Starbucks, for example, lists earnings before income taxes, net earnings, and earnings per share of outstanding stock (see Table 14.4). Like most companies, Starbucks presents not only the current year's results but also the previous two years' income statements to permit comparison of performance from one period to another.

Temporary Nature of the Income Statement Accounts Companies record their operational activities in the revenue and expense accounts during an accounting period. Gross profit, earnings before interest and taxes, and net income are the results of calculations made from the revenues and expenses accounts; they are not actual accounts. At the end of each accounting period, the dollar amounts in all the revenue and expense accounts are moved into an account

called "Retained Earnings," one of the owners' equity accounts. Revenues increase owners' equity, while expenses decrease it. The resulting change in the owners' equity account is exactly equal to the net income. This shifting of dollar values from the revenue and expense accounts allows the firm to begin the next accounting period with zero balances in those accounts. Zeroing out the balances enables a company to count how much it has sold and how many expenses have been incurred during a period of time. The basic accounting equation (Assets = Liabilities + Owners' equity) will not balance until the revenue and expense account balances have been moved or "closed out" to the owners' equity account.

One final note about income statements: You may remember that corporations may choose to make cash payments called dividends to shareholders out of their net earnings. When a corporation elects to pay dividends, it decreases the cash account (in the assets category of the balance sheet) as well as a capital account (in the owners' equity category of the balance sheet). During any period of time, the owners' equity account may change because of the sale of stock (or contributions/withdrawals by owners), the net income or loss, or from the dividends paid.

The Balance Sheet

The second basic financial statement is the **balance sheet**, which presents a "snapshot" of an organization's financial position at a given moment. As such, the balance sheet indicates what the organization owns or controls and the various sources of the funds used to pay for these assets, such as bank debt or owners' equity.

The balance sheet takes its name from its reliance on the accounting equation: Assets *must* equal liabilities plus owners' equity. Table 14.5 provides a sample balance sheet with line-by-line explanations. Unlike the income statement, the balance sheet does not represent the result of transactions completed over a specified accounting period. Instead, the balance sheet is,

debts that management does not expect to collect. The bad-debts adjustment is normally based on historical collections experience and is deducted from the accounts receivable balance to present a more realistic view of the payments likely to be received in the future, called net receivables. Inventory may be held in the form of raw materials, work-in-progress, or finished goods ready for delivery.

Long-term, or fixed assets represent a commitment of organizational funds of at least one year. Items classified as fixed include long-term investments, plant and equipment, and intangible assets, such as corporate "goodwill," or reputation, as well as patents and trademarks.

Liabilities As seen in the accounting equation, total assets must be financed either through borrowing (liabilities) or through owner investments (owners' equity). **Current liabilities** include

> **balance sheet**
> a "snapshot" of an organization's financial position at a given moment
>
> **current assets**
> assets that are used or converted into cash within the course of a calendar year
>
> **accounts receivable** money owed a company by its clients or customers who have promised to pay for the products at a later date

> "The balance sheet takes its name from its reliance on the accounting equation: Assets *must* equal liabilities plus owners' equity."

by definition, an accumulation of all financial transactions conducted by an organization since its founding. Following long-established traditions, items on the balance sheet are listed on the basis of their original cost less accumulated depreciation, rather than their present values.

Balance sheets are often presented in two different formats. The traditional balance sheet format placed the organization's assets on the left side and its liabilities and owners' equity on the right. More recently, a vertical format, with assets on top followed by liabilities and owners' equity, has gained wide acceptance. Starbucks' balance sheet for 2009 and 2010 is presented in Table 14.6. In the sections that follow, we'll briefly describe the basic items found on the balance sheet; we'll take a closer look at a number of these in Chapter 16.

Assets All asset accounts are listed in descending order of *liquidity*—that is, how quickly each could be turned into cash. **Current assets**, also called short-term assets, are those that are used or converted into cash within the course of a calendar year. Cash is followed by temporary investments, accounts receivable, and inventory, in that order. **Accounts receivable** refers to money owed the company by its clients or customers who have promised to pay for the products at a later date. Accounts receivable usually includes an allowance for bad

This type of machinery would be considered a long-term asset on the balance sheet.

▼ **TABLE 14.5** Sample Balance Sheet

The following exhibit presents a balance sheet in word form with each item defined or explained.

Typical Company December 31	
Assets	This is the major category for all physical, monetary, or intangible goods that have some dollar value.
Current assets	Assets that are either cash or are expected to be turned into cash within the next 12 months.
Cash	Cash or checking accounts.
Marketable securities	Short-term investments in securities that can be converted to cash quickly (liquid assets).
Accounts receivable	Cash due from customers in payment for goods received. These arise from sales made on credit.
Inventory	Finished goods ready for sale, goods in the process of being finished, or raw materials used in the production of goods.
Prepaid expense	A future expense item that has already been paid, such as insurance premiums or rent.
Total current assets	The sum of the above accounts.
Fixed assets	Assets that are long term in nature and have a minimum life expectancy that exceeds one year.
Investments	Assets held as investments rather than assets owned for the production process. Most often the assets include small ownership interests in other companies.
Gross property, plant, and equipment	Land, buildings, and other fixed assets listed at original cost.
Less: Accumulated depreciation	The accumulated expense deductions applied to all plant and equipment over their life. Land may not be depreciated. The total amount represents in general the decline in value as equipment gets older and wears out. The maximum amount that can be deducted is set by the U.S. Federal Tax Code and varies by type of asset.
Net property, plant, and equipment	Gross property, plant, and equipment minus the accumulated depreciation. This amount reflects the book value of the fixed assets and not their value if sold.
Other assets	Any other asset that is long term and does not fit into the above categories. It could be patents or trademarks.
Total assets	The sum of all the asset values.
Liabilities and Stockholders' Equity	This is the major category. Liabilities refer to all indebtedness and loans of both a long-term and short-term nature. Stockholders' equity refers to all money that has been contributed to the company over the life of the firm by the owners.
Current liabilities	Short-term debt expected to be paid off within the next 12 months.
Accounts payable	Money owed to suppliers for goods ordered. Firms usually have between 30 and 90 days to pay this account, depending on industry norms.
Wages payable	Money owned to employees for hours worked or salary. If workers receive checks every two weeks, the amount owed should be no more than two weeks' pay.
Taxes payable	Firms are required to pay corporate taxes quarterly. This refers to taxes owed based on earnings estimates for the quarter.
Notes payable	Short-term loans from banks or other lenders.
Other current liabilities	The other short-term debts that do not fit into the above categories.
Total current liabilities	The sum of the above accounts.
Long-term liabilities	All long-term debt that will not be paid off in the next 12 months.
Long-term debt	Loans of more than one year from banks, pension funds, insurance companies, or other lenders. These loans often take the form of bonds, which are securities that may be bought and sold in bond markets.
Deferred income taxes	This is a liability owed to the government but not due within one year.
Other liabilities	Any other long-term debt that does not fit the above two categories.
Stockholders' equity	The following categories are the owners' investment in the company.
Common stock	The tangible evidence of ownership is a security called common stock. The par value is stated value and does not indicate the company's worth.
Capital in excess of par (a.k.a. contributed capital)	When shares of stock were sold to the owners, they were recorded at the price at the time of the original sale. If the price paid was $10 per share, the extra $9 per share would show up in this account at 100,000 shares times $9 per share, or $900,000.
Retained earnings	The total amount of earnings the company has made during its life and not paid out to its stockholders as dividends. This account represents the owners' reinvestment of earnings into company assets rather than payments of cash dividends. This account does not represent cash.
Total stockholders' equity	This is the sum of the above equity accounts representing the owner's total investment in the company.
Total liabilities and stockholders' equity	The total short-term and long-term debt of the company plus the owner's total investment. This combined amount *must* equal total assets.

▼ **TABLE 14.6**   Starbucks Corporation Consolidated Balance Sheet (in thousands, except per share data)

Fiscal Year Ended	10/03/2010	09/27/2009
Assets		
Current assets		
Cash and cash equivalents	$ 1,164.0	$ 599.8
Short-term investments—available-for-sale securities	236.5	21.5
Short-term investments—trading securities	49.2	44.8
Accounts receivable, net	302.7	271.0
Inventory	543.3	664.9
Prepaid expenses and other current assets	156.5	147.2
Deferred income taxes, net	304.2	286.6
Total current assets	2,756.4	2,035.8
Long-term investments—available-for-sale securities	191.8	71.2
Equity and cost investments	341.5	352.3
Property, plant and equipment, net	2,416.5	2,536.4
Other assets	346.5	253.8
Other intangible assets	70.8	68.2
Goodwill	262.4	259.1
Total assets	$ 6,385.9	$ 5,576.8
Liabilities and shareholders' equity		
Current Liabilities:		
Accounts payable	282.6	267.1
Accrued compensation and related costs	400.0	307.5
Accrued occupancy costs	173.2	188.1
Accrued taxes	100.2	127.8
Insurance reserves	146.2	154.3
Other accrued expenses	262.8	147.3
Deferred revenue	414.1	388.7
Current portion of long-term debt	—	0.2
Total current liabilities	1,779.1	1,581.0
Long-term debt	549.4	549.3
Other long-term liabilities	375.1	389.6
Total liabilities	2,703.6	2,519.9
Shareholders' equity:		
Common stock	0.7	0.7
Additional paid-in capital	106.2	147.0
Other additional paid-in capital	39.4	39.4
Retained earnings (accumulated deficit)	3,471.2	2,793.2
Accumulated other comprehensive income (loss)	57.2	65.4
Total shareholders' equity	3,674.7	3,045.7
Noncontrolling Interests	7.6	11.2
Total shareholders' equity	3,682.3	3,056.9
Total liabilities and shareholders' equity	$ 6,385.9	$ 5,576.8

Source: *2010 Starbucks Annual Report,* page 40.

current liabilities
a firm's financial obligations
to short-term creditors,
which must be repaid
within one year

accounts payable
the amount a company
owes to suppliers for goods
and services purchased
with credit

accrued expenses
an account representing all
unpaid financial obligations
incurred by the organization

**statement of cash
flows** explains how the
company's cash changed
from the beginning of the
accounting period to the
end

a firm's financial obligations to short-term creditors, which must be repaid within one year, while long-term liabilities have longer repayment terms. **Accounts payable** represents amounts owed to suppliers for goods and services purchased with credit. For example, if you buy gas with a BP credit card, the purchase represents an account payable for you (and an account receivable for BP). Other liabilities include wages earned by employees but not yet paid and taxes owed to the government. Occasionally, these accounts are consolidated into an **accrued expenses** account, representing all unpaid financial obligations incurred by the organization.

Owners' Equity Owners' equity includes the owners' contributions to the organization along with income earned by the organization and retained to finance continued growth and development. If the organization were to sell off all of its assets and pay off all of its liabilities, any remaining funds would belong to the owners. Not surprisingly, the accounts listed as owners' equity on a balance sheet may differ dramatically from company to company. Corporations sell stock to investors, who then become the owners of the firm. Many corporations issue two, three, or even more different classes of

common and preferred stock, each with different dividend payments and/or voting rights. Because each type of stock issued represents a different claim on the organization, each must be represented by a separate owners' equity account, called contributed capital.

The Statement of Cash Flows

The third primary financial statement is called the **statement of cash flows**, which explains how the company's cash changed from the beginning of the accounting period to the end. Cash, of course, is an asset shown on the balance sheet, which provides a snapshot of the firm's financial position at one point in time. However, many investors and other users of financial statements want more information about the cash flowing into and out of the firm than is provided on the balance sheet in order to better understand the company's financial health. The statement of cash flows takes the cash balance from one year's balance sheet and compares it with the next while providing detail about how the firm used the cash. Table 14.7 presents Starbucks' statement of cash flows.

The change in cash is explained through details in three categories: cash from (used for) operating activities, cash from (used for) investing activities, and cash from (used for) financing

▼ **TABLE 14.7** Starbucks Corporation Consolidated Statements of Cash Flows (in millions)

Report Date	10/03/2010	09/27/2009	09/28/2008
Net earnings	$ 948.3	$ 390.8	$ 315.5
Adjustments to reconcile net earnings to net cash provided by operating activities:			
Depreciation and amortization	540.8	563.3	604.5
Provision for impairments and asset disposals	67.7	224.4	325.0
Deferred income taxes	(42.0)	(69.6)	(117.1)
Equity in income of investees	(108.6)	(78.4)	(61.3)
Distributions of income from equity investees	91.4	53.0	52.6
Stock-based compensation	113.6	83.2	75.0
Tax benefit from exercise of stock options	13.5	2.0	3.8
Excess tax benefit from exercise of stock options	(36.9)	(15.9)	(14.7)
Other	(15.3)	5.4	(0.1)
Cash provided/(used) by changes in operating assets and liabilities:			
Inventories	123.2	28.5	(0.6)
Accounts payable	(3.6)	(53.0)	(63.9)
Accrued taxes	(12.9)	57.2	7.3
Deferred revenue	24.2	16.3	72.4
Other operating assets	(16.1)	120.5	(11.2)
Other operating liabilities	17.6	61.3	71.5

(*continued*)

▼ **TABLE 14.7** *continued*

Report Date	10/03/2010	09/27/2009	09/28/2008
Net cash provided by operating activities	1,704.9	1,389.0	1,258.7
Investing Activities:			
Purchase of available-for-sale securities	(549.0)	(129.2)	(71.8)
Maturities and calls of available-for-sale securities	209.9	111.0	20.0
Sales of available-for-sale securities	1.1	5.0	75.9
Acquisitions, net of cash acquired	(12.0)	—	(74.2)
Net purchases of equity, other investments and other assets	1.2	(4.8)	(52.0)
Additions to property, plant and equipment	(440.7)	(445.6)	(984.5)
Proceeds from sale of property, plant and equipment	0	42.5	—
Net cash used by investing activities	(789.5)	(421.1)	(1,086.6)
Financing Activities:			
Proceeds from issuance of commercial paper	0	20,965.4	65,770.8
Repayments of commercial paper	0	(21,378.5)	(66,068.0)
Proceeds from short-term borrowings	0	1,338.0	528.2
Repayments of short-term borrowings	0	(1,638.0)	(228.8)
Purchase of noncontrolling interest	(45.8)	—	—
Proceeds from issuance of common stock	127.9	57.3	112.3
Excess tax benefit from exercise of stock options	36.9	15.9	14.7
Principal payments on long-term debt	(6.6)	(0.7)	(0.6)
Cash dividends paid	(171.0)	—	—
Repurchase of common stock	(285.6)	—	(311.4)
Other	(1.8)	(1.6)	(1.7)
Net cash used by financing activities	(346.0)	(642.2)	(184.5)
Effect of exchange rate changes on cash and cash equivalents	(5.2)	4.3	0.9
Net increase (decrease) in cash and cash equivalents	564.2	330.0	(11.5)
Cash and Cash Equivalents:			
Beginning of Period	599.8	269.8	281.3
End of Period	1,164.0	599.8	269.8
Supplemental Disclosure of Cash Flow Information:			
Cash paid during the period for:			
Interest, net of capitalized interest	32.0	39.8	52.7
Income taxes	527.0	162.0	259.5

Source: *Starbucks 2010 Annual Report.*

activities. *Cash from operating activities* is calculated by combining the changes in the revenue accounts, expense accounts, current asset accounts, and current liability accounts. This category of cash flows includes all the accounts on the balance sheet that relate to computing revenues and expenses for the accounting period. If this amount is a positive number, as it is for Starbucks, then the business is making extra cash that it can use to invest in increased long-term capacity or to pay off debts such as loans or bonds. A negative number may indicate a business that is in a declining position with regards to operations.

Negative cash flow is not always a bad thing, however. It may indicate that a business is growing, with a very negative cash flow indicating rapid growth.

Cash from investing activities is calculated from changes in the long-term or fixed asset accounts. If this amount is negative, as is the case with Starbucks, the company is purchasing long-term assets for future growth. A positive figure indicates a business that is selling off existing long-term assets and reducing its capacity for the future.

ratio analysis calculations that measure an organization's financial health

profitability ratios ratios that measure the amount of operating income or net income an organization is able to generate relative to its assets, owners' equity, and sales

profit margin net income divided by sales

return on assets net income divided by assets

stated goals, that really matters. Remember, while the profitability, asset utilization, liquidity, debt ratios, and per share data we'll look at here can be very useful, you will never see the forest by looking only at the trees.

Profitability Ratios

Profitability ratios measure how much operating income or net income an organization is able to generate relative to its assets, owners' equity, and sales. The numerator (top number) used in these examples is always the net income after taxes. Common profitability ratios include profit margin, return on assets, and return on equity. The following examples are based on the 2010 income statement and balance sheet for Starbucks, as shown in Tables 14.4 and 14.6. Except where specified, all data are expressed in millions of dollars.

Finally, *cash from financing activities* is calculated from changes in the long-term liability accounts and the contributed capital accounts in owners' equity. If this amount is negative, the company is likely paying off long-term debt or returning contributed capital to investors. As in the case of Starbucks, if this amount is positive, the company is either borrowing more money or raising money from investors by selling more shares of stock.

RATIO ANALYSIS: ANALYZING FINANCIAL STATEMENTS

The income statement shows a company's profit or loss, while the balance sheet itemizes the value of its assets, liabilities, and owners' equity. Together, the two statements provide the means to answer two critical questions: (1) How much did the firm make or lose? and (2) How much is the firm presently worth based on historical values found on the balance sheet? **Ratio analysis**, calculations that measure an organization's financial health, brings the complex information from the income statement and balance sheet into sharper focus so that managers, lenders, owners, and other interested parties can measure and compare the organization's productivity, profitability, and financing mix with other similar entities.

As you know, a ratio is simply one number divided by another, with the result showing the relationship between the two numbers. Financial ratios are used to weigh and evaluate a firm's performance. An absolute value such as earnings of $70,000 or accounts receivable of $200,000 almost never provides as much useful information as a well-constructed ratio. Whether those numbers are good or bad depends on their relation to other numbers. If a company earned $70,000 on $700,000 in sales (a 10 percent return), such an earnings level might be quite satisfactory. The president of a company earning this same $70,000 on sales of $7 million (a 1 percent return), however, should probably start looking for another job!

Ratios by themselves are not very useful. It is the relationship of the calculated ratios to both prior organizational performance and the performance of the organization's "peers," as well as its

The **profit margin**, computed by dividing net income by sales, shows the overall percentage profits earned by the company. It is based solely upon data obtained from the income statement. The higher the profit margin, the better the cost controls within the company and the higher the return on every dollar of revenue. Starbucks' profit margin is calculated as follows:

$$\text{Profit margin} = \frac{\text{Net income (Net earnings)}}{\text{Sales (Total net revenues)}}$$
$$= \frac{\$945.6}{\$10,707.4}$$
$$= 8.83\%$$

Thus, for every $1 in sales, Starbucks generated profits of 8.8 cents.

Return on assets, net income divided by assets, shows how much income the firm produces for every dollar invested in assets. A company with a low return on assets is probably not using its assets very productively—a key managerial failing. For its construction, the return on assets calculation requires data from both the income statement and the balance sheet.

$$\text{Return on assets} = \frac{\text{Net income (Net earnings)}}{\text{Total assets}}$$
$$= \frac{\$945.6}{\$6385.9}$$
$$= 14.81\%$$

In the case of Starbucks, every $1 of assets generated a return of around 14.8 percent, or profits of around 14.81 cents per dollar.

> "Profitability ratios measure how much operating income or net income an organization is able to generate relative to its assets, owners' equity, and sales."

return on equity net income divided by owners' equity; also called return on investment (ROI)

asset utilization ratios ratios that measure how well a firm uses its assets to generate each $1 of sales

receivables turnover sales divided by accounts receivable

inventory turnover sales divided by total inventory

total asset turnover sales divided by total assets

liquidity ratios ratios that measure the speed with which a company can turn its assets into cash to meet short-term debt

current ratio current assets divided by current liabilities

Stockholders are always concerned with how much money they will make on their investment, and they frequently use the return on equity ratio as one of their key performance yardsticks. **Return on equity** (also called return on investment [ROI]), calculated by dividing net income by owners' equity, shows how much income is generated by each $1 the owners have invested in the firm. Obviously, a low return on equity means low stockholder returns and may indicate a need for immediate managerial attention. Because some assets may have been financed with debt not contributed by the owners, the value of the owners' equity is usually considerably lower than the total value of the firm's assets. Starbucks' return on equity is calculated as follows:

$$\text{Return on equity} = \frac{\text{Net income}}{\text{Stockholders' equity}}$$
$$= \frac{\$945.6}{\$3,674.7}$$
$$= 25.73\%$$

For every dollar invested by Starbucks stockholders, the company earned around a 25.7 percent return, or 25.73 cents per dollar invested.

Asset Utilization Ratios

Asset utilization ratios measure how well a firm uses its assets to generate each $1 of sales. Obviously, companies using their assets more productively will have higher returns on assets than their less efficient competitors. Similarly, managers can use asset utilization ratios to pinpoint areas of inefficiency in their operations. These ratios (receivables turnover, inventory turnover, and total asset turnover) relate balance sheet assets to sales, which are found on the income statement.

The **receivables turnover**, sales divided by accounts receivable, indicates how many times a firm collects its accounts receivable in one year. It also demonstrates how quickly a firm is able to collect payments on its credit sales. Obviously, no payments means no profits. Starbucks collected its receivables 35 to 36 times per year. The reason the number is so high is that most of Starbucks' sales are for cash and not credit.

Receivables turnover
$$= \frac{\text{Sales (Total net revenues)}}{\text{Receivables}}$$
$$= \frac{\$10,707.4}{\$302.7}$$
$$= 35.37\text{X}$$

Inventory turnover, sales divided by total inventory, indicates how many times a firm sells and replaces its inventory over the course of a year. A high inventory turnover ratio may indicate great efficiency but may also suggest the possibility of lost sales due to insufficient stock levels. Starbucks' inventory turnover indicates that it replaced its inventory approximately 20 times last year, or almost twice a month.

Inventory turnover
$$= \frac{\text{Sales (Total net revenues)}}{\text{Inventory}}$$
$$= \frac{\$10,707.4}{\$543.3}$$
$$= 19.71\text{X}$$

Total asset turnover, sales divided by total assets, measures how well an organization uses all of its assets in creating sales. It indicates whether a company is using its assets productively. Starbucks generated $1.68 in sales for every $1 in total corporate assets.

Total asset turnover
$$= \frac{\text{Sales (Total net revenues)}}{\text{Total assets}}$$
$$= \frac{\$10,707.4}{\$6,385.9}$$
$$= 1.68\text{X}$$

Liquidity Ratios

Liquidity ratios compare current (short-term) assets to current liabilities to indicate the speed with which a company can turn its assets into cash to meet debts as they fall due. High liquidity ratios may satisfy a creditor's need for safety, but ratios that are too high may indicate that the organization is not using its current assets efficiently. Liquidity ratios are generally best examined in conjunction with asset utilization ratios because high turnover ratios imply that cash is flowing through an organization very quickly—a situation that dramatically reduces the need for the type of reserves measured by liquidity ratios.

The **current ratio** is calculated by dividing current assets by current liabilities. Starbucks's current ratio indicates that for every $1 of current liabilities, the firm had $1.55 of current assets on hand. This number improved from previous years, and indicates that Starbucks has increased its liquidity as it restructures its business. Although current liabilities increased from 2009 to 2010, current assets also increased during this period, making for a much improved current ratio. Additionally, accounts receivable has increased over the same time period.

$$\text{Current ratio} = \frac{\text{Current assets}}{\text{Current liabilities}}$$
$$= \frac{\$2,756.4}{\$1,779.1}$$
$$= 1.55X$$

The **quick ratio** (also known as the **acid test**) is a far more stringent measure of liquidity because it eliminates inventory, the least liquid current asset. It measures how well an organization can meet its current obligations without resorting to the sale of its inventory. In 2010, Starbucks had 1.24 cents invested in current assets (after subtracting inventory) for every $1 of current liabilities, an increase over previous years.

$$\text{Quick ratio} = \frac{\text{Current assets} - \text{Inventory}}{\text{Current liabilities}}$$
$$= \frac{\$2,213.1}{\$1,779.1}$$
$$= 1.24X$$

Debt Utilization Ratios

Debt utilization ratios provide information about how much debt an organization is using relative to other sources of capital, such as owners' equity. Because the use of debt carries an interest charge that must be paid regularly regardless of profitability, debt financing is much riskier than equity. Unforeseen negative events such as recessions affect heavily indebted firms to a far greater extent than those financed exclusively with owners' equity. Because of this and other factors, the managers of most firms tend to keep debt-to-asset levels below 50 percent. However, firms in very stable and/or regulated industries, such as electric utilities, often are able to carry debt ratios well in excess of 50 percent with no ill effects.

The **debt to total assets ratio** indicates how much of the firm is financed by debt and how much by owners' equity. To find the value of Starbucks' total debt, you must add current liabilities to long-term debt and other liabilities.

$$\text{Debt to total assets} = \frac{\text{Debt (Total liabilities)}}{\text{Total assets}}$$
$$= \frac{\$2,703.6}{\$6,385.9}$$
$$= 42.3\%$$

Thus, for every $1 of Starbucks' total assets, 42.3 percent is financed with debt. The remaining 55 percent is provided by owners' equity.

The **times interest earned ratio**, operating income divided by interest expense, is a measure of the safety margin a company has with respect to the interest payments it must make to its creditors. A low times interest earned ratio indicates that even a small decrease in earnings may lead the company into financial straits. Because Starbucks has more interest income than interest expense, it would appear that their times interest earned ratio is not able to be calculated by using the income statement. However, in the statement of cash flows in Table 14.7 on the second line from the bottom, we can see that Starbucks paid $32.7 million in interest expense, an amount that was covered nearly 43.4 times by income before interest and taxes. A lender would probably not have to worry about receiving interest payments.

$$\text{Time interest earned} = \frac{\text{EBIT (Operating income)}}{\text{Interest}}$$
$$= \frac{\$1,419.4}{\$32.7}$$
$$= 43.4X$$

Per Share Data

Investors may use **per share data** to compare the performance of one company with another on an equal, or per share, basis. Generally, the more shares of stock a company issues, the less income is available for each share.

Earnings per share is calculated by dividing net income or profit by the number of shares of stock outstanding. This ratio is important because yearly changes in earnings per share, in combination with other economywide factors, determine a company's overall stock price. When earnings go up, so does a company's stock price—and so does the wealth of its stockholders.

$$\text{Diluted earnings per share} = \frac{\text{Net income}}{\text{Number of shares outstanding (diluted)}}$$
$$= \frac{\$945.6}{764.2}$$
$$= \$1.24$$

We can see from the income statement that Starbucks' basic earnings per share increased from $0.53 in 2009 to $1.27 in 2010. Notice that Starbucks lists diluted earnings per share, calculated here, of $0.52 per share in 2009 and $1.24 per share in 2010. You can see from the income statement that diluted earnings per share include more shares than the basic calculation; this is because diluted shares include potential shares that could be issued due to the exercise of stock options or the conversion of certain types of debt into common stock. Investors generally pay more attention to diluted earnings per share than basic earnings per share.

Dividends per share are paid by the corporation to the stockholders for each share owned. The payment is made from earnings after taxes by the corporation but is taxable income to the stockholder. Thus, dividends result in double taxation: The corporation pays tax once on its earnings, and the stockholder pays tax a second time on his or her dividend income. Starbucks paid dividends of $171 million in 2010. For each share owned, Starbucks paid a 23-cent dividend.

Dividents per share paid*

$$= \frac{\text{Dividents paid}}{\text{Number of shares outstanding}}$$

$$= \frac{\$171}{746.2}$$

$$= \$0.23$$

*The income statement shows $0.36 declared but not necessarily paid in 2010.

Industry Analysis

We have used McDonald's as a comparison to Starbucks because there are no real national and international coffee houses that compete with Starbucks on the same scale. While McDonald's is almost four times larger than Starbucks in terms of sales, they both have a national and international presence and to some extent compete for the consumer's dollars. Table 14.8 shows that McDonald's dominates Starbucks in areas of profitability. Since 2007, McDonald's has doubled its profitability. Starbucks stumbled somewhat during the recession years but has since rebounded. Both companies have very little accounts receivable relative to the size of their sales, and so the ratios are very high, indicating a lot of cash sales and credit card sales. McDonald's pushes off much of its inventory holding costs on its suppliers, and so has much less inventory per sales dollar compared with Starbucks and, therefore, has a much higher inventory turnover ratio. Both have current ratios about the same, but because McDonald's has less inventory, its quick ratio is higher than Starbucks. Fortunately for Starbucks, its inventory is highly liquid and can be turned into cash quickly. The difference in the quick ratios is of little consequence to the financial analyst or lender because both companies have high times interest earned ratios. The return of Starbucks founder Howard Schultz and

the introduction of new Starbucks products has helped Starbucks recover from its lower earning levels during the 2008–2009 recession. Its earnings per share has increased from $0.52 in 2009 to $1.24 a year later. On the other hand, McDonald's has increased its earnings per share from $1.93 in 2007 to $4.58 in 2010. McDonald's has also increased its dividend over this time period from $1.50 per share to $2.26 per share, whereas Starbucks paid its first dividends in 2010 after years of reinvesting in the company's expansion and debt

earnings per share net income or profit divided by the number of stock shares outstanding

dividends per share the actual cash received for each share owned

▼ **TABLE 14.8** Industry Analysis, Year Ending 2010

	Starbucks	McDonald's
Profit margin	8.83%	20.55%
Return on assets	14.81%	15.47%
Return on equity	25.73%	33.80%
Receivables turnover	35.37X	20.41X
Inventory turnover	19.71X	219.05X
Total asset turnover	1.68X	0.75 X
Current ratio	1.55X	1.49 X
Quick ratio	1.24X	1.46 X
Debt to total assets	42.3%	54.23%
Times interest earned	43.4 X	16.57X
Diluted earnings per share	$1.24	$4.58
Dividends per share paid	$0.23	$2.26

Source: Data calculated from 2010 annual reports.

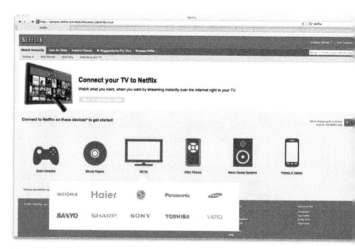

Many of Netflix's financial ratios were higher than the industry average. However, after the company raised the price on one of its most popular rental plans, the value of its stock price fell significantly. This could impact Netflix's future financial ratios.

CERTIFIED FRAUD EXAMINERS REPORT ON FRAUDSTERS

A recent survey reported bad news for business owners. Despite regulations, corporate scandals, and external controls, fraud is still lurking among businesses. In a survey of 1,842 global fraud investigators, the Association of Certified Fraud Examiners (ACFE) revealed that fraud remains difficult to spot. In fact, it can take almost two years on average to recognize that fraud is taking place.

Accounting controls alone are not reliable for catching fraudulent behavior. Instead, it is often up to employees to blow the whistle. The ACFE states that "tip-offs" remain the most effective means of catching a thief, revealing fraud three times as often as traditional reviews and accounting checks and balances. Unfortunately, many employees fear that if they reveal fraud, they will face reprisals from supervisors or fellow employees. This is not totally unjustified; whistleblowers at Enron, for example, were threatened with firing. Only 7.4 percent of companies praise employees who come forward with information.

To curb fraud, therefore, managers must find ways to encourage employees to step forward. One way is to set up anonymous employee hotlines and to ask all employees, no matter how senior, to submit to routine screenings and attend trainings. To be safe, employers should also keep an eye out for lifestyle changes among employees. An upturn in an employee's fortunes may point to fraud.

Fraud is not disappearing anytime soon. In the meantime, it is costing U.S. companies median losses of anywhere from $80,000 to $150,000. To keep fraud from taking over, companies would be wise to alter their cultures to provide employees with safe methods for reporting suspected fraud. Vigilant accounting is simply not enough to catch every fraudster.[7]

Discussion Questions

1. Why do you think fraud is a significant financial issue in most businesses?
2. What is the best way to prevent fraud?
3. As a manager, how would you try to detect fraud?

---

reduction. Both companies are in good financial health, but McDonald's is winning the race for stockholder returns. One thing is for sure: If Starbucks could earn the same profit margin as McDonald's, it would improve its other profitability ratios and its stock price.

ACCOUNTING AND THE IMPACT OF THE FINANCIAL CRISIS

The financial crisis of 2007–2009 provided another example of failed accounting audits. Banks and other financial institutions often held assets off their books by manipulating their accounts. In 2010, the examiner for the Lehman Brothers' bankruptcy found that the most common example of removing assets or liabilities from the books was entering into what is called a "repurchase agreement." In a repurchase agreement, assets are transferred to another entity with the contractual promise of buying them back at a set price. In the case of Lehman Brothers and other companies, repurchase agreements were used as a method of "cooking the books" that allowed them to manipulate accounting statements so that their ratios looked better than they actually were. If the accountants, the SEC, and the bank regulators had been more careful, these types of transactions would have been discovered and corrected. The public discovered that the audit system failed with Lehman Brothers and many other major financial firms during the 2008 crisis on Wall Street.

Banks and other financial companies blamed much of the problem on the accounting rule of mark-to-market, which was also used by Enron to make it look more profitable. This rule meant that assets on the books have to be carried on the books at the current market price. As the financial markets deteriorated, the value of many assets (such as mortgages) could not be valued accurately. What happens when a market is so unhealthy that it basically ceases to function? Is the asset worth zero? Because the value of the assets held on their books determined a bank's capital adequacy ratios, the decline in value that resulted from using the mark-to-market accounting method made banks' capital appear to shrink dramatically. Investors determined that these banks were suddenly risky investments. The government determined that it had to step in and allow banks to revalue assets. Many think this was helpful in stemming the deterioration of banks' capital. Some accountants, however, argued that the mark-to-market rule creates a more honest balance sheet and true value of a company's worth. This may be true under normal circumstances, where markets are not frozen and investors continue to trade and trust the financial stability of their trading partners. These issues will continue to be addressed by the government in future financial reform.

Banks were not the only institutions engaging in high-risk behavior. During the global financial crisis, it was revealed that Greece had also been engaging in deceptive

TEAM EXERCISE

You can look at websites such as Yahoo! Finance (http://finance.yahoo.com/), under the company's "'key statistics'" link, to find many of its financial ratios, such as return on assets and return on equity. Have each member of your team look up a different company, and explain why you think there are differences in the ratio analysis for these two ratios among the selected companies.

accounting practices, with the help of U.S. investment banks. Greece was using financial techniques that hid massive amounts of debt from its public balance sheets. Eventually, the markets figured out that the country was up to its ears in debt and might not be able to pay off its creditors. The European Union and the International Monetary Fund came up with a plan to give Greece some credit relief, but tied to this was the message to "get your financial house in order."

To top this off, *The New York Times* reported that many states, such as Illinois and California, seem to have the same problems as Greece—debt overload. These states have "budgets that will not balance, accounting that masks debt, the use of derivatives to plug holes, and armies of retired public workers who are counting on benefits that are proving harder and harder to pay." Clearly, the financial crisis will have some lasting effects that need clear accounting solutions.[8] ▪

SO YOU WANT TO BE // an Accountant /

Do you like numbers and finances? Are you detail oriented, a perfectionist, and highly accountable for your decisions? If so, accounting may be a good field for you. If you are interested in accounting, there are always job opportunities available no matter the state of the economy. Accounting is one of the most secure job options in business. Of course, becoming an accountant is not easy. You will need at least a bachelor's degree in accounting to get a job, and many positions require additional training. Many states demand coursework beyond the 120 to 150 credit hours collegiate programs require for an accounting degree. If you are really serious about getting into the accounting field, you will probably want to consider getting your master's in accounting and taking the CPA exam. The field of accounting can be complicated, and the extra training provided through a master's in accounting program will prove invaluable when you go out looking for

a good job. Accounting is a volatile discipline affected by changes in legislative initiatives.

With corporate accounting policies changing constantly and becoming more complex, accountants are needed to help keep a business running smoothly and within the bounds of the law. In fact, the number of jobs in the accounting and auditing field are expected to increase 22 percent between 2008 and 2018, with more than 1.5 million jobs in the United States alone by 2018. Jobs in accounting tend to pay quite well, with the national average salary standing at just over $59,000 annually. If you go on to get your master's degree in accounting, expect to see an even higher starting wage. In 2009, accountants with a bachelor's degree received an average opening offer of $48,993, while employees with master's degrees were offered $49,786 starting. Of course, your earnings could be higher or lower than these averages, depending on where you work, your level of experience, the firm, and your particular position.

Accountants are needed in the public and the private sectors, in large and small firms, in for-profit and not-for-profit organizations. Accountants in firms are generally in charge of preparing and filing tax forms and financial reports. Public-sector accountants are responsible for checking the veracity of corporate and personal records in order to prepare tax filings. Basically, any organization that has to deal with money and/or taxes in some way or another will be in need of an accountant, either for in-house service or occasional contract work. Requirements for audits under the Sarbanes-Oxley Act and rules from the Public Company Accounting Oversight Board are creating more jobs and increased responsibility to maintain internal controls and accounting ethics. The fact that accounting rules and tax filings tend to be complex virtually ensures that the demand for accountants will never decrease.[9]

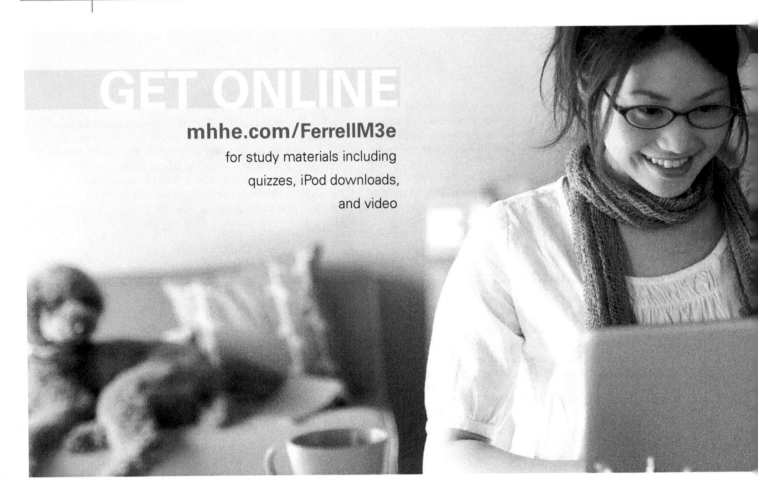

GET ONLINE

mhhe.com/FerrellM3e

for study materials including
quizzes, iPod downloads,
and video

chapter fourteen

active review card
Accounting and Financial Statements

in a nutshell

The use of accounting information and the accounting process is important in making business decisions. Understanding simple financial statements and accounting tools is useful in analyzing organizations worldwide.

The following statements will test your take-away knowledge from this chapter. Do your best to explain each one in the space provided below.

LO.1 Define accounting, and describe the different uses of accounting information.

LO.2 Demonstrate the accounting process.

LO.3 Examine the various components of an income statement in order to evaluate a firm's "bottom line."

LO.4 Interpret a company's balance sheet to determine its current financial position.

LO.5 Analyze the statement of cash flows to evaluate the increase and decrease in a company's cash balance.

368 Introduction to Business

Did your answers include the following important points?

LO.1. Define accounting, and describe the different uses of accounting information.

- Accounting is the language businesses and other organizations use to record, measure, and interpret financial transactions.
- Financial statements are used internally to judge and control an organization's performance and to plan and direct its future activities and measure goal attainment.
- External organizations such as lenders, governments, customers, suppliers, and the Internal Revenue Service are major consumers of the information generated by the accounting process.

LO.2. Demonstrate the accounting process.

- Assets are an organization's economic resources; liabilities are debts the organization owes to others; owners' equity is the difference between the value of an organization's assets and liabilities.
- This principle can be expressed as the accounting equation: Assets = Liabilities – Owners' equity.
- The double-entry bookkeeping system is a system of recording and classifying business transactions in accounts that maintain the balance of the accounting equation.
- The accounting cycle involves recording transactions in a journal, posting transactions, and preparing financial statements on a continuous basis throughout the life of the organization.

LO.3. Examine the various components of an income statement in order to evaluate a firm's "bottom line."

- The income statement indicates a company's profitability over a specific period of time. It shows the "bottom line," the total profit (or loss) after all expenses have been deducted from revenue.

- The cash flow statement details how much cash is moving through the firm and adds insight to the firm's "bottom line."

LO.4. Interpret a company's balance sheet to determine its current financial position.

- The balance sheet, which summarizes the firm's assets, liabilities, and owners' equity since its inception, portrays its financial position as of a particular point in time.
- Major classifications included in the balance sheet are current assets, fixed assets, current liabilities, long-term liabilities, and owners' equity.

LO.5. Analyze the statement of cash flows to evaluate the increase and decrease in a company's cash balance.

- The statement of cash flows explains how the company's cash changed from the beginning of the accounting period to the end.
- The change in cash is explained through details in three categories: cash from (used for) operating activities, cash from (used for) investing activities, and cash from (used for) financing activities.
- Ratio analysis consists of calculations that measure an organization's financial health and bring the complex information from the income statement and balance sheet into sharper focus so that managers, lenders, owners, and other interested parties can measure and compare the organization's productivity, profitability, and financing mix with other similar entities.

Practical Application

LO.1.

- A(n) _____ is an individual who has been state-certified to provide accounting services ranging from the preparation of financial records and the filing of tax returns to complex audits of corporate financial records.
- An internal financial plan that forecasts expenses and income over a set period of time is known as an organization's _____.
- A(n) _____ is a summary of the firm's financial information, products, and growth plans for owners and potential investors.

LO.2.

- Trendy, an organization that specializes in hand-stitched clothes, owes money to its suppliers and to the Small Business Administration. The money owed is an example of Trendy's _____.
- The system of recording and classifying business transactions in separate accounts in order to maintain the balance of the accounting equation is called _____.
- A(n) _____ is a book or computer program with separate files for each account.

LO.3.

- The _____ is the amount of money the firm spent to buy and/or produce the products it sold during the accounting period.

- _____ is the process of spreading the costs of long-lived assets such as buildings and equipment over the total number of accounting periods in which they are expected to be used.
- The _____ shows the profit or loss once all taxes and expenses have been deducted from the revenue.

LO.4.

- Short-term assets that are used or converted into cash within the course of a calendar year are also known as _____.
- _____ represents amounts owed to suppliers for goods and services purchased with credit.
- All unpaid financial obligations of a company are kept in the _____ account.

LO.5.

- The _____ explains how the company's cash changed from the beginning of the accounting period to the end.
- Cash from _____ is calculated by combining the changes in the revenue accounts, expense accounts, current asset accounts, and current liability accounts.
- Cash from _____ is calculated from changes in the long-term liability accounts and the contributed capital accounts in owners' equity.

ANSWERS LO1 •certified public accountant •budget •annual report LO2 •liabilities •double-entry bookkeeping •ledger LO3 •cost of goods sold •Depreciation• net income LO4 •current assets •Accounts payable •accrued expenses LO5 •statement of cash flows •operating activities •financing activities •

chapter fifteen

money +
the financial
system

From Wall Street to Main Street, both overseas and at home, money is the one tool used to measure personal and business income and wealth. **Finance** is the study of money: how it's made, how it's lost, and how it's managed. This chapter introduces you to the role of money and the financial system in the economy. Of course, if you have a checking account, automobile insurance, a college loan, or a credit card, you already have personal experience with some key players in the financial world.

We begin our discussion with a definition of money and then explore some of the many forms money may take. Next, we examine the roles of the Federal Reserve Board and other major institutions in the financial system. Finally, we explore the future of the finance industry and some of the changes likely to occur over the course of the next several years.

LEARNING OBJECTIVES

LO1 Define money, its functions, and its characteristics.

LO2 Describe various types of money.

LO3 Specify how the Federal Reserve Board manages the money supply and regulates the American banking system.

LO4 Compare and contrast commercial banks, savings and loan associations, credit unions, and mutual savings banks.

LO5 Distinguish among nonbanking institutions such as insurance companies, pension funds, mutual funds, and finance companies.

LO6 Investigate the challenges ahead for the banking industry.

finance the study of
money; how it's made,
how it's lost, and how it's
managed

money anything
generally accepted in
exchange for goods and
services

MONEY IN THE FINANCIAL SYSTEM

Strictly defined, money, or *currency*, is anything generally accepted in exchange for goods and services. Materials as diverse as salt, cattle, fish, rocks, shells, cloth, as well as precious metals such as gold, silver, and copper have long been used by various cultures as money. Most of these materials were limited-supply commodities that had their own value to society (for example, salt can be used as a preservative and shells and metals as jewelry). The supply of these commodities therefore determined the supply of "money" in that society. The next step was the development of "IOUs," or slips of paper that could be exchanged for a specified supply of the underlying commodity. "Gold" notes, for instance, could be exchanged for gold, and the money supply was tied to the amount of gold available. While paper money was first used in North America in 1685 (and even earlier in Europe), the concept of *fiat money*—a paper money not readily convertible to a precious metal such as gold—did not gain full acceptance until the Great Depression in the 1930s. The United States abandoned its gold-backed currency standard largely in response to the Great Depression and converted to a fiduciary, or fiat, monetary system. In the United States, paper money is really a government "note" or promise, worth the value specified on the note.

Functions of Money

No matter what a particular society uses for money, its primary purpose is to enable a person or organization to transform a desire into an action. These desires may be for entertainment actions, such as party expenses; operating actions, such as paying for rent, utilities, or employees; investing actions, such as buying property or equipment; or financing actions, such as for starting or growing a business. Money serves three important functions: as a medium of exchange, a measure of value, and a store of value.

Medium of Exchange Before fiat money, the trade of goods and services was accomplished through *bartering*—trading one good or service for another of similar value. As any school-age child knows, bartering can become quite inefficient—particularly in the case of complex, three-party transactions involving peanut butter sandwiches, baseball cards, and hair barrettes. There had to be a simpler way, and that was to decide on a single item—money—that can be freely converted to any other good upon agreement between parties.

Measure of Value As a measure of value, money serves as a common standard or yardstick of the value of goods and services. For example, $2 will buy a dozen large eggs and $25,000 will buy a nice car in the United States. In Japan, where the currency is known as the yen, these same transactions would cost about 185 yen and 2.3 million yen, respectively. Money, then, is a common denominator that allows

> ## No matter what a particular society uses for money, its primary purpose is to enable a person or organization to transform a desire into an action.

For centuries people on the Micronesian island of Yap have used giant round stones, like the ones shown here, for money. The stones aren't moved, but their ownership can change.

people to compare the different goods and services that can be consumed on a particular income level. While a star athlete and a "burger-flipper" are paid vastly different wages, each uses money as a measure of the value of their yearly earnings and purchases.

Store of Value As a store of value, money serves as a way to accumulate wealth (buying power) until it is needed. For example, a person making $500 per week who wants to buy a $500 computer could save $50 per week for each of the next 10 weeks. Unfortunately, the value of stored money is directly dependent on the health of the economy. If, due to rapid inflation, all prices double in one year, then the purchasing power value of the money "stuffed in the mattress" would fall by half. On the other hand, "mattress savings" buy more when prices fall as they did for more than 52 months in Hong Kong between 1999 and 2005.

Characteristics of Money

To be used as a medium of exchange, money must be acceptable, divisible, portable, stable in value, durable, and difficult to counterfeit.

Acceptability To be effective, money must be readily acceptable for the purchase of goods and services and for the settlement of debts. Acceptability is probably the most important characteristic of money: If people do not trust the value of money, businesses will not accept it as a payment for goods and services, and consumers will have to find some other means of paying for their purchases.

Divisibility Given the widespread use of quarters, dimes, nickels, and pennies in the United States, it is no surprise that the principle of divisibility is an important one. With barter, the lack of divisibility often makes otherwise preferable trades impossible, as would be an attempt to trade a steer for a loaf of bread. For money to serve effectively as a measure of value, all items must be valued in terms of comparable units—dimes for a piece of bubble gum, quarters for laundry machines, and dollars (or dollars and coins) for everything else.

Portability Clearly, for money to function as a medium of exchange, it must be easily moved from one location to the next. Large colored rocks could be used as money, but you couldn't carry them around in your wallet. Paper currency and metal coins, on the other hand, are capable of transferring vast purchasing power into small, easily carried (and hidden!) bundles. Few Americans realize it, but more U.S. currency is in circulation outside the United States than within. Currently, about $829 billion of U.S. currency is in circulation, and the majority is held outside the United States.[1]

Stability Money must be stable and maintain its declared face value. A $10 bill should purchase the same amount of goods or services from one day to the next. The principle of stability allows people who wish to postpone purchases and save their money to do so without fear that it will decline in value. As mentioned earlier, money declines in value during periods of inflation, when economic conditions cause prices to rise. Thus, the same amount of money buys fewer and fewer goods and services. In some countries, people spend their money as fast as they can in order to keep it from losing any more of its value. Instability destroys confidence in a nation's money and its ability to store value and serve as an effective medium of exchange. Ultimately, people faced with spiraling price increases avoid the increasingly worthless paper money at all costs, storing all of their savings in the form of real assets such as gold and land.

Durability Money must be durable. The crisp new dollar bills you trade at the music store for the hottest new CD will make their

TABLE 15.1 The Life Expectancy of Paper Currency

Denomination of Bill	Life Expectancy (Years)
$1	1.8
$5	1.3
$10	1.5
$20	2.0
$50	4.6
$100	7.4

Source: "How Currency Gets into Circulation", Federal Reserve Bank of Bank of New York, www.newyorkfed.org/aboutthefed/fedpoint/fed01.html (accessed March 31, 2010).

?

DID YOU KNOW?

Around 75 percent of counterfeit currency is found and destroyed before it ever reaches the public.[2]

way all around town for about 20 months before being replaced (see Table 15.1). Were the value of an old, faded bill to fall in line with the deterioration of its appearance, the principles of stability and universal acceptability would fail (but, no doubt, fewer bills would pass through the washer!). Although metal coins, due to their much longer useful life, would appear to be an ideal form of money, paper currency is far more portable than metal because of its light weight. Today, coins are used primarily to provide divisibility.

Difficulty to Counterfeit Finally, to remain stable and enjoy universal acceptance, it almost goes without saying that money must be very difficult to counterfeit—that is, to duplicate illegally. Every country takes steps to make counterfeiting difficult. Most use multicolored money, and many use specially watermarked papers that are virtually impossible to duplicate. Counterfeit bills represent less than 0.03 percent of the currency in circulation in the United States,[3] but it is becoming increasingly easier for counterfeiters to print money with just a modest inkjet printer. This illegal printing of money is fueled by hundreds of people who often circulate only small amounts of counterfeit bills. To thwart the problem of counterfeiting, the U.S. Treasury Department redesigned the U.S. currency, starting with the $20 bill in 2003, the $50 bill in 2004, the $10 bill in 2006, the $5 bill in 2008, and the $100 bill in 2010. For the first time, U.S. money includes subtle colors in addition to

The U.S. government redesigns currency in order to stay ahead of counterfeiters and protect the public.

checking account money stored in an account at a bank or other financial institution that can be withdrawn without advance notice; also called a demand deposit	**savings accounts** accounts with funds that usually cannot be withdrawn without advance notice; also known as time deposits	**money market accounts** accounts that offer higher interest rates than standard bank rates but with greater restrictions	**certificates of deposit (CDs)** savings accounts that guarantee a depositor a set interest rate over a specified interval as long as the funds are not withdrawn before the end of the period—six months or one year, for example	**credit cards** means of access to preapproved lines of credit granted by a bank or finance company

the traditional green, as well as enhanced security features, such as a watermark, security thread, and color-shifting ink.[4]

Although counterfeiting is not as much of an issue with coins, metal coins have their own problems. The value of certain coins is less than the money it costs to produce them. In 2006 the new Jefferson nickel was introduced, showing a profile of the nation's third president. Due to the increased price of metals, it costs 5.79 cents to make the 5-cent piece.[5] President Lincoln was the first president to appear on a coin when the Lincoln penny was introduced in 1909. As Figure 15.1 indicates it costs more than a penny to manufacture a penny, resulting in a call to discontinue it.

Types of Money

While paper money and coins are the most visible types of money, the combined value of all of the printed bills and all of the minted coins is actually rather insignificant when compared with the value of money kept in checking accounts, savings accounts, and other monetary forms.

You probably have a **checking account** (also called a *demand deposit*), money stored in an account at a bank or other financial institution that can be withdrawn without advance notice. One way to withdraw funds from your account is by writing a *check,* a written order to a bank to pay the indicated individual or business the amount specified on the check from money already on deposit. Figure 15.2 explains the significance of the numbers found on a typical U.S. check. As legal instruments, checks serve as a substitute for currency and coins and are preferred for many transactions due to their lower risk of loss. If you lose a $100 bill, anyone who finds or steals it can spend it. If you lose a blank check, however, the risk of catastrophic loss is quite low. Not only does your bank have a sample of your signature on file to compare with a suspected forged signature, but you can render the check immediately worthless by means of a stop-payment order at your bank.

There are several types of checking accounts, with different features available for different monthly fee levels or specific minimum account balances. Some checking accounts earn interest (a small percentage of the amount deposited in the account that the bank pays to the depositor). One such interest-bearing checking account is the *NOW (Negotiable Order of Withdrawal) account* offered by most financial institutions. The interest rate paid on such accounts varies with the interest rates available in the economy but is typically quite low (ranging between 2 and 5 percent).

Savings accounts (also known as *time deposits*) are accounts with funds that usually cannot be withdrawn without advance notice and/or have limits on the number of withdrawals per period. While seldom enforced, the "fine print" governing most savings accounts prohibits withdrawals without two or three days' notice. Savings accounts are not generally used for transactions or as a medium of exchange, but their funds can be moved to a checking account or turned into cash.

Money market accounts are similar to interest-bearing checking accounts, but with more restrictions. Generally, in exchange for slightly higher interest rates, the owner of a money market account can write only a limited number of checks each month, and there may be a restriction on the minimum amount of each check.

Certificates of deposit (CDs) are savings accounts that guarantee a depositor a set interest rate over a specified interval of time as long as the funds are not withdrawn before the end of the interval—six months, one year, or seven years, for example. Money may be withdrawn from these accounts prematurely only after paying a substantial penalty. In general, the longer the term of the

FIGURE 15.1
Cost to Produce a Penny

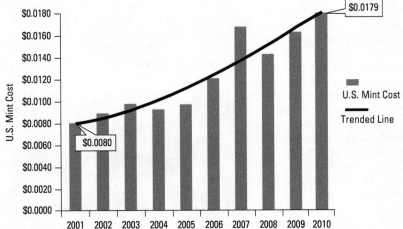

$0.0179

$0.0080

U.S. Mint Cost
Trended Line

2001 2002 2003 2004 2005 2006 2007 2008 2009 2010

Source: "Cost to Make Penny and Nickel Rises for US Mint," *Coin Update News*, January 10, 2011, http://news.coinupdate.com/cost-to-make-penny-nickel-0619/ (accessed January 18, 2011).

▼**FIGURE 15.2**
A Check

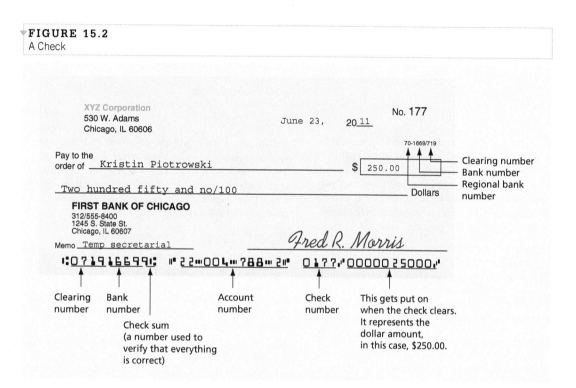

CD, the higher is the interest rate it earns. As with all interest rates, the rate offered and fixed at the time the account is opened fluctuates according to economic conditions.

Credit cards allow you to promise to pay at a later date by using preapproved lines of credit granted by a bank or finance company. They are a popular substitute for cash payments because of their convenience, easy access to credit, and acceptance by merchants around the world. The institution that issues the credit card guarantees payment of a credit charge to merchants and assumes responsibility for collecting the money from the cardholders. Card issuers charge a transaction fee to the merchants for performing the credit check, guaranteeing the payment and collecting the payment. The fee is typically between 2 and 5 percent, depending on the type of card. American Express fees are usually higher than Visa and MasterCard.

The original American Express cards require full payment at the end of each month, but American Express now offers credit cards similar to Visa, MasterCard, and Discover that allow cardholders to make installment payments and carry a maximum balance. There is a minimum monthly payment with interest charged on the remaining balance. Some people pay off their credit cards monthly, while other make monthly payments. Charges for unpaid balances can run 18 percent or higher at an annual rate, making credit card debt one of the most expensive ways to borrow money.

Besides the major credit card companies, many stores— Target, Saks Fifth Avenue, Macy's, Bloomingdales,

Sears, and others—have their own branded credit cards. They use credit rating agencies to check the credit of the cardholders and they generally make money on the finance charges.

In May 2009, President Obama signed the Credit CARD (Card Accountability Responsibility and Disclosure) Act of 2009 into law, primarily to regulate the practices of credit card companies that were coming under attack by consumers during the recession of 2007–2009. Without going into the details, the law limited the ability of card issuers to raise interest rates, limited credit to young adults, gave people more time to pay

High interest rates on credit cards and the most recent recession have led the bulk of Americans to reduce credit card balances for the first time in years.

debit card a card that looks like a credit card but works like a check; using it results in a direct, immediate, electronic payment from the cardholder's checking account to a merchant or third party

Federal Reserve Board an independent agency of the federal government established in 1913 to regulate the nation's banking and financial industry

monetary policy means by which the Fed controls the amount of money available in the economy

open market operations decisions to buy or sell U.S. Treasury bills (short-term debt issued by the U.S. government) and other investments in the open market

bills, required that if there were various levels of interest rates that the balances with the highest rate would be paid off first, and made clearer due dates on billing cycles, along with several other provisions. For college students, the most important part of the law is that young adults under the age of 21 will have to have an adult co-signer or show proof that they have enough income to handle the debt limit on the card.

This act is important to all companies and cardholders. There were approximately 180 million credit cardholders in the United States in 2010, and the average cardholder has 3.5 cards. One study indicated that 41 percent of college students have credit cards, and 65 percent of them paid off their bills in full at the end of each month, which is a higher rate than the general population.[6]

A **debit card** looks like a credit card but works like a check. The use of a debit card results in a direct, immediate, electronic payment from the cardholder's checking account to a merchant or other party. While they are convenient to carry and profitable for banks, they lack credit features, offer no purchase "grace period," and provide no hard "paper trail." Debit cards are gaining more acceptance with merchants, and consumers like debit cards because of the ease of getting cash from an increasing number of ATMs. Financial institutions also want consumers to use debit cards because they reduce the number of teller transactions and check processing costs. Some cash management accounts at retail brokers like Merrill Lynch offer deferred debit cards. These act like a credit card but debit to the cash management account once a month. During that time, the cash earns a money market return.

Traveler's checks, money orders, and cashier's checks are other common forms of "near money." Although each is slightly different from the others, they all share a common characteristic: A financial institution, bank, credit company, or neighborhood currency exchange issues them in exchange for cash and guarantees that the purchased note will be honored and exchanged for cash when it is presented to the institution making the guarantee.

THE AMERICAN FINANCIAL SYSTEM

The U.S. financial system fuels our economy by storing money, fostering investment opportunities, and making loans for new businesses and business expansion as well as for homes, cars, and college educations. This amazingly complex system includes banking institutions, nonbanking financial institutions such as finance companies, and systems that provide for the electronic transfer of funds throughout the world. Over the past 20 years, the rate at which money turns over, or changes hands, has increased exponentially. Different cultures place unique values on saving, spending, borrowing, and investing. The combination of this increased turnover rate and increasing interactions with people and organizations from other countries has created a complex money system. First, we need to meet the guardian of this complex system.

The Federal Reserve System

The guardian of the American financial system is the **Federal Reserve Board**, or "the Fed," as it is commonly called, an independent agency of the federal government established in 1913 to regulate the nation's banking and financial industry. The Federal Reserve System is organized into 12 regions, each with a Federal Reserve Bank that serves its defined area (Figure 15.3). All the Federal Reserve banks except those in Boston and Philadelphia have regional branches. The Cleveland Federal Reserve Bank, for example, is responsible for branch offices in Pittsburgh and Cincinnati.

The Federal Reserve Board is the chief economic policy arm of the United States. Working with Congress and the president, the Fed tries to create a positive economic environment capable of sustaining low inflation, high levels of employment, a balance in international payments, and long-term economic growth. To this end, the Federal Reserve Board has four major responsibilities: (1) to control the supply of money, or monetary policy; (2) to regulate banks and other financial institutions; (3) to manage regional and national checking account procedures, or check clearing; and (4) to supervise the federal deposit insurance programs of banks belonging to the Federal Reserve System.

Monetary Policy The Fed controls the amount of money available in the economy through **monetary policy**. Without this intervention, the supply of and demand for money might not balance. This could result in either rapid price increases (inflation) because of too much money or economic recession and a slowdown of price increases (disinflation) because of too little growth in the money supply. In very rare cases (the depression of the 1930s) the United States has suffered from deflation, where the actual purchasing power of the dollar has increased as prices declined. To effectively control the supply of money in the economy, the Fed must have a good idea of how much money is in circulation at any given time. This has become increasingly challenging because the global nature of our economy means that more and more U.S. dollars are circulating overseas. Using several different measures of the money supply, the Fed establishes specific growth targets that, presumably, ensure a close balance between money supply and money demand. The Fed fine-tunes money growth by using four basic

▼ FIGURE 15.3
Federal Reserve System

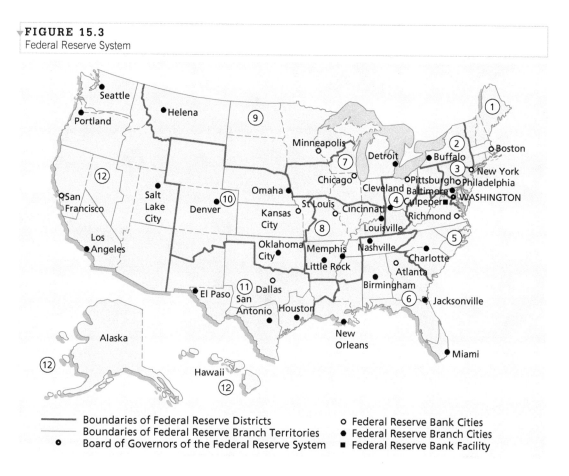

——— Boundaries of Federal Reserve Districts
——— Boundaries of Federal Reserve Branch Territories
  ⊙ Board of Governors of the Federal Reserve System
○ Federal Reserve Bank Cities
● Federal Reserve Branch Cities
■ Federal Reserve Bank Facility

▼ TABLE 15.2 Fed Tools for Regulating the Money Supply

Activity	Effect on the Money Supply and the Economy
Buy government securities	The money supply increases; economic activity increases.
Sell government securities	The money supply decreases; economic activity slows down.
Raise discount rate	Interest rates increase; the money supply decreases; economic activity slows down.
Lower discount rate	Interest rates decrease; the money supply increases; economic activity increases.
Increase reserve requirements	Banks make fewer loans; the money supply declines; economic activity slows down.
Decrease reserve requirements	Banks make more loans; the money supply increases; economic activity increases.
Relax credit controls	More people are encouraged to make major purchases, increasing economic activity.
Restrict credit controls	People are discouraged from making major purchases, decreasing economic activity.

tools: open market operations, reserve requirements, the discount rate, and credit controls (see Table 15.2). There is generally a log of 6 to 18 months before the effect of these charges shows up in economic activity.

Open market operations refer to decisions to buy or sell U.S. Treasury bills (short-term debt issued by the U.S. government; also called T-bills) and other investments in the open market.

The actual purchase or sale of the investments is performed by the New York Federal Reserve Bank. This monetary tool, the most commonly employed of all Fed operations, is performed almost daily in an effort to control the money supply.

When the Fed buys securities, it writes a check on its own account to the seller of the investments. When the seller of the investments (usually a large bank) deposits the check, the Fed

One of the roles of the Federal Reserve is to use its policies to keep money flowing. Money is the lifeblood of the economy. If banks become too protective of their funds and stop lending money, the economy can grind to a halt.

transfers the balance from the Federal Reserve account into the seller's account, thus increasing the supply of money in the economy and, hopefully, fueling economic growth. The opposite occurs when the Fed sells investments. The buyer writes a check to the Federal Reserve, and when the funds are transferred out of the purchaser's account, the amount of money in circulation falls, slowing economic growth to a desired level.

The second major monetary policy tool is the **reserve requirement**, the percentage of deposits that banking institutions must hold in reserve ("in the vault," as it were). Funds so held are not available for lending to businesses and consumers. For example, a bank holding $10 million in deposits, with a 10 percent reserve requirement, must have reserves of $1 million. If the Fed were to reduce the reserve requirement to, say, 5 percent, the bank would need to keep only $500,000 in reserves. The bank could then lend to customers the $500,000 difference between the old reserve level and the new lower reserve level, thus increasing the supply of money. Because the reserve requirement has such a powerful effect on the money supply, the Fed does not change it very often, relying instead on open market operations most of the time.

The third monetary policy tool, the **discount rate**, is the rate of interest the

> The Fed establishes and enforces banking rules that affect monetary policy and the overall level of the competition between different banks.

Fed charges to loan money to any banking institution to meet reserve requirements. The Fed is the lender of last resort for these banks. When a bank borrows from the Fed, it is said to have borrowed at the "discount window," and the interest rates charged there are often higher than those charged on loans of comparable risk elsewhere in the economy. This added interest expense, when it exists, serves to discourage banks from borrowing from the Fed.

When the Fed wants to expand the money supply, it lowers the discount rate to encourage borrowing. Conversely, when the Fed wants to decrease the money supply, it raises the discount rate. The increases in interest rates that occurred in the United States from 2003 through 2006 were the result of more than 16 quarter-point (0.25 percent) increases in the Fed discount rate. The purpose was to keep inflation under control and to raise rates to a more normal level as the economy recovered from the recession of 2001. During the most recent recession, which started in 2007, the Fed lowered interest rates to nearly zero in order to encourage borrowing. In an environment where credit markets were nearly frozen, the Fed utilized monetary policy to stimulate spending. Not surprisingly, economists watch changes in this sensitive interest rate as an indicator of the Fed's monetary policy.

reserve requirement the percentage of deposits that banking institutions must hold in reserve

discount rate the rate of interest the Fed charges to loan money to any banking institution to meet reserve requirements

credit controls the authority to establish and enforce credit rules for financial institutions and some private investors

commercial banks the largest and oldest of all financial institutions, relying mainly on checking and savings accounts as sources of funds for loans to businesses and individuals

The final tool in the Fed's arsenal of weapons is **credit controls**—the authority to establish and enforce credit rules for financial institutions and some private investors. For example, the Fed can determine how large a down payment individuals and businesses must make on credit purchases of expensive items such as automobiles, and how much time they have to finish paying for the purchases. By raising and lowering minimum down payment amounts and payment periods, the Fed can stimulate or discourage credit purchases of "big ticket" items. The Fed also has the authority to set the minimum down payment investors must use for the credit purchases of stock. Buying stock with credit—"buying on margin"—is a popular investment strategy among individual speculators. By altering the margin requirement (currently set at 50 percent of the price of the purchased stocks), the Fed can effectively control the total amount of credit borrowing in the stock market.

Regulatory Functions The second major responsibility of the Fed is to regulate banking institutions that are members of the Federal Reserve System. Accordingly, the Fed establishes and enforces banking rules that affect monetary policy and the overall level of the competition between different banks. It determines which nonbanking activities, such as brokerage services, leasing, and insurance, are appropriate for banks and which should be prohibited. The Fed also has the authority to approve or disapprove mergers between banks and the formation of bank holding companies. In an effort to ensure that all rules are enforced and that correct accounting procedures are being followed at member banks, surprise bank examinations are conducted by bank examiners each year.

Check Clearing The Federal Reserve provides national check processing on a huge scale. Divisions of the Fed known as check clearinghouses handle almost all the checks written against a bank in one city and presented for deposit to a bank in a second city. Any banking institution can present the checks it has received from others around the country to its regional Federal Reserve Bank. The Fed passes the checks to the appropriate regional Federal Reserve Bank, which then sends the checks to the issuing bank for payment. With the advance of electronic payment systems and the passage of the Check Clearing for the 21st Century Act (Check 21 Act), checks can now be processed in a day. The Check 21 Act allows banks to clear checks electronically by presenting an electronic image of the check. This eliminates mail delays and time-consuming paper processing.

Depository Insurance The Fed is also responsible for supervising the federal insurance funds that protect the deposits of member institutions. These insurance funds will be discussed in greater detail in the following section.

Banking Institutions

Banking institutions accept money deposits from and make loans to individual consumers and businesses. Some of the most important banking institutions include commercial banks, savings and loan associations, credit unions, and mutual savings banks. Historically, these have all been separate institutions. However, new hybrid forms of banking institutions that perform two or more of these functions have emerged over the last two decades. The following all have one thing in common: They are businesses whose objective is to earn money by managing, safeguarding, and lending money to others. Their sales revenues come from the fees and interest that they charge for providing these financial services.

Commercial Banks The largest and oldest of all financial institutions are **commercial banks**, which perform a variety of financial services. They rely mainly on checking and savings accounts as their major source of funds and use only a portion of these deposits to make loans to businesses and individuals. Because it is unlikely that all the depositors of any one bank will want to withdraw all of their funds at the same time, a bank can safely loan out a large percentage of its deposits.

JPMorgan Chase is the second largest commercial bank in the United States behind Bank of America.

Today, banks are quite diversified and offer a number of services. Commercial banks make loans for virtually any conceivable legal purpose, from vacations to cars, from homes to college educations. Banks in many states offer *home equity loans,* by which home owners can borrow against the appraised value of their already purchased homes. Banks also issue Visa and MasterCard credit cards and offer CDs and trusts (legal entities set up to hold and manage assets for a beneficiary). Many banks rent safe deposit boxes in bank vaults to customers who want to store jewelry, legal documents, artwork, and other valuables. In 1999 Congress passed the Financial Services Modernization Act, also known as the Gramm-Leach-Bliley Bill. This act repealed the Glass Stegal Act, which was enacted in 1929 after the stock market crash and prohibited commercial banks from being in the insurance and investment banking business. This puts U.S. commercial banks on the same competitive footing as European banks and provides a more level playing field for global banking competition. As commercial banks and investment banks have merged, the financial landscape has changed. Consolidation remains the norm in the U.S. banking industry. For example, JPMorgan Chase completed a merger with Bank One in 2004, making it the second largest bank in the United States behind Citigroup. JPMorgan was created through a merger with Chase Manhattan Bank and JPMorgan, and Bank One acquired many Midwestern banks, with its biggest acquisition being First Chicago Corp. The financial crisis and the economic recession only accelerated the consolidation as large,

healthy banks ended up buying weak banks that were in trouble. JPMorgan Chase bought Washington Mutual; Wells Fargo bought Wachovia; PNC bought National City Bank; and Bank of America bought Countrywide and Merrill Lynch. Most of these purchases were made with financial help from the U.S. Treasury and Federal Reserve.

Savings and Loan Associations **Savings and loan associations (S&Ls),** often called "thrifts," are financial institutions that primarily offer savings accounts and make long-term loans for residential mortgages. A mortgage is a loan made so that a business or individual can purchase real estate, typically a home; the real estate itself is pledged as a guarantee (called *collateral*) that the buyer will repay the loan. If the loan is not repaid, the savings and loan has the right to repossess the property. Prior to the 1970s, S&Ls focused almost exclusively on real estate lending and accepted only savings accounts. Today, following years of regulatory changes, S&Ls compete directly with commercial banks by offering many types of services.

Savings and loans have gone through a metamorphosis since the early 1990s, after having almost collapsed in the 1980s. Today, many of the largest savings and loans have merged with commercial banks. This segment of the financial services industry plays a diminished role in the mortgage lending market.

Credit Unions A **credit union** is a financial institution owned and controlled by its depositors, who usually have a

> "Banks are quite diversified and offer a number of services."

ARE CREDIT UNIONS A BETTER DEAL THAN BANKS?

Is it time to ditch the bank for the credit union? After the most recent financial crisis led to the closure of several banks, credit unions began looking better and better. Credit unions have several advantages over banks. Because they are nonprofit institutions, and therefore do not have to pay shares or executive salaries, the money that credit unions earn goes back to members in the form of dividends. The lack of pressure to make a profit also allows credit unions to offer more attractive rates on items like CDs, mortgages, credit

cards, and car loans. For example, in May 2010 credit unions charged an average 5.73 percent for a four-year new-car loan, while banks charged an average of 6.98 percent.

Some consumers also feel that credit unions offer more quality services, such as taking the time to help customers set up financial plans. Additionally, most credit unions offer free checking and lower penalty fees than banks. With 91.5 million members, credit unions are becoming a popular alternative to traditional banking.

Of course, credit unions have their downsides as well. Unlike banks, consumers must meet requirements to become members of credit unions. Banks also offer more diverse products and services than many credit unions do. Additionally,

although credit unions did not require as much of a government bailout as banks did, regulators did have to bail out the wholesale credit union sector. These downsides have led analysts to recommend that consumers carefully investigate financial institutions, be it bank or credit union, before investing. However, for those consumers who constantly get frustrated with their banks, credit unions might be the way to go.[7]

Discussion Questions

1. What are the advantages of credit unions over banks?
2. What are the disadvantages of credit unions over banks?
3. Given a choice, would you rather deal with a bank or a credit union?

| savings and loan associations (S&Ls) financial institutions that primarily offer savings accounts and make long-term loans for residential mortgages; also called "thrifts" | credit union a financial institution owned and controlled by its depositors, who usually have a common employer, profession, trade group, or religion | mutual savings banks financial institutions that are similar to savings and loan associations but, like credit unions, are owned by their depositors | Federal Deposit Insurance Corporation (FDIC) an insurance fund established in 1933 that insures individual bank accounts | National Credit Union Association (NCUA) an agency that regulates and charters credit unions and insures their deposits through its National Credit Union Insurance Fund |

common employer, profession, trade group, or religion. The Aggieland Credit Union in College Station, Texas, for example, provides banking services for faculty, employees, and current and former students of Texas A&M University. A savings account at a credit union is commonly referred to as a share account, while a checking account is termed a share draft account. Because the credit union is tied to a common organization, the members (depositors) are allowed to vote for directors and share in the credit union's profits in the form of higher interest rates on accounts and/or lower loan rates.

While credit unions were originally created to provide depositors with a short-term source of funds for low-interest consumer loans for items such as cars, home appliances, vacations, and college, today they offer a wide range of financial services. Generally, the larger the credit union, the more sophisticated its financial service offerings will be.

Mutual Savings Banks

Mutual savings banks are similar to savings and loan associations, but, like credit unions, they are owned by their depositors. Among the oldest financial institutions in the United States, they were originally established to provide a safe place for savings of particular groups of people, such as fishermen. Found mostly in New England, they are becoming more popular in the rest of the country as some S&Ls have converted to mutual savings banks to escape the stigma created by the widespread S&L failures in the 1980s.

Insurance for Banking Institutions

The **Federal Deposit Insurance Corporation (FDIC)**, which insures individual bank accounts, was established in 1933 to help stop bank failures throughout the country during the Great Depression. Today, the FDIC insures personal accounts up to a maximum of $250,000 at nearly 8,000 FDIC member institutions.[8] While most major banks are insured by the FDIC, small institutions in some states may be insured by state insurance funds or private insurance companies. Should a member bank fail, its depositors can recover all of their funds, up to $250,000. Amounts over $250,000, while not legally covered by the insurance, are in fact usually covered because the Fed understands very well the enormous damage that would result to the financial system should these large depositors withdraw their money. When the financial crisis occurred, the FDIC was worried about people taking their money out of banks, so they increased the deposit insurance amount from $100,000 to $250,000. The amount is scheduled to revert back to $100,000 on December 31, 2013. The *Federal Savings and Loan Insurance Corporation (FSLIC)* insured thrift deposits prior to its

insolvency and failure during the S&L crisis of the 1980s. Now, the insurance functions once overseen by the FSLIC are handled directly by the FDIC through its Savings Association Insurance Fund. The **National Credit Union Association (NCUA)** regulates and charters credit unions and insures their deposits through its National Credit Union Insurance Fund.

When they were originally established, Congress hoped that these insurance funds would make people feel secure about their savings so that they would not panic and withdraw their money when news of a bank failure was announced. The "bank run" scene in the perennial Christmas movie *It's a Wonderful Life,* when dozens of Bailey Building and Loan depositors attempted to withdraw their money (only to have the reassuring figure of Jimmy Stewart calm their fears), was not based on mere fiction. During the Great Depression, hundreds of banks failed and their depositors lost everything. The fact that large numbers of major financial institutions failed in the 1980s and 1990s—without a single major banking panic—underscores the effectiveness of the current insurance system. While the future may yet bring unfortunate surprises, most depositors go to sleep every night without worrying about the safety of their savings.

Nonbanking Institutions

Nonbank financial institutions offer some financial services, such as short-term loans or investment products, but do not accept deposits. These include insurance companies, pension funds, mutual funds, brokerage firms, nonfinancial firms, and finance companies. Table 15.3 lists some other diversified financial services firms.

▼ **TABLE 15.3** Diversified Financial Services Firms

Company	Revenues (in Millions)
General Electric	$156,779.0
International Assets Holding	43,604.4
Freddie Mac	37,614.0
Fannie Mae	29,065.0
Marsh & McLennan	10,493.0
Ameriprise Financial	7,946.0
Aon	7,595.0
SLM	6,144.7
H&R Block	4,213.4

Source: "Industry: Diversified Financials," *Fortune* 500 2010, *Fortune,* http://money.cnn.com/magazines/fortune/fortune500/2010/industries/31/index.html (accessed January 19, 2011).

insurance companies
businesses that protect their clients against financial losses from certain specified risks (death, accident, and theft, for example)

pension funds
managed investment pools set aside by individuals, corporations, unions, and some nonprofit organizations to provide retirement income for members

Diversified Firms Recently, a growing number of traditionally nonfinancial firms have moved onto the financial field. These firms include manufacturing organizations, such as General Motors and General Electric, that traditionally confined their financial activities to financing their customers' purchases. GE was once so successful in the financial arena that its credit subsidiary accounted for more than 40 percent of the company's revenues and earnings. Unfortunately, GE Capital became a liability to GE during the financial crisis, and the stock price fell from $42 per share to less than $8 per share. It is in the process of recovery as GE cuts the size of its finance unit and writes off billions of dollars in bad loans. Other nonfinancial firms have been also been unsuccessful in their financial ventures. Sears, the retail giant, once commanded an imposing financial network composed of real estate (Coldwell Banker), credit card (Discover Card), and brokerage (Dean Witter Reynolds) companies, but losses of hundreds of millions of dollars forced Sears to dismantle its network. The very prestigious brokerage firm Morgan Stanley acquired Dean Witter Discover, thus creating one of the largest investment firms in the country—in a league with Smith Barney and Merrill Lynch. Perhaps the moral of the story for firms like Sears is "stick to what you know."

Insurance Companies Insurance companies are businesses that protect their clients against financial losses from certain specified risks (death, injury, disability, accident, fire, theft, and natural disasters, for example) in exchange for

a fee, called a premium. Because insurance premiums flow into the companies regularly, but major insurance losses cannot be timed with great accuracy (though expected risks can be assessed with considerable precision), insurance companies generally have large amounts of excess funds. They typically invest these or make long-term loans, particularly to businesses in the form of commercial real estate loans.

Pension Funds Pension funds are managed investment pools set aside by individuals, corporations, unions, and some nonprofit organizations to provide retirement income for members. One type of pension fund is the *individual retirement account (IRA)*, which is established by individuals to provide for their personal retirement needs. IRAs can be invested in a variety

State Farm Insurance allows users to input their information on its website to receive an auto insurance quote quickly and conveniently.

> "A growing number of traditionally nonfinancial firms have moved onto the financial field."

THRUST FUND FOUNDERS ENCOURAGE INVESTMENTS IN THEMSELVES

It takes a daring individual to gamble on the uncertainty of one's future earnings, but young entrepreneurs Kjerstin Erickson, Jon Gosier, and Saul Garlick are doing just that. They've co-founded the Thrust Fund, an organization through which they are seeking investments of $300,000 to $600,000 in exchange for 3 to 6 percent of their future earnings. Is this idea feasible? Some fear the three entrepreneurs may be selling themselves short by asking for too little, while others worry that receiving upfront funding may reduce the entrepreneurial drive. On the other hand, many entrepreneurs rack up tremendous debt or risk their homes to fund their ventures. Therefore, 3 to 6 percent of future earnings may be the safer bet. Investors face risk as well. What happens if these three fail to earn much money in the future? The fact that all three already run successful organizations may quell some concerns. Should they prosper, investors may net well beyond their initial investments. Only time will tell whether this new type of investing will pay off.[9]

of financial assets, from risky commodities such as oil or cocoa to low-risk financial "staples" such as U.S. Treasury securities. The choice is up to each person and is dictated solely by individual objectives and tolerance for risk. The interest earned by all of these investments may be deferred tax-free until retirement.

In 1997, Congress revised the IRA laws and created a Roth IRA. Although similar to a traditional IRA in that investors may contribute $5,000 per year, the money in a Roth IRA is considered an after-tax contribution. When the money is withdrawn at retirement, no tax is paid on the distribution. The Roth IRA is beneficial to young people who can allow a long time for their money to compound and who may be able to have their parents or grandparents fund the Roth IRA with gift money.

Most major corporations provide some kind of pension plan for their employees. Many of these are established with bank trust departments or life insurance companies. Money is deposited in a separate account in the name of each individual employee, and when the employee retires, the total amount in the account can be either withdrawn in one lump sum or taken as monthly cash payments over some defined time period (usually for the remaining life of the retiree).

Social Security, the largest pension fund, is publicly financed. The federal government collects Social Security funds from payroll taxes paid by both employers and employees. The Social Security Administration then takes these monies and makes payments to those eligible to receive Social Security benefits—individuals who are retired or disabled, and the young children of deceased parents.

Mutual Funds

A **mutual fund** pools individual investor dollars and invests them in large numbers of well-diversified securities. Individual investors buy shares in a mutual fund in the hope of earning a high rate of return and in much the same way as people buy shares of stock. Because of the large numbers of people investing in any one mutual fund, the funds can afford to invest in hundreds (if not thousands) of securities at any one time, minimizing the risks of any single security that does not do well. Mutual funds provide professional financial management for people who lack the time and/or expertise to invest in particular securities, such as government bonds. While there are no hard-and-fast rules, investments in one or more mutual funds are one way for people to plan for financial independence at the time of retirement.

A special type of mutual fund called a *money market fund* invests specifically in short-term debt securities issued by governments and large corporations. Although they offer services such as check-writing privileges and reinvestment of interest income, money market funds differ from the money market accounts offered by banks primarily in that the former represent a pool of funds, while the latter are basically specialized, individual checking accounts. Money market funds usually offer slightly higher rates of interest than bank money market accounts.

Brokerage Firms and Investment Banks

Brokerage firms buy and sell stocks, bonds, and other securities for their customers and provide other financial services. Larger brokerage firms like Merrill Lynch, Charles Schwab, and Edward Jones offer financial services unavailable at their smaller competitors. Merrill Lynch, for example, offers the Merrill Lynch Cash Management Account (CMA), which pays interest on deposits and allows clients to write checks, borrow money, and withdraw cash much like a commercial bank. The largest of the brokerage firms (including Merrill Lynch) have developed so many specialized services that they may be considered financial networks—organizations capable of offering virtually all of the services traditionally associated with commercial banks.

Most brokerage firms are really part financial conglomerates that provide many different kinds of services besides buying and selling securities for clients. For example, Merrill Lynch also is an investment banker, as is Morgan Stanley, Smith Barney, and Goldman Sachs. The **investment banker** underwrites new issues of securities for corporations, states, and municipalities needed to raise money in the capital markets. The new issue market is called a *primary market* because the sale of the securities is for the first time. After the first sale, the securities trade in the *secondary markets* by brokers. The investment banker advises on the price of the new securities and generally guarantees the sale while overseeing the distribution of the securities through the selling brokerage houses. Investment bankers also act as dealers who make markets in securities. They do this by offering to sell the securities at an asked price (which is a higher rate) and buy the securities at a bid price (which is a lower rate)—the difference in the two prices represents the profit for the dealer.

Finance Companies

Finance companies are businesses that offer short-term loans at substantially higher rates of interest than banks. Commercial finance companies make loans to businesses, requiring their borrowers to pledge assets such as equipment, inventories, or unpaid accounts as collateral for the loans. Consumer finance companies make loans to individuals. Like commercial finance companies, these firms require some sort of personal collateral as security against the borrower's possible inability to repay their loans. Because of the high interest rates they charge and other factors, finance companies typically are the lender of last resort for individuals and businesses whose credit limits have been exhausted and/or those with poor credit ratings.

mutual fund an investment company that pools individual investor dollars and invests them in large numbers of well-diversified securities

brokerage firms firms that buy and sell stocks, bonds, and other securities for their customers and provide other financial services

investment banker underwrites new issues of securities for corporations, states, and municipalities

finance companies businesses that offer short-term loans at substantially higher rates of interest than banks

electronic funds transfer (EFT) any movement of funds by means of an electronic terminal, telephone, computer, or magnetic tape

automated teller machine (ATM) the most familiar form of electronic banking, which dispenses cash, accepts deposits, and allows balance inquiries and cash transfers from one account to another

automated clearinghouses (ACHs) a system that permits payments such as deposits or withdrawals to be made to and from a bank account by magnetic computer tape

▼ **TABLE 15.4** Facts about ATM Use

- The first ATM was introduced in 1969.
- 17 percent of Americans use ATMs as their primary banking method.
- The United States has more than 425,000 ATMs.
- More than 11.8 billion ATM transactions take place annually.
- The top five ATM owners are Cardtronics, Payment Alliance, Bank of America, JPMorgan Chase, and Wells Fargo.

Source: Tyler Metzger, "ATM Use in the United States," *CreditCards.com*, www.creditcards .com/credit-card-news/atm-use-statistics-3372.php (accessed April 2, 2010).

Electronic Banking

Since the advent of the computer age, a wide range of technological innovations has made it possible to move money all across the world electronically. Such "paperless" transactions have allowed financial institutions to reduce costs in what has been, and continues to be, a virtual competitive battlefield. **Electronic funds transfer (EFT)** is any movement of funds by means of an electronic terminal, telephone, computer, or magnetic tape. Such transactions order a particular financial institution to subtract money from one account and add it to another. The most commonly used forms of EFT are automated teller machines, automated clearinghouses, and home banking systems.

Automated Teller Machines Probably the most familiar form of electronic banking is the **automated teller machine (ATM)**, which dispenses cash, accepts deposits, and allows balance inquiries and cash transfers from one account to another. ATMs provide 24-hour banking services—both at home (through a local bank) and far away (via worldwide ATM networks such as Cirrus and Plus). Rapid growth, driven by both strong consumer acceptance and lower transaction costs for banks (about half the cost of teller transactions), has led to the installation of hundreds of thousands of ATMs worldwide. Table 15.4 presents some interesting statistics about ATMs.

Automated Clearinghouses

Automated clearinghouses (ACHs) permit payments such as deposits or withdrawals to be made to and from a bank account by magnetic computer tape. Most large U.S. employers, and many others worldwide, use ACHs to deposit their employees' paychecks directly to the employees' bank accounts. While direct deposit is used by only 50 percent of U.S. workers, nearly 100 percent of Japanese workers and more than 90 percent of European workers utilize it. The largest user of automated clearinghouses in the United States is the federal government, with 99 percent of federal government employees and 65 percent of the private workforce receiving their pay via direct deposit. More than 82 percent of all Social Security payments are made through an ACH system.

The advantages of direct deposits to consumers include convenience, safety, and potential interest earnings. It is estimated that more than 4 million paychecks are lost or stolen annually, and FBI studies show that 2,000 fraudulent checks are cashed every day in the United States. Checks can never be lost or stolen with direct deposit. The benefits to businesses include decreased check-processing expenses and increased employee productivity. Research shows that businesses that use direct deposit can save more than $1.25 on each payroll check processed. Productivity could increase by $3 to $5 billion annually if all employees were to use direct deposit rather than taking time away from work to deposit their payroll checks.

Some companies also use ACHs for dividend and interest payments. Consumers can also use ACHs to make periodic (usually monthly) fixed payments to specific creditors without ever having to write a check or buy stamps. The estimated number of bills paid annually by consumers is 20 billion, and the total number paid through ACHs is estimated at only 8.5 billion. The average consumer who writes 10 to 15 checks each month would save $41 to $62 annually in postage alone.[10]

Online Banking Many banking activities are now conducted on a computer at home or at work, or through wireless devices such as cell phones and PDAs anywhere there is a wireless "hot point." Consumers and small businesses can now make a bewildering array of financial transactions at home or

Computers and handheld devices have made online banking extremely convenient. However, hackers have stolen millions from banking customers by tricking them into visiting websites and downloading malicious software that gives the hackers access to their passwords.

on the go 24 hours a day. Functioning much like a vast network of personal ATMs, companies like Google and Apple provide online banking services through mobile phones, allowing subscribers to make sophisticated banking transactions, buy and sell stocks and bonds, and purchase products and airline tickets without ever leaving home or speaking to another human being. Many banks allow customers to log directly into their accounts to check balances, transfer money between accounts, view their account statements, and pay bills via home computer or other Internet-enabled devices. Computer and advanced telecommunications technology have revolutionized world commerce; 25 percent of adults list Internet banking as their preferred banking method, making it the most popular banking method in the United States.[11]

Banking in the Future and the Impact of the Financial Crisis

Rapid advances and innovations in technology are challenging the banking industry and requiring it to change. As we said earlier, more and more banks, both large and small, are offering electronic access to their financial services. ATM technology is rapidly changing, with machines now dispensing more than just cash. Online financial services, ATM technology, and bill

presentation are just a few of the areas where rapidly changing technology is causing the banking industry to change as well.

The premise that banks will get bigger over the next 10 years is uncertain. During 2007–2008, the financial markets collapsed under the weight of declining housing prices, subprime mortgages (mortgages with low-quality borrowers), and risky securities backed by these subprime mortgages. Because the value of bank assets declined dramatically, most large banks like CitiBank, Bank of America, and Wachovia had a shrinking capital base. That is, the amount of debt in relation to their equity was so high that they were below the minimum required capital requirements. This was a financial environment where banks did not trust the counterparties to their loans and asset-backed securities. In this environment, the markets ceased to function in an orderly fashion. To keep the banking system from total collapse, the U.S. Treasury and the Federal Reserve created the TARP program, an acronym for Troubled Asset Relief Program. This program allowed the Treasury to purchase up to $250 billion of senior preferred shares of bank securities.[12]

Most of the big banks either needed to take the cash infusion from the U.S. Treasury or were forced to sell preferred stock to the Treasury. The rationale from the government's point of view was that it didn't want

CONSUMER FINANCIAL PROTECTION BUREAU TO UNDERTAKE FINANCIAL REFORM

Financial products can be hard to comprehend. This inability to understand the risks of financial products and lending practices contributed to the 2008–2009 financial meltdown. To try to prevent similar problems in the future, the U.S. government has formed the Consumer Financial Protection Bureau (CFPB).

The CFPB became a reality as a component of the Dodd-Frank Act signed into law in July 2010. Established by Harvard Law Professor Elizabeth Warren, the bureau is designed to mimic the independent Consumer Product Safety Commission, which aims to keep unsafe consumer products

out of the hands of individuals. Instead of consumer products, however, the CFPB's authority involves financial products and services. The CFPB has rule-making authority and supervisory power over the credit market. Its goal is to make financial products and services easy to understand in terms of costs, risks, and product/service comparisons. It also aims to curtail unfair lending and credit card practices, to check the safety of financial products before they are launched into the market, and to require changes to those financial products deemed to be too"dangerous" or risky. According to Warren, the CFPB works proactively to supervise lenders by regularly checking their books and working together with both the attorneys general and the American people. When necessary, the CFPB will step in to enforce new rules on those not complying.

Although the CFPB sounds like a good idea, critics point out potential problems.

Banks are worried that the CFPB might increase costs and inhibit their decision-making authority to serve the market effectively. Warren and her team admit the bureau is merely in the beginning stages of functionality, but over time they believe it will have a strong positive impact on lenders and borrowers throughout the credit world.[13]

Discussion Questions

1. Why was it considered necessary to create the Consumer Financial Protection Bureau?
2. Is there any danger that the Consumer Financial Protection Bureau could abuse its decision-making authority and damage consumer access to some financial products?
3. Will the Consumer Financial Protection Bureau be able to identify and deal with all the financial products that are"dangerous" or"risky"?

to signal to the financial community which banks were strong and which ones were weak for fear that depositors would move massive amounts of money from weak banks to strong banks. This phenomenon actually occurred several times and forced banks like Wachovia to be merged with Wells Fargo.

During this period, the Federal Reserve took unprecedented actions that included buying up troubled assets from the banks and lending money at the discount window to nonbanks such as investment banks and brokers. The Fed also entered into the financial markets by making markets in commercial paper and other securities where the markets had ceased to function in an orderly fashion. Additionally, the Fed began to pay interest on reserves banks kept at the Fed and kept interest rates low to stimulate the economy and to help the banks regain their health. Because banks make money by the spread between their borrowing and lending rates, the Fed managed the spread between long- and short-term rates to generate a fairly large spread for the banks.

The Federal Deposit Insurance Corp. also took action. The institution adopted rules that require banks to share the risks of the securities they sell. Starting January 1, 2011, banks were required to hold 5 percent of securities on their books. The hope is that this will encourage banks to be more careful in screening their borrowers to prevent future financial meltdowns. The FDIC also created new rules over what information banks must disclose to regulators and over the documents that borrowers must submit to be eligible for loans.[14]

Lastly, the future of the structure of the banking system is in the hands of the U.S. Congress. In reaction to the financial meltdown and severe recession, politicians are passing new financial regulations that will limit the ability of banks to create this type of problem again. The greatest of these regulations to date is the Dodd-Frank Wall Street Reform and Consumer Protection Act passed in 2010. The purpose of the Dodd-Frank Act is to reform the financial industry, end "too big to fail" businesses, create greater transparency and accountability, and protect consumers from deceptive or complex financial products. One of the agencies created by Dodd-Frank is the Consumer Financial Protection Bureau, discussed in our boxed feature. Dodd-Frank has 16 major provisions that cover nearly every aspect of the finance industry, including new agencies to ensure financial stability; debit card fees; mortgage reform; insurance; predatory lending; the Federal Reserve; and more. The legal appendix to Chapter 2 goes into further detail on these new laws. Other financial reform proposals being discussed include placing limits on bank sizes and eliminating the Graham-Leach-Bliley Act, which did away with some major consumer protections and contributed to the deregulation of the financial and banking industries. Only time will tell what is in store for the U.S. banking system. ▪

SO YOU'RE INTERESTED // in Financial Systems or Banking /

You think you might be interested in going into finance or banking, but it is so hard to tell when you are a full-time student. Classes that seem interesting when you take them might not translate into an interesting work experience after you graduate. A great way to see if you would excel at a career in finance is to get some experience in the industry. Internships, whether they are paid or unpaid, not only help you figure out what you might really want to do after you graduate but they are also a great way to build up your résumé, put your learning to use, and start generating connections within the field.

For example, for the past four years, Pennsylvania's Delaware County District Attorney's Office has been accepting business students from Villanova University for a six-month internship. The students work in the economic-crime division, analyzing documents of people under investigation for financial crimes ranging from fraud to money laundering. The students get actual experience in forensic accounting and have the chance to see whether this is the right career path. On top of that, the program has saved the county an average of $20,000 annually on consulting and accounting fees, not to mention that detectives now have more time to take on larger caseloads. Michael Busby, a student who completed the program, spent his six months investigating a case in which the owner of a sewage treatment company had embezzled a total of $1 million over the course of nine years. Busby noted that the experience helped him gain an understanding about how different companies handle their financial statements, as well as how accounting can be applied in forensics and law enforcement.

Internship opportunities are plentiful all over the country, although you may need to do some research to find them. To start, talk to your program advisor and your professors about opportunities. Also, you can check company websites where you think you might like to work to see if they have any opportunities available. City, state, or federal government offices often provide student internships as well. No matter where you end up interning, the real-life skills you pick up, as well as the résumé boost you get, will be helpful in finding a job after you graduate. When you graduate, commercial banks and other financial institutions offer major employment opportunities. In 2008–2009, a major downturn in the financial industry resulted in mergers, acquisitions, and financial restructuring for many companies. While the immediate result was a decrease in job opportunities, as the industry recovers, there will be many challenging job opportunities available.[15]

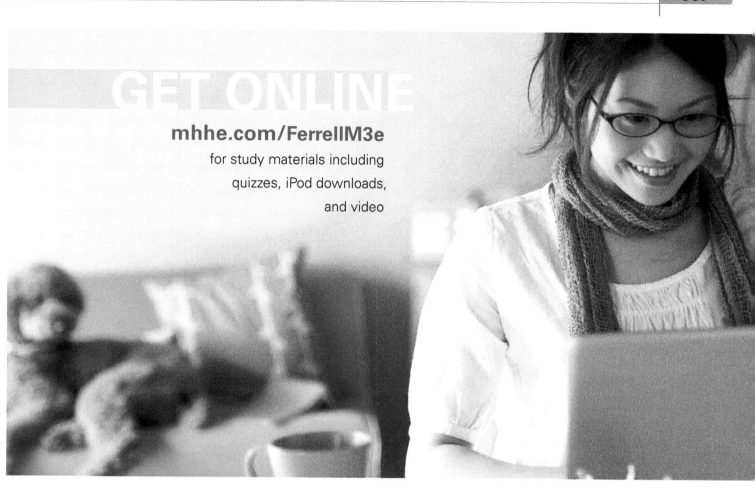

GET ONLINE

mhhe.com/FerrellM3e

for study materials including
quizzes, iPod downloads,
and video

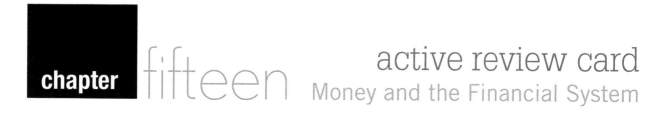

chapter fifteen

active review card
Money and the Financial System

in a nutshell

The Federal Reserve and other major financial institutions play significant roles in the financial system. In understanding finance, you need to consider the definition of money and the forms money may take. You also need to consider the future of the finance industry and the changes likely to occur over the course of the next several years.

The following statements will test your take-away knowledge from this chapter. Do your best to explain each one in the space provided below.

LO.1 Define money, its functions, and its characteristics.

LO.2 Describe various types of money.

LO.3 Specify how the Federal Reserve Board manages the money supply and regulates the American banking system.

LO.4 Compare and contrast commercial banks, savings and loan associations, credit unions, and mutual savings banks.

LO.5 Distinguish among nonbanking institutions such as insurance companies, pension funds, mutual funds, and finance companies.

LO.6 Investigate the challenges ahead for the banking industry.

Did your answers include the following important points?

LO.1. Define money, its functions, and its characteristics.

- Money is anything generally accepted as a means of payment for goods and services. Money serves as a medium of exchange, a measure of value, and a store of wealth.
- To serve effectively in these functions, money must be acceptable, divisible, portable, durable, stable in value, and difficult to counterfeit.

LO.2. Describe various types of money.

- Money may take the form of currency, checking accounts, or other accounts.
- Checking accounts are funds left in an account in a financial institution that can be withdrawn without advance notice.
- Other types of accounts include savings accounts, money market accounts, certificates of deposit, credit cards, and debit cards, as well as traveler's checks, money orders, and cashier's checks.

LO.3. Specify how the Federal Reserve Board manages the money supply and regulates the American banking system.

- The Federal Reserve Board regulates the U.S. financial system. The Fed manages the money supply by buying and selling government securities, raising or lowering the discount rate, raising or lowering bank reserve requirements, and adjusting down payment and repayment terms for credit purchases.
- It also regulates banking practices, processes checks, and oversees federal depository insurance for institutions.

LO.4. Compare and contrast commercial banks, savings and loan associations, credit unions, and mutual savings banks.

- Commercial banks are financial institutions that take and hold deposits in accounts for and make loans to individuals and businesses.
- Savings and loan associations are financial institutions that primarily specialize in offering savings accounts and mortgage loans. Mutual savings banks are similar to S&Ls, except that they are owned by their depositors.
- Credit unions are financial institutions owned and controlled by their depositors.

LO.5. Distinguish among nonbanking institutions such as insurance companies, pension funds, mutual funds, and finance companies.

- Insurance companies are businesses that protect their clients against financial losses due to certain circumstances, in exchange for a fee.
- Pension funds are investments set aside by organizations or individuals to meet retirement needs.
- Mutual funds pool investors' money and invest in large numbers of different types of securities, while brokerage firms buy and sell stocks and bonds for investors and finance companies make short-term loans at higher interest rates than banks.

LO.6. Investigate the challenges ahead for the banking industry.

- Future changes in financial regulations are likely to result in fewer but larger banks and other financial institutions.

Practical Application

LO.1.

- Trading one good or service for another of similar value is known as _____.
- When a dollar bill is handled hundreds of times and is still being used, it has _____.
- When inflation is very high, people no longer believe that money is _____.

LO.2.

- Another name for a savings account is a(n) _____.
- In general, the longer the term of a certificate of deposit, the higher its _____.
- The acronym NOW, when used in financial circles, stands for _____.

LO.3.

- To carry out its functions of controlling the supply of money, the Federal Reserve Board uses its _____.
- When the Federal Reserve buys securities, it _____.

LO.4.

- If employees of a local school district conduct their financial business through the same financial institution that they own and only they are allowed to join, the institution is probably a(n) _____.

- _____ are the oldest and largest of all financial institutions.
- The _____ was established in 1933 to help stop bank failures throughout the country during the Great Depression and has nearly 8,000 member institutions at present.

LO.5.

- Insurance companies invest premiums from insured individuals and businesses or make short-term loans, particularly to businesses in the form of _____.
- _____ permits home computer users to conduct banking activities through their personal computers.

LO.6.

- The Federal Reserve and the U.S Treasury created the _____ to save the banking system from total collapse.
- The future of the structure of the American banking system is largely in the hands of the _____.

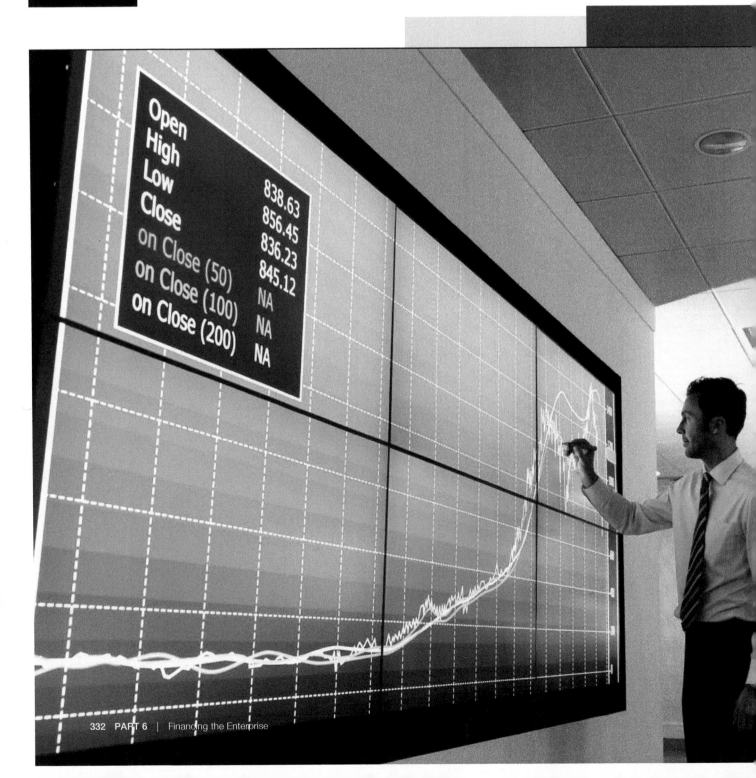

financial management
+ securities markets

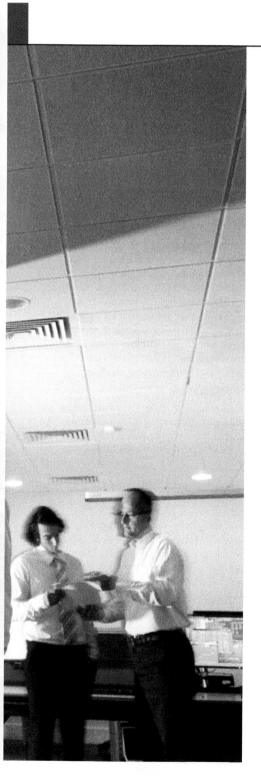

introduction

While it's certainly true that money makes the world go around, financial management is the discipline that makes the world turn more smoothly. Indeed, without effective management of assets, liabilities, and owners' equity, all business organizations are doomed to fail—regardless of the quality and innovativeness of their products. Financial management is the field that addresses the issues of obtaining and managing the funds and resources necessary to run a business successfully. It is not limited to business organizations: All organizations, from the corner store to the local nonprofit art museum, from giant corporations to county governments, must manage their resources effectively and efficiently if they are to achieve their objectives.

In this chapter, we look at both short- and long-term financial management. First, we discuss the management of short-term assets, which companies use to generate sales and conduct ordinary day-to-day business operations.

Next, we turn our attention to the management of short-term liabilities, the sources of short-term funds used to finance the business. Then, we discuss the management of long-term assets such as plants, equipment, and the use of common stock (equity) and bonds (long-term liability) to finance these long-term corporate assets. Finally, we look at the securities markets, where stocks and bonds are traded.

LEARNING OBJECTIVES

LO1 Describe some common methods of managing current assets.

LO2 Identify some sources of short-term financing (current liabilities).

LO3 Summarize the importance of long-term assets and capital budgeting.

LO4 Specify how companies finance their operations and manage fixed assets with long-term liabilities, particularly bonds.

LO5 Discuss how corporations can use equity financing by issuing stock through an investment banker.

LO6 Describe the various securities markets in the United States.

working capital management the managing of short-term assets and liabilities

transaction balances cash kept on hand by a firm to pay normal daily expenses, such as employee wages and bills for supplies and utilities

lockbox an address, usually a commercial bank, at which a company receives payments in order to speed collections from customers

MANAGING CURRENT ASSETS AND LIABILITIES

Managing short-term assets and liabilities involves managing the current assets and liabilities on the balance sheet (discussed in Chapter 14). Current assets are short-term resources such as cash, investments, accounts receivable, and inventory. Current liabilities are short-term debts such as accounts payable, accrued salaries, accrued taxes, and short-term bank loans. We use the terms *current* and *short term* interchangeably because short-term assets and liabilities are usually replaced by new assets and liabilities within three or four months, and always within a year. Managing short-term assets and liabilities is sometimes called **working capital management** because short-term assets and liabilities continually flow through an organization and are thus said to be "working."

Managing Current Assets

The chief goal of financial managers who focus on current assets and liabilities is to maximize the return to the business on cash, temporary investments of idle cash, accounts receivable, and inventory.

Managing Cash
A crucial element facing any financial manager is effectively managing the firm's cash flow. Remember that cash flow is the movement of money through an organization on a daily, weekly, monthly, or yearly basis. Ensuring that sufficient (but not excessive) funds are on hand to meet the company's obligations is one of the single most important facets of financial management.

Idle cash does not make money, and corporate checking accounts typically do not earn interest. As a result, astute money managers try to keep just enough cash on hand, called **transaction balances**, to pay bills—such as employee wages, supplies, and utilities—as they fall due. To manage the firm's cash and ensure that enough cash flows through the organization quickly and efficiently, companies try to speed up cash collections from customers.

To facilitate collection, some companies have customers send their payments to a **lockbox**, which is simply an address for receiving payments, instead of directly to the company's main address. The manager of the lockbox, usually a commercial bank, collects payments directly from the lockbox several times a day and deposits them into the company's bank account. The bank can then start clearing the checks and get the money into the company's checking account much more quickly than if the payments had been submitted directly to the company. However, there is no free lunch: The costs associated with lockbox systems make them worthwhile only for those companies that receive thousands of checks from customers each business day.

Large firms with many stores or offices around the country, such as HSBC Finance Corporation, formerly known as Household International, frequently use electronic funds transfer to speed up collections. HSBC Finance Corporation's local offices deposit checks received each business day into their local banks and, at the end of the day, HSBC Finance Corporation's corporate office initiates the transfer of all collected funds to its central bank for overnight investment. This technique is especially attractive for major international companies, which face slow and sometimes uncertain physical delivery of payments and/or less-than-efficient check-clearing procedures.

More and more companies are now using electronic funds transfer systems to pay and collect bills online. Companies generally want to collect cash quickly but pay out cash slowly. When companies use electronic funds transfers between buyers and

MISSION MOTORS LICENSES THE FASTEST E-BIKES TO RAISE FUNDS

What do software and motorcycles have in common? They are both licensed by Mission Motors. Mission Motors is a software company that combines lithium-ion batteries with its own cooling and management technology to create electric power systems. In order to entice investors to fund its electric power systems, Mission Motors plans to sell a limited number of its $68,995 e-motorcycles, equipped with its battery system.

Why motorcycles? The current financial environment is making it difficult for start-ups to acquire funding. For this reason, companies such as Mission Motors are pursuing licensing rather than doing their own manufacturing. The motorcycles might also give it an edge over the 20 other lithium-ion battery start-ups out there. Mission's motorcycles have certainly gained attention, particularly after they achieved an e-motorcycle record speed of 150 miles per hour. To date, Mission has raised over $3 million and may link up with China's largest motorcycle maker Zongshen Power Machinery.[1]

suppliers, the speed of collections and disbursements increases to one day. Only with the use of checks can companies delay the payment of cash by three or four days until the check is presented to their bank and the cash leaves their account.

Investing Idle Cash As companies sell products, they generate cash on a daily basis, and sometimes cash comes in faster than it is needed to pay bills. Organizations often invest this "extra" cash, for periods as short as one day (overnight) or for as long as one year, until it is needed. Such temporary investments of cash are known as **marketable securities**. Examples include U.S. Treasury bills, certificates of deposit, commercial paper, and eurodollar deposits. Table 16.1 summarizes a number of different marketable securities used by businesses and some sample interest rates on these investments as of June 23, 2006, and April 15, 2011. The safety rankings are relative. While all of the listed securities are very low risk, the U.S. government securities are the safest. You can see from the table that interest rates have declined during the two periods presented.

You may never see interest rates this low in your lifetime. The Fed used monetary policy to lower interest rates to stimulate borrowing and investment during the severe recession of 2007–2009 and continued to maintain low rates into 2011 in order to stimulate employment and economic growth.

Many large companies invest idle cash in U.S. **Treasury bills (T-bills)**, which are short-term debt obligations the U.S. government sells to raise money. Issued weekly by the U.S. Treasury, T-bills carry maturities of between one week to one year. U.S. T-bills are generally considered to be the safest of all investments and are called risk free because the U.S. government will not default on its debt.

Commercial certificates of deposit (CDs) are issued by commercial banks and brokerage companies. They are available in minimum amounts of $100,000 but are typically in units of $1 million for large corporations investing excess cash. Unlike consumer CDs (discussed in Chapter 15), which must be held until maturity, commercial CDs may be traded prior to maturity. Should a cash shortage occur, the organization can simply sell the CD on the open market and obtain needed funds.

One of the most popular short-term investments for the largest business organizations is **commercial paper**—a written promise from one company to another to pay a specific amount of money. Because commercial paper is backed only by the name and reputation of the issuing company, sales of commercial paper are restricted to only the largest and most financially stable companies. As commercial paper is frequently bought and sold for durations of as short as one business day, many "players" in the market find themselves buying commercial paper with excess cash on one day and selling it to gain extra money the following day.

During 2007 and 2008, the commercial paper market simply stopped functioning. Investors no longer trusted the IOUs of even the best companies. Companies that had relied on commercial paper to fund short-term cash needs had to turn to the banks for borrowing. Those companies who had existing lines of credit at their bank were able to draw on their line of credit. Others were in a tight spot. Eventually, the Federal Reserve entered the market to buy and sell commercial paper for its own portfolio. This is something the Fed was not in the habit of doing. But it rescued the market.

Some companies invest idle cash in international markets such as the **eurodollar market**, a market for trading U.S. dollars in foreign countries. Because the eurodollar market was originally developed by London banks, any dollar-denominated deposit

marketable securities temporary investment of "extra" cash by organizations for up to one year in U.S. Treasury bills, certificates of deposit, commercial paper, or eurodollar loans

Treasury bills (T-bills) short-term debt obligations the U.S. government sells to raise money

commercial certificates of deposit (CDs) certificates of deposit issued by commercial banks and brokerage companies, available in minimum amounts of $100,000, which may be traded prior to maturity

commercial paper a written promise from one company to another to pay a specific amount of money

eurodollar market a market centered in London for trading U.S. dollars in foreign countries

▼ **TABLE 16.1** Short-Term Investment Possibilities for Idle Cash

Type of Security	Maturity	Seller of Security	Interest Rate 6/23/2006	Interest Rate 4/15/2011	Safety Level
U.S. Treasury bills	90 days	U.S. government	4.80%	0.06%	Excellent
U.S. Treasury bills	180 days	U.S. government	5.05	0.12	Excellent
Commercial paper	30 days	Major corporations	5.14	0.16	Very good
Certificates of deposit	90 days	U.S. commercial banks	5.40	0.23	Very good
Certificates of deposit	180 days	U.S. commercial banks	5.43	0.32	Very good
Eurodollars	90 days	European commercial banks	5.48	0.42	Very good

Source: "Selected Interest Rates," *Federal Reserve Statistical Release,* April 18, 2011, www.federalreserve.gov/releases/h15/current (accessed April 20, 2011).

Firms and individuals can buy and redeem T-bills and other government securities from the U.S. Department of the Treasury at www. treasurydirect.com.

in a non-U.S. bank is called a eurodollar deposit, regardless of whether the issuing bank is actually located in Europe, South America, or anyplace else. For example, if you travel overseas and deposit $1,000 in a German bank, you will have "created" a eurodollar deposit in the amount of $1,000. Because the U.S. dollar is accepted by most countries for international trade, these dollar deposits can be used by international companies to settle their accounts. The market created for trading such investments offers firms with extra dollars a chance to earn a slightly higher rate of return with just a little more risk than they would face by investing in U.S. Treasury bills.

Maximizing Accounts Receivable

After cash and marketable securities, the balance sheet lists accounts receivable and inventory. Remember that accounts receivable is money owed to a business by credit customers. For example, if you charge your Shell gasoline purchases, until you actually pay for them with cash or a check, they represent an account receivable to Shell. Many businesses make the vast majority of their sales on credit, so managing accounts receivable is an important task.

Each credit sale represents an account receivable for the company, the terms of which typically require customers to pay the full amount due within 30, 60, or even 90 days from the date of the sale. To encourage quick payment, some businesses offer some of their customers discounts of between 1 to 2 percent if they pay off their balance within a specified period of time (usually between 10 and 30 days). On the other hand, late payment charges of between 1 and 1.5 percent serve to discourage slow payers from sitting on their bills forever. The larger the early payment discount offered, the faster customers will tend to pay their accounts. Unfortunately, while discounts increase cash flow, they also reduce profitability. Finding the right balance between the added advantages of early cash receipt and the disadvantages of reduced profits is no simple matter. Similarly, determining the optimal balance between the higher sales likely to result from extending credit to customers with less than sterling credit ratings and the higher bad-debt losses likely to result from a more lenient credit policy is also challenging. Information on company credit ratings is provided by local credit bureaus, national credit-rating agencies such as Dun and Bradstreet, and industry trade groups.

Optimizing Inventory

While the inventory that a firm holds is controlled by both production needs and marketing considerations, the financial manager has to coordinate inventory purchases to manage cash flows. The object is to minimize the firm's investment in inventory without experiencing production cutbacks as a result of critical materials shortfalls or lost sales due to insufficient finished goods inventories. Every dollar invested in inventory is a dollar unavailable for investment in some other area of the organization. Optimal inventory levels are determined in large part by the method of production. If a firm attempts to produce its goods just in time to meet sales demand, the level of inventory will be relatively low. If, on the other hand, the firm produces materials in a constant, level pattern, inventory increases when sales decrease and decreases when sales increase. One way that companies are attempting to optimize inventory is through the use of radio frequency identification (RFID) technology. Companies such as Walmart are attempting to better manage their inventories by using RFID tags. An RFID tag, which contains a silicon chip and an antenna, allows a company to use radio waves to track and identify the products to which the tags are attached. These tags are primarily used to track inventory shipments from the manufacturer to the buyer's warehouses and then to the individual stores.

The automobile industry is an excellent example of an industry driven almost solely by inventory levels. Because it is inefficient to continually lay off workers in slow times and call them back in better times, Ford, General Motors, and Chrysler try to set and stick to quarterly production quotas. Automakers typically try to keep a 60-day supply of unsold cars. During particularly slow periods, however, it is not unusual for inventories to exceed 100 days of sales.

Although less publicized, inventory shortages can be as much of a drag on potential profits as too much inventory. Not having an item on hand may send the customer to a competitor—forever. Complex computer inventory models are frequently employed to determine the optimum level of inventory a firm should hold to support a given level of sales. Such models can indicate how and when parts inventories should be ordered so that they are available exactly when required—and not a day before. Developing and maintaining such an intricate production and inventory system is difficult, but it can often prove to be the difference between experiencing average profits and spectacular ones.

Managing Current Liabilities

While having extra cash on hand is a delightful surprise, the opposite situation—a temporary cash shortfall—can be a crisis. The good news is that there are several potential sources of short-term funds. Suppliers often serve as an important source through credit sales practices. Also, banks, finance companies, and other organizations offer short-term funds through loans and other business operations.

Accounts Payable Remember from Chapter 14 that accounts payable is money an organization owes to suppliers for goods and services. Just as accounts receivable must be actively managed to ensure proper cash collections, so too must accounts payable be managed to make the best use of this important liability.

The most widely used source of short-term financing, and therefore the most important account payable, is **trade credit**—credit extended by suppliers for the purchase of their goods and services. While varying in formality, depending on both the organizations involved and the value of the items purchased, most trade credit agreements offer discounts to organizations that pay their bills early. A supplier, for example, may offer trade terms of "1/10 net 30," meaning that the purchasing organization may take a 1 percent discount from the invoice amount if it makes payment by the 10th day after receiving the bill. Otherwise, the entire amount is due within 30 days. For example, pretend that you are the financial manager in charge of payables. You owe Ajax Company $10,000, and it offers trade terms of 2/10 net 30. By paying the amount due within 10 days, you can save 2 percent of $10,000, or $200. Assume you place orders with Ajax once per month and have 12 bills of $10,000 each per year. By taking the discount every time, you will save 12 times $200, or $2,400, per year. Now assume you are the financial manager of Gigantic Corp., and it has monthly payables of $100 million per month. Two percent of $100 million is $2 million per month. Failure to take advantage of such trade discounts can add up to large opportunity losses over the span of a year.

Bank Loans Virtually all organizations—large and small—obtain short-term funds for operations from banks. In most instances, the credit services granted these firms take the form of a line of credit or fixed dollar loan. A **line of credit** is an arrangement by which a bank agrees to lend a specified amount of money to the organization upon request—provided that the bank has the required funds to make the loan. In general, a business line of credit is very similar to a consumer credit card, with the exception that the preset credit limit can amount to millions of dollars.

In addition to credit lines, banks also make **secured loans**—loans backed by collateral that the bank can claim if the

trade credit credit extended by suppliers for the purchase of their goods and services

line of credit an arrangement by which a bank agrees to lend a specified amount of money to an organization upon request

secured loans loans backed by collateral that the bank can claim if the borrowers do not repay them

---

Y COMBINATOR GIVES BOOST TO STARTUP COMPANIES

Although thousands of companies failed during the most recent recession, Y Combinator and the companies it assists were among those thriving. Founder Paul Graham (famous in tech circles for creating Viaweb—sold to Yahoo! for $49 million) launched Y Combinator in 2005. His method is somewhat like a school for startups, and his funding somewhat like financial aid. Graham gathers entrepreneurs for three-month periods, during which time he provides them with small loans (typically under $20,000) to meet basic needs, allowing them to focus on developing their fledgling companies. In exchange, Y Combinator receives a 2 to 10 percent company stake.

Graham offers something more valuable than a simple loan—an experienced eye, solid advice, and a positive and creative environment. Y Combinator focuses on tech startups, with an emphasis on Web-based applications. Graham's experience allows him to help direct, or redirect, founders toward workable concepts attractive to larger investors. His business motto is "Make something people want." Graham also addresses running businesses, handling investors, and dealing with acquisitions. Y Combinator was rated number eleven in *BusinessWeek's* top angel investors.

Small businesses like those funded by Y Combinator are making some *Fortune* 500 companies nervous. For example, eBay, for all of its success, does not often update its auction system. This leaves room for a small startup to gain market share if it can provide a superior service. These small companies are often less expensive and more flexible, making them better equipped to do well in a recession. Although Graham takes a risk with each startup, graduates such as Scribd (which partnered with literary giants and received over $12 million in venture capital funding) and Omnisio (purchased by Google for more than $15 million) make it worthwhile. Some of the companies flourish—and when they do, Graham makes a substantial profit.[2]

Discussion Questions
1. Why has Y Combinator succeeded while many other firms in the financial industry have failed?
2. What are the risks involved in creating a business like Y Combinator?
3. What are the rewards for Graham in taking a risk in small tech startups?

Because both businesses and individuals want to keep their financing costs to a minimum, when interest rates drop, their investment in assets tends to increase.

borrowers do not repay the loans—and **unsecured loans**—loans backed only by the borrowers' good reputation and previous credit rating. Both individuals and businesses build their credit rating from their history of borrowing and repaying borrowed funds on time and in full. The three national credit-rating services are Equifax, TransUnion, and Experian. A lack of credit history or a poor credit history can make it difficult to get loans from financial institutions. The *principal* is the amount of money borrowed; *interest* is a percentage of the principal that the bank charges for use of its money. As we mentioned in Chapter 15, banks also pay depositors interest on savings accounts and some checking accounts. Thus, banks charge borrowers interest for loans and pay interest to depositors for the use of their money. In addition, these loans may include origination fees.

One of the complaints from borrowers during the financial meltdown and recession was that banks weren't willing to lend. There were several causes. Banks were trying to rebuild their capital, and they didn't want to take the extra risk that lending offers in an economic recession. They were drowning in bad debts and were not sure how future loan losses would affect their capital. The banks' lack of lending caused problems for small businesses.

The **prime rate** is the interest rate commercial banks charge their best customers (usually large corporations) for short-term loans. While for many years, loans at the prime rate represented funds at the lowest possible cost, the rapid development of the market for commercial paper has dramatically reduced the importance of commercial banks as a source of short-term loans. Today, most "prime" borrowers are actually small- and medium-sized businesses.

The interest rates on commercial loans may be either fixed or variable. A variable, or floating-rate, loan offers an advantage when interest rates are falling but represents a distinct disadvantage when interest rates are rising. Between 1999 and 2004, interest rates plummeted, and borrowers refinanced their loans with low-cost fixed-rate loans. Nowhere was this more visible than in the U.S. mortgage markets, where homeowners lined up to refinance their high-percentage home mortgages with lower-cost loans, in some cases as low as 5 percent on a 30-year loan. These mortgage interest rates had returned to 6.5 percent by mid-2006, but by the end of 2009 they had declined to less than 5.0 percent and were still hovering around 5 percent in spring of 2011. Individuals and corporations have the same motivation: to minimize their borrowing costs.

Nonbank Liabilities Banks are not the only source of short-term funds for businesses. Indeed, virtually all financial institutions, from insurance companies to pension funds, from money market funds to finance companies, make short-term loans to many organizations. The largest U.S. companies also actively engage in borrowing money from the eurodollar and commercial paper markets. As noted earlier, both of these funds' sources are typically slightly less expensive than bank loans.

In some instances, businesses actually sell their accounts receivable to a finance company known as a **factor**, which gives the selling organizations cash and assumes responsibility for collecting the accounts. For example, a factor might pay $60,000 for receivables with a total face value of $100,000 (60 percent of the total). The factor profits if it can collect more than what it paid for the accounts. Because the selling organization's customers send their payments to a lockbox, they may have no idea that a factor has bought their receivables.

Additional nonbank liabilities that must be efficiently managed to ensure maximum profitability are taxes owed to the government and wages owed to employees. Clearly, businesses are responsible for many different types of taxes, including federal, state, and local income taxes, property taxes, mineral rights taxes, unemployment taxes, Social Security taxes, workers' compensation taxes, excise taxes, and more. While the public tends to think that the only relevant taxes are on income and sales, many industries must pay other taxes that far exceed those levied against their income. Taxes and employees' wages represent debt obligations of the firm, which the financial manager must plan to meet as they fall due.

MANAGING FIXED ASSETS

Up to this point, we have focused on the short-term aspects of financial management. While most business failures are the result of poor short-term planning, successful ventures must also consider the long-term financial consequences of their

approach is leasing assets such as equipment, machines, and buildings. Leasing involves paying a fee for usage rather than owning the asset. There are two kinds of leases: capital leases and operating leases. A capital lease is a long-term contract and shows up on the balance sheet as an asset and liability. The operating lease is a short-term cancelable lease and does not show up on the balance sheet. We'll take a closer look at long-term financing in a moment, but first let's address some issues associated with fixed assets, including capital budgeting, risk assessment, and the costs of financing fixed assets.

Capital Budgeting and Project Selection

One of the most important jobs performed by the financial manager is to decide what fixed assets, projects, and investments will earn profits for the firm beyond the costs necessary to fund them. The process of analyzing the needs of the business and selecting the assets that will maximize

> **All assets and projects must be continually reevaluated to ensure their compatibility with the organization's needs.**

actions. Managing the long-term assets and liabilities and the owners' equity portion of the balance sheet is important for the long-term health of the business.

Long-term (fixed) assets are expected to last for many years—production facilities (plants), offices, equipment, heavy machinery, furniture, automobiles, and so on. In today's fast-paced world, companies need the most technologically advanced, modern facilities and equipment they can afford. Automobile, oil refining, and transportation companies are dependent on fixed assets.

Modern and high-tech equipment carry high price tags, and the financial arrangements required to support these investments are by no means trivial. Leasing is just one approach to financing. Obtaining major long-term financing can be challenging for even the most profitable organizations. For less successful firms, such challenges can prove nearly impossible. One

Although pharmaceutical manufacturers may want to undertake many projects, the costs involved require them to use capital budgeting to determine which projects will lead to the greatest profits. The company Allergan used capital budgeting to determine the potential profitability of the eye medication Restasis.

its value is called **capital budgeting**, and the capital budget is the amount of money budgeted for investment in such long-term assets. But capital budgeting does not end with the selection and purchase of a particular piece of land, equipment, or major investment. All assets and projects must be continually reevaluated to ensure their compatibility with the organization's needs. Financial executives believe most budgeting activities are occasionally or frequently unrealistic or irrelevant. If a particular asset does not live up to expectations, then management must determine why and take necessary corrective action. Budgeting is not an exact process, and managers must be flexible when new information is available.

Assessing Risk

Every investment carries some risk. Figure 16.1 ranks potential investment projects according to estimated risk. When considering investments overseas, risk assessments must include the political climate and economic stability of a region. The decision to introduce a product or build a manufacturing facility in England would be much less risky than a decision to build one in the Middle East, for example.

The longer a project or asset is expected to last, the greater its potential risk because it is hard to predict whether a piece of equipment will wear out or become obsolete in 5 or 10 years. Predicting cash flows one year down the road is difficult, but projecting them over the span of a 10-year project is a gamble.

The level of a project's risk is also affected by the stability and competitive nature of the marketplace and the world economy as a whole. IBM's latest high-technology computer product is far more likely to become obsolete overnight than is a similar $10 million investment in a manufacturing plant. Dramatic changes in the marketplace are not uncommon. Indeed, uncertainty created by the rapid devaluation of Asian currencies in the late 1990s wrecked a host of assumptions in literally hundreds of projects worldwide. Financial managers must constantly consider such issues when making long-term decisions about the purchase of fixed assets.

Pricing Long-Term Money

The ultimate profitability of any project depends not only on accurate assumptions of how much cash it will generate, but also on its financing costs. Because a business must pay interest on money it borrows, the returns from any project must cover not only the costs of operating the project but also the interest expenses for the debt used to finance its construction. Unless an organization can effectively cover all of its costs—both financial and operating—it will eventually fail.

Clearly, only a limited supply of funds is available for investment in any given enterprise. The most efficient and profitable companies can attract the lowest-cost funds because they typically offer reasonable financial returns at very low relative risks. Newer and less prosperous firms must pay higher costs to attract capital because these companies tend to be quite risky. One of the strongest motivations for companies to manage their financial resources wisely is that they will, over time, be able to reduce the costs of their funds and in so doing increase their overall profitability.

In our free-enterprise economy, new firms tend to enter industries that offer the greatest potential rewards for success. However,

FIGURE 16.1
Qualitative Assessment of Capital Budgeting Risk

as more and more companies enter an industry, competition intensifies, eventually driving profits down to average levels. The digital music player market of the early 2000s provides an excellent example of the changes in profitability that typically accompany increasing competition. The sign of a successful capital budgeting program is that the new products create higher than normal profits and drive sales and the stock price up. This has certainly been true for Apple. It introduced the first iPod in 2001, and after many enhancements it continued to sell 8.3 million iPods in 2007. Its sales have grown from $6.2 billion in 2003 to $65.2 billion in 2010, while its earnings per share have increased from $0.10 per share to $15.25 during the same time frame. From a low price of $6.36 per share in 2003, its stocks rose to a high of $350 on April, 8, 2011. Note that $1,000 invested in Apple at its low point in 2003 would be worth approximately $55,000 on April, 8, 2011, at $350 per share.[3]

The success of the iPod and iTunes was followed up with the introduction of the iPhone in 2007. The iPhone was followed by the successful introduction of the iPad tablet in April 2010. The combination of these products and the ease of synchronization with the iMac computers caused a complementary sales effect for Apple computers. Even with a well-planned capital budgeting program, it may be difficult for Apple to stay ahead of the competition because it is difficult to maintain market dominance in the consumer electronics industry for extended periods of time.

The same is true in the personal computer market. With increasing competition, prices have fallen dramatically since the 1990s. Even Dell, with its low-cost products, has moved into other markets such as servers and televisions in order to maintain growth in a maturing market. Weaker companies have failed, leaving the most efficient producers/marketers scrambling for market share. The expanded market for personal computers dramatically reduced the financial returns generated by each dollar invested in productive assets. The "glory days" of the personal computer industry—the time in which fortunes

could be won and lost in the space of an average-sized garage—have long since passed into history. Personal computers have essentially become commodity items, and profit margins for companies in this industry have shrunk as the market matures. With sales falling and profits falling faster, Hewlett-Packard and Compaq merged to gain the economies of scale that saved money and created efficiencies.

> **long-term liabilities** debts that will be repaid over a number of years, such as long-term loans and bond issues
>
> **bonds** debt instruments that larger companies sell to raise long-term funds

FINANCING WITH LONG-TERM LIABILITIES

As we said earlier, long-term assets do not come cheaply, and few companies have the cash on hand to open a new store across town, build a new manufacturing facility, research and develop a new life-saving drug, or launch a new product worldwide. To develop such fixed assets, companies need to raise low-cost long-term funds to finance them. Two common choices for raising these funds are attracting new owners (*equity financing*), which we'll look at in a moment, and taking on long-term liabilities (*debt financing*), which we'll look at now.

Long-term liabilities are debts that will be repaid over a number of years, such as long-term bank loans and bond issues. These take many different forms, but in the end, the key word is *debt*. Companies may raise money by borrowing it from commercial banks or other financial institutions in the form of lines of credit, short-term loans, or long-term loans. Many corporations acquire debt by borrowing money from pension funds, mutual funds, or life-insurance funds.

Companies that rely too heavily on debt can get into serious trouble should the economy falter; during these times, they may not earn enough operating income to make the required interest payments (remember the times-interest-earned ratio in Chapter 14). In severe cases when the problem persists too long, creditors will not restructure loans but will instead sue for the interest and principal owed and force the company into bankruptcy.

Bonds: Corporate IOUs

Much long-term debt takes the form of **bonds**, which are debt instruments that larger companies sell to raise long-term funds. In essence, the buyers of bonds (bondholders) loan the issuer of the bonds cash in exchange for regular interest payments until the loan is repaid on or before the specified maturity date. The bond itself is a certificate, much like an IOU, that represents the company's debt to the bondholder. Bonds are issued by a wide variety of entities, including corporations; national, state, and local governments; public utilities; and nonprofit corporations. Most bondholders need not hold their bonds until maturity; rather, the existence of active secondary markets of brokers and dealers allows for the quick and efficient transfer of bonds from owner to owner.

As a public corporation, one way in which Dell takes on long-term debt is in the form of bonds. The company sells bonds to raise long-term funds.

unsecured bonds debentures, or bonds that are not backed by specific collateral	**secured bonds** bonds that are backed by specific collateral that must be forfeited in the event that the issuing firm defaults	**serial bonds** a sequence of small bond issues of progressively longer maturity	**floating-rate bonds** bonds with interest rates that change with current interest rates otherwise available in the economy	**junk bonds** a special type of high-interest-rate bond that carries higher inherent risks

The bond contract, or *indenture,* specifies all of the terms of the agreement between the bondholders and the issuing organization. The indenture, which can run more than 100 pages, specifies the basic terms of the bond, such as its face value, maturity date, and the annual interest rate. Table 16.2 briefly explains how to determine these and more things about a bond from a bond quote, as it might appear in *The Financial Times.* The face value of the bond, its initial sales price, is typically $1,000. After this, however, the price of the bond on the open market will fluctuate along with changes in the economy (particularly, changes in interest rates) and in the creditworthiness of the issuer. Bondholders receive the face value of the bond along with the final interest payment on the maturity date. The annual interest rate (often called the *coupon rate*) is the guaranteed percentage of face value that the company will pay to the bond owner every year. For example, a $1,000 bond with a coupon rate of 7 percent would pay $70 per year in interest. In most cases, bond indentures specify that interest payments be made every six months. In the example above, the $70 annual payment would be divided into two semiannual payments of $35.

In addition to the terms of interest payments and maturity date, the bond indenture typically covers other important topics, such as repayment methods, interest payment dates, procedures to be followed in case the organization fails to make the interest payments, conditions for the early repayment of the bonds, and any conditions requiring the pledging of assets as collateral.

Types of Bonds

Not surprisingly, there are a great many different types of bonds. Most are **unsecured bonds**, meaning that they are not backed by collateral; such bonds are termed *debentures.* **Secured bonds**, on the other hand, are backed by specific collateral that must be forfeited in the event that the issuing firm defaults. Whether secured or unsecured, bonds may be repaid in one lump sum or with many payments spread out over a period of time. **Serial bonds**, which are different from secured bonds, are actually a sequence of small bond issues of progressively longer maturity. The firm pays off each of the serial bonds as they mature. **Floating-rate bonds** do not have fixed interest payments; instead, the interest rate changes with current interest rates otherwise available in the economy.

In recent years, a special type of high-interest-rate bond has attracted considerable attention (usually negative) in the financial press. High-interest bonds, or **junk bonds** as they are popularly known, offer relatively high rates of interest because they have higher inherent risks. Historically, junk bonds have been associated with companies in poor financial health and/or startup firms with limited track records. In the mid-1980s, however, junk bonds became a very attractive method of financing corporate mergers; they remain popular today with many investors as a result of their very high relative interest rates. But higher risks are associated with those higher returns (upward of 12 percent per year in some cases) and the average investor would be well-advised to heed those famous words: Look before you leap!

▼ **TABLE 16.2** Bonds—Global Investment Grade Quoted in US $

30-Mar-10	Red Date [a]	Coupon[b]	S[c]	M[c]	F[c]	Bid Price[d]	Bid Yield[e]	Spread vs. Govts.[f]
GE Capital	01/16	5.00	AA+	Aa3	AA−	103.7	4.01	1.56
AT&T Wireless	03/31	8.75	A	A2	A	128.2	6.3	1.53
Goldman Sachs	02/33	6.13	A	A1	A+	98.29	6.27	1.49

[a]Red Date—the month and year that the bond matures and must pay back the borrowed amount.

[b]Coupon—the percentage in interest payment that the bond pays based on a $1,000 bond. For example, the GE Capital bond pays 5 percent on $1,000 or $50 per year while the AT&T bond pays $87.50.

[c]S-M-F—the ratings provided by the three major rating agenices: S (Standard and Poor's), M (Moody's), and F (Fitch). Using Standard and Poor's as an example, a rating of AAA would be the highest quality and lowest risk bond. Any bond in the A category is investment grade and considered high quality.

[d]Bid Price—the price as a percentage of par value ($1,000) that investors are willing to pay for a bond. For example, the GE capital bond has a bid price of 103.69, which would translate into 103% of $1,000 or a price of $1,036.90.

[e]Bid Yield—the annual rate of return the investor would receive if he or she held the bond to maturity. For example, with the GE bond you would get $50 per year until the bond matured in January 2016, and you would receive $1,000 par value at maturity. Because you paid $1,036.90, you would lose $36.90 on your investment. The 4.01 percent bid yield reflects both the income from the interest payment and the loss on the investment.

[f]Spread vs. Govts.—represents the premium yield the corporate bond pays over a U.S. government bond of equal maturity. Because corporate bonds are riskier than government bonds, an investor would expect the corporation to pay more than a risk-free government bond. In the case of GE Capital, the premium the company pays is an extra 1.56 percent.

Source: *The Financial Times,* March 31, 2010, p. 23.

SHAREHOLDERS ENJOY GROWTH AT DICK'S SPORTING GOODS

What began in 1948 as a small bait and tackle shop is now the multi-billion-dollar national sporting goods chain Dick's Sporting Goods. Founded by Richard Stack with $300 from his grandmother's cookie jar, the company is currently run by second-generation Ed Stack (CEO). Annual revenues in 2010 soared beyond the $4 billion mark, landing the company on the *Fortune* 500. Since the company's public debut in 2002, share value has increased over 600 percent. Analysts continue to predict growth for the company.

Such growth may be attributed in part to Ed Stack and the lessons that he has learned as CEO. With a personal stake in two-thirds of the voting shares and one-fourth of the common stock, Stack wins or loses significantly based on the company's performance. Early on Stack led the company on a path of rapid expansion, nearly causing the company's failure. When firms expand too rapidly, this creates financial pressure as expenses become greater than revenue. Today Stack grows the company slowly, focusing on regional customers throughout its over 400 stores. For example, the company pays attention to each region's seasons to ensure that products are stocked at exactly the right times. This allows products to quickly leave the shelves, thereby increasing revenue. Stack also focuses heavily on customer experience in an effort to create repeat customers willing to pay Dick's prices.

With an eye toward 800 stores, Stack is building relationships with professional athletes, sports fishermen, and more. He also views financial performance as the key to shareholder support. Of course, as with all companies, success hinges in part on events outside the company's control. For example, Dick's Sporting Goods depends heavily on the seasons, which can be unpredictable. However, Stack is driven and determined to control all in his power, steering Dick's Sporting Goods toward continued success for shareholders.[4]

Discussion Questions

1. How has Dick's Sporting Goods grown to be so financially successful?

2. Why does too rapid growth of a company cause a stress on finances?

3. What could be some financial challenges in growing Dick's Sporting Goods to 800 stores?

> ## A second means of long-term financing is through equity.

FINANCING WITH OWNERS' EQUITY

A second means of long-term financing is through equity. Remember from Chapter 14 that owners' equity refers to the owners' investment in an organization. Sole proprietors and partners own all or a part of their businesses outright, and their equity includes the money and assets they have brought into their ventures. Corporate owners, on the other hand, own stock or shares of their companies, which they hope will provide them with a return on their investment. Stockholders' equity includes common stock, preferred stock, and retained earnings.

Common stock (introduced in Chapter 4) is the single most important source of capital for most new companies. On the balance sheet, the common stock account is separated into two basic parts—common stock at par and capital in excess of par. The *par value* of a stock is simply the dollar amount printed on the stock certificate and has no relation to actual *market value*—the price at which the common stock is currently trading. The difference between a stock's par value and its offering price is called *capital in excess of par*. Except in the case of some very low-priced stocks, the capital in excess of par account is significantly larger than the par value account. Table 16.3 briefly explains how to gather important information from a stock quote, as it might appear in *The Wall Street Journal* or on the NASDAQ website.

Preferred stock was defined in Chapter 14 as corporate ownership that gives the stockholder preference in the distribution of the company's profits but not the voting and control rights accorded to common stockholders. Thus, the primary advantage of owning preferred stock is that it is a safer investment than common stock.

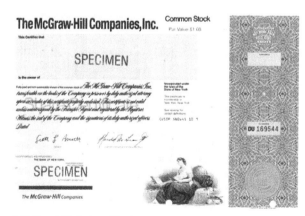

A McGraw-Hill stock certificate.

retained earnings
earnings after expenses and taxes that are reinvested in the assets of the firm and belong to the owners in the form of equity

All businesses exist to earn profits for their owners. Without the possibility of profit, there can be no incentive to risk investors' capital and succeed. When a corporation has profits left over after paying all of its expenses and taxes, it has the choice of retaining all or a portion of its earnings and/or paying them out to its shareholders in the form of dividends. **Retained earnings** are reinvested in the assets of the firm and belong to the owners in the form of equity. Retained earnings are an important source of

funds and are, in fact, the only long-term funds that the company can generate internally.

When the board of directors distributes some of a corporation's profits to the owners, it issues them as cash dividend payments. But not all firms pay dividends. Many fast-growing firms retain all of their earnings because they can earn high rates of return on the earnings they reinvest. Companies with fewer growth opportunities typically pay out large proportions of their earnings in the form of dividends, thereby allowing their stockholders to reinvest their dividend payments in higher-growth

▼ **TABLE 16.3** A Basic Stock Quote

1		2	3	4	5	6	7	8
Stock Price	52 Week							
High	Low	Stock	Symbol	Dividend	Yield (%)	Volume	Close	Net Change
92.49	60.89	Nike	NKE	1.24	1.50%	1,517,318	83.71	−0.35
44.90	19.00	Skechers USA	SKX	0.00	0.00	426,524	21.28	−0.47
27.37	15.07	Timberland	TBL	0.00	0.00	580,105	27.20	+0.31
33.00	23.51	Wolverine Worldwide	WWW	0.44	1.40%	89,870	31.35	−0.31

1. The **52-week high and low**—the highest and lowest prices, respectively, paid for the stock in the last year; for Nike stock, the highest was $92.49 and the lowest price, $60.89.

2. **Stock**—the name of the issuing company. When followed by the letters "pf," the stock is a preferred stock.

3. **Symbol**—the ticker tape symbol for the stock; NKE.

4. **Dividend**—the annual cash dividend paid to stockholders; Nike paid a dividend of $1.24 per share of stock outstanding.

5. **Dividend yield**—the dividend return on one share of common stock; 1.50 percent.

6. **Volume**—the number of shares traded on this day; Nike, 1,517,318

7. **Close**—Nike's last sale of the day was for $83.71.

8. **Net Change**—the difference between the previous day's close and the close on the day being reported; Nike was down $0.35.

Source: Yahoo! Finance, http://finance.yahoo.com/q?s (accessed January 19, 2011).

▼ **TABLE 16.4** Estimated Common Stock Price-Earnings Ratios and Dividends for Selected

Ticker Symbol	Company Name	Price per Share	Dividend per Share	Dividend Yield	Earnings per Share (*)	Price Earnings Ratio P/E
AEO	American Eagle	$14.50	$0.44	3.10%	$ 0.54	26.73
AXP	American Express	45.19	0.72	1.60	3.06	14.71
AAPL	Apple	342.34	0.00	0.00	15.15	22.59
CPB	Campbell Soup	34.82	1.16	3.30	2.36	14.73
DIS	Disney	39.11	0.40	1.00	2.03	19.28
F	Ford	18.12	0.00	0.00	1.89	9.60
HOG	Harley-Davidson	36.17	0.40	1.10	−0.10	N/A (**)
HD	Home Depot	35.64	0.95	2.60	$1.85	19.26
MCD	McDonald's	75.25	2.44	3.30	$4.53	16.61
PG	Procter & Gamble	65.52	1.93	2.90	$4.06	16.09
LUV	Southwest Airlines	12.92	0.02	0.10	0.59	21.93
SBUX	Starbucks	33.02	0.52	1.60	1.24	26.63

*Earnings per share are for the latest 12-month period and do not necessarily match year-end numbers.

**N/A—not applicable because of negative earnings.

Source: http://finance.yahoo.com/q?s (accessed January 19, 2011).

companies. Table 16.4 presents a sample of companies and the dividend each paid on a single share of stock. As shown in the table, when the dividend is divided by the price the result is the **dividend yield**. The dividend yield is the cash return as a percentage of the price but does not reflect the total return an investor earns on the individual stock. If the dividend yield is 3.2 percent on Campbell Soup and the stock price increases by 10 percent from $34.92 to $38.41, then the total return would be 13.2 percent. It is not clear that stocks with high dividend yields will be preferred by investors to those with little or no dividends. Most large companies pay their stockholders dividends on a quarterly basis.

INVESTMENT BANKING

A company that needs more money to expand or take advantage of opportunities may be able to obtain financing by issuing stock. The first-time sale of stocks and bonds directly to the public is called a *new issue*. Companies that already have stocks or bonds outstanding may offer a new issue of stock to raise additional funds for specific projects. When a company offers its stock to the public for the very first time, it is said to be "going public," and the sale is called an *initial public offering*.

New issues of stocks and bonds are sold directly to the public and to institutions in what is known as the **primary market**—the market where firms raise financial capital. The primary market differs from **secondary markets**, which are stock exchanges and over-the-counter markets where investors can trade their securities with other investors rather than the company that issued the stock or bonds. Primary market transactions actually raise cash for the issuing corporations, while secondary market transactions do not.

Investment banking, the sale of stocks and bonds for corporations, helps such companies raise funds by matching people and institutions who have money to invest with corporations in need of resources to exploit new opportunities. Corporations usually employ an investment banking firm to help sell their securities in the primary market. An investment banker helps firms establish appropriate offering prices for their securities. In addition, the investment banker takes care of the myriad details and securities regulations involved in any sale of securities to the public.

Just as large corporations such as IBM and Microsoft have a client relationship with a law firm and an accounting firm, they also have a client relationship with an investment banking firm. An investment banking firm such as Merrill Lynch, Goldman Sachs, or Morgan Stanley Smith Barney can provide advice about financing plans, dividend policy, or stock repurchases, as well as advice on mergers and acquisitions. Many now offer additional banking services, making them "one-stop

shopping" banking centers. When Pixar merged with Disney, both companies used investment bankers to help them value the transaction. Each firm wanted an outside opinion about what it was worth to the other. Sometimes mergers fall apart because the companies cannot agree on the price each company is worth or the structure of management after the merger. The advising investment banker, working with management, often irons out these details. Of course, investment bankers do not provide these services for free. They usually charge a fee of between 1 and 1.5 percent of the transaction. A $20 billion merger can generate between $200 and $300 million in investment banking fees. The merger mania of the late 1990s allowed top investment bankers to earn huge sums. Unfortunately, this type of fee income is dependent on healthy stock markets, which seem to stimulate the merger fever among corporate executives.

THE SECURITIES MARKETS

Securities markets provide a mechanism for buying and selling securities. They make it possible for owners to sell their stocks and bonds to other investors. Thus, in the broadest sense, stocks and bonds markets may be thought of as providers of liquidity—the ability to turn security holdings into cash quickly and at minimal expense and effort. Without liquid securities markets, many potential investors would sit on the sidelines rather than invest their hard-earned savings in securities. Indeed, the ability to sell securities at well-established market prices is one of the very pillars of the capitalistic society that has developed over the years in the United States.

Unlike the primary market, in which corporations sell stocks directly to the public, secondary markets permit the trading of previously issued securities. There are many different secondary markets for both stocks and bonds. If you want to purchase 100 shares of Google common stock, for example, you must purchase this stock from another investor or institution. It is the active buying and selling by many thousands of investors that establishes the prices of all financial securities. Secondary market trades may take place on organized exchanges or in what is known as the over-the-counter market. Many brokerage houses exist to help investors with financial decisions, and many offer their services

dividend yield the dividend per share divided by the stock price

primary market the market where firms raise financial capital

secondary markets stock exchanges and over-the-counter markets where investors can trade their securities with others

investment banking the sale of stocks and bonds for corporations

securities markets the mechanism for buying and selling securities through the Internet. One such broker is Charles Schwab. Its site offers a wealth of information and provides educational material to individual investors.

Stock Markets

Stock markets exist around the world in New York, Tokyo, London, Frankfort, Paris, and other world locations. The two biggest stock markets in the United States are the New York Stock Exchange (NYSE) and the NASDAQ market. The American Stock Exchange is now part of the New York Exchange, and NASDAQ bought both the Boston and Philadelphia regional exchanges. The Chicago Stock Exchange still exists as a regional exchange, but it has a difficult time justifying its existence as a stand-alone exchange.

Exchanges used to be divided into organized exchanges and over-the-counter markets, but during the last several years, dramatic changes have occurred in the markets. Both the NYSE

The New York Stock Exchange is the world's biggest stock exchange in terms of market capitalization.

and NASDAQ became publicly traded companies. They were previously not-for-profit organizations but are now for-profit companies. Additionally, both exchanges bought or merged with electronic exchanges, the NYSE with Archipelago and the NASDAQ with Instinet. Electronic trading is faster and less expensive than floor trading (where brokers meet to transact business) and now accounts for most of the stock trading done worldwide.

In an attempt to expand their markets, NASDAQ acquired the OMX, a Nordic stock exchange headquartered in Sweden, and the New York Stock Exchange merged with Euronext, a large European electronic exchange that trades options and futures contracts as well as common stock. Both the NYSE and NASDAQ have expanded their reach, their product line, and their ability to trade around the world. What we are witnessing is the globalization of the world's financial markets.

Traditionally, the NASDAQ market has been an electronic market, and many of the large technology companies such as Microsoft, Oracle, and Apple trade on the NASDAQ market. The NASDAQ operates through dealers who buy and sell common stock (inventory) for their own accounts. The NYSE has traditionally been a floor-traded market, where brokers meet at trading posts on the floor of the New York Stock Exchange to buy and sell common stock. The brokers act as agents for their clients and do not own their own inventory. This traditional division between the two markets is becoming less significant as the exchanges become electronic.

The Over-the-Counter Market

Unlike the organized exchanges, the **over-the-counter (OTC) market** is a network of dealers all over the country linked by computers, telephones, and Teletype machines. It has no central location. Today, the OTC market consists of small stocks, illiquid bank stocks, penny stocks, and companies whose stocks trade on the "pink sheets." Once NASDAQ was classified as an exchange by the SEC, it was no longer part of the OTC market. Further, because most corporate bonds and all U.S. securities are traded over the counter, the OTC market regularly accounts for the largest total dollar value of all of the secondary markets.

Measuring Market Performance

Investors, especially professional money managers, want to know how well their investments are performing relative to the market as a whole. Financial managers also need to know how their companies' securities are performing when compared with their competitors'. Thus, performance measures—averages and indexes—are very important to many different people. They not only indicate the performance of a particular securities market but also provide a measure of the overall health of the economy.

Indexes and averages are used to measure stock prices. An *index* compares current stock prices with those in a specified base period, such as 1944, 1967, or 1977. An *average* is the average of certain stock prices. The averages used are usually

"Many investors follow the activity of the Dow Jones Industrial Average to see whether the stock market has gone up or down."

not simple calculations, however. Some stock market averages (such as the Standard & Poor's Composite Index) are weighted averages, where the weights employed are the total market values of each stock in the index (in this case 500). The Dow Jones Industrial Average is a price-weighted average. Regardless of how they are constructed, all market averages of stocks move together closely over time.

Many investors follow the activity of the Dow Jones Industrial Average to see whether the stock market has gone up or down. Table 16.5 lists the 30 companies that currently make up the Dow. Although these companies are only a small fraction of the total number of companies listed on the New York Stock Exchange, because of their size they account for about 25 percent of the total value of the NYSE.

The numbers listed in an index or average that tracks the performance of a stock market are expressed not as dollars but as a number on a fixed scale. If you know, for example, that the Dow Jones Industrial Average climbed from 860 in August 1982 to a high of 11,497 at the beginning of 2000, you can see clearly that the value of the Dow Jones Average increased more than 10 times in this 19-year period, making it one of the highest rate of return periods in the history of the stock market.

Unfortunately, prosperity did not last long once the Internet bubble burst. Technology stocks and new Internet companies were responsible for the huge increase in stock prices. Even companies with few sales and no earnings were selling at prices that were totally unreasonable. It is always easier to realize that a bubble existed after it has popped. By September 2002, the

Dow Jones Industrial Average hit 7,461. The markets stabilized and the economy kept growing; investors were euphoric when the Dow Jones Industrial Average hit an all time high of 14,198 in October 2007. However, once the housing bubble burst, the economy and the stock market went into a free fall. The Dow Jones Industrial Average bottomed out at 6,470 in March 2009. The market entered a period of wild fluctuations, and by April 2010, it hit a new high for the year of 10,975 and continued up to 12,453 by April 20, 2011. Perhaps this roller coaster ride indicates why some people are afraid to enter the market and buy common stocks. If you look at the long-term trend and long-term returns in common stocks, they far outdistance bonds and government securities. When you are young, you should be playing the long-term trends, and as you get older your investments should become more conservative.

Recognizing financial bubbles can be difficult. It is too easy to get caught up in the enthusiasm that accompanies rising markets. Knowing what something is worth in economic terms is the test of true value. During the housing bubble, banks made loans to subprime borrowers to buy houses. (Remember that the prime rate is the rate for the highest quality borrowers and subprime loans are generally made to those who do not qualify for regular ones.) As more money poured into the housing market, the obvious supply and demand relationship from economics would indicate that housing prices would rise. As prices rose, speculators entered the real estate market trying to make a fast buck. States such as Florida, Arizona, Nevada, and California were the favorite speculative spots and the states with the largest decline in house prices. To make matters worse, banks had created the home equity loan years ago so that borrowers could take out a second mortgage against their house and deduct the interest payment for tax purposes. Many homeowners no longer thought about paying off their mortgages but instead used the increase in the price of their houses to borrow more money. This behavior was unsustainable.

The bankers engaged in risky financial behavior packaged up billions of dollars of mortgages into securitized assets. In other words, an investor could buy a pool of assets and collect the interest income and eventually get a payment at the end of the life of the product. This technique allowed banks to make a mortgage, collect a fee,

▼ **TABLE 16.5** The 30 Stocks in the Dow Jones Industrial Average

3M Co	DuPont	McDonald's
Alcoa Inc.	ExxonMobil	Merck
American Express Co	General Electric	Microsoft
AT&T Inc.	Hewlett-Packard	Pfizer
Bank of America	Home Depot	Procter & Gamble
Boeing	Intel	Travelers Companies
Caterpiller	IBM	United Technologies
Chevron	Johnson & Johnson	Verizon
Cisco Systems	JPMorgan Chase	Walmart
Coca-Cola	Kraft Foods	Walt Disney

Source: "Dow Jones Industrial Average," *Yahoo! Finance,* http://finance.yahoo.com/q/cp?s=^DJI (accessed April 20, 2011).

FIGURE 16.2

Long-Term Performance of Stock Market and Dow Jones Industrial Average (^DJI)

Source: "Dow Jones Industrial Average," *Yahoo! Finance,* http://finance.yahoo.com/charts?s=%5EDJI#symbol=%5Edji;range=20010402,20110401;compare=;indicator=volume;charttype=area;crosshair=on;ohlcvalues=0;logscale=off;source=; (accessed April 21, 2011).

package the mortgage, and collect another fee. These securitized mortgages were sold to the market as asset-backed securities with a AAA credit rating off their books and replaced with cash to make more loans. In this case, when the bubble burst, it had extremely severe consequences for the economy, workers, and investors.

People defaulted on loans when they could no longer afford to pay the mortgage. Many of these people shouldn't have been able

to borrow in the first place. The defaults caused housing prices to fall, and some people who had home equity loans no longer had any equity left in their house. Some homeowners owed the bank more than the house was worth, and they started walking away from their mortgages. As the same time, investors realized that the mortgage-backed securities they owned were probably not worth what they thought they were worth, and prices of these assets plummeted. Banks and other financial service firms that had these assets on their books suffered a double whammy. They had loan losses and losses on mortgage-backed securities that another division of the bank had bought for investment purposes. Soon, many banks were close to violating their capital requirement, and the U.S. Treasury and Federal Reserve stepped in—with the help of funding from Congress—to make banks loans, buy securities that were illiquid, and invest in the capital of the banks by buying preferred stocks.

SO YOU WANT TO WORK // in Financial Management or Securities /

Taking classes in financial and securities management can provide many career options, from managing a small firm's accounts receivables to handling charitable giving for a multinational to investment banking to stock brokerage. We have entered into a less certain period for finance and securities jobs, however. In the world of investment banking, the past few years have been especially challenging. Tens of thousands of employees from Wall Street firms have lost their jobs. This phenomenon is not confined to New York City either, leaving the industry with a lot fewer jobs around the country. This type of phenomenon is not isolated to the finance sector. In the early 2000s, the tech sector experienced a similar downturn, from which it has subsequently largely recovered. Undoubtedly, markets will bounce back and job creation in finance and securities will increase again—but until that happens the atmosphere

across finance and securities will be more competitive than it has been in the past. However, this does not mean that there are no jobs. All firms need financial analysts to determine whether a project should be implemented, when to issue stocks or bonds, or when to initiate loans. These and other forward-looking questions such as how to invest excess cash must be addressed by financial managers. Economic uncertainty in the financial and securities market has made for more difficulty in finding the most desirable jobs.

Why this sudden downturn in financial industry prospects? A lot of these job cuts came in response to the subprime lending fallout and subsequent bank failures such as Bear Stearns, which alone lost around 7,000 employees. All of these people will be looking for new jobs in new organizations, increasing the competitive level in a lot of different employment areas. For young jobseekers with relatively

little experience, this may result in a great deal of frustration. On the other hand, by the time you graduate, the job market for finance majors could be in recovery and rebuilding with new employees. Uncertainty results in hiring freezes and layoffs, but leave firms lean and ready to grow when the cycle turns around, resulting in hiring from the bottom up.

Many different industries require people with finance skills. So do not despair if you have a difficult time finding a job in exactly the right firm. Most students switch companies a number of times over the course of their careers. Many organizations require individuals trained in forecasting, statistics, economics, and finance. Even unlikely places like museums, aquariums, and zoos need people who are good at numbers. It may require some creativity, but if you are committed to a career in finance, look to less obvious sources—not just the large financial firms.[6]

▼ **TABLE 16.6** Top Companies: Best Investments

1 Year	Annual Rate %
Avis Budget Group	$ 1,774.3
Dana Holdings	1,364.9
TRW Automotive Holdings	563.3
Tenneco	501.0
Rite Aid	387.1
Dillard's	374.1
Tenet Healthcare	368.7
Unisys	353.6
Advanced Micro Devices	348.1
Ford Motor	336.7
5 Years	**Annual Rate % (2004–2009)**
Apple	$ 45.6
Express Scripts	35.2
Western Digital	32.4
FMC Technologies	30.5
Mosaic	30.4
Flowserve	28.8
Precision Castparts	27.6
Google	26.3
Cameron International	25.5
Monsanto	25.4
10 Years	**Annual Rate % (1999–2009)**
XTO Energy	$ 43.0
Holly	34.2
Precision Castparts	33.0
World Fuel Services	31.9
DaVita	29.4
Consol Energy	29.0
Gilead Sciences	29.0
Reynolds American	28.4
Chesapeake Energy	28.0
EOG Resources	27.8

Source: "Top Companies: Best Investments," *Fortune,* http://money.cnn.com/magazines/fortune/fortune500/2010/performers/companies/bestinv/index.html (accessed March 2, 2011).

The consensus of most economists is that through the actions of the U.S. Treasury, and the Federal Reserve, the U.S. economy escaped what might have been another depression equal to or worse than the depression of the 1930s. The recession of 2007–2009 lasted 18 months and was the longest recession since the 1930s. Hundreds of banks went bankrupt during 2008–2009, and the Federal Deposit Insurance Corporation closed these banks and reopened them as part of another healthy bank with no losses for the depositors. Most of the big banks have paid back their loans, but many of the smaller banks still owe the Treasury money. Unemployment that had hit over 10.4 percent was down to 9.7 percent and the economy was growing again. Given that the stock market is a leading indicator, it has been rising since the bottom in March 2009, and everyone—from investors to people relying on pensions tied to the market—hopes we can eventually get back to the 2007 high of more than 14,000 on the Dow Jones Industrial Average. Now you know why investing in the stock market takes discipline, knowledge, and the willingness to weather out economic storms. (See Figure 16.2.)

For investors to make sound financial decisions, it is important that they stay in touch with business news, markets, and indexes. Of course, business and investment magazines, such as *Bloomberg BusinessWeek, Fortune,* and *Money,* offer this type of information. Many Internet sites, including the CNN/*Money, Business Wire, USA Today,* other online newspapers, and *PR Newswire,* offer this information as well. Many sites offer searchable databases of information by topic, company, or keyword. However investors choose to receive and review business news, doing so is a necessity in today's market. Table 16.6 provides information about total shareholder return by company over the past 10 years. ■

TEAM EXERCISE

Compare and contrast financing with long-term liabilities such as bonds versus financing with owners' equity, typically retained earnings, common stock, and preferred stock. Form groups and suggest a good mix of long-term liabilities and owners' equity for a new firm that makes wind turbines for generating alternate energy and would like to grow quickly.

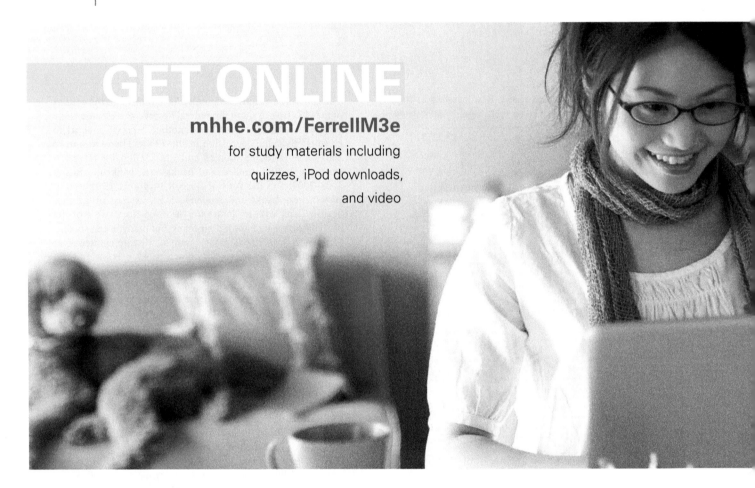

GET ONLINE

mhhe.com/FerrellM3e

for study materials including
quizzes, iPod downloads,
and video

chapter sixteen

active review card
Financial Management and
Securities Markets

in a nutshell

Companies use short-term assets to generate sales and conduct ordinary day-to-day business operations and short-term liabilities to finance business. They also use long-term assets such as plant and equipment and long-term liabilities such as stocks and bonds to finance corporate assets. Financial management is dependent on the management of these assets and liabilities, as well as the trade of stocks and bonds.

The following statements will test your take-away knowledge from this chapter. Do your best to explain each one in the space provided below.

LO.1 Describe some common methods of managing current assets.

LO.2 Identify some sources of short-term financing (current liabilities).

LO.3 Summarize the importance of long-term assets and capital budgeting.

LO.4 Specify how companies finance their operations and manage fixed assets with long-term liabilities, particularly bonds.

LO.5 Discuss how corporations can use equity financing by issuing stock through an investment banker.

LO.6 Describe the various securities markets in the United States.

Did your answers include the following important points?

LO.1. Describe some common methods of managing current assets.

- Current assets are short-term resources such as cash, investments, accounts receivable, and inventory.
- Financial managers focus on minimizing the amount of cash kept on hand and increasing the speed of collections through lockboxes and electronic funds transfer and by investing in marketable securities.
- Marketable securities include U.S. Treasury bills, certificates of deposit, commercial paper, and money market funds.
- Managing accounts receivable requires judging customer creditworthiness and creating credit terms that encourage prompt payment.
- Inventory management focuses on determining optimum inventory levels that minimize the cost of storing the ordering inventory without sacrificing too many lost sales due to stockout.

LO.2. Identify some sources of short-term financing (current liabilities).

- Current liabilities are short-term debt obligations that must be repaid within one year, such as accounts payable, taxes payable, and notes payable.
- Trade credit is extended by suppliers for the purchase of their goods and services, whereas a line of credit is an arrangement by which a bank agrees to lend a specified amount of money to a business whenever the business needs it.
- Secured loans are backed by collateral; unsecured loans are backed only by the borrower's good reputation.

LO.3. Summarize the importance of long-term assets and capital budgeting.

- Long-term or fixed assets are expected to last for many years, such as production facilities, offices, and equipment. Businesses need modern up-to-date equipment to succeed in today's competitive environment.

- Capital budgeting is the process of analyzing company needs and selecting the assets that will maximize its value; a capital budget is the amount of money budgeted for the purchase of fixed assets.

LO.4. Specify how companies finance their operations and manage fixed assets with long-term liabilities, particularly bonds.

- Two common choices for financing are equity financing and debt financing. Long-term liabilities are debts that will be repaid over a number of years, such as long-term bank loans and bond issues.
- A bond is a long-term debt security that an organization sells to raise money. The bond indenture specifies the provisions of the bond contract—maturity date, coupon rate, repayment methods, and others.

LO.5. Discuss how corporations can use equity financing by issuing stock through an investment banker.

- Owners' equity represents what owners have contributed to the company and includes common stock, preferred stock, and retained earnings.
- To finance operations, companies can issue new common and preferred stock through an investment banker that sells stocks and bonds to corporations.

LO.6. Describe the various securities markets in the United States.

- Securities markets provide the mechanism for buying and selling stocks and bonds. Primary markets allow companies to raise capital by selling new stock directly to investors through investment bankers.
- Secondary markets allow the buyers of previously issued shares of stock to sell them to other owners. Major secondary markets are the New York Stock Exchange, the American Stock Exchange, and the over-the-counter market.
- Investors measure stock market performance by watching stock market averages and indexes.

Practical Application

LO.1.
- A(n) _____ is an address for receiving payments from customers.
- _____ are short-term debt obligations that the U.S. government sells to raise money.
- Good financial managers minimize the amount of cash available to pay bills in _____.

LO.2.
- A finance company to which businesses sell their accounts receivable, usually for a percentage of the total face value, is a(n) _____ .
- The most widely used source of short-term financing is _____.

LO.3.
- Plants, offices, and equipment are considered _____ assets.
- The process of analyzing the needs of the business and selecting the assets that will maximize its value is called _____ .
- In general, the longer the expected life of a project or asset, the _____ the potential risk.

LO.4.
- _____ are a sequence of small bond issues of progressively longer maturity.
- Items such as a bond's value, date, and rate are specified in the _____.
- A method of long-term financing that requires repaying funds with interest is _____ .

LO.5.
- The first-time sale of stocks and bonds to the public directly is called _____.
- If a company retains all of its earnings, it will not pay _____.
- Corporations usually employ an investment banking firm to help sell their securities in the _____.

LO.6.
- A(n) _____ is a network of dealers rather than an organized exchange.
- A(n) _____ compares current stock prices with those in a specified base period.

notes

CHAPTER 1

1. Debbie Thorne, O. C. Ferrell, and Linda Ferrell, *Business and Society* (Mason, OH: South-Western Cengage Learning, 2011), p. 304; "The Chiefs Children's Fund and Charity Game," Kansas City Chiefs, **www.kcchiefs.com/community/programs/childrens-fund.html** (accessed January 3, 2010).

2. "GMAC® Diversity Initiatives," The Graduate Management Admissions Council, **www.gmac.com/gmac/SchoolServices/Diversity/GMACDiversityInitiatives.htm** (accessed February 22, 2010).

3. Liz Clarke, "While Nascar Takes Stock, Racing's Popularity Wanes," *The Washington Post*, November 4, 2007, p. D3.

4. Mariko Sanchanta, "Starbucks Plans Big Expansion in China," *The Wall Street Journal*, April 14, 2010, p. B10; Claire Cain Miller, "Starbucks Still Sees Growth, as Well as Dividends," *The New York Times*, March 24, 2010, **http://dealbook.blogs.nytimes.com/2010/03/24/starbucks-still-sees-growth-as-well-as-dividends** (accessed June 7, 2010); **www.starbucks.co.jp/en/company.html** (accessed June 12, 2010); "Asia Pacific," **http://news.starbucks.com/about+starbucks/starbucks+coffee+international/asia+pacific/** (accessed June 12, 2010); David Teather, "Starbucks legend delivers recovery by thinking smaller," *The Guardian*, January 21, 2010, **www.guardian.co.uk/business/2010/jan/21/starbucks-howard-schultz** (accessed June 12, 2010); "How Starbucks Colonised the World," *The Sunday Times*, February 17, 2008, **http://business.timesonline.co.uk/tol/business/industry_sectors/leisure/article3381092.ece** (accessed June 13, 2010); John Jannarone, "The Stars Could Be Aligned for Growth at Starbucks," *The Wall Street Journal*, June 14, 2010, **http://online.wsj.com/article/SB10001424052748704463504575301182988291248.html?mod=WSJ_Heard_LeadStory** (accessed June 14, 2010); "Starbucks to Enter China's Tea Drinks Market," China Retail News, March 11, 2010, **www.chinaretailnews.com/2010/03/11/3423-starbucks-to-enter-chinas-tea-drinks-market** (accessed June 14, 2010); "Greater China," **http://news.starbucks.com/about+starbucks/starbucks+coffee+international/greater+china** (accessed June 14, 2010); "2010 World's Most Ethical Companies," *Ethisphere*, October 1, 2010, pp. 30–33.

5. Craig Torres and Anthony Field, "Campbell's Quest for Productivity," *Bloomberg Businessweek*, November 2–December 5, 2010, pp. 15–16.

6. Miriko Yash, "Sony and Samsung Strategic Split," *Bloomberg Businessweek*, January 18, 2010, p. 52.

7. Elizabeth M. Whelan, "Kellogg's: A Sad Cereal Sellout," *The New York Post*, June 17, 2007, **www.nypost.com/seven/06172007/postopinion/opedcolumnists/kelloggs__a_sad_cereal_sellout_opedcolumnists_elizabeth_m__whelan.htm** (accessed February 23, 2010).

8. Bruce Horowitz, "Unilever Gets All the Trans Fat Out of Its Margarines," *USA Today*, July 27, 2009, **www.usatoday.com/money/industries/food/2009-07-26-trans-fat-unilever_N.htm?csp=34** (accessed February 23, 2010).

9. "Got Milk?" **www.whymilk.com/celeb.php** (accessed February 25, 2010).

10. "About Bill Daniels," **www.danielsfund.org/BillDaniels/index.asp** (accessed February 23, 2010).

11. "Venecuba, A Single Nation," *Economist*, February 13–19, 2010, p. 40.

12. "Reforms Please Cubans, But Is It Communism?" Associated Press, April 2, 2008, **www.msnbc.msn.com/id/23925259** (accessed April 18, 2008).

13. James T. Areddy and Craig Karmin, "China Stocks Once Frothy, Fall by Half in Six Months," *The Wall Street Journal*, April 16, 2008, pp. 1, 7.

14. John D. Sutter and Doug Gross, "Apple Unveils the 'Magical' iPad," *CNN Tech*, January 28, 2010, **www.cnn.com/2010/TECH/01/27/apple.tablet/index.html?section=cnn_latest** (accessed February 3, 2010); Geoffrey A. Fowler and Nick Wingfield, "Apple's Showman Takes the Stage," *The Wall Street Journal*, March 3, 2011, **www.nytimes.com/2010/08/08/arts/television/08foodcart.html?_r=1** (accessed March 17, 2011).

15. *Solid State Technology*, "China Patent Filings could Overtake US, Japan in 2011," ELECTROIQ, October 11, 2010, **www.electroiq.com/index/display/semiconductors-article-display/1436725261/articles/solid-state-technology/semiconductors/industry-news/business-news/2010/october/china-patent_filings.html** (accessed January 3, 2011).

16. "Zimbabwe," *CIA—The World Factbook*, **https://www.cia.gov/library/publications/the-world-factbook/geos/zi.html#** (accessed February 3, 2010).

17. Jennifer Wang, "Patagonia, from the Ground Up," *Entrepreneur*, June 2010, pp. 24–32; "A Little Enlightened Self-Interest," *Inc.*, June 2010, pp. 56–60; **www.patagonia.com** (accessed August 1, 2010).

18. "Monthly Statement of the Public Debt of the United States," Treasury Public Debt, December 31, 2010, **www.treasurydirect.gov/govt/reports/pd/mspd/2010/opds122010.pdf** (accessed January 18, 2011).

19. Mick Vann, "Mobile Food," *The Austin Chronicle*, August 20, 2010, **www.austinchronicle.com/gyrobase/Issue/story?oid=oid:1070852** (accessed September 17, 2010); Emily Gertz, "Nouvelle Food Trucks Make Fast food with Slow Values," *Grist*, August 11, 2010, **www.grist.org/article/food-nouvelle-food-trucks-make-fast-food-with-slow-values** (accessed September 17, 2010); "The Great Food Truck Race," The Food Network, **www.foodnetwork.com/the-great-food-truck-race/index.html** (accessed September 17, 2010); Kate Linthicum, "Miracle Mile Lunch Trucks Prompt Food Fight," *The Los Angeles Times*, June 17, 2010, **http://articles.latimes.com/2010/jun/17/local/la-me-0617-food-truck-20100617/2** (accessed September 17, 2010).

20. Haya El Nasser, Gregory Korte, and Paul Overberg, "308.7 Million," *USA Today*, December 22, 2010, p. 1A.

21. "Facts about Working Women," *Women Employed*, **www.womenemployed.org/index.php?id=20** (accessed February 23, 2010).

22. Liz Welch, "Wolfgang Puck: From Potato Peeler to Gourmet-Pizza Tycoon," *Inc.*, October 2009, pp. 87–88; "Restaurants," Wolfgang Puck, **www.wolfgangpuck.com/restaurants** (accessed March 17, 2011); "The Hershey Company," The United States Securities and Exchange Commission Form 10-K, February 18, 2011, **http://phx.corporate-ir.net/phoenix.zhtml?c=115590&p=irol-SECText&TEXT=aHR0cDovL2lyLmludC53ZXN0bGF3YnVzaW5lc3MuY29tL2RvY3VtZW50L3YxLzAwMDExMjEtMDM5Nzg5L3htbA%3d%3d** (accessed March 17, 2011).

23. "About the Hershey Company," The Hershey Company, **www.thehersheycompany.com/** (accessed February 15, 2010).

24. "Fortune Global 500," **http://CNNMoney.com, money.cnn.com/ magazines/fortune/global500/2009/snapshots/2255.html** (accessed February 19, 2010); Anthony Bianco and Wendy Zellner, "Is Wal-Mart Too Powerful?" *BusinessWeek*, October 6, 2003, pp. 100–10; "Wal Mart Stores, Inc. Business Information, Profile, and History," **http://companies.jrank.org/pages/4725/ Wal-Mart-Stores-Inc.html** (accessed February 23, 2010); *Walmart 2010 Financial Report*, **http://cdn.walmartstores.com/ sites/AnnualReport/2010/PDF/01_WMT%202010_Financials .pdf** (accessed March 23, 2011).

25. Dennis Schaal, "100 Best Corporate Citizens 2008," *The CRO*, **www.thecro.com/node/615** (accessed February 23, 2010).

26. 2003 National Business Ethics Survey (n.d.), **www.ethics.org/ nbes/2003/1003nbes_summary.html** (accessed January 6, 2004); "2007 National Business Ethics Survey: An Inside View of Private Sector Ethics," Ethics Resources Center, 2007.

27. Lindsey Gerdes, "Where Undergrads Dream of Working," *BusinessWeek Online*, May 23, 2008, **www.businessweek .com/managing/content/may2008/ca20080523_988667 .htm?chan=search** (accessed June 19, 2008).

CHAPTER 2

1. "The 2010 World's Most Ethical Companies—Company Profile: T-Mobile USA," *Ethisphere*, Q1, p. 33.

2. Thomas Catan, "Drug Firms Agree to Pay $421 Million to Settle Claims," *The Wall Street Journal*, December 18, 2010, p. B4.

3. Ronald Alsop, "Corporate Scandals Hit Home," *The Wall Street Journal*, February 19, 2004, via **www.driversofloyalty .com/services/pubs/The_Wall_Street_Journal_Corporate ScandalsHitHome_2004.pdf** (accessed February 5, 2010).

4. Sandra Block, "Visa, MasterCard Agree to Settle Antitrust Suit," *USA Today*, October 15, 2010, p. 1B. Courtney Rubin, "Visa, MasterCard Settle Antitrust Suit Over Fees," *Inc.*, October 5, 2010, **www.inc.com/news/articles/2010/10/visa-and-mastercard-to-let-businesses-reveal-processing-fees.html** (accessed January 6, 2011).

5. O. C. Ferrell, John Fraedrich, and Linda Ferrell, *Business Ethics: Ethical Decision Making and Cases*, 8th ed. (Mason, OH: South-Western Cengage Learning, 2011), p. 7.

6. David Callahan, as quoted in Archie Carroll, "Carroll: Do We Live in a Cheating Culture?" *Athens Banner-Herald*, February 21, 2004, **www.onlineathens.com/stores/022204/bus_20040222028 .shtml** (accessed February 25, 2010).

7. Jenny Anderson, "3 Executives Under Fire on Exit Pay," *The New York Times*, March 8, 2008, pp. B1, B4.

8. Catalina Camia, "DeLay Gets 3-Year Sentence for Corruption," *USA Today*, January 11, 2011, p. 2A.

9. Michael McCarthy, "Gillette Ends Endorsement Deal with Tiger Woods," *USA Today*, December 24, 2010, **www.usatoday .com/communities/gameon/post/2010/12/tiger-woods-dropped-as-endorser-by-gillette/1** (accessed January 6, 2011).

10. Vic Marks, "Pakistan Embroiled in No-Ball Betting Scandal against England," August 29, 2010, guardian.co.uk, **www.guardian.co.uk/sport/2010/aug/29/pakistan-cricket-betting-allegations** (accessed January 6, 2011); "Cricket Chiefs Consider Lie-Detectors to Fight Corruption," *CNN*, December 15, 2010, **www.cnn.com/2010/SPORT/12/15/cricket.lie .detector.corruption/** (accessed January 6, 2011).

11. Ferrell, Fraedrich, and Ferrell, *Business Ethics*.

12. Bobby White, "The New Workplace Rules: No Video Watching," *The New York Times*, March 3, 2008, p. B1.

13. "Proper Use of Company, Customer, and Supplier Resources," Boeing, November 19, 2009, **www.boeing.com/companyoffices/ aboutus/ethics/pro10.pdf** (accessed January 28, 2010).

14. Laura Petrecca, "Bullying in Workplace Is Common, Hard to Fix," *USA Today*, December 28, 2010, pp. 1B–2B.

15. Peter Lattman, "Boeing's Top Lawyer Spotlights Company's Ethical Lapses," *The Wall Street Journal*, Law Blog, January 30, 2006, **http://blogs.wsj.com/law/2006/01/31/boeings-top-lawyerrips-into-his-company/tab/article/**(accessed February 25, 2010).

16. Barbara Kiviat, "A Bolder Approach to Credit-Agency Rating Reform," *Time*, September 18, 2009, **http://curiouscapitalist. blogs.time.com/2009/09/18/a-bolder-approach-tocredit-rating-agency-reform/** (accessed January 28, 2010).

17. "New York Merchant Bank Pleads Guilty to FCPA Violation; Bank Chairman Pleads Guilty to Failing to Disclose Control of Foreign Bank Account," The United Department of Justice, August 6, 2010, **www.justice.gov/opa/pr/2010/August/ 10-crm-909.html** (accessed March 17, 2011).

18. "Corruption Perceptions Index 2010," Transparency International, **www.transparency.org/policy_research/surveys_indices/ cpi/2010/results** (accessed January 6, 2011).

19. "National Survey Reveals Truth Behind Disappearing Office Supplies," OfficeMax, PR Newswire, June 8, 2010, **http://multivu .prnewswire.com/mnr/officemax/44541/** (accessed January 6, 2011).

20. David Whelan, "Only the Paranoid Resurge," *Forbes*, April 10, 2006, **www.forbes.com/forbes/2006/0410/042.html** (accessed March 23, 2011).

21. *Reuters*, "Intel Pays AMD $1.25 billion to Settle All Disputes," *Wired*, November 12, 2009, **www.wired.com/epicenter/ 2009/11/intel-paysamd-125-billion-to-settle-all-disputes/** (accessed January 29, 2010); Jordan Robertson, "Intel Hit with More Antitrust Charges in FTC Suit," Yahoo! Finance, December 16, 2009, **http://finance.yahoo.com/news/Intel-hit-with-moreantitrust-apf-642649616.html?x=0**, (accessed January 29, 2010); David Goldman, "FTC Settles Antitrust Suit with Wrist Slap," CNN Money, August 4, 2010, **money.cnn .com/2010/08/04/technology/intel_ftc_settlement/index.htm** (accessed January 7, 2011).

22. Jennifer Corbett Dooren, "Regulators Turn Cautious on Bisphenol A," *The Wall Street Journal*, January 16, 2010, **http:// online.wsj.com/article/SB10001424052748703657604575 005211658393810.html** (accessed January 28, 2010).

23. Michael Josephson, "The Ethics of American Youth 2008," Josephson Institute of Ethics, press release, **http://charactercounts .org/programs/reportcard/2008/index.html** (accessed February 25, 2010).

24. "Teens Respect Good Business Ethics." *USA Today*, Snapshots, December 12, 2005, p. 13-1.

25. Al Lewis, "Lying, Cheating, Violence—All Ingredients for Success, Teen Survey Says," *Denver Post*, December 5, 2007, **http://blogs .denverpost.com/lewis/2007/12/05/lying-cheatingviolence-all-ingredients-for-successteen-survey-says/** (accessed February 25, 2010).

26. Associated Press, "Justice Investigation Shows FBI Agents Cheated on Test," *USA Today*, September 28, 2010, p. 10A.

27. Michael Schmidt, "Guilty Plea in Sale of Products with Steroids," *The New York Times*, January 20, 2010, **www .nytimes.com/2010/01/21/business/21steroids.html** (accessed January 28, 2010).

28. "Campaign Warns about Drugs from Canada," *CNN*, February 5, 2004, **www.cnn.com**; Gardiner Harris and Monica Davey, "FDA Begins Push to End Drug Imports," *The New York Times,* January 23, 2004, p. C1.

29. Rita Rubin, "FDA Plans New Cigarette Warnings," *USA Today,* November 11, 2010, p. 3A.

30. Marc C. Willemsen, "The New EU Cigarette Health Warnings Benefit Smokers Who Want to Quit the Habit: Results from the Dutch Continuous Survey of Smoking Habits," *The European Journal of Public Health* 15, no. 4 (2005), pp. 389–92.

31. Ethics Resource Center, *2005 National Business Ethics Survey* (Washington, DC: Ethics Resource Center, 2005), p. 43.

32. Thomas M. Jones, "Ethical Decision Making by Individuals in Organizations: An Issue-Contingent Model," *Academy of Management Review* 2 (April 1991), pp. 371–73.

33. Sir Adrian Cadbury, "Ethical Managers Make Their Own Rules," *Harvard Business Review* 65 (September–October 1987), p. 72.

34. David Leonhardt, "Spillonomics: Underestimating Risk," *The New York Times,* May 31, 2010, **www.nytimes.com/2010/06/06/magazine/06fob-wwln-t.html**, (accessed June 22, 2010); Robert Mackey, "Rig Worker Says BP Was Told of Leak in Emergency System Before Explosion," June 21, 2010, *The New York Times,* **http://thelede.blogs.nytimes.com/2010/06/21/rig-worker-claims-bp-knew-of-leak-in-emergency-system-before-explosion/?scp=5&sq=BP&st=cse** (accessed June 22, 2010); "BP and the Gulf of Mexico Alliance Announce Implementation of BP's $500 Million Independent Research Initiative," BP, September 29, 2010, **www.bp.com/genericarticle.do?categoryId=2012968&contentId=7065262** (accessed October 27, 2010); "BP Pledges Collateral for Gulf of Mexico Oil Spill Trust," BP, October 1, 2010, **www.bp.com/genericarticle.do?categoryId=2012968&contentId=7065280** (accessed October 27, 2010); Russell Gold and Tom McGinty, "BP Relied on Cheaper Wells," *The Wall Street Journal,* June 19, 2010, **http://online.wsj.com/article/NA_WSJ_PUB:SB10001424052748704289504575313010283981200.html** (accessed October 27, 2010); Joel K. Bourne, Jr., "The Deep Dilemma," *National Geographic,* October 2010, pp. 40–53.

35. Ferrell, Fraedrich, and Ferrell, *Business Ethics,* pp. 174–75.

36. Ethics Resource Center, *2009 National Business Ethics Survey* (Washington, DC: Ethics Resource Center, 2009), p. 41.

37. "The 2010 World's Most Ethical Companies—Company Profile: Granite Construction," *Ethisphere,* Q1, p. 33.

38. Ethics Resource Center, *2009 National Business Ethics Survey* (Washington, DC: Ethics Resource Center, 2009), p. 9.

39. Skadden, Arps, Slate, Meagher & Flom LLP & Affiliates, *The Dodd Frank Act: Commentary and Insights,* July 12, 2010, **www.skadden.com/Cimages/siteFile/Skadden_Insights_Special_Edition_Dodd-Frank_Act1.pdf** (accessed January 7, 2011).

40. Ferrell, Fraedrich, and Ferrell, *Business Ethics,* p. 13.

41. John Galvin, "The New Business Ethics," *SmartBusinessMag.com,* June 2000, p. 99.

42. Archie B. Carroll, "The Pyramid of Corporate Social Responsibility: Toward the Moral Management of Organizational Stakeholders," *Business Horizons* 34 (July/August 1991), p. 42.

43. Bryan Walsh, "Why Green Is the New Red, White and Blue," *Time,* April 28, 2008, p. 46.

44. Adam Shriver, "Not Grass-Fed, but at Least Pain-Free," *The New York Times,* February 18, 2010, **www.nytimes.com/2010/02/19/opinion/19shriver.html?scp=4&sq=animal%20rights&st=cse** (accessed February 25, 2010).

45. Walsh, "Why Green Is the New Red, White and Blue," p. 54.

46. Alan Beattie, "Countries Rush to Restrict Trade in Basic Foods," *Financial Times,* April 2, 2008, p. 1.

47. Laura Petrecca, "Marketing Efforts May End Up in a Green Blur," *USA Today,* April 22, 2008, p. 10B.

48. Alexandra Zendrian, "Workers: Employers Not Green Enough," *Inc.,* April 17, 2008, **www.inc.com/news/articles,2008/04/green.html** (accessed February 25, 2010).

49. "2010 World's Most Ethical Companies," *Ethisphere,* **http://ethisphere.com/wme2010/** (accessed March 17, 2011).

50. Indra Nooyi, "The Responsible Company," *The Economist, The World in 2008 Special Edition,* March 2008, p. 132.

51. Ferrell, Fraedrich, and Ferrell, *Business Ethics,* pp. 13–19.

52. Matthew Dolan, "Ford to Begin Hiring at New Wages," *The New York Times,* January 26, 2010, **http://online.wsj.com/article/SB10001424052748704762904575025420550494324.html** (accessed January 28, 2010).

53. Jeff Harrington, "Outback Steakhouse Settle Class-Action Sex Discrimination Case for $19M," *St. Petersburg Times,* December 30, 2009, **www.tampabay.com/news/business/corporate/outback-steakhouse-settlesclass-action-sex-discrimination-casefor-19m/1061920** (accessed May 4, 2010).

54. "Year after Fatal Walmart Stampede, Black Friday Gets Makeover," Associated Press, November 25, 2009, via **www.nola.com/business/index.ssf/2009/11/year_after_walmart_stampede_bl.html** (accessed January 28, 2010).

55. Todd Littman, "Win-Win Emissions Reductions Strategies," Victoria Transport Policy Institute, **www.vtpi.org/wwclimate.pdf** (accessed February 25, 2010).

56. Lauren Etter, "Earth Day: 36 Years on, Plenty of Concerns Remain," *The Wall Street Journal,* April 22–23, 2006, p. A7.

57. Cornelia Dean, "Drugs Are in the Water, Does It Matter?" *The New York Times,* April 3, 2007, HEALTH, **www.nytimes.com/2007/04/03/science/earth/03water.html?_r=1&scp=55&sq=%22cornelia+dean%22&st=nyt&oref=slogin** (accessed February 25, 2010).

58. Kristina Dell, "The Promise and Pitfalls of Bioplastic," *Time,* May 3, 2010, **www.time.com/time/magazine/article/0,9171,1983894,00.html** (accessed June 2, 2010); **www.natureworksllc.com** (accessed July 2, 2010); Cheryl Long, "The Truth About Biodegradable Plastics," Mother Earth News, June/July 2010, **www.motherearthnews.com/nature-community/the-truth-about-biodegradable-plastics.aspx** (accessed June 3, 2010); William F. Brinton and Gretchen K. Stuart, "Degradation of Bioplastics in Industrial Composting Environments vs. Home Composting Environments," Woods End Laboratories Inc., **www.motherearthnews.com/uploadedFiles/articles/issues/2010-06-01/MotherEarthBioPlasticsFinalReport(1).pdf** (accessed October 27, 2010); Bruce Horowitz, "SunChips Sends Its Bag to Dump," *The Wall Street Journal,* October 5, 2010, 3B; "SunChips Unveils New Less-Noisy Eco-Friendly Bag [VIDEO]," AOL News, February 24, 2011, **www.aolnews.com/2011/02/24/sunchips-unveils-new-less-noisy-eco-friendly-bag-video/** (accessed March 17, 2011).

59. "Diamant Corporation Furthers National Consumer Awareness Efforts as British Prime Minister Gordon Brown Announces Tougher Measures to Drastically Reduce the Society's Dependence on Single-Use Plastic Bags," *CNN Money,* March 25, 2008, **money.cnn.com/news/newsfeeds/articles/marketwire/0379140.htm** (accessed February 25, 2010).

60. Matthew Knight, "Plastic Bags Fly into Environmental Storm," *CNN.com,* March 17, 2008, **http://edition.cnn.com/2007/**

TECH/11/14/fsummit.climate.plasticbags/index.html (accessed February 25, 2010).

61. "Whole Foods to Sack Disposable Plastic Grocery Bags," January 22, 2008, **www.wholefoodsmarket.com/cgi-bim/print10pt .cgi?url=/pressroom/pr_01-22-08.html** (accessed February 25, 2010).

62. Josh Glasser, "T. Boone Pickens on Natural Gas: You Can't Beat It," *Fortune*, July 14, 2009, **http://bigtech.blogs.fortune. cnn.com/2009/07/14/news/economy/pickens_natural_gas. fortune/?postversion=2009071415** (accessed January 28, 2010); Brian Merchant, "The US Imports $1.5 Billion Barrels of Oil a Year from 'Dangerous or Unstable' Nations," Treehugger.com, January 14, 2010, **www.treehugger.com/files/2010/01/us-imports-1-5-billion-barrels-oil-year-dangerous-unstable-nations .php** (accessed January 7, 2011); "US Spent Over $30 Billion for Foreign Oil in April," *BusinessWire*, May 17, 2010, **www. businesswire.com/news/home/20100517006122/en/U.S.- Spent-30-Billion-Foreign-Oil-April** (accessed January 7, 2011).

63. "U.S. Stimulus Boosts Renewables, Energy Efficiency, and Smart Grids," Energy Envirofinland." Source originally taken from *Reuters*, February 14, 2009, **www.energy-enviro.fi/index .php?PAGE=2427** (accessed January 28, 2010).

64. Alan K. Reichert, Marion S. Webb, and Edward G. Thomas, "Corporate Support for Ethical and Environmental Policies: A Financial Management Perspective," *Journal of Business Ethics* 25 (2000), pp. 53–64.

65. David J. Lynch, "Corporate American Warms to Fight Against Global Warming," *USA Today*, June 1, 2006, p. B1.

66. Jim Rogers, "Point of View: A New Model for Energy Efficiency," *The News & Observer*, February 19, 2008, **www.newsobserver .com/print/tuesday/opinion/story/951188.html** (accessed February 25, 2010).

67. "GreenChoice: The #1 Green Power Program in America," Austin Energy (n.d.), **www.austinenergy.com/Energy%20Efficiency/Programs/Green%20Choice/index.htm** (accessed February 25, 2010).

68. "Certification," Home Depot, **www.homedepot.com/HDUS/EN_ US/corporate/corp_respon/certification.shtml** (accessed February 25, 2010).

69. Chiquita, Bananalink, **www.bananalink.org.uk/content/view/62/ 22/lang,en/** (accessed February 25, 2010).

70. "Majora Carter, Founder, Majora Carter Group," "The 100 Most Creative People in Business 2010," *FastCompany*, June 2010, p. 101; **www.majoracartergroup.com** (accessed July 13, 2010); Mary Landers, "Majora Carter Tells How to Green the Urban Jungle," Savannah Morning News, February 15, 2010, **http:// savannahnow.com/news/2010-02-15/majora-carter-tells-how-green-urban-jungle** (accessed July 13, 2010).

71. "US Charitable Giving Estimated to Be $307.65 Billion in 2008," Press Release, Giving USA, **www.aafrc.org/press_ releases/gusa/GivingReaches300billion.pdf** (accessed February 25, 2010).

72. Mark Calvey, "Profile: Safeway's Grants Reflect Its People," *San Francisco Business Times*, July 14, 2003, **http://sanfrancisco .bizjournals.com/sanfrancisco/stories/2003/07/14/focus9.html** (accessed February 25, 2010).

73. "About Avon," Avon, **www.avoncompany.com/about/** (accessed February 25, 2010); "The Avon Breast Cancer Crusade," Avon, **www .avoncompany.com/women/avoncrusade/** (accessed February 25, 2010); Avon Foundation for Women website, **www.avonfoundation .org/breast-cancer-crusade/** (accessed March 23, 2011).

74. "Take Charge of Education," Target (n.d.), **http://target.com/ common/page.jhtml;jsessionid=GWORM5AQSLBLDLARAAVW**

W4FMCEACU1IX?content=target_cg_take_charge_of_education (accessed February 25, 2010).

75. "The 2010 World's Most Ethical Companies—Company Profile: **http://Salesforce.com**," *Ethisphere*, Q1, p. 32.

76. "Who Really Pays for CSR Initiatives," *Environmental Leader*, February 15, 2008, **www.environmentalleader.com/2008/02/15/ who-really-paysfor-csr-initiatives/** (accessed February 25, 2010); "Global Fund," **www.joinred.com/globalfund** (accessed February 25, 2010); Reena Jana, "The Business of Going Green," *Business-Week Online*, June 22, 2007, **www.businessweek.com/innovate/ content/jun2007/id20070622_491833.htm?chan=search** (accessed June 19, 2008).

77. M.P. McQueen, "Agency Misses Chance to Curb Lead in Jewelry," *The Wall Street Journal*, February 12, 2008, p. D1.

78. Dana Mattioli, "At Kodak, Patents Hold the Key to the Future," *The Wall Street Journal*, April 20, 2010, p. B8; Grant Gross, "ITC to Investigate Apple's Patent Complaint against Kodak," *ComputerWorld*, May 14, 2010, **www.computerworld.com/s/ article/9176792/ITC_to_investigate_Apple_s_patent_complaint_ against_Kodak** (accessed June 15, 2010); Franklin Paul, "UPDATE 3-Kodak Growth Concerns Overshadow Patent Riches," *Reuters*, April 29, 2010, **www.reuters.com/article/idUSN2923844820100429** (accessed June 15, 2010); United States Patent and Trademark Office, **www.uspto.gov** (accessed October 15, 2010); Geoff Duncan, "Samsung and Kodak Reach Patent Settlement," *Digital Trends*, December 23, 2009, **www.digitaltrends.com/mobile/samsung-and-kodak-reach-patent-settlement/** (accessed October 16, 2010).

79. "5 Major Corporate Bankruptcies of 2009," BankruptcyHome.com, **www.bankruptcyhome.com/Five-Major-Corporate-Bankruptcies-2009.htm** (accessed January 28, 2010).

80. Sara Murray, "Bankrupt Filings Leapt 9% Last Year," *The Wall Street Journal*, January 4, 2011, p. A1.

81. Jessica E. Vascallero, "Google Book-Search Pact Draws Antitrust Scrutiny," *The Wall Street Journal*, April 29, 2009, **http://online. wsj.com/article/SB124095639971465549.html** (accessed January 28, 2010); Catherine Holahan, "Google's Antitrust Trouble," *BusinessWeek*, September 15, 2008, **www.businessweek .com/bwdaily/dnflash/content/sep2008/db20080914_683068 .htm** (accessed January 28, 2010); "Ending Our Agreement with Yahoo!," The Official Google Blog, November 5, 2008, **http:// googleblog.blogspot.com/2008/11/ending-our-agreement-with-yahoo.html** (accessed January 28, 2010).

82. Maureen Dorney, "Congress Passes Federal Anti-Spam Law: Preempts Most State Anti-Spam Laws," *DLA Piper*, December 3, 2003, **http://franchiseagreements.com/global/publications/ detail.aspx?pub=622** (accessed February 25, 2010).

83. Larry Barrett, "Data Breach Costs Surge in 2009: Study," *eSecurityPlanet*, January 26, 2010, **www.esecurityplanet.com/ features/article.php/3860811/Data-Breach-Costs-Surge-in-2009-Study.htm** (accessed January 28, 2010).

84. Jean Eaglesham and Ashby Jones, "Whistle-blower Bounties Pose Challenges," *The Wall Street Journal*, December 13, 2010, pp. C1, C3.

85. "Durbin Statement on His Debit Card Swipe Fee Amendment," United States Senator Dick Durbin, May 13, 2010, **http://durbin.senate.gov/showRelease.cfm?releaseId=324958** (accessed February 22, 2011).

86. "Office of Financial Research," *U.S. Department of Treasury*, **www.treasury.gov/initiatives/Pages/ofr.aspx** (accessed February 22, 2011); "Initiatives: Financial Stability Oversight Council," *U.S. Department of Treasury*, **www.treasury.gov/initiatives/Pages/FSOC-index.aspx** (accessed February 22, 2011).

CHAPTER 3

1. Tim Kelly, "Squash the Caterpillar," *Forbes,* April 21, 2008, p. 136.

2. "Julie Jargon, "Subway Runs Past McDonald's Chain," *The Wall Street Journal,* March 9, 2011, p. B4.

3. Bruce Horowitz and Howard Schultz, "Starbucks Hits 40 Feeling Perky," *USA Today,* March 7, 2011, pp. 1B, 3B.

4. Elisabeth Sullivan, "Choose Your Words Wisely," *Marketing News,* February 15, 2008, p. 22.

5. Ellen Byron, "P&G Turns Febreze into a $1 Billion Brand," *The Wall Street Journal,* March 8, 2011, **http://online.wsj.com/article/ SB10001424052748704076804576180683371307932 .html** (accessed March 10, 2011).

6. Sullivan, "Choose Your Words Wisely."

7. Michelle Yun and Kathy Chu, "Philippines May Answer Call," *USA Today,* January 10, 2011, pp. 1B–2B.

8. "Goods and Services Deficit Increases in 2010," U.S. Census Bureau, February 11, 2011, **www.census.gov/indicator/www/ ustrade.html** (accessed March 2, 2011).

9. Dexter Roberts and David Rocks, "China Let a Thousand Brands Bloom," *Bloomberg BusinessWeek,* October 17, 2005, **www .businessweek.com/magazine/content/05_42/b3955084.htm** (accessed November 27, 2011).

10. Joseph O'Reilly, "Global Logistics: In China, Bigger Bull's-Eye Better," *Inbound Logistics,* April 2008, p. 26.

11. "Goods and Services Deficit Increases in 2010," U.S. Census Bureau, February 11, 2011, **www.census.gov/indicator/www/ ustrade.html** (accessed March 2, 2011).

12. Ibid.

13. "Trade in Goods (Imports, Exports and Trade Balance) with China," U.S. Census Bureau: Foreign Trade Statistics, **www.census.gov/ foreign-trade/balance/c5700.html** (accessed March 2, 2011).

14. Sky Canaves, "China Slams Luxury Goods' Quality," The Wall Street Journal, March 17, 2010, p. B2; Astrid Wendlandt, "Bain Sees 2010 Global Luxury Goods Sales Up 4 Pct," *Reuters,* April 15, 2010, **www.reuters.com/article/idUSLDE63E2EA20100415** (accessed June 8, 2010); Joel Backaler, "What Are China's Luxury Consumers Buying?," Forbes, May 16, 2010, http:// **blogs.forbes.com/china/2010/05/16/what-are-chinas-luxury- consumers-buying** (accessed June 8, 2010); Sheppard Mullin, "International Luxury Brands May Face Product Quality Enforcement in China," Fashion & Apparel Law Blog, April 5, 2010, **www .fashionapparellawblog.com/2010/04/articles/enforcement- of-fashion-laws/international-luxury-brands-may-face-product- quality-enforcement-in-china** (accessed June 8, 2010); Jonathan Tepperman, "Classic to the Core," Newsweek, March 19, 2010, **www.newsweek.com/2010/03/18/classic-to-the-core.html** (accessed June 8, 2010); Carol Matlack, "High-End Tailor Zegna's Marco Polo Moment," *Bloomberg Businessweek,* June 10, 2010, **www.businessweek.com/magazine/content/10_25/ b4183018327399.htm** (accessed October 27, 2010).

15. Jeanne Whalen, "Novartis Invests in Chinese Vaccines," *The Wall Street Journal,* November 5, 2009, p. B2.

16. Summer Said, "Pact Keeps BlackBerrys Running," *The Wall Street Journal,* August 9, 2010, p. B3; "Forbidden Telecoms Fruit," *The Economist,* August 7, 2010, pp. 46–47; "Indonesia Joins Countries Mulling BlackBerry Ban," CBS News, August 4, 2010, **www .cbsnews.com/stories/2010/08/04/tech/main6742774.shtml** (accessed January 7, 2011); "United Arab Emirates Will Not Ban BlackBerries," BBC News, October 8, 2010, **www.bbc.co.uk/ news/technology-11499755** (accessed January 7, 2011).

17. O'Reilly, "Global Logistics: New Tax Treaty Raises U.S. Stakes in Belgium's Lowlands," p. 24.

18. "The Restricted Zone in Mexico," Penner & Associates—Mexico Law Firm and Business Consulting for Mexico, **www.mexicolaw .com/LawInfo17.htm** (accessed January 10, 2011).

19. "Sixth Annual BSA and IDC Global Software Piracy Study," Business Software Alliance, May 2009, **http://global.bsa.org/ globalpiracy2008/index.html** (accessed February 20, 2010).

20. Jose De Cordoba and Nicholas Casey. "Cuba Unveils Huge Layoffs in Tilt toward Free Market," *The Wall Street Journal,* September 14, 2010, pp. A1, A15; Tim Padgett, "Cuba's Big Layoffs: What to Do with the Unemployed?" *Time,* September 14, 2010, **www.time.com/time/world/article/0,8599,2019225,00.html** (accessed September 20, 2010); WSJ Staff Reporter, "Cubans Dip a Toe in Capitalist Waters," *The Wall Street Journal,* October 6, 2010, p. A18.

21. Kitty Bean Yancey and Laura Bly, "Door May Be Inching Open for Tourism," *USA Today,* February 20, 2008, p. A5; Sue Kirchhoff and Chris Woodyard, "Cuba Trade Gets 'New Opportunity,'" *USA Today,* February 20, 2008, p. B1.

22. "Obama Move on China Tires Could Spur More Requests," *Reuters,* September 14, 2009, **www.reuters.com/article/ idUKTRE58D3Y120090914** (accessed February 23, 2010).

23. Julie Bennett, "Product Pitfalls Proliferate in Global Cultural Maze," *The Wall Street Journal,* May 14, 2001, p. B11.

24. Ann Blackman Moscow, "Moscow's Big Mac Attack," *Time,* February 5, 1990, **www.time.com/time/magazine/article/ 0,9171,969321,00.html** (accessed March 8, 2010).

25. "Slogans Gone Bad," Joe-ks, **www.joe-ks.com/archives_ apr2004/slogans_gone_bad.htm** (accessed March 3, 2010).

26. David Ricks, *Blunders in International Business,* 4th ed. (Malden, MA: Blackwell Publishing, 2006), p. 70. Downloaded from Google Books, **http://books.google.com/books?id = S4L3ntwgs-8C&pg = PA68&lpg = PA68&dq = Mountain + Bell + company, + Saudi+advertisement&source=bl &ots= 9apNX6s3hy&sig= Z5BEVaLe4-2p39kNYMIBd5sOX- GA&hl= en&ei=XJGFS6rfNpPKsAODk5zEDw&sa = X&oi = book_result&ct= result&resnum=5&ved = 0CBcQ6AEwBA#v = onepage&q = airline&f= false** (accessed February 24, 2010).

27. J. Bonasia, "For Web, Global Reach Is Beauty—and Challenge," *Investor's Business Daily,* June 13, 2001, p. A6.

28. Matthew Wilkins, "Dell Retakes Second Rank in Global PC Market as Acer Stumbles," iSuppli, September 2, 2010, **www .isuppli.com/Home-and-Consumer-Electronics/News/Pages/ Dell-Retakes-Second-Rank-in-Global-PC-Market-as-Acer- Stumbles.aspx** (accessed January 10, 2011).

29. "What Is the WTO," World Trade Organization (n.d.), **www.wto .org/english/thewto_e/whatis_e/whatis_e.htm** (accessed March 3, 2010).

30. Bao Chang, "Steel Fastener Makers Hope EU Sales Can Recover on WTO Ruling," China Daily, December 7, 2010, **www.chinadaily .com.cn/bizchina/2010-12/07/content_11662675.htm** (accessed January 10, 2011).

31. International Monetary Fund, **www.imf.org/external/pubs/ft/ weo/2010/02/weodata/weorept.aspx?sy=2008&ey=2011&scs m=1&ssd=1&sort=country&ds=.&br=1&c=156&s=PPPGDP% 2CPPPPC&grp=0&a=&pr.x=42&pr.y=6** (accessed January 10, 2011).

32. "Trade in Goods (Imports, Exports and Trade Balance) with Canada," U.S. Census Bureau, **www.census.gov/foreign-trade/ balance/c1220.html** (accessed February 24, 2010); "North

America: Canada," *CIA—World Factbook,* **https://www.cia.gov/library/publications/the-world-factbook/geos/ca.html** (accessed February 24, 2010).

33. "America's Biggest Partners," *CNBC.com,* **www.cnbc.com/id/31064179?slide = 11** (accessed February 24, 2010).

34. "North America: Mexico," *CIA World Factbook,* **https://www.cia.gov/library/publications/the-world-factbook/geos/mx.html** (February 24, 2010); International Monetary Fund, **www.imf.org/external/pubs/ft/weo/2010/02/weodata/weorept.aspx?sy=2008&ey=2015&scsm=1&ssd=1&sort=country&ds=.&br=1&c=273&s=PPPGDP%2CPPPPC&grp=0&a=&pr.x=67&pr.y=13 6** (accessed January 10, 2011).

35. "North America: Mexico," *CIA—World Factbook,* **https://www.cia.gov/library/publications/the-worldfactbook/geos/mx.html** (February 24, 2010); "Trade in Goods (Imports, Exports and Trade Balance) with Mexico," U.S. Census Bureau, **www.census.gov/foreign-trade/balance/c2010.html#2009** (accessed February 24, 2010).

36. U.S. Census Bureau, **http://factfinder.census.gov/servlet/DTTable?_bm=y&-geo_id=01000US&-ds_name=ACS_2009_1YR_G00_&-_lang=en&-redoLog=true&-mt_name=ACS_2009_1YR_G2000_B03001&-format=&-CONTEXT=dt** (accessed March 18, 2011).

37. Pete Engardio and Geri Smith, "Business Is Standing Its Ground," *BusinessWeek,* April 20, 2009, pp. 34–39.

38. "Country Comparison: GDP (purchasing power parity)," *CIA—World Factbook,* **https://www.cia.gov/library/publications/the-worldfactbook/rankorder/2001rank.html?countryName=United%20States&countryCode = us&regionCode = na&rank = 2#us** (accessed February 3, 2010).

39. "A Tale of Two Mexicos: North and South," *The Economist,* April 26, 2008, pp. 53–54.

40. "Antecedents of the FTAA Process," Free Trade Area of the Americas (n.d.), **www.ftaa-alca.org/View_e.asp** (accessed March 10, 2010); "FTAA Fact Sheet," Market Access and Compliance, U.S. Department of Commerce (n.d.), **www.mac.doc.gov/ftaa2005/ftaa_fact_sheet.html** (accessed November 3, 2003).

41. Josh Mitchell, "U.S. Jump-Starts Bid to End Truck Dispute With Mexico," *The Wall Street Journal,* January 7, 2011, **http://online.wsj.com/article/SB10001424052748704415104576065924125822128.html** (accessed January 10, 2011); Elizabeth Williamson, "U.S., Mexico Agree to Settle Truck Feud," *The Wall Street Journal,* March 4, 2011, **online.wsj.com/article/SB10001424052748703300904576178511087875924.html** (accessed March 18, 2011).

42. Geri Smith and Cristina Lindblad, "Mexico: Was NAFTA Worth It?," *BusinessWeek,* December 23, 2003, **www.businessweek.com/magazine/content/03_51/b3863008.htm** (accessed May 5, 2010).

43. Pete Engardio and Geri Smith, "Business Is Standing Its Ground," *BusinessWeek,* April 20, 2009, pp. 34–39.

44. "Europe in 12 Lessons," **http://europa.eu/abc/12lessons/lesson_2/index_en.htm** (accessed March 3, 2010).

45. "Europe: European Union," *CIA—World Factbook,* **https://www.cia.gov/library/publications/the-worldfactbook/geos/ee.html** (accessed February 25, 2010); "European Countries," Europa, **http://europa.eu/abc/european_countries/candidate_countries/index_en.htm** (accessed March 18, 2011).

46. Stanley Reed, with Ariane Sains, David Fairlamb, and Carol Matlack, "The Euro: How Damaging a Hit?" *BusinessWeek,* September 29, 2003, p. 63; "The Single Currency," *CNN* (n.d.),

www.cnn.com/SPECIALS/2000/eurounion/story/currency/ (accessed July 3, 2001).

47. Abigail Moses, "Greek Contagion Concern Spurs European Sovereign Default Risk to Record," *Bloomberg,* April 26, 2010, **www.bloomberg.com/news/2010-04-26/greek-contagion-concern-spurs-european-sovereign-default-risk-to-record.html** (accessed March 18, 2011).

48. James G. Neuger and Joe Brennan, "Ireland Weighs Aid as EU Spars Over Debt-Crisis Remedy," *Bloomberg,* **www.bloomberg.com/news/2010-11-16/ireland-discusses-financial-bailout-as-eu-struggles-to-defuse-debt-crisis.html** (accessed March 18, 2011).

49. "Spreading Infection," *The Economist,* March 3, 2011, **www.bloomberg.com/news/2010-04-26/greek-contagion-concern-spurs-european-sovereign-default-risk-to-record.html** (accessed March 18, 2011).

50. "About EFSF," EFSF, **www.efsf.europa.eu/about/index.htm** (accessed March 18, 2011).

51. "About APEC," Asia-Pacific Economic Cooperation, **www.apec.org/apec/about_apec.html** (accessed February 25, 2010).

52. Smith and Lindblad, "Mexico: Was NAFTA Worth It?"

53. "China Economic Growth Accelerates," *BBC News,* October 22, 2009, **http://news.bbc.co.uk/2/hi/business/8319706.stm** (accessed February 25, 2010).

54. Kathy Chu and Michelle Yun, "Workers Are Finding Their Voice in China," *USA Today,* November 19, 2010, pp. 1B–2B; Elizabeth Holmes, "U.S. Apparel Retailers Turn Their Gaze Beyond China," *The Wall Street Journal,* June 16, 2010, p. B1.

55. James T. Areddy, James Hookway, John Lyons, and Marcus Walker, "U.S. Slump Takes Toll Across Globe," *The Wall Street Journal,* April 3, 2008, p. A1; Pam Woodall, "The New Champions," *The Economist,* November 15, 2008, p. 55; Matt Jenkins, "A Really Inconvenient Truth," *Miller-McCune,* April/May 2008, p. 42.

56. Holmes, "U.S. Apparel Retailers Turn Their Gaze Beyond China," p. B1.

57. Rebecca Christie, "IMF Says Greek Program Doing Well, Approves New Loan Payment," *Bloomberg Businessweek,* December 17, 2010, **www.businessweek.com/news/2010-12-17/imf-says-greek-program-doing-well-approves-new-loan-payment.html** (accessed January 10, 2011); Bruno Waterfield, "Ireland Forced to Take EU and IMF Bail-Out Package," *The Telegraph,* November 22, 2010, **www.telegraph.co.uk/finance/financetopics/financialcrisis/8150137/Ireland-forced-to-take-EU-and-IMF-bail-out-package.html** (accessed January 10, 2011).

58. David J. Lynch, "The IMF is . . . Tired Fund Struggles to Reinvent Itself," *USA Today,* April 19, 2006. p. B1.

59. Ilan Brat and Paul Kiernan, "Heinz Seeks to Tap Mexico's Taste for Ketchup," *The Wall Street Journal,* November 24, 2009, pp. B1–B2.

60. Ben Worthen, "The Crazy World of Outsourcing," *WSJ.com,* February 25, 2008. **http://blogs.wsj.com/biztech/2008/02/25/the-crazy-world-ofoutsourcing/?mod = relevancy** (accessed May 6, 2008).

61. Walter B. Wriston, "Ever Heard of Insourcing?" Commentary, *The Wall Street Journal,* March 24, 2004, p. A20.

62. Nick Heath, "Banks: Offshoring, Not Outsourcing," *BusinessWeek,* March 10, 2009, **www.businessweek.com/globalbiz/content/mar2009/gb20090310_619247.htm** (accessed February 25, 2010); Coomi Kapoor, "What Now after the Satyam Fraud?" *Asia News Network,* December 1, 2009, **www.asianewsnet.net/news.php?id= 3368&sec = 3&t=** (accessed February 25, 2010).

63. Keith B. Richburg, "Chinese films look to team up with Hollywood," *The Washington Post,* September 6, 2010, **www.washingtonpost .com/wp-dyn/content/article/2010/09/03/AR2010090302853_2 .html?sid=ST2010090305799** (accessed October 29, 2010); Jonathan Watts, "Chinese film industry aims to challenge Hollywood," *The Guardian,* September 13, 2010, **www.guardian .co.uk/world/2010/sep/13/chinese-film-industry-rival-hollywood** (accessed October 29, 2010); Ronald Grover and Michael White, "Hollywood Looks to China for Movie Money," *Bloomburg Businessweek,* October 14, 2010, **www.businessweek.com/magazine/content/10_43/b4200023890594.htm** (accessed October 29, 2010).

64. Barclays Wealth, **www.census.gov/hhes/www/cpstables/032009/ hhinc/new01_009.htm** (accessed March 3, 2010); Heath, "Banks: Offshoring, Not Outsourcing."

65. "About Us," Carrefour: Arab Republic of Egypt, **www.carrefour .com.eg/aboutus.aspx** (accessed February 25, 2010).

66. Matt O'Sullivan, "Virgin Blue mines fly-in, fly-out boom," *The Sydney Morning Herald,* January 10, 2011, **www. smh.com.au/business/virgin-blue-mines-flyin-flyout-boom-20110110-19kb3.html** (accessed January 10, 2011); Matt O'Sullivan, "Virgin Blue hooks up with regional Skywest," *The Sydney Morning Herald,* January 11, 2011, **www.smh .com.au/business/virgin-blue-hooks-up-with-regional-skywest-20110110-19l7d.html** (accessed January 11, 2011).

67. Sharon Silk Carty, "Ford Plans to Park Jaguar, Land Rover with Tata Motors," *USA Today,* March 26, 2008, p. B1.

68. O. C. Ferrell, John Fraedrich, and Linda Ferrell, *Business Ethics,* 6th ed. (Boston: Houghton Mifflin, 2005), pp. 227–230.

69. Export.gov, **www.export.gov/about/index.asp** (accessed March 3, 2010); CIBER Web, **http://CIBERWEB.msu.edu** (accessed March 3, 2010).

CHAPTER 4

1. Stella & Dot website, **www.stelladot.com** (accessed October 19, 2010); "*Inc.* 500: # 67 Stella & Dot," *Inc.,* 2010, **www.inc .com/inc5000/profile/Stella-dot** (accessed October 19, 2010); Max Chafkin, "And the Winners Are ...," *Inc.,* October 2010, pp. 27–28.

2. The Entrepreneurs' Help Page, **www.tannedfeet.com/sole_ proprietorship.htm** (accessed March 16, 2010); Kent Hoover, "Startups Down for Women Entrepreneurs, Up for Men," *San Francisco Business Times,* May 2, 2008, **http://sanfrancisco .bizjournals.com/sanfrancisco/stories/2008/05/05/smallb2 .html** (accessed March 16, 2010).

3. Maggie Overfelt, "Start-Me-Up: How the Garage Became a Legendary Place to Rev Up Ideas," *Fortune Small Business,* September 1, 2003, **http://money.cnn.com/magazines/fsb/fsb_ archive/2003/09/01/350784/index.htm** (accessed March 16, 2010).

4. Digital Artists Agency, **www.da-a.com/clients/clientindexframe .html** (accessed March 18, 2011).

5. Christian Sylt, "Cirque du Soleil may leap for new partner," *The Telegraph,* January 30, 2011, **www.telegraph.co.uk/finance/ newsbysector/banksandfinance/privateequity/8290380/Cirque-du-Soleil-may-leap-for-new-partner.html#** (accessed March 18, 2011).

6. "THE AM LAW 100: Davis Polk Leads the New York Pack; Sullivan, Cleary Hang In," The AM LAW Daily, March 12, 2010, **http://amlawdaily.typepad.com/amlawdaily/2010/03/ al100nyfirms.html** (accessed March 18, 2011).

7. Laura Petrecca, "A partner can give your business shelter or a storm," *USA Today,* October 9, 2009, **www.usatoday .com/money/smallbusiness/startup/week4-partnerships.htm** (accessed January 11, 2011).

8. Clarissa French, "Diversification accounts for BKD revenue results," sbj.net, March 5, 2010, **http://sbj.net/main.asp?SectionID =48&SubSectionID=108&ArticleID=86481** (accessed March 18, 2011); "About BKD," BKD website, **www.bkd.com/about/ AtaGlance.htm** (accessed March 18, 2011).

9. N. Kane Bennett, "Dispute between Business Partners Ends in Dissolution and Double Damages under Connecticut Wage Act," *Connecticut Business Litigation Blog,* September 13, 2009, **www.connecticutbusinesslitigation.com/2009/09/arti-cles/employment-1/dispute-between-business-partnersends-in-dissolution-and-doubledamages-under-connecticut-wage-act** (accessed March 8, 2010).

10. "Facts & History," Kiva, **www.kiva.org/about/facts** (accessed March 18, 2011); David M. Ewalt, "Low-Dose Capitalism," *Forbes,* November 2, 2009, p. 40; Leena Rao, "Kiva Brings Microlending Home to U.S. Entrepreneurs in Need," *TechCrunch,* June 10, 2009, **www.techcrunch.com/2009/06/10/kiva-brings-microlending-home-tous-entrepreneurs-in-need** (accessed December 19, 2009); Peter Greer and Phil Smith, *The Poor Will Be Glad* (Grand Rapids, MI: Zondervan, 2009), pp. 99, 107.

11. *Warren Buffett's Berkshire Hathaway Letter to Shareholders,* **www .berkshirehathaway.com/letters/2010ltr.pdf** (accessed March 14, 2011).

12. "America's Largest Privately-Owned Companies," *Forbes.com,* October 28, 2009, **www.forbes.com/lists/2009/21/private-companies-09_Cargill_5ZUZ.html** (accessed March 2, 2010).

13. "Global Brands," Mars, **www.mars.com/global/global-brands .aspx** (accessed March 8, 2010); Scott DeCarlo, Andrea D. Murphy and John J. Ray, "America's Largest Private Companies," November 3, 2010, *Forbes,* **www.forbes.com/lists/ 2010/21/private-companies-10_land.html** (accessed January 10, 2011).

14. Deborah Orr, "The Secret World of Mars," *Forbes,* April 28, 2008, **www .forbes.com/2008/04/28/billionaires-mars-wrigley-bizbilliescz_ do_0428marsfamily.html** (accessed March 16, 2010).

15. "Fortune 500," **CNNMoney.com, http://money.cnn.com/magazines/ fortune/fortune500/2010/full_list/** (accessed January 11, 2011).

16. Jay Hart, "Not His father's CEO," *Yahoo! Sports,* January 22, 2010, **http://sports.yahoo.com/nascar/news?slug=jhfrance012209** (accessed March 2, 2010).

17. Scott DeCarlo, "The World's Leading Companies," *Forbes,* April 21, 2010, **www.forbes.com/2010/04/20/global-2000-leading-world-business-global-2000-10-intro.html** (accessed January 11, 2011).

18. Chris Isidore, "GM IPO biggest ever," *CNNMoney.com,* November 18, 2010, **http://money.cnn.com/2010/11/17/news/ companies/gm_ipo_pricing/index.htm** (accessed January 11, 2011); Clare Baldwin and Jonathon Spicer, "GM IPO now world's biggest," *Reuters,* November 26, 2010, **www.reuters .com/article/idUSTRE6AP50E20101127** (accessed January 11, 2011).

19. Niraj Sheth and Jeff McCracken, "RCN Is Sold to Firm in $535 Million Deal," *The Wall Street Journal,* March 5, 2010, **http:// online.wsj.com/article/SB1000142405274870391520457510 3362665861820.html?KEYWORDS= private+equity+buy+out** (accessed March 9, 2010).

20. O. C. Ferrell, John Fraedrich, and Linda Ferrell, *Business Ethics: Ethical Decision Making and Cases,* 8th ed. (Mason, OH: South-Western Cengage Learning, 2011), p. 109.

21. Floyd Norris, "For Boards, S.E.C. Keeps the Bar Low," *The New York Times*, March 3, 2011, **www.nytimes.com/2011/03/04/business/04norris.html?pagewanted=1&_r=1&src=busln** (accessed March 4, 2011).

22. Gary Strauss, "$228,000 for a part-time job? Apparently, that's not enough," *USA Today*, March 4-6, 2011, 1A.

23. "Board Composition," P&G, **www.pg.com/en_US/company/global_structure_operations/governance/board_composition.shtml** (accessed March 18, 2011).

24. Joseph Nathan Kane, *Famous First Facts,* 4th ed. (New York: The H. W. Wilson Company, 1981), p. 202.

25. "How an Employee Stock Ownership Plan (ESOP) Works," NCEO—The National Center for Employee Ownership," **www.nceo.org/main/article.php/id/8** (accessed June 8, 2010); **www.bobsredmill.com** (accessed June 8, 2010); Dana Tims, "Founder of Bob's Red Mill Natural Foods transfers business to employees," *OregonLive.com*, February 16, 2010, **www.oregonlive.com/clackamascounty/index.ssf/2010/02/bobs_red_mill_natural_foods_ro.html**(accessed June 8, 2010); Christine Brozyna, "American Heart: Owner of Multi-Million Dollar Company Hands Over Businesses to Employees," *ABC News*, February 18, 2010, **http://abcnews.go.com/WN/owner-multi-million-dollar-company-hands-business-employees/story?id=9875038** (accessed June 8, 2010); John Brant, "Bob Moore, Bob's Red Mill, Integrity is Baked In," *Inc.*, May 2010, pp. 83-84.

26. David Kaplan, "Dow Jones in Joint Venture to Launch WSJ Japan Site," *The Washington Post,* May 7, 2009, **www.washingtonpost.com/wp-dyn/content/article/2009/05/07/AR2009050703543.html** (accessed March 3, 2010).

27. Robert D. Hisrich and Michael P. Peters, *Entrepreneurship,* 5th ed. (Boston: McGraw-Hill, 2002), pp. 315–16.

28. Russell Gold, "Biomass Power Generates Traction," *The Wall Street Journal*, June 1, 2009, p. A4.

29. Kerry Capell and Dermot Doherty, "What Novartis Sees in Eye Care," *Bloomberg Businessweek*, January 18, 2010, p. 26; Katie Reid, "Novartis wins Alcon with cash sweetener," *Reuters*, December 15, 2010, **www.reuters.com/article/idUSTRE6BE10Q20101215** (accessed January 11, 2011).

30. "CKE Restaurants Adopts Poison Pill Plan," January 5, 2009, **www.thestreet.com/story/10456052/ckerestaurants-adopts-poison-pill-plan.html** (accessed March 9, 2010).

CHAPTER 5

1. "FAQs," U.S. Small Business Administration, **http://web.sba.gov/faqs/faqindex.cfm?areaID =24** (accessed March 9, 2010).

2. "Let a million flowers bloom," *The Economist*, March 12–18, 2011, pp. 79–81.

3. "Environmentalism: What We Do," Patagonia, **www.patagonia.com/web/us/patagonia.go?assetid = 2329** (accessed March 9, 2010).

4. "FAQs," U.S. Small Business Administration, **http://web.sba.gov/faqs/faqindex.cfm?areaID=24** (accessed March 18, 2011).

5. "Nation's Women-Owned Firms Contribute Nearly $3 Trillion to U.S. Economy According to Groundbreaking Research," Center for Women's Business Research, October 2, 2009, **www.womensbusinessresearchcenter.org/Data/newsroom/pressreleases/2009pressreleases/economicimpactmeas/cfwbreconomicimpact.release.100209.pdf** (accessed March 9, 2010).

6. Ilan Brat, "Start-Up Seeks Profits in Mounds of Garbage," *The Wall Street Journal,* May 3, 2010, p. B8; **www.terracycle.net** (accessed June 9, 2010); "How I Saved My Company: TerraCycle," You're the Boss—*The New York Times* blog, June 2, 2010, **http://boss.blogs.nytimes.com/2010/06/02/how-i-saved-my-company-terracycle** (accessed June 9, 2010); Jonathan Bardelline, "TerraCycle Turns Pens into Trash Cans," *Greener Design*, February 16, 2010, **www.greenbiz.com/news/2010/02/16/terracycle-turns-pens-trash-cans** (accessed June 9, 2010); "Entrepreneur's Annual 100 Brilliant Ideas," "Don't Call It Garbage," *Entrepreneur*, June 2010, **www.entrepreneur.com/magazine/entrepreneur/2010/june/206722-5.html** (accessed June 11, 2010); Lucie Young, "TerraCycle: The Google of Garbage?," *Telegraph*, June 17, 2010, **www.telegraph.co.uk/earth/businessandecology/recycling/7832655/TerraCycle-The-Google-of-garbage.html** (accessed July 11, 2010).

7. "Estimates of Business Ownership by Gender, Ethnicity, Race, and Veteran Status: 2007," U.S. Census Bureau: Survey of Business Owners (SBO), **www.census.gov/econ/sbo/** (accessed March 18, 2011).

8. "FAQs," U.S. Small Business Administration, **web.sba.gov/faqs/faqindex.cfm?areaID=24** (accessed March 18, 2011).

9. Ibid.

10. "Bittersweet Synergy: Domestic Outsourcing in India," *The Economist,* October 22, 2009, p. 74.

11. Joseph Schumpeter, "Brand Royalty," *The Economist,* November 26, 2009, p. 78.

12. "Small Biz Stats & Trends," SCORE®, **www.score.org/small_biz_stats.html** (accessed March 21, 2011).

13. "How to Finance a New Business," *Consumer Reports*, April 2008, **www.consumerreports.org/cro/money/credit-loan/how-to-finance-a-newbusiness/overview/how-to-finance-anew-business-ov.htm** (accessed March 9, 2010).

14. "Moms 'Can't Live Without' the Boppy ® Pillow," Boppy website, Press Release, October 6, 2009, **www.boppy.com/news-releases/the-boppypillow-wins-1** (accessed March 16, 2010).

15. Associated Press, "Service Sector Grew in June, but More Slowly Than in May," *The New York Times*, July 6, 2010, **www.nytimes.com/2010/07/07/business/economy/07econ.html** (accessed January 11, 2011).

16. Lindsay Blakely, "One Man Brands," *Money.CNN.com*, July 6, 2007, **http://money.cnn.com/galleries/2007/biz2/0706/gallery.building_brands.biz2/2.html** (accessed March 16, 2010).

17. "Seven U.S. Organizations Honored with the 2010 Baldrige National Quality Award," National Institute of Standards and Technology, November 23, 2010, **www.nist.gov/baldrige/baldrige_recipients2010.cfm** (accessed January 11, 2011).

18. "Statistics of U.S. Businesses (SUSB)" U.S. Census Bureau, Updated December 21, 2010, **www.census.gov/econ/susb/** (accessed January 11, 2011).

19. "Press Room," Facebook, **www.facebook.com/press/info.php?statistics** (accessed January 11, 2011).

20. Dana Knight, "Big-Headed Guy Gets a Big Idea for Sunglasses Business," *USA Today*, March 21, 2006, p. 4B; Fatheadz, **www.fatheadz.com** (accessed March 9, 2010); Dana Hunsinger, "Fatheadz Founder Thrilled That Retail Giant Wal-Mart Has Taken a Shine to His Sunglasses for Bigger Noggins," *The Indianapolis Star*, July 27, 2009, **www.fatheadz.com/pressselect.php?sid = 16** (accessed March 9, 2010).

21. "FAQs," U.S. Small Business Administration.

22. "Let's Hear Those Ideas," *The Economist*, August 14, 2010, pp. 55–57; "The New Heroes," "What Is Social Entrepreneurship," PBS, **www.pbs.org/opb/thenewheroes/whatis** (accessed December 3, 2010).

23. Jennifer Martin, "From Cow Pies to Cow Pots: A Creative Way to Manage Farm Waste," Cooperative State Research, Education, and Extension Service, July 17, 2007, **www.csrees.usda .gov/newsroom/research/2007/cowpots.html** (accessed March 16, 2010).

24. Jena McGregor, "Second Acts: Trading Textbooks for Triple Crème," *Fortune,* February 19, 2010, **http://money.cnn .com/2010/02/18/news/companies/fifth_town_cheese.fortune** (accessed March 16, 2010).

25. "Keep an Eye on These: Greentech Media's Top 50 Cleantech Startups," *eBoom,* March 8, 2010, **www.energyboom.com/ emerging/keepeye-these-greentech-medias-top-50-cleantech-startups** (accessed March 9, 2010).

26. Thomas W. Zimmerer and Norman M. Scarborough, *Essentials of Entrepreneurship and Small Business Management,* 6th ed. (Upper Saddle River, NJ: Pearson Prentice Hall, 2005), pp. 118–24.

27. Ibid.

28. "Media Fact Sheet," SCORE, **www.score.org/media_fact_sheet .html** (accessed January 11, 2011).

29. Adapted from "Tomorrow's Entrepreneur," *Inc. State of Small Business* 23, no. 7 (2001), pp. 80–104.

30. Nanci Hellmich, "Baby Boomers by the Numbers: Census Reveals Trends," *USA Today,* November 10, 2009, **www.usatoday .com/news/nation/census/2009-11-10-topblline10_ST_N.htm** (accessed March 9, 2010).

31. Molly Smith, "Managing Generation Y as They Change the Workforce," *Reuters,* January 8, 2008, **www.reuters.com/ article/pressRelease/idUS129795+ 08-Jan-2008+ BW20080108** (accessed March 16, 2010).

32. Jeffrey Passal and D'Vera Cohn, "Immigration to Play Lead Role in Future U.S. Growth," Pew Research, February 11, 2008, **http://pewresearch.org/pubs/729/united-states-population-projections** (accessed March 16, 2010).

33. Guitar Syndicate website, **www.guitarsyndicate.com** (accessed June 8, 2010); **www.facebook.com/home.php?#!/pages/Guitar-Syndicate/110953749034?v=wall&ref=search** (accessed June 8, 2010); "Guitar Retailer Offers Inventory on Facebook," Practical ecommerce, April 27, 2010, **www.practicalecommerce .com/articles/1855-Guitar-Retailer-Offers-Inventory-on-Face-book** (accessed June 8, 2010); Sarah E. Needleman, "Merchants Push Sales Through Social Media," *The Wall Street Journal,* June 1, 2010, p. B6; Kermit Pattison, "How to Market Your Business With Facebook," *The New York Times,* November 12, 2009, **www.nytimes.com/2009/11/12/business/ smallbusiness/12guide.html** (accessed November 18, 2009); **www.facebook.com** (accessed December 20, 2009); Kyle Austin, "5 Tips for Marketing on Facebook's New Pages," *Fast Company,* March 12, 2009, **www.fastcompany.com/blog/kyle-austin/channeling-media/5-tips-marketing-facebooks-new-pages** (accessed December 20, 2009); "Have You Tried Marketing Your Business With Facebook," *The New York Times,* November 16, 2009, **http://boss.blogs.nytimes.com/2009/11/16/ have-you-tried-marketing-your-business-with-facebook** (accessed December 20, 2009); Dan Fost, "Facebook a Friend to Small Businesses," *Chicago Tribune,* October 28, 2009, p. 47.

34. Daniel McGinn, "How I Did It: Arianna Huffington," *Inc.,* February 10, 2010, p. 65, **www.inc.com/magazine/20100201/ how-i-did-itarianna-huffington.html** (accessed March 16, 2010); "AOL Agrees to Acquire The Huffington Post," *The Huffington Post,* February 7, 2011, **www.huffingtonpost .com/2011/02/07/aol-huffington-post_n_819375.html** (accessed March 21, 2011).

35. Gifford Pinchott III, *Intrapreneuring* (New York: Harper & Row, 1985), p. 34.

36. Paul Brown, "How to Cope with Hard Times," *The New York Times,* June 10, 2008, **www.nytimes.com/2008/06/10/business/ smallbusiness/10toolkit.html?_r=1&ref=smallbusiness&oref=sl ogin** (accessed March 10, 2010).

CHAPTER 6

1. "Ford Fiesta," *Automobile,* April 2010, p. 14.

2. Leigh Buchanan, "More Than a Moving Company," Inc., December 1, 2010, **www.inc.com/magazine/20101201/more-than-a-moving-company.html** (accessed December 17, 2010); Jim Witkin, "Despite Struggles, Entrepreneurs Find Ways to Give Back," *The New York Times*, September 15, 2010, **www .nytimes.com/2010/09/16/business/smallbusiness/16sbiz.html** (accessed January 12, 2011); Gentle Giant Movers website, **www.gentlegiant.com** (accessed January 12, 2011).

3. "Letter to Stakeholders," General Electric Ecomagination, **http:// ge.ecomagination.com/annual-reports/letter-to-stakeholders .html** (accessed March 22, 2011).

4. "Celestial Difference," Celestial Seasonings, **www.celestialseasonings .ca/en/index.php/celestial** (accessed March 22, 2011).

5. "2010 Corporate Engagement Award of Excellence," Points of Light Institute, **www.handsonnetwork.org/corporateawards** (accessed January 12, 2011).

6. G. Tomas, M. Hult, David W. Cravens, and Jagdish Sheth, "Competitive Advantage in the Global Marketplace: A Focus on Marketing Strategy," *Journal of Business Research* 51 (January 2001), p. 1.

7. Telis Demos, "Bag Revolution," *Fortune,* May 12, 2008, p. 18.

8. "BP's Spill Contingency Plans Vastly Inadequate," *CBS News*, June 9, 2010, **www.cbsnews.com/stories/2010/06/09/national/ main6563631.shtml** (accessed January 12, 2011); Joel K. Bourne, Jr., "The Deep Dilemma," *National Geographic*, October 2010, pp. 40–53.

9. Catherine Larkin and Molly Peterson, "J&J Faces More Scrutiny from FDA on McNeil Consent Decree," *Bloomberg Business-week,* March 11, 2011, **www.businessweek.com/news/2011-03-11/j-j-faces-more-scrutiny-from-fda-on-mcneil-consent-decree .html** (accessed March 21, 2011).

10. Stanley Reed, "Media Giant or Media Muddle," *BusinessWeek,* May 12, 2008, p. 47.

11. John Barfield, "Staffing Up for Growth," *Fortune,* May 5, 2008, p. S10; "Bartech Group Recognized by Eaton as Premier Supplier Award Winner," Bartech Group Talent Solutions, March 22, 2010, **www.bartechgroup.com/news/PDFs/pressReleases/ Bartech_Wins_Eaton_Premier_Supplier_Award_2009.pdf** (accessed January 12, 2011); "About Us," Bartech Group, **www.bartechgroup.com/aboutUs/index.html** (accessed March 21, 2011).

12. "Labor Force Statistics from the Current Population Survey," Bureau of Labor Statistics, **http://data.bls.gov/PDQ/servlet/ SurveyOutputServlet?series_ id=LNS14000000** (accessed March 2, 2010).

13. "The Big Picture," *BusinessWeek,* July 16, 2001, p. 12.

14. Brian Womack and Douglas MacMillan, "Facebook Is Said to Be Worth $60 Billion in Employee Offering," *Bloomberg,* February 10, 2011, **www.bloomberg.com/news/2011-02-10/**

facebook-said-to-be-worth-60-billion-in-employee-offering.html (accessed March 21, 2011).

15. "About the IAPP," IAPP, **https://www.privacyassociation.org/about_iapp/** (accessed January 12, 2011).

16. "Women CEOs," May 3, 2010, **http://money.cnn.com/magazines/fortune/fortune500/2010/womenceos/** (accessed January 12, 2011).

17. Angeline Benoit and Elena Berton, "2nd UPDATE: PAI to Sell Yoplait Stake to General Mills," *The Wall Street Journal*, March 18, 2011, **http://online.wsj.com/article/BT-CO-20110318-705804.html** (accessed March 21, 2011).

18. Joe Bel Bruno and Jessica Papini, "Morgan Stanley's Gorman: No Bonus, but $9 Million Package," *The Wall Street Journal*, January 23, 2010, **http://online.wsj.com/article/SB10001424052748703822404575019650173532966.html** (accessed March 22, 2011).

19. Annie Finnigan, "Different Strokes," *Working Woman*, April 2001, p. 44.

20. W. Garrison Jackson, "Multicultural Advertising," *Fortune*, May 5, 2008, p. S23.

21. Kim Reynolds, "Spark Versus Ignition: In Which the Tiny Electric Car Company from San Carlos, California, Takes on What May Be Zuffenhausen's Best Open Sports Car Ever. It Wins to 60 mph," *Motor Trend*, February 2010, pp. 40–48.

22. "Chevy Volt FAQs," GM-Volt.com, **http://gm-volt.com/chevy-volt-faqs** (accessed March 22, 2011).

23. Google Management," **www.google.com/intl/en/corporate/execs.html** (accessed March 22, 2011); "The Engineer's Life at Google," **www.google.com/intl/en/jobs/lifeatgoogle/englife** (accessed March 22, 2011).

24. Bo Burlingham, "Lessons From a Blue-Collar Millionaire," Inc., February 2010, pp. 57–63; **www.nickspizzapub.com** (accessed March 22, 2011); Bo Burlingham, "Lessons of a Blue-Collar Millionaire—Addendum," Small Giants Community, February 1, 2010, **www.smallgiants.org/article.php?article_id=2** (accessed March 22, 2011).

25. Dan Wilchins and Jonathan Stempel, "Citigroup CEO to Resigns: Reports," *Reuters*, November 2, 2007, **www.reuters.com/article/idUSN0233640620071103** (accessed January 12, 2011); Chuck Prince, Citigroup memo, February 14, 2005, **http://specials.ft.com/spdocs/launchmemo14205.pdf** (accessed January 12, 2011).

26. Miguel Bustillo and Timothy W. Martin, "Beyond the Big Box: Wal-Mart Thinks Smaller," *The Wall Street Journal*, April 28, 2010, p. B1; Jane Hodges, "Shopping in a Big Way: Warehouse vs. Big Box," *The Wall Street Journal*, May 27, 2010, p. D4; Jeff Reeves, "Three Ways Walmart Wins by Going Small and Urban," Blogging Stocks, April 29, 2010, **www.bloggingstocks.com/2010/04/29/walmart-small-urban-stores** (accessed March 22, 2011); "In Brief," "Wal-Mart Stores Sales Fall at Home, Surge Abroad," *Bloomberg Businessweek*, May 24–30, 2010, p.24; Stephanie Clifford, "Wal-Mart Gains in Its Wooing of Chicago," June 24, 2010, *The New York Times*, **www.nytimes.com/2010/06/25/business/25walmart.html** (accessed March 22, 2011); "Fortune 500: Our Annual Ranking of America's Largest Corporations," "1. Wal-Mart Stores," *Fortune*, 2010, **http://money.cnn.com/magazines/fortune/fortune500/2010/snapshots/2255.html** (accessed March 22, 2011).

27. Kerrie Unsworth, "Unpacking Creativity," *Academy of Management Review* 26 (April 2001), pp. 289–97.

28. Pallavi Gogoi, "A Bittersweet Deal for Wrigley," *BusinessWeek*, May 12, 2008, p. 034.

29. *Harvard Business Review* 60 (November–December 1982), p. 160.

30. Kris Maher, "The Jungle," *The Wall Street Journal*, May 29, 2001, p. B16.

31. "The Passion to Perform," The Nierenberg Group, **www.selfmarketing.com/about.html** (accessed March 22, 2011).

32. "Salary After Taxes," *Employment Spot*, **www.employmentspot.com/employment-articles/salary-after-taxes** (accessed March 22, 2011).

33. Ibid.

CHAPTER 7

1. Mina Kimes, "What Admired Firms Don't Have in Common," *CNNMoney.com*, March 6, 2009, **http://money.cnn.com/2009/03/06/news/companies/hay.survey.fortune/index.htm** (accessed March 22, 2011).

2. Richard McGill Murphy, "Why Doing Good Is Good for Business," *CNNMoney.com*, February 2, 2010, **http://money.cnn.com/2010/02/01/news/companies/dov_seidman_lrn.fortune/index.htm** (accessed March 22, 2011).

3. "A New Future for Toms Shoes, Tweed Shire and Room to Read," *Reputation Report*, August 7, 2009, **www.reputationreport.com.au/2009/08/a-new-future-by-toms-shoes-tweed-shire-and-room-to-read/** (accessed March 22, 2011); "Our Movement," TOMS Shoes, **www.tomsshoes.com/content.asp?tid = 271** (accessed March 22, 2011).

4. Kasey Wehrum, "An Office of Rock Stars," *Inc.*, November 2010, pp. 115–116.

5. Joe Light, "Finance and Tech Signal Bold Attitudes on Ethics," *The Wall Street Journal*, March 7, 2011, **http://online.wsj.com/article/SB10001424052748704728004576176711042012064.html** (accessed March 21, 2011).

6. Alina Dizik, "Education for Executives: Sustainability Is a Growing Theme," *The Wall Street Journal*, March 4, 2010, p. B10; Amy Westervelt, "IBM, Professors Team Up to Train 'Smart' Students for a Green Jobs Future," solveclimate, April 21, 2010, **http://solveclimate.com/blog/20100421/ibm-professors-team-train-smart-students-green-jobs-future** (accessed March 22, 2011); **http://careers.campbellsoupcompany.com/interns.aspx** (accessed June 9, 2010); Diana Middleton, "Where M.B.A.s Are Finding Jobs," *The Wall Street Journal*, March 3, 2010, **online.wsj.com/article/NA_WSJ_PUB:SB10001424052748704541304575099792424392362.html** (accessed March 22, 2011).

7. FSB 100, *CNNMoney.com*, **http://money.cnn.com/magazines/fsb/fsb100/2009/snapshots/72.html** (accessed March 21, 2011); "Nathan's Famous, Inc. Reports Year End Results," Nathan's Famous, June 11, 2010, **http://phx.corporate-ir.net/phoenix.zhtml?c=113414&p=irol-newsArticle&ID=1437140&highlight=** (accessed March 21, 2011); "A Treasured Tradition," Nathan's Famous, **http://nathansfamous.com/PageFetch/getpage.php?pgid=31** (accessed March 21, 2011).

8. Adam Smith, *Wealth of Nations* (New York: Modern Library, 1937; originally published in 1776).

9. "Profile: Campbell Soup Company (CPB)," *Reuters*, **www.reuters.com/finance/stocks/companyProfile?symbol=CPB** (accessed March 21, 2011).

10. Leigh Buchanan, "The Way I Work: 'I Have to Be the Worrywart So My Son Feels Free to Exercise His Imagination,'" *Inc.*, May 2010, pp. 125–128; Johnny Cupcakes website, **www.johnnycupcakes.com** (accessed July 26, 2010).

11. Ella Ide, "Italy Critics Trash McDonald's Nationalist Food Bid," **http://af.reuters.com/article/oddlyEnoughNews/idAFTRE61431720100205** (accessed March 22, 2011).

12. "Why Work Here?" **www.wholefoodsmarket.com/careers/work-here.php** (accessed March 3, 2010).

13. "PepsiCo Unveils New Organizational Structure, Names CEOs of Three Principle Operating Units," PepsiCo Media, November 5, 2007, **www.pepsico.com/PressRelease/PepsiCo-Unveils-New-Organizational-Structure-Names.html** (accessed March 22, 2011); "The PepsiCo Family," PepsiCo, **www.pepsico.com/Company/The-Pepsico-Family/PepsiCo-Americas-Beverages.html** (accessed January 12, 2011).

14. Jon R. Katzenbach and Douglas K. Smith, "The Discipline of Teams," *Harvard Business Review* 71 (March–April 1993), 19.

15. Ibid.

16. Leah Buchanan, "When Absence Makes the Team Grow Stronger," *Inc.*, June 2008, p. 40; Joe Albanese, "Commodore People," Commodore Builders, **www.commodorebuilders.com/people/JosephAlbanese.html** (accessed January 12, 2011).

17. "How to Build a (Strong) Virtual Team," *CNNMoney.com*, **http://money.cnn.com/2009/11/19/news/companies/ibm_virtual_manager.fortune/index.htm** (accessed March 22, 2011).

18. Jenna Goudreau, "Ford's Green Team," Forbes, February 9, 2010, **www.forbes.com/2010/02/09/ford-green-technology-forbes-woman-leadership-cars.html**(accessed October 28, 2010); Carol Costello, "Ford's 'Green' Team of Female Engineers," *CNN*, June 1, 2010, **http://am.fix.blogs.cnn.com/2010/06/01/fords-green-team-of-female-engineers** (accessed December 2, 2010); Stephen Calogera, "Ford Making Greener Vehicles by Using Renewable, Recycled Materials," egmCarTech, April 20, 2010, **www.egmcartech.com/2010/04/20/ford-making-greener-vehicles-by-using-renewable-recyclable-materials/** (accessed December 11, 2010).

19. "Toyota Motor Corporation President Akio Toyoda Announces Global Quality Task Force," Toyota Newsroom, February 5, 2010, **http://pressroom.toyota.com/pr/tms/toyota-motor-corporation-president-153566.aspx** (accessed March 22, 2011).

20. Jerry Useem, "What's That Spell? TEAMWORK," *Fortune*, June 12, 2006, p. 66.

21. Jia Lynnyang, "The Power of Number 4.6," *Fortune*, June 12, 2006, p. 122.

22. "School of Food Science Student Groups," Washington State University, **www.sfs.wsu.edu/student_groups/FoodProdDevTeam.html** (accessed January 12, 2011).

23. Richard S. Wellins, William C. Byham, and Jeanne M. Wilson, *Empowered Teams: Creating Self-Directed Work Groups That Improve Quality, Productivity, and Participation* (San Francisco: Jossey-Bass Publishers, 1991), p. 5.

24. Matt Krumrie, "Are Meetings a Waste of Time? Survey Says Yes," *Minneapolis Workplace Examiner*, May 12, 2009, **www.examiner.com/workplace-in-minneapolis/are-meetings-a-waste-of-time-survey-says-yes** (accessed March 21, 2011).

25. "Top 10 Ideas: Making the Most of Your Corporate Intranet," **www.claromentis.com/blog/2009/04/top-10-ideas-making-the-most-of-yourcorporate-intranet** (accessed March 22, 2011).

26. "Corporate America vs. Workers: Companies Do More with Fewer Employees," *NY Daily News*, November 5, 2009, **www.nydailynews.com/money/2009/11/05/2009-11-05_corporate_america_vs_workers_companies_do_more_with_fewer_employees.html** (accessed March 22, 2011).

27. Kim Komando, "Why You Need a Company Policy on Internet Use," **www.microsoft.com/business/en-us/resources/management/employee-relations/why-you-need-a-company-policy-on-internet-use.aspx?fbid=abWQUsC20hw#WhyyouneedacompanypolicyonInternetuse** (accessed March 22, 2011).

CHAPTER 8

1. Guy Chazan, "Clean-Fuels Refinery Rises in Desert," *The Wall Street Journal*, April 16, 2010, p. B8; Stanley Reed & Robert Tuttle, "Shell Aims for 'New Nigeria' as Qatari Plant Starts (update 2)," *Bloomberg Businessweek*, March 4, 2010, **www.businessweek.com/news/2010-03-04/shell-aims-for-new-nigeria-as-qatari-plant-starts-update1-.html** (accessed June 9, 2010).

2. Rina Rapuano, "Check Please!," *The Washingtonian Blog*, February 18, 2010, **www.washingtonian.com/blogarticles/restaurants/bestbites/15008.html** (accessed March 22, 2011).

3. Leonard L. Berry, *Discovering the Soul of Service* (New York: The Free Press, 1999), pp. 86–96.

4. Valerie A. Zeithaml and Mary Jo Bitner, *Services Marketing*, 3rd ed. (Boston: McGraw-Hill Irwin, 2003), pp. 3, 22.

5. Bernard Wysocki, Jr., "To Fix Health Care, Hospitals Take Tips from the Factory Floor," *The Wall Street Journal*, April 9, 2004, via **www.chcanys.org/clientuploads/downloads/Clinical_resources/Leadership%20Articles/LeanThinking_ACF28EB.pdf** (accessed March 22, 2011); Julie Weed, "Factory Efficiency Comes to the Hospital," *The New York Times*, July 10, 2010, **www.nytimes.com/2010/07/11/business/11seattle.html?pagewanted=all** (accessed January 12, 2011).

6. "Success Story," Google AdWords, **https://www.google.com/intl/en_us/adwords/select/success/cordarounds.html** (accessed March 22, 2011).

7. Faith Keenan, "Opening the Spigot," *BusinessWeek* e.biz, June 4, 2001, **www.businessweek.com/magazine/content/01_23/b3735616.htm** (accessed March 22, 2011).

8. Ryan Underwood, "Dear Customer . . . Managing E-Mail Campaigns," *Inc.*, March 2008, p. 59.

9. "Making Chocolate," Hershey's, **www.hersheys.com/discover/tour_printv.htm** (accessed January 12, 2011).

10. "Environmental Stewardship," PNM, **www.pnm.com/environment/home.htm** (accessed March 22, 2011); "Climate Change: PNM's Position," PNM, **www.pnm.com/climate/position.htm** (accessed March 22, 2011).

11. "Top 10 Solar Friendly States," *Cooler Planet*, **http://solar.coolerplanet.com/Articles/top-10-solar-friendly-states.aspx** (accessed March 22, 2011).

12. "IFR Statistics Report Optimistic about Robotics Industry Growth in 2011-12," Robotics & Automation Society, June 18, 2010, **www.ieee-ras.org/news/236/IFR-Statistics-report-optimistic-about-robotics-industry-growth-in-2011-12.html** (accessed January 12, 2011).

13. Gina Kolata, "Results Unproven, Robotic Surgery Wins Converts," *The New York Times*, February 13, 2010, **www.nytimes.com/2010/02/14/health/14robot.html?pagewanted=1** (accessed March 22, 2011).

14. "Sustainability," Walmart, **http://walmartstores.com/sustainability** (accessed March 22, 2011).

15. Bryan Walsh, "Why Green Is the New Red, White and Blue," *Time*, April 28, 2008, p. 53.

16. "Introducing Chevrolet Volt," Chevrolet, **www.chevrolet.com/pages/open/default/future/volt.do** (accessed March 22, 2011).

17. Megan Kamerick, "How to Go Green," *New Mexico Business Weekly*, May 23–29, 2008, p. 3.

18. O. C. Ferrell and Michael D. Hartline, *Marketing Strategy* (Mason, OH: South-Western, 2011), p. 215.

19. John Edwards, "Orange Seeks Agent," *Inbound Logistics,* January 2006, pp. 239–42.

20. Ferrell and Hartline, *Marketing Strategy,* p. 215.

21. Trader Joe's website, **www.traderjoes.com** (accessed October 2, 2010); Beth Kowitt, "Inside the Secret World of Trader Joe's-Full Version," *Fortune,* August 23, 2010, **http://money.cnn .com/2010/08/20/news/companies/inside_trader_joes_full_ version.fortune/index.htm#joe** (accessed October 1, 2010); "2010 World's Most Ethical Companies," *Ethisphere,* 2010, **http://ethisphere.com/wme2010** (accessed October 1, 2010).

22. Bob Daniell, John Tracy, and Simon Kaye, "Made in China: Perspectives on the Global Manufacturing Giant," *Inbound Logistics,* March 2008, pp. 46–49.

23. Scott McCartney, "The Big Guys Finish Last in 2010 Airline Rankings," *USA Today,* January 13, 2011, pp. D1, D4.

24. Susan Carey, "Airlines Play Up Improvements in On-Time Performance," *The Wall Street Journal,* February 10, 2010, p. B6.

25. "Seven U.S. Organizations Honored with the 2010 Baldrige National Quality Award," National Institute of Standards and Technology, November 23, 2010, **www.nist.gov/ baldrige/baldrige_recipients2010.cfm** (accessed January 11, 2011).

26. Christopher Lawton, "The War on Product Returns," *The Wall Street Journal,* May 8, 2008, p. D1.

27. K.W., "The Dog Lover," *Inc.,* October 2010, pp. 68–70; Rebecca Konya, "Marie Moody: Women of Influence 2010," *The Business Journal,* 2010, **www2.bizjournals.com/milwaukee/ events/2010/women_of_influence/marie_moody_women_of_ influence_2010.html** (accessed October 19, 2010); **www .stellaandchewys.com** (accessed October 19, 2010).

28. Philip B. Crosby, *Quality Is Free: The Art of Making Quality Certain* (New York: McGraw-Hill, 1979), pp. 9–10.

29. Nigel F. Piercy, *Market-Led Strategic Change* (Newton, MA: Butterworth-Heinemann, 1992), pp. 374–85.

30. "Compuware Gomez Introduces Free Web Performance Benchmarking Tool," Gomez, February 16, 2010, **www.gomez .com/compuware-gomez-introduces-free-web-performance-benchmarking-tool/** (accessed March 22, 2011).

31. "Employment Opportunities," Careers in Supply Chain Management, **www.careersinsupplychain.org/career-outlook/empopp.asp** (accessed March 22, 2011).

CHAPTER 9

1. Elaine Appleton Grant, "Next Health: Better Office Health Through Employee's Diet," *FastCompany,* June 2010, **www.fastcompany.com/magazine/146/cookie-monster.html** (accessed July 10, 2010); **www.thefullyield.com** (accessed July 11, 2010); "The Grocery Cart: Essential in the Fight Against Rising Healthcare Costs," Core Source, **www.coresource .com/427.htm** (accessed July 15, 2010); Aaron Kagan, "Making a Lifestyle of Healthier Choices," *The Boston Globe,* February 10, 2010, **www.boston.com/lifestyle/food/articles/2010/02/10/ danvers_start_up_coaches_clients_on_making_healthier_ choices** (accessed July 15, 2010).

2. Dan Heath and Chip Heath, "Business Advice from Van Halen," *Fast Company,* March 1, 2010, **www.fastcompany.com/ magazine/143/made-to-stick-thetelltale-brown-mampm.html** (accessed March 11, 2010).

3. "100 Best Companies to Work For 2010," *Fortune,* **http:// money.cnn.com/magazines/fortune/bestcompanies/2010/ snapshots/4.html** (accessed February 18, 2010); "Benefits,"

Google Jobs, **www.google.com/support/jobs/bin/static.py?page= benefits.html** (accessed February 18, 2010).

4. "How Much Does Absenteeism Cost Your Business," Success Performance Solutions, December 10, 2008, **www.super-solutions .com/CostofAbsenteeism.asp** (accessed March 11, 2010).

5. "Careers," Nikebiz.com, **www.nikebiz.com/careers/benefits/other/ whq_campus.html** (accessed February 9, 2010).

6. "CEO Compensation," *Forbes,* April 28, 2010, **www.forbes. com/lists/2010/12/boss-10_CEO-Compensation_Rank .html** (accessed January 12, 2011).

7. Charisse Jones, "Great Work. Now Hit the Road—on Us," *USA Today,* May 12, 2010, pp. 1B–2B; V. Dion Haynes, "Washington-Baltimore Benefits Survey: Part-Timers Getting More Perks," *The Washington Post,* June 8, 2010, **www.washingtonpost.com/ wp-dyn/content/article/2010/06/07/AR2010060704513.html** (accessed June 10, 2010); Kim Covert, "Travel Perks One Way to Keep Employees Engaged," *The Vancouver Sun,* April 27, 2010, **www.vancouversun.com/life/Travel+perks+keep+employees+ engaged/2956071/story.html** (accessed June 10, 2010); **www.pointsoflight.org** (accessed May 2, 2010); "Best Places to Work 2009," crain's, **www.crainsnewyork.com/apps/pbcs.dll/ gallery?Site=CN&Date=20091207&Category=GALLERIES&Art No=120209998&Ref=PH&Params=Itemnr=31** (accessed May 2, 2010); **www.patagonia.com** (accessed July 10, 2010).

8. "L.L. Bean Named #1 in NRF Foundation Customer Service Survey," L.L. Bean News, February 21, 2008, **www .llbean.com/customerService/aboutLLBean/newsroom/ stories/02212008_LLBean_News.html** (accessed March 12, 2011); Jena McGregor, "Customer Service Champs 2010," *Bloomberg Businessweek,* **http://images.businessweek.com/ss/ 10/02/0218_customer_service_champs/2.htm** (accessed January 13, 2011).

9. Douglas McGregor, *The Human Side of Enterprise* (New York: McGraw-Hill, 1960), pp. 33–34.

10. Ibid.

11. Jon L. Pierce, Tatiana Kostova, and Kurt T. Kirks, "Toward a Theory of Psychological Ownership in Organizations, *Academy of Management Review* 26, no. 2 (2001), p. 298.

12. "2009 National Business Ethics Survey: Ethics in the Recession," Ethics Resource Center, p. 33.

13. Archie Carroll, "Carroll: Do We Live in a Cheating Culture?" *Athens Banner-Herald,* February 21, 2004, **www.onlineathens.com/ stories/022204/bus_20040222028.shtml,** accessed March 12, 2010.

14. Geoff Colvin, "Ursula Burns launches Xerox into the future," *CNNMoney.com,* April 22, 2010, **http://money.cnn.com/ 2010/04/22/news/companies/xerox_ursula_burns.fortune/index. htm** (accessed October 7, 2010); Ella L. J. Edmondson Bell, PhD, "Ursula Burns: Managing With Heart and Some Soul," *The Huffington Post,* March 16, 2010, **www.huffingtonpost .com/ella-l-j-edmondson-bell-phd/urusual-burns-managing-wit_b_498944.html** (accessed June 10, 2010); Adam Bryant, "Xerox's New Chief Tries to Redefine Its Culture," *The New York Times,* February 20, 2010, **www.nytimes.com/2010/02/21/ business/21xerox.html** (accessed June 10, 2010); Heidi Evans, "Ursula Burns to Head Xerox, Will Be the First Black Woman to Be CEO for *Fortune* 500 Company," nydailynews.com, May 23, 2010, **www.nydailynews.com/money/2009/05/23/2009- 05-23_1st_black_woman_xerox_ceo.html** (accessed June 14, 2009); Jenny A. DiColo, "With Ursula Burns As CEO, Xerox Gets Tough Operator," Dow Jones Newswire, May 21, 2009, **www .smartmoney.com/news/on/?story=ON20090521-000817-1629** (accessed June 11, 2009); Nanette Byrnes and Roger O. Crockett,

"An Historic Succession at Xerox," *BusinessWeek*, June 8, 2009, pp. 018–022.

15. Geoff Colvin, "How Top Companies Breed Stars," September 20, 2007, **http://money.cnn.com/magazines/fortune/fortune_archive/2007/10/01/100351829/index.htm** (accessed March 12, 2010).

16. MyGuides, USA.com, "Which Jobs Offer Flexible Work Schedules?" **http://jobs.myguidesusa.com/answers-to-myquestions/which-jobs-offer-flexiblework-schedules?/** (accessed March 12, 2010).

17. Robert Preidt, "Workplace Flexibility Can Boost Healthy Behaviors," Wake Forest University Baptist Medical Center, news release, December 10, 2007, via **http://yourtotalhealth.ivillage.com/workplaceflexibility-can-boost-healthy-behaviors.html** (accessed March 12, 2010).

18. My Guides, USA.com, "Which Jobs Offer Flexible Work Schedules?"

19. "Telework Revs Up as More Employers Offer Work Flexibility," *WorldatWork*, February 17, 2009, **www.workingfromanywhere.org/news/pr021609.html** (accessed February 9, 2010).

20. "Telecommuting Benefits," **www.telecommutect.com/content/benefits.htm** (accessed March 12, 2010).

21. "HR Executives Split on Telecommuting," *USA Today*, March 1, 2006, p. B1.

22. Kurt Badenhausen, "The Best Places for Business and Careers," *Forbes*, April 14, 2010, **www.forbes.com/2010/04/13/best-places-for-business-beltway-business-places-10_lander.html** (accessed April 13, 2011).

CHAPTER 10

1. "Careers," P&G, **www.pg.com/en_US/careers/hiring_process.shtml** (accessed April 14, 2011); "Procter & Gamble: Employment, Jobs, Career & Work," JobBankUSA, **www.jobbankusa.com/employment_jobs_career/proctor_gamble.html** (accessed April 14, 2011).

2. Burgerville website, **www.burgerville.com** (accessed April 14, 2011); Sarah E. Needleman, "Burger Chain's Health-Care Recipe," *The Wall Street Journal*, August 31, 2009, **http://online.wsj.com/article/SB125149100886467705.html** (accessed April 14, 2011); Adam Ghassemi, "Burgerville Aims to Change Fast-Food Trash," *Katu.com*, February 9, 2010, **www.katu.com/news/local/83982017.html** (accessed April 14, 2011).

3. "What Does Employee Alcohol & Drug Use Cost Your Business," DWI Resource Center, **www.dwiresourcecenter.org/bizcenter/workplace/cost.shtml** (accessed April 14, 2011).

4. Associated Press, "Food Network Chef Fired After Resume Fraud," *USA Today*, March 3, 2008, **www.usatoday.com/news/nation/2008-03-03-chef-fired_N.htm** (accessed April 14, 2011).

5. Christopher T. Marquet and Lisa J.B. Peterson, "Résumé Fraud: The Top Ten Lies," Marquet International, Ltd., **www.marquetinternational.com/pdf/Resume%20Fraud-Top%20Ten%20Lies.pdf** (accessed April 14, 2011).

6. "Charge Statistics FY 1997 Through FY 2010," U.S. Equal Employment Opportunity Commission, **www.eeoc.gov/eeoc/statistics/enforcement/charges.cfm** (accessed January 13, 2011); "EEOC Reports Job Bias Charges Hit Record High of Nearly 100,000 in Fiscal Year 2010," U.S. Equal Employment Opportunity Commission, January 11, 2011, **www.eeoc.gov/eeoc/newsroom/release/1-11-11.cfm** (accessed January 13, 2011).

7. Joseph Daniel McCool, "Diversity Picture Rings Hollow," *BusinessWeek*, February 5, 2008, **www.businessweek.com/managing/content/feb2008/ca2008025_080192.htm?chan=search** (accessed April 14, 2011).

8. "America's Changing Workforce: Recession Turns a Graying Office Grayer," Pew Research Center: A Social and Demographic Trends Report, September 3, 2009, **http://pewsocialtrends.org/assets/pdf/americas-changing-workforce.pdf** (accessed April 14, 2011).

9. Dennis Cauchon, "American Workforce Growing Grayer," *USA Today*, December 15, 2010, p. 1A.

10. Stephen Bastien, "12 Benefits of Hiring Older Workers," *Entrepreneur.com*, September 20, 2006, **www.entrepreneur.com/humanresources/hiring/article167500.html** (accessed April 14, 2011).

11. Catherine Rampell, "The Gender Wage Gap, Around the World," March 9, 2010, **http://economix.blogs.nytimes.com/2010/03/09/the-gender-wage-gap-around-the-world/** (accessed April 14, 2011).

12. Sue Shellenbarger, "New Workplace Equalizer: Ambition," *The Wall Street Journal*, March 25, 2009, **http://online.wsj.com/article/SB123801512551141207.html** (accessed April 14, 2011).

13. "Our Curriculum," Hamburger University, **www.aboutmcdonalds.com/mcd/careers/hamburger_university/our_curriculum.html** (accessed April 14, 2011).

14. Doug Stewart, "Employee-Appraisal Software," *Inc.*, **www.inc.com/magazine/19940615/3288_pagen_2.html** (accessed April 14, 2011).

15. Maury A. Peiperl, "Getting 360-Degree Feedback Right," *Harvard Business Review*, January 2001, pp. 142–48.

16. Chris Musselwhite, "Self Awareness and the Effective Leader," *Inc.com*, October 1, 2007, **www.inc.com/resources/leadership/articles/20071001/musselwhite.html** (accessed April 14, 2011).

17. Laura Lorber, "A Corporate Culture Makeover," *The Wall Street Journal*, April 15, 2008, **http://online.wsj.com/article/SB120827656392416609.html** (accessed April 14, 2011).

18. Marcia Zidle, "Employee Turnover: Seven Reasons Why People Quit Their Jobs," **http://ezinearticles.com/?Employee-Turnover:-Seven-Reasons-Why-People-Quit-Their-Jobs&id = 42531** (accessed April 14, 2011).

19. "GM, Chrysler to Cut 50,000 Jobs," *CBC News*, February 17, 2009, **www.cbc.ca/money/story/2009/02/17/carbailout.html** (accessed April 14, 2011); "2009 Chrysler Will Shed 789 Dealers," **www.carpictures.com/vehicle/09EDD063625060.html** (accessed April 14, 2011).

20. "Chrysler to Rehire 376 Workers at Kokomo Plants," *The Seattle Times*, May 11, 2010, **http://seattletimes.nwsource.com/html/businesstechnology/2011835839_apuschryslerkokomo.html?syndication=rss** (accessed January 13, 2011).

21. Kelly K. Spors, "Top Small Workplaces 2008," *The Wall Street Journal*, February 22, 2009, **http://online.wsj.com/article/SB122347733961315417.html** (accessed April 14, 2011); King Arthur Flour website, **www.kingarthurflour.com** (accessed April 14, 2011); "King Arthur Flour Leads the Way with B-Corp Logo," CSRwire, February 15, 2008, **www.csrwire.com/press/press_release/14672-King-Arthur-Flour** (accessed April 14, 2011); "Best Place to Work in Vermont," 2010, **http://bestplacestoworkinvt.com/index.php?option=com_content&task=view&id=43** (accessed April 14, 2011); "About

the White House: Presidents," "1. George Washington," **www.whitehouse.gov/about/presidents/georgewashington/** (accessed April 14, 2011).

22. "Wage and Hour Division (WHD)," U.S. Department of Labor, **www.dol.gov/whd/flsa/index.htm** (accessed April 14, 2011).

23. Associated Press, "Santa Fe Not Likely to Raise Minimum Wage," kvia.com, December 22, 2009, **www.connectamarillo.com/news/money/story.aspx?id=393245** (accessed April 14, 2011).

24. "Kele & Co: First Innovative Jewelry Company in Direct Sales," Press Exposure, May 5, 2008, **http://pressexposure.com/Kele_and_Co_-_The_First_Innovative_Jewelry_Company_In_Direct_Sales-16878.html** (accessed March 16, 2010).

25. Sharon Jayson, "Working at Home: Family-friendly?," *USA Today*, April 15, 2010, p. 1A; "Is Working from Home the New Calling in Sick?," *msnbc*, March 2, 2010, **www.msnbc.msn.com/id/35676647/ns/business-careers** (accessed April 14, 2011); Emili Vesilind, "The Home Office Is Humming," *Entrepreneur*, June 2010, **www.entrepreneur.com/magazine/entrepreneur/2010/june/206662.html** (accessed April 14, 2011); Max Chafkin, "The Office Is Dead. Long Live the Office; The Case, and the Plan, for the Virtual Company," *Inc.*, April 2010, pp. 62–73; Joel Stein, "Where the Copy Machine Never Jams...," *Bloomberg Businessweek*, June 28–July 4, 2010, pp.73–75; Anna Jane Grossman, "Freelancers Forgo Office Space for Casual Coworking," *WIRED*, July 20, 2007, **www.wired.com/techbiz/people/news/2007/07/coworking** (accessed April 14, 2011); Carrie Sloan, "Office Space for the Self-Employed: Working Away from Home Helps Freelancers, Entrepreneurs Succeed," *NY Daily News*, July 13, 2009, **www.nydailynews.com/money/2009/07/13/2009-07-13_office_space_for_the_selfemployed_working_away_from_home_helps_freelancers_entre.html** (accessed April 14, 2011).

26. Chris Casacchia, "Employee-Owned Stock Outperforms Wall Street," *Phoenix Business Journal*, July 31, 2009, **www.bizjournals.com/phoenix/stories/2009/08/03/story2.html?page=all** (accessed November 27, 2011).

27. "Employer Costs for Employee Compensation," U.S. Bureau of Labor Statistics, March 10, 2010, **www.bls.gov/news.release/ecec.nr0.htm** (accessed April 14, 2011).

28. Jamie Page, "Pensacola City Employees' Benefits Cut," *Pensacola News Journal*, March 17, 2010, **www.pnj.com/article/20100317/NEWS01/3170329/1006/news01/Pensacola-city-employees—benefits-cut** (accessed March 17, 2010).

29. John Schmitt, "The Unions of the States, Center for Economic and Policy Research," February 2010, **www.cepr.net/documents/publications/unions-states-2010-02.pdf** (accessed April 14, 2011).

30. "Pension Rallies Hit French Cities," *BBC News*, September 7, 2010, **www.bbc.co.uk/news/world-europe-11204528** (accessed April 14, 2011).

31. Matthew Futterman, "NFL Girds for Fight, Says Loss Is Covered," *The Wall Street Journal*, March 14, 2011, pp. B1, B5.

32. National Population Projections 2010–2050, U.S. Census Bureau, released 2009, **www.census.gov/population/www/projections/2009cnmsSumTabs.html** (accessed April 14, 2011).

33. Pamela Babcock, "Diversity Accountability Requires More Than Numbers," Society for Human Resource Management, April 13, 2009, **www.shrm.org/hrdisciplines/Diversity/Articles/Pages/MoreThanNumbers.aspx** (accessed April 14, 2011).

34. Taylor H. Cox Jr., "The Multicultural Organization," *Academy of Management Executives* 5 (May 1991), pp. 34–47; Marilyn Loden and Judy B. Rosener, *Workforce America! Managing Employee Diversity as a Vital Resource* (Homewood, IL: Business One Irwin, 1991).

CHAPTER 11

1. Adapted from Pride and O.C. Ferrell, "Value-Driven Marketing," *Foundations of Marketing*, 4th ed. (Mason, OH: South-Western Cengage Learning), pp. 13–14.

2. Mike Esterl, "Can This Chip Be Saved?" *The Wall Street Journal*, April 24, 2011, pp. D1, D5.

3. "Beauty Queen," *People*, May 10, 2004, p. 187.

4. Michael Treacy and Fred Wiersema, *The Discipline of Market Leaders* (Reading, MA: Addison-Wesley, 1995), p. 176.

5. "2009 Form 10-K/A Filed January 25, 2010," Apple Investor Relations, **http://phx.corporateir.net/phoenix.zhtml?c=107357&p=irol-index** (accessed March 25, 2010); "Apple Stores," AAPL Investors, **http://aaplinvestors.net/marketing/applestores/** (accessed January 14, 2011).

6. Venky Shankar, "Multiple Touch Point Marketing," American Marketing Association, Faculty Consortium on Electronic Commerce, Texas A&M University, July 14–17, 2001.

7. Bruce Horovitz, "Consumer Products Giant Looks beyond U.S. Borders," *USA Today*, March 18, 2010, pp. B1–B2; Jon Newberry, "Aisles of Opportunity," portfolio.com, April 7, 2010, **www.portfolio.com/companies-executives/2010/04/07/proctor-and-gamble-is-aiming-to-expand-its-marketshare-in-india/** (accessed April 14, 2011); Dyan Machan, "Q&A: Procter & Gamble CEO Bob McDonald," SmartMoney, May 26, 2010, **www.smartmoney.com/invest/stocks/interview-with-procter-gamble-ceo-bob-mcdonald** (accessed April 14, 2011); Anjali Cordeiro, "P&G Targets India for Expansion Push," *The Wall Street Journal*, June 23, 2010, **http://online.wsj.com/article/NA_WSJ_PUB:SB20001424052748704123604575322751934618996.html** (accessed August 16, 2010).

8. Bruce Horovitz, "Tween Years Prove to Be Rewarding for Toymakers," *USA Today*, December 22, 2010, p. 1B; "Crayola Targets Tween Girls with Pop Art Pixies Launch," August 1, 2010, **www.crayola.com/mediacenter/download/news/press_release_316.pdf** (accessed April 7, 2011).

9. Jan Norman, "Calif Tops in U.S. in Women-Owned Firms," *The Orange County Register*, April 5, 2011, **http:// jan.ocregister.com/2011/04/05/calif-tops-in-u-s-in-women-owned-firms/57141/** (accessed April 6, 2011).

10. Laurel Wentz, "Olive Garden and Don Francisco Go to Tuscany," *Advertising Age*, March 25, 2010, **http:// adage.com/hispanic/article?article_id=142977** (accessed March 30, 2010).

11. Hope Yen, "U.S. Minority Population Could Be Majority by Mid-Century, Census Shows," *Huffington Post*, June 10, 2010, **www.huffingtonpost.com/2010/06/10/us-minority-population-co_n_607369.html** (accessed April 6, 2011).

12. Moon Ihlwan, "Samsung's Plan to Widen Its Range," *BusinessWeek*, August 24 and 31, 2009, p. 30.

13. Charisse Jones, "Airlines Get Ready for Return of Elite Fliers," *USA Today*, March 16, 2010, p. 6B.

14. Lauren Bans, "Social Networking Searching for Twitter Treasure: An Online Game Gets Customers to Shop," *Inc.*, May 2010, pp. 114–116; Andrea Koskey, "Twitter Treasure Hunt Promotes Local Shopping," *San Francisco Examiner*, November 11, 2009, **www.sfexaminer.com/local/Twitter-treasure-hunt-promotes-local-shopping-69816932.html** (accessed June 13, 2010).

15. "The Coca-Cola Company Fact Sheet," **www.thecoca-colacompany .com/ourcompany/pdf/Company_Fact_Sheet.pdf** (accessed April 7, 2011).

16. Hannah Elliott, "Most Fuel-Efficient Cars for the Buck," *Forbes,* March 30, 2009, **www.forbes.com/2009/03/30/fuel-efficient-carslifestyle-vehicles-efficient-cars.html** (accessed March 30, 2010).

17. Valerie Bauerlein, "U.S. Soda Sales Fell at Slower Rate Last Year," *The Wall Street Journal,* March 25, 2010, **http://online .wsj.com/article/SB1000142405274870426650457514171 0213338560.html** (accessed April 8, 2010).

18. "MSPA North America," Mystery Shopping Providers Association, **www.mysteryshop.org/index-na.php** (accessed April 1, 2010); Paula Andruss, "Missing Research Insights," *Marketing News,* May 20, 2010, pp. 23–25; "MSPA North America," Mystery Shopping Providers Association, **www.mysteryshop.org/ index-na.php** (accessed April 1, 2010).

19. Mya Frazier, "CrowdSourcing," *Delta Sky Mag,* February 2010, via **http://msp.imirus.com/Mpowered/imirus.jsp?volume= ds10&issue=2&page=72** (accessed February 18, 2010), p. 73.

20. Yelp website, **www.yelp.com** (accessed August 10, 2010); "Yelp Adds a Tiny Bit of Transparency...And Inches Away from Pay for Placement," The Entrepreneur's Corner, TechDirt, **www.tech-dirt.com/blog/entrepreneurs/articles/20100330/1539268795 .shtml** (accessed August 20, 2010); Peter Burrows & Joseph Galante, "Yelp: Advertise or Else?," *Bloomberg Businessweek,* March 3, 2010, **www.businessweek.com/magazine/ content/10_11/b4170027355708.htm** (accessed August 10, 2010); Jeremy, YELP CEO, "Additional Thoughts on Last Week's Lawsuit, or How a Conspiracy Theory Is Born," Yelp Web Log, **http://officialblog.yelp.com/2010/03/additional-thoughts-on-last-weeks-lawsuit-or-how-a-conspiracy-theory-is-born-.html** (accessed August 10, 2010); Kermit Pattison, "Talking to the Chief of Yelp, the Site That Businesses Love to Hate," *The New York Times,* March 24, 2010, **www.nytimes.com/2010/03/25/ business/smallbusiness/25sbiz.html** (accessed August 10, 2010); Bill Chappell, "Yelp Goes Unfiltered. Let the Arguments Begin," all tech CONSIDERED, NPR, April 6, 2010, **www.npr .org/blogs/alltechconsidered/2010/04/06/125631274/yelp-goes-unfiltered—let-the-arguments-begin** (accessed August 10, 2010); Jessica Guynn, "Restaurant Review Site Yelp and Reservation Booking Site OpenTable Team Up," *The Los Angeles Times,* June 3, 2010, **http://latimesblogs.latimes.com/technology/ 2010/06/restaurant-review-site-yelp-and-reservationbooking-site-opentable-team-up.html** (accessed August 10, 2010).

21. Leslie Eaton and Ann Zimmerman, "Dollar Stores Hold on to the Trade-Down Set," *The Wall Street Journal,* December 22, 2010, pp. B1, B8.

22. "Shopping Behavior to Change as a Result of New Marketplace Realities, According to PricewaterhouseCoopers and Kantar Retail," *PR Newswire,* March 9, 2010, **www.prnewswire.com/ news-releases/shopping-behavior-to-change-as-aresult-of-new-marketplace-realitiesaccording-to-pricewaterhousecoopersand-kantar-retail-87104307.html** (accessed March 30, 2010).

23. "DOE Report: U.S. Will Remain Coal-Dependent in 2035, Carbon Emissions Rise," *Reuters,* December 23, 2010, **http://blogs .reuters.com/environment/2010/12/23/doe-report-u-s-will-remain-coal-dependent-in-2035-carbon-emissions-rise/** (accessed April 7, 2011); "Some Coal-Fired Power Plants Were Built Last Year—A New Trend?" Institute for Energy Research, September 1, 2010, **www.instituteforenergyresearch.org/2010/09/01/some-coal-fired-power-plants-were-built-last-year-is-this-the-start-of-a-new-trend-or-are-new-coal-plants-dead/** (accessed April 7, 2011).

24. Bryan Walsh, "Why Green Is the New Red, White and Blue," *Time,* April 28, 2008, pp. 45–58; Denis Ryan, "Taking the Green Change," *The Vancouver Sun,* May 31, 2008, pp. 136–37.

25. "Harvesting the Air," *The Economist,* April 3, 2010, p. 32.

CHAPTER 12

1. Narendra Rao, "The Keys to New Product success (Part 1)—Collecting Unarticulated & Invisible Customer-Needs," *Product Management & Strategy,* June 19, 2007, **http://productstrategy. wordpress.com/2007/06/19/the-keys-tonew-product-successpart-1-collectingunarticulated-invisible-customer-needs/** (accessed April 1, 2010).

2. Gwendolyn Cuizon, "SWOT Analysis of Dell Computers," Suite101 .com, March 5, 2009, **http://strategic-businessplanning. suite101.com/article.cfm/swot_analysis_of_dell_computers** (accessed March 31, 2010).

3. "Coke Blak Goes Black," *BevNet,* August 31, 2007, **www .bevnet.com/news/2007/08-31-2007-Blak_coca-cola.asp** (accessed April 1, 2010).

4. "Nissan Leaf Electric Car Wins 2010 Green Car Vision Award," Green Car, January 26, 2010, **www.greencar.com/articles/ nissan-leaf-electric-car-wins-2010-green-car-vision-award.php** (accessed April 7, 2011); "Nissan Unveils "Leaf"—The World's First Electric Car Designed for Affordability and Real-World Requirements," Nissan, August 2, 2009, **www.nissan-global .com/EN/NEWS/2009/_STORY/090802-02-e.html** (accessed April 7, 2011).

5. "Vision and Innovation: The Shuffle Master Story," ShuffleMaster Incorporated, **www.shufflemaster.com/01_company/history/ index.asp** (accessed April 1, 2010).

6. Faith Keenan, "Friendly Spies on the Net," *BusinessWeek e.biz,* July 9, 2001, p. EB27.

7. Anjali Cordeiro, "P&G Ends Tide Basic Test," *The Wall Street Journal,* June 24, 2010, **http://online.wsj.com/article/SB10 001424052748704629804575324940521990382.html** (accessed November 19, 2010).

8. "McDonald's Opens First McCafe in U.S.," *Entrepreneur,* May 14, 2001, **www.entrepreneur.com/franchises/franchisezone/ thisjustin/article40494.html** (accessed April 2, 2010); "McDonald's Poised to Rival Starbucks Nationwide Starting Today," *QSR,* May 5, 2009, **www.qsrmagazine.com/articles/ news/story.phtml?id=8625** (accessed April 2, 2010).

9. Susan Berfield, "The Man Behind The Bandz," *Bloomberg Businessweek,* June 14–20, 2010, pp. 62–67; Emily Maltby, "Silly Bandz Seek to Stretch Popularity," *The Wall Street Journal,* July 8, 2010, **http://online.wsj.com/article/SB10001424 052748703636404575353060497299790.html** (accessed July 4, 2010); "Silly Bandz Could Be 'Hottest Toy of the Year,'" *Chicago Sun Times,* July 2, 2010, **www.suntimes.com/ business/2456678,CST-NWS-bandz02.article** (accessed July 4, 2010); "Brand Central Joins the Craze with Silly Bandz," The Licensing Blog, **http://licensingblog.com/brand-central-joins-the-craze-with-sillybandz** (accessed July 6, 2010); Bruce Horovitz, "Silly Bandz Stretch into a Trend as Copycat Rivals Hop on Board," *USA Today,* July 1, 2010, **www.usatoday.com/money/ smallbusiness/2010-07-01-sillybandz01_CV_N.htm** (accessed July 30, 2010); **www.crazyfads.com** (accessed August 10, 2010); "Beanie Babies," Wikipedia, **http://en.wikipedia.org/wiki/ Beanie_Baby** (accessed August 10, 2010); Bruce Horovitz, "Silly Bandz Fad Fades Out," *USA Today,* December 17, 2010, p. B1.

10. "Electric Cars for 2010," *Clean Fleet Report,* December 14, 2009, **www.cleanfleetreport.com/electric-vehicles/**

electric-car-for-2010/ (accessed April 8, 2010); Jim Motavelli, "Demand Will Exceed Supply of Electric Cars," *Forbes,* August 23, 2010, **www.forbes.com/2010/08/21/electric-cars-chelsea-technology-sexton.html** (accessed April 7, 2011).

11. Jo Piazza, "It's Pancakes. In a Can. It's Made $15 Million," *CNNMoney.com,* January 1, 2010, **http://money.cnn .com/2009/12/23/smallbusiness/batter_blaster.fsb/index .htm** (accessed January 6, 2010); "How to Market a Product That Doesn't Have a Niche," *BNET,* October 29, 2010, **www .batterblaster.com/BNet_10.29.2010.pdf** (accessed April 7, 2011).

12. "iPod + iTunes Timeline," Apple Press Info, **www.apple.com/pr/ products/ipodhistory/** (accessed January 14, 2010).

13. Bruce Horovitz, "Snacks: Does This Bag Make Me Look Fat?" *USA Today,* February 20, 2008, p. B1.

14. "Product Life Cycle," Answers.com, **www.answers.com/topic/ productlife-cycle** (accessed March 31, 2010).

15. Ann Zimmerman, "Are Mattel's New Dolls Black Enough?" *The Wall Street Journal,* December 3, 2009, pp. B11, B14; Ann Zimmerman, "Mattel Hopes Barbie Facelift Will Show Up Younger Rivals," *The Wall Street Journal,* December 21, 2009, pp. A1, A20.

16. "Private Label Gets Personal," *Shopper Culture,* **www.shop-perculture.com/shopper_culture/2009/10/privatelabel-gets-personal.html** (accessed April 2, 2010).

17. Mona Doyle, "What Packaging Will Consumers Pay More For?" *Food & Beverage Packaging,* August 1, 2008, **www.foodandbeveragepackaging .com/Articles/Article_Rotation/BNP_GUID_9-5-2006_A_10000000000000401665** (accessed January 14, 2011).

18. Mike Barris, "20-Ounce Sales Lose Fizz, Sinking Coke Enterprises," *The Wall Street Journal,* May 28, 2008, **http://online.wsj .com/article/SB121197848027325835.html** (accessed April 8, 2010).

19. "ASCI Scores—National, Sector, & Industry," ASCI, **www .theacsi.org/images/stories/ACSI_TREE_12_10.pdf** (accessed January 14, 2011); "About ACSI," ACSI, **www.theacsi. org/index.php?option=com_content&task=view&id=49&Ite mid=28** (accessed January 14, 2011); "December 2010 and Historical ACSI Scores," The American Customer Satisfaction Index, **www.theacsi.org/index.php?option=com_content &task=view&id=207&Itemid=225** (accessed January 14, 2011).

20. Scott McCartney, "The Big Guys Finish Last in 2010 Airline Rankings," *The Wall Street Journal,* January 13, 2011, p. D1.

21. "American Demographics 2006 Consumer Perception Survey," *Advertising Age,* January 2, 2006, p. 9. Data by Synovate.

22. Rajneesh Suri and Kent B. Monroe, "The Effects of Time Constraints on Consumers' Judgments of Prices and Products," *Journal of Consumer Research* 30 (June 2003), p. 92.

23. "Talisman," De Beers, **www.debeerseu.com/Collections/Talisman/ icat/maintalisman** (accessed April 5, 2010); Andy Stone, "Drill Bits Are Forever," *Forbes,* December 10, 2007, p. 200.

24. Rags Srinivasan, "Instant Coffee Price Is About Skimming," *Iterative Path,* September 30, 2009, **http://iterativepath.wordpress .com/2009/09/30/instant-coffee-price-is-about-skimming/** (accessed April 5, 2010).

25. David Luhnow and Chad Terhune, "Latin Pop: A Low-Budget Cola Shakes Up Markets South of the Border," *The Wall Street Journal,* October 27, 2003, pp. A1, A18.

26. "Top Threats to Revenue," *USA Today,* February 1, 2006, p. A1.

27. Bruce Horovitz, "Baby Carrots Take on Junk Food with Hip Marketing Campaign," August 29 2010, **www.usatoday.com/ money/industries/food/2010-08-29-baby-carrots-marketing_N .htm** (accessed October 4, 2010); Tom Laskawy, "Carrot Vending Machines a Surprise Success," grist, September 21, 2010, **www.grist.org/article/food-2010-09-21-schools-carrot-vending-machines-a-success/** (accessed October 4, 2010); Emily Fredrix, "Oh Snap! New Baby Carrot Campaign Mimics Junk Food," *msnbc .com,* September 2, 2010, **www.msnbc.msn.com/id/38972945/ ns/business-consumer_news/** (accessed October 4, 2010).

28. Brad Howarth, "Hear This, iPods from a Vending Machine," *The Sydney Morning Herald,* November 14, 2006, **www .smh.com.au/news/biztech/hear-this-ipods-from-a-vending-machine/ 2006/11/13/1163266481869.html** (accessed April 8, 2010).

29. "Welcome to the Future of Shopping," Zoom Systems, **www .zoomsystems.com/zoomshops/zs_index.html** (accessed April 5, 2010).

30. Laura Petrecca and Christine Dugas, "Going Truly Green Might Require Detective Work," *USA Today,* April 22, 2010, pp. 1B–2B; Laura Petrecca and Christina Dugas, "Groups Help Consumers Find 'Real' Green Products," *USA Today,* April 22, 2010, p. 2B; Julie Deardorff, "How to Spot Greenwashing," *Chicago Tribune,* May 7, 2010, **http://featuresblogs.chicagotribune.com/features_ julieshealthclub/2010/05/how-to-spot-greenwashing.html** (accessed June 13, 2010); Sarah Mahoney, "H&M Introduces Its First Organic Skincare," MarketingDaily, March 3, 2010, **www.mediapost.com/publications/?fa=Articles.showArticle&art_ aid=123424** (accessed June 13, 2010); Leslie Berkman, "Efforts Spread to Verify Claims of Businesses Who Market Themselves as Environmentally Friendly," *The Press-Enterprise,* January 31, 2010, **www.pe.com/business/local/stories/PE_New_Local_W_ green01.46c7f14.html** (accessed June 13, 2010); **www.green-washingindex.com** (accessed June 13, 2010); Julie Deardorff, "Eco-friendly Claims: When Is 'Green' Really Green?," *Chicago Tribune,* May 7, 2010, **http://featuresblogs.chicagotribune .com/features_julieshealthclub/2010/05/ecofriendly-claims-when-is-green-really-green.html** (accessed December 12, 2010).

31. Abbey Klaassen, "Even Google Has to Advertise," *Advertising Age,* June 2, 2008, p. 4.

32. Bruce Horowitz, "Super Bowl Ads Play to Social Media," *USA Today,* December 13, 2010, p. 1B.

33. Alex Konrad, "Mad Men Is back, and So Is Product Placement," *CNNMoney,* July 27, 2010, **http://money.cnn.com/gal-leries/2010/fortune/1007/gallery.mad_men_products.fortune/ index.html** (accessed April 8, 2011); "New York's Gone Mad—AMC *Mad Men* Season 4 World Premiere Screening Event," *AMC,* **http://blogs.amctv.com/mad-men/2010/07/season-4-premiere-party.php** (accessed April 8, 2011).

34. Gerry Khermouch and Jeff Green, "Buzz Marketing," *Business-Week,* July 30, 2001, pp. 50–56.

35. Andrew Romano, "Now 4 Restaurant 2.0," *Newsweek,* February 28, 2009, **www.newsweek.com/id/187008** (accessed April 5, 2010).

36. Abigail Bassett, "Beat the Recession, One Penny at a Time," *CNNMoney.com,* April 29, 2009, **http://money.cnn.com/2009/ 04/28/pf/coupon_savings/index.htm** (accessed April 5, 2010).

37. Kate MacArthur, "Sierra Mist: Cie Nicholson," *Advertising Age,* November 17, 2003, p. S-2.

38. "Kimberly Clark: Becoming the Indispensable Partner for Retailers," *Retail Solutions,* **www.t3ci.com/pdfs/Retail_Solutions_Kimberly_ Clark_Case_Study_2009-01.pdf** (accessed April 5, 2010).

39. Bruce Horovitz, "Bud's Latest Ad Strategy: Free Beer," *USA Today,* September 22, 2010, p. 1B.

CHAPTER 13

1. This material in this chapter is reserved for use in the authors' other textbooks and teaching materials.

2. Brad Stone and Bruce Einhorn, "Baidu China," *Bloomberg Businessweek,* November 15–21, 2010, pp. 60–67; Loretta Chao, "China's Baidu Brings App Craze to Web," *The Wall Street Journal*, September 3, 2010, p. B8.

3. "Fortune 500," CNNMoney, **http://money.cnn.com/magazines/fortune/fortune500/2010/full_list/** (accessed January 17, 2011).

4. "Fortune 500: Amazon.com," *Fortune,* 2009, **http://money.cnn.com/magazines/fortune/fortune500/2009/snapshots/10810.html** (accessed April 13, 2011); Josh Quitter, "How Jeff Bezos Rules the Retail Space," *Fortune,* May 5, 2008, pp. 127–132.

5. "Media Info," Hulu, **www.hulu.com/about** (accessed April 13, 2011).

6. Bobby White, "The New Workplace Rules: No Video-Watching," *The Wall Street Journal,* March 4, 2008, p. B1.

7. "A World of Connections," *The Economist,* January 28, 2010, **www.economist.com/node/15351002** (accessed January 27, 2011).

8. "Internet Usage Statistics," Internet World Stats, **www.Internetworldstats.com/stats.htm** (accessed April 13, 2011).

9. Michael V. Copeland. "Tapping Tech's Beautiful Mind," *Fortune,* October 12, 2009, pp. 35–36.

10. Emily Steel, "Nestlé Takes a Beating on Social-Media Sites," *The Wall Street Journal,* March 29, 2010, p. B5; "World's Most Admired Companies 2010," *Fortune,* **http://money.cnn.com/magazines/fortune/mostadmired/2010/full_list** (accessed April 13, 2011); Augie Ray, "Seven Things Your Organization Must Do Because of Social Media," Forrester, May 11, 2010, **http://blogs.forrester.com/augie_ray/10-05-11-seven_things_your_organization_must_do_because_social_media** (accessed April 13, 2011); Jennifer Van Grove, "Nestle Meets Greenpeace's Demand Following Social Media Backlash," mashable, May 2010, **http://mashable.com/2010/05/17/nestle-social-media-fallout** (accessed April 13, 2011); Caroline McCarthy, "Nestle Mess Shows Sticky Side of Facebook Pages," cnet news, March 9, 2010, **http://news.cnet.com/8301-13577_3-20000805-36.html** (accessed April 13, 2011).

11. Miguel Bustillo and Geoffrey A. Fowler, "Walmart Uses Its Stores to Get an Edge Online," *The Wall Street Journal,* December 15, 2009, p. B1.

12. Aaron Back, "China's Big Brands Tackle Web Sales," *The Wall Street Journal,* December 1, 2009, p. B2.

13. "2009 Digital Handbook," *Marketing News,* April 30, 2009, p. 13.

14. Cameron Chapman, "The History and Evolution of Social Media." *WebDesigner Depot,* October 7, 2009, **www.webdesignerdepot.com/2009/10/the-history-and-evolution-of-social-media/** (accessed April 19, 2011).

15. Danah M. Boyd and Nicole B. Ellison,"Social Network Sites: Definition, History, and Scholarship," *Journal of Computer-Mediated Education,* 2007, **http://jcmc.indiana.edu/vol13/issue1/boyd.ellison.html** (accessed April 19, 2011).

16. Emily Schmall, "Growing Pains," *Forbes,* August 11, 2008, pp. 60–63.

17. Zachary Karabell, "To Tweet or Not to Tweet," April 12, 2011, *Time,* p. 24.

18. "2009 Digital Handbook," p. 11.

19. Charlene Li and Josh Bernoff, *Groundswell* (Boston: Harvard Business Press, 2008), p. 43.

20. A.C. Nielsen, "Global Faces and Networked Places: A Nielsen Report on Social Networking's New Global Footprint," March 2009, **http://blog.nielsen.com/nielsenwire/wp-content/uploads/2009/03/nielsen_globalfaces_mar09.pdf** (accessed April 19, 2011).

21. "Couldn't Stop the Spread of the Conversation in Reactions from Other Bloggers," from Hyejin Kim's May 4, 2007, blog post "Korea: Bloggers and Donuts" on the blog Global Voices at **http://groundswell.forrester.com/site1-16** (accessed April 19, 2011).

22. Randy Tinseth, "Randy's Journal," Boeing, **http://boeingblogs.com/randy/** (accessed April 13, 2011).

23. Drake Bennett, "Assessing Wikipedia, Wiki-Style, on Its 10th Anniversary," *Bloomberg Businessweek*, January 10–16, 2011, pp. 57–61.

24. Li and Bernoff, *Groundswell,* pp. 25–26.

25. "2009 Digital Handbook," p. 11.

26. David Meerman Scott, *The New Rules of Marketing & PR* (Hoboken, NJ: John Wiley & Sons, Inc., 2009), p. 224; "Mainframe: The Art of the Sales, Lesson One," YouTube, **www.youtube.com/watch?v= MSqXKp-00Hm** (accessed April 13, 2011); Ryan Rhodes, "The Mainframe: It's Like a Barn," IBM Systems, March–April 2007, **www.ibmsystemsmag.com/mainframe/marchapril07/stoprun/11984p1.aspx** (accessed April 13, 2011).

27. "Get Involved in Our Film Making competition," Unilever, April 2010, **www.unilever.com/sustainability/news/news/getinvolvedinourfilmmakingcompetition.aspx** (accessed April 15, 2011); Ben Bold, "Unilever Declares Vaseline Ad Winner in UGC Competition," Marketing, October 26, 2010, **www.marketingmagazine.co.uk/news/1037195/Unilever-declares-Vaseline-ad-winner-UGC-competition/** (accessed April 15, 2011).

28. "Search Giant Google to Buy YouTube for $1.65B," *FoxNews.com,* October 10, 2006, **www.foxnews.com/story/0,2933,218921,00.html** (accessed April 13, 2011).

29. Zeke Camusio, "Flickr Marketing—6 Awesome Tactics to Promote Your Website on Flickr," The Outsourcing Company, February 19, 2009, **www.theoutsourcingcompany.com/blog/social-media-marketing/flickr-marketing-6-awesome-tactics-to-promote-your-website-on-flickr/** (accessed April 19, 2011).

30. Bianca Male, "How to Promote Your Business on Flickr," *The Business Insider,* December 1, 2009, **www.businessinsider.com/how-to-promote-your-business-on-flickr-2009-12?utm_source=feedburner&utm_medium=feed&utm_campaign=Feed%3A+businessinsider+(The+Business+Insider)** (accessed on April 13, 2011).

31. "How to Market on Flickr," Small Business Search Marketing, **www.smallbusinesssem.com/articles/marketing-on-flickr/#ixzz0cLlpJUTW** (accessed April 13, 2011).

32. "About GM Blogs," Flickr, **www.flickr.com/people/gmblogs/** (accessed April 13, 2011).

33. Sage Lewis, "Using Flickr for Marketing," YouTube, uploaded February 13, 2007, **www.youtube.com/watch?v= u2Xyzkfzlug** (accessed January 11, 2010).

34. "2009 Digital Handbook," p. 14.

35. Christopher S. Penn, "About the Financial Aid Podcast," *FinancialAidNews.com,* **www.financialaidnews.com/about-2/** (accessed April 13, 2011).

36. "2009 Digital Handbook," p. 13.

37. Li and Bernoff, *Groundswell,* p. 22.

38. "2009 Digital Handbook," p. 13.

39. Dawn C. Chmielewski, "MySpace, Google Renew Search and Advertising Deal," *Los Angeles Times*, December 16, 2010, **http://latimesblogs.latimes.com/entertainmentnews-buzz/2010/12/myspace-google-renew-search-deal.html** (accessed April 11, 2011).

40. MySpace website, **www.myspace.com/** (accessed April 11, 2011).

41. "Facebook: Largest, Fastest Growing Social Network," *Tech Tree*, August 13, 2008, **www.techtree.com/India/News/Facebook_Largest_Fastest_Growing_Social_Network/551-92134-643.html** (accessed April 13, 2011).

42. Dan Macsai and Zachary Wilson, "When Brands Go Social," *Fast Company*, December 2009/January 2010, p. 77; Brad Stone, "Ads Posted on Facebook Strike Some as Off-Key," *The New York Times*, March 3, 2010, **www.nytimes.com/2010/03/04/technology/04facebook.html** (accessed April 13, 2011); Emily Bryson York, "McDonald's to Use Facebook's Upcoming Location Feature," *AdvertisingAge*, May 6, 2010, **http://adage.com/digital/article?article_id=143742** (accessed April 13, 2011); Benny Evangelista, "Twitter Puts Ads in Mix of Tweets," Sfgate, April 14, 2010, **http://articles.sfgate.com/2010-04-14/business/20848338_1_twitter-users-tweets-biz-stone** (accessed April 13, 2011); "Hello World," April 13, 2010, **http://blog.twitter.com/2010/04/hello-world.html** (accessed June 4, 2010); John Yates, "Using Twitter, Facebook to Submit Consumer Complaints," *Chicago Tribune*, April 23, 2010, **http://newsblogs.chicagotribune.com/the-problem-solver/2010/04/social-media-as-a-consumercomplaint-avenue.html** (accessed April 13, 2011); Kit Eaton, "Fox's Twitter TV Experiment Tweets Its Way to Epic Failure," Fast Company, September 4, 2009, **www.fastcompany.com/blog/kit-eaton/technomix/foxs-twitter-tv-overlays-tweet-their-way-epic-failure** (accessed April 13, 2011); "Twitter Snags over 100 Million Users, Eyes Money-Making," *The Economic Times*, April 15, 2010, **http://economictimes.indiatimes.com/infotech/internet/Twitter-snags-over-100-million-users-eyes-money-making/articleshow/5808927.cms** (accessed April 13, 2011).

43. "2009 Digital Handbook," p. 13.

44. Nick Summers, "Heated Rivalries:#9 Facebook vs. MySpace," *Newsweek*, **www.2010.newsweek.com/top-10/heated-rivalries/facebook-vs-myspace.html** (accessed April 13, 2011).

45. "2009 Digital Handbook," p. 13.

46. AlphaGraphics Franklin, "State Farm Insurance Will Run Facebook Contest," Facebook, **www.facebook.com/note.php?note_id=201261566562422** (accessed April 12, 2011).

47. Hansen's Cakes, **http://hansencakes.blogspot.com/** (accessed April 13, 2011); **www.facebook.com/pages/Hansens-Cakes/171578118691** (accessed April 13, 2011).

48. "Pepsi Refresh Project," **www.refresheverything.com/index** (accessed April 13, 2011); Stuart Elliot, "Pepsi Invites the Public to Do Good," *The New York Times*, January 31, 2010, **www.nytimes.com/2010/02/01/business/media/01adco.html** (accessed April 13, 2011).

49. "Facebook Needs to Be a Marketing Destination, Not Just a Conduit," *Marketing News*, March 15, 2011, p. 12.

50. "2009 Digital Handbook," p. 13; "Top 15 Most Popular Social Networking Websites," *eBizMBA*, April 2011, **www.ebizmba.com/articles/social-networking-websites** (accessed April 13, 2011).

51. Alison Doyle, "LinkedIn and Your Job Search," *About.com*, **http://jobsearch.about.com/od/networking/a/linkedin.htm** (accessed April 13, 2011).

52. Laura Petrecca, "More Grads Use Social Media to Job Hunt," *USA Today*, April 5, 2011, p. 3B.

53. "LinkedIn's Newest Features Allow for Corporate Networking and Business Promotion," *Marketing News*, March 15, 2011, p. 12.

54. Jefferson Graham, "Cake Decorator Finds Twitter a Tweet Recipe for Success," *USA Today*, April 1, 2009, p. 5B.

55. "2009 Digital Handbook," p. 11.

56. Gregory L. White, "Medvedev Sets Kremlin Atwitter," *The Wall Street Journal*, September 1, 2010, p. A12.

57. Claire Cain Miller, "Twitter Loses Its Scrappy Start-Up Status," *The New York Times*, April 15, 2010, **www.nytimes.com/2010/04/16/technology/16twitter.html** (accessed April 13, 2011).

58. Bruce Horowitz, "Marketers Step Up Their Rewards for Twitter Buzz," *USA Today*, November 17, 2010, p. 2B.

59. Suzanne Vranica, "Tweeting to Sell Cars," *The Wall Street Journal*, November 15, 2010, p. B12.

60. Josh Tyrangiel, "Bing vs. Google: The Conquest of Twitter," *Time*, October 22, 2009, **www.time.com/time/business/article/0,8599,1931532,00.html** (accessed April 13, 2011).

61. "As Twitter Grows and Evolves, More Manpower Is Needed," *Marketing News*, March 15, 2011, p. 13.

62. "Real Cars Drive into Second Life," *CNNMoney.com*, November 18, 2006, **http://money.cnn.com/2006/11/17/autos/2nd_life_cars/index.htm** (accessed April 13, 2011).

63. Alice Truong, "Q&A: A Real Study of Virtual Worlds," *The Wall Street Journal*, May 4, 2010, **http://blogs.wsj.com/digits/2010/05/04/qa-a-real-study-ofvirtual-worlds/** (accessed May 6, 2010).

64. "CNN Enters the Virtual World of Second Life," November 12, 2007, *CNN.com*, **www.cnn.com/2007/TECH/11/12/second.life.irpt/index.html** (accessed April 13, 2011).

65. Roger Yu, "Smartphones Help Make Bon Voyages," *USA Today*, March 5, 2010, p. B1.

66. Mickey Alam Khan, "Jiffy Lube Mobile Coupons Bring 50 Percent New Households," *Mobile Marketer*, January 30, 2009, **www.mobilemarketer.com/cms/news/commerce/2551.html** (accessed April 13, 2011).

67. Umika Pidaparthy, "Marketers Embracing QR Codes, for Better or Worse," *CNN Tech*, March 28, 2011, **http://articles.cnn.com/2011-03-28/tech/qr.codes.marketing_1_qr-smartphone-users-symbian?_s=PM:TECH** (accessed April 11, 2011).

68. Li and Bernoff, *Groundswell*, p. 41.

69. Ibid., pp. 41–42.

70. Ibid., p. 44.

71. Ibid., pp. 44–45.

72. Melissa Harris, "Viewpoints Network Snags Client, Enhances Its Long-Term Outlook," *Chicago Tribune*, May 23, 2010, **http://articles.chicagotribune.com/2010-05-23/business/ct-biz-0523-confidential-viewpoints-20100523_1_autistic-adults-business-plan-venture-capitalists** (accessed April 13, 2011); Michael Krauss, "Moog Synthesizes Social Media," *Marketing News*, September 30, 2010, pp. 10.

73. Mya Frazier, "CrowdSourcing," *Delta Sky Mag*, February 2010, p. 70.

74. Li and Bernoff, *Groundswell*, pp. 26–27.

75. Sarah Nassauer, "'I Hate My Room,' The Traveler Tweeted. Ka-Boom! An Upgrade!" *The Wall Street Journal*, June 24, 2010, p. D1.

76. John W. Miller, "Yahoo Cookie Plan in Place," *The Wall Street Journal*, March 19, 2011, **http://online.wsj.com/article/SB10 00142405274870351240457620870081381555 70.html** (accessed April 11, 2011).

77. Jon Swartz, "Facebook Changes Its Status in Washington," *USA Today*, January 13, 2011, pp. 1B–2B; "Details of 100 Million Facebook Users Published Online," *MSNBC.com*, July 29, 2010, **www.msnbc.msn.com/id/38463013/ns/technology_and_science/?GT1=43001** (accessed July 29, 2010); Julia Angwin and Steve Stecklow, "'Scrapers' Dig Deep for Data on Web," *The Wall Street Journal*, October 12, 2010, pp. A1, A18.

78. Quentin Hardy, "In Mark We Trust," *Forbes*, October 11, 2010, pp. 81–86; Swartz, "Facebook Changes Its Status in Washington," pp. 1B–2B.

79. Jennifer Valentino-DeVries, "Ad Industry Takes Another Look At 'Do-Not-Track' in Browers," *The Wall Street Journal*, March 31, 2011, p. B5.

80. "About TRUSTe," TRUSTe, **www.truste.com/about_TRUSTe/index.html** (accessed April 13, 2011).

81. Better Business Bureau Online, **www.bbbonline.org/** (accessed April 13, 2011).

82. Larry Barrett, "Data Breach Costs Surge in 2009: Study," *eSecurityPlanet*, January 26, 2010, **www.esecurityplanet.com/features/article.php/3860811/Data-Breach-Costs-Surgein-2009-Study.htm** (accessed April 13, 2011).

83. Sarah E. Needleman, "Social-Media Con Game," *The Wall Street Journal*, October 12, 2009, p. R4.

84. "Facebook Takes Strong Stance Against Haiti Fraud," *Media Street*, January 19, 2010, **www.www.media-street.co.uk/blog/facebook-takes-strong-stance-against-haiti-fraud** (accessed April 19, 2011).

85. Brad Stone and Bruce Einhorn, "Baidu China," *Bloomberg Businessweek*, November 15–21, 2010, pp. 60–67.

86. Abigail Field, "Viacom v. YouTube/Google: A Piracy Case in Their Own Words," *Daily Finance*, March 21, 2010, **www.dailyfinance.com/story/company-news/viacom-v-youtubegoogle-a-piracy-case-in-their-ownwords/19407896/** (accessed April 13, 2011).

87. Kevin Shanahan and Mike Hyman "Motivators and Enablers of SCOURing," *Journal of Business Research* 63 (September–October 2010), pp. 1095–1102.

88. Seventh Annual BSA and IDC Global Software Piracy Study," BSA, **http://portal.bsa.org/globalpiracy2009/index.html** (accessed April 13, 2011).

89. Max Chafkin, "The Case, and the Plan, for the Virtual Company," *Inc.*, April 2010, p. 68.

CHAPTER 14

1. "Break Up the Big Four?" *CFO Magazine*, June 1, 2004, **www.cfo.com/article.cfm/3014059** (accessed April 26, 2011).

2. Michael Repoport, "Citi Explains How It Hid Risk from the Public," *The Wall Street Journal*, July 16, 2010, p. C1.

3. *Report to the Nations: 2010 Global Fraud Study*, **www.acfe.com/rttn/rttn-2010.pdf** (accessed April 26, 2011).

4. "About the ACFE," Association of Certified Fraud Examiners, **www.acfe.com/about/about.asp** (accessed April 26, 2011).

5. Kate O'Sullivan, "From Adversity, Better Budgets," *CFO Magazine*, June 2010, pp. 45–47; Jack Sweeny, "UPS CFO Spies a Silver Lining," *Business Finance*, March 10, 2010, **www.businessfinancemag.com/article/ups-cfo-spies-silver-lining-0310** (accessed October 8, 2010)

6. Julie Schmit, "Clean, Cheap Power from Fuel Cells in a Box?," *USA Today*, February 24, 2010, p. 1B; **www.bloomenergy.com** (accessed September 15, 2010); Todd Woody, "Short on Roof Space? Adobe Plants Fuel Cells," *The New York Times*, September 28, 2010, **www.usatoday.com/tech/news/2010-02-24-fuel-cell_N.htm** (accessed October 13, 2010).

7. Marie Leone, "Something Wicked This Way Comes," *CFO Magazine*, June 2010, pp. 14–15; Sarah E. Needleman, "Business Owners Get Burned by Sticky Fingers," *The Wall Street Journal*, March 11, 2010, **http://online.wsj.com/article/SB10 00142405274870386270457509966179356831 0.html** (accessed September 1, 2010); **www.acfe.com** (accessed September 13, 2010); Will Deener, "Whistle-Blowers Find More Corporate Fraud Than Regulators, Study Finds," *dallasnews*, March 22, 2010, **www.dallasnews.com/sharedcontent/dws/bus/columnists/wdeener/stories/DN-Deener_22bus.ART.State.Edition1.3dafd6c.html#slcgm_comments_anchor** (accessed September 13, 2010).

8. Mary Williams Walsh, "State Woes Grow Too Big to Camouflage," *The New York Times*, March 29, 2010, **www.nytimes.com/2010/03/30/business/economy/30states.html** (accessed March 31, 2010).

9. Bureau of Labor Statistics, "Accountants and Auditors," Occupational Outlook Handbook 2010–2011, **www.bls.gov/oco/ocos001.htm** (accessed April 26, 2011).

CHAPTER 15

1. "How Currency Gets into Circulation," Federal Reserve Bank of New York (n.d.), **www.newyorkfed.org/aboutthefed/fedpoint/fed01.html** (accessed April 26, 2011).

2. "Weird and Wonderful Money Facts and Trivia," *Happy Worker*, **www.happyworker.com/magazine/facts/weird-and-wonderful-money-facts** (accessed April 26, 2011).

3. Ibid.

4. "Redesigned Currency," NewMoney.gov, **www.newmoney.gov/currency/default.htm** (accessed April 26, 2011).

5. "US Mint Cost to Produce the Penny and Nickel," *Coin Update News*, **http://news.coinupdate.com/us-mint-cost-to-produce-the-penny-and-nickel-0137/** (accessed April 26, 2011).

6. Credit Card Statistics, Industry Facts, Debt Statistics," *CreditCards.com*, **www.creditcards.com/credit-card-news/credit-card-industry-facts-personal-debt-statistics-1276.php** (accessed January 18, 2011).

7. Jane J. Kim, "Credit Unions: A Better Bet Than Banks?" *The Wall Street Journal*, June 5–6, 2010, p. B8; Bankrate.com, "Are Credit Unions Better Than Banks?" Bankrate.com, **www.bankrate.com/finance/savings/are-credit-unions-better-than-banks.aspx** (accessed November 15, 2010); Mark Maremont and Victoria McGrane, "Credit Unions Bailed Out," *The Wall Street Journal*, September 25, 2010, **http://online.wsj.com/article/SB1000142 40527487034996045755122540636822 36.html** (accessed November 15, 2010).

8. "Deposit Insurance Simplification Fact Sheet," FDIC website, **www.inbk.com/pdf/FDIC_Deposit_Insurance_Coverage.pdf** (accessed April 26, 2011).

9. Sarah Kessler, "For Sale: A Young Entrepreneur's Future Income," *Inc.*, May 2010, p. 23; **www.thrustfund.com** (accessed April 26, 2011); Kim-Mai Cutler, "Entrepreneurs Offer Their Life's Future Earnings for an Investment," Deals & More, March 3, 2010,

deals.venturebeat.com/2010/03/03/life-investment (accessed April 26, 2011); Marcia Stepanek, "Three Social Entrepreneurs Sell Shares in Selves to Scale," Stanford Social Innovation, January 14, 2010, **www.ssireview.org/opinion/entry/three_social_entrepreneurs_sell_shares_in_selves_to_scale** (accessed April 26, 2011); Saul Garlick, "Invest in Me, Take My Equity," social edge, January 2010, **www.socialedge.org/discussions/funding/invest-in-me-take-my-equity** (accessed April 26, 2011).

10. "NACHA Reports More Than 18 Billion ACH Payments in 2007," NACHA: The Electronic Payments Association, May 19, 2008, **http://admin.nacha.org/userfiles/File/Stats/Volume_Final.pdf** (accessed April 26, 2011).

11. Tyler Metzger, "ATM Use in theUnited States," *CreditCards.com*, **www.creditcards.com/credit-card-news/atm-use-statistics-3372.php** (accessed April 26, 2011).

12. Federal Deposit Insurance Corporation website, **www.fdic.gov** (accessed April 26, 2011).

13. Sudeep Reddy, "Elizabeth Warren's Early Words on a Consumer Financial Protection Bureau," *The Wall Street Journal*, September 17, 2010, **http://blogs.wsj.com/economics/2010/09/17/elizabeth-warrens-early-words-on-a-consumer-financial-protection-bureau/** (accessed April 26, 2011); Jennifer Liberto and David Ellis, "Wall Street Reform: What's in the Bill," *CNN*, June 30, 2010); **http://money.cnn.com/2010/06/25/news/economy/whats_in_the_reform_bill/index.htm** (accessed April 26, 2011); **www.whitehouse.gov** (accessed December 15, 2010).

14. Associated Press, "New FDIC Rules Kick In for Bank Securities," *USA Today,* September 28, 2010, 5B.

15. "CSI Pennsylvania," *CFO Magazine,* March 2008, p. 92.

CHAPTER 16

1. Brian Dumaine, "A Motorcycle on a Mission," *Fortune,* June 14, 2010, p. 30; "The Mission One Motorcycle," *FastCompany,* April 2010, p. 59; Julie Klein, "Mission Motors Races Ahead with $3.4M for Electric Motorcycles," Deals & More, *VentureBeat,* June 10, 2010, **http://deals.venturebeat.com/2010/06/10/mission-motors-races-ahead-with-3-4m-for-electric-motorcycles** (accessed August 10, 2010)

2. **http://ycombinator.com** (accessed September 15, 2010); Ira Sager, Kimberly Weisul, and Spencer Ante, "Tech Investing: How Smart Is the Smart Money?" *Bloomberg Businessweek*, February 2010, **http://images.businessweek.com/ss/10/02/0225_angel_investors/12.htm** (accessed October 7, 2010); Om Malik, "Notes From a Conversation With Y Combinator's Paul Graham," *Gigaom*, February 1, 2010, **http://gigaom.com/2010/02/01/ycombinator-paul-graham/** (accessed September 20, 2010); Paul Graham, "A New Venture Animal," March 2008, **www.paulgraham.com/ycombinator.html** (accessed June 20, 2009); Sean Ellis, "Y Combinator Hatches Brilliant Entrepreneurs," Start Up Marketing Blog by Sean Ellis," December 2, 2008, **http://startup-marketing.com/y-combinator-hatches-brilliant-entrepreneurs/** (accessed June 20, 2009); Andy Louis-Charles, "Ignore Y Combinator at Your Own Risk," *The Motley Fool*, April 28, 2009, **www.fool.com/investing/general/2009/04/28/ignore-y-combinator-at-your-own-risk.aspx** (accessed June 20, 2009); Josh Quittner, "The New Internet Start-Up Boom: Get Rich Slow," *Time,* April 9, 2009, **www.time.com/time/magazine/article/0,9171,1890387-1,00.html** (accessed June 20, 2009).

3. Financial information, Apple, Inc., **http://finance.yahoo.com/q?s = AAPL** (accessed April 8, 2011).

4. Marc Gunther, "Retail's Rising Star," *Fortune*, May 3, 2010, pp. 165–168; **www.dickssportinggoods.com** (accessed June 14, 2010); Cynthia Lin, "Dick's Sporting Goods Posts Higher Profit," Market Watch—*The Wall Street Journal*, August 19, 2010, **www.marketwatch.com/story/dicks-sporting-goods-posts-higher-profit-2010-08-19** (accessed October 16, 2010); Viraj Nair, "UPDATE 2—Dick's Sporting Q3 Profit View Disappoints; Shares Dip," *Reuters*, August 19, 2010, **www.reuters.com/article/idUSSGE67I0G220100819** (accessed October 16, 2010).

5. "Company Research," *The Wall Street Journal*, **http://online.wsj.com** (accessed June 17, 2004); Selena Maranjian, "The Math of the Dow," *The Motley Fool,* January 29, 2004, **www.fool.com/investing/general/2004/01/29/the-math-of-the-dow.aspx** (accessed April 26, 2011).

6. Vincent Ryan, "From Wall Street to Main Street," *CFO Magazine,* June 2008, pp. 85–86.

photo credits

FRONTMATTER

Page v: © Alex Slobodkin/iStockphoto; **vi (t):** © Dan Tero/iStockphoto, **(b):** © Kadir Barcin/iStockphoto; **vii:** © fanelie rosier/iStockphoto; **viii (t):** © Joe Belanger/iStockphoto, **(b):** © TommL/iStockphoto; **ix:** © Tomislav Forgo/iStockphoto.

CHAPTER 1

Pages 2–3: © Gregor Schuster/Getty Images/DAL; **4:** Courtesy of Seventh Generation, Inc.; **7:** © PR NewsFoto/Milk Processor Education Program; **13:** Courtesy of the U.S. Department of the Treasury Bureau of the Public Debt.

CHAPTER 2

Page 22: © The McGraw-Hill Companies, Inc./Jill Braaten, photographer/DAL; **25:** © Sandy Huffaker/Bloomberg via Getty Images; **26:** © Bill Greenblatt/UPI/Landov; **28:** © Chuck Hodes/CBS via Getty Images; **36:** © Dave M. Bennett/Getty Images; **38:** Courtesy of The Home Depot; **40:** © Paul Edmondson/Getty Images/DAL; **42:** © Shawn O'Connor/Tetra Images/Getty Images/DAL; **46:** © Steve LaBadessa Photography; **55:** © The McGraw-Hill Companies, Inc./Jim Flournoy, photographer/DAL.

CHAPTER 3

Pages 60–61: © Brand X Pictures/Jupiterimages/DAL; **63:** © Imaginechina via AP Images; **66:** Courtesy of AT&T; **68:** Courtesy of Aktion Plagarius (www.plagarious.com); **71:** © The McGraw-Hill Companies, Inc./Barry Barker, photographer/DAL; **74:** © Imaginechina via AP Images; **77:** © PR NewsFoto/Yogen Fruz; **78:** © AP Photo/Shizuo Kambayashi.

CHAPTER 4

Page 82: © John Anthony Rizzo/Getty Images/DAL; **88:** © AP Photo/Paul Sakuma; **93 (t):** UNCLE BEN'S®, M&Ms®, SNICKERS®, TWIX®, DOVE®, MARS®, PEDIGREE®, and WHISKAS® are registered trademarks of Mars, Incorporated and its affiliates. These trademarks and product images are used with permission. Mars, Incorporated and its affiliates are not associated with McGraw-Hill Higher Education, **(b):** © Jonathan Alcorn/Bloomberg via Getty Images; **94:** © Stockbyte/Getty Images/DAL; **96:** © AP Photo/Gene J. Puskar; **99:** © Roberts Publishing Services. All rights reserved.

CHAPTER 5

Pages 102–103: © Siri Stafford/Getty Images/DAL; **106:** © AP Photo/Alaska Journal of Commerce, Claire Chandler; **107:** © Joshua Lutz/Redux; **109:** © Imagestate Media (John Foxx)/DAL; **112:** Courtesy of 1-800-GOT-JUNK?; **115:** Jack Dorsey/© jack.

CHAPTER 6

Pages 118–119: © John Rowley/Getty Images/DAL; **122:** © PRNewsFoto/AirTran Airways; **123:** © Michele Limina/AFP/Getty Images; **126:** © AP Photo/Paul Sakuma; **132 (l):** Courtesy of Southwest Airlines, **(r):** © Aaron M. Sprecher/Bloomberg via Getty Images; **136:** © LinkedIn Corporation.

CHAPTER 7

Page 138: © Ingram Publishing/DAL; **141:** © PRNewsFoto/TOMS Shoes; **143:** © Library of Congress/DAL; **146:** © AP Photo/Mel Evans; **153:** © RI Screenshots/Alamy.

CHAPTER 8

Pages 158–159: © Monty Rakusen/Getty Images/DAL; **162:** © Alexi Boitsov/Bloomberg via Getty Images; **163:** © Jonathan Nackstrand/AFP/Getty Images; **166:** © Christof Stache/AFP/Getty Images; **168:** © Susan Van Etten/PhotoEdit Inc.; **170:** Courtesy of FAC; **171:** © Katie N. Gardner for the Washington Post via Getty Images; **173:** © AP Photo/Richard Vogel; **177:** © Kent Knudson/PhotoLink/Getty Images/DAL.

CHAPTER 9

Pages 180–181: Royalty-Free/CORBIS; **183:** © AP Photo/Ann Heisenfelt; **184:** © Amy Uratsu/Stockbyte/Getty Images; **185:** © Sarah M. Golonka/Brand X Pictures/PunchStock; **189:** © Discovery Channel/Photofest; **194:** © AP Photo/Chris O'Connor; **195:** © Noel Hendrickson/Digital Vision/Getty Images.

CHAPTER 10

Page 198: Tom Merton/OJO Images/Getty Images; **200:** David Lees/Digital Vision/Getty Images; **201:** Screenshot © Copyright 2011 TheLadders; **204 (t):** Jeffrey Coolidge/Digital Vision/Getty Images, (b)Copyright © 2006 Info Cubic—A Leading Nationwide Pre Employment Screening Company, All Rights Reserved; **208:** (t)Qilai Shen/Bloomberg via Getty Images, (b)PRNewsFoto/Manpower Inc.; **211:** Simon Belcher/Alamy; **213:** AP Photo/Richmond Times-Dispatch, Cindy Blanchard; **216:** Michael Dwyer/Alamy; **218:** Kai Chiang/Golden Pixels LLC/Corbis.

CHAPTER 11

Page 222: Andrew Burton/Getty Images; **225:** Christopher Polk/Getty Images for PCA; **226:** Richard Levine/Alamy; **228:** (l)Jim West/Alamy, (r)Eric Charbonneau/Le Studio/Wireimage; **230:** Product photo used with permission of The Procter & Gamble Company. All rights reserved; **233:** Justin Sullivan/Getty Images; **234:** (l)Allison Rocks! Photography, (r)*Marketing News* Cover Reprinted with permission of the American Marketing Association. All rights reserved; **236:** Emily Anne Epstein/Corbis; **237:** Photo courtesy of the Advertising Archives.

CHAPTER 12

Page 240: Kim White/Bloomberg via Getty Images; **242:** Ramin Talaie/Corbis; **244:** culture-images GmbH/Alamy; **248:** Tetra Images/Alamy; **249:** Michael Maloney/San Francisco Chronicle/Corbis; **250:** Eric Carr/Alamy; **251:** Screenshot courtesy of Century Link; **252:** Morgan Gaunt/www.fortheloveofskinny.com; **256:** (t)© Steve Crise/BNSF Railway, (b)PR NEWSWIRE; **259:** Advertisement reprinted with permission of Ogilvy & Mather. All rights reserved; **260:** Nelson Ching/Bloomberg via Getty Images; **261:** Copyright © 2010–2011 WhaleShark Media, Inc. All rights reserved.

CHAPTER 13

Pages 266–267: Najlah Feanny/Corbis; **269:** Screenshot © 1999–2011, Nextag, Inc.; **270:** © Benjamin Moore & Co. Used with permission; **272:** Screenshot reprinted Courtesy of Walmart.com; **273:** Screenshot Courtesy of the Chicago Bulls; **275:** Old Spice screenshot used with permission of The Procter & Gamble Company. All rights reserved; **276:** Andrew Cutraro/Getty Images; **279:** Screenshot courtesy of Second Life. Copyright Linden Research, Inc. All rights reserved; **280:** © 2009–2011 Yowza!! All rights reserved; **282:** Flying Colours Ltd/Getty Images; **286:** Screenshot © Bittorrent.com.

CHAPTER 14

Pages 288-289: Adam Gault/OJO Images/Getty Images; **290:** VIEW Pictures Ltd/Alamy; **293:** Patrick La Roque/Alamy; **294:** AP Photo/Paul Sakuma; **295:** Courtesy of Rendezvous BBQ; **301:** Mikhail Kondrashov "fotomik"/Alamy; **309:** Screenshot courtesy of Netflix

CHAPTER 15

Page 314: Stock Connection Blue/Alamy; **316:** Courtesy Yap Tourism Bureau; **317:** The Bureau of Engraving and Printing; **319:** Lana Sundman/Alamy; **322:** Corbis Premium RF/Alamy; **323:** Andre Babiak Photography/Alamy; **326:** Net-Photos/Alamy; **328:** Royalty-Free/CORBIS

CHAPTER 16

Pages 332-333: Monty Rakusen/Cultura/Getty Images; **336:** Screenshot courtesy of Treasury-Direct.gov; **338:** Phillip Spears/Getty Images; **339:** Jeff Greenberg/Alamy; **341:** Courtesy of Dell Inc.; **343:** The McGraw-Hill Companies, Inc.; **346:** vario images GmbH & Co.KG/Alamy.

index

Online Supplements

ConnectPlus Business with LearnSmart One-Semester Online Access for Business, Third Edition

McGraw-Hill ConnectPlus® provides an online eBook and immediate feedback on online assignments, quizzes, and practice tests, providing a learning experience that is personalized for YOU. Study more efficiently and engage with your learning process – Connect with future success!

HOW TO REGISTER

Using a <u>Print Book</u>?

To register and activate your ConnectPlus account, simply follow these easy steps:

1. **Go to the ConnectPlus course web address provided by your instructor or visit the Connect link set up on your instructor's course within your campus learning management system.**
2. **Click on the link to register.**
3. **When prompted, enter the ConnectPlus code found on the inside back cover of your book and click Submit. Complete the brief registration form that follows to begin using Connect.**

Using an <u>eBook</u>?

To register and activate your ConnectPlus account, simply follow these easy steps:

1. **Upon purchase of your eBook, you will be granted automatic access to ConnectPlus.**
2. **Go to the ConnectPlus course web address provided by your instructor or visit the Connect link set up on your instructor's course within your campus learning management system.**
3. **Sign in using the same email address and password you used to register on the eBookstore. Complete your registration and begin using Connect.**

Note: Access Code is for one use only. If you did not purchase this book new, the access code included in this book is no longer valid.

Need help? Visit mhhe.com/support